A HISTORY (
THE NATIONAL
GRAPHICAL
ASSOCIATION

A HISTORY OF THE NATIONAL GRAPHICAL ASSOCIATION

JOHN GENNARD

Professor of Industrial Relations
Strathclyde Business School

London
UNWIN HYMAN
Boston   Sydney   Wellington

Published by the Academic Division of
Unwin Hyman Ltd
15/17 Broadwick Street, London W1V 1FP, UK

Unwin Hyman Inc.,
8 Winchester Place, Winchester, Mass. 01890, USA

Allen & Unwin (Australia) Ltd,
8 Napier Street, North Sydney, NSW 2060, Australia

Allen & Unwin (New Zealand) Ltd in association with the
Port Nicholson Press Ltd,
Compusales Building, 75 Ghuznee Street, Wellington 1, New Zealand

First published in 1990

British Library Cataloguing in Publication Data
Gennard, John
A history of the National Graphical Association.
1. Great Britain. Printing industries. Trade Unions.
National Graphical Association (1982), history
I. Title
331.8818620941
ISBN 0–04–445811–8

Library of Congress Cataloging in Publication Data
Gennard, John.
A history of the National Graphical Association / John Gennard.
p.   cm
Includes bibliographical references
ISBN 0–04–445811–8.
1. National Graphical Association (Great Britain)—History.
2. Trade-unions—Printing industry—Great Britain—History.
I. Title.
Z243.G7G46   1990   90–12201
338.8′2616862—dc20   CIP

Typeset in 11/13 Times Roman by Columns of Reading Ltd.
and printed in Great Britain by The University Press, Cambridge

CONTENTS

CONTENTS

CONTENTS

CONTENTS

CONTENTS

CONTENTS

LIST OF FIGURES AND TABLES

Plate section
appears between
pages 302 and 303

PREFACE

Towards the end of 1982 I approached Mr J.F.Wade, the then General Secretary of the NGA (1982) with reference to writing a history of the Association. The intention was to update Musson's history of the Typographical Association and Howe and Waite's history of the London Society of Compositors and record the development of the NGA over the first twenty years of its existence. The NGA agreed to my request and I began an interesting task.

However, neither party at this stage could have predicted the momentous events that were to affect the NGA over the period 1983–87. These centred around 'an industrial revolution' in the provincial and national newspaper industry and involved the NGA in major industrial disputes with the Messenger Group, the *Wolverhampton Express and Star* and News International over that company's transfer of production from Fleet Street to Wapping. Although its members employed in newspapers have never exceeded around 15 per cent of the NGA total membership, it was agreed that the history should be extended to cover the first twenty-five years of the NGA's existence and the momentous events of the 1980s.

My objective has been to describe and analyse the evolution and development of the NGA over the period 1948–89. The Association has given me open access to all its records and an entirely free hand to write the history as I found it. Any views expressed in this history are entirely my own, without any influence or censorship by the NGA.

I have arranged the history in four parts. The first deals with the NGA and its founding unions' relationships with other printing unions and the formation of the NGA in 1964 and the NGA (1982) in March 1982. The second part deals with the decision-making and financial structure of the Association, whilst the third part analyses its relationship with the Printing and Kindred Trades Federation, the International Graphical Federation, the Trades Union Congress and the Labour Party. The final part deals with relationships with employers and covers *inter alia* wages, hours of work, holidays, pensions and women's issues. This approach, however, is not without its limitations in that it involves overlapping and any division into separate compartments is unreal historically.

The history has been written from the Association's official records – National Council minutes, delegate meeting reports, branch circulars, rulebooks and monthly journals, etc. – and interviews with present and past leading officials. In addition, the annual reports of the Printing and Kindred Trades Federation, the International Graphical Federation, the Trades Union Congress and the Labour Party have provided a great deal of information, as have the monthly journals of the British Printing Industries Federation (formerly the British Federation of Master Printers) and the Newspaper Society. The reports of the three post Second World War Royal Commissions on the Press, Courts of Inquiry into printing industry disputes and government and quasi-government bodies have also been important sources of information. A.E. Musson's history of the Typographical Association has been a rich and indispensable source of reference for the early chapters of this history.

I have to thank the University of Strathclyde Research and Development Committee and the Economic and Social Research Council, which over the period October 1982 to October 1985 provided financial support to enable me to undertake the writing of this history. I must also express my thanks to the late Professor John Ward of the History Department, University of Strathclyde. He and I worked together on the history until his untimely death in 1987. He was a constant source of encouragement and advice and his death was a sad loss to the project. I also wish to express my great appreciation of the kindness and constant helpfulness of Joe Wade, Tony Dubbins, the late Les Dixon, Bryn Griffiths, John Ibbotson and all other national and branch officials of the NGA.

I also wish to express my sincere thanks for the constant and unstinting help received from Mr Hayward, the NGA Research Officer, who acted as the link between myself and the Association during the writing of this history.

A debt of gratitude is owed to Miss Hazel Gordon who diligently and cheerfully typed numerous drafts of the manuscript.

Lastly, research work inevitably impinges upon family life and thanks for understanding in this matter are due to Anne, John and Julie Gennard.

JOHN GENNARD

A. D. Dubbins – General Secretary

FOREWORD

By Tony Dubbins

Ever since the NGA came into existence in 1964, its growth and development have been characterised by amalgamations and mergers. Twenty-five years on, only three unions out of the prewar thirty-five are left in the industry: the NGA, which caters for skilled and professional workers; Sogat, which, although having some skilled workers, primarily organises the non-craft side of the industry; and the NUJ – the journalists' union.

Way back in 1984, talks seemed to be well on the way to achieving an amalgamation with Sogat and the establishment of a single production union for the industry. It appeared therefore that the NGA might be reaching the end of its life as an independent organisation and that the time was opportune to record the events that had taken place within the printing industry, and particularly in the development of the craft and skilled unions, since 1948 – the date Musson concluded his definitive study of the Typographical Association. At the time of writing now that the package of proposals for the merger of the NGA and Sogat is completed and in all probability will be voted on in November of this year, it seems even more appropriate to publish this history.

The National Council were approached by two distinguished academics from the University of Strathclyde to carry out a feasibility study, aimed at establishing whether a history of the NGA would have interest and appeal to a wider audience other than our own members. Professor John Gennard, Dean of the Strathclyde Business School, along with his colleague, the late Professor John Ward, author of the inimitable exposition on the nineteenth-century factory system and the 'Ten Hour Movement', carried out the study and reported that the richness and uniqueness of the industry and the union, and in particular the evolution and development of the NGA, would indeed have considerable appeal to students and scholars of labour history and industrial relations.

The National Council therefore decided that Professors Gennard and

Ward should write something more than an internal commemorative history of the NGA. They were to produce a serious piece of scholarship which provided a true and factual account of the union's history.

Unfortunately, Professor Ward died early in the life of the project, but Professor Gennard continued the work and I am delighted to say in this Foreword that he has achieved a remarkable book, which examines critically, but sympathetically, the history of an industry, a movement and a union.

Every assistance has been given to Professor Gennard, and the very rich material housed in the NGA's Archives at Warwick University and Graphic House have also been freely available.

One of the conditions on which Professor Gennard accepted this mammoth task, and indeed which helped him to raise the necessary funding from the academic world, was an undertaking by us that we would not seek to interfere, edit or influence the content or analysis contained within the final manuscript. For our part we have honoured that obligation and we as a union are proud to be associated with such a well-written and researched piece of work, which I have no doubt will stand the test of time and will be an ever-present obligatory text on the reading list of students engaged within the field of industrial relations or labour history.

CHAPTER I

THE PRINTING INDUSTRY IN 1950 AND 1989

The National Graphical Association (NGA) came into being on 1 January 1964 with the amalgamation of the London Typographical Society and the Typographical Association. The former had been created by an amalgamation in 1955 of the Printing Machine Managers Trade Society, founded in 1839, and the London Society of Compositors, formed in 1848. The Typographical Association had been formed in 1849. Centenary histories of the London Society of Compositors and the Typographical Association were written but no comprehensive studies exist of their post centenary year developments.[1]

Although this history examines the progress of the NGA in its first twenty-five years, this cannot be done without references to events between 1948 and its formation in 1964. Today the printing industry is very different than in 1950. As background to the evolution and development of the NGA I start by comparing the printing industry of 1950 with that of today.

THE INDUSTRY IN 1950

Product Sectors, Processes and Tasks

The printing industry covered a wide range of sectors. There was the 'general trade', which included firms that produced security printing, packaging and stationery, catalogues, bank notes, maps, cards, tickets, etc., as well as books, magazines and periodicals. Some 3,500 periodicals were published in the United Kingdom. A second sector was national newspapers in which ten national daily morning newspapers had a total circulation of 17 million[2] and ten national Sunday papers

1

had a total circulation of 30.5 million.[3] Most national morning newspapers were controlled by three groups – those headed by Lords Beaverbrook and Rothermere and that by the Daily Mirror. National Sunday press ownership was also dominated by three groups – Beaverbrook, Mirror and News of the World Ltd. In addition to national daily and Sunday newspaper circulation, three London evening papers had a total circulation of 3.5 million. A third sector was the provincial press, which contained companies producing daily morning and evening papers, and bi-weekly and tri-weekly newspapers. There were in Great Britain twenty-five daily morning provincial newspapers selling in total 3 million copies and seventy-five daily evening provincial papers with a total circulation of 7 million. The majority of the provincial press nevertheless belonged to four national chains – Lord Rothermere, Lord Thomson, Cowdray and Drayton.

Although there were significant differences between the product sectors, they had much in common in their production techniques and the workpeople they employed. Of the three main printing processes – letterpress, lithography and gravure – by which print products were produced, the dominant one was letterpress. For example, in 1950, 83,000 out of a total of 102,000 craft printing trade union members were employed in letterpress, which uses type or blocks to produce the image to be printed, which stands out on a raised surface. Lithographic printing uses a plate on which the printing and non-printing parts are on the same level but the latter is kept damp and free from ink. Photogravure printing uses cylinders on which the image is etched. Letterpress and lithographic printing were carried out either on flat-bed machines, in which the type or plate remained stationary, or on rotary machines, in which the type was attached to revolving cylinders. Photogravure printing was almost always by rotary machines. Printing machines were fed by single sheets of paper or by a web of paper, which after printing could be cut into individual sheets, or folded by a folder into sections of a book or periodical.

Whatever the printing process used, the main tasks involved fell into five departments – composing, process and foundry, machine room, finishing, warehousing and despatch, and office and general management. Two main types of compositors were involved in preparing material to be printed by the letterpress process. Hand compositors arranged the separate letters to form the words and the lines of texts. However, the predominant form of composition was mechanical, which entered the industry at the beginning of this century.[4] The keyboards used in

2

machine composition either operated a casting machine (for example, the linotype and intertype machine), which produced each line of type in one metal slug, or produced paper tape which operated a caster (for example, the monotype machine) outputting lines made up of separate letters. The compositor's work was checked and corrected by the reader. In newspapers the make-up of pages was also done in the composing department.

Although the gravure process was not widely used, it was expanding. Composition tasks were different from those in letterpress in that the type was usually set in small areas and not laid down in page form. The compositor took proofs of this type and made a final page or area paste-up. The reader corrected the work, which was then passed to the process department.

The process and foundry department produced the printing surfaces for blocks, plates or cylinders. A plate was required for all litho work, whereas for much letterpress work the metal type could be used as the printing surface. Some of the larger letterpress printers and most newspapers made their own blocks and plates, but for most companies such work was contracted out to specialist trade houses. Tasks in preparation for letterpress printing included retouching of blocks and gravure cylinders, etching or hand-engraving, routing out surplus metal, mounting letterpress blocks and the making of moulded duplicate blocks or plates (stereotyping or electrotyping). In the litho area, the preparation process included the making of art work, the production of positive or negative film and separation of primary colours for full colour work.

The actual printing took place in the machine department. The predominance of letterpress was seen in that, taking all sectors of printing, some 85 per cent of machine managers were in charge of letterpress machines. In newspapers the percentage was over 90. Litho machines were most common in general printing. Letterpress and litho machines were operated by machine managers who worked with assistants. On average, litho presses employed almost twice as many assistants per minder as did letterpress.

Employment, Trade Unions and Employers' Organisations

Small firms dominated the industry. Nearly 70 per cent of firms in membership of the British Master Printers' Federation had fewer than twenty-five employees. Fewer than 3 per cent of its member firms employed 300 or more. Newspaper firms were larger than those in the general trade and nearly two-thirds of establishments had over twenty-five employees. London was the dominant printing centre with some 1,000 firms undertaking general print work. Of 83,000 letterpress craftsmen in the industry, 24,000 worked in London, as did 32 per cent of litho craftsmen.

There were in total 338,000 employees in the printing industry, of whom 29 per cent were employed in the printing and publishing of newspapers and periodicals; 45 per cent of all employees were employed in London and the South East. Of 97,000 employed in newspapers and periodicals, 40 per cent were skilled operatives (compositors, plate-makers, machine managers), 41 per cent were administrative, technical and clerical workers, and 20 per cent were semi-skilled or unskilled operators. In the general printing trade, however, 62 per cent of employees were skilled, 14 per cent were non-craft employees and 24 per cent were administrative, technical and clerical personnel.

There were thirteen major trade unions in the industry with a total membership of 273,000. The demarcation of the jobs between the unions was clear. In letterpress, the craft composing and reading functions involved five unions, of which two were confined to London and one to Scotland.[5] The London Society of Compositors (LSC) organised compositors and readers in London, which was defined as a 15 mile radius from Charing Cross. The Association of the Correctors of the Press (ACP)[6] also organised readers in London. Its members became readers by passing the Association's entrance examination and had previously been readers' assistants and as such members of the National Society of Operative Printers and Assistants (Natsopa). The Monotype Casters and Typefounders' Society (MCTS) catered for monotype caster attendants in London and parts of England and Wales.[7] Monotype keyboard operators were members of the LSC, the Typographical Association and the Scottish Typographical Association. The Typographical Association (TA) organised compositors, caster attendants and readers in the English provinces, Wales, Northern Ireland and the Irish Republic (except for Dublin). The Scottish Typographical Association (STA) catered for the same groups in Scotland.[8]

The transmission and receiving of text and pictures by electronics for inclusion in newspapers and journals was the preserve of the National

Union of Press Telegraphists (NUPT)[9] whose members were employed in national newspapers, provincial newspapers and news agencies. The production of written information for inclusion in newspapers, journals and periodicals was the province of the National Union of Journalists (NUJ), which, unlike the unions previously mentioned, did not operate a closed shop.

The production of letterpress printing plates was undertaken by members of the National Society of Electrotypers and Stereotypers (NSES), which operated a pre-entry closed shop and an apprenticeship system of entry into the trade. Letterpress printing took place in the machine room, where machine managers in London were organised in the Printing Machine Managers Trade Society (PMMTS), in Scotland in the STA and in the rest of the UK and the Irish Republic (excluding Dublin) in the TA. The PMMTS operated a closed shop and an apprenticeship system and operated only within a 15 mile radius of Charing Cross. It did not control all the machine rooms in London; in some houses, for example the *News of the World*, control lay with Natsopa and in others with the National Union of Printing, Bookbinding and Paperworkers (NUPB&PW). These situations had arisen because the PMMTS initially regarded rotary and platen machines as being outwith the province of the craftsman. As a result, Natsopa (in the case of rotary presses) and NUPB&PW (in the case of platens) gained control in some houses and by the time the PMMTS realised the situation neither unions nor the employers were prepared to relinquish what had been gained.[10]

On the non-craft side of letterpress printing there were two unions – Natsopa and the NUPB&PW.[11] The former mainly organised readers' assistants, machine room assistants, warehouse workers and clerical employees. However in London it had machine manager members. Outside printing it organised employees in ink manufacturing. NUPB&PW's main sections of membership were bookbinders and rulers, who were predominantly female but apprenticed trained, warehousemen, cutters and general assistants, and employees in paper and board mills. There were, however, small but important groups of NUPB&PW members in traditional craft areas, viz. its printing machine interests.

The two lithographic craft unions were national and not confined solely to London. Origination was controlled by the Society of Lithographic Artists, Designers, Engravers and Process Workers

(Slade),[12] which operated a pre-entry closed shop and an apprentice entry system. It controlled the allocation of labour and wage levels through a 'white card system', under which a vacancy in a branch was offered first to an unemployed member in that branch, then to an unemployed member in another branch and finally to employed members in the branch where the vacancy existed.

Plate-making and printing in lithography were controlled by the Amalgamated Society of Lithographic Printers and Auxiliaries of Great Britain and Ireland (ASLP),[13] which operated a closed shop and an apprentice entry system. As in letterpress, non-craft manual workers were organised by Natsopa and the NUPB&PW. There were four main trade unions with an interest in lithographic printing compared with eleven in letterpress. The non-craft unions organised across the main printing processes. The craft unions, on the other hand, organised around particular jobs within the main printing processes. Of the eight letterpress craft unions, three had memberships confined to London and one to Scotland. Of the two national unions, their London branches accounted for a significant proportion of their total membership.

Although the printing unions jealously guarded their autonomy, they recognised the need to speak collectively on many matters and to have a means of resolving their inter-union difficulties. In 1901 the printing unions formed the Printing and Kindred Trades Federation (P&KTF) to coordinate their activities.[14] In 1950 the Federation had seventeen affiliated unions and a total membership of 233,733.[15] Its objectives included the establishment of uniform working conditions in different branches of the industry, the coordination of union policies, the prevention and settlement of disputes and securing unity of action amongst its affiliates. It spoke collectively for them to the TUC and to government and conducted research and enquiry work for its affiliated unions either collectively or individually. However, the Federation's constitution clearly stated that 'the Federation shall not interfere in the internal management of any union, nor its rules and customs'. Nevertheless, it had powers to deal with demarcation disputes between affiliated unions via an Arbitration Board whose decision was binding on the parties.

The major employers' organisations in the United Kingdom were the British Federation of Master Printers (BFMP), the Newspaper Society (NS) and the Newspaper Proprietors' Association (NPA). The BFMP, founded in 1900, was the largest of these organisations.[16] Its members were engaged in general printing but, as well as negotiating on labour matters, the Federation was a commercial trade association. It comprised twelve regional bodies, known as 'Alliances', which varied greatly in the number of associations and firms they represented. The London Alliance, for example, comprised six associations and some 750 firms, whilst the North West Alliance had four associations but only forty-two firms. In 1950 the Federation had over 4,000 members in the United Kingdom, who employed over 85 per cent of the total employees engaged in general printing.

The Newspaper Society, whose roots go back to 1895, represented the provincial morning, evening and weekly newspapers in England, Wales and Northern Ireland, including weekly newspapers published in London.[17] The Society had some 350 members, of whom about 50 had their newspapers printed under contract. It represented 290 newspaper plants, including 60 daily newspaper houses, most of whom also printed weekly newspapers. Some Newspaper Society members undertook general printing and were also members of the BFMP. In 1950, NS member firms employed 20,000 production employees.

The Newspaper Proprietors' Association, formed in 1906, represented the national newspapers published in London and Manchester.[18] In 1950 its member firms employed some 18,000 regular operative staff. Although the NPA maintained informal contacts with the BFMP and the NS on labour matters, it conducted separate negotiations with the unions. NPA members considered their product was so specialised that they could not afford, by being associated with other branches of the industry, the risk of a stoppage. They saw themselves vulnerable to union action in that they produced a highly perishable product, which did not apply to the general trade employers.

In Ireland there were a multitude of employers' associations. In Belfast there was the Belfast Newspaper Society and the Belfast Printing Trades Employers' Association. In Cork there was the Cork Master Printers' Association, whilst the Cork *Examiner* negotiated a company agreement directly with the TA. In Scotland, the Scottish Daily Newspaper Society, established in 1915, represented the interest of daily newspapers in Scotland, whilst the Scottish Newspaper Proprietors' Association represented the interests of Scottish weekly and bi-weekly newspaper publishers. There was also the Scottish Alliance of the BFMP, which retained control of all matters affecting the industry in Scotland; collective agreements were made directly between the Scottish Alliance and the unions concerned.

Industrial Relations Machinery and Procedures

No formal machinery existed for negotiating agreements. Ad hoc arrangements prevailed whereby if one side wished to change the agreement it approached the other and if mutually agreed the agreement would be renegotiated. In the general trade and the provincial newspapers, the BFMP and Newspaper Society negotiated jointly with the individual unions over wages. The P&KTF negotiated on behalf of its affiliated unions with BFMP and NS over apprentices' wages, hours of work, annual holidays, pensions and sick pay. The standard working week in 1950 was 43½ hours over five days and annual holidays were two weeks. This had been achieved in 1946. In that year the P&KTF claimed a 40 hour week to replace the 45 hours agreed in 1937. Although the settlement was 43½ hours, both sides agreed in principle to work towards a 42½ hour week when the industry's recruitment problems had been overcome.[19]

In the general trade and provincial newspapers, individual unions negotiated national minimum wages for the various classes and grades of workers in different sectors of the industry. Between 1947 and 1951 the BFMP and the NS failed to persuade the unions to coordinate their wages claims through the P&KTF, rather than submit separate and unrelated claims, so as to produce a wage structure which would bring stability to the industry. Although the unions supported the desirability of a wage structure they were unable to reach agreement amongst themselves on such a structure. They were divided over provincial craft parity, the London/provincial craft differential, provincial grading, the craft/non-craft differential and the system of voting within the P&KTF to determine any coordinated wage claim.

In 1950, however, as a result of a dispute between the LSC and the London Master Printers' Association (LMPA) over a wage claim to re-establish the London/provincial craft differential to that awarded in January 1948 by a National Arbitration Tribunal, a wage structure of a kind emerged.[20] The settlement of the dispute included a London craft rate of £7.75 per week, wages and conditions stabilised for five years, and a cost-of-living bonus related to changes in the Index of Retail

8

Prices. This agreement formed the basis in 1951 of agreements between the BFMP and the NS and all other print unions. The TA craft rate was set at £7.17½, giving a London/provincial craft differential of 57½p and a provincial craft/non-craft differential of £1.50. By early 1951 the general trade and provincial newspapers had agreed stability of wages and conditions for the following five years.

In 1919 a Joint Industrial Council for the printing industry (JIC), consisting of forty members elected by the BFMP and the NS and forty members elected by the P&KTF, had been established. The Council had no authority to negotiate wage agreements but its constitution provided machinery for settling disputes via conciliation committees, for the selection and training of apprentices and learners and for the provision of health and safety in the industry.

The arrangements for the selection and training of apprentices were supervised by the Apprenticeship Authority, a standing committee of the JIC. The majority of apprenticeships were filled by boys leaving school, although arrangements for adult apprenticeships existed in certain occupations. The period of apprenticeship was in general six years, but the procedure for selection varied throughout the country. Some firms recruited from school but in some parts of the country potential apprentices were screened by joint district committees, and employers then made their selection from those recommended by these committees.

In national newspapers there was also no formal machinery for negotiating agreements. Ad hoc arrangements existed for the negotiation of agreements. The P&KTF frequently conducted negotiations on wages and conditions on behalf of its affiliates with the NPA and acted on its own behalf on hours, holidays and other matters. The P&KTF coordinated individual unions' claims prior to presenting a collective claim on their behalf. Each union retained its autonomy and right to individual approach to the NPA. Any agreement reached as a result of P&KTF negotiations had to be approved by the members of the unions concerned. The agreements were thus between the individual union and the NPA. Usually the unions submitted their own domestic claims in addition to the general P&KTF claims.

In 1951 the NPA and the LSC signed a three-year agreement providing for percentage increases in basic rates, a cost-of-living bonus based on movements in the Index of Retail Prices and a basic craft rate of £9.67½ per week. The chapels then negotiated additional payments to and based on this basic rate, which in reality bore little relationship to what was actually paid. In 1951 NPA collective agreements covered over 100 different minimum rates. In London, minimum terms and conditions of employment were fixed between the unions and the NPA, but in Manchester the TA negotiated with the Manchester Managers Committee of the NPA. Manchester chapels then negotiated pluses on this rate. The Manchester Managers Committee had authority to negotiate separate agreements from London, but final authority lay with the NPA Council.

There was no Joint Industrial Council for national newspapers. In 1919 the NPA opposed the JIC for the printing industry, arguing that its interests were distinct from those of general printers and that, unlike provincial newspaper owners, it did not have commercial printing interests. However, in 1949 consideration was given to the establishment of a JIC for national newspapers. This followed a dispute in 1948 in Manchester over a disturbance in the differentials between rates received by TA members employed in NPA offices and its members employed in NS offices. It was felt that if conciliation machinery as operated by the JIC for the printing industry had existed, the strike might have been avoided. A draft JIC constitution was submitted to the unions for consideration. Seven unions, including the LSC, supported the formation of a JIC, but three, including the TA, were against. Since these three unions represented the majority of employees in national newspapers, steps to establish a JIC ended.

The high earnings in national newspapers meant no shortage of applicants for jobs. Some argued that the restriction of labour to national newspapers, despite an increase in demand for all kinds of printing since the end of the Second World War, was due to apprentice quotas applied by the craft unions and to excessive staffing levels in certain establishments. The unions argued that apprentice quotas existed to regulate entry into the industry and provide a balanced labour force. National newspapers depended on provincial newspapers and the general printing trade for their supply of trained craftsmen. Few apprentices were allowed in national newspaper offices as the unions considered such offices could not provide a sufficiently wide training.

In the Irish Republic provinces there were three grades of pay for letterpress craftsmen. The top rate was £6.87½ per week. In Cork the minimum craft rate in the general trade was £7.42½ per week, which was the same as in Dublin, where the main letterpress craft union was the Dublin Typographical Provident Society.

The Economic Environment

The immediate post Second World War years saw rising production and employment in the printing industry. In 1950 industrial production in paper and print increased by 18 per cent, compared with 8 per cent for all industries. In the same year the LSC's total payments on unemployment benefit amounted to £160. The TA spent £1,300 on unemployment benefit out of a total expenditure on all benefits in 1950 of £13,000.

In 1950 there was an acute shortage of skilled labour in the industry. The employers sought to overcome this by persuading the unions to accept increases in the number of apprenticeships and the more effective use of existing labour via incentive schemes. A January 1948 agreement between the BFMP and the NS and the TA provided for a wage increase in return for concessions on the apprentice ratio and the establishment of a joint committee to formulate incentive payments for use in TA areas. A 1949 wage agreement had seen further wage increases for TA members in return for a bonus intake of apprentices, cooperation in the introduction of payment by results schemes, the acceptance of dilutees and the working of overtime. The 1951 TA wages agreement also gave wage increases in return for increases in the labour force in terms of both numbers and effort. The 1950 agreement between the LSC and the LMPA also traded wage increases for additional supplies of labour. The employer policy of trading wage increases for manpower concessions was to be a feature of wage agreements in the industry for the next twenty years.

However, the increased demand in the immediate post Second World War era for print work also brought problems for the print unions which were beginning to surface in 1950. The London Master Printers' Association told the 1950 Court of Inquiry that delays in completing printing orders because of manpower shortages were resulting in work being sent abroad and firms establishing in-plant printing arrangements.[21] Both the LSC and the TA reacted quickly to the growth of miniature litho printing processes (e.g. multigraph and varitypers) in local authorities, nationalised industries, banks and insurance companies, realising the threat they posed to letterpress printing. In response to the growth of small office printing machines, the LSC established an Allied Process Department in 1951 to organise persons engaged on processes producing work that had hitherto been that of the compositor. It had little success in organising employees working on miniature printing machines within the industry let alone outside it. The TA was no more successful than the LSC in organising such workers, who were normally enjoying pay and conditions superior to those in the general printing industry. The problem of small litho printing machines accelerated in subsequent years but remained 'hidden' whilst the conventional printing industry experienced over-full employment.

THE INDUSTRY IN 1989

Product Sectors, Processes and Tasks

In 1989 the general printing industry covered a wide range of products, including packaging, advertising materials, security printing, business forms, books, periodicals, magazines, stationery and catalogues. Although books, periodicals and magazines are sold to the general public, this is the case with only a small proportion of the total output from this sector. However in 1989, unlike 1950, the general printing industry operated in an increasingly international market. Limitations on the import or export of print products which had existed forty years previously had been removed, bringing increased competition from foreign printers in both UK and export markets. Book printers were suffering from this competition to a greater extent than the rest of the printing industry. This is particularly so in the case of glossy colour hardbound books, which are printed mainly in Holland or Italy or increasingly in Singapore.

In 1989 there were ten national daily morning newspapers with a total circulation of 14 million and eight national Sunday papers with a total circulation of 20 million. Compared with 1950 the *Daily Herald*, the *News Chronicle* and the *Daily Sketch* had ceased publication. Of the Sunday titles, the *Dispatch*, the *Reynolds News*, the *Graphic* and the *Chronicle* had closed,[22] whilst the *Sunday Pictorial* had become the *Sunday Mirror*. The early 1980s saw new daily morning newspapers appear, e.g. the *Independent*, the *Star* and *Today*. The *Sun* is now the largest-selling daily newspaper with a circulation of over 5 million. However, national newspaper ownership remains concentrated in a small number of large groups – Beaverbrook Newspaper Ltd, the Mirror Group Newspapers and News International. It was no longer only the 'Press Lords' who dominated but also entrepreneurs like Rupert Murdoch and Robert Maxwell.[23] By the end of 1989 no national newspapers were printed in Fleet Street. The printing of the *Sun*, *The Times*, the *Sunday Times* and the *News of the World* moved to Wapping in 1986, and in the following year the *Guardian*, the *Daily Telegraph*, the *Daily Mail*, and the *Financial Times* moved to the London Docklands. By 1989 national newspapers had decentralised their printing arrangements by separating their editorial and origination departments from the actual printing process. A further contrast between 1989 and 1950 was that virtually all national newspapers now included some colour printing.

In 1989 there were some 1,300 separate provincial weekly and daily newspaper titles with a total circulation of 16 million. The industry still consisted of a large number of companies varying in terms of ownership, control, size, organisation and products. Nevertheless, the bulk of the separate titles were owned by large groups such as the Westminster Press, Thomson Regional News, United Newspapers and Associated News.

The late 1970s saw the rise of freesheet newspapers, which depended solely on advertising revenue, rather than cover price plus advertising revenue, to meet their costs. Such newspapers had the advantage that the customer receives a copy free of charge, no large-scale distribution operation is required and young people are hired to deliver copies to every household. The entrepreneurs starting these 'freesheet' news-papers had backgrounds in information, sales and general business. Freesheets were expected to fold under competition from traditional papers which launched their own 'free' papers. However, many prospered and in the early 1980s there were over 600 free news sheets throughout the country. The majority are today owned by the large provincial groups and there are few remaining independent freesheets. These independents are new to the printing industry and not steeped in its conventions. They contract out their printing and employ few journalists.

By 1989, letterpress, which was the dominant printing process in 1950, had ceased to be a significant printing process. The National Council report to the 1986 Delegate Meeting reported that the NGA's new equipment survey showed that the introduction of new letterpress equipment, both typesetting and printing, was almost nil. Gravure had a larger share of the total print market than in 1950, having achieved competitive advantages from improved reproduction systems and the ability to produce acceptance standards of print on lower-quality materials. However, its share of the market was considerably lower than in the 1960s and the 1970s.

The dominant printing process in 1989 was lithography. Its growth was linked to photocomposition replacing hot metal systems in the late 1960s and early 1970s as the dominant mode of origination. Hot metal composition and litho printing techniques were incompatible, but photocomposition and litho were not. The advantages of litho over letterpress include a higher quality of printing, particularly colour printing. The introduction of litho into letterpress houses in the late 1960s led to disputes between the letterpress and litho craft unions.[24] In the 1990s lithography is predicted to grow further and its machines to have robotics and electronic attachments which are expected to eliminate many ancillary jobs in the press room.[25]

These changes in the distribution of printing process in 1989 relative to 1950 are also reflected in the industry's current occupational structure. Today there are few hand and mechanical compositors. In the mid-1950s mechanical composition was replaced by photocomposition, which was subsequently replaced in the mid-1970s by computerised composition. Photocomposition involved setting on film or paper rather than the manipulation of metal type. It changed the nature of the work rather than the numbers of compositors required, but output was considerably increased. The tasks of the hand compositor, for example, changed from the assembly of metal type and blocks to paste-up or assembling film on a transparent backing. Mechanical compositors found that photocomposition created new jobs for them as Qwerty keyboard operators or as photocomposer operators.

By 1989 computerised composition was the dominant form, particularly in newspapers, where it enabled three previously separate tasks – editorial, advertising and composition – to be combined. The journalist and advertising employees are now able to typeset, correct and do area but in the main are not yet full page make-up, all of which had previously been the preserve of compositors. In magazine and periodical publishing, computerised composition merged previously clearly demarcated tasks to the detriment of the compositor. Under previous technology the work of the author (creative origination) and typesetting were separated, but now the author could perform both tasks. Direct entry reduced the number of compositors employed in the industry, particularly in newspapers where the number employed between 1985 and 1989 fell by several thousand.

The expansion of litho impacted on jobs in the process and foundry departments. The decline of letterpress meant that by 1989 there were few photo-engravers and letterpress plate-makers in the industry. In

1967 the NSES had 5,000 members, but if it were in existence today its membership would certainly be fewer than 1,000. Litho process tasks have expanded relative to 1950. The introduction of new technology into the repro and litho print areas means that employees are responsible for operating expensive and sophisticated equipment.

In the machine room the dominance of litho meant that relative to 1950 press speeds were faster. There were also substantially more single and multi-colour litho printing machines than in 1950. In the machine room the litho machine manager predominated in every printing product sector. There were also acute skill shortages for the operation of the larger web-fed machines.

Employment, Trade Unions and Employers' Organisations

In 1989 the general printing trade was still dominated by small establishments, 90 per cent of which had fewer than fifty employees. Only 1 per cent employed 500 or more. The majority of firms remained family businesses. Relatively few were public companies. However, takeovers and mergers were a feature of the latter half of the 1980s. The British Printing and Communications Corporation (BPCC), St Ives and Norton Opax were particularly active in this regard, which has led to an increasing concentration of ownership and control in the industry. Another late-1980s trend was the takeover of printing companies by basically 'non-print' organisations, for example, the takeover of Senews by Ladbrokes. Newspaper firms remained larger than general trade firms and by 1989 multinational companies had a presence in national newspapers, for example News International Ltd.

In 1989, 349,000 employees were employed in all sectors of the printing industry. A major difference in the industry's workforce relative to 1950 was the number of women employees in craft occupations. In 1989, some 10,000 women were employed in areas that in 1950 were traditional journeymen areas.[26] There was also a greater proportion of non-manual employees, e.g. administrators, supervisors, scientists and technicians, in the industry's workforce. In 1971, the proportion of white-collar workers in printing and publishing was some 18 per cent. By 1989 the percentage exceeded 25 per cent. By 1989 London had ceased to be the dominant printing centre in the UK. The NGA London Region, for example, was by this time only the third largest region of the union in terms of membership, whereas at the formation of the NGA it was the largest. The London Master Printers'

Association, which in 1950 conducted independent negotiations with the London-based unions, ceased to exist in 1985 when it merged, because of falling membership, into the British Printing Industries Federation's South East Alliance.

By 1989 there were three main unions in the printing industry – the NGA(1982), the Society of Graphical and Allied Trades (82) and the NUJ – with a total membership of 355,000. In 1966, the NUPB&PW and Natsopa merged to form the Society of Graphical and Allied Trades (Sogat).[27] Attempts to determine a common rulebook after the merger failed and in 1970 the marriage was dissolved. The former NUPB&PW retained the name Sogat but Natsopa adopted the title National Society of Operative Printers, Graphical and Media Personnel. In 1975, Sogat and the Scottish Graphical Association (SGA) merged to form Sogat(75) in which the SGA was given autonomous trade section status.[28] In 1982, Natsopa and Sogat(75) merged to form Sogat(82).[29]

The NGA(1982) is the result of the merger of ten previously separate societies. In 1955 the LSC and the PMMTS amalgamated to form the LTS, which in 1964 merged with the TA to create the NGA. In 1965 the ACP and the NUPT transferred their engagements into the NGA and in 1967 the NSES did the same In 1969 the ASLP joined the NGA and ten years later the National Union of Wallcoverings, Decorative and Allied Trades (NUWDAT) did the same. The family tree was completed when NGA and Slade amalgamated to form the NGA(1982).

The P&KTF was dissolved in April 1974. Mergers amongst printing unions had reduced the need for a body to coordinate common policy. However there existed the TUC Printing Industries Committee (PIC), established in 1975, whose membership included not only the printing unions but the Amalgamated Engineering Union (AEU) and the Electrical, Electronic Telecommunications Plumbing Union (EETPU), which organised maintenance workers in the industry. These had been excluded from the P&KTF. The PIC is not an authoritative body but a forum for information exchange. Its activities cover health and safety, industrial training and monitoring developments affecting the industry.

In 1989 the major employers' organisation remained that of the general printing trade employers. However, the BFMP changed its name in April 1974 to the British Printing Industries Federation (BPIF). It felt that the words Federation of Master Printers were an inaccurate description, in that they did not reflect that the industry had changed from a master and servant relationship to one of management and employee. The Newspaper Society still represented provincial newspaper employers' interests, but the NPA, which changed its name in 1968 to the Newspaper Publishers' Association, had dismantled its involvement in industrial relations matters. In Scotland the main employers' organisations were the Society of Master Printers of Scotland, which had adopted this title in 1962, and the Scottish Newspaper Publishers Association. The Scottish Daily Newspaper Society had disbanded in 1982. In Ireland the multiplicity of employers' associations, for example the Irish Master Printers' Association and the Cork Master Printers' Association, remained. Relative to 1950 there was also now an employers' organisation on the island of Jersey. Another employers' organisation emerged in 1972, namely the Reproduction and Graphics Association (RAGA) representing the interests of those employers in the ad-setting industry not in membership of the Advertising, Typesetting and Foundry Employers' Federation (ATFEF).[30] Since 1950, employers' organisations for the advertising agencies had also been created, namely the Association of Scottish Advertising Agencies, the Association of Northern Advertising Agencies and the Association of Midland Advertising Agencies, and the Metal Packaging Manufacturers Association still has an agreement with the NGA.

Industrial Relations Machinery and Procedures

In 1989 no formal negotiating machinery existed in the general printing and provincial and national newspaper sectors of the industry. The ad hoc arrangements of 1950 remained. The BPIF and the Newspaper Society now negotiated separately with the printing unions. However, unlike in the 1950s, the basis wage agreements were no longer characterised by stabilisation, cost-of-living bonuses and wage increases for manpower concessions. A system of annual negotiations with BPIF and the NS has existed since 1969.

In 1989 the standard working week in the general trade and provincial newspapers in the UK was 37½ hours and had been achieved following a major industrial stoppage in 1980. However, well over 10,000 NGA members had achieved a 35 hour working week. Three weeks' annual paid holidays had been achieved in the mid-1960s, four weeks in the early 1970s and then a progressive increase to five weeks in 1989. In 1989 the basic minimum rate for craftsmen in the UK was £133 per week. Provincial grade rates had been abolished in the 1960s. A voluntary industry-wide transferable money purchase pension scheme for the general trade was introduced in 1986. The bargaining power of the unions in provincial newspapers relative to the general trade had declined by 1989. This change was reflected in that in 1988/9 and 1989/90 the new money increases gained in the annual wage negotiations were higher in the general trade than in provincial newspapers. In 1989 the minimum weekly earnings for craft workers in provincial newspapers were £126.64 and for non-craft employees £119.20 per week.

A significant change by 1989 relative to 1950 was that in the general trade the apprenticeship system no longer existed. This ended in 1983 when the BPIF and the NGA(1982) signed a recruitment, training and retraining agreement. Although the apprenticeship had served the industry well, the dramatic technological and organisational changes in the industry post mid-1970s questioned its value. The need now was for skilled workers regularly to update their skills to keep pace with changes in technology. The main principles of the new training agreements for the general printing industry are training to standards, joint management and chapel manpower planning, a modular system of training, comprehensive coverage of all skilled production workers with open age entry to skilled occupations, and national certification. In provincial newspapers, Scotland and Ireland, the apprenticeship system still prevails but its length had been reduced to three years.

In national newspapers, wages and conditions were in 1989 negotiated on a company basis, and wages in the machine area had moved to the point where they were on a par with the origination areas. However, the introduction of direct entry into national newspapers resulted in declines in employment in the composing process, plate-making and telegraphist areas. The NGA National Council report to the 1988 Biennial Delegate Meeting claimed that the introduction of direct input had reduced staffing levels in composing rooms by half to two-thirds of their previous size.[31] It had a significant impact on the printing of national newspapers in Manchester in that the centralisation of editorial departments in London brought the elimination, with one exception, of all the composing departments in Manchester. By 1989 newspapers in Scotland and Ireland had also suffered the winds of change with a considerable effect on employment. The bargaining power of skilled origination craftsmen in newspapers had declined out of all recognition relative to 1950. Provincial newspapers were now able to recruit new – usually non-union and often female – employees to the origination area at minimum wage rates. To prevent these workers from using NGA rates in the origination areas as bench marks for equal pay claims, provincial newspaper employers were able to impose considerable wage cuts on NGA craft origination workers. This would have been impossible in 1950.

The Economic Environment

The early 1980s saw a sharp increase in unemployment in the printing industry, but by 1989 the general trade was suffering from an acute skills shortage, particularly colour originators and litho printers. The Printing and Publishing Industry Training Board, established in the mid-1960s, had been disbanded in 1982. However, in 1989 the NGA and a number of employers were seeking to establish a jointly funded national training centre to help overcome this problem.

In 1989 the printing industry was facing intensified competition from foreign imports, the growth of in-plant printing departments in many companies across a wide spectrum of industries, the growth of instant print shops, and the expansion of advertising and art studios.[32] However the industry was also facing a threat from the growth of an alternative communications industry based on electronic devices. Electronic information systems, such as Oracle, Ceefax and Prestel, offered an alternative way of communicating information, whilst audio visual discs and cassettes offered mail order, holiday and travel companies the means of reaching their customers via TV screens. New cable methods which give households direct access to information and entertainment are also likely to compete with traditional printing methods. Publishers of books and magazines are also attracted to these new systems, particularly desk top publishing.

Over the period 1950–89 the printing industry underwent a major industrial revolution which is not yet complete. The origination areas were affected by first photocomposition and then direct entry becoming the dominant mode of origination when for over fifty years mechanical composition had held this position. The process and foundry departments have been affected by the virtual demise of letterpress over the last forty years and by the increased demand for colour printing in all sectors of the industry. The machine departments have also been dramatically affected by the decline of letterpress, the rapid rise of lithography and the slower increase in gravure. Hot metal composition and letterpress printing, which dominated the industry in 1950, were virtually non-existent by 1989. Computerised composition and litho printing processes are now dominant. The compositor was the dominant occupation in 1950 in terms of control of the production systems. This was not so in 1989, especially in newspapers where control of origination now lay with those in the editorial and advertising areas. Work which originally passed through the composing room could now be done by less skilled people and be performed off the premises. The number of trade unions in the industry has fallen from thirteen in 1950 to three today. The industry faces more intense competition than in 1950 from imports, in-plant printing, art and advertising studios, instant print shops and alternative modes of communications based on electronic devices.

The formation in 1964 of the NGA and its development over the next twenty-five years, at which point it was still a dominant force in the industry, can only be explained against this industrial revolution.

NOTES

1. See E. Howe and H.E. Waite, *The London Society of Compositors*, Cassell, 1948, and A.E. Musson, *The Typographical Association*, Oxford University Press, 1954.

2. These papers were: the *Daily Mirror*, *Daily Express*, *Daily Mail*, *Daily Herald*, the *News Chronicle*, the *Daily Telegraph*, the *Daily Sketch*, *The Times*, the *Guardian* and the *Financial Times*.

3. These papers were: the *News of the World*, the *Sunday Pictorial*, the *Sunday Dispatch*, the *Sunday Times*, the *Observer*, *Reynolds News*, the *Empire News*, the *Sunday Graphic*, the *Sunday Chronicle* and the *Sunday Express*.

4. See E. Howe and H.E. Waite, *The London Society of Compositors*, Cassell, 1948, Part II, Ch. XIII, and A.E. Musson, *The Typographical Society*, Oxford University Press, 1954, Ch. XI.

5. The letterpress unions also organised craftsmen in the photogravure process. The struggle for control of gravure by the letterpress and lithographic unions was settled in favour of the former in 1938. See A.E. Musson, *The Typographical Society*, Oxford University Press, 1954, Ch. XIX, pp. 437–9.

6. The centenary history of the Association of the Correctors of the Press was published in 1954. See T. Shane, *Passed for Press*, ACP, 1954. In the early 1950s the union introduced an apprenticeship entry system in addition to its examination system. However, the bulk of its intake of new members remained from the examination system.

7. For a detailed account of the first sixty years of this union see *Monotype Casters and Typefounders' Society, Diamond Jubilee, 1889–1949, Sixtieth Annual Report 1949*.

8. For a detailed account of the history of this union during its first 100 years existence (1848–1948), see S.C. Gillespie, *The Scottish Typographical Society*, Maclehose, 1953.

9. For a detailed account of the origins and development of this union from 1909 to 1959, see *Jubilee Souvenir of the National Union of Press Telegraphists, 1909–1959*, NUPT, London, 1959.

10. For fuller accounts of these events see J. Moran, *Natsopa: Seventy-five Years*, London, 1964, Ch. 6, pp. 51–6 and C.J. Bundock, *The National Union of Printing, Bookbinding and Paperworkers*, Oxford, 1959, Chs 25, 26, 27 and 30, especially pp. 246–9, 255–7 and 282–3

11. For the histories of these unions, see ibid.

12. For an account of the evolution of Slade, see *Society of Lithographic Artists, Designers, Engravers and Process Workers: A Record of Fifty Years, 1885–1935*, Slade, London, 1935.

13. For an account of the evolution and development of the ASLP from 1880 to 1930, see *The History and Progress of the Amalgamated Society of Lithographic Printers, 1880–1930*, ASLP, 1930.

14. For a fuller description of the events surrounding the formation of the P&KTF, see A.E. Musson, *The Typographical Association*, Oxford University Press, 1954, Ch. XII, pp. 285–99; J. Child, *Industrial Relations in the British Printing Industry*, Allen & Unwin, 1967, Ch. XII, pp. 194–7 and *Sixty Years of Service, 1901–1961*, Printing and Kindred Trades Federation, 1961. For a description of its work during the Second World War years, see J. Fletcher, *Team Work*, P&KTF, undated.

15. The four other unions in addition to those already mentioned were: the Pattern Card Members' Society (334 members); the Sign and Display Trade Union (449 members); the London Society of Music Engravers (40 members); and the Map and Chart Engineers Association (32 members).

16. For an account of the development of the British Federation of Master Printers, see E. Howe, *The British Federation of Master Printers, 1900–1950*, 1950.

17. In 1895 the Linotype Users' Association was formed as the first national organisation with the expressed purpose of negotiation with the TA a national agreement which would standardise working conditions throughout the provinces. It quickly established itself as the most important negotiating body in the provincial newspaper industry. In 1920 the Linotype Users' Association was reconstituted as the Newspaper Society and absorbed the other newspaper organisations.

18. In 1906 the LSC reached deadlock with the London Master Printers' Association (LMPA) in negotiations on overtime limits, night shifts and the monotype scale. At the same time the PMMTS and Natsopa became involved in a dispute with the London firm of Hampton's, which reacted by declaring themselves a non-union shop. The LSC told the LMPA that if Hampton's did not reinstate its members then there would be a ballot for a strike of all compositors in London. Alarmed at the prospect of a 'general strike' of London compositors, a group of daily newspaper owners approached the LSC and agreed to withdraw from the LMPA and conduct separate negotiations with the compositors on the understanding that the Society would not involve the daily newspapers in any dispute with the masters in the general printing industry. The Hampton's dispute thus gave birth to the NPA. For a fuller account, see E. Howe and H. Waite, *The London Society of Compositors*,

21

Cassell, London, 1954, Ch. XIX, pp. 316–17, and J. Child, *Industrial Relations in the British Printing Industry*, Allen & Unwin, 1967, Ch. XII, p. 202.

19. See *Report of a Court of Inquiry into the nature and circumstances of a dispute between the British Federation of Master Printers and the Printers and Kindred Trades Federation*, Cmnd 6912, HMSO, London, 1946; J. Child, *Industrial Relations in the British Printing Industry*, Allen & Unwin, 1967, Ch. XVIII, pp. 299–303, and A.E. Musson, *The Typographical Association*, Oxford University Press, 1954, Ch. XXIV, pp. 492–7.

20. See *Report of a Court of Inquiry into the causes and circumstances of a dispute between the London Master Printers' Association and the London Society of Compositors*, Cmnd 8074, HMSO, London, 1950.

21. ibid., p. 13, para. 48.

22. A Royal Commission on the Press had been appointed in 1947 and had reported in 1949 that 'the present degree of concentration of ownership in the Newspaper Press as a whole or in any important class of it is not so great as to prejudice the free expression of opinion or the accurate presentation of news or to be contrary to the best interests of the public'. See *Royal Commission on the Press: Report*, Cmnd 7700, HMSO, London, 1949. However, between 1949 and 1961, seventeen daily and Sunday newspapers ceased publication in London and the provinces and the ownership of those that remained became concentrated in fewer hands. Public concern about the state of the press was brought home by two events – the deaths of the long-respected *News Chronicle* and the *Star*, and the acquisition by Daily Mirror Newspapers Ltd of Odhams Press Ltd, which published the *Daily Herald* and the *People* as well as controlling a large number of periodicals. Against this background another Royal Commission on the Press was appointed in 1961 to inquire into the economic factors affecting the press generally. See *Report of the Royal Commission on the Press, 1961–62*, Cmnd 1811, HMSO, London, 1962. By the mid-1970s there was concern that economic difficulties facing national newspapers were lowering editorial standards in pursuit of increased circulation and that the solution of the industry's economic difficulties might require direct or indirect government action. This led in 1974 to the establishment of a third post Second World War Royal Commission on the Press, which produced an *Interim Report* (Cmnd 6433) in 1976 and a *Final Report* (Cmnd 6810, HMSO, 1977) in 1977.

23. In 1989 Rupert Murdoch owned *The Times, Sunday Times*, the *Sun*, the *News of the World* and *Today*.

24. See *Report of a Court of Inquiry into the problems caused by the introduction of web-offset machines in the printing industry and the problems arising from the introduction of other modern printing techniques and the arrangements which should be adopted within the industry for dealing with them*, Cmnd 3184, HMSO, London, 1967; and *Report of the Committee of Inquiry into the Dispute at Odhams (Watford) Ltd*, HMSO, London, 1974.

25. See C. Harding, 'Press room of the future – Now', *NGA Focus*, No. 3, September 1988.

26. For a less than objective analysis of the attitude of craft compositors in national newspapers towards women, see C. Cockburn, *Brothers: Male Dominance and*

Technological Change, Pluto Press, 1983. This book is based on ex-post hypothesis and contains numerous historical factual errors.

27. In 1962 the Monotype Casters and Typefounders' Society had merged with the NUPB&PW. In the following year the Pattern Card Makers' Society, a non-craft union, also merged with the Paperworkers.

28. The Scottish Typographical Association had changed its name to the Scottish Graphical Association in 1970.

29. In 1972 the Sign and Display Trades Union merged into Natsopa.

30. ATFEF had come into being in 1960. The advertising setting houses provide a service to the general printing trade and both national and provincial newspapers. The ad-setting firms were in membership of the BFMP and were concerned that when that body was in dispute with the unions they could not continue to supply the national newspapers. During the 1959 dispute the BFMP would not accept a separate agreement for ad-setters so these employers approached the LTS themselves and made a separate agreement, after which they formed the ATFEF. Not all ad-setting houses affiliated to ATFEF, but they paid the conditions established by the ATFEF agreement. However, during 1972 the NGA sought a 36 hour working week from the ad-setters. The ATFEF members were only prepared to offer a 37½ hour week spread over 12 months. However, the non-federated firms were prepared to concede the 36 hour week. These firms formed themselves into the Reproduction and Graphics Association and concluded an agreement which provided for the 37½ hour working week from October 1972 to October 1974 but, unlike the ATFEF agreement, accepted a 36 hour working week from the end of the agreement, i.e. November 1974.

31. See *National Council Report*, National Graphical Association, 1988, para 11, p. 19.

32. See *Report of Inquiry into Certain Trade Union Recruitment Activities*, Cmnd 7706 HMSO, London, 1979, and NGA Discussion Paper, *Work from Unrecognised Sources*, NGA, June 1978.

PART I

INTER-UNION RELATIONSHIPS

CHAPTER 2

THE FORMATION OF THE NGA: ITS CAUSES

In 1950 the printing craft unions were organised around particular jobs between and within the main printing processes of letterpress, lithography and photogravure. The non-craft printing unions organised across all the main printing techniques. The demarcation between the job boundaries of the unions was clear and relatively unchallenged. In addition there was a clear division between the interests of provincial and London-based print unions. The P&KTF coordinated the activities of its seventeen member unions and could resolve demarcation and/or organisational problems that arose between its affiliates. The stability of the situation was captured by Howe and Waite, who recorded in 1948, '. . . at the close of its century the LSC seems as far away from any form of amalgamation with either or both the TA or the ACP as it ever had been . . .'[1]

Within fifteen years of this observation, London and English provincial and Irish and Welsh compositors, readers and machine managers had done what they had long aspired to do but had nevertheless resisted, namely amalgamated into one union.[2] This union was the National Graphical Association.

A number of factors explain why the NGA came into being. First, in the 1950s and the early 1960s the printing industry experienced the implementation of technological developments which blurred, or threatened to blur, the clear, and relatively unchallenged, demarcation between jobs within and between the main printing processes. These developments centred around an expansion in the use of lithographic printing techniques at the expense of a relative and absolute decline in the use of the letterpress process. They presented a challenge to inter-craft and craft/non-craft union job control in the composing, process, foundry and printing departments.

27

Second, the 1950s and early 1960s saw the growth of substitute print products. These years witnessed the continued growth of miniature printing machines in local authorities, nationalised industries, the civil service and the financial sector. They were also years of accelerating growth in the imports of printed matter and in alternative outlets to newspapers and magazines for advertising, which was a major source of revenue from which newspapers at least covered their costs.

Third, the late 1950s and the early 1960s saw a relative decline of London as a printing centre. Work was lost during this period from the closure of printing establishments and from the merger of and the takeover of printing firms operating in London. Work was also being lost from the capital in that printing firms were relocating outside of London, often in response to financial incentives from central government.

Fourth, events surrounding the unions' demands for wage advances in 1955/6 illustrated that in the changing circumstances of the industry no one craft union could successfully prosecute an improvement in wages and conditions in isolation from other craft unions or non-craft unions. The employers had made it clear that with respect to improvements in employment conditions they would strongly resist conceding to one union more than they were prepared to grant to other unions. In 1959 the printing unions, for the first time since the end of the Second World War, presented a collective claim for an increase in wages and a reduction in hours of work. The same happened in the 1962 wages movement.

These four factors – technological change, increasing product market competition, the relative decline of London as a printing centre, and the need for collective approaches to the employers for improvements in employment conditions – meant that the letterpress and London-based craft unions became fearful of redundancy, of increasing employment insecurity, and of loss of control and influence in the industry to the litho craft unions and/or the non-craft unions. The craft unions, but the TA and LTS in particular, realised by the mid-1950s that the idea of any one union independently of the others successfully influencing and controlling the changes taking place in the industry was highly unlikely. They accepted that, if the craft unions were to influence the future development of the industry, they had to find common ground between each other and this would best be achieved by amalgamation. The union structure that had existed relatively unchallenged in the industry for nearly 120 years was now considered inappropriate for the changes taking place, and those anticipated to take place.

THE TECHNOLOGICAL CHANGE AND DEVELOPMENTS OF THE 1950s AND EARLY 1960s

During this period the traditional methods of reproducing the printed word were revolutionised. The pace of the introduction of change accelerated throughout the period. Not only were new machines produced, but completely new techniques were introduced. These were based on the lithographic process, and the traditional lines of demarcation between the unions not only changed but in many cases disappeared. The TA, the London typographical unions, the STA and the lithographic craft unions realised that to continue with the traditional lines of demarcation, based on processes of the past, would be impossible. In 1962 the LTS warned its members 'that the traditional ways of the letterpress compositor and machine manager, whilst they will continue for many years, are nonetheless on the way out'.[3] The rise of lithographic printing techniques at the expense of letterpress affected the dominance of the letterpress craft unions in the composing, process, foundry and printing departments. Hot metal composition was incompatible with lithographic techniques, whilst composition based on film or paper was incompatible with letterpress techniques. The growth of lithographic techniques increased the opportunities for employers to introduce composition based on film rather than type, which was controlled by unions other than the LTS, the TA and the STA.

In the mid to late 1950s some printing firms inclined to give preference to the litho process when buying new machinery, particularly in houses in which litho printing departments already existed. Technical developments in litho made it now more economical than the letterpress process for a great many kinds of work and especially for colour work of medium to long printing runs. Relatively higher speeds of production and relatively less standing time than on letterpress machines were now available with litho. The process had a number of attractions to magazine and periodical publishers. First, it offered the end of set-off pages which were previously an inhibition to editorial and advertising departments. Second, it could produce colour work of the highest quality, whilst third, since it needed merely a black image on an opaque or transparent background, it could accept not only type proofs or original art work but the output of all photosetting equipment.

29

The impact of the rise of lithography on the composing department was the gradual introduction of phototypesetting techniques (e.g. photosetter, protype and dalcopier), which were based on film, at the expense of hot metal mechanical composition techniques. In 1953 phototypesetting was being used in the industry only for experimental purposes. By 1960, however, it was well out of this stage and it was apparent that photocomposition would be widely used in the industry. Phototypesetting presented particular demarcation problems as it involved the use of film or paper instead of type. The LTS and the TA claimed that, in accordance with past custom of the trade, their members should not only operate the photocomposing keyboards and output units but should also make the corrections and do the make-up before handing over these material to other unions.

Slade, on the other hand, argued that typographical union members should handle jobs only up to the production of the undeveloped film or paper, after which all operations should be carried out by Slade and ASLP members. They contended that when an individual tapped the keyboard instead of tapping out type they tapped out pulses that became photographic film. Slade, and not LTS or TA, members should do the developing, the cutting up of film, the make-up of pages and the putting it down for plates. Photosetting was, claimed Slade, photography and had nothing to do with typography. They saw no point in allowing the typographical unions to handle a medium that had always been the preserve of Slade. They claimed that the handling of film was the exclusive right of litho unions and, because no metal type was involved, TA and LTS members forfeited their traditional rights of correction, make-up and imposition of their own composition.

The LTS and the TA argued that, if all that was left to them was the operation of the keyboard, they would lose nearly one-third of their respective memberships. The LTS General Secretary told his 1956 annual conference: 'Our argument has been, to put it in very simple language, that we claim to do with film whatever we would have done with hot metal . . .'[4] The following year he told delegates that Slade had been told that using a photographic composing machine was not just a question of preparing some film to paste-up somewhere in another department. It was a question of having knowledge of typography, all the background of make-up and layout which was a compositor's training and should remain his craft.[5] The TA and LTS both saw dangers to their members' future employment from the introduction of photocomposition techniques.

The introduction of lithographic techniques into the machine room caused tensions between the TA and the LTS on the one hand and the ASLP on the other, particularly over dry relief offset and sheet and web-fed offset. The LTS and the TA disputed the ASLP claim that dry relief offset (also referred to as letterpress offset) was a lithographic process, even though it was being introduced into litho departments and on litho machines converted for that purpose. This process was one in which plates in relief print onto an offset cylinder covered with an offset blanket and from the offset cylinder onto the sheet. The sheet to be printed did not make direct contact with the printing plates but received the image from the offset cylinder. The ASLP claimed that these machines should be manned by their members by virtue of their use of an offset cylinder and that the only way one could print from film was the litho process. The TA and the LTS, however, persisted in their view that, since printing on these machines was from deep-etch chrome-faced brass plates fitted round a cylinder inked up by rollers and the ink image was then transferred to a rubber blanket, which in turn transferred the image to the paper or other materials that might be being used, the process was letterpress. In short, the process was letterpress because the printing image came from a relief plate, and the depth of etching required was deeper than that required for half tone.

The web-offset used the lithographic offset process in connection with reel-fed machines. Lithographic printing, whether direct or offset, had been carried out on sheet-fed rotaries for many years. It had not previously been considered possible or practical to use web-fed machines in this field. However, by the late 1950s and early 1960s these technical problems had been overcome and web-fed machines were being installed in the provincial newspaper industry, often in association with film composition. The problem for the TA and the LTS was that letterpress employers, who employed the bulk of their members, might replace that process with litho machines, which the ASLP claimed were their preserve. The major problem arose in newspapers in the early 1960s with the introduction of web-offset into a number of weekly news offices. The printing of newspapers had traditionally belonged to the typographical unions and they were naturally concerned about the possible entry of ASLP into newspapers. They claimed the retention of newspaper production, notwithstanding the fact that in the commercial field web-offset belonged to the ASLP.

The 1950s saw a steady expansion in the photogravure side of the industry and the early 1960s saw coloured feature pages and advertisements produced by this process appearing in national newspapers. These were pre-printed in photogravure, re-reeled and then used on the newspaper rotary presses for the normal monochrome pages all kept in register by electronic control.

The 1950s also saw new developments in teletypesetters being introduced into newspaper offices. These led to demarcation problems between the typographical unions and the NUPT. These machines could be used as a teleprinter (NUPT areas) as well as a typesetter. Teletypesetting equipment consisted of a keyboard, not unlike a typewriter, and an attachment to a high-speed linotype and intertype machine. The keyboard or perforator punched tape, which, when fed into the attachment, operated the line-casting machine at a much greater speed than could be achieved by manual operation. The tape from the perforator could be used for transmission by wire to line-casting machines fitted with attachments installed in other offices or to machines in the same office. Since the teletypesetter could be used for the transmission of news, it was an innovation which could have had far-reaching effects.

In the early 1950s the machine was in use in London, the provinces and Scotland. By the late 1950s the TA and the LTS were concerned that newspaper employers were beginning to use keyboard perforators for transmitting not inside the office itself but to another town. By using the teletypesetter keyboard it was possible for a compositor in London to work a linotype machine in Manchester or vice versa. The LTS and the TA argued that the operation of keyboards was their work, but the NUPT contended with equal firmness that the keyboard was 'sending' equipment and belonged to its members. The NUPT argued that the job of the printer was to communicate facts and ideas through the printed word. The job of the telegraphist was to communicate the same facts and ideas in a way which made extreme distances negligible. The basis for almost all telegraphic systems was the punched tape, which was produced on a perforator and when passed through a transmitter sent electrical impulses to a receiver, which in turn operated a machine that reproduced the information at the distant end. The NUPT argued that for many years its members had produced punched tape to operate machines at a distant print location and such work was the main source of their livelihood. The letterpress compositors argued that their livelihood was the setting of type and they could not allow members of another union to perform such work from a distance or otherwise.

The introduction of web-offset into newspapers, the extension of teletypsetting and developments in photocomposition and offset printing all disturbed the previously clear job demarcations between the letterpress craft and the lithographic craft unions. Blurring was also caused in the previously clear distinction between the transmission of and the typesetting of text. The LTS was of the view that a lasting solution for these demarcation problems could only come from an amalgamation of unions. Prior to its successful merger with the TA in 1963, the LTS was involved in two unsuccessful merger attempts. The first was an attempt, together with the TA, in the late 1950s to merge six letterpress unions into one craft union.[6] In September 1959 the LTS withdrew from these amalgamation talks. In the following year it became involved in merger talks with the NUPB&PW, but these ended unsuccessfully in 1961.

The General Secretary of the TA told its 1963 Delegate Meeting that the pressure towards amalgamation was coming from developments in the technical field and the demarcation issues to which they were giving rise. He stressed that the biggest development and threat to TA members' future were the advances of lithography at the expense of letterpress.[7] The TA considered that the existing union set-up in the industry was inadequate to cope with the technical changes being implemented and believed that only by the amalgamation of the craft unions could the problems these changes presented to the various unions be overcome. Such mergers would give the craft unions some influence and control over the expansion or contraction of the labour force in each of the crafts according to the demands for the various skills and thereby reduce the fear of redundancy which lay behind inter-union differences over demarcation of tasks.

The TA 1953 Delegate Meeting approved a motion from the Newcastle branch 'that this conference, conscious of the changing circumstances and developments in the printing industry, is convinced that only through amalgamation of all craft unions can the interests of members of all the unions be safeguarded and enhanced and instructs the Executive Council to take action immediately towards this end.'[8] Before its successful merger with the LTS, the TA, responding to the blurring of demarcation lines in the industry, was involved in two unsuccessful merger attempts: in 1954 it had amalgamation talks with the PMMTS and Natsopa, and between 1956 and 1960 it was involved in the six letterpress craft union amalgamation attempt.

A further pressure on the TA and the LTS was the claims of Natsopa and the NUPB&PW that their members should now be able to undertake 'craft' work since the changes were blurring demarcation not only between crafts but between the tasks of craft and non-craft groups. The typographical unions feared that as letterpress declined they would have to cope with increasing redundancy amongst their members. The litho craft unions, on the other hand, would have to expand to cope with the new developments. If the litho craft unions could not meet the increased demand for labour there was the danger that employers might be tempted to meet the labour shortage by offering to up-grade the members of the non-craft unions. The litho and letterpress unions shared a common interest in ensuring control over the expansion of litho craft jobs. In examining the general factors as to why the NGA was formed, one cannot ignore the position of the non-craft unions, whose memberships in the 1950s were growing much faster than the letterpress craft unions. Over the period 1955–63 the total membership of the letterpress craft unions increased from 90,000 to 97,000 – an addition of some 8 per cent. The corresponding figures for the litho unions were an increase from 22,000 to 26,000 – an increase of about 18 per cent. The total combined membership of Natsopa and the NUPB&PW rose from 196,000 in 1955 to 216,000 in 1963, an increase of over 10 per cent.

THE GROWTH OF ALTERNATIVE PRODUCTS TO THE PRINT INDUSTRY

By the time of the formation of the NGA the printing industry had ceased to be the 'sheltered industry' it was in 1950.[9] In the period 1950–63 the industry experienced greater product market competition from three sources – the expansion of in-plant printing, increased import penetration, and the rise of competitive outlets to newspapers and magazines for advertising, particularly the advent of independent television in the mid-1950s. The first two sources were a threat to the general printing trade, whilst the third was a challenge to the newspaper and periodical sectors of the industry. Although this alternative 'general' printing industry was producing lower-quality products at a lower price than the conventional industry, the quality was more than adequate for customers' needs.

The increased competition to the printing industry in the 1950s was due to a continuing expanding demand for printed matter, which the industry could not meet. There were long delays in the completion of orders such that some customers began to place their orders abroad and others to establish their own in-plant printing capacity. The BFMP and the NS argued that they could not meet the expanding market requirements because of an acute shortage of labour in the industry as the craft unions would not agree adequate manpower concessions (for example, the admission of adult trainees) to enable them to obtain sufficient labour to meet the expanding demands of customers.

The TA and the LTS did not deny the 1950s' acute manpower shortage, but they had different views from the employers as to how the manpower gap might be bridged. They considered the solution lay in a better utilisation of existing craft labour, for example through the introduction of incentive schemes, and by the modification of trade practices, such as limitations on overtime and the period of notice necessary to transfer employees from one kind of machine to another. LTS and TA members viewed the growth of product market competition in the 1950s as a potential threat to employment security rather than an actual one. Although it represented a loss of work from the industry, there was still more than enough work to go round given the acute shortages of composing labour. There was a strong feeling amongst compositors and machine managers that these emerging alternative printing products would never be a real threat to their employment security. However, this was not the case with the national leadership of the LTS and TA, who sought to combat the actual and potential threat of this increased market competition to the industry and to their members' livelihoods.

Miniature Office Printing Machines

The main types of these machines were multigraph, rotaprint and multilith and they enabled organisations outside the industry to establish their own printing capacity rather than satisfy their printing requirements from the jobbing trade. From the end of the Second World War there was a constant increase in the introduction of miniature printing machines into the offices of local government, nationalised industries, banks, insurance companies and other private firms. The growth was the result of the industry being unable to cope with all the demands for its products and because the production of certain kinds of printing was cheaper on office offset machines than machines used in the printing industry for that class of work. In addition they had the advantage that their output was not subject to purchase tax like that from conventional printing machines. In 1959 the number of miniature office printing machines in use in the UK was about 15,000, of which 15 per cent were in organisations outside the printing industry. Some 5,000 were estimated to be in London.[10]

These office printing machines were taking bread and butter work from the letterpress jobbing printer. Although most of them were small offset litho, and were accepted internationally as the preserve of the litho unions (and the ASLP in particular), the LTS and the TA considered the loss of letterpress work made it important to insist they should control office printing machines and take every opportunity to gain this class of work. The ASLP on the other hand was concerned to protect its internationally agreed organisational rights with respect to small offset litho.

The LSC recognised, as early as 1948, the threat that miniature printing processes posed to the jobbing sector of the industry. In 1951 it established the Allied Process Department to organise and represent the interests of workers employed on miniature printing processes. In a further effort to increase membership awareness of the threat of these processes and to convince employers introducing them of its desire to embrace them within the industry, the LSC in 1953 held a miniature printing machine exhibition. The TA also attempted to organise office machine operators both within and outside the industry and like the LSC, and subsequently the LTS, it had little success in establishing organisation amongst these groups. Where organisation was achieved it was usually outside the printing industry and by non-print unions.

In the early 1950s both the LSC (subsequently the LTS) and the TA adopted the policy that the only practical way of tackling the threat of office printing machines was to bring them into the industry. This proved easier said than done. Within the industry, before the TA could make an accommodation with the employers over the manning of these machines, it needed to resolve the demarcation issue with ASLP. In December 1952 the two unions reached an accommodation over the manning of office printing machines. TA members were to be allowed to operate them on the condition they became associate members of the ASLP (see Chapter 3). Whilst this agreement enabled the printing craft unions to have some control over the operation of miniature printing machines in the printing industry, it did little to solve the real difficulty, namely the control of these machines in private and public organisations outside the industry.

Here the problems were that non-print unions claimed the right to recruit individuals operating office printing machines, that such operators so often had employment conditions more favourable than those in the general printing industry, and that there were distinct anti-trade union attitudes amongst the operators, many of whom were female. There was the added problem that the typographical unions had difficulty in finding out exactly where these machines existed. In local authorities, the attitude adopted by the LSC (subsequently the LTS) and the TA was to persuade councils not to install miniature printing machines but to have their printing work done in traditional printing shops. If persuasion failed, the unions tried to ensure that local authorities employed only printing union members on such machines. This policy brought conflicts with Nalgo (National and Local Government Officers), which was prepared to recruit any non-manual workers employed by a local authority. Attempts to resolve jurisdictional disputes with Nalgo via the P&KTF and the TUC failed. Nalgo kept firmly to its policy that it organised all 'Town Hall' staffs from the office boy to the town clerk, that its members were operating office printing machines because much of the work had been done previously on office duplicating machines, and that their members working these machines had more favourable terms and conditions of employment than existed in the general printing industry.

In private organisations the LTS and the TA clashed with the Clerical and Administrative Workers' Union (CAWU) over the union membership of miniature printing machines. The typographical unions were claiming not office machines that reproduced by means of stencils cut by typewriters but only those that produced work by orthodox letterpress and lithographic processes. They further argued that the installation of miniature printing machines was usually followed by the introduction of ancillary machines, such as wire-stitchers and guillotines, the effect of which was to take even more work from the printing trade. CAWU argued that the printing unions should devise a formula distinguishing the circumstances in which miniature printing machines were to be regarded as office machines to be operated by office staff and when they were to be seen as printing machines to be operated by print workers. The print unions were unable to agree an acceptable demarcation formula and continued, with little success, to pursue their own policies to organise workers on small printing machines.

The introduction of miniature printing machines into the industry and into organisations outside it in the 1950s and 1960s took work away from the letterpress side of the industry. They represented a significant challenge, along with technological change, to the dominance of the printing industry by the letterpress process and to the control in the industry exercised by the TA and the LTS. But for the period of full employment experienced by the industry in the 1950s and early 1960s a situation could have developed whereby a considerable number of letterpress operators were unemployed whilst lithographers were in short supply, but at the same time considerable numbers of newcomers were entering the industry. However, the leaderships of the typographical unions had difficulty in getting their members to appreciate this.

Increased Import Penetration

By the early 1960s the printing industry faced competition from imported print matter on a much larger scale than in 1950. The competition was coming from Holland, France, Germany, Japan, Poland and Finland. During the 1959 wage negotiations, the BFMP, in setting out the economic situation of the industry, referred to the loss of work arising from serious competition from Holland and Czechoslovakia. It pointed out that in 1958 the total value of book imports into the UK was some £3.7 million. From Holland alone the figure was £500,000, which was three times as much as in 1948. The employers stressed that with respect to Czechoslovakia the price of imported books printed there was below the basic cost of production in the UK. By 1957 the value of imports of books from this source was nearly £200,000. Technical and medical books were increasingly being set in Holland. Books with heavy setting were also being increasingly done abroad and British printers were finding it difficult to win back this work. Customers were telling the print employers that this work, most of which was produced by the letterpress process, was being lost on price.

The printing unions did not deny that the amount of work being done abroad was increasing. However, throughout the 1950s the TA and the LTS stressed that the employers were silent about the industry's success in print exports. They pointed out to employers that, for every piece of print being imported, between three and four were being exported by British printing firms. Although by the early 1960s the balance of trade in printing products was still in the UK's favour, it was smaller than in the 1950s and there was clear evidence that the industry had lost work to overseas producers. These competitive pressures were leading employers to consider ways of reducing their costs and, against a background of labour shortages, the introduction of new printing techniques offered many attractions.

Advertisement Outlets

Receipts from advertising were an important source of revenue for provincial and national newspapers, magazines and periodicals. The rate charged to advertisers was related to circulation. The higher the circulation of a newspaper or a magazine, the higher the rate that could be charged, and vice versa. In the early 1950s there was little competition to newspapers and magazines as outlets for advertisers. However, the introduction of commercial television in 1956 changed this and advertising in printed matter began to be lost to this medium.

Given the importance of advertising revenue to newspapers in covering their costs, the late 1950s and early 1960s meant attention had to be given to containing the costs of newspaper production. With increased competition for advertising, newspapers could no longer automatically increase advertising rates by an appropriate amount to cover increased production costs. At the same time, newspapers had to give consideration to offsetting lost advertising revenues by increasing their cover prices. To do this carried the danger of loss of circulation, which in turn made the paper less attractive to advertisers and reduced the possibility of increasing advertising rates. The same applied to magazines.

By the late 1950s the impact of competition from television for advertising was seen in the closure of periodicals and newspapers and/or their amalgamation. This trend accelerated in the early 1960s with the closure amongst others of the *News Chronicle*, the *Empire News*, the *Sunday Dispatch*, the *Bristol Evening World* and the *Birmingham Evening Dispatch*. By 1963 Glasgow was the only city outside London with two evening newspapers. All this contributed to a loss of work in newspapers, which were areas of letterpress dominance. Increases in costs of production could only intensify this trend. In provincial and London papers labour costs were the biggest factor in production costs. If the competitiveness of newspapers was to be re-established then employers were attracted to consider ways in which production costs might be reduced. The introduction of new production techniques based on lithographic processes was seen as a means of doing this. The employers told the unions in 1959:

We are fighting now in our joint interests against foreign competition, against expansion of customers' own printing, against transfers to non-traditional printing, against inroads made by television into the field of printed advertisements. And our one weapon is good printing at reasonable cost. . .[11]

THE DECLINE OF LONDON AS A PRINTING CENTRE

In the late 1950s the LTS began to face a problem of a loss of work for its members in London. The need to 'follow' this work into the provinces was an important factor in its decision to seek an amalgamation with the TA. The loss of work took the form of firms in London closing down, of firms transferring productive capacity from London into the provinces and of redundancy amongst its members stemming from takeovers of and mergers between firms within London.

Over the period 1958–62 companies with which the Society lost work included:

Hazel, Watson and Viney	– work transferred to its Slough and Bedford establishments
W. Speaght and Sons	– work transferred to the gravure process
George Reveirs	– work transferred to Southend
The Times	– discontinued its general trade printing office
Star and *News Chronicle*	– ceased publication
Sunday Graphic	– ceased publication
May and Wilbourne	– went into liquidation
Waterlow and Sons	– bank note department taken over by De La Rue
Mirror Group and Odhams	– a merger resulting in a fall-off in London work
Sunday Dispatch	– ceased publication
Chiswick Press	– transferred operations to the provinces
Abbey Press	– closure
Hendon Times	– closure of its machine department
Augenar Ltd	– transferred work to Yarmouth
Patina Press	– transferred work to the provinces
Dettoner and Piggot	– went into liquidation

Ramsayer Group	– bought printing firms in London, closed them down for sale on the property market, transferring such work as might be done to firms that were mainly controlled outside of London
Waterlows (Dagenham)	– closure
Martlet Press	– closure
Wickes & Andrews	– closure
Spencer Press	– closure
Merivale Press	– work transferred to the provinces
Islington Gazette	– closure
Potters Press	– closure of its jobbing department
Harrison and Sons	– closure of its central London establishment
Samuel Stephen	– redundancies from fall-off in work
IPC Group	– closure of the periodical printing department at Odhams Press, Long Acre, London

The LTS General Secretary told delegates to its 1963 annual conference that between 1958 and 1962 the number of members who had had to find jobs as a result of closures, mergers and removals from the Fairs List (i.e. firms which applied LTS terms and conditions to their employees) was 1,176 and that in addition from January to June 1963 a further fifteen firms had either closed or merged with other firms.[12] By 1963 London had lost the bulk of its photogravure work to Watford. The 1961 takeover battle for Odhams between Thomson Allied Newspapers and the Mirror Group, won by the latter, was of great concern to the LTS. When Odhams took over George Newnes and the Hulton Press, two fortnightly magazines ceased publication immediately and four monthlies and two weeklies were transferred from London to the provinces. The union feared that if the Mirror Group gained control of Odhams there would be further closures, since when the Mirror Group took over Amalgamated Press in 1959 eight weeklies, four monthlies and seven annuals ceased publication. Between 1958 and 1960, 135 periodicals printing in London either ceased publication or amalgamated. The majority had gone out of business. The LTS was also concerned about the possible effect of the takeover of Odhams by the Mirror Group on the *Daily Herald* and the *Sunday People*, since a successful bid would have brought eight newspapers under the control of that organisation.[13] Following the Mirror Group's takeover of Odhams, the *Women's Illustrated* was merged with *Woman* and *Woman's Day* with *Woman's Own* and a number of LTS members were declared redundant, although others were redeployed. During 1962 the Mirror Group transferred more existing work from London to the provinces.

Employers justified their ending of work in London and/or transferring it to the provinces on the grounds that production costs in London were some 40 per cent above those in the provinces and that manning levels were higher on machines in London than in the provinces. These higher costs were attributed to alleged excessive overtime, staffing and working practices in London relative to the provinces. The LTS General Secretary warned its 1962 annual conference that 'half nights and fat overtime are as much contributory factors to work going out of London as anything'. In early 1963 the Mirror Group (now the International Publishing Corporation) presented a memorandum to the P&KTF entitled 'Factors Contributing to High London Printing Costs'. It sought discussions with the unions on this document, stressing that such talks were crucial as the objective was to jointly agree economies that would allow, as far as IPC was concerned, London to survive as a print centre. By the time of the formation of the NGA these talks had not been concluded. The IPC's plans for the survival of London as a major print centre included the introduction of web-offset techniques, in place of letterpress, for the production of many of its periodicals, re-equipping some existing letterpress factories, the withdrawal of periodical and general printing from Odham's central London factory and a smaller workforce. The whole plan, the company argued, represented an effort, with trade union cooperation, to reverse the trend away from London in periodical and general printing. However, this did not prevent IPC in 1963, whilst these talks were proceeding, from transferring one of its publications (*Amateur Gardening*) from London to Aldershot on the grounds of high London printing costs.

The problems of closures and takeovers in national newspapers in 1960 came as a shock to the LTS and other printing unions. The threat of possible further closures led the government to establish a Royal Commission on the Press in February 1961 'to examine the economic and financial factors affecting the production and sales of newspapers, magazines and other periodicals in the UK'. In 1963 the NPA presented the P&KTF with a memorandum entitled 'Efficiency of Production' setting out how it envisaged employment security in national newspapers in London could be improved. It proposed a smaller and higher-paid labour force, 'realistic' staffing, a reduction in the number of wage categories, the basic wage to be related more closely to take-home pay, a reduction in casual working, provision for compensation for redundancy and a sickness scheme. Discussions between the LTS and the NPA over this document were still going on at the time of the formation of the NGA (see Chapter 15). The implementation of these measures would have meant a further loss of work to LTS members but the NPA considered them necessary if national newspapers were to continue to be produced in London on a significant scale.

As the number of firms leaving London continued to increase the LTS frequently warned its members that their labour market position had changed radically from the halcyon days of full employment and that for the first time since 1945 it was necessary to speak somewhat grimly of the prospects for the future. In the short run, the LTS was able to minimise the effects of the loss of printing work in London by placing affected members in alternative jobs. However, this policy could not be sustained in the longer run. Its members would eventually need 'to follow the work' from London into the provinces. It needed to gain a stake in the provinces where other print unions had a considerable influence. The LTS needed to make an accommodation with one of these unions. The obvious one was the TA. The need to expand from London was spelt out by its General Secretary to its 1963 annual conference,

> I referred yesterday to one chapel father who wrote in asking for an assurance that the wall built around London will be maintained to keep people out. My reply was that we will be anxious to get out ourselves and there is a danger that the wall might be used to keep us in, and indeed it would be used to keep us in if we did not have the right to move out which amalgamation could give us.[14]

COLLECTIVE APPROACHES TO IMPROVED EMPLOYMENT CONDITIONS

By 1956 both the TA and the LTS had realised that the possibility of their advancing the wage interests of their members independently of other craft and non-craft print unions was less likely than in the

43

previous decade.[15] Since the end of the Second World War the BFMP and the NS had urged the unions to approach them on a collective basis with respect to wages claims rather than to submit wide-ranging and unrelated claims, the result of which was simply that a settlement with one union became the basis of a claim by another.

By the mid-1950s the employers had become determined that they would concede to one union only what they were prepared to concede to all. Both the TA and the LTS accepted the desirability of a wage structure for the industry covering London/provincial craft differentials and craft/non-craft relativities, but given the multiplicity of union interests the problem was the practicalities of devising such a structure. Both in 1951 and in 1956 the industry had arrived at a form of wage structure somewhat fortuitously from separate negotiations by various unions or groups of unions, often with conflicting claims. However, on both these occasions it had been the LSC and LTS respectively that had been the leaders, and previous settlements with other unions were adjusted in the light of the London settlement. However post-1956 saw the print unions taking positive steps to arrive at a mechanism of agreeing a wage structure amongst themselves before entering negotiations again with the employers. A factor in the decision of the TA and the LTS in 1956 to try and bring six letterpress craft unions together in an amalgamation was their realisation that if a coordinated approach to wages advance was to be achieved then the number of trade unions in the industry needed to be reduced.

In 1919 a series of National Wage Basis Agreements established minimum rates for craftsmen in London at 12½p higher than for similar craftsmen in provincial grade 1 towns. When wage reductions took place in the early 1920s, the London compositors did not suffer to the same extent as those in the provinces, with the result that the differential increased to 57½p per week. The NSES also secured better terms for its members in the provinces, thereby disturbing provincial craft parity. The TA pledged itself to restore the 1919 relativities at the earliest opportunity. However, from 1923 to 1940 there was no alteration in the minimum craftsmen's rate throughout the industry. During the war and up to 1946 wage claims were presented to employers on behalf of all printing unions by the P&KTF and settlements took the form of flat-rate wage increases for all groups in the industry.

In 1947 the BFMP and the NS received a series of claims for wage increases and for changes to conditions of work from thirteen unions that were seeking to advance their own interests regardless of those of other unions. The claims varied in amount and character and had little or no relationship to one another. The TA claimed an increase of 45p a week plus any increase that might be given to other unions (namely, the LSC and the NSES) already enjoying better rates than the TA. The objective was to re-establish provincial craft parity and the London/provincial craft differential as in the 1919 agreements. In January 1948, simultaneously with the acceptance of a 45p per week increase by the TA, the LSC accepted an increase of 75p per week, which caused the London and provincial compositors' differential to become 87½p. When the employers conceded a 42½p increase to the NSES, the TA immediately presented a claim to re-establish provincial craft parity. The employers conceded this in November 1949, and the LSC immediately told the employers it would be making a new wage demand to restore the London/provincial percentage differential to that established by the 1948 agreement. However, it did not make this claim until April 1950; following an unsatisfactory offer from the employers and the National Arbitration Tribunal (NAT), its members undertook industrial action. The dispute was referred to a Court of Inquiry, which reported in October 1950.[16]

The Court's report provided the basis for an agreement between the LSC and the LMPA in which a £7.75 per week basic London craft rate was established, a cost-of-living bonus based on movements in the Index of Retail Prices introduced, and the union made concessions on the supply of craft labour and a stabilisation period of five years. It was clear this London settlement could not remain in isolation. It became the basis for separate settlements with the other unions. The TA and the other letterpress craft unions accepted weekly increases of 57½p for London craftsmen, 62½p for provincial craftsmen and 50p for non-craft workers. The ASLP also signed a similar agreement. By 1951, from separate negotiations in which various unions or groups of unions attempted to advance their interests independently of other unions, a wage structure for the industry had been achieved.

The employers continued to argue that wage differentials could only be settled by a joint conference of both sides of the industry. The Court of Inquiry urged that a coordinated wage structure applicable to all grades in the industry be established. However, its suggestion that separate wage-negotiating committees of the Joint Industrial Council be established (a) for craftsmen only and (b) for semi-skilled and unskilled workers, and that the committees' decisions should not be subject to review by the Council as a whole, was naive. During the wage stabilisation period of 1951–5 there were no attempts to proceed along the lines suggested by the Court.

When the time came to review the 1951 wage agreements, union autonomy on wage issues still remained strong. In 1955 the P&KTF consulted its affiliates to see if a coordinated approach to the BFMP and the NS was possible. The LTS and the ACP preferred to pursue their own claims. Six unions, including the TA, agreed to participate in a collective effort and presented their claim to the employers in July 1955. The TA subsequently withdrew from this collective approach, but the ASLP joined it. In November 1955 the six unions agreed to accept increases of 92½p for craftsmen, 77½p for non-craft members, a cost-of-living bonus scheme, stabilisation for three years and arrangements for increases in the supply of labour to the industry. In January 1956 five unions' members accepted these terms, but ASLP members rejected them.

By January 1956 the separate negotiations between the LMPA and the LTS and the ACP had broken down. In February, LTS and ACP members were locked out and the Minister of Labour established a Court of Inquiry into the dispute.[17] The TA had also imposed sanctions on the employers but an initial decision by the Ministry of Labour to establish a Court of Inquiry was dropped when the TA agreed to resume negotiations as soon as the Court of Inquiry report into the London dispute was published. The TA was prepared to let the LTS be the pacemaker in advancing the craftsmen's rate. The Court recommended a London craft rate of £10.77½, a cost-of-living sliding scale bonus, three years' stabilisation and national machinery on a two-tier basis for the negotiation of wages and conditions in the industry.[18]

Following the Court's report, four craft unions (the LTS, TA, ASLP and ACP) came together and negotiated a final deal with the employers covering the London/provincial and the craft/non-craft differentials. The agreement provided *inter alia* for a London craft rate of £11, for a grade 1 provincial towns' rate of £10.27½, a cost-of-living bonus, stabilisation for three years and increases in the craft labour force. This settlement meant that the agreements made with the six unions in January 1956 needed adjustment. It was the old problem. A settlement with one union or group of unions became the basis of a claim by another union or group of unions. The January unions now requested craft parity, 87.5 per cent of the craft rate for semi-skilled operators and 85 per cent for general assistants. Craft parity was achieved, but difficulties arose with increases for non-craft employees. It was

September 1956 before negotiations for agreements to replace those expiring in November 1955 were finally completed.

The 1955/6 negotiations had taken a long time to complete and prominent amongst the reasons was the complicated union structure in the industry and the wide range of claims of the individual unions or groups of unions. The TA was now convinced that it was inconceivable that one union could pursue its own wages policy independently of that of other unions. It accepted that, if there was to be a stable relationship between the pay and conditions of craft and non-craft employees, then the claims put forward by individual unions would have to be coordinated. It considered this could be best achieved by amalgamations. The September 1956 issue of the *Typographical Circular*, in reviewing the 1955/6 wage negotiations, stated this view clearly:

> But if craft unions found it necessary to make common cause in order to secure basic wage rates commensurate with the skills of their members – which is, after all, their primary function – the question necessarily arises as to whether there are any longer cogent reasons for their continued existence as separate organisations. And that raises the further question as to whether multiplicity of unions is in the interests of the industry as a whole.[19]

The events surrounding the 1955/6 wage negotiations led the NUPB&PW to submit a motion to the 1956 P&KTF Administrative Council urging a meeting of representatives from each union to attempt to devise a wage structure. The LTS tabled an amendment favouring a two-tier wage structure, one for craft and one for non-craft. In April 1957 a set of proposals, which were largely the work of the LTS, were agreed whereby, before a wage claim was put to the BFMP and the NS to replace the 1956 agreements, there be a conference of all unions with craft members to discuss the amount to be claimed by these unions. There would be a conference of unions with non-craft members for the same purpose. A conference of all unions would then be held at which agreement would be reached on the percentage of the craft rate to be claimed by the non-craft unions. The negotiations between the employers and the craft and non-craft unions would then proceed side by side. There would be consultation and report on progress by both sections, with the P&KTF acting as the liaison between the unions.

Using this machinery, nine unions devised a coordinated wages and hours claim in 1959 to the BFMP and the Newspaper Society. They claimed a 40 hour working week and a 5.5 per cent increase in pay. Progress with this claim, the events leading up to the stoppage of work in June 1959, the strike itself and the eventual settlement are described in Chapter 12. However, the significance of the 1959 dispute from the point of view of the unions was its confirmation that the days of individual union action independently of the rest of the printing unions were over. It illustrated that a collective approach could be successful. In the 1956 negotiations the craft unions had tried acting together but it had not been completely successful. Between 1947 and 1951 individual union action had been even less successful. When the time came in 1962 to renegotiate the 1959 agreements, a collective approach was again undertaken.

By the 1960s the TA and the LTS accepted that the long tradition of tight union organisation which had made it possible for individual unions to do better on their own than they could do in association with others was over. Leap-frogging wage claims were now strongly resisted by the employers, who were now facing the unions with a common front. In preparing for the 1959 wage negotiations the BFMP and the NS stated in a letter to their members that they proposed to follow a joint policy and to aim to reach settlements with all unions at one time, and that they realised this would involve the responsibility to give support to any area or section of their membership which might be subjected to pressure from the unions. The employers wanted to keep the London and the provincial negotiations in step and not allow London to become the spearhead. The 1950 and 1956 disputes in London had forced the BFMP and the NS to make concessions to other unions which they would not otherwise have made. Twice in five years (1959 and 1962) ten unions had jointly negotiated with the employers improved employment conditions in the industry. This was not really as satisfactory, the LTS and the TA contended, as was one organisation.

The general trends and developments in the industry in the 1950s and early 1960s that led the LTS and the TA to merge to form the NGA have been reviewed. The typographical unions feared increased employment insecurity for their members as lithographic printing techniques advanced at the expense of letterpress. They were particularly fearful that letterpress houses would increasingly convert to litho techniques. The previously clear demarcation between litho and letterpress was blurred and there was the additional fear that employers might meet labour shortages in litho by upgrading existing assistants. The typographical unions needed to gain a foothold in litho. Technical developments also blurred the distinction between the transmission of text and pictures and the composition of text. In addition, the London-based unions, fearing the loss of work from London to the provinces, needed to gain a foothold in the provinces. As printing companies and newspapers experienced increasing competition from imports, the growth of in-plant printing and alternative outlets for advertisements, they saw the re-establishment of competitiveness coming from the introduction of new printing techniques. Newspapers, which had always been produced by letterpress techniques, were turning to the web-offset process, which was controlled by the litho unions which had no presence in newspaper production. These changes meant the trade union structure of the industry of 1950 was now no longer relevant. The implementation of new technology and the overcoming of fears of employment loss by the letterpress craft unions led those unions to realise that these problems would best be dealt with by amalgamation. Attempts to form one letterpress craft union began in 1956 but these broke down in 1961 and led the LTS and the TA to merge in 1963 in the hope that other letterpress craft unions would quickly join them. The November/December 1963 issue of the *Typographical Circular* remarked,

> The theme of amalgamation amongst the printing unions now seems as old as the hills. But little enough has been done about it. Now economic and technological trends make this not merely desirable but essential.
>
> The amalgamation of two unions with such long traditions of independence is achievement enough. What we must hope is that this will be but the beginning of a continuing movement towards a much wider amalgamation of unions in our industry.

NOTES

1. See E. Howe and H. Waite, *The London Society of Compositors: A Centenary History*, Cassell, 1948, Part III, Ch. XVII, p. 284.

2. For example, a conference had been held in April 1908 between representatives of the TA, LSC, PMMTS and the STA to consider the question of amalgamation. At this conference the principle was unanimously adopted 'that the societies should amalgamate into one association' and a constitutional framework was provisionally

agreed. However, attempts to form a 'Typographical Union' had failed by 1910. The TA desired genuine merger but the London unions and the STA wanted – though they did not say so – merely federation. The fundamental difference proved unbridgeable. See A.E. Musson, *The Typographical Association*, Oxford University Press, 1954, Part II, ch. XII, pp. 276–8.

3. See *The Changing Face of Print*, London Typographical Society, 1962, p. v.

4. See *1st Annual Conference Report*, London Typographical Society, 1956, p. 12.

5. See *2nd Annual Conference Report*, London Typographical Society, 1957, p. 6.

6. This was known as the 'six union movement' and included the LTS, the TA, the ACP, NUPT, NSES and the MCTS.

7. See *Delegate Meeting Report 1963*, Typographical Association, p. 45.

8. See *Delegate Meeting Report 1953*, Typographical Association, p. 71.

9. In presenting a case to the BFMP in 1946 for the introduction of the 40 hour working week the spokesman for the unions had said, 'We believe the printing industry is in a favourable position to institute a forty hour working week as it is to a considerable extent a sheltered industry'. See *Typographical Circular*, March 1959, p. 43.

10. See *Typographical Circular*, March 1959, p. 43.

11. ibid., p. 47.

12. See *8th Annual Conference Report*, London Typographical Society, 1963, p. 59.

13. These were the *Daily Mirror, Sunday Pictorial, Women's Mirror, Daily Record and Mail, Sunday Mail, Daily Herald*, the *People* and the *Sporting Life*.

14. See *8th Annual Conference Report*, London Typographical Society, 1963, pp. 58–9.

15. See *Typographical Circular*, September 1956, p. 165.

16. See *Report of a Court of Inquiry into the causes and circumstances of a dispute between the London Master Printers' Association and the London Society of Compositors*, Cmnd 8074, HMSO, London, 1950.

17. See *Report of a Court of Inquiry into the causes and circumstances of disputes between the London Master Printers' Association and the London Typographical Society and the Association of the Correctors of the Press*, Cmnd 9717, HMSO, London, March 1956.

18. ibid., pp. 18–19, para. 70.

19. See *Typographical Circular*, September 1956, p. 165.

CHAPTER 3

THE FOUNDING UNIONS OF THE NGA: RELATIONSHIPS WITH OTHER PRINT UNIONS

THE LONDON SOCIETY OF COMPOSITORS

The Association of the Correctors of the Press (ACP)

The LSC faced competition from the Association of the Correctors of the Press (ACP) for the organisation of readers in London, which was defined as a 15 mile radius from the London General Post Office. The bulk of the ACP's 1,500 members had become readers through passing an entrance examination[1] and had previously been revisers or copyholders and as such members of Natsopa. This contrasted with LSC readers who had become readers as a result of their composing background.

There was a fundamental philosophical difference between the ACP and the LSC in their attitude towards reading. The LSC considered that an efficient reader required a composing room training and a familiarity with the ways of the compositor. Every compositor was a potential reader and reading was a craft. The ACP viewed reading as a profession and not an extension of the composing function. It admitted into membership only those who could display sufficient professional reading competence, as judged by passing the ACP's reading examination. Unlike the traditional apprenticeship system, which the ACP viewed as an artificial limitation on entry to the occupation, the examination system was open to all who had worked beside a reader for at least six continuous years. There were no restrictions on the numbers who could sit the examination or who could pass it. The ACP, unlike the LSC, was concerned not to restrict the supply of labour to the employer but to

51

uphold and enhance the professional standards of reading. Successful examination candidates, although automatically admitted to ACP membership, could not work on a national newspaper until they had completed three years' membership. Their first employment placing in the general printing trade had to be through the ACP's call system.[2]

In the late 1940s the ACP and the LSC attempted to reach agreement on their respective jurisdiction over readers working in the London area. The LSC proposed a division of reading boxes between the two societies, on the basis that the union having the majority of members in the box would control that particular office for all time, that all readers retain membership of their parent society but pay a weekly sum of 2½p to the union controlling the firm in which they worked, and that all readers employed in recognised houses at the time of the agreement continue to be so employed. The ACP claimed that the LSC should recognise it as controlling all readers in London, that reader-compositors should be permitted to be members of the LSC, but that LSC members over the age of 55 should be allowed to become members of the ACP without having to pass its readers' examination. It also proposed that compositors offered jobs as full-time readers in the firms in which they were currently employed should be allowed to continue such employment for six months without an ACP card providing no ACP reader was available and that all other LSC members would have to apply for membership of the ACP before accepting work as a reader. Such applications were to be accepted only provided the LSC members passed the ACP examination and there were no unemployed ACP members. The LSC rejected these proposals and restated its policy that LSC compositors should be accepted as readers wherever offered such positions.

In 1952 the two unions returned to the question of their respective jurisdiction over readers in London. In May 1952 a census to see which offices were controlled by the ACP and which by the LSC showed ninety-eight offices to be under ACP control and sixty-seven under the LSC. In September 1953 the two unions signed an agreement concerning the organisation of readers in London. It was based on the principle that if one union was unable to fill a vacancy in an office under its control then the other union had the opportunity to supply the required labour.

Under the agreement the union control of the reading department was decided by which union had the preponderance of members as at May 1952 in that office. For this purpose those who were members of both unions were treated as LSC members. In offices where the majority of members of either union showed a substantial change lasting for at least twelve months then transfer of control from one union to the other, subject to mutual agreement, could take place. A joint consultative committee, established to develop closer working relationships between the unions, dealt with any problems arising from the operation of the agreement. The agreement worked well. It continued when the LTS was formed and lapsed only when the ACP transferred its engagements into the NGA in 1965.

In the early 1950s new techniques entering the industry began to cause demarcation problems between the LSC and other craft unions. To minimise these difficulties the LSC concluded three *Closer Working Agreements* designed to establish demarcation lines between itself and three craft unions in London – the PMMTS (1953), the NSES London Branch (1953) and the NUPT (1954).

The Printing Machine Managers Trade Society (PMMTS)

The LSC had amicable relationships with the PMMTS, although in the late 1940s and early 1950s the issue of job demarcations between their respective members began to emerge. The PMMTS, formed in 1839, organised machine managers in London. However, the demarcation problems were not extensive. The February 1953 Closer Working Agreement recognised as a basic principle that imposition was the work of the compositor. The LSC made no claim to the imposition of cylindrical plates and accepted the right of the machine manager to impose plates used for repetition work. The agreement recognised that where Honeycombe mountings and similar bases were used they were the work of the LSC but where bases were clamped on machines as a permanent fixture the work was of the PMMTS. In printing offices introducing plate-laying imposition operations the work was the LSC unless the bases were clamped on machines as a permanent fixture. The Closer Working Agreement operated smoothly and, within eighteen months of the signing of the agreement, the LSC and the PMMTS amalgamated.

The National Society of Electrotypers and Stereotypers (NSES)

In August 1953 the LSC concluded a Closer Working Agreement with the London branch of the NSES, whose members made letterpress plates in the foundry departments of newspapers, general printing departments and advertising houses. The agreement accepted as a basic principle that the mounting of plates was the work of the stereotyper and imposition that of the compositor. Guidelines were established for settling jurisdictional boundaries. These accepted that for the mounting of plates on Parker Boards or similar mounting bases, twelve pages and under was the work of the stereotyper but all such work involving over twelve pages that of the LSC. Another situation covered by the Closer Working Agreement was cornerstone mounting bases. Here it was recognised that where such bases were used for six pages and under the work was that of the stereotyper but anything over six pages was the work of LSC members. All unfolioed work was accepted to be that of the stereotyper but where the pages followed a definite scheme of imposition for the purposes of folding it was LSC work. The operation of the Closer Working Agreement was overseen by a joint committee.

The National Union of Press Telegraphists (NUPT)

A Closer Working Agreement between the LSC and the NUPT was concluded in January 1954. The NUPT, which had come into being on 1 October 1909,[3] had members employed in three areas – national newspapers, provincial newspapers and news agencies – transmitting and receiving text and pictures.[4] Many NUPT members did not operate in a conventional printing industry environment and had probably never seen a composing or machine room. Under the Closer Working Agreement all matters of mutual interest to the LSC and the NUPT, including issues affecting the industry in general, were to be the subject of joint consultation as to the action to be taken by the two unions. On matters affecting the particular interests of one union, before either laid claim to any new developments in the industry there was to be joint consultation and, until mutual agreement was reached, the process concerned was to be placed in 'quarantine' by both unions. To protect the mutual interests of the two unions, the agreement provided that both the LSC and the NUPT would claim, without prejudice to subsequent discussion, any developments regarding teletypesetting. A joint consultative committee supervised the agreement, which was general in character, and the two unions recognised they would have to meet periodically to review the agreement in the light of changed circumstances.

The Typographical Association (TA)

Relationships between the LSC and the TA were, to say the least, prickly and centred around three issues – the London/provincial craft differential, the movement of TA members into London and LSC members in to the provinces, and the movement of work into and out of London. As we saw in the last chapter, the LSC sought to maintain an appropriate London/provincial craft differential and was prepared to take industrial action to achieve this. Table 3.1 shows the London/provincial craft differential over the period 1919–51.

Table 3.1
London/provincial craft differential

	London rate	Provincial grade (grade I)	money differential	% differential
1919 agreements	£3.87½	£3.75	12½p	3.3
1922 wage reductions	£4.45	£3.87½	57½p	14.8
1948 TA agreement	£4.45	£4.32½	12½p	2.9
National Arbitration Tribunal award (London) 1948	£7.00	£6.12½	87½p	14.2
Employers' proposals (1948)	£7.00	£6.50	50p	7.6
1949 TA agreement	£7.00	£6.55	45p	6.8
1950 LSC/TA agreements	£7.75	£7.17½	57½p	7.4

TA members seeking employment in London experienced difficulties in obtaining LSC membership. Historically those who slipped through the net suffered harsh treatment from the LSC and the PMMTS. This had led in 1907 to the TA establishing a branch in London, but by agreement with the LSC in 1919 it was disbanded.[5] However, in 1920 the TA re-established the branch, which remained in existence until the formation of the NGA. Between 1949 and 1955 full branch membership fell from 470 to 442, whilst the branch secretary was over retiring age and was part time. The branch provided advice to members if any particular difficulties arose and acted as a useful liaison for TA members who came to London without following the recognised procedures.

Although the TA London branch was small in terms of numbers, its psychological impact was significant. It enabled the TA on appropriate occasions to argue it was a national union and that it could protect its members who came to London. However, in reality the branch had no effective industrial strength since TA members working in London could not have their own chapels and LSC membership was necessary under the 1919 agreement. On the other hand, it was a source of annoyance to the LSC, which felt its existence was unnecessary.

The LSC exclusion policy towards TA members was designed to prevent an influx into London of TA members competing with LSC members for work and thus being a downward pressure on wages. The LSC refused to recognise TA cards, insisted TA members gaining work in London joined the LSC and attempted to prevent TA members securing London situations.[6] The exclusionist policy operated despite a 1919 agreement between the two unions under which the London radius remained at 15 miles, the TA disbanded its London branch, the LSC abolished its Home Counties branches and TA/LSC members obtaining employment in the area of the other society were to become full members of the society in whose area they worked. In retaliation against the exclusion policy the TA told its branches to debar from membership LSC members whilst unemployed TA members existed.

In March 1950 the two unions met to discuss TA complaints against the LSC's exclusion policy. The LSC replied that it could not open its doors to new members – whether they came from the TA or were non-union. It stressed that this attitude was necessitated by the Society's peculiar position as a London union, the restricted geographical area in which its members worked, the high rates of benefit paid to members, and the need to strike a balance between membership of the LSC and the number of jobs available in London. The LSC also expressed concern that when organising 'non-union' houses it sometimes found TA members working in such offices. This usually arose from TA members responding to advertisements appearing in the national press for London jobs.

The TA considered that London was suffering an acute labour shortage and that the LSC fears of admitting TA members were invalid. They pointed out that the LSC admitted new members if only to cover loss of membership by natural wastage, e.g. superannuation, deaths, etc., and that some new entrants were non-unionists. The TA argued that the least the LSC might do was that, in taking in new members, priority be given to TA members over non-unionists. In reply to the LSC complaint that TA members took vacancies in non-union firms, it argued that in such cases they had received assurances that the office was an 'open shop' and therefore individual TA members did not feel they were wrong to accept employment in such houses.

The talks brought agreement concerning the admission of TA members into the LSC. TA members were to be admitted into LSC membership providing vacancies existed and the likelihood of unemployment was remote. TA members were not to answer advertised vacancies in London placed in the national press and all applications for admission to the LSC were to be made through a TA branch secretary. The TA agreed to issue a statement to all its members employed as compositors in London urging them to report to the LSC the office in which they were employed. Where the office was non-union the LSC agreed to organise it or alternatively to provide TA members with an LSC card and a job in a recognised office. After a date to be agreed, any TA member found working in a non-union office was to be reported to the TA and disciplinary action taken against them. Such individuals would be barred for all time from admission into membership of the LSC. The agreement also obliged any LSC members seeking work in a TA area to furnish a letter from the LSC to the appropriate TA branch secretary. In accepting these arrangements the LSC did not depart from its policy of replacing only members lost through natural wastage. The only change was that in implementing this policy TA members would be given priority of admission over non-unionists.

Although this agreement repaired relationships between the LSC and the TA over the latter's members taking employment in London, there was still tension between the two unions over the movement of printed matter into and out of London. These surfaced during the 1950 LSC–LMPA dispute when the TA refused an LSC request to 'black' work transferred from London to the provinces to circumvent the effects of the dispute. The LSC had, during the 1950 dispute, reimposed its ban on imported matter from the provinces which had been relaxed in the late 1940s. As a result of this relaxation, many firms in the provinces, and especially those with offices around the London perimeter and who were associates of firms in the capital, had increased their interchange of printed matter between London and the provinces. The TA claimed that 'blacking' would have a detrimental effect on the employment of its members, in that work might be removed from the provinces into non-union London houses. The LSC argued that it rigidly applied its rule on handling imported matter and if the TA was correct about an increase in the interchange of printed matter between London and the provinces this was through a desire by the LSC to achieve closer working than previously existed between the two unions.

The LSC anger at the TA's behaviour was seen in the June 1950 editorial of the LSC's journal:

> It may well be when our difficulties with the London Master Printers reach a successful conclusion that as a union we shall have to consider whether we can accept into membership members of a union that apparently is so reluctant to assist its colleagues when negotiating in a struggle for better conditions.

It went on to say that in future, in deciding on the movement of printed matter or on admitting new members, the LSC would be guided by self-interest and not by a desire to secure cooperation and closer working with the TA.[7]

The Formation of the London Typographical Society (LTS)

In December 1953 the Executive Committees of the PMMTS and the LSC agreed 'That we, the Joint Executives of the PMMTS and the LSC, recommend to our respective membership that we amalgamate into one craft union with recognition of the equal status of both organisations.[8] Amalgamation would extend to London the same uniting of the compositor and the machine manager as operated in the TA and the STA. The marriage was unusual in that it was to be based on 'recognition of the equal status of both organisations'. This was to remove fears PMMTS members might have that their interests would be swamped in the new union by LSC, whose membership was three and a half times greater than the PMMTS. In February 1954 amalgamation panels were established.

The rulebook of the London Typographical Society captured the 'equal status' principle in a number of ways. First, where the two unions had the same officer positions they were to be held on a dual basis and they would act jointly. Hence the LTS had joint Financial Secretaries and joint General Secretaries. On the retirement or the termination of office of one of the individuals the joint principle would cease. Second, the Executive Committee was to consist of equal numbers of former LSC members and former PMMTS members. Third, former members of the two unions would have their own separate quarterly delegate meetings. Fourth, the LTS was to have a policy-making annual conference at which there would be equal representation of former LSC members and former PMMTS members. The 'equality' principle operated throughout the LTS structure, except where it could not, for example in membership ballots. LSC members voted by 7,602 votes to 932 to merge with the PMMTS, whose members voted by 3,330 votes to 543 to amalgamate with the LSC. The LTS came into being in March 1955.

Why had this amalgamation taken place? Although there were favourable factors at work, in that the two unions' organisation and financial structures were practically the same, deeper forces were at work. The LSC had been particularly concerned at attempts in autumn 1953 by the TA, the PMMTS and Natsopa to merge. These three unions saw this merger not only solving immediate difficulties in the machine room over the transfer of the printing of the *Daily Sketch* (see below) but resolving longer-term craft and non-craft union difficulties over the manning of newspaper machine rooms throughout the country. The fear that a provincial craft union and a national non-craft union might gain footholds in London machine rooms and might then challenge the LSC in the composing room led the LSC to warn,

> if, however, one large union catering only for a section of the country were to amalgamate with another large union catering for the whole country including Scotland and covering London, then there could be – and possibly would be – repercussions of a most serious kind. Lines of demarcation have over the years been laid down with a reasonable degree of agreement and a clear division of labour. If, however, the situation which we envisage were to arise – of a large union catering for the provinces amalgamating with a national union covering London – then it is unthinkable that London would be prepared to stand by and watch changes being effected which might well affect the welfare and well-being of their members.[9]

The LSC feared that, if the London craft unions did not start to come together, the non-craft unions would claim jobs currently the preserve of craft unions on the basis that they should be open, via promotion, to everyone and not just journeymen. For the LSC to have a link with the PMMTS was natural. Its membership would not have entertained an amalgamation with a non-craft union. The existence of a sister craft union in London, a marriage with which would create a parallel organisation to the TA, enabled the LSC to present a logical justification to its members for a merger.

The events of 1953 surrounding the transfer of the printing of the *Daily Sketch* to the offices of the *News of the World* heightened PMMTS concerns as to its vulnerability to the behaviour of Natsopa in machine rooms.[10] The antagonism between the two unions over the manning of rotary presses went back to the turn of the century. Unlike the TA, the PMMTS did not have an agreement with Natsopa over filling vacancies in the machine room. However, it was party to an agreement made in 1918 with the NPA, whereby the manning of all printing presses was PMMTS work although it accepted that where Natsopa controlled the machine room, e.g. the *News of the World*, this would remain the position.

Although this agreement gave some stability to PMMTS and Natsopa relationships, there was often open conflict between them. Natsopa members were bitter they could not gain machine managers' jobs simply because they lacked an apprenticeship training which they regarded as largely irrelevant to managing rotary presses. The PMMTS resented Natsopa's control of certain houses and was concerned it could not supply the employers with sufficient labour given full employment in the industry. Natsopa members' aspirations, and the absence of any agreement between the two unions over the filling of machine manager vacancies, meant that there was the possibility the employers might collaborate with Natsopa to undermine PMMTS control by upgrading Natsopa machine assistants to fill vacancies.

PMMTS's fears of Natsopa surfaced in 1953 when Associated Newspapers announced the transfer of the printing of the *Daily Sketch*, on which the machine managers were PMMTS members, to the offices of the *News of the World*, where machine managers were Natsopa members. PMMTS argued that the *Daily Sketch* should continue to be printed by its members as they should be allowed to 'follow the jobs'. Natsopa rejected this claiming that the 'custom of the house' determined which union's members should print the *Daily Sketch* in its new offices. However, Natsopa was prepared to accept PMMTS's members continuing to print the *Daily Sketch* if they transferred to Natsopa membership.[11] The dispute illustrated the PMMTS's vulnerability if it remained a separate union and Natsopa persisted with its aggressive attitude.[12] Given its members' concerns about Natsopa, a link with the LSC was natural.

THE LONDON TYPOGRAPHICAL SOCIETY

Throughout its history the LTS found itself involved in work demarcation problems with nearly every printing union. It had amicable relations with the Monotype Casters and Typefounders' Society,[13] but in 1955 began discussions with that union over the control of the 'sortmaster machine'. The MCTS had some 900 members, of whom over 75 per cent were employed in London. The union had come into existence because the LSC and, initially the TA, refused to organise casters on monotype machines. However, by 1950 the majority of type casters in the provinces were in the TA.

The LTS considered the 'sortmaster' machine to be auxiliary to the compositors' work. The MCTS rejected this view but, following P&KTF intervention, the two unions reached a demarcation agreement whereby the machine was to be at the disposal of both unions' members. However the production of mounting bases other than normally produced by members of the MCTS was to be LTS work in offices where no members of the NSES existed.

The National Union of Press Telegraphists

Relationships with NUPT centred around which union should control the use of the teletypesetter. Between 1955 and the formation of the NGA the two unions were unable to reach an agreement on this issue but, while negotiations continued, arrangements concerning the operation of the teletypesetters' perforator unit were dealt with by house agreements. The LTS concluded agreements with Bemrose, *The Times* and many other newspapers, in all of which their members operated the perforator. However, in the *Guardian* operation was on a shared basis, agreed mutually so as to avoid redundancy for press telegraphists. The *Guardian* was the only establishment in which all the perforators were not handled by the LTS.

Electrotypers and Stereotypers

In the late 1950s a number of rotary machines using rubber plates were introduced into the industry and led to demarcation problems between the LTS and the NSES. In cases where these machines had mounting plates on a spare cylinder, the NSES claimed the work. Although the

LTS challenged this view, agreement was reached between the two unions under which the rights of LTS machine managers to lay down plates on a spare cylinder were recognised.

The Typographical Association

Relationships between TA machine managers and the LTS (machine department) were governed by the same reciprocity agreement as had existed between the PMMTS and the TA. Under this agreement any members seeking or obtaining employment in towns within the area of either union had to present their credentials to the secretary of the society in that area. Reciprocity members were entitled to either unemployment benefit or strike allowance under the rules of their parent association, which refunded such payments to the reciprocating society. Any members of a reciprocating society working in the area of another society became associate members of the adopted society but continued to have full membership rights in their parent society. Associate members received all the privileges of membership of the adopted society and were subject to the industrial control of the adopted society. Disagreements over the operation of the reciprocity agreement were dealt with by the P&KTF.

By the early 1960s some complications had arisen with the operation of the 1950 agreement over the admission of TA members into the LSC and vice versa. The two unions reviewed the workings of the agreement and changed it so that an LTS compositor seeking employment in the TA area had to seek employment through a TA branch. London compositors seeking employment in the provinces were now in the same position as TA compositors seeking work in London. Antagonism had built up in Home Counties' TA branches over the admission of LTS compositors, and it was hoped this would now be reduced. A further change, designed to avoid misunderstanding between the respective memberships, was for the union rejecting an application for membership to report to the applicant's union the reason for the rejection. These revised arrangements emphasised that, if a member of either union failed to comply with their provisions, the union in whose area employment was sought was relieved of any obligation to admit them to membership, and that any member seeking employment by direct application to a firm in the area of the other union was not to be admitted to that union.

Like the LSC, the LTS was concerned to maintain an appropriate

London/provincial craft differential. The stabilisation agreements of 1950/1 provided for flat-rate cost-of-living bonus increases to the basic rate. By the time the 1950/1 agreements terminated in November 1955 the cost-of-living bonus stood at £1.65 per week. Although these flat-rate increases left the money differential between London and provincial craftsmen unchanged at 57½p, the percentage differential fell from 7.4 to 6.2. In the 1955/6 wage negotiations the LTS sought to widen the differential again. This was an important factor in its decision to pursue these negotiations in isolation from other printing unions. In defense of its £12 per week basic rate for London craftsmen, the LTS again claimed that the 1948 NAT award had established a percentage differential of 17.7 per cent over TA members in grade 1 provincial towns. It told the Court of Inquiry into its 1956 wage dispute with the LMPA that 'the current offer of £9.75 to the TA would give the Society a basic rate of about £11.30 without considering the extra manpower "concessions" which the Society was making'.[14] The Court rejected the LTS argument that the differential between London and provincial craftsmen had a traditional percentage basis. In negotiations that followed the Court's report the London/provincial craft differential settled at 72½p, or 6.6 in percentage terms.

The Lithographic Craft Unions – ASLP and SLADE

During 1956, meetings involving the LTS, TA, STA, MCTS, ASLP and Slade[15] were held to discuss the photosetter. Following this, joint talks with BFMP resulted in an agreement to an experiment at McCorquodales where for a period of four months the photosetter was to be shared between Slade and the LTS. At the end of this trial period an agreement was reached on photocomposing demarcation problems between the lithographic unions and the typographical unions. The operation of photocomposition keyboards and output units, correction of errors up to galley proof stage, and the make-up of pages and advertisements was to be typographical union work, i.e. the bulk of the hot metal compositor's work. The insertion of half tones and illustrations was to be the work of Slade members. The control of imposition from photocomposition remained to be negotiated. The formula, endorsed by the BFMP, ensured the avoidance of large-scale inter-union disputes over claims to control photosetting.

In 1960 the typographical unions and Slade also agreed a demarcation formula covering the protype machine, whereby if the machine was installed in a composing department it would be LTS work but if installed in a studio it would be the preserve of Slade. Similar agreements were made between the two unions with respect to three other small photosetting devices – filmtype, typro-units and the varityper-headliners. In 1961 the LTS and Slade agreed a demarcation formula for the operation of the dalcopier. Where the machine was used for proofing purposes it came under the control of the LTS, but where negatives, positives and bromides were required it was the work of Slade members.

The LTS disputed with ASLP[16] that dry relief offset machines were a lithographic process. It considered control of these machines should be shared until a demarcation agreement could be worked out. The ASLP rejected this view, claiming the machines in their entirety, and stated that if LTS were concerned about possible redundancies this could be handled by LTS machine managers taking ASLP membership. Eventually the two unions reached agreement over the manning of dry relief offset machines on a shared basis. Where the machines were installed in a letterpress house converting to lithographic techniques they were to be operated by LTS members, but where installed in a litho house staffing was to be by ASLP members. Where such machines were introduced into mixed houses they were to be operated alternately by members of the ASLP and LTS, i.e. the first machine ASLP, the second machine LTS, and from then on in strict rotation.

The National Union of Printing, Bookbinding and Paperworkers (NUPB&PW)

Differences existed between the LTS and the Printing Machine Branch of the Paperworkers' union over certain issues.[17] In May 1957 the two unions reached an agreement over the manning of composing presses other than slipgalley proofing presses, which were recognised as the work of the LTS. Its objective was to promote closer working relationships between the two unions whilst conserving their respective interests. Under the agreement, where a PMB member was employed compositors were not to pull more than six proofs. Where no PMB members were employed or available, compositors were required to proof.

In machine rooms the LTS and the PMB operated an 'associate agreement' whereby members of either union could be employed on printing machines claimed by each other, on the condition that the operating society had no members available for such work at that particular time. In 1957 the PMB requested changes to the agreement so that both unions exercised equal control over small cylinder machines up to demy size. The LTS would not agree, claiming it would represent encroachment on a field traditionally covered by its members, a position which had been confirmed by a decision of a P&KTF Arbitration Board of 1931.[18] When accommodation could not be reached, the PMB gave notice to terminate the agreement, fearing its members would be adversely affected by the growing tendency of some employers to replace platen machines with small cylinder machines.

The NUPB&PW requested that the matter be referred to arbitration by the P&KTF. In December 1962 the P&KTF ruled in favour of the LTS, despite the fact that the 1931 agreement had not been observed and several PMB members were currently working machines which, under the 1931 agreement, belonged to LTS members.[19] However, the award urged the parties to draw up a new associate agreement to provide for associate membership status of the LTS for PMB members who at the date of the 1962 award were employed on machines that under the 1931 agreement belonged to the LTS. It also awarded that PMB members currently operating these machines be allowed to continue to do so and that if any machines which belonged to the PMB were replaced by small cylinder machines then PMB members be allowed to operate them. However, when these PMB members ceased employment on these replacement machines, the manning was to revert back to the LTS.

When the award was rejected by the Paperworkers, the TUC invited both unions to talks and after a lengthy session it was agreed that an associate agreement as suggested in the 1962 award should be made. The LTS agreed to amend the terms of the award to cover men working small cylinder machines that had replaced platens so that they could seek work elsewhere on similar machines provided they held an associate card.

THE TYPOGRAPHICAL ASSOCIATION

The Association of the Correctors of the Press

The TA's post Second World War relationships with the ACP were amicable. Although the ACP operated an exclusionist policy against provincial readers seeking employment in London, the TA custom and practice was to admit into membership, free of any entrance fees, any applicants who could show they were members of the ACP. This arrangement worked well until the early 1960s when the TA discovered that some individuals who had not served an apprenticeship, and who on those grounds had been refused admission to the TA, were obtaining membership of the ACP by taking that union's examination and then applying to a TA branch for TA membership. To overcome the problem, the TA and the ACP agreed that there should be a period of two years' London qualification before ACP members were automatically accepted into TA membership. However, the two unions also agreed that 'special cases' could be accepted and that the qualification criteria should not operate as an automatic embargo on all applicants.

The Monotype Casters and Typefounders' Society (MCTS)

TA relationships were amicable with the MCTS despite this union insisting it was national and did not accept the TA's claim to represent provincial caster operators. In 1959 the two unions agreed that no dual members of both unions could resign or drop their membership of the MCTS when employed as caster operators in London or the provinces. The Monotype Casters' Union occasionally complained to the TA that pressure was being brought to bear on its members working in the provinces to resign and join the TA. In 1960 the TA assured the MCTS that such pressure was no part of TA policy and advised its branches that no pressure was to be put upon members of the MCTS to resign from that union.

Press Telegraphists

Musson, reviewing the TA's relationship with print unions in the inter-war years, remarked that if teletypesetting developed it would almost certainly cause serious inter-union disputes. This happened in the 1950s and led to demarcation problems between the TA and the NUPT, in Scotland between the STA and the NUPT, and in London between the LSC/LTS and the NUPT. In 1954 the TA began talks with the Newspaper Society over the operation of teletypesetter (TTS) equipment, which some newspapers were hoping to introduce. Agreement in principle was reached in mid-1954 for the operation of 'single-office' installations of teletypesetting equipment. The trial period was to end on 31 December 1954, after which either party could re-open discussions with a view to reaching a firm agreement or an extension of the trial period. During this experimental period all perforators and casting units were manned by TA members on the condition they were not responsible for more than two casting units. Simultaneously a demarcation agreement between the TA and NUPT was struck on the basis of a 'standstill arrangement' until further experience with the equipment had been gained.

In 1955 the final terms of an interim agreement between the TA and the Newspaper Society covering conditions for the operation of single-office installations of teletypesetter equipment in provincial newspapers were agreed. It would operate for six months. Both the perforator and the casting unit would be operated by the TA only. In February 1957 the TA and the Newspaper Society accepted that the interim agreement should continue, subject to three months' notice by either party. However, the main clash between the TA and the NUPT was over the operation of teletypesetting keyboards. Both unions, with equal firmness, claimed it was the work of their members. Discussions between the two unions were along the lines that TA and NUPT members might hold dual cards or that associate membership of the TA be granted to allow telegraphists to operate keyboards on a 50/50 basis with TA members.

At the end of 1958 the two unions issued a Joint Declaration which permitted the transmission of news by teletypesetter between two provincial newspaper offices, namely that of the *Cumberland Evening News* at Carlisle to that of the *Workington Star*, a subsidiary of the *Cumberland News*. The agreement provided that two perforators at Carlisle be operated by TA members and that TTS equipment be maintained solely by NUPT members. The provisions related only to transmission between the two offices named and were without prejudice to any other teletypesetting situations that might arise. The Joint Declaration contained a number of principles. First, the NUPT and the TA would cooperate in the use of TTS for transmission of news only by mutual consent. Second, the two unions would support each other in measures necessary to avoid redundancy of members of either or both unions arising from the introduction of TTS for transmission of news.

Despite the Joint Declaration, the issue of principle between the two unions remained unresolved. The NUPT continued to insist that traditionally its members had transmitted news telegraphically and should operate TTS perforators when they were used for telegraphic transmission. The TA claimed that typesetting was the traditional work of its members and emphasised that perforators should be operated by its members. The unions had merely found an interim formula to allow transmission by TTS to proceed in the provinces but at the same time protect their members against possible redundancy.

In 1961 the *Manchester Guardian* became a national newspaper called the *Guardian*. This was welcomed by the TA as it meant the expansion of national newspapers. However, the paper's plan to introduce TTS to and from London caused difficulties between the LTS, the TA and the NUPT. Despite the desire of each union to safeguard the continued employment of its members, an agreement was reached with the *Guardian* over the matter. All three were satisfied it provided the necessary immediate and future protection. The agreement operated satisfactorily to all concerned.

The National Society of Electrotypers and Stereotypers

During the period 1948–64 the TA faced claims from the NSES that that union's members should imposition plates. The TA rejected this, claiming it was the work of the compositor. The TA discovered, especially in firms which had transferred out of London into the provinces, that stereotypers were doing this work. A number of meetings were held with the NSES on individual cases and normally a settlement acceptable to both sides was reached, usually on the basis that where NSES members by tradition and custom were engaged on the imposition of plates they should continue to do so. Otherwise it was TA work.

The 1960s saw the development of a variety of small moulding presses using rubber stereo plates. These presses were attractive to general printing firms which had no facilities for plate-making. While the P&KTF accepted in principle that this process belonged to the stereotyper, the difficulty of keeping track of its installations prompted the NSES to approach the TA to secure an understanding so that control over the situation could be exercised. In 1963 the TA and the NSES reached agreement under which rubber stereo plate production was to be craft work. However where the volume of production did not justify the employment of a full-time stereotyper the TA was responsible for such work, provided management cleared this in advance with the NSES. In such cases the TA member concerned became an associate member of the NSES.

Scotland and Ireland

The TA's relationships with the STA were based on a reciprocity agreement made in 1900.[20] However relations with the Dublin Typographical Provident Society, which refused to admit TA members seeking jobs in Dublin, were cool. For many years after the end of the Second World War some TA members in the Irish Republic, influenced by nationalist feelings, favoured breaking from the TA to form a purely Irish union. The TA suspected these activities were encouraged by the Dublin Typographical Provident Society. An attempt in 1952 by some TA members to conduct a ballot on a breakaway union failed when a number of Irish branches boycotted it.

The union's first counter to these unofficial moves was to authorise a tour of Irish branches by the General Secretary, after which the TA decided to ballot its Irish membership. In May 1953 the Irish membership were given the opportunity to vote in favour of (a) continuation of the present form of organisation whereby Irish provincial craftsmen were members of the TA, or (b) an Irish Typographical Union with headquarters in Ireland, separate and apart from the TA. The members voted by 1,106 to 324 to remain in the TA. This majority was not confined to Northern Ireland, as the greater part of TA members in the Irish Republic voted to stay with the TA. The July 1953 *Typographical Circular* commented that in effect Irish members had given priority to everyday industrial problems, being content to leave nationalist politics to the politicians.

The Lithographic Craft Unions – SLADE and ASLP

The TA's relationship with the ASLP centred around the organisation of office printing machines, the development of dry lithography, the expansion of the lithographic printing process at the expense of letterpress and the introduction of web-offset processes into newspapers. In 1951 the BFMP sought an agreement with the TA for the manning of office machines installed in printing offices. The TA felt it could not make an agreement with the employers until it had done so with the ASLP. In December 1952 the two unions reached an agreement whereby TA members could operate small litho office printing machines. It was based on TA members becoming associate members of the ASLP, but made it possible for employers to introduce small offset printing machines manned by TA members where no ASLP members were available.

This agreement for the manning of multilith, rotaprint and similar machines was based on three principles: first, that workers in charge of one or more office machines must be members of the appropriate craft union; second, that multilith, rotaprint and similar machines were the prerogative of the ASLP, which was responsible for negotiating manning and wages for those operating these machines; third, that where assistants were employed they must be members of the appropriate assistants' union. The agreement provided for associate membership of ASLP where it was unable to supply the labour. TA members operating small printing machines were to become associate members of the ASLP in its Multilith and Rotaprint Section. For each associate member the TA paid a weekly contribution of 2½p for men and 1p for women into the funds of the ASLP. Any associate member who was a TA member could become a full member of the M & R Section only upon resigning from the TA. Operators of small offset printing machines capable of multicolour work and who held craft status in their own union plus ASLP associate membership were eligible for full membership of the M & R Section. Either union could terminate the agreement by giving three months' notice.

Whilst this agreement provided for the manning of office machines in printing plants, it did little to solve the problem of controlling these machines outside the industry. However, it did simplify procedures within the industry and satisfied the ASLP desire to maintain jurisdiction for small offset litho machines.

Conscious of the threat to its members of the rise of litho at the expense of letterpress, the TA approached the ASLP for discussions. The outcome, in 1961, was an agreement known as the Retraining and Transfer of Membership Agreement, designed to safeguard the employment of members in an office where one process was declining by making provision for training in the expanding process and the transfer of members of one union to the other subject to no qualified members in that process being available to accept vacancies. The BFMP and the Newspaper Society accepted the principles embodied in the agreement and became signatories. Under the agreement, in establishments where expansion of printing by the lithographic process involved the contraction of printing by letterpress, photogravure or the aniline processes, or vice versa, the two unions, with the cooperation of the employers' organisations and the management at the establishment concerned, were to take all measures to avoid as far as possible members of either union becoming redundant as a result of the contraction of the process in which they were engaged. Measures to avoid the discharge of employees were to include the retraining of craftsmen from the declining process to the expanding process and the transfer of members of one union to the other. The period of retraining was normally to be three years, the wages of the 'retrainee' were not to be less at any stage than the minimum grade for the craft in which retraining was being given, and no craftsmen qualified in the process for which the member of the other union was being retrained were to be available for employment.

There were conditions attached to the transfer of members under the agreement. During the period of retraining, the union to which the trainee belonged paid to the other union an annual associate membership of £2.10. At the beginning of the retraining period, the qualified retrainee transferred union membership to the union within whose area their new process came. An ASLP member transferred to the TA under the agreement and who at the time of the transfer qualified for the ASLP superannuation benefit had to continue the necessary contributions to the ASLP to retain entitlement to the benefit. Members transferred from one union to the other were to have the membership of their first union credited for the purpose of qualifying for unemployment benefit in their new union.

In the early 1960s the introduction by the Heidelberg company of a rotary litho press attracted TA attention because of its potential as an alternative to letterpress. By substituting a flexible wrap-around plate for the normal litho plate, the machine could produce work by indirect letterpress. Furthermore, the attachment of a rubber blanket to the first cylinder and the use of a wrap-around plate on the second cylinder enabled conventional letterpress work to be produced. The machine was attractive to letterpress printers anxious to enter the litho field. The TA and the ASLP agreed that, where the machine was introduced into letterpress houses, consultations should take place with the ASLP branch secretary to establish the process into which the machine fell, and the head offices should be kept informed of arrangements made.

The introduction of the web-offset process in newspapers in the early 1960s caused considerable difficulties between the TA, STA and LTS on the one hand and the ASLP on the other. The first company to inform the TA of its intention to introduce the web-offset process was Q.B. (Newspaper Printers) of Colchester. In 1962 agreement was reached between the company, the TA and the ASLP by which TA members' employment at the company was protected. The introduction of web-offset saw two ASLP members recruited and some TA members transferred into membership of the ASLP. Similar arrangements for the introduction of the web-offset printing processes were agreed with the *Banbury Guardian* and Parrett and Neves of Chatham.

Web-offset was a printing process and composing room methods were not necessarily affected by its use. Although traditional composing methods continued initially at Colchester, Banbury and Chatham, the process lent itself to the use of photocomposing or justifying typewriters or a combination of both. When film-based composing techniques were introduced at Colchester and Banbury they remained under the control of TA members and there were no redundancies. Indeed, these two conditions were fundamental if employers wanted TA cooperation over the introduction of web-offset. By 1963 the introduction into weekly news offices of web-offset without an agreement or any consultation with the TA had happened in only two offices. These were the *Shrewsbury Chronicle*, to which TA members never returned after the 1959 dispute, and the *Welwyn Times*, which was a fully organised office until web-offset was introduced and was not reorganised until 1968/9. Although by mid-1962 the introduction of web-offset into newspapers was confined to weekly news offices, it was recognised that it was only a matter of time before it was introduced into provincial daily newspapers.

In trying to negotiate an agreement at Parrett and Neves similar to those at Banbury and Colchester, two factors emerged which were to change the TA's approach to the acceptance of the introduction of web-offset into newspapers. First, the introduction of ASLP members into the company would have caused TA redundancies. Second, the TA was dealing for the first time with an office where the web-offset process would be used solely for newspaper production. The ASLP initially proposed that the TA find alternative employment for its redundant members to make way for ASLP members, but subsequently proposed that the TA members concerned transfer to the ASLP.

By December 1962 the TA faced not only the development of web-offset in a manner which threatened redundancy to its members but also its spread into the daily newspaper field. It was apparent these trends would spread to London and Scotland. The TA, LTS and the STA formulated a common policy for an understanding with the ASLP over the introduction of web-offset into daily newspaper houses. Initially the ASLP indicated little interest in accommodating the typographical unions but ultimately it agreed to meet with them.

When the four unions met little progress was made. The ASLP insisted that the typographical unions concede jurisdiction over the process before it would consider any proposals. However, the ASLP agreed to consider proposals suggested by the typographical unions. First, the typographical unions were willing to give firm assurances that they had no intention to invade the traditional province of the ASLP in commercial printing. Second, newspaper production should remain the prerogative of the typographical unions, reflecting that lithography was but one element in web-offset and the practical difficulties associated with the entry of another union into newspaper production. Third, the typographical unions were prepared to establish an agreed definition of the newspaper field with the ASLP and to underwrite its position in regard to magazine and commercial printing.

Eventually the possibility of an agreed formula on the introduction of web-offset into newspapers emerged. However, in January 1963 the ASLP rejected the typographical unions' proposed formula under which purely newspaper offices would remain the prerogative of the typographical unions, but in commercial offices web-offset machines would be manned by ASLP members. In weekly newspaper houses where there was 'mixed production', a system of 'sharing' should be agreed. When in June 1963 ASLP rejected a second formula, the issue was referred to the P&KTF, but before it could consider the matter the ASLP referred the question to the TUC. By the time of the formation of the NGA, the Federation was still considering the matter.

These demarcation problems between the ASLP and the TA led to calls for amalgamation between the two unions. The TA Manchester branch moved a resolution to the TA 1963 Delegate Meeting: 'That this Triennial Delegate Meeting instructs the officers of our Association to approach the ASLP with a view to complete amalgamation of the two Associations into one grand organisation.'[21] It was argued that the ASLP was making inroads into processes traditionally belonging to the TA, that ASLP members were displacing TA members, and that the Retraining and Transfer of Membership Agreement was difficult to implement. Others argued that the TA was only seeking an amalgamation with the LTS to defend itself against the ASLP and this could be a misguided strategy if the ASLP's then merger talks with the Paper-workers were successful.[22] However the motion was referred to the Executive Council on a number of grounds, including that it would be impossible to approach the ASLP at such a late stage in the LTS/TA merger talks.

For most of the period 1948–63 there was little contact between the TA and Slade. This was due not to hostility, but simply that their paths seldom crossed. However, towards the latter part of the period demarcation problems between the two unions revolving around the introduction of electronic engraving machines and photocomposition began to arise. Nevertheless relationships remained good and were helped in that, although the TA accepted that some of its traditional work was now that of Slade, that union supported the principle that nobody from the two unions should suffer redundancy and was prepared to adjust demarcation lines with the TA to ensure this.

In 1958 the TA and Slade made an agreement over the introduction of electronic engraving machines into provincial newspaper offices that previously had no process departments. Slade was concerned about these machines because, in many cases, the newspapers had insufficient work to justify the full employment of a Slade member. Under the agreement where TA members in provincial newspapers were to take charge on a part-time basis of electronic engraving machines, the arrangement required the approval of Slade. The TA members were able to take up associate membership of Slade so that, when the production of blocks by electronic engraving machines increased to justify a full-time operator and thus a possible TA redundancy, TA members had the opportunity to transfer to Slade membership.

In 1958, after two years of negotiations, the ASLP, LTS, MCTS, STA, Slade and the TA agreed a photocomposition demarcation formula. The details of the agreement have been described above. However, between 1958 and 1961 photocomposition technology advanced rapidly and the early 1960s saw the advent of the linofilm machine, which was a radical departure from the traditional linotype machine. It comprised a keyboard on which tape was perforated, a second unit on which the composition was transmitted from tape to film, and third a correcting and a make-up and display unit. Post-1958 photocomposition developments put the demarcation formula under strain. Experience of the operation of photocomposition showed that the formula failed to meet a number of production requirements. In 1961 the unions met to consider TA proposals for modification to the

1958 formula. Revisions were agreed in 1962 and included a procedure for the transfer of members from one union to another.[23] The blurring of work demarcations between TA and Slade led to pressures from TA members for closer relationships with Slade to be established.

The National Union of Printing, Bookbinding and Paperworkers

Relationships between the TA and the PMB of the Paperworkers' Union over the period 1948–63 were governed by a Reciprocity Agreement. For many years the PMB had sought to include vertical miehle machines in the agreement so as to establish uniformity with that between itself and the LTS. Until the 1950s the TA opposed any extension of the scope of the agreement and insisted it be confined to platen machines. However, by the mid-1950s feelings had grown in the TA that little would be lost by allowing vertical miehle machines to be included in the Reciprocity Agreement. In April 1955 the agreement was widened to give effect to this.

The National Society of Operative Printers and Assistants (Natsopa)

In 1918 the TA and Natsopa had signed a 50/50 agreement over filling vacancies in newspapers. The operation of this agreement caused difficulties in the inter-war years and post Second World War period. The TA interpreted the agreement as meaning that, when no unemployed TA rotary machinemen were available, vacancies should be filled alternately by TA flat-bed minders and Natsopa members on a 50/50 basis. Natsopa considered the agreement meant equal opportunities and it was for employers to determine the filling of vacancies. There were similar difficulties within news reading departments concerning the promotion of Natsopa copyholders and revisers. This agreement, similar to that covering rotary machine rooms, had been made in 1936.

Over the period 1948–63 the shortage of newspaper rotary minders meant that under the 50/50 agreement many Natsopa members were promoted in daily newspapers. Natsopa opposed the introduction of TA flat-bed machine minders, whilst the employers were unwilling to place expensive machinery in the charge of TA new entrants with no rotary experience. With the TA normally unable to provide men for vacancies, about 95 per cent were going to Natsopa members. This was distasteful to TA craft feelings and demands were made for the strict observance of the agreement. Some members suggested a limited apprenticeship system be introduced in rotary newspaper departments to give the TA some chance of providing qualified minders. Natsopa opposed this. The TA was forced to accept the existing facts and tolerate larger numbers of Natsopa members becoming rotary machine minders.

The TA 1950 Delegate Meeting carried a motion 'that this Conference calls upon the EC to take the necessary steps to abrogate the Fifty-Fifty Agreement as applied to the TA rotary and reading departments in newspaper offices with Natsopa, such agreements being detrimental to the best interests of the TA membership in so far as the advantages of these agreements are all against TA members in general'. Those favouring the motion repeated the arguments outlined above.

Those opposing the motion stressed three problems with regard to the 50/50 agreements. First, there was a shortage of TA labour, in that there were few rotary minders or readers available who had served their time in a newspaper office. Second, there was the reluctance of newspaper employers to accept anyone other than people who had had experience in handling rotary machines. Third, there was the reluctance of TA members to accept opportunities open to them under the agreements.

In November 1950 the TA met Natsopa to discuss abrogation of the agreements. They pointed to the resentment in many branches to Natsopa's aggressive attitude and to a growing feeling that Natsopa sought to eliminate TA jobbing machinemen from access to newspaper rotary machines. Natsopa claimed that abrogation of the agreements would cause chaos. The TA was in a dilemma. On the one hand, there was the instruction of its delegate meeting. On the other, there was the likely state of affairs if the agreements were ended. Eventually the TA decided in 1952 to remit the issue to its 1953 Delegate Meeting for a more mature consideration and to seek the membership's approval of its decision not to implement the 1950 Delegate Meeting decision. In a ballot taken in February 1952, the membership voted by 18,437 to 4,566 votes to approve the executive's action.

At the 1953 Delegate Meeting the General Secretary defended the executive's action. He stressed that the agreements were confined to daily newspaper offices and that demand for abrogation was greatest in Manchester where the presence of national and Sunday newspapers made newspaper work lucrative and meant a queue of jobbing machinemen to take such work. However the Manchester situation did not apply in the rest of the country. Here the TA had difficulty in persuading members to take their share of vacancies. Whilst in Manchester the TA could fill every vacancy, the position elsewhere was the reverse and Natsopa could gain control of machine rooms. A problem was that no apprentices were permitted by the TA on newspaper rotary presses, whilst Natsopa assistants, some of whom had worked such presses for over twenty years, wanted upgrading. The General Secretary argued that the possibility of Natsopa agreeing to abrogate the 50/50 agreements was remote. A unilateral abrogation risked a period of intense rivalry with Natsopa, one result of which was the possibility of TA elimination from rotary press rooms. The delegates accepted the executive's action and rejected attempts by the Manchester branch to have the 1950 Delegate decision accepted forthwith.

The 1953 Delegate Meeting also rejected a motion seeking an amendment to the 50/50 agreement in the reading department. It was suggested that Natsopa members seeking reader positions should pass an examination set by the TA. This would prevent the senior copyholder being promoted rather than the best person for the job. The motion was defeated on the argument that Natsopa members had the right to promotion irrespective of TA members' willingness to fill reading room vacancies.

The 1957 Delegate Meeting also considered the 50/50 agreements. It rejected a motion proposing 'that the TA Executive Council consider the desirability of opening discussions with Natsopa on the question of the 50/50 Agreement with a view to terminating the present arrangement, and for the TA and the Newspaper Society to substitute an apprenticeship system, which would ultimately result in ending the inter-union friction which has been responsible in the past for so much unrest in news offices of the provincial press'. It was argued that the 50/50 agreements operated against the interests of the TA and perpetuated a system whereby the training of rotary minders was in the hands of Natsopa. The resolution sought acceptance of the principle of apprenticeships in newspaper machine rooms, that rotary minder jobs were those of TA members, that the TA choose the most favourable time for introducing an apprenticeship system, and that when it could supply adequate amounts of labour to rotary machines it consider withdrawal from the agreement.

The 50/50 agreements were again raised at the 1960 Delegate Meeting when it was proposed 'that negotiations be opened with a view to the ending of the 50/50 Agreement and the substitution therefore of recruitment by apprenticeship'. The EC argued that the termination of the 50/50 agreements was impractical. Natsopa would not agree to termination, or to the introduction of an apprenticeship system, whilst abrogation carried the risk of the elimination of the TA from rotary presses in certain daily newspaper offices. These arguments were repeated at the 1963 Delegate Meeting when it was proposed that, in the light of technological developments, the time for abrogation of the 50/50 agreements was clear. Whether the members liked them or not they were there and had to be honoured. Abrogation held too great a risk.

NOTES

1. In November 1950 the ACP concluded an agreement with the London Master Printers' Association which provided for increases in pay and an apprenticeship system for readers. This apprenticeship system and the examination system existed side by side until the provision of journeymen readers by way of apprenticeships was sufficient to meet the requirements of the industry. However the agreement stated clearly, 'It is not the intention that the Apprenticeship Scheme shall replace our normal method of recruitment'.

2. This practice was designed to prevent several new members rushing after one job and to protect them from being rejected by employers on the grounds that they were too inexperienced as readers.

3. For a detailed account of the origins and development of the NUPT from 1909 to 1959, see *Jubilee Souvenir of the National Union of Press Telegraphists*, NUPT, London, 1959.

4. In addition to transmitting and receiving text and pictures, NUPT members also transmit and receive information via the news agencies to betting shops and to television – for example, the football results and latest scores on the Saturday afternoon sports programmes of the BBC and ITV.

5. For a more comprehensive account of the events leading to the establishment of the London branch of the TA, see E. Howe and H.E. Waite, *The London Society of Compositors*, Cassell, 1948, Ch. XVII, pp. 272–82, and A.E. Musson, *The Typographical Association*, Oxford University Press, 1954, chs XII and XX, pp. 271–81 and 447–8.

6. The TA also sought the help of the TUC against this LSC policy, but a decision of a TUC Disputes Committee in October 1924 upheld the LSC policy 'in view of the large amount of unemployment that now exists amongst members of the LSC'.

7. See *London Typographical Circular*, June 1950, p. 6.

8. See *London Typographical Circular*, March 1954, p. 9.

9. See *London Typographical Circular*, January 1954.

10. See *Report of a Court of Inquiry into an apprehended dispute affecting the National Society of Operative Printers and Assistants, the Printing Machine Managers Trade Society, Associated Newspaper Ltd and the Newspaper Proprietors Association*, Cmnd 8931, HMSO, 1953, and J. Moran, *Natsopa, Seventy-five Years*, Heinemann, London, 1963, Ch. 14, pp. 110–13.

11. The PMMTS regarded this as a less than generous offer. Indeed, they told the Court of Inquiry into the dispute that 'to offer membership of Natsopa to craftsmen of thirty to forty years standing was not compatible with their self respect'. See *Court of Inquiry*, ibid., para. 50, p. 19.

12. The dispute between Natsopa and the PMMTS over the transfer of the printing of the *Daily Sketch* to the offices of the *News of the World* was eventually settled by the two unions agreeing that its printing in its new offices would be on a shared basis.

13. In 1962, the Monotype Casters and Typefounders' Society amalgamated with the NUPB&PW.

14. See *Report of a Court of Inquiry into the causes and circumstances of Disputes between the London Master Printers' Association and the London Typographical Society and the Association of the Correctors of the Press*, Cmnd 9717, HMSO, London, 1956, para. 44, p. 14.

15. The Society of Lithographic Artists, Designers, Engravers and Process Workers had been formed in 1885 and represented the interests of all craftsmen employed in the various processes by which the graphic image is produced as a printing medium. For an account of the evolution of Slade, see *Society of Lithographic Artists, Designers, Engravers and Process Workers: A Record of Fifty Years, 1885–1935*, Slade, London, 1935.

16. The Amalgamated Society of Lithographic Printers and Auxiliaries was formed in 1880. It was a national union with members in the Irish Republic. Its members operated lithographic machines to print not only on paper but also on tin. For an account of the evolution and development of the ASLP from 1880 to 1930, see *The History and Progress of the Amalgamated Society of Lithographic Printers, 1880–1930*, ASLP, 1930.

17. For a detailed account of the evolution and development of this union from its origins to the late 1950s, see C.J. Bundock, *The National Union of Printing, Bookbinding and Papermakers*, Oxford University Press, 1959.

18. See 'P&KTF Arbitration Decision: Manning of Small Cylinder Machines', *London Typographical Journal*, January 1963, p. 17.

19. ibid.

20. See A.E. Musson, *The Typographical Association*, Oxford University Press, 1954, Ch. XII, p. 272.

21. See *Report of the Delegate Meeting, Morecambe, 1963*, Typographical Association, p. 56.

22. In 1963 an agreement between the NUPB&PW and the ASLP involving the transfer of engagements from the latter to the former was put to their respective members. Although both sets of members voted in favour of 'The Alliance', the size

of the majority and the size of the turnout in the election did not meet the requirements of the 1913 Trade Union (Amalgamation) Act. The marriage, therefore, could not take place. Had it done so then the history of the NGA would have taken a very different course.

23. See *Typographical Circular*, March 1962, pp. 46–7.

CHAPTER 4

THE ACTUAL FORMATION OF
THE NGA

In the late 1950s and early 1960s the TA and the LSC/LTS, in response
to the blurring of boundaries between their interests and those of other
print unions, sought to establish new foundations for such relationships.
In addition to long-standing relationships based on reciprocity agreements,[1] there were attempts to build new understandings based on
closer working relationships,[2] demarcation formulas[3] and joint declara-
tions.[4]

The TA and the LSC/LTS saw these at best as 'holding' arrangements
and that new relationships of a lasting character could come only from
union amalgamations. The 1953 TA Delegate Meeting had accepted a
motion from the Newcastle branch,

> that this Conference, conscious of the changing circumstances
> and developments in the printing industry, is convinced that
> only through amalgamation of all craft unions can the interests
> of members of all unions be safeguarded and enhanced and
> instructs the Executive Council to take action immediately
> towards this end.[5]

Apart from the amalgamation of the LSC and the PMMTS in 1955 and
of the NUPB&PW and the MCTS in 1962, there were no print mergers
until the formation of the NGA in 1964. The period, however,
witnessed unsuccessful attempts. The LTS was involved in two abortive
attempts, first with five other craft unions between 1956 and 1960, and
then with NUPB&PW between 1960 and 1962. The TA was also
involved in two unsuccessful merger attempts. In 1954 a proposed

marriage with the PMMTS and Natsopa failed, whilst an attempt to merge with five other craft unions, which started in 1956, ended in failure in 1961. Within five years of the formation of the NGA, four other unions – the ACP, the NUPT, the NSES and the ASLP – had joined.

THE PROPOSED TA/PMMTS/NATSOPA AMALGAMATION, 1953–4

In 1953 the transfer of the printing of the *Daily Sketch* to the premises of the *News of the World* brought the London printing industry to the brink of conflagration. The *Sketch* had been printed on machines in charge of the PMMTS, which expected not only to 'follow the job' when the paper transferred but that any replacements or additions to the machine staff would be by its members. Since 1912 the *News of the World* machine room had been staffed by Natsopa minders and assistants who claimed that the 'custom of the house' should prevail and that Natsopa should be solely responsible for the printing of the *Daily Sketch* in its new premises.

For weeks the possibility of a major dispute between the two unions existed. In July 1953 a Court of Inquiry was appointed to inquire into the dispute. Although its findings gave some satisfaction to both unions, neither was entirely satisfied. Bad feeling continued despite the Court's recommendation of 'a shared house' being implemented. A threat that the dispute might flare up again and affect the whole London printing industry could not be discounted.

Against this background the TA General Secretary Harry Riding approached Mr P. Astins (General Secretary of the PMMTS) and Mr R.W. Briginshaw (General Secretary of Nasopa) and suggested an amalgamation of their three unions. He argued that such a merger would settle the immediate London difficulties and the long-standing differences between the machine managers' unions and Natsopa over the manning of newspaper machine rooms throughout the country. They agreed that amalgamation was practical and desirable. Each agreed to report their conversations to their executives and to keep in touch.

The October 1953 meeting of the TA Executive Council agreed that the TA should be represented at any official meetings to explore the possibility of an amalgamation between the three unions. The Natsopa executive also approved the principle of amalgamation. A meeting was arranged for 25 November 1953, but the PMMTS, whose executive had not approved further discussions, was absent.

Despite the absence of the PMMTS, the TA and Natsopa sent a joint statement to the P&KTF and its affiliated unions informing them of the discussions. The two unions began exploring the practicality of merger and agreed steps by which a marriage might be forged. The two unions were to meet again, with a further invitation to the PMMTS, to consider proposals for submission to the respective memberships.

The TA agreed a further meeting on 27 January 1954. However, on 14 January the LSC and the PMMTS issued the joint statement of their intention to merge. The TA immediately wrote to Natsopa stating that 'this development is bound to affect the negotiations proceeding between Natsopa and the TA as our preliminary unofficial discussions and subsequent official proceedings all envisaged arrangements embracing the PMMTS as well as our two organisations.' It suggested that the 27 January meeting be postponed, since, as Natsopa had a large London membership, any new union would also have to embrace the PMMTS if constant and increasing friction over the manning of newspaper machine rooms was to be avoided. The TA was in an invidious position. If the amalgamation attempt continued, the TA risked conflict with its fellow craftsmen in London. In February 1954 the TA advised Natsopa that the changed circumstances made it inadvisable to proceed further with amalgamation negotiations. However, it reaffirmed its commitment to the principle of amalgamation among printing trade unions.

THE PROPOSED SIX CRAFT UNION MERGER, 1956–61

In July 1956 a joint meeting of the TA and LTS executives pledged their support to merger. The meeting was at the invitation of the LTS following informal talks on amalgamation at the May 1956 P&KTF Administrative Council held in Edinburgh. The meeting established a small committee of representatives from each union to examine the rules of the two unions and to explore the practicalities of an amalgamation.

However, before the committee began its work a joint invitation was sent to all other print craft unions to meet with the TA and LTS to consider the desirability of a wider amalgamation of craft unions. Why had the LTS and the TA decided to seek a wider craft amalgamation? The TA saw three reasons.[6] First, the events surrounding wage movements in the industry in 1955/6 had illustrated that no one craft union could successfully prosecute a wage claim in isolation from the rest. The employers would not concede to one union more than they were prepared to give to others. Second, technical changes were causing serious demarcation problems for the craft unions and the current union structure was inadequate to cope with these changes. An all-embracing craft union could regulate the expansion or contraction of the labour force in each craft according to the demand for the various skills. Third, Natsopa and the NUPB&PW were claiming the 'right' to do craft work. It was feared that, if insufficient craft labour were supplied to the new and expanding printing techniques, employers would be attracted to fill any 'gaps' by up-grading members of the non-craft unions.

Nine craft unions attended a conference in September 1956 to consider the formation of an all-embracing craft union. The TA and LTS emphasised that it was their intention not to absorb the others but to effect a genuine merger in which all interests would be safeguarded. The meeting established a committee to examine the practicality of amalgamation and to formulate a plan whereby this could be achieved. None of the unions participating in the drafting of the general plan would be committed to amalgamation. When an outline plan had been formulated the unions would decide whether or not to proceed further. Those unions deciding to do this would be committed to amalgamation subject to an adverse vote by their members in a ballot on the final proposals.

In November 1956 the STA decided to take no further part in the amalgamation talks, arguing that they preferred to rely upon the P&KTF providing more coordinated activity between the printing trade unions. A subcommittee of three – John Bonfield of the TA, Bob Willis of the LTS and Alf Buckle of the NSES – prepared a blueprint, which was presented in March 1957 to interested unions. A conference of union executives held in April 1957 appointed one representative from each union to form a drafting committee to devise a constitution for the new union. In May 1957 Slade and ASLP indicated that they wished no further part in the amalgamation talks. The six letterpress unions (TA, LTS, ACP, MCTS, NUPT and NSES), which had a total membership of 80,000, decided to continue merger talks.

Merging six unions was never going to be easy. There were many potential problems. Each union had cherished traditions and was reluctant to surrender them. Some of the unions had superannuation schemes, whilst other didn't. There was also the problem of matching the administrative structures and the positions occupied by the officers and staffs of the six unions. The talks were not between unions that were impoverished and desperately seeking new strengths from closer alliances. They were between unions that were wealthy, strong in their independence, firm on traditions and with memberships satisfied with the services provided by their unions. The challenge to achieve a successful merger was to preserve traditions and independence but at the same time ensure a control of the organisation as a whole that could supersede, where necessary, ideas and prejudices. Despite these challenges, the 1956 LTS Annual Report remarked,

> But there can be little doubt that these problems can and must be solved given goodwill for it is becoming increasingly evident that the only hope of avoiding continued inter-union clashes and disputes on lines of demarcation is by some form of amalgamation of the present craft societies.[7]

The task of drafting the new union's rules was given to the LTS Research Department. The TA provided a breakdown of membership on an area basis on which representation on the new union's Executive Council would be decided.

Under the proposed constitution the new union was to have an Executive Council of twenty area representatives, of which twelve were to be appointed from trade groups. The Council's Executive Committee was to comprise six area representatives and six trade group representatives. In addition, the decision-making structure of the new union was to consist of trade groups, area committees, branches, chapels, a triennial delegate conference and an annual trade delegate conference to deal with trade matters. The senior national officers were to be the General Secretary and Assistant General Secretaries and there were to be trade group secretaries, area secretaries and branch secretaries. The chapels were to be the linchpin of the system and the link to the branches, the area committees, the trade groups and the Executive Committee.

The LTS also played a major part in shaping the proposed financial structure of the new union. It devised one scheme for benefits for all members of the new union on a subscription rate lower than that currently paid by LTS members. Each union would pay into a common pool for benefit purposes three-quarters of their existing funds to form a capital fund from which all provident benefits (superannuation, funeral, unemployment, etc.) would be paid. The unions currently paying superannuation benefit would continue to pay the benefit provided for in their current rules. Unions without superannuation schemes would pay an enhanced subscription, although their members would not draw benefit for three years. The LTS estimated that by that time there would be an accumulation of some £4 million in reserves, thus making it possible to pay uniform benefits to all members of the new union. Although the proposed weekly subscription to the new union was lower than existing LTS subscriptions, it was higher than that paid by most of the unions in the proposed merger.

An alternative financial structure, involving the establishment of a superannuation department within the new union to take over the assets and commitments of the existing unions' superannuation schemes, was also proposed. There would be a uniform subscription for all members of the new union entitling them to all other benefits. The complication of the provision of a superannuation benefit in the new union was illustrated in that it was impossible to allow voluntary participation in any proposed schemes or else the fund would quickly become bankrupt. The proposed decision-making and financial structure of the new union was submitted to the drafting committee, which began the process of reaching some measure of agreement between the six unions.

Progress was slow. Delays were caused by the heavy commitments of the General Secretaries of the unions involved, the wages and hours movement of 1959, demarcation difficulties over teletypesetting and photocomposition and negotiations with the BFMP and the NS on bonus apprentices. The unions had members scattered throughout the country, different locations for their head offices and a multiplicity of rules to be matched. A major obstacle to progress was the LTS's insistence that any merged union must continue to pay a superannuation benefit. A good deal of time was spent on this issue, but fundamental differences proved difficult to reconcile.

The slow progress of the talks carried the risk that unions' members would begin to lose interest in amalgamation. The talks continued for nearly three years without any conclusion being reached and even one rule being drafted. In September 1959 a specially convened delegate meeting of the LTS voted to withdraw from the amalgamation movement. Its reasons were spelt out to the 1962 conference:

It was too complicated a job; it was setting up too big a machine. It meant creating a special superannuation scheme.

> We could not agree on the benefits. We could not agree on the subscription. We could agree on hardly anything because there were 6 unions each clinging to their own particular traditions all the time. In other words we wanted to get married but we still wanted to stay with mother.[8]

Following the LTS withdrawal the TA felt it premature to announce that the craft union amalgamation attempt had failed. It invited the remaining unions to continue the merger on a five union basis, which they unanimously decided to do. To avoid further delays they established a drafting committee at which the attendance of all General Secretaries would not be necessary.

By March 1960 the drafting committee had made some progress, including agreement on provident benefits. The superannuation benefit was taken out of the comprehensive scheme and a separate fund established from which superannuation liabilities would be met. In May 1961 the five unions finally accepted that amalgamation attempts had failed. The notice of termination of the talks said:

> With five unions involved, all with differing constitutional and benefit provisions, it was necessary to devise a new structure which would take into account all those differences if the five unions were to amalgamate on an equal footing. It has now become clear that not all the executives feel that they can carry their members with them on the scheme of amalgamation such as was proposed. In these circumstances, it has been agreed that no useful purpose would be served in continuing the talks.

Why did the amalgamation attempt fail? First, in retrospect, most of the unions felt the effort was too ambitious. The TA accepted the responsibility for this. It was their idea at the July 1956 meeting that all the craft unions be invited to a meeting to consider a wider craft merger. Although initially all the unions responded positively, it was soon clear some were there simply for information. Delays and the attempt to do too much caused the LTS to withdraw. Second, a serious obstacle was the LTS demand that superannuation provisions be extended to all members. The TA opposed this, arguing that there was the prospect of a compulsory government superannuation scheme being introduced, and its members would not pay an additional weekly subscription of 27½p for a union superannuation benefit as well. The TA had seen its own superannuation scheme collapse in 1947 and was not prepared to commit its members into another scheme about which there were serious doubts. Third, it might have been wiser when the LTS withdrew to have accepted that the initiative had failed. The proposed constitution of the new union, with its complex provisions for trade boards, area committees, etc., was going to be costly with a total membership of 60,000, as opposed to the 80,000 envisaged in 1956 when a nine union amalgamation was anticipated. As the remaining sponsoring union, the TA, at the time of the LTS withdrawal, felt it inappropriate to do anything that might have ended the merger moves. Fourth, by 1960 further complications had arisen. It was apparent that the chances of the litho unions joining the new union were remote, although they constantly suggested they might. It was also clear that the probability of ACP members accepting the merger was low.

THE PROPOSED LTS/NUPB&PW MERGER, 1960–1

Following its withdrawal from the craft amalgamation talks, the LTS was approached by the NUPB&PW with a proposal that the two unions merge. In exploratory talks the LTS became satisfied that in any merger it could retain considerable autonomy, that its rules would change little, and that a basis for merger existed. Anxious that the greatest possible number of members be consulted, the LTS decided not to have a normal delegate meeting at which 500 might attend, but to have one at which representation would be on the basis of one delegate for every six members.

This special delegate meeting was held on 11 March 1960. The General Secretary, Bob Willis, advocated merger on three grounds. First, it was society policy that mergers be pursued by any course offering a prospect of success. The Paperworkers would not present an obstacle to amalgamation because a large measure of autonomy was possible within its constitution. Second, there was the financial position of the LTS. The increase of superannuation benefit to £2 per week had a marked effect on the union's finances and serious deficits in its Provident and Superannuation Fund were predicted for future years. An amalgamation, under which the head office of the merged union would bear the administrative responsibilities and liabilities of benefits and services to members, would bring a substantial improvement in the present funds of the LTS.

Third, the LTS was to have a unique position in the new union in that a London Typographical Division would be created. The manner in which the division would conduct its business would be entirely a matter for itself in accordance with the desires of its membership subject to national rules. The changes required to the LTS rulebook would be of a consequential character. The division would have four representatives on the union's national council, whilst the LTS General Secretary would become Joint General Secretary of the national union. The merger was to be based on a recognition of the LTS's position in the industry and on preserving the links with its officers and current meeting procedures. The LTS would be linking not only with the largest union in the printing industry but with one which had 40,000 craftsmen in membership and which had the bulk of its membership in the provinces. The proposed Paperworkers' amalgamation would give the LTS a route to the provinces and a means of 'following the work leaving London'. It would also give it protection from an encroachment on its territory by the five craft union amalgamation if that were to come about.

The special delegate meeting voted by 901 votes to 802, with many abstentions, that merger talks should not continue. It was considered that the LTS with its long and splendid tradition was capable of fighting future battles on its own, that the proposed merger would not help future demarcation problems and that only four representatives on the National Council would mean a swamping of LTS interests.

The LTS wrote to the NUPB&PW expressing regret that the merger talks had ended abruptly. The Paperworkers hoped that the decision would 'not close the door on what is regarded as a potentially profitable and wise partnership'. The LTS waited twelve months before convening a members' meeting to reconsider amalgamation with the NUPB&PW. A special conference held in March 1961 voted by 289 votes to 168 in favour of restarting merger talks with the Paperworkers. It is difficult to know why views had changed since the previous meeting, but the LTS 1960 Annual Report suggested, 'It could be that take-over bids, the general situation in the printing industry and the obvious over-lapping that is taking place as between union and union have been contributory factors.'[9]

Work began on devising the rules for the new union. Although agreement was reached on the duties and salaries for the officials, considerable discussion took place over the issues of superannuation and a per capita payment by the LTS into the general funds of the NUPB&PW. The LTS was to be exempt from the Paperworkers' superannuation scheme and was to hand over £68,000 as a per capita fee to that union. The LTS balloted its members on the £68,000 payment as a means of gaining some indication of its members' feelings on the proposed amalgamation. The ballot produced a majority of over 1,000 against the payment. The LTS interpreted this as a vote against continuing amalgamation talks with NUPB&PW.

The attempt to merge with the NUPB&PW had failed. The amalgamation would have preserved LTS autonomy, given it a stake in the provinces and helped resolve the difficulties between the two unions over the operation of small cylinder machines. However, these industrial advantages were insufficient to overcome the LTS members' reservations that the NUPB&PW was an inappropriate partner for them.

THE LTS/TA MARRIAGE

Following the failure of the craft union amalgamation movement, the TA accepted that a less ambitious approach to future amalgamations was needed. In June 1962 the TA approached the LTS with a view to an amalgamation. The 1962 LTS Annual Conference approved an emergency motion,

> that this Conference, having discussed the problems of amalgamation, the movements taking place within the industry and in particular the invitation from the Typographical Association that an amalgamation shall be effected, instructs the Executive Council to go ahead with talks on the amalgamation of our two societies. That this conference recognises that in such a combination between two great craft unions, adequate funds will have to be provided to cover essential benefits, but not withstanding this, insists that the Superannuation Fund of the London Typographical Society, as it is now, should be retained within the Group, Branch and Division for the membership of the London Typographical Society and that in providing an allocation of funds sufficient monies should be set aside to cover the liabilities in this regard. . .[10]

In December 1962 the two unions agreed three basic principles for the merger. First, there would be as little interference as possible with the rules of the two unions. The TA rules would become the general rules of the new union. The LTS rules would continue as the rules of the London Typographical Society (London Region) and change only to conform to the rules operated by the new national union. The rulebooks of the two unions were to be 'welded together' rather than their existing constitutions dispensed with.

The second principle recognised that, where an existing TA benefit was better than that of an existing LTS benefit, the new union would adopt the TA benefit, and vice versa. Provident benefits would be at the most advantageous of the existing rates of the two unions. The subscriptions to the new union were to be those of the TA. Within the merged union the former LTS would maintain its existing superannuation benefits and subscriptions and sufficient of its existing funds to support its superannuation benefit. The best provident benefits of each union were to be preserved, whilst no member of either union would be required to pay increased subscriptions.

The third principle was that, once draft rules had been agreed, it would be impracticable to make amendments, as this would involve a lengthy and complex process which would make amalgamation an almost endless task. Members were to be asked to accept the draft rules as they stood. This was felt to be practical since merger was the overriding consideration and the rules of the two unions were being left intact as far as possible. To ensure that the will of the members of the new union would ultimately prevail, a special rules revision conference was to be held within two years of the new union coming into being. At this conference opportunity would be given to examine all the rules in the light of experience and not merely on the basis of speculation. Immediately following the conference there would be a London regional conference to consider the London Region rules.

The 'politics' of the TA/LTS merger required both unions' members to see it as a marriage of equal partners and not one of one union taking over the other. The LTS sought an organisationial structure for the new union which reflected this. It insisted on the same number of national officers in the new union as the TA, although it accepted that the General President of the TA should become the General President of the new union.[11] Of the ten other national officers, five were to be former LTS officials. The LTS insisted it could not be merely a branch of the new union. It was to be the London Region and the London branch of the new union.

The LTS also sought to have autonomy as a region, not only in terms

91

of decision-making structure but also in terms of its officers, its own premises, the retention of its superannuation, removal and emigration benefits and the retention of the name London Typographical Society, if necessary. The office of General Secretary was to be held jointly by the existing General Secretaries of the LTS and the TA as from the date of amalgamation until the retirement of either officer, when the remaining one would become sole General Secretary.

The LTS could not accept the location of the head office of the new union in Manchester, which was the site of the TA head office. Nevertheless, it accepted that if the new union were to have its head office in London then it could not be the LTS premises. To allay the fears of LTS members that their interests would be swamped by those of the larger TA (62,000 members to the LTS's 20,000) the constitution of the new union was to provide for the LTS to be represented on the Executive Council in proportion to its share of the total membership of the new union. Former LTS representation at the triennial delegate meeting of the new union was designed to give proportional representation. London would send 109 delegates out of the 460 total number.

The TA members also had to be assured that the amalgamation was not a London takeover. It successfully insisted that the TA rulebook, which embraced a national framework, should be taken as the basis for the rules of the new union, that there be a joint General Secretaryship, and that the head office of the new union not be located in London. In addition, TA members expected that the new union would make it easier for them to gain jobs in London. Although the proposed merger would help break down barriers between London and the provinces, restrictions on access to national newspaper employment would remain, in that two years' employment in the London printing trade was and would remain a necessary precondition for employment in 'Fleet Street'.

The draft constitution drawn up by the Amalgamation Panel was unanimously approved by the executives of both unions and in June 1963 by the TA Delegate Meeting and the LTS Annual Conference. When put to the memberships of the two unions it was overwhelmingly carried. LTS members voted by 11,250 votes to 1,750 in favour of amalgamation with the TA, whose members voted by 35,943 votes to 5,200 in favour of merger. Not one TA branch voted against and even the narrowest branch majority would have met the requirements of the Trade Union (Amalgamation) Act 1917, namely at least a 50 per cent turnout of members and that the number of votes cast in favour of merger must exceed by 20 per cent those votes cast against. The NGA thus came into being. The name National Graphical Association was selected as it was felt desirable to move away from the word 'typographical' given the rapidly changing techniques entering the industry and the need to associate with the graphic arts. The name was also seen as appropriate in that it would leave the door open for subsequent amalgamation with unions not purely typographical or not even typographical at all.

The marriage of the LTS and the TA had been achieved. The belief was that the two organisations were complementary, that their coming together would provide greater bargaining strength, that the new organisation would provide a stable financial background for both sets of members and that the London–provincial divide would narrow and hopefully disappear. However, there were deeper reasons for merging. London was under pressure in economic terms. With work leaving London, a marriage with the TA would make it easier for London members to follow work from London. The background to the marriage talks was the changed balance between London and the provinces in terms of printing work. The Londoners regarded themselves as 'elite' print workers and often looked down on the TA, which in turn regarded the LTS with envy and distrust. However, these prejudices were overcome through, on the one hand, the mechanics of the amalgamation and, on the other, the futuristic argument about the advance of new technology combined with the need for craftsmen to protect themselves against encroachments from other unions and employers. The LTS General Secretary told its 1963 Annual Conference, 'We are amalgamating not in order to say how many members we have got. We are amalgamating crafts in order to save what industrial power we have got . . .'[12]

Both the TA and the LTS saw the formation of the NGA as a first step and hoped other unions would quickly join the NGA. For both unions the future maintenance of control and influence in the industry lay in one union for the printing industry. However, following the experiences of the six craft union amalgamation attempt, they realised that one union for the industry could not happen overnight. For the moment the amalgamation of the LTS and the TA was achievement enough. The formation of the NGA was envisaged as the beginning of print union mergers on a wider scale. This proved to be the case.

THE FAMILY GROWS, 1965–69

On 28 June 1965 the NGA was joined, via the transfer of engagements procedure, by the NUPT and the ACP.[13] In autumn 1963 the LTS and the TA had written to these unions stating that if their own amalgamation efforts were successful they would approach them with a view to merger. Both the NUPT and the ACP replied that if the TA/LTS merger were achieved they would welcome an approach to join the new union.

The NUPT

This union came into being on 1 October 1909 but its founding meeting had been held at the Clarion Club in Manchester on 29 August 1909. It was a national union with seventeen branches, including three in Scotland and one in the Irish Republic. It had a membership of 1,300, of whom 800 were in its London branch. The head office had been moved from Manchester to Fleet Street in 1929. Its General Secretaryship had been established on a full-time basis only in 1942.

The union had participated in the affairs of the P&KTF and in 1923 had affiliated to the TUC. It had affiliated to the Labour Party shortly after the passing of the 1913 Trade Union Act, but disaffiliated in 1927 when the Chief Registrar of Friendly Societies told the union it was failing to comply with the 1913 Act. A ballot held in 1947 to re-establish the NUPT's political fund and to affiliate to the Labour Party resulted in a 3 to 1 majority against such action.

The NUPT's members were employed in three areas – national and provincial newspapers and news agencies such as Reuters and the Press Association. They received and transmitted text and pictures to newspapers, to the news agencies, to betting shops and to television. Its wire and tele-photo operators were found not only in newspapers and agency offices but also in such places as the House of Commons, the floor of the Stock Exchange and in mobile tents established to cover important events and from which photographs could be wired to a newspaper or other outlet. In addition to operators, the NUPT also organised mechanics, technicians and those who maintained and repaired the electrical and electronic equipment used by press telegraphists.

Why was the NUPT prepared to join the NGA? It was motivated by considerations that the union structure in the printing industry was outdated, inefficient and prevented unions from functioning effectively as individual organisations. It saw the NGA as providing a more effective and powerful organisation for dealing with print employers.

The outdated union structure had, the NUPT believed, been exposed by the introduction of new techniques into the industry. It felt that the only effective way for the unions to deal with developments like the increasing use of tape, computers and teletypesetting machines was the creation of one union. The TA, LTS and the NUPT had not found permanent solutions to the vexed question of the operation of keyboards on teletypesetting machines. Both the NGA and the NUPT considered the issue was so important to their respective members that, short of merger, a lasting solution to teletypesetting transmission was unlikely.[14] Both unions also realised, with techniques in the industry changing so rapidly, that if union structure did not change then the unions would spend most of their time arguing over 'who does what?' instead of controlling the introduction of new processes.

The NUPT believed that, in moving to one union for the industry, the first step had to be the amalgamation of the TA and the LTS. This had happened and it saw merger with the NGA as a small but significant step to achieving one union for the printing industry. In speaking at the 1964 NUPT's General Conference, its General Secretary remarked,

> When I say 'in one organisation' I mean that we must forget that we are press telegraphists, or compositors or machine minders, that what affects one affects everyone, and that the interests of all workers must be looked at as a whole instead of, as at present, each unit looking solely at its own sectional interests. That is why we are convinced amalgamation is necessary.[15]

The attraction of the NUPT to the NGA did not lie solely in reducing union demarcation problems. Telecommunications and electronics were expanding and playing an increasing role in the industry. The NUPT had members in this expanding area, whilst NGA members were confined to letterpress, a declining printing process. The inclusion in the NGA of employees already in the telecommunications and electronics sector of the industry would assist its future growth. The press telegraphist opened to the NGA a new field. For NUPT members the merger offered job opportunities in a wider field of the printing industry.

Under the transfer of engagements, NUPT members assigned to the London Region of the NGA could choose whether to participate in that region's superannuation fund. But new members would have no choice. All NUPT assets (£47,000) were merged with NGA funds and represented a per capita figure of some £31, which was similar to that of LTS and the TA when they amalgamated. The NGA was to form a Telecommunications and Electronics Trade Group, whilst a consultative committee in this area was to be established by the NGA National Council. The chairman of the consultative committee was to sit on the NGA executive as an *ex officio* member. In NGA branch areas where the NUPT had thirty or more members, those members could appoint a consultative committee whose secretary was to sit on the NGA branch committee. In London, former NUPT members were to form a consultative committee with rights of representation on the London Region News Committee and the London Regional Executive Council. Where existing NUPT chapels had fewer than four members they became part of the NGA composing chapel. Where there were four or more members they could form their own chapels, coming under the Imperial Father and with representation on the main composing chapel committee. Former NUPT delegations to the NGA triennial delegate meetings were to be on the basis of one delegate for each 149 full-time members. The NUPT General Secretary became the national trade group officer of the T & E Trade Group. NUPT members voted by 865 votes to 345 to transfer their engagements to the NGA.

The entry of the NUPT took the NGA for the first time into Scotland and Dublin. The TA's Dublin branch functions had been restricted to administrating members working in an area for which it was not industrially responsible. The NGA now had members working in Dublin whose industrial conditions were its concern and the NGA Dublin branch was reconstituted to include former NGA and former NUPT members.

The ACP

The ACP, formed in 1854, organised readers in a 15 mile radius from the London General Post Office. The bulk of its members had become readers through passing an entrance examination, having previously been Natsopa revisers or copyholders. The ACP had 1,500 members, of whom 1,000 were employed in the general periodical and trade typesetting houses.

It had no branches and its decision-making machinery consisted of chapels, general meetings, an annual meeting and an Executive Committee. The policy of the union was determined by the quarterly general meetings, which were open to all members. On financial matters the ultimate authority was a ballot of the membership. It was affiliated to the TUC, the P&KTF, the International Graphical Federation (IGF) and the London Trades Council. It had a political fund and affiliated to the Labour Party.

Most of the candidates for the ACP entrance examination were copyholders and revisers who had worked beside readers for at least six continuous years. The examination took place annually. Of the usual 120–130 candidates about 25 per cent passed. The examination covered *inter alia* composing theory, the collating of style and the correction of galley proofs. The papers were set and marked by the Committee members.

The ACP was an attraction to the NGA because, if it could be persuaded to join, the reader position in London would be tidied up. The NGA would have extended control over the terms and conditions of employment of all readers in England and Wales. The ACP favoured a link with the NGA because its members' employment security was threatened as print work left London. The NGA would provide the bridge for its members to follow work into the provinces. The NGA, in contrast to the ACP, considered every compositor was a potential reader. Although in 1965 only 30 per cent of readers in London were in the NGA, the ACP feared that the NGA might begin to challenge its presence in London reading rooms. The ACP considered that independence and isolation were a second-best option.

Some ACP members feared that by joining the NGA their interests would become swamped. The transfer of engagements arrangements went a long way to remove this fear. Former ACP members became members of the NGA London Region. A sum equal to the costs of two years' benefits to cover existing ACP superannuation commitments was paid into that region's superannuation fund from ACP assets. In addition, ACP paid into the NGA General Fund a per capita sum of £32 per full working member. The balance of the ACP total assets formed an ACP superannuation reserve fund to pay supplementary allowances to existing retired members of the ACP or those due to retire within five years of the transfer of engagements.

Former ACP chapels become part of NGA chapels but existing ACP chapels could continue, by mutual arrangements, as separate entities under Imperial Fathers of Chapels and with representation on the main composing room chapel committee. The NGA London Region altered its rules to provide for representation of readers on their Compositors' Trade Committee, their News Committee and their Regional Council. At national level the NGA established a Readers' Consultative Committee whose chairman would serve on the National Council as an *ex officio* member. This consultative committee was to be serviced by the readers' national trade group officer, who was to be the ACP General Secretary. In respect of representation at the NGA triennial conference, under existing procedures there was no guarantee that readers would be elected as London Region/branch delegates. It was therefore agreed that the London Region, in electing its delegates to the triennial conference, would ensure that no fewer than eight reader members would be included in their delegation. It was also accepted that if there were no NGA members to fill reader vacancies then the NGA would continue the entrance examination for suitable revisers, copyholders and other candidates.

Despite these safeguards for the interests of former ACP members in the NGA, the ballot to transfer engagements to the NGA was carried by only 51 votes. There were 580 votes in favour as opposed to 529 against.

The NSES

In 1966 the NSES approached the NGA, suggesting that the two unions examine the possibility of a merger. The NSES had 5,000 members who made letterpress printing plates in the foundry departments of newspapers, general printing companies and ad-setting trade houses. Although many stereotypers could be found in newspaper chapels, the more common situation was their employment in ones or twos. Many printing establishments did not have the volume of work to justify employing a stereotyper. However, most had stereotyping equipment which was operated by TA members. The undertaking of NSES work by the TA in small companies caused ill-feeling between the two unions.

The decision-making structure of the NSES consisted of chapels, branches, a National Council, a subcommittee of the National Council, a triennial delegate conference and referendums of the membership. Of its twenty-five branches, London was the largest with over 1,500 members. It was affiliated to the TUC and the P&KTF, had a political fund and affiliated to the Labour Party.

The NSES saw a merger with the NGA offering a solution to the falling employment opportunities for its members stemming from the decline in the use of letterpress printing techniques. The NSES members were trained only to produce letterpress printing plates. Given the growing trend of letterpress printers to change to lithographic techniques, the demand for NSES members was threatened while that of the ASLP, whose members made lithographic plates, was increasing. Unless the NSES could find a bridge into lithography its members would face serious redundancy problems against which it could do little to protect them. The NGA was party to a Retraining and Transfer of Membership Agreement with the ASLP with respect to letterpress machine managers and this agreement could easily be extended to plate-making. The ASLP and NGA were talking seriously about a merger.

Employment opportunities for NSES members in ad-setting houses were also declining. The advent of independent television in the mid-1950s resulted in a loss of advertising material for newspapers, magazines and periodicals. The NSES needed to find alternative employment opportunities for these members. A merger with the NGA again presented such a possibility since that union had interests in a wide spectrum of printing occupations. Given that its members' skills were becoming moribund and that there had been abortive merger discussions with the ASLP and Slade, a link with the NGA offered the NSES members the only possible route to alternative employment opportunities. Its plight was described by a delegate at its 1967 Triennial Conference:

> There has been talk through the years that the stereotyper will always be here: there will always be stereotypers. This was the cry I heard when I was young. But everyone must know now that the future of our trade is in jeopardy, so say the least of it, with all the new techniques, the processes, the materials and all the rest of it that have overtaken us, especially offset printing, we cannot do anything else in all reason but to marry ourselves to a more powerful organisation.[16]

NSES members voted to transfer their engagements into the NGA with effect from 30 October 1967. The terms of the transfer of engagement protected the interests of former NSES members within the NGA. In England, Ireland and Wales NSES chapels containing fewer than four members became part of the relevant NGA chapels, but those containing four or more members could have separate E & S chapels under Imperial Fathers of Chapels and with representation on the appropriate NGA chapel committees. Where there were twenty-five or more former NSES members in an NGA branch they could appoint their own consultative committee, the secretary of which would be a member of the NGA branch committee. In Scotland, T & E and NSES chapels combined to form NGA chapels though, where either former T & E or NSES chapels contained four or more members, they were entitled to separate chapels under Imperial Fathers of Chapels and representation on the NGA chapel committee.

At national level the NGA established an Electrotypers and Stereotypers Consultative Committee whose chairman served on the executive as an *ex officio* member. The committee was serviced by the E & S Trade Group officer, who was the Assistant General Secretary of the NSES. In respect of representation at the NGA triennial delegate meeting, the E & S Trade Group elected its own delegates on the basis of one delegate for each 149 full working members.

Within four years, five letterpress unions had come together to form one union with a membership of 90,000. Of the remaining letterpress unions the STA remained aloof. Its June 1967 Delegate Meeting voted to abrogate the STA/NGA Reciprocity Agreement as from 30 December 1967. The MCTS had, on the collapse of the six craft union amalgamation talks, joined the NUPB&PW. In December 1965 the NGA and the Monotype Casters' and Typefounders' branch of the Paperworkers' union signed an agreement on monotype casters which defined their respective spheres of membership. From 1 January 1966 the monotype caster membership in London was to be the MCTB and in the provinces the NGA. However, the NGA's real need was to gain a stake in the expanding area of lithography. To this end it sought a merger with the ASLP.

The ASLP

In 1964 the NGA invited the ASLP to discuss merger. Talks proceeded for twelve months but in late 1965 the ASLP felt unable to proceed any further. However, it did say amalgamation was not only desirable but inevitable and accepted the NGA's invitation to put forward its own merger proposals. Talks recommenced in November 1966 and, on 20 June 1968, despite various obstacles, the two unions agreed a common basis for the ASLP to transfer its engagements into the NGA, which was subsequently accepted by a majority of nearly 2 to 1 by ASLP members.

The ASLP had been formed in 1880. It was a national union with members in the Irish Republic and a head office in Manchester. Its members operated lithographic printing processes that printed not only on paper but also on tin. The major tasks of its members were litho plate-making and managing litho machines. In addition it had two other sections – the Plate Preparers and the Small Offset, which consisted of male and female operators of small offset printing machines.

It had forty-six branches, including two in the Irish Republic (Dublin and Cork). Of its 11,000 members, one-third were in its London branch in 1968. Its branches were assigned to six districts, which held meetings immediately after those of the National Council. District meetings were the consultative mechanism between the National Council and the branches. Between the National Council meetings the administration of the union lay with an Executive Committee, whose members were elected not from across the country but from the ASLP Manchester branch. The ASLP policy-making body was its triennial General Council. It was affiliated to the TUC and P&KTF but had no political fund.

The problem for the ASLP in the late 1950s and early 1960s was that lithography developed so quickly that it could not provide sufficient labour to meet this expansion. To remain an independent union carried the risk of loss of control of the litho production process to either the NGA, Sogat Division 1 (formerly Natsopa)[17] or the large field of non-union personnel operating lithographic processes particularly in small offset. In addition, to remain an independent union the ASLP needed a massive injection of new resources, which its members might have found difficult to meet. Remaining independent was not a viable long-term option. The NGA with its craft background seemed the best merger partner. The issue for the ASLP was not merger or no merger, but could it negotiate an acceptable deal from the NGA.

Merger offered to the two unions the best solution to their demarcation problems, which centred around dry offset, sheet-fed offset and the introduction of web-offset, particularly in the field of newspapers but later also in magazines and periodicals. The NGA was not prepared to tolerate a situation in which there was unemployment of letterpress plate-makers and machine managers but an acute shortage of equivalent litho labour. There was also the threat that the spread of litho might result in composition based on film replacing that based on metal, and if this were to happen redundancy would become a reality amongst its compositor and reader members. Letterpress employers converting their plants to litho were concerned that another union would be entering their plants. They preferred the ASLP and the NGA to join forces.

Against this background, the existing arrangements between the two unions to control the expansion of litho and the decline of letterpress could only be 'holding' operations. Dry offset machines were jointly controlled by the two unions following an agreement made in 1966, whilst in the general printing industry the 1959 Retraining and Transfer of Membership Agreement allowed letterpress machine managers to be retrained in litho and then transfer membership from the NGA to the ASLP. The NGA could not allow this agreement ultimately to bring about its virtual disappearance from plate-making and printing in the general trade. As provincial newspapers introduced web-offset machines the majority continued to be manned by NGA machine managers previously employed in the offices concerned on rotary letterpress machines. In a few instances ASLP members were also working with these NGA members. If this situation continued the ASLP would find its control of the lithographic process undermined. The NGA was unlikely to change its position that newspaper production was its preserve. Varying arrangements for the introduction of web-offset machines into provincial newspapers had been made, but, to bring some uniformity, the two unions established a joint committee at the end of 1965 to deal with future web-offset installations in newspaper and periodical offices. Although this was a significant step forward, it did not resolve the issues of principle involved. A lasting solution short of amalgamation seemed difficult to envisage.

However, in later 1965 another factor pushing the two unions towards merger surfaced when Natsopa claimed that in the manning of web-offset presses its members should have equal opportunities with those of the ASLP and NGA to operate such presses as machine managers.[18] The ASLP and the NGA immediately declared jointly that the operational control of web-offset presses was the exclusive right of the craft lithographer and the machine manager members of the two unions. Natsopa claimed adult promotion for their members in the provincial press, the photogravure periodicals trade and national newspapers on the grounds that their merger with the NUPB&PW to form Sogat made them an all-graphical union. These claims by Natsopa for equal access to machine manager jobs led to disputes between the NGA and Natsopa at Southwark Offset Limited in London, the Co-operative Press in Manchester,[19] the Thomson Organisation at Hemel Hempstead and the *Daily Mirror* in Belfast. The ASLP and NGA asserted that, although former Natsopa members had experience of both lithographic and letterpress machines, it did not include craft operations on these machines. In their view, members of Sogat 1 did not have sufficient knowledge to operate a lithographic press without training under a lithographic printer. The NGA and ASLP also rejected the Sogat view that in letterpress houses assistants transferring to web-offset should not perform on the new press – using completely different technology – the duties they performed on letterpress machines. The two crafts could not concede the Sogat claim. To do so would restrict the employment opportunities available to their members whilst extending these to the non-craft union.

Sogat claimed that, without some retraining, members of the NGA and the ASLP had insufficient knowledge to manage web-offset or rotary offset processes. ASLP members required retraining in the techniques involved in web handling, whilst NGA machine minders required instruction in lithography. Sogat saw no reason why its members should not receive the necessary retraining to enable them to manage these presses. The traditional division of responsibilities on presses between Sogat members and those of the NGA and the ASLP were undesirable given the operational and technical requirements of web-offset machines.[20] The NGA considered the purpose of Sogat's behaviour was not to meet the aspiration of their members with regard to security of employment in the future or their aspirations for opportunities to achieve craft status but to advance Sogat as a union into the craft field.[21]

The Sogat threat made both the NGA and the ASLP realise that, if they remained separate organisations, control over the development of litho might pass from their hands. As separate organisations they would not have the support of each other in their efforts to ensure that craft duties on web-offset machines remained the preserve of craft unions. If Sogat gained a foothold on web-offset machines it would be used as a base from which to claim traditional craft areas. The NGA was therefore happy to agree to the ASLP request during the merger talks that in any merged union all NGA litho members and all ASLP members be brought together into a Lithographic Trade Group controlled by lithographers.

Although the main forces behind the efforts to promote an NGA–ASLP merger involved rival union claims to control new technological developments on the machine side, there were other factors at work. ASLP realised that 'going it alone' would call for substantial reorganisation and additional resources. A possible re-organisation considered included the wider provision of clerical assistance in branches, the appointment of three or four new full-time officers with a primary function for organisation and recruitment, and the establishment of a national position of full-time General President. Although soundings amongst the membership indicated support for a doubling or trebling of subscriptions to support such a reorganisation, this examination of the practical implications of remaining a separate union gave a further impetus to merger. The review had illustrated that the union would need to be more businesslike in its operation and administration. The NGA already possessed an efficient administration. Merger with it would give this gain to ASLP members without additional cost.

Under the terms of the transfer of engagement the ASLP received assurances that the interests of its members would be protected in the NGA. ASLP chapels containing fewer than four members became part of the appropriate NGA chapel. Where chapels contained four or more former ASLP members they could establish separate litho trade groups at chapel level under Imperial Fathers of Chapels and with representation on the appropriate NGA chapel committees. In completely litho houses ASLP members would form an NGA Lithographers' Trade Group chapel. In houses that were predominantly litho with a small number of NGA members the latter became members of the Litho Trade Group chapel if fewer than four in number, or of their own chapel if four or more in number, with representation on the chapel committee, and both coming under an Imperial FOC.

For trade group purposes, where there were twenty-five or more former full ASLP members in any NGA branch they could form a local Lithographers' Trade Group Committee and elect their own trade group secretary, unless they already had a full-time ex-ASLP branch secretary, to deal with their trade group matters. If they chose not to exercise this option they could refer a problem to the nearest Lithographers' Trade Group Committee via the appropriate NGA branch secretary. Existing NGA branch committees were reconstituted to provide for representation of lithographers. Where a local Lithographers' Trade Group Committee referred a local matter to the national level it was dealt with by the national trade group officer, who could refer the matter to the National Trade Group Board, which in turn could refer it to National Council.

The former ASLP branches were allocated to the appropriate NGA Region, although a new region for Scotland, taking in the former ASLP Scottish branches, was established. In addition, a Scottish Regional Council was created with a part-time Scottish Regional Secretary. At the national level, lithographers were to be represented by a Lithographers' National Trade Group Board, which would appoint four of its members to serve on the NGA National Council, which in turn would appoint one lithographer member to serve on its Executive Committee. For representation at the NGA's triennial delegate meeting the Litho Trade Group elected one delegate for each 149 full working members in the Lithographers' Trade Group.[22]

Because of the wide differences between the 1968 per capita figures of the NGA (£52) and the ASLP (£25), for five years former ASLP members would receive only half the rates of NGA benefits, except for dispute benefit. The sickness and superannuation benefits of the ASLP were retained, but former ASLP members paid additional weekly subscriptions for this purpose. Six full-time branch secretaries of the ASLP became Lithographer Trade Group secretaries responsible for litho members in those branches. The existing London branch and assistant branch secretaries took responsibility for lithographers in London. The salaries of former ASLP branch officers were paid centrally by the NGA, whilst the ASLP General Secretary became the national trade group secretary.

The merger arrangements also dealt with ASLP fears that they would lose out in employment terms to NGA members. Transfers of members from one trade group to another would not be permitted except by the approval of the appropriate National Trade Group Committee or the National Council and then only in special circumstances such as redundancy. A priority for filling vacancies was also agreed. The first priority in filling letterpress or litho vacancies was the avoidance of redundancy, after which vacancies would become available to suitably trained members of the appropriate sections of the trade, and thereafter vacancies would be filled at the discretion of the National Council, according to the labour situation in the area. If craftsmen were unavailable to fill vacancies, the upgrading of auxiliary members would be considered.

By 1969 six craft societies had come together in the NGA, which now had a membership of 101,000.[23] Only Slade and the STA remained outside. It had been matched on the non-craft side by the formation of Sogat (1966) when Natsopa and the Paperworkers merged. The NGA viewed these two groupings as desirable in the light of its longer-term objective of one union for the printing industry.[24] However, its short-term objective remained the creation of one union for printing craftsmen. The merger of the NGA and the ASLP was significant since the NGA was no longer a typographical union.[25] It now had a stake in the litho field. Had the NGA not achieved this merger, its historical development would have been much different.

NOTES

1. For example, those between the TA and STA, between the TA and the PMMTS and then the Machine Department of the LTS, between the TA and the Printing Machine Branch of the NUPB&PW, and between the PMMTS and the STA.

2. For example, between the LSC and the ACP, between the LSC and the NUPT, between the LSC and the London branch of the NSES and between the LTS (Machine Department) and the Printing Machine Branch of the NUPB&PW. Those agreements signed in the name of the LSC applied to the LTS (Composing Department) on the creation of the LTS.

3. For example, the Photocomposition-Demarcation Formula of Lithographic and Typographical Unions, made in 1958 and amended in 1962.

4. For example, the 1958 TA–NUPT Join Declaration on Teletypesetting transmission.

5. See *Report of the Delegate Meeting, Douglas, 1953*, Typographical Association, p. 71.

6. See 'Craft Amalgamation', *Typographical Circular*, September 1956, pp. 165–6.

7. See *2nd Annual Report*, London Typographical Society, 1956, p. 11.

8. See *7th Annual Conference Report*, London Typographical Society, 1962, p. 19.

9. See *6th Annual Report*, London Typographical Society, 1960, p. 5.

10. See *7th Annual Conference Report*, London Typographical Society, 1962, p. 18.

11. The office of General President did not exist in the LTS.

12. See *8th Annual Conference Report*, London Typographical Society, 1963, p. 40.

13. A transfer of engagements is a legal device to avoid unions wishing to merge having to entirely revise their rules and bring the two set of rules together and then ballot their respective members. Under the Trade Union (Amalgamations etc) Act (1964)

a transfer of engagements of one union to another is permissible by a simple majority of members of the union seeking to merge in this way, provided that the other union is willing to accept them. The union accepting the transfer may agree to amendments to its rules to meet the wishes of the transferring union and these changes, once authorised by the Registrar, become binding on the union.

14. The NGA and the NUPT were parties to the Joint Declaration of 1958 which had allowed the transmission of news between two offices of Cumberland Newspapers Ltd. In 1964 the NGA, NUPT, Newspaper Society and the Press Association agreed a pilot scheme whereby the Press Association could transmit by teletypesetting edited copy from its London centre to its subsidiaries in the provinces.

15. See 'A Summarised Discussion and Debate on Amalgamation', *35th General Delegate Conference*, NUPT, April 1964.

16. See *Debate on Amalgamation, Triennial Conference, National Society of Electrotypers and Stereotypers*, May 1967. p. 57.

17. The Society of Graphical and Allied Trades (Sogat) had been formed in 1966 by an amalgamation of Natsopa and the NUPB&PW. Sogat was organised in two divisions – Division 1 (the former Natsopa) and Division A (the former NUPB&PW).

18. See 'Trouble looms with Natsopa', *The Graphical Journal*, vol. 2, no. 12, December 1965, pp. 372–3.

19. The disputes at Southwark Offset Limited and the Co-operative Press at Manchester, and the general problems caused by the introduction of web-offset machines in the printing industry were the subject of a Court of Inquiry under the chairmanship of Lord Cameron. The Court's report supported the views of the ASLP and the NGA. See *Report of a Court of Inquiry into the problems caused by the introduction of web-offset machines in the printing industry, and the problems arising from the introduction of other modern printing techniques and the arrangements which should be adopted within the industry for dealing with them*, Cmnd 3184, HMSO, London, January 1967.

20. Although Sogat was stressing concerns about the denial of opportunities for its members to advance to craft status, there were other factors at work. Not least of these was that the traditional positions of Sogat members on newspaper rotary presses were in danger of being virtually eliminated by the introduction of web-offset machines.

21. *Report of the Delegate Meeting 1969*, National Graphical Association, pp. 34 and 187.

22. The members of the ASLP Small Offset Section and of their Plate Preparers' and Metal Varnishers' Section were to continue to be covered by separate sections of the NGA and their supplementary rules included as appendices to the NGA rules.

23. At the end of 1968, following the successful ASLP ballot for merger with the NGA, two challenges arose from individual members representing two small chapels. One challenge led to a court appearance in which the appellant lost the case. The substance of the complaint was that the ASLP had no right under its rules to merge

with the NGA. It was established, however, that such a right existed, providing the procedure was observed. The other challenge led to an appearance before the Registrar on the grounds that no proper opportunity had been given to voting on the merger issue. The ASLP established to the satisfaction of the Registrar that all that could be done had been done by the union to give an opportunity for all members to vote in the ballot. The Registrar therefore rejected the complaint.

24. The 1966 NGA Delegate Meeting approved two motions on amalgamation. One proposed one craft union for the industry and the other one union for the industry. The NEC expressed support for both motions, but argued that the first step to one union for the industry was one craft union. It considered the two motions complemented each other.

25. This led the NGA to advise its branches that, if they had not already done so, they could change their title to 'Graphical Society' or to 'Branch of the National Graphical Association'.

CHAPTER 5

THE FORMATION OF THE NGA (1982): GENERAL CAUSES

By 1982 the number of print unions was reduced to three. In March 1982 the NGA and Slade amalgamated to form NGA (1982), whilst in the July Sogat(75) and Natsopa merged to create Sogat(82). The late 1970s saw an unsuccessful attempt to form the Graphic Arts Union by an amalgamation of NGA, Slade, Natsopa and the National Union of Wallcoverings, Decorative and Allied Trades.

There were many pressures leading the NGA to seek mergers. The 1966 Delegate Meeting committed the union to achieve one union for the printing industry. Continuing developments in technological change, for example film-setting and computerised composition, blurred the traditional distinction between NGA jobs and those of other unions, particularly Slade. Related to these developments was the growth of sources of origination work outside of the industry, for example art and advertising studios and word processors. These developments enabled work to bypass the composing room. The compositor, on the whole, escaped the effects of technological change in the 1950s and 1960s, but in the 1970s the impact of technical change adversely affected the compositor, the major occupational group within the NGA.

A third factor causing the NGA to seek mergers in the 1970s was the growth of import penetration of UK printing markets. The technological developments of the 1970s removed many previous technical limitations on the import or export of print work. Imports rose particularly sharply in book manufacturing, manufactured stationery and packaging. The sharp rise in the UK inflation rate and in the level of unemployment in the printing industry in the late 1970s and early

1980s were further pressures towards the formation of NGA (1982). The unemployment of NGA members arising from closures, mergers and redundancy caused severe financial difficulties and led the NGA to feel that declining employment opportunities should be tackled by union mergers.

A further pressure was the significant changes in the early 1980s in the legal environment surrounding the UK industrial relations system. The Employment Acts of 1980 and 1982 outlawed important NGA and Slade industrial practices, for example the 'blacking' of work not produced by unionised labour. Potentially this legislation made it difficult for unions in isolation to resist the implementation of changing techniques in the industry. Its impact would best be countered by one union for the industry.

TECHNOLOGICAL CHANGE AND DEVELOPMENTS: 1970s AND EARLY 1980s

During this period traditional composing methods were revolutionised by photocomposition and by computer-based composing techniques. These made it possible for employees outside the industry, after relatively short periods of training, to produce print origination work at standards acceptable to the customer. By opening up print origination to a wider world they threatened NGA control of the industry and the wages and conditions of composing craftsmen.

The late 1960s saw the introduction of typewriter keyboards and attempts by employers to employ females on these. Although the NGA opposed the employment of women, a number of employers presented the union with a *fait accompli* by introducing both typewriter keyboards and female operators, often at the minimum BPIF keyboard rate rather than the keyboard rate for the area. The NGA was hampered in dealing with this industrial threat in that there were either no members available to take jobs or alternatively no members willing to transfer to keyboards. To retain this work for make-up compositors in the short run the NGA issued 'Recognition Cards' to females until proposals could be presented to the employers to avoid the introduction of females. The employers did not respond positively to the NGA proposals, which included that, if no NGA operators were available to work the keyboard, retraining opportunities should be offered to existing NGA staff within the firm or other NGA members in the branch and that arrangements be made for specialised apprentices indentured as keyboard compositors.[1]

Dispensations to the policy were made only after exhaustive attempts to secure qualified NGA labour or suitable male labour from outside the industry had failed. Employers were required to advertise in the national, local and trade press and in the columns of *Print* and then to examine the possibility of engaging males with the appropriate experience, such as telex operators. If this failed employers were to attempt to recruit disabled males. Only when all these avenues had been explored would the NGA accept the employment of women on keyboards and then on the condition they were paid the keyboard rate for the area and not the minimum in the BPIF agreement. However, keeping females off keyboards was difficult given the reluctance of existing compositors to undertake keyboard duties and the general shortage of labour in this section of the industry.

The National Council report to the 1976 Delegate Meeting claimed that, whilst government legislation covering discrimination against females could present the NGA with problems, the equal pay legislation had reinforced the union's policy of opposing the employment of females on keyboards, since all things being equal the employers would now opt to employ a man rather than a woman. The London delegation had unsuccessfully challenged this NGA males-only policy at the 1974 Delegate Meeting.[2] They did so again at the 1976 meeting and succeeded in referring back to National Council the paragraph dealing with females on keyboards. Delegates accepted that, although the union should resist unskilled labour coming into a department, it was unacceptable to say 'we would have deaf, dumb, blind or crippled men rather than accept any women'.[3] Following this the Association changed its policy to one of recognising no distinction between males and females and that entry into the NGA be solely on the basis of craft ability, and receiving the rate for the job.

The increasing use of cold composition led to demarcation disputes between NGA and Slade over the use of Letraset and page-planning or make-up operations. Letraset entered the industry in about 1966. It is a type image produced in the form of a paper transfer, which can be stripped in as individual letters to form words for purposes of producing headings, sub-heading and drop capitals. The process was attractive where an editor required a heading in a typeface not available in hot metal. Its flexibility attracted its use, particularly in studios, whether the typeface required was in stock in the printing house or not. The NGA adopted the policy that where the process was introduced to replace work hitherto undertaken by compositors it should remain their work. The NUJ claimed an interest in the process and, in April 1967, NGA, Slade and the NUJ made a tripartite agreement covering the operation of the process. Where Letraset was used to replace or as part of work normally done by an artist, the operation would belong to Slade. If Letraset was used in substitution for work normally done by the compositor, then the work would be performed by the NGA.

However, within a few months of the agreement coming into operation Slade claimed an interpretation of it which virtually meant that NGA members were prevented from handling Letraset if it replaced normal typesetting. Slade told the NGA and the NUJ that if they could not accept this interpretation then it would withdraw from the agreement. Difficulties continued over the interpretation of the 1967 agreement, especially in newspapers, and were dealt with on a far from ideal case-by-case basis. Although the use of Letraset in the industry increased steadily, it did so at a relatively slow rate and because of this never really significantly threatened the employment prospects of NGA and Slade members[4] as its introduction could be managed by the two unions on a case-by-case basis.

The use of Letraset was superseded by the typositor photocomposition machines which allowed the production of strips of letters by photographic methods. The produced strips were black on white and were ready for photographing and enabled any photographic work required on these strips to be done without any involvement of the composing room. The typositor machine led to a number of disputes between the NGA and Slade over page 'make-up' or page 'planning'. One such dispute at Odhams (Watford) Ltd led the Department of Employment to establish a Committee of Inquiry.[5] They were not disputes over who should operate the machine, as this was accepted as NGA work where it was situated in a composing room. The disputes were around the subsequent operations of make-up or planning, in that the typositor allowed a choice in work allocation that did not exist previously.

In the gravure printing process, page make-up or page planning traditionally involved three stages. The composing department prepared a 'doc' print for submission to the publisher for approval by first running an impression of whatever had been set in hot metal and second pasting on the 'doc' positives of illustrations prepared by the camera operators and sent to the composing department for that purpose. Following the publisher's approval of the proof, the composing department produced a 'type repro' of what had been set in hot metal for the process department. The planners in the process department added the reproductions of illustrations to produce a complete page of printed matter onto which were positioned any other components. What was disputed was whether, in planning the page, Slade members should be permitted to stick on to the 'repro print' the main headings, sub-headings and drop capitals when these had not been produced by artists in the first place but by NGA members using a typositor machine.

The difference which the exercise of this choice made was simple. Slade argued that if all the 'lettering' on a page were set in letterpress by compositors then all that would remain to be added would be the illustrations 'pure and simple'. If the compositors then 'made up' the page 'complete' for photographing there would be nothing but illustrations for Slade members to add. If only the text of the page were set in hot metal by the compositors, and if the repro-proof sent to the process department for make-up contained no more than text, the compositors would be mere setters of text and the Slade members would assemble the page. Both the NGA and Slade argued that their members were able to carry out fuller responsibilities.

The 1967 tripartite agreement was meant to secure agreement on a local basis on demarcation and relevant procedures in respect of both Letraset and typositor material. However, there were difficulties of interpretation with this agreement, and differences between the NGA and Slade over page-planning or make-up operations were resolved on a case-by-case basis. These pragmatic responses by the two unions led to a partial rather than a lasting solution to the fundamental problem. A merger offered a lasting solution.

There were also particular problems between the NGA and Slade over the insertion of illustrations and the imposition of filmset pages. The NGA would not surrender insertion of illustrations and made it clear that, if necessary, it would secede from the 1958 photocomposition formula and make its own arrangements with employers. However, in April 1967 the two unions agreed a supplementary interpretation to the 1958 formula which permitted local arrangements for either unions' members to undertake insertion of illustrations, separately or jointly, provided approval of such arrangements was obtained at national level. A number of local agreements on the basis of mixed NGA and Slade teams were made to remove the problem of 'who does what' on film page make-up. They fell short of a permanent settlement to the problem, but were a measure of some progress. During the 1970s the number of photocomposing installations continued to grow and with it the degree of sophistication of the equipment, and bromide paper rather than film became the main material output from the system. This increased the role of NGA members and reduced that of Slade members as the make-up of bromide pages had not been covered in the original 1958 photocomposition agreement. The NGA sought to influence this growth through photocomposition agreements with the BPIF and the Newspaper Society.

Another technical development of the 1970s that threatened NGA control of the composing room was optical character recognition (OCR) equipment, which made it possible, for example, for tele-ad staff to undertake the copy-preparation of the small ads and then place them directly through the OCR scanning equipment, completely bypassing the composing room. However, the NGA had nothing to fear from the process, providing its members set the hard copy for scanning as well as being responsible for the scanning equipment. In 1972 one company – T.Bailey Foreman Ltd – unilaterally introduced OCR equipment to its *Guardian-Journal/Evening Post*. Tele-ad staff were to place their work directly into the equipment, but in January 1973 the company agreed that small ads be prepared by NGA members even though this meant duplicating the setting. However, the use of OCR turned out to be less than feared in both the newspapers and the commercial field.[6] In this latter sector the NGA established, in the four companies concerned, the principle that all hard copy fed into the equipment would be NGA originated and the equipment itself would be under the control of an NGA member. The scanner became a peripheral piece of composing equipment.

In 1975 the NGA and the Newspaper Society agreed that a controlled experiment should take place in the use of OCR in four newspaper offices. However it was delayed when the NGA became involved in a dispute with Sharman's of Peterborough (see Chapter 14). After the end of the dispute the controlled experiment went ahead. However, the equipment did not take off because of technical problems associated with its operation.

The introduction of the computer into the printing industry over the period 1966–83 also threatened the traditional composing room. In the late 1960s and early 1970s the NGA faced problems where computers were installed for dual purposes, i.e. clerical end-product and a typesetting end-product. The difficulties were with the programming and operational stage, but following discussions with Sogat it wasagreed that when a programme was required for clerical tasks it would be Sogat work but where the end-product was printing it would be done by a member of the NGA. If, as often happened, a job combined both functions, joint union consultation determined the work allocation. In the period there was a significant increase in computers in newspaper offices for both typesetting and multi-purposes. In accommodating the use of computers in these circumstances the NGA sought guarantees from the employers in terms of redundancy, earnings and retraining.

From the mid-1970s the introduction of new technology on the composing side of newspapers became of concern to the NGA. The *Daily Mirror* became in 1977 the first national daily to introduce a fully integrated computerised photocomposition system. However, the NGA maintained control over the input to the system and this agreement formed the basis for the subsequent introduction of computerised photocomposition systems in other national daily newspapers.[7] The biggest potential threat to newspaper composing rooms was the introduction of direct entry/front end systems for the typesetting, editorial and advertising functions. In reality these systems made it possible to dispense with the traditional compositor by giving direct input to composition and automatic typesetting units.

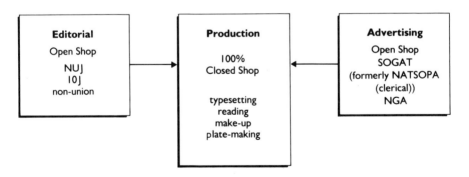

Figure 5.1   Newspaper production processes: hot metal

This potential threat to the NGA compositor is shown in Figures 5.1, 5.2 and 5.3, which illustrate the newspaper production processes under hot metal, photocomposition and direct entry composing systems.

Under hot metal (Figure 5.1), the functions and occupations involved in producing a newspaper fell into separate and easily definable categories. In the editorial department, journalists, who were either in membership of the NUJ or in some cases in no union at all, created the copy, usually with the aid of a typewriter; this copy was subsequently processed and prepared by sub-editors. Hard copy was usually sent straight through to the sub-editor prior to being passed to the NGA compositor for typesetting. In the advertising department, advertising copy, whether received by telephone or as space sold by advertising staff, was drafted in either handwritten or typewritten form and then sent to the composing room for typesetting. Employees in the advertising department were in many cases unorganised or members of the clerical section of Natsopa (subsequently Sogat(82)).

All contents of a newspaper, whether news or adverts, were typeset in hot metal by NGA compositors, who also corrected their work and then assembled it in page form. Unlike the editorial and advertising departments the composing room was 100% NGA organised. The compositor's work was then sent to the foundry, where NGA stereotyper members produced a plate for the printing press. The machine room was controlled by NGA machine managers, who also operated a closed shop.

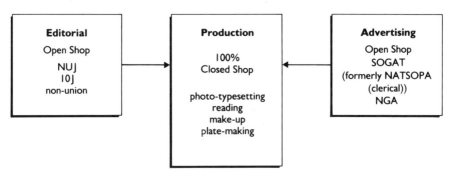

Figure 5.2　Newspaper production processes: photocomposition

The processes involved in photocomposition (see Figure 5.2) were not radically different from those which characterised hotmetal. With photocomposition, typesetting was undertaken by NGA members. Compositors, by the use of VDUs on line to the photocomposition system, manipulated and recalled that copy and corrected it. The output from photocomposing units was a bromide paper, which was subsequently assembled and made up into pages by NGA compositors. The made up pages were then reproduced as a lithographic plate which was used for printing. In the late 1970s/early 1980s electronic photocomp 'area' assembling devices were introduced in newspapers, but these were mainly operated by NGA members. Electronic page make-up had the advantage that it reduced the amount of film and photographic paper required, allowing the compositor to undertake full page make-up on a VDU screen.

Figure 5.3 shows that 'direct entry' ('single keystroking') brings a

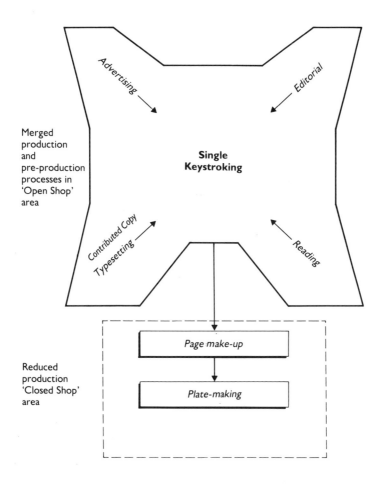

Figure 5.3   Newspaper production processes: direct entry

radical change by introducing into the editorial area VDUs which are directly linked with a typesetting computer. The creative function of the journalist can be combined with the typesetting and correction function which has traditionally been that of the compositor. It transfers keystroking from an NGA area to an area which is the province of the NUJ or non-unionists. Figure 5.3 shows that exactly the same relocation and merging of processes takes place with the composing area (fully NGA) and the advertisement/tele-ad area (former Natsopa [clerical] or non-unionised). Direct entry means that the traditionally separated editorial, advertising and production functions are merged and NGA control of the production process undermined. The implications of direct entry for the NGA newspaper compositors were far-reaching. If an accommodation could not be made with Natsopa (subsequently Sogat(82)) and the NUJ, the NGA's bargaining power in the industry would change dramatically and, given the relatively low degree of unionisation in editorial and advertising areas, the newspaper industry could become de-unionised.

A merger with one or both of these unions offered the best way of retaining some control for the NGA in the newspaper industry. What has been described above for newspapers was equally true of magazines and periodicals where direct entry meant that 'creative origination' by authors and journalists could bypass the composing room. The NGA was determined to protect its interests in the face of the threat of direct entry. The then Assistant General Secretary of the NGA told its 1978 Delegate Meeting, 'Our policy will remain that, except in the broader context of a possible amalgamation, we cannot concede control of the original keystroke to other than compositors.'[8]

The crunch for the NGA over direct entry did not finally materialise until the mid-1980s, but nevertheless it was faced in 1978/9 with a direct challenge by Times Newspapers, which insisted that its new production system must be operated on the basis of direct input involving journalists and advertising staff (see Chapter 14).[9] The potential threat of direct entry systems was an important factor pushing the NGA, Slade, Natsopa and NUWDAT to amalgamation talks in 1976.

A further threat to the NGA compositor in the 1970s was the development of facsimile transmission, which allowed NGA (T&E) members to send complete pages from one centre or town to another, where the production of a paper could take place without the need of the traditional composing room. The process did not, however, develop as anticipated. The *Daily Mirror* experimented with the process in 1969 by sending complete pages from Manchester to Belfast. Inter-union difficulties arose but the experiment was abruptly ended in 1971 when the IRA blew up the *Mirror*'s plant in Belfast.

There were also pressures from technological change in the foundry and machine room fuelling the NGA's amalgamation objectives. The 1970s saw the change-over from flat-bed rotary letterpress machines to sheet-fed letterpress rotary machines capable of printing more than two colours. Throughout the 1970s lithographic printing continued to expand in England, Wales and Northern Ireland. However some respite for letterpress printing came from the introduction of deep-etched wrap-around plates which re-established the potential for letterpress printing over a wide range of work.

The introduction of photoresponsive plates caused demarcation difficulties between Slade and the NGA. In 1973 the two unions reached an agreement on the production of photopolymer plates under which NGA members would make the plates for the printing of provincial newspapers and Slade members the plates produced in provincial news offices to print commercial work. In all other offices Slade members would make the original plates for commercial work, although it was recognised that where problems arose over Slade members producing duplicate plates, as an alternative to stereotyping, they should be resolved on a house-to-house basis by agreement of the two unions. In short, the NGA was to make photopolymer plates to go on the presses whilst Slade members would make the original pattern plates. Out of this provincial newspaper agreement on photopolymer plates was born an agreement, along similar lines, for the national newspapers in 1974. Whilst the agreement provided some protection for NGA members in national newspaper offices, it did not cover the commercial and trade house fields. As employment opportunities in national newspapers fell in the 1970s the NGA looked towards the general trade for redeployment opportunities for its members, particularly former electrotypers and stereotypers, and this was likely to bring further difficulties between the two unions. The photopolymer plates agreement was a short-term solution which was not viable in the long term. A long-term solution lay with a merger of NGA and Slade.

The introduction of laser plate-making in the 1970s also led to disagreements between Slade and the NGA. Laser plate-making offered significant changes in preparation techniques, in that it avoided the use of photosensitive emulsions in the plate-making process. Both unions recognised that to 'fight' each other over the control of laser plate-making was likely to be beneficial only to the employers. This was a further factor pushing towards the merger of the two unions.

WORK BYPASSING THE COMPOSING ROOM

The issues of work bypassing the composing room and the implementation of new technology were closely related. The vast changes in techniques introduced in the printing industry in the 1970s and 1980s blurred the boundaries not only between it and other industries but also between the skills needed to perform traditional composing tasks. At the time of the formation of the NGA, if employers wanted to produce origination work for print on a viable basis, they had to employ NGA craft composing members. Without a five- or six-year apprenticeship a person did not possess the skills to operate hot metal systems, to set type, and to assemble advertisements or pages. Cold composition techniques meant that Slade members could also produce complete origination. However, the growth of computers meant origination work could be done outside the industry, by non-unionists or members of other trade unions, and then sent to a printing firm for printing, thereby bypassing the composing room.

There were a number of sources from which origination work could be done outside the printing industry. Computers allowed copy which would conventionally have gone to the composing room to be put on a magnetic tape which could be transmitted straight through the composing machine, bypassing the intertype or monotype operator. Magnetic tapes were attractive to producers of directories and indexes since they enabled updating to take place more easily than before. Magnetic tapes also led publishers, authors and automatic data-processing (ADP) establishments to produce their own punched tape. The implications of the rise of magnetic tapes for NGA compositors were stated by a delegate to the 1972 Delegate Meeting:

> If this process continues the logical outcome will be that the whole of the telephone directories, one of the largest printing productions not only in this country, but in the world, will be on a tape produced by non-society labour, and all the stationery offices will do, and there are quite a few of them throughout the country, will be to print the things; the comps, the operators, will be completely superfluous. Surely the correct thing to do is

to insist that all these tapes are produced by NGA labour and if this does not happen we will refuse to handle them.[10]

Another source of origination work from outside the industry was microfilm. In the mid-1970s the NGA decided it was essential to attempt to establish itself in microfilm. The ADP industry normally used film for record purposes, but microfilm and microfiche could be put to other uses which impinged upon work previously done by the printing industry. By late 1975 it was becoming common for parts catalogues, price lists, library lists and other work of this kind to be produced on microfilm. The NGA accepted that, although it might have to lose the printing of these catalogues, it was essential to retain the composition despite the ADP field being organised largely by non-printing unions. Each time a data basis was compiled by non-printing labour a threat was posed to the printing industry. The National Council report to the 1980 Delegate Meeting stated,

> The lines of demarcation between data processing and printing are becoming increasingly blurred, and it will be in our interests to seek to move into this field and to assist in the compilation of data basis and the production of microfilm and microfiche. This has been the policy of the Association for a number of years, and whilst progress has been modest, no attempts to gain recognition have been lost.[11]

Additionally, the development of direct impression keyboards, combined with the use of Letraset was making it possible for non-craft labour to produce origination of standards and costs perfectly acceptable to most customers. In the late 1970s the word processor appeared as another technique whereby origination work could be produced without the involvement of NGA members. By linking a typewriter through a mini-computer and a visual display terminal, an inexpensive composition system was produced. Word processing offered the opportunity for authors, publishers and printers to use machines which threatened disastrous consequences for compositors in the book publishing industry. By 1978 large typesetting companies were requesting agreements with the NGA to use facilities on their photosetters to process cassettes produced on word processing systems.

When all these simplifications of composing techniques are taken with the wider availability of litho printing, reasons for an expansion of in-plant printing in the 1970s are not hard to find. In-plant printing in local government, nationalised industries and other parts of the public sector had long been a problem for printing craft unions. The 1970s saw the spread of in-plant printing into food processing and engineering companies as well as building societies, banks and other financial companies. NGA attempts to establish some control over in-plant print and origination work brought it into disagreements with many non-print unions, notably the Association of Professional and Executive Staffs (APEX), Nalgo, Technical and Supervisory Staffs (TASS) and the Association of Scientific, Technical and Managerial Staff (ASTMS), and led it to propose alterations to the TUC Disputes Principles and Procedures (see Chapter 10).

Direct impression keyboards and relatively cheap, and easy to operate photocomposing systems meant that certain work which originally passed through the composing room could now be undertaken to standards acceptable to the customer in art and advertising studios. Slade also faced problems from changing technology. The significant development took place in the production of transparencies. Previously much of the work that needed to be reproduced in colour was flat copy (artwork). In the upsurge in the use of transparencies, each picture could be reproduced in ratio to each other. As a consequence it was possible to montage the transparencies together and, in some instances, assemble those into pages. This work was sometimes carried out in the photographic laboratory as opposed to the reproduction house, and thereby created a loss of work to the repro studios. It was this development and the preparation of artwork within the studios outside of Slade control which led both the NGA and Slade to decide to try and organise employees in advertising and art studios and, as we show below, become involved in a bitter conflict with each other.

The 1970s and early 1980s were also the period in which non-paper modes of communications began to develop and give rise to a communications industry based on electronic devices – for example, Teletext, Viewdata, Prestel, Ceefax, video cassettes, video discs and cable television. This new world of communications offered a threat to the NGA and it needed a foothold there if it was to have an influence on developments in it. Other than the NUJ, the trade unions existing in these new information technology industries were non-print unions. Many other unions, like the NGA without a presence in this new world, were in the early and mid-1980s attempting to establish their presence there. This brought the NGA into inter-union difficulties with many unions, including the National Communications Union, the Union of Communications Workers, the Electrical, Electronic Telecommunications Plumbing Union and the Amalgamated Engineering Union.

The NGA viewed work that bypassed the composing room as work from unrecognised sources, which under its rules its members were obliged not to handle when it came into a printing shop. It was this concern about the increase in work from unrecognised sources that led the London Region to submit successfully a motion to the 1974 Delegate Meeting requiring the National Council to take steps to organise advertising agencies and studios, that, if camera-ready copy came into an NGA office and if the source was unrecognised and it proved not possible to organise the employees concerned, the work be blacked in future, and that all employers be given three months' notice that camera-ready copy from unrecognised sources be refused.[12]

Following this delegate meeting the NGA gave notice in January 1975 that work from unrecognised sources would not be handled and a labelling system would be introduced to identify the source of copy. Early in 1975 there were informal meetings between the NGA, the BFMP and the NS which culminated in the withdrawal of the blacking notice, restoration of the status quo and the establishment of a joint committee to investigate the 'work bypassing' problem in an endeavour to agree a solution. The work of the joint committees was unable to prevent the 1976 Delegate Meeting confirming that unrecognised work would not be handled by NGA members.[13] Despite continued discussions between the NGA, BPIF and the NS, the ban came into effect in August 1976. However, it rapidly developed into a clash between NGA and Slade (see below). Between September 1976 and the end of 1978 the NGA ban on work from unrecognised sources continued to interrupt normal working, although the employers claimed that the union's action was spasmodic and unevenly applied. Although the 1979 wage agreement included a joint statement on work from 'unrecognised sources' and further discussions on the matter, these never took place because of a general deterioration in the relationships between the BFIP and the NS which culminated in the 1980 wages and hours dispute. Nevertheless, in a number of cases where difficulties arose over work from unrecognised sources interim arrangements were secured and these worked reasonably well. The 1982 Delegate Meeting accepted a Bristol resolution that the work bypassing the composing room campaign should be re-examined as to whether it was sufficient to safeguard the union's interests in the future.[14]

However, the NGA was not inactive in trying to return work to the composing room. It adopted a flexible and pragmatic approach in an effort to retain work. In 1972 the NGA made an agreement with the BFMP and the NS that its members would accept work from magnetic tapes by seeking recognition of input of a typographical nature. However, by 1978 this policy had become outdated and impractical. The NGA thus amended its policy towards magnetic tapes to one based on three parts. First, where work came from a data bank and had no original print intention it was to be accepted subject to approval from head office. Second, where work came from a data bank and had a print end but could be used for other purposes the NGA would try where possible to obtain control of origination and processing. It was recognised that this might not be possible in all cases and in such cases the work should be handled only if a dispensation was given by the National Council. Third, where there was a 100 per cent intention for the origination to be used to produce a print end product, or for a database to be used for retrieval purposes, the NGA should control all origination and processing. Further, in an attempt to control the use of magnetic tapes, the NGA sought to widen its membership base, for example admitting computer operators and programmers into membership.

The NGA adopted a policy of controlled acceptance of work originated on word processors from non-traditional sources provided specific benefits and safeguards could be secured for the members concerned. In February 1982 an agreement was made between the NGA and RAGA covering the introduction of word processors, under which all typographical instructions on materials to be subsequently used for operation of computers or typesetters were to be inserted by NGA members. Word processors were to be used only to produce copy for setting which was not justified or hyphenated. All other operations were to be performed at the typesetting stage by NGA members. If work was initially set by non-NGA labour on word processors and then printed in Britain by NGA members, it became a formal condition of accepting word processing output that it continue to be printed in the UK by NGA members. A detailed monthly analysis of word processing work handled by RAGA members was to be supplied to the NGA. The minimum rates and conditions and the general principles and objectives contained within the agreement could be adapted to meet the needs of employers wishing to secure NGA cooperation in word processing utilisation. In the BPIF sector, the NGA adopted a policy of negotiating the acceptance of work originated on a word processor on an individual company basis but on the terms contained in the RAGA Agreement.

In response to the expansion of in-plant printing the NGA sought, with little success, to persuade non-printing unions organising there to transfer their members and negotiating rights to it. However, an agreement was reached with APEX that when vacancies arose in establishments where APEX members held the negotiating rights and were involved in print origination work they would be offered to the NGA to fill. Any NGA member filling these vacancies retained NGA membership but was required to take out APEX membership. In addition, APEX agreed to cease organising any more print origination or printing departments, whether they be independent studios or company in-plant operations.

By the late 1970s TASS members were not only producing copy for technical booklets and pamphlets but were now typesetting and assembling pages. The NGA and TASS agreed the contract draughts-men, involved in the production of print origination, should be in membership of the NGA but that the negotiating rights should be retained by TASS. The engineering employers refused, however, to accept these arrangements. In the engineering industry the Confedera-tion of Shipbuilding and Engineering Unions was unwilling to accept the NGA and work from TASS members remained 'blacked'. ASTMS agreed that where their members were involved in producing origina-tion work in in-plant shops they should transfer membership to the NGA. However, in publishing, where ASTMS had a considerable number of members, the NGA failed to persuade it to transfer members or to enter into any kind of agreement over the membership issue.[14] The NGA also held discussions on membership and negotiating rights transfers in in-plant printing establishments with the Union of Shop, Distributive and Allied Workers (USDAW), the Transport Salaried Staffs Association (TSSA), the National Union of Public Employees (NUPE), the Civil and Public Services Association (CPSA), the Institute of Professional Civil Servants (IPCS) and the Greater London Council Staff Association. In some cases, for example USDAW, agreements were reached to transfer members and negotiat-ing rights to the NGA, but with most stalemate prevailed.

Of some 7,600 employees in local government employed on printing work, over 1,400 were members of Nalgo and generally received pay and conditions below those prevailing in the traditional printing industry. The NGA failed to persuade Nalgo to transfer these workers to the Association. Nalgo contended that if it agreed to transfer printers to the NGA it could be faced with claims from other unions for sections to be transferred to other appropriate craft unions. An attempt to reach an understanding with Nalgo on the basis of dual membership for all existing local government employees employed on in-plant printing activities also failed.

The NGA policy towards the transfer of membership and negotiating rights surrounding the growth of print origination work away from traditional printing offices was influenced by a desire to avoid the TUC's Disputes Principles and Procedures criteria for determining membership rights. The NGA considered that these worked unfairly against single-industry unions and contended that a criterion of 'prescribing the rights of members of particular unions to particular work' was a better basis for dealing with inter-union membership problems stemming from the introduction of new technology. It therefore submitted to the 1978 TUC Congress a successful resolution calling for a review of the TUC Disputes Principles and Procedures (see Chapter 10.)

The ban on work from unrecognised sources put the NGA into dispute with Slade when the Association adopted the policy that all make-up and assembly of advertisements, publications, etc., should be the prerogative of NGA composing members. The NGA's policy created a situation where much of the paste-up and origination work, which was sometimes produced by Slade artist members in studios, agencies, publishers, etc., was no longer acceptable to the NGA. The difference in philosophy centred around whether the ban on work from unrecognised sources was intended, as the NGA insisted, primarily to maintain and return work to the printing industry, or whether, as Slade was proposing, it should be a question solely of organising the establishments in which this work was performed, as it was imprac-ticable to return the work to the printing industry. Although the NGA priority was the return of work, it did accept that some organisation in art and advertising studios, etc., was inevitable.

A competitive position existed between the two unions concerning how many members could be recruited, and what areas each union should control. The NGA was driven into a recruitment drive to protect its composing interests.[16] Through the intervention of the TUC Printing Industries Committee, agreement was reached in December 1976 over membership rights. The joint jurisdictional agreement provided for typography to be handled by NGA members, visualising and design work to be handled by Slade members, and for a 50/50 situation between NGA and Slade members in the make-up and assembly area. The agreement related only to the agency and studio field, in which the NGA had previously had virtually no involvement although several hundred Slade members had been involved for a number of years.

In June 1977 a joint Fairs List was issued with a joint Slade/NGA labelling system for identifying work from recognised sources and a 'model' agreement for terms and conditions to be achieved in the studio and agency areas. The model agreement aimed to ensure that advertising agency employers, even if not employing NGA members, paid rates and conditions comparable to those existing in the RAGA and ATFEF agreements if their work was to be 'recognised' when it arrived at a traditional print shop. In this way it was hoped there would be an equitable competitive position between the agencies and studios and the traditional typesetting area. Following Slade members' rejection in 1979 of proposals to amalgamate with the NGA, the joint Fairs List and labelling system were discontinued and the NGA substituted a rubber stamp system to identify 'recognised' work.

Both the NGA and Slade recognised that fighting each other for control of agencies and studios was not in their best interests. However in the absence of an agreement between themselves they had no choice but to crudely defend their own self-interests. Fear and self-interest drew them together and both unions recognised that short of a full merger the joint jurisdictional agreement and a joint Fairs List and labelling system could only be a temporary expedient. The dispute between the two unions highlighted the fact that the changes in techniques presently being introduced in the industry made it impossible to continue drawing demarcation lines on a traditional basis. This was a major factor in Slade and the NGA initiating amalgamation talks towards the end of 1976. Slade also acknowledged that tribal warfare between the separate unions was not advisable because both unions' members' work was disappearing in one way or another because of new materials, new techniques and new methods under the control of the publisher and the customer, rather than the printer. In a bitter conflict over membership in agencies and studios the two unions had fought themselves to a position of stalemate, despite Slade organising some ten members to every one recruited to the NGA. By late 1976 Slade was willing to enter amalgamation talks and conflict between the two unions over work from unrecognised sources was undoubtedly a catalyst of the four union amalgamation talks that began in 1976.

THE GROWTH OF IMPORT PENETRATION

The 1970s saw a sharp increase in the amount of imported print work into the UK. Although the value of exported printing goods exceeded that of imported goods throughout the whole of the 1970s and the early 1980s, the trade balance for the industry declined. The share of imports in the UK printing market rose steadily over the period 1972–82, from 9.4 per cent to 16.4 per cent.

The book manufacturing industry was particularly affected by the loss of work abroad. By the mid-1970s a number of books, particularly children's, were being typeset and printed in Hong Kong, Spain, the Canary Islands and Czechoslovakia. Throughout the 1970s an increasing volume of mail order catalogues, cardboard cartons and travel brochures were printed abroad. There were many reasons for the expansion of imported print matter into the UK, but among the more significant were technological change, the higher inflation rate in the UK relative to other countries in the 1970s, the 'strong' value of the pound in foreign exchanges in the early 1980s, the high interest rate policy adopted by the incoming Conservative government in 1979, and the high cost of energy in the UK relative to other countries.[17] The printing employers also blamed the NGA's ban on handling work from unrecognised sources. They argued that publishers seeking to re-establish their competitiveness were turning to lower-cost non-traditional methods of origination. The increasing use of word processors and of author-generated copy meant that an increasing amount of origination work for books was being produced as camera-ready copy. The employers said that whilst all this work was subject to the NGA ban it was increasingly likely that more of it would be sent overseas.

Cold composition developments meant that it was now possible to have a book typeset in one country and printed and bound in another. A growing number of companies were importing origination and print from places like South-east Asia and India, having established their own typesetting and origination departments in those parts of the world. If the challenge of increasing imports of printed matter was to be overcome, it would be better if the unions could come together and agree a common strategy and set of policies to deal with the problem. Although this could be achieved by loose associations (for example, the TUC Printing Industries Committee), a merger of unions offered a more permanent solution. Amalgamation offered the advantage that job losses from increased imports could be more easily managed via redeployment and retraining, and so on, since the barriers of individual unions defending their self-interest would be removed.

INCREASING UNEMPLOYMENT AND INFLATION

A further threat to the NGA in the 1970s and early 1980s was increasing unemployment amongst its members and the increasing rate of inflation in the UK. The oil price shock of 1973/4 plunged the British economy into recession from which the printing industry did not escape. During the period 1974–6 the industry witnessed an unprecedented number of closures of firms, which in turn led to large-scale redundancies, and unemployment amongst the NGA membership rose to 2 per cent. This was the highest level since the formation of the NGA and the highest in the post Second World War period of any of the constituent unions of the Association. This compared with a national average of 5 per cent. In the latter half of the 1970s, however, unemployment amongst NGA members fell whilst the national average unemployment figure continued to rise. In June 1978, 1 per cent of NGA members were unemployed and this had fallen to below 0.5 per cent by June 1980. Two years later the British economy found itself in severe recession with 3 million people (12.1 per cent of the working population) out of work. Unemployment in the printing industry in mid-1982 stood at 4 per cent. This rising unemployment stemmed from rationalisation of company structures following corporate takeovers and mergers, closures, companies declaring redundancies to survive in the market place, and increased foreign competition. The highest proportion of redundancies took place in the book sector of the industry and in 1980 unemployment in this sector stood at 8 per cent compared with 2 per cent for the industry as a whole. In the three and a half years from January 1979 to June 1982, 185 closures of printing firms, involving 27,500 redundancies, were reported to the Department of Employment. In mid-1975 there had been some 315,000 employees in the industry, but by 1982 this figure had fallen to 249,000. In addition to increasing unemployment amongst its members stemming from economic recession, there was also the threat of unemployment from technological change.

Although even at its highest point the overall level of unemployment amongst NGA members was low, it was not evenly spread. It was much greater amongst letterpress members and compositors than amongst litho printers, and in the large printing cities – London, Manchester and Birmingham – rather than in the towns. The rising unemployment also put financial strains on the NGA. In 1980 it paid an unemployment benefit of £29 per week for 26 weeks, which with a 4 per cent unemployment rate meant a liability of £2.6 milion in the six-month period. The liability was met in the 1980s but required the membership to pay a levy of £1 per week to provide sufficient funds.

The early 1970s saw a sharp rise in the UK inflation rate, which peaked at 25 per cent in mid-June 1975. From mid-1975 to mid-1979, as a result of the government's incomes and prices policy, the inflation rate fell steadily to around 10 per cent. However, in the early 1980s inflation surged again, reaching 21 per cent in the summer of 1980, after which it fell steadily. Throughout the 1970s and the early 1980s the wage increases of NGA members just kept pace with inflation. This was also the experience of Slade, Natsopa, Sogat and NUJ members.

Rising unemployment and inflation were additional factors pushing the NGA to accept that the union organisation established in 1969 could not continue. Merger with one or all of Slade, Natsopa, NUJ and Sogat would make adjustment to the changed circumstances and environment surrounding the industry easier, although it would nevertheless be a difficult adjustment to make. In a larger union it would be easier to deal with change, for example via redeployment and other measures, than if the unions continued as independent bodies protecting their own self-interest regardless of that of other unions.

THE CHANGED LEGAL ENVIRONMENT

A further pressure pushing the NGA to consider mergers with other print unions was the Employment Acts (1980 and 1982), which were designed to reform alleged abuse of union power and to adjust an alleged imbalance in bargaining power against the employer. Some of the provisions in these Acts were direct challenges to the industrial practices of the NGA.

The 1980 Act severely restricted the circumstances in which a trade union could gain immunity from legal action when involved in secondary industrial action. The NGA had used such action to good effect in the 1980 wages and hours dispute and in a number of disputes in the late 1970s revolving around the introduction of new technology. The Act also removed immunity for those who organised or took part in so-called 'secondary' picketing, namely picketing at a place other than the pickets' own place of work. Controlled mass picketing had also been used effectively by the NGA in industrial disputes in the 1970s. The closed shop had been central to the NGA activities and those of its constituent unions for centuries. The 1980 Act sought to regulate the circumstances in which new closed shops could be established and also challenged existing closed shops in that it made the dismissal of an employee in a closed shop situation on the grounds of non-union membership automatically unfair if the individual had conscientious grounds or other deeply held personal convictions against being a member of any trade union whatsoever or of a particular union.

The 1982 Employment Act built on the process started by the 1980 Act. It narrowed the definition of a lawful trade dispute to disputes between workers and their own employers and to matters wholly or mainly employment related, for example pay and work allocation. One effect of this was to remove legal immunity for trade unions involved in an inter-union dispute. This had consequences for printing unions in influencing the implementation of technical change in the industry. The Act also provided for those damaged by unlawful industrial action to gain compensation from the union or unions involved, although the amount of such compensation was limited depending on the membership size of the union. The 1982 Act also outlawed the refusal of employees to handle goods from another firm because the goods were produced by non-union employees. This made the NGA rule on work from unrecognised offices unlawful if implemented. The Act extended the 1980 Employment Act closed shop provisions. Dismissal on grounds of non-union membership in a closed shop became automatically unfair unless the closed shop had been approved in a ballot of those working under the arrangements in the last five years. Those dismissed in these circumstances could receive large compensation payments, which the trade union enforcing the closed shop could be made to pay. The NGA adopted a policy of non-participation in ballots for the approval of closed shops. The 1982 Employment Act permitted circumstances in which non-unionists could continue to work in a closed shop and this was in contradiction of one of the objects of the NGA, namely, 'to assist in securing 100 per cent trade unionism throughout the industry to the extent that it shall be the duty of members to refuse to co-operate with non-trade unionists (male or female) who have been given the opportunity of joining their respective trade unions and have refused to do so.'

This changed legal environment, designed to undermine effective trade union action, together with the changing technological environment of the printing industry meant that the ability of the NGA to protect and advance the interests of its members in isolation from other unions was most difficult. A common printing union policy towards the Employment Acts would be helpful but would always carry the possibility that one or more might break ranks over policy differences. A merger offered a more stable situation.

We have seen that a number of developments in the 1970s and early 1980s motivated the NGA to realise that the union organisation in the printing industry established by 1969 was inappropriate. Changing technology, work bypassing the composing room, increasing import penetrating into the UK printing industry, rising unemployment and inflation and a changed legal environment surrounding the UK industrial relations system all played a part in this. Although the relative significance of each of these factors varied, they were nevertheless all interrelated.

NOTES

1. See *Report of the Delegate Meeting, 1969*, National Graphical Association, pp. 95–7.

2. See *Report of the Delegate Meeting, 1974*, National Graphical Association, pp. 81–3.

3. See *Report of the Delegate Meeting, 1976*, National Graphical Association, pp. 24 and 81–2.

4. See *Report of the Delegate Meeting, 1976*, National Graphical Association, para. 32, p. 25.

5. See *Report of the Committee of Inquiry into the Dispute at Odhams (Watford) Limited involving the International Publishing Corporation, the Society of Lithographic Artists, Designers, Engravers and Process Workers and the National Graphical Association over the handling of photo-composed material*, Department of Employment, HMSO, London, 1974.

6. For example, there were only four installations in the commercial field, each of which was completely under the control of the NGA.

7. For an account of the introduction of photocomposition systems into the national newspapers, see R. Martin, *New Technology and Industrial Relations in Fleet Street*, Oxford University Press, 1981.

8. See *Report of the Delegate Meeting, 1978*, National Graphical Association, p. 247.

9. For a fuller account of this Times Newspapers dispute, see E. Jacobs, *Stop Press*, Deutsch, 1979, and 'Work and New Technology – The Disputes at Times Newspapers Ltd, 1978–79' in S. Meredeen, *Managing Industrial Conflict: Seven Major Disputes*, Hutchinson, 1988, Ch. 5.

10. See *Report of the Delegate Meeting, 1972*, National Graphical Association, p. 103.

11. See *Report of the Delegate Meeting, 1980*, National Graphical Association, p. 23.

12. See *Report of the Delegate Meeting, 1974*, National Graphical Association, pp. 199–205.

13. See *Report of the Delegate Meeting, 1976*, National Graphical Association, pp. 148–56.

14. See *Report of the Delegate Meeting, 1982*, National Graphical Association, pp. 208–10.

15. Here ASTMS was influenced by its membership's competitive position with the NUJ in the design and origination departments of a number of publishing houses.

16. For full accounts of the inter-union difficulties between the NGA and Slade, see *Report of Inquiry into certain Trade Union Recruitment Activities*, Cmnd 7706, HMSO, 1979, Ch. 4, and Discussion Paper, *Work from Unrecognised Sources (work bypassing the Composing Room)*, NGA Delegate Meeting, June 1978.

17. See *The Future of the Printing Industries*, Report to the National Economic Development Council, Printing Industries Sector Working Party, HMSO, 1983, Table 8, p. 13.

CHAPTER 6

THE ACTUAL FORMATION OF THE NGA (1982)

RELATIONSHIPS BETWEEN THE NGA AND OTHER PRINT UNIONS

The Scottish Typographical Association

Relationships with this Society were less than cordial. On 31 December 1969 a Reciprocity Agreement which had existed between the two unions since 1901 was abrogated by the STA. In the early 1970s the two unions challenged each others' claims to jurisdiction over litho machines introduced into letterpress houses in Scotland. Attempts to reach agreement with the STA to cover this development failed, following the STA reaching an understanding in 1972 with the Society of Master Printers of Scotland (SMPS) that where there were conflicting claims as to rights to lithographic equipment the STUC should adjudicate.

The NGA responded to this by stating that if the STA was not prepared to accept the traditional demarcation lines then neither was the NGA and it intended to recruit in Scotland amongst compositors and letterpress machine managers. However, in December 1973 the NGA proposed that the two unions enter talks with a view to amalgamation and improving the deterioration that had taken place in their relationships, particularly since the STUC, without reference to the NGA, informed the SMPS that the jurisdiction of litho machines in Scotland should go to the STA.[1] In February 1974 the STA formally rejected the NGA proposal that the two unions enter amalgamation talks, as it was involved in amalgamation discussions with Sogat and it would be dishonourable to conduct amalgamation talks with more than one union at a time.

In October 1974 new discussions opened between the two unions to resolve their differences over litho printing. The NGA stressed that these difficulties could be resolved on a long-term basis only by an amalgamation. The STA (by now the Scottish Graphical Association) said it could not respond to this proposal because its merger talks with Sogat had reached an advanced stage. Nevertheless the NGA proposed an interim agreement to deal with the immediate problems. It proposed that a joint committee should have responsibility for dealing with litho installation in Scotland and have the maximum flexibility to deal with all the situations that might arise. It would act within agreed guidelines. First, both unions would adhere at all times to the TUC Disputes Principles and Procedures with regard to the transfer of members. Second, SGA members currently operating litho machines and those required to operate them in the future would be given the opportunity to become members of the NGA. Third, the NGA would bring pressure to bear with respect to NGA membership on SGA members operating litho machines in solely letterpress houses or those required to operate them in future who declined to join the NGA. The understanding would operate for twelve months, but could be terminated earlier by agreement between the two unions. However, it proved impossible to gain mutual acceptance of these proposals and, in the last months of its independent existence before amalgamating with Sogat on 1 October 1975, the SGA declined to acknowledge, let alone reply, to NGA correspondence.[2]

The differences between the NGA and SGA over the manning of litho machines remained and after the Sogat merger became more acute. The NGA continued to reserve the right to recruit in Scotland all those categories of worker for whom it catered elsewhere in Britain unless Sogat (75) agreed to recognise and respect the NGA's traditional rights in the litho field. However, in the spring of 1976 the NGA and Sogat (75) reached agreement on jurisdictional rights in the lithographic printing field. Under the agreement the traditional NGA areas of Scotland were recognised and accepted by Sogat. Where existing letterpress houses changed to litho printing, members of the former SGA so affected were to remain in membership of Sogat but Sogat would pay a licence fee of 15p in respect of each of such members. If members of the SGA covered by the licence fee wished to go to a traditional litho establishment under the control of the NGA, Sogat agreed they must transfer to the NGA. Sogat also said it did not wish to intrude into the litho agreement held between the NGA and the SMPS.

Under this 1976 agreement, any matters arising in the future concerning its operation were to be referred to the head office of both unions.

The Irish Graphical Society/Irish Print Union

As lithographic printing techniques were introduced into former letterpress printing houses in Dublin problems arose as to the jurisdiction of litho machines. The Dublin Typographical Provident Society changed its name in 1964 to the Irish Graphical Society which claimed jurisdiction over litho machines in Dublin, which traditionally were the preserve of the ASLP. However, the issue was complicated by the IGS claim to become a single Irish Republic union for graphical workers. As a result, post-1964 relationships between the NGA and the IGS took a turn for the worse, although relationships in Dublin between NGA members and IGS members remained cordial. The differences between the two unions over the manning of litho machines in Dublin proved impossible to resolve.

Arising from the NGA policy in respect of work from unrecognised sources it was necessary to have discussions between the IGS, Slade and the NGA. The IGS supported the NGA's campaign. However, problems arose with the Irish Transport and General Workers' Union (IT&GWU), which mounted a successful organising campaign in art studios and advertising agencies. In late 1977 the IT&GWU suggested that the Slade Southern Ireland Branch transfer membership on attractive terms to the IT&GWU Print Branch. Consideration was given to the offer, in the light of which urgent talks took place between IGS, Slade and NGA concerning the implications arising from the IT&GWU offer. They agreed that a committee of the three unions be set up without delay to combat the IT&GWU threat to resolve any disputes between the three societies. The committee met on several occasions, but in 1980 the IGS withdrew from the committee in protest against the NGA organising supervisory employees in a Dublin company. The end of the decade saw the establishment of an NUJ–NGA–Irish Print Union (IPU) committee and significant developments towards the amalgamation of the IPU and the NUJ.

The Wallpaper Workers' Union

The Wallpaper Workers' Union was an industrial union and had cordial relationships with the NGA. Transfers of membership between the two unions was easy and the officials of the Wallpaper Workers' Union knew the NGA would talk amalgamation with it whenever it wanted. In 1969 the Wallpaper Workers' Union requested that the NGA organise wallpaper workers in a new factory in Southern Ireland on the understanding that if the Wallpaper Workers' Union found it possible to undertake the organisation and to negotiate for the employees in the future the NGA would accept their prior rights.[3] The establishment was manned by NGA members as it were under licence from the Wallpaper Workers' Union.

The NGA Manchester branch submitted a motion to the 1972 Delegate Meeting requesting the NGA to proceed with merger discussions with the Wallpaper Workers' Union. The motion was amended to include Slade and remitted to the National Council.[4] Relationships between the two unions remained good and there was informal talks on the subject of amalgamation. In 1975 the Wallpaper Workers' Union retitled itself the National Union of Wallcoverings, Decorative and Allied Trades (NUWDAT), but in 1976 it joined amalgamation talks together with the NGA and Natsopa, attracted by the proposed link-up between two unions of which one was predominantly craft oriented and the other predominantly non-craft. A merged NGA/Natsopa union would have contained both craft and non-craft workers, as was the case with the Wallpaper Workers' Union.

Slade

Relationships between the NGA and Slade prior to their entering a four union amalgamation attempt have been described in the previous chapter. The disappointing results of the Slade ballot in 1978 on the proposals to form the Graphic Arts Union nevertheless meant that dialogue and cooperation between the two unions had to continue if the problems that occurred in 1976 were to be avoided. However, in March 1978 Slade informed the NGA that it was no longer prepared to be joint parties in the Fairs List and identity label system. This made it more difficult for the two unions to find common policy on many points, including the inter-union problems surrounding the introduction of new technology and changing techniques. In 1981, in the face of increasing industrial and political problems, Slade approached the NGA and suggested that amalgamation discussions should be re-opened. These talks were to prove successful.

The organisational efforts of Slade and the NGA in the advertising agency and studio field were subjected in 1979 to a Report of Inquiry conducted by Andrew Leggat QC. The two unions decided, as did all of the other print unions and the TUC, not to participate in the inquiry. It was considered that, given the government's criticisms of the two unions' organising activities, the outcome of the inquiry was predetermined. As things turned out, the inquiry was particularly damning as far as Slade was concerned; the condemnation of the NGA was considerably more restrained. In certain parts of the inquiry's report the NGA was vindicated as having pursued organisation in art and advertising studios with the intention of protecting the traditional interests of its existing members.[5] Nevertheless the Conservative government used the inquiry findings to justify making illegal, under the 1980 Employment Act, the blacking of non-union produced goods and services with the explicit purpose of recruiting workers into a certain union or unions unless the action was aimed at other workers employed by the same employer or workers who worked at the same place.

Natsopa/Sogat (Division I)/Natsopa

In September 1964 Natsopa sought a meeting with the NGA to discuss closer working between the two unions or even some form of amalgamation. A meeting for this purpose took place on 4 November 1964 at which Natsopa indicated that it was prepared to amalgamate with the NGA on a 'divisional basis' but would wish to retain its existing rules and practices. The NGA considered this impractical but did agree to further talks, although it had no mandate from its members for an amalgamation with other than craft unions. However, in early 1965 Natsopa informed the NGA that it had decided not to proceed further with talks and had initiated amalgamation discussions with the NUPB&PW.

Following this, the relationship between the two unions deteriorated rapidly, particularly when Natsopa claimed a share of the control of web-offset presses and adult promotion for their members in national and provincial newspapers and the photogravure periodical industry. In 1966 the NGA and Sogat (Division 1) set up a Joint Liaison Committee to resolve their differences and explore the possibility of amalgamation. However, it soon became obvious that little progress could be made towards amalgamation whilst the issue of control of web-offset presses remained unresolved. An opportunity to do so arose with the report of the Cameron Court of Inquiry, which came down on the side of the NGA (and the ASLP) in its dispute with Sogat over the manning of web-offset presses. Although the NGA accepted the Court's findings, Sogat did not and continued to pursue its policy of integrated staffing on web-offset presses. Towards the end of 1967, in a further attempt to resolve the problem, the NGA proposed a joint web-offset committee on which representatives of NGA, ASLP and Sogat (Division 1) would sit to deal with all future web-offset installations. An essential part of the proposal was an undertaking by the NGA and the ASLP to participate in discussions about opportunities for the progression of Sogat members in the industry and an undertaking by Sogat to withdraw its claim for integrated staffing.

Although the three unions approved the proposals, problems quickly arose. ASLP had reservations about the inclusion of general printing web-offset installations into the committee's terms of reference whilst Sogat announced that its cooperation was subject to national newspapers being outside the committee's remit. Sogat also intimated that, if it withdrew its claim for integrated staffing in the national newspaper field, it would negotiate independently on rates and staffing. The final break came when Sogat refused to attend a meeting of the three unions at which the terms of reference for the committee would be agreed. However, significant factors did emerge from the discussions. For the first time Sogat pinpointed the two main considerations which motivated its policy with regard to the manning of web-offset presses. The first was that the traditional positions of Sogat members on newspaper rotary presses were in danger of being virtually eliminated by the introduction of web-offset machines. Second, it was concerned that its members were denied opportunities for advancement to craft status.

In an effort to meet these two points, the NGA early in 1968 suggested to Sogat that there should be one union for all machine and composing rooms, and that this should be the NGA. It was further proposed that a formula be worked out jointly by the two unions whereby there was progression from non-craft to craft in these fields. However, Sogat rejected these proposals unless they were implemented within the context of amalgamation.

Although the door for further discussions between the NGA and Sogat (Division 1) to establish closer working and, ultimately, an amalgamation remained open, it was unrealistic to assume in the summer of 1969 that any real progress could be made until Sogat withdrew its demand for jurisdiction over web-offset machines. The NGA was also concerned that Sogat was failing to honour its obligations under the terms of the P&KTF clerical formula with regard to NGA members transferring to clerical and administrative work by virtue of their technical knowledge. In addition, Sogat resisted the transfer of its members employed on small offset machines to the NGA under the terms of an agreement between the former ASLP and Sogat. The NGA regarded Sogat's main motive in this behaviour as its advancement as a union into the craft field rather than concern to meet its members' aspirations with regard to employment security or with regard to opportunities for them to achieve craft status.

Relationships with Sogat (Division 1) and Natsopa remained strained during the early 1970s and were not helped by the NGA resignation from the TUC in 1972 (see Chapter 10) and Natsopa's support for the P&KTF being dissolved whilst the NGA considered it should continue. The NGA General Secretary, John Bonfield, told the 1974 Delegate Meeting that relationships with other print unions were just about as bad as they had ever been in all his experience and that the only consolation was that they were so bad that they could only get better.[6]

By mid-1975 relationships with Natsopa were beginning to improve. They were further helped in 1976 by the new General Secretaries – Wade (NGA) and O'Brien (Natsopa) – of the two unions adopting policy stances to improve the relationships between their respective unions. Both the NGA and Natsopa 1976 Delegate Meetings approved resolutions committing them to the concept of one union for the industry.[7] Following its 1976 Delegate Meeting, the NGA concluded that any attempt to bring all the printing unions together at one fell swoop would be doomed to failure and decided on a 'step-by-step' approach. It therefore decided to approach Natsopa to examine the possibility of amalgamation. Merger talks began in 1976 and subsequently Slade and NUWDAT joined them, but in 1977 Natsopa was unable to provide certain financial information to the respective amalgamation panels and was advised that unless and until it could provide this information the amalgamation talks should continue on a three union basis. In April 1978 Natsopa sought to rejoin the merger talks but was told that the three union movement would continue until either a new union was formed or one or all three unions' members rejected amalgamation. As a result, Natsopa began to discuss amalgamation with Sogat, but in the summer of 1979 these were shelved. The NGA and Sogat then explored the possibility of amalgamation talks but, given that subsequently the NGA entered formal merger talks with the NUJ and Sogat with Natsopa, it was decided that to continue discussions with Sogat would be inappropriate. In July 1982 Sogat and Natsopa amalgamated to form Sogat (82).

NUPB&PW/Sogat (Division A)/Sogat

Developments in the litho field led to disputes between the NGA and Sogat (Division A). One such problem occurred towards the end of 1969 in connection with the operation of multilith machines engaged on the personalisation of cheques. This arose when a firm – where the work had previously been performed by the PMB of Sogat (A) on vertical miehles – closed down and the work was transferred to another office. At the time of this transfer, new multilith machines were introduced and because of the threat of redundancies Sogat claimed the right of its members to follow the job. It also challenged the right of NGA litho members to operate small offset machines. After a series of meetings a formula was reached that no redundancies would occur and that the machines would be operated on a 50/50 basis. In addition, any new machines were to be operated by NGA members, or by PMB Sogat (A) members issued with NGA cards. The formula, however, firmly established recognition of the jurisdictional rights of the NGA in this particular field.

Early in 1970 discussions took place between the NGA and Sogat (A) to resolve difficulties which had arisen over the operation of lithographic proofing equipment in hitherto letterpress process houses. It had been customary for PMB Sogat members to carry out proofing. However, with the change-over to litho, the NGA claimed that it should now be done by their litho members. An additional complication was that this NGA attitude would mean redundancies amongst PMB members. Eventually an agreement acceptable to the two unions was reached. Under this, Sogat recognised Art Reproductions Limited as a litho house under NGA jurisdiction; the restriction of the provisions made to ·PMB proven members consisted of 500–600 members in Federation of Master Process Engravers Houses; in the event of an expansion of litho proofing opportunities, this was to be clearly recognised as the province of the NGA, and where technical change caused possible redundancy to PMB proofers they were to be allowed to operate these machines with associate cards. In drawing up this formula the negotiators endorsed the view of Sogat and NGA that one union for the printing industry was the ultimate aim and that closer working between the two unions would be a contribution to achieving this.

In the early 1970s relationships between the two unions deteriorated. The problems arose from differences over the manning of printing machines in peripheral areas of the industry, the NGA resignation from the TUC, and challenges to the NGA's position in London over the manning of litho machines and the operation of the latest types of film-setters. The NGA regarded all these issues as Sogat intensifying an overt attack on its craft position begun by Natsopa in the 1960s with its claim to shared jurisdiction over the managing of web-offset machines. The NGA laid the main cause of the deterioration of its relationships with the non-craft unions over the period 1966–76 at the door of the non-craft unions themselves.[8]

In an endeavour to resolve its differences with Sogat, the NGA agreed in April 1975 to joint talks under the auspices of the Advisory, Conciliation and Arbitration Service (ACAS), on the basis that Sogat gave a prior undertaking to recognise the traditional jurisdictional rights of the NGA. In return the NGA would cooperate with Sogat in protecting the employment of any of its members threatened by technological developments. The only proviso to this guideline was that NGA members whose employment might similarly be threatened would have priority and those Sogat members who might transfer to recognised NGA operations would take up some form of NGA membership. Sogat refused to give such an undertaking and indicated that it intended to carve out its own future jurisdictional position in the industry regardless of other unions. The NGA concluded that Sogat was more concerned for its status and size than for its members' individual interests and saw no alternative but to withdraw from the ACAS talks in September 1975.

In 1976 relationships between the two unions changed dramatically, helped by the NGA's return to the TUC and the desire of the new NGA General Secretary, Joe Wade, to set in train informal discussions with Sogat and Natsopa with the objective of improving cooperation amongst the printing unions. Such cooperation was seen as vital if the unions were adequately to defend their members' interests in the face of economic and technological change. This NGA initiative met with almost instant success in that in May 1976 the union announced new understandings with Sogat in London and Scotland. In London the PMB of Sogat, the Monotype Casters, Filmsetters and Typefounders Branch and the NGA London Region were to be brought together in a new structure. A joint NGA/Sogat committee was quickly established which made it possible to introduce photocomposing equipment to the benefit of both unions' members. In Scotland the two unions agreed the jurisdictional rights on lithographic printing techniques outlined above.

The new cordial relationship with Sogat enabled a series of jurisdictional and demarcation problems between the two unions to be the subject of agreement. The NGA/Sogat joint committee assisted in alleviating difficulties arising from new technology between the NGA London Region and Sogat's PMB and Monocasters Branch. The NGA/Sogat (Scottish Graphical Division) joint committee continued to discuss problems over litho printing in Scotland and organisational difficulties were generally resolved to the satisfaction of both unions.[9] However, difficulties were to emerge again with Sogat in the PMB area, over the Monocasters' agreement and the Perth agreement over the introduction of litho in Scotland, although prior to this the NGA and Sogat agreed in 1979 to enter immediate talks about the possibility of finding common ground to begin formal amalgamation discussions. These talks continued into 1981, at which point the NGA decided that, since it was involved in formal amalgamation discussions with the NUJ, and Sogat was in a likewise position with Natsopa, talks should end.

The National Union of Journalists

Between 1969 and 1982 the NGA's relationship with the NUJ varied between at times good and others hostile. Although the NGA had an agreement with the NUJ relating to the transmission of pictures whereby any freelance journalist who installed a tele-photo transmitter signed an agreement providing for payments to NGA members who worked on a full- and/or part-time basis, no such agreement existed in respect of freelance journalists who installed telex machines to wire copy into newspaper offices. In the 1970s the practice of wiring copy increased and the NGA claimed that such work should be carried out by its members. The NUJ initially rejected this view but subsequently conceded the work to the NGA.

In the mid-1970s the NUJ was involved in a number of industrial stoppages up and down the country and called upon the assistance of the NGA, since the reaction of NGA compositors was usually the key to the success or otherwise of NUJ disputes. However, the NGA limited its support in most of these strikes. Had it not done so, the number of strikes in itself might well have closed down the provincial newspaper industry for long periods. In addition, in two NGA disputes (Parrett and Neves and Sharman's), the results of which were of vital concern to large numbers of its members, the support of the NUJ members had not been forthcoming. The NUJ was reluctant to enter consultations with the NGA before embarking on industrial disputes affecting NGA members and those of other unions, whether those disputes concerned the closed shop or an improvement in wages and working conditions.

This dichotomy was particularly highlighted in the dispute at North of England Newspapers in Darlington in 1977 where the NGA supported the NUJ claim for the establishment of a closed shop in the editorial area. During the dispute the NGA presented proposals to the NUJ for closer working in respect of new technology and a closed shop strategy for editorial departments. The proposals included the settlement of the NUJ dispute at Darlington and were unacceptable to that union. The NGA considered that the chance of achieving mutually beneficial agreements with the NUJ on a closed shop strategy and new technology had not been taken up.

Nevertheless, relationships between the two unions improved and a working relationship was achieved. During 1980, the NUJ was involved in a major dispute in the London area, which also affected a number of newspaper companies in the provinces, over an increase in the NUJ London weighting allowance. Support was given by the NGA to the extent that only advertising copy was handled and the dispute was eventually satisfactorily resolved. In early 1981, the NUJ was also involved in a dispute with the *Camden Journal*. The NGA tried to conciliate between the parties, but, following a rejection by the company of an offer by the NUJ to accept binding arbitration, the NGA agreed to strike against the company. As a result the company reconsidered the arbitration proposal and the matter was resolved through that process.

The 1980 NUJ Annual Delegate Meeting approved a motion suggesting amalgamation talks with the NGA. The result of these talks was the creation of a permanent subcommittee between the two unions and part of its terms of reference require either union to consult before embarking upon disputes that could involve members of the other union. A 'Letter of Association' was also drawn up between the two unions covering a commitment from both organisations to work together and give mutual support in areas of common interest, such as disputes, new technology[10] and the reporting of racial issues. The Letter of Association was regarded by both unions as an important statement of intent and as a step towards amalgamation between the two unions.

ATTEMPTS TO FORM THE GRAPHIC ARTS UNION (GAU)

The NGA envisaged one union for the industry being achieved in two stages. First a single craft union would be created and then one industry-wide union. The 1976 NGA Delegate Meeting instructed the National Council to approach the other print unions to bring about one union for the industry. The achievement of one union in the industry would not be easy or straightforward and a phased approach was thought desirable.

In August 1976 the NGA approached Natsopa to examine the possibility of amalgamation between the two unions. The NGA made it clear that if a successful merger were achieved it must be seen as the first step towards the ultimate goal of one union for the industry. Natsopa had come to the same conclusion and preliminary discussions were started immediately. Why had the NGA chosen Natsopa, a non-craft union, for the first step and not a craft union? In 1976 Slade was not really in the amalgamation game since, unlike the NGA, Natsopa and Sogat, it was not committed by conference decision to the concept of one union for the industry. The compelling reason for a link-up with Natsopa was the introduction of direct entry and web-offset into national and provincial newspapers. These techniques enabled advertising staffs to undertake typesetting, reading and page make-up functions which had traditionally been controlled by the NGA. Although advertising staffs were mostly non-union, the appropriate union for such staff was the clerical section of Natsopa. If the NGA was to retain some control in the newspaper world of direct entry systems and protect the interests of its compositor members, it needed a presence in the advertising departments. An amalgamation with Natsopa would give this. The stark alternative was involvement in major conflicts on an ever-increasing scale with Natsopa.

Before the NGA/Natsopa talks had progressed very far a request was received from the NUWDAT to participate in the amalgamation discussions. NUWDAT saw the proposed link-up between a union predominantly craft oriented and one predominantly non-craft as the ideal basis for an involvement on its part. Although to admit NUWDAT to the amalgamation talks required amendment to the background work which had already been done, both the NGA and Natsopa reacted favourably to the NUWDAT request.

An indication of the size and scope of the amalgamation task was that it took many months of painstaking research merely to establish the factual position about each union's finances, structure, constitution, rules and policies. Much progress was made but events were also moving in another direction which was to bring Slade into the amalgamation movement. The decision of the NGA to impose a ban on work from unrecognised sources inevitably led it into a recruiting campaign in advertising agencies and art studios. Against this background Slade decided at the end of 1976 to enter the amalgamation talks. Although the NGA, Natsopa and NUWDAT realised that widening the amalgamation to cover four unions would inevitably mean a fresh start and that a great deal of work which had already been done would have to be abandoned, they accepted that this was a price worth paying. The four unions coming together would give effective union control over origination and printing in the industry for the first time.

Problems arose during the months of painstaking discussion. The first setback came when Natsopa was unable to provide essential financial information to allow a proper costing exercise to be carried out. In the circumstances the other three unions felt they had no alternative but to advise Natsopa that, unless and until it could provide this financial information, amalgamation would go ahead on a three union basis. This is what happened from December 1977. A second hitch arose when two members of the Slade Art Union were granted an injunction in January 1978 to stop Slade introducing special rules to cover its art union section, which had 8,000 members out of a total membership of 23,000. Slade attempted to resolve the problem within the terms of the injunction, but the three unions decided that if Slade was unable to resolve the problem before amalgamation then the new union would tackle the problem. A third 'crisis' arose in April 1978 when Natsopa finally told the other unions that it now had the financial information required and would produce it at the next amalgamation meeting. The three unions replied that so much progress had been made that it was impossible to re-start four union talks. The three unions stressed that the new union would be willing to continue discussions with Natsopa with a view to a merger once the new union came into being.[11]

Natsopa, however, was never to return to the amalgamation talks and in 1982 amalgamated with Sogat. Had Natsopa been able to provide the missing financial information in late 1977, or earlier than May 1978, it would have re-entered the merger talks. If this had happened and the merger had been successful then the story of the implementation of direct entry in the newspaper sector of the industry might have been very different. Such are the 'accidents of history'.

In May 1978 the proposals for amalgamating the NGA, Slade and NUWDAT to form the new National Graphical Union were unveiled and accepted at the 1978 NGA Delegate Meeting. Delegates were asked to approve the proposals without amendments on the condition that the first conference of the new union would be a rules revision conference at which amendments to the constitution could be submitted in the light of practical experience.

The new union was to be based on constitutional principles acceptable to the three unions. The existing NGA rulebook formed the basis of the rulebook of the new union, whilst the present NGA financial structure was to be the basis of its financial structure. A third principle was that the name for the new union would have to be a significant change from NGA or else both Slade and NUWDAT members would see the amalgamation as a virtual NGA takeover. Eventually agreement was reached on the name of the Graphic Arts Union. A fourth principle was that, as far as representation was concerned at National Council, delegate meetings, trade group boards, regions and branches, proportional representation should apply. This was proposed on the condition that both Slade and the NUWDAT accepted that there should be no special trade group boards to cover their particular interests.

Given that some 25 per cent of NUWDAT members were in clerical, technical and administrative jobs it was decided to set up a new trade group board – Art, Clerical, Technical and Administrative (ACTA) – consisting of NUWDAT members in clerical and administrative positions, Slade and NGA members working in the agency and studio field, NGA members in the clerical and administrative field, most of whom presently had no representational rights in the NGA, and the existing Executive, Technical and Overseers section of the NGA. The bulk of NUWDAT members were in the North of England and to take account of this its former members were to have special representation rights in the northern region decision-making structures of the new union.

With respect to region and branch representation, Slade and NUWDAT accepted that the existing NGA regional and branch officers would remain as at present and that in effect in each region and branch the existing NGA branch or regional officer would become the regional/branch secretary in overall control industrially and administratively of the branch or region. However a former Slade full-time officer was to be sited at all regional offices to ensure that, should branches require special industrial assistance on particular problems, a former Slade officer would be available.

In addition to ensuring that they had adequate representation in the decision-making structure of the new union, Slade and NUWDAT also sought 'guarantees and understandings' on their industrial practices. The new union was to accept the operation of the house agreement policy in the Slade litho and gravure areas. Slade did not hold national agreements in those areas but sought house agreements in accordance with policy decided by a national conference of FOCs and branch officials. Slade house agreements were not like those in the NGA areas, where they were additions to the minimum conditions set out in national agreements and represented extras for some and not all. It was also accepted that Slade policy in respect of shift and overtime working would be contained within the appendices to the new rulebook, and that the 'white card' system of obtaining employment in the Slade area would continue, although it would be under the control of branch secretaries.

NUWDAT also had certain problems in that, unlike the NGA and Slade, it did not operate a pre-entry closed shop. However, NUWDAT was assured that this would not be a difficulty, for in a number of NGA and Slade areas, notably agencies, studios and small offset establishments, a post-entry rather than a pre-entry closed shop system operated. The existing NGA policy did not permit balancing of time and it was proposed to retain this policy in the new union. A number of agreements were held with employers by NUWDAT which permitted balancing time. In fact a number of agreements also existed in some NGA areas, particularly in the litho field, allowing balancing of time. All three unions agreed that these agreements would continue in the new union, but that in line with the overall policy of the union there would be attempts, through negotiation, to remove these over a period of time.

In addition to representational and industrial practices protection,

NUWDAT and Slade sought to maintain the continuation of their cherished democratic practices. For example, the NGA elected its national officials by a first past the post electoral system. Slade elected its national officials by exhaustive ballot. In the new union, a system similar to that of an exhaustive ballot was to be introduced for the election of national officials.

Although there were differences in the per capita values of the three unions, it was agreed that all members of the new union should achieve an equal financial status. To bring the Slade per capita fee up to that of the NGA, Slade members were to pay a levy of 10p per week over and above the basic subscription for a period of three years from 2 April 1979. As for NUWDAT, equalisation would be achieved by its members paying subscriptions at 60 per cent of the full rate in the first year, progressing by 10 per cent annual stages up to the full 100 per cent over five years from 2 April 1979. During this period NUWDAT members would receive certain benefits at half the rate provided for in the rules.

The Graphic Arts Union was to come into being on 2 April 1979. So that all members would have an early opportunity to discuss the industrial policy of the new union, its first delegate meeting was to be held in September 1980 and confined solely to industrial issues. As it was desirable to allow members to gain some experience of the way the rules and constitution of the new union operated before involving themselves in changing the rules, a rules revision conference would not be held until June 1981.

The general principles of the draft constitution of the Graphic Arts Union were approved by delegates at the Slade Triennial Conference in May 1978, at the NGA Biennial Delegate Meeting in June 1978 and at a special delegate meeting called by NUWDAT in September 1978. Subsequently the executives of the three unions approved the proposed rules of the new union. In December 1978 the members of the three unions voted on the proposed formation of the Graphic Arts Union, which was designed to retain the best of the traditions, customs and practices of each of the three unions and yet be broad and modern enough in structure, constitution and outlook to meet the ever-changing situation of the industry. However, in January 1979 the three unions announced that their plans to form the Graphic Arts Union had failed. Although NGA and NUWDAT members had voted in favour of merger by substantial majorities, there was a small majority against in the Slade ballot. Voting figures were:

	In favour	Against	Majority
NGA	44,888	13,755	31,133
NUWDAT	1,987	950	1,037
Slade	5,589	6,667	1,078

Because under the Trade Union Amalgamation Act (1964) each union's members had to have their own majority, the rejection by Slade meant that the Graphic Arts Union, which would have had 140,000 members, could not come into existence. The failure of the amalgamation attempt was a disappointment to the three unions, all of whom saw the Graphic Arts Union as vital to the protection of their members' interests given the technological and economic changes occurring and expected to occur in the industry.

THE NGA/NATIONAL UNION OF WALLCOVERINGS, DECORATIVE AND ALLIED TRADES (NUWDAT) MERGER

Both the NGA and NUWDAT felt that the rejection of the Graphic Arts Union by Slade in no way invalidated the reasons for the merging of their two unions. Proposals for a transfer of engagements from NUWDAT to the NGA were presented to NUWDAT members in July 1979 and carried by 1,758 votes to 813 against. NUWDAT members were to be represented as a separate section at NGA delegate meetings, to have two members on the National Council elected on a national basis, and to have representation on the Letterpress Trade Group Board and on all the regional councils except Scotland and Ireland. Former NUWDAT members were to join the appropriate NGA branch and were to be represented on its committee in direct proportion to their strength in the branch, with a minimum of one representative. Where there were thirty or more former NUWDAT members in two or more chapels in any branch they could form a local consultative committee. Given the concentration of former NUWDAT members in the North of England the existing part-time NGA branches of Accrington and Stockport became full-time.

One of the bigger changes which the NGA/NUWDAT merger brought was the setting up of a new trade group board – the Art, Technical, Clerical and Administrative – to cater for art, technical and

NGA white-collar members. The board was to be responsible for negotiating with employers on behalf of all clerical and administrative members. The General Secretary of the NUWDAT was to become an NGA national officer, its Assistant General Secretary a Northern Region Officer, and its one national officer would become an officer at NGA head office with particular responsibilities for organising. NUWDAT also received certain industrial assurances. Recruiting of labour within the wallcoverings industry was by a post-entry closed shop, as opposed to a pre-entry closed shop in NGA areas, and this practice would continue. The NUWDAT's existing negotiating and consultative arrangements with the major wallcoverings employers were to continue. Where provisions in the current NUWDAT agreements were at variance with NGA rules, they were to be honoured, subject to negotiating changes in line with general NGA policy.

All NUWDAT assets were incorporated into those of the NGA. Full members of NUWDAT were to pay 60 per cent of NGA full subscriptions for the first year, progressing by 10 per cent each year until the 100 per cent was reached. During this five-year period NUWDAT members were to receive certain benefits, e.g. unemployment benefit, at half the rate provided for in the rules. The NGA/NUWDAT merger became effective from 1 October 1979.

NUWDAT was a different type of union from those with which the NGA had previously merged. These had been craft unions. NUWDAT, with some 4,000 members, was an industrial union. It organised and represented all the production workers in the wallcoverings industry, the unskilled workers, the semi-skilled and the skilled on the origination side of the industry, the machine production and also the finishing, warehousing and despatch side. It also organised the salaried employees of the industry. Some 25 per cent of its membership was in clerical, administrative and technical areas. It claimed to have in membership 95 per cent of the wallcoverings industry workforce. The union operated juvenile and adult apprentices, and a progressive system of attaining skills, but all under its control.

NUWDAT saw many advantages in a link with the NGA. The wallcoverings industry was declining with the increasing use of emulsion paint as a substitute for wallpaper, and the rising popularity of plastic-coated wallcoverings. These trends reduced the demands for wallcoverings, which led to a decline in NUWDAT membership. However, this declining membership required increasing and more sophisticated servicing in response to the increasing concentration of the ownership of the industry and external pressures stemming from legal changes covering pensions and health and safety at work, etc. The NUWDAT lacked sufficient resources to provide the quality of servicing now required by its members. A link with the NGA would provide this.

Why then should the NGA favour a link with NUWDAT? The union offered the NGA at least two advantages. Technological developments were dictating that the NGA expand its membership. The expansion of word processors, direct entry systems, photocomposition, camera-ready copy, etc., was moving the traditional control of the printing industry away from the NGA compositor. Origination work was moving into staff and salaried employees' areas, etc. The NGA had few white-collar members. Natsopa (clericals) was generally accepted as the appropriate non-manual union in the industry. A merger with Natsopa at this time was by no means a possibility let alone a certainty. If the NGA moved into non-manual areas it faced the prospect that not only would employers resist this but Natsopa might invoke the TUC Disputes Principles and Procedures on the grounds that the NGA had no claim to organise non-manuals and had few, if any, in membership. As some 25 per cent of NUWDAT membership was non-manual, a merger with that union would get the NGA into the non-manual area and allow it to argue that it had an established white-collar section. It would also enable the NGA to begin recruiting amongst advertising staffs in newspapers. Natsopa, on the whole, had done little, outside London and the Home Counties, to organise these employees. Organisation amongst such employees was vital to the NGA if it was to have any influence on the introduction of direct entry composing systems in the newspaper field.

The NUWDAT link-up also offered the NGA expertise it did not currently possess. If non-manual employees were to join the NGA they would have to be persuaded of the advantages of doing so and be confident that the union could service their needs in terms of job evaluation and performance appraisal systems, etc. The NGA in 1979 possessed few chapel and branch officials with membership recruitment skills. The operation of the apprenticeship system and the pre-entry closed shop meant that employees automatically joined the NGA. It was not necessary to persuade individuals of the value of trade union membership. If the NGA was to gain a significant foothold amongst non-manual employees it needed to persuade these workers of the benefits of joining. By linking with NUWDAT the NGA would gain access to the organising skills of NUWDAT officials. These officials would be able to train NGA chapel and branch officials in the skills and knowledge required to persuade non-manual employees to join the NGA. Job evaluation, appraisal systems, grading-based pay structures, promotion procedures, etc. were another world to NGA officials. To NUWDAT officials they were everyday facts of life. The NGA/ NUWDAT merger was thus a significant link-up in that it provided the NGA with the opportunity to broaden its membership base into the industry's clerical, administrative and technical workers.

THE NGA/SLADE MARRIAGE

In the spring of 1980 Slade decided to approach the NGA to re-open amalgamation discussions. The Slade approach was received favourably and by March 1981 proposals for an amalgamation had been agreed and were submitted to a ballot of the respective memberships. Slade members were to vote first and, provided they voted in favour, NGA members were then to be balloted.

Providing there was a majority vote in favour by members of both unions, the new union would come into existence on 29 March 1982. The 1984 Delegate Meeting would determine the name of the new union, but in the meantime the title National Graphical Association (1982) was to be used. That delegate meeting confirmed the title NGA (1982) on the grounds that the union's stand in 1983 against the Employment Acts (1980 and 1982) and the attacks mounted against its members, its funds and its officials by the Conservative government and the courts had established the NGA (1982) prominently within the trade union and labour movement, that the cost of changing the interim title would be considerable, and that many branches had incorporated direct references to the NGA (1982) into their branch rules.[12]

The arrangements for NGA (1982) were based on the Graphic Arts Union proposals but with certain changes suggested by Slade. The structure, constitution and rules of the new union were designed to cause the minimum of dislocation to existing practices. The industrial policies and practices developed by Slade over the years, such as the house agreement policies and the 'white card' employment procedures, were to continue for former Slade members in the new union. The election of the principal officials in NGA (1982) was to be conducted on an amended form of exhaustive ballot principle limited to no more than three ballots for any officer position.

Existing NGA and Slade branches were to continue in separate operations but governed by the rules of the new union and its National

Council, whilst they worked towards integrating into amalgamated branches. It was agreed that this integrating process needed to be progressed as quickly as possible and completed not later than the 1984 Delegate Meeting. In any area where this had not taken place by 1984 the National Council was to place proposals before the 1984 Delegate Meeting to instruct those branches not already amalgamated to take immediate steps to do so with the intention of full branch amalgamation by January 1985.

One of the reasons why Slade members had rejected the Graphic Arts Union proposals was a dislike of the immediate integration of the branches of the three unions on vesting day. However, many matter concerning branch arrangements had been left outstanding and resulted in many Slade members having reservations about the level of involvement they would have at branch level in the Graphic Arts Union. To avoid this mistake with the formation of NGA (1982) it was agreed that, while the union at regional and national level would be fully integrated from vesting day, at branch level Slade branches would continue to operate side by side with NGA branches, whilst discussions between them took place with a view to forming integrated branches at the earliest opportunity after vesting day. However, it was not an open-ended commitment and a maximum period for these discussions to be completed had been set. By November 1983 the majority of former Slade branches had been totally merged into the appropriate NGA (1982) branches. Of the 22,388 members of Slade at the time of the formation of NGA (1982), some 21,700 had been merged into NGA (1982) branches by the end of December 1983.

The NGA branches formed the basis of the merged union, although Edinburgh was to become a branch with a full-time secretary and a new branch was created at Dundee. Existing NGA full-time branch secretaries were to continue to run the new branches. Former Slade full-time branch secretaries who did not become regional officers within NGA (1982) would become full-time branch officials. Unless former NGA and former Slade members agreed to the contrary, former NGA and Slade members were to be represented on the branch committee in proportion to their respective numbers in the branch, with a minimum of at least one former Slade member (or former NGA) on each branch committee. Where there were thirty or more former Slade members in a branch they could, if they wished, have a local consultative committee to deal with technical and related matters affecting them.

The NGA's regional structure and full-time regional officers were to be retained. The Scottish Region was to have two regional officials until one vacated office. The NGA's regional councils and trade group boards were to be increased in size to accommodate representatives elected by former Slade members. The National Council of the NGA (1982) was to have forty members, including six former Slade members. The Slade General Secretary was to become joint Assistant General Secretary, whilst the Slade Assistant General Secretary was to be appointed to a new post in the new union of National Secretary. The National Assistant Secretary and National Organiser of Slade were to become national officers of NGA (1982), whilst Slade's Financial Secretary was to become Assistant Financial Secretary of the new union.

It was agreed that the contribution of both former NGA and former Slade members towards financing the new union would be fair and equitable, with neither group gaining advantage at the expense of the other. Slade assets, measured on a per capita basis, were less than those of the NGA. It was therefore agreed that former Slade members would pay a special levy of 35p per week for whatever period was necessary to make up the difference and to allow Slade members to enjoy the higher unemployment and disputes benefits of the NGA immediately.

Slade recommended its members to vote for merger with the NGA on the grounds that Slade branches would continue to function separately whilst they worked towards amalgamated branches with the NGA at local level, that fair and proportional representation for Slade at all levels of decision-making in the NGA (1982) had been achieved, that Slade chapels and main industrial practices would continue unchanged, and that contributions in the NGA (1982) would be less than Slade would pay on its own and unemployment benefit in the new union would be higher. Slade members voted in July 1981 by 6,726 votes to 3,499 in favour of amalgamation with the NGA. In October 1981, NGA members voted by 46,481 to 16,777 in favour of merger with Slade. In December 1981, Slade, following a complaint to the Certification Officer that the distribution of amalgamation ballot papers in the London area had not been done properly, declared the amalgamation ballot null and void. It decided to hold a further ballot on amalgamation with the NGA. This too was in favour of merger and the NGA (1982) came into being on 29 March 1982.

In accepting the 1976 NGA Delegate Meeting resolution calling on the NGA to seek the cooperation of other printing unions for the concept of one union for the industry, the then General Secretary said that the path would not be straightforward. This is exactly how it turned out. Over the period 1976–81 the NGA had had separate discussions with Natsopa, bipartite discussions with Natsopa and Slade, tripartite discussions with Natsopa, Slade and NUWDAT, and more recently discussions with Sogat. Unfortunately, until the autumn of 1981 all this activity proved abortive with the exception in October 1979 of the transfer of engagements of the NUWDAT into the NGA.

The formation of NGA (1982) was one of the most important print union amalgamations. It provided a significant platform to protect the future of the members of the two unions involved in the origination area. It also offered the potential means to establish a considerable degree of control over future technological developments in origination areas. The two unions separately were having to struggle against economic recession, high inflation rates, declining real wages for their members, new technology, work from unrecognised sources, competition from abroad, high levels of unemployment and an increasingly hostile political environment. Amalgamation would enable the two unions to tackle these problems in a constructive manner. The alternative was each union defending its economic interests in a series of disruptive inter-union battles. However, the forces that had helped to create the National Graphical Association (1982) equally affected the two remaining major print unions – the National Union of Journalists and Sogat (1982) – and moves by the NGA (1982) to achieve further rationalisation of the printing union structure were inevitable

RELATIONS WITH THE NATIONAL UNION OF JOURNALISTS

Amalgamation talks between the NGA and NUJ began in June 1980. Slade was also represented at these discussions but the creation of NGA (1982) provided a better environment in which to conduct these amalgamation talks. A merger made industrial sense for both unions. In provincial newspapers it was anticipated that the 1980s would see the introduction of direct entry systems which would blur the division between the functions of the journalists and compositors thus raising the spectre of bitter inter-union battles between the two unions.

Amalgamation offered a possibility to ensure job security and reasonable conditions for NGA members. A link with the NUJ also had the attraction that it offered a route into the 'new world' of communications based on information technology, for example local radio, Ceefax, Oracle, Prestel cable television, etc. In this 'new world' in 1982 the NGA had only a precarious foothold through its telecommunication and electronics members (former NUPT). It was a world predicted to expand at an exponential rate whilst the old world of communications based on paper and ink which the NGA (1982) dominated was expected to decline. The NUJ was in both worlds. In 1982, 40 per cent of its membership was employed by national or provincial newspapers. The other 60 per cent were found in magazines, public relations, radio, television, and as freelance operators who were usually self-employed. The NUJ offered the NGA a bridge from the old world of communications into the new world of communications.

For the NUJ the attraction of a merger with the NGA was far from confined to avoidance of inter-union disputes over the introduction of direct entry systems in provincial and national newspapers. The NUJ was not strongly organised in many sections of the provincial newspaper industry. Few if any closed shops existed in editorial areas and journalists could resign from the NUJ at any time. If such individuals did not wish to become non-unionists then they could join the Institute of Journalists (IOJ). The NUJ found it difficult to conduct successful industrial disputes without the support of the NGA. The industrial strength of the NGA should be used to obtain increased organisation in the editorial departments in the provincial press and in some areas to gain the establishment of the closed shop.

The introduction of direct entry systems into newspapers would not change the NUJ into a strong united force overnight, able to prosecute a successful dispute without the help and assistance of the NGA. The reality was that if the NUJ was not well organised before new technology was introduced, all that technology would do would make it even more difficult for the NUJ to obtain a strong organisational base, with the inevitable result that the only winners would be the employers. The NGA Assistant Secretary told the 1982 Delegate Meeting,

> For the NUJ in the future to be able to use technology to improve the wages and conditions of their members, they need the NGA. Without the NGA, particularly in the provincial newspaper industry over the period of the next few years, the NUJ will find it increasingly difficult to exist as an effective trade union. The continuing strength of the NGA is vital, therefore, for the NUJ. With or without new technology we are their first line of defence. Only together can we ensure that with the

introduction of new technology, employers are forced to pay the full social price for our joint co-operation. This has already been recognised by the Newspaper Society who have expressed concern about what has been described as the unhealthy relationship developing between us.[13]

There was a strong industrial case for the marriage of the two unions. If an amalgamation was to be successful it would not only be a further step towards one union for the printing industry but also a major step towards one union for the media industry. However, there were major problems to be overcome if a successful NGA/NUJ merger was to be achieved.

First, NGA members had to realise that an amalgamation with the NUJ would be unlike any of the other previous mergers involving the NGA. It would not be a merger of two craft unions, which had been the basis of previous NGA marriages. It would be an amalgamation between a predominantly skilled manual worker union and a union which, although it considered itself to be creative and professionally oriented, required to be able to represent its members industrially. The NUJ had a role in ensuring that journalists observed certain professional and ethical standards. To accommodate this the amalgamation panels of the two unions considered the possibility of separating its industrial role from the professional and ethical role which journalists would want to retain.

Second, in previous mergers, the traditional structure of the NGA had remained relatively unchanged. Most of the other craft mergers had been integrated into the existing NGA structure, mainly because the craft industry and traditions of those unions were similar to those of the NGA. This would not be the case with the NUJ and a successful amalgamation would require NGA members to accept a radical alteration of the NGA (1982) structure.

Third, the NUJ had several thousand members involved in broadcasting and was not solely involved in the printing industry. It had working arrangements and agreements with the broadcasting authorities and broadcasting unions. Any amalgamation between the NUJ and the NGA was only likely to be supported by the NUJ broadcasting members if it was seen in the context of a major step towards creating one union for the media.

Fourth, the financial positions of the two unions were very different. There were considerable differences in the per capita figures. If any amalgamation was to be successful, the NGA's traditional approach to merger of insisting on the establishment of equal per capita values would have to be relaxed and a different or combined per capita and benefits approach adopted.

It was important that NGA (1982) members realised at the outset that a successful NGA/NUJ amalgamation would not result in a bigger but still traditional NGA. Merger would produce a radically new union, which it was hoped, through its structures, would represent the interests of all its members and act as a catalyst for the formation of one union for the media industry.

However, the NGA/NUJ amalgamation panel was unable to produce an amalgamation package which could be placed before their respective memberships and merger talks were terminated in January 1983. A number of problems proved insoluble even after eleven lengthy and protracted meetings. The issues included the structure of the London Region/branch; the editor of the journal; the qualification period for office; the Professional Council/Appeals Body; the frequency of delegate meetings; and the question of National Council seats. In addition, the NGA was concerned about the composition of the NUJ amalgamation panel. The NGA panel found it frustrating to find itself in discussions with an NUJ panel which had a significant number of representatives elected by their conference in addition to representatives from their executive. The dual responsibilities of NUJ representatives had an adverse effect on the discussions in terms of both making it more difficult to obtain from the NUJ a definitive position on many issues and also the momentum of discussions. The NGA found negotiating with an NUJ amalgamation panel accountable to two different masters too big a hindrance to productive progress. The NGA reluctantly decided that until it could be sure who was the ultimate source of authority on the NUJ panel – the executive members or the conference representatives – there was little to be gained by continuing the talks.

At branch level the NUJ operates a part-time branch system which does not play a dominant role in supporting its members industrially. NUJ branches are centrally funded and their rules and practices are very similar. Their function is mainly a representative one within the union structure. NGA branches, on the other hand, have an industrial role, can raise their own subscriptions and have different rules and practices. They are the first line of industrial defence. The NGA was reluctant to reduce the industrial role of its branches and insisted that its full-time structure be retained. There was little prospect of the NGA branches giving up the right to raise their own finances, to appoint their own officers and to determine their own branch rules. The NUJ sought agreement that in any new union there would be guidelines providing minimum guarantees for branch procedures, e.g. the frequency of meetings, which would be included in branch rules.

In respect of qualification for branch office the NUJ found it understandable that somebody should be a member of a union for a certain period of time before they could stand as General Secretary of the union, but it could not see why the same individual also had to be a member of the branch for varying periods of time before they qualified to become branch secretary. The NGA felt it essential that full-time officers knew the branch, knew the members locally, and had experience of the local chapels. The NUJ pointed out that their members were generally more mobile than those of the NGA and this meant that, if the NGA system was maintained, a considerable number of NUJ members would be prevented from taking up branch office. The NUJ saw the NGA system protecting local interests rather than advancing the concept of best-person government. Although the NGA was prepared to make compromises on the issue, agreement could not be reached.

A further difficulty was the question of attendance and voting at branch meetings. The NUJ rulebook provides that all members are entitled to attend branch meetings, to speak and to vote. In the NGA, branches operate on a delegate system. The NGA was not willing to impose an impractical system on its branches in any merged union, although it was prepared to accept provisions for special branch meetings to be called to discuss particular problems. The NUJ branch structure combined geographically based branches with industrial ones. This gave particular problems to the NGA London Region since the vast majority of NUJ members in industrial branches worked within the London Region. Consideration was given to establishing six 'trade' branches in London but it proved impossible to find a solution to the NUJ industrial branches/NGA London Region problem.

On the surface, the amalgamation talks had failed because the constitutional arrangements for the new union could not be agreed. The NGA considered that the structure proposed by the NUJ, whilst desirable in terms of lay participation and democracy, would never have been industrially credible.[14] The NGA had found the discussions with the NUJ amalgamation panel particularly confusing. The NGA

National Council was responsible for the amalgamation discussions and was accountable to the delegate meeting. The NGA thought the NUJ was operating on the same basis. However, the NUJ amalgamation panel did not take collective responsibility and its ADM representatives made reports, upon which individual or groups of amalgamation panel or NEC representatives could indicate their support or otherwise of sections of the amalgamation package. During the amalgamation talks, it often appeared to the NGA that it was negotiating not with the NUJ NEC but with factions within the NUJ.

However, there were deeper factors at work.[15] Technological developments in newspapers made the NGA realise that a link with the journalists would protect the interests of its members. However, many NUJ members in newspapers saw direct inputting increasing the bargaining power of the NUJ without the necessity of NGA support. They argued that the transfer of keystroking from composing to editorial areas would automatically transfer power to editorial areas. The NGA did not see the situation this way. Its power in the composing room stemmed not from keystroking but from its 100 per cent union organisation enforced by a closed shop. The NGA considered that the introduction of new technology into editorial departments which were poorly organised, with Institute of Journalist members and non-unionists present, would do nothing to strengthen the NUJ. Without strong unionisation, any benefits arising from new technology would go mainly to the employers.

There was also the problem that NUJ members in broadcasting and television found it difficult to see the necessity for relationships between print and broadcasting unions. The NGA saw that the advent of electronic media created mutual interests between broadcasting unions and print unions. Origination produced for a print end-product was often exactly the same origination used for Viewdata, Prestel and other electronic media. For the NGA, the involvement of newspaper proprietors and publishers in the ownership of cable TV and local broadcasting created the need for print and media unions to merge, otherwise the same employers would exploit one part of the media and one group of workers to the detriment of another. The underlying reason for the NGA/NUJ talks failing was that although the NGA was motivated by factors that push unions to accommodate each other – namely, fear (loss of employment opportunities and bargaining power) and self-interest (the need to provide new employment opportunities) – the NUJ was not. From its own self-interest the NUJ considered that single keystroking and developments in the media industry would enhance its bargaining power and its members' terms and conditions of employment without the need of the NGA.

Following the breakdown of the amalgamation talks, relationships between the two unions were governed by the 'Letter of Association', but the industrial realities often made it difficult for the NGA to comply with the terms of the Letter on each and every occasion. However, in 1983 the Newspaper Society launched 'Project Breakthrough', outlining proposals for the introduction of single keystroking into the provincial newspaper industry. Broadly, the Society wished to negotiate a national enabling agreement laying down guidelines for the introduction of single keystroking from both editorial and advertising staff, leaving NGA members to set contributed copy and counter advertisements (see Chapter 14).

The NGA feared that, if the three unions involved – itself, NUJ and Sogat – could not agree a common policy for the acceptance of the implementation of new technology in the provincial newspapers, the industry might become de-unionised. It therefore issued a document in March 1984 entitled, *The Way Forward – New Technology in the Provincial Newspaper Industry: An NGA (82) Initiative*, which sought to provide all parties – employees, unions and employers – with a stake in the industry's future and a share of the benefits arising from the implementation of new technology. It hinged on four principles. The first principle was the need for the three unions to be united. The second was that 'unity of action' could be achieved only if all parties saw gains from cooperating with the introduction of new technology. The third principle was that a new concept of the 'origination area' was required since direct entry would combine advertising, editorial and composing functions. It proposed that origination should comprise advertising, marketing, administration, editorial and composing as a single entity, in which union membership would be distributed equally on a 'one-third/one-third/one-third' basis between Sogat, the NUJ and the NGA. The fourth principle was that typesetting remain a unionised operation, with only union members operating the new technology systems.

The NGA was unable to persuade Sogat and the NUJ that *The Way Forward* should be the agreed approach for the acceptance of direct entry systems in provincial newspapers. In November 1984 negotiations between Sogat and the NGA produced an agreed division of union membership in advertising departments on a 50/50 basis except where either union already had 100 per cent membership. The agreement was, however, rejected by the Sogat National Executive. The NUJ responded to *The Way Forward* in October 1984. It accepted the principles that only union members should operate new technology, that there be a united union approach to cooperation with the introduction of new technology, and that there be unity of action by the unions. It considered the one-third/one-third/one-third approach to recruitment in the new origination are to be arbitrary and doubted whether the proposed wider definition of origination could be established. It reasserted its sole right to organise and represent journalists, stating that NGA members retrained for editorial jobs must join and be represented by the NUJ.

The three unions had not agreed a common approach to the acceptance of new technology when in December 1984 the Newspaper Society decided that negotiations over the introduction of new techniques should shift to the local level. In the absence of a common approach the NGA (1982) found itself in a position where it would have to protect its own corner when necessary and come to agreements with employers on new technology independently of the NUJ. This is exactly what happened at Portsmouth and Sunderland Newspapers in early 1985 when that company and the NGA signed an agreement which provided *inter alia* for the redeployment of NGA members into the editorial area where they would retain NGA membership and that union would continue to negotiate for them. The NUJ opposed the agreement by strike action, arguing that it was the union with rights to represent all employees in the editorial area (see Chapter 14).

Early in 1985 the NGA found itself in dispute with *Wolverhampton Express and Star* over the introduction of single keystroking and full-page make-up from the advertising and editorial areas. Before NGA chapels could consider the company's terms, management imposed direct entry from the advertising area and suspended NGA members at its Wolverhampton, West Bromwich and other businesses. The NGA's position was not helped in that the NUJ and Sogat refused to respect its picket lines. NGA–NUJ relations became even worse when in April 1985 NUJ chapels at the company agreed to accept direct inputting from the editorial area. They sank even lower when in the summer of 1985 the NUJ cooperated with the *Kent Messenger* in the installation of new computer equipment which enabled the company to continue the production of the paper even though it was in dispute with the NGA (See chapter 14).

The outcome of these three disputes had been a salutary lesson for both unions. The NUJ now realised what the NGA had argued, namely, if the two unions could not agree a joint basis for the introduction of new technology then companies would simply play them off against each other to management's advantage. However, these experiences probably did more than anything else to bring about in October 1985 what is known as the 'Joint Accord' between the NGA and the NUJ.

The TUC, concerned about the deteriorating relationship between the two unions, arranged talks in April 1985 under the chairmanship of Lord McCarthy to see if a formula could be agreed for a joint policy for acceptance of new technology in the provincial press. After numerous meetings an agreement was reached between the two unions in October 1985. Under this agreement, entitled *NGA '82/NUJ Agreement/Direct Input in Provincial Newspapers*, direct entry from the editorial departments would be accepted only on the basis of a prior joint agreement with an employer and that those negotiations for the implementation of new technology had been undertaken jointly by both unions at national officer level with branch and chapel involvement. It also committed both unions to maintain and increase union membership, to reach agreed training programmes for NGA members transferred to editorial work, to avoid compulsory redundancies, to wherever possible allow union members only access to direct input and to no diminution of employment conditions for journalists or NGA members. In addition, NGA members transferred into the editorial area are represented by the NUJ for collective and individual bargaining purposes but continue to retain membership of, and to continue to pay their subscriptions to, the NGA. Nevertheless, they become full members of the NUJ subject to its industrial control from national, branch and chapel level. These memberships and subscription arrangements are to operate to at least October 1990.

In the period July 1986 to December 1987 relationships between the NGA and the NUJ improved, which could partly be credited to the Accord.[6] Whilst this did not eliminate all problems between the two unions, it did at least provide the prospect of resolving them on a firm trade union basis. Further illustrations of the developing closer working relationships between the two unions were the January 1987 agreement over guidelines for the training of NGA members who transfer to editorial work and cooperation with the NGA policy for dealing with the development of new technology in publishing offices and an organisation policy in those publishing companies on an 'as and when' basis.

In 1989 NUJ and NGA relationships were very close and stable. Regular fortnightly meetings between the senior officers of the unions take place to discuss policy and action over matters of mutual interest. Present NGA/Sogat merger talks are continuing and the NGA membership has given a clear indication that a merger with the NUJ has priority for the future. In response to the growing cross-ownership of newspapers, magazines, television and satellite television, in 1988 the NGA, ACTT, BETA and the NUJ set up machinery for quarterly meetings to discuss problems of mutual interest. The unions are represented by their General Secretaries and General Presidents.

THE PROPOSED NGA (1982)/Sogat (82) AMALGAMATION

Following the failure of merger talks with the NUJ, the NGA entered amalgamation talks with Sogat(82), which at the time of writing are still continuing. The approach was consistent with the NGA's policy of achieving one union for the industry as the most advantageous way of protecting its members' jobs and jurisdictional rights as the introduction of new technology in all areas of the printing industry continued to eradicate traditional demarcation lines. The alternative was damaging conflicts between the different unions.

In considering an amalgamation with Sogat the main motivating factor for the NGA was the introduction of direct entry systems in provincial newspapers, as these merged the functions of those working in advertising departments and those employed in the composing department. Although the NGA and Sogat might have sought an accommodation short of amalgamation, the changes in the industry were so radical that no agreement was likely to be permanent without the unions being able to consolidate that temporary accommodation by amalgamation. An NGA/Sogat merger also made sense in terms of the machine rooms, where there had been regular demarcation disputes between the two unions. The merger would also assist the NGA in Scotland, where as the minority union it often found itself in conflict with Sogat over developments in plate-making and lithographic printing techniques.[17] The antipathy that existed between the NGA and the SGB Division of Sogat over the control of the litho printing process in Scotland in the 1980s was illustrated in disputes between the two unions at Holmes McDougall and Waddie. These disputes were referred to

TUC disputes committees which made awards favourable to the NGA (see Chapter 10).

The proposed merger had other attractions. New technology, by blurring demarcation lines and altering skill content, was swinging the balance of bargaining power in favour of the employers. If the two unions remained separate the employers would simply use their enhanced bargaining power to the detriment of Sogat and NGA members. To engage in mutually destructive inter-union conflict would simply increase the bargaining power of the employers even further. In addition, the balance of power was being steadily tipped against the printing unions by the Conservative government's employment legislation of the early 1980s. This gave added impetus to the NGA and Sogat to merge. The ability of the NGA and Sogat to influence the Labour Party and the TUC both generally and specifically in those organisations' policies for the printing and newspaper industry would be generally enhanced through amalgamation.

Although the industrial logic of a merger between the NGA and Sogat was clear, there were many problems to be overcome if a marriage was to be achieved. First, any merged union would not simply be a bigger NGA. Sogat has a different organisational structure from the NGA and also some fundamental problems would have to be reconciled at the branch level. Unlike the NGA's other successful mergers it would not be politically possible for the amalgamation simply to absorb members of one union into the existing branch structure of the other. NGA members are unlikely to be prepared to go into Sogat branches and vice versa. Associated with this is the question of who is going to be the senior official within a branch after the amalgamation. These branch issues were to be a significant factor in the merger talks. There were potential branch problems in Scotland, bearing in mind that the Scottish Graphical Branch membership is still partly separate from those of the traditional Sogat members, and London where there were nine separate Sogat branches and one NGA branch. Non-manual employees in membership of Sogat are in its Art, Technical, Administrative, Executive and Sales (ATAES) branch, which is a national one, whilst such members of the NGA are in its geographically based branches.

Second, this was the first amalgamation movement in which the NGA had been involved in which it was numerically the smaller union. At the beginning of the talks, Sogat had some 170,000 working members, of whom 30,000 were working in paper-making. The NGA claimed a working membership of 107,000. If an amalgamation were to be achieved, the NGA would have to convince its members that within the new union their interests would not be swamped by Sogat's greater numbers, which are mainly non-craft and that craft interest will be protected. However, during the five years of the NGA/Sogat merger talks Sogat's membership fell much faster than that of the NGA such that there is today a much smaller difference in membership numbers. A marriage based on parity and equality is more possible now than when the talks began in 1984.

Third, the history and separate development of the two unions on a craft and industrial basis were recognised as a major problem not only by the memberships but by the entire industry. There exist in sections of the NGA membership deep prejudices against the members of Sogat and its constituent unions, particularly Natsopa. Such feelings are equally felt by some Sogat members against the NGA. A successful merger required not only constructive compromise on the part of the two unions but a major reassessment of long-held attitudes and prejudices by both sets of members. The NGA General Secretary warned delegates to the 1986 Delegate Meeting,

> Having said that, I believe that we now really have the last chance and nothing must be allowed to stand in the way of this amalgamation, not personalities at national level, not history and prejudice at local level and not vested interests at branch or any other level within the union.[18]

A fourth problem to overcome was contributions and benefits in the new union. There was a large difference between the per capita figures of the two unions. In September 1987 that for the NGA stood at £143, compared with £112 when the merger talks first began. In September 1987 the per capita figure for Sogat was £35.60. In 1984, the total subscription for Sogat members, national and branch, was around 80–90p per week lower than that paid by NGA members. The benefits the two unions paid were also significantly different. The NGA dispute benefit is some three times higher than that of Sogat. Sogat returns to its branches 40 per cent of national subscription income compared with 21 per cent for the NGA. Sogat members pay a lower national subscription rate than NGA members and again the NGA suggested that parity be achieved over a period of time and not on the vesting day of the new union.

The amalgamation panels met regularly in 1983 and 1984 and made some progress. However, from the autumn of 1984 to February 1986 there were no meetings of the amalgamation panels. During this period the relationship between the two unions reached an all-time low, mainly because of the attitude of Sogat on new technology in provincial newspapers and publishing.

Over the period 1984–7 in provincial newspapers the issue of direct inputting from advertising departments caused difficulties between the NGA and Sogat despite their merger talks. Sogat rejected *The Way Forward* and relationships severely deteriorated when it refused to respect NGA picket lines in the *Wolverhampton Express and Star* and *Kent Messenger* disputes and then actively cooperated with those managements to undermine the NGA position in those disputes. Matters were not improved when, during a dispute that the NGA was involved in with Boxfoldia in Birmingham, Sogat not only crossed NGA picket lines but allowed its machine assistants to be retrained to operate the company's lithographic presses.

Matters got worse as a result of Sogat's behaviour at the *Liverpool Post and Echo*. In October 1985 the paper announced that it would introduce direct entry systems from the editorial and advertising departments. Sogat refused to participate in a tripartite response with the NGA and NUJ, and became involved in discussions with management to reach an agreement allowing its members to perform functions traditionally carried out by NGA members. Over the period 1986 until the end of December 1987 Sogat continued to conclude direct entry agreements with a number of employers in the provincial newspaper industry which effectively transferred NGA work to its members without NGA agreement.

Sogat frequently assisted provincial newspaper employers who found themselves in difficulty when introducing direct entry from the editorial areas in direct challenge to the NGA/NUJ Accord. This role of Sogat resulted in the NGA lodging formal complaints under the TUC's Disputes Principles and Procedures. The TUC established a committee chaired by Professor Kessler to consider the matter. The committee recommended a formula which identified the division of work between the two unions, and provided for joint negotiations and closer working relationships at chapel levels. The formula was accepted by the NGA but rejected by Sogat, whereupon the NGA demanded a formal TUC Disputes Committee hearing on its complaints against Sogat. In 1988 the Committee issued an award supportive of the NGA's contentions on the issue of direct entry from the advertising area. It recommended that neither the NGA nor Sogat should sign an agreement or reach an understanding with any provindial newspaper about the introduction of new technology within the advertising area unless it is with the agreement of the other union. Although the award was helpful to the NGA it was impossible to turn the clock back in provincial newspapers where so many NGA members had lost employment and suffered reductions in wages which could have been offset had Sogat been prepared to work jointly with the NGA.

In August 1986 the NGA, Sogat and the NUJ agreed to the establishment of a Joint Publishing Committee to discuss the development of technology in unorganised publishing offices and the pursuit of a tripartite approach to trade union organisation and recruitment in the publishing industry. The NGA submitted a document for discussion setting out its views on how to approach the dual problems of technology and union organisation in publishing houses. The NUJ supported the NGA's approach, which was rejected by Sogat which agreed to produce its own paper. It took Sogat some eight months to do this. The paper indicated that there was no union membership role for the NGA in publishing. Given this the three unions decided the Committee could serve no further useful purpose. The denial by Sogat of a 'stake' for the NGA in publishing companies did little to improve NGA–Sogat relationships.

Why had Sogat adopted this anti-NGA stance with respect to the introduction of new technology into provincial newspapers and publishing? Sogat was motivated by a number of factors. It considered the NGA's real motive in *The Way Forward* was to take over its members' jobs in the advertising departments of newsapers, despite the fact that this was an area where a national agreement with the Newspaper Society recognised Sogat as the appropriate union. The NGA argument that its members should 'follow the work' into the advertising department was regarded by Sogat as a cover for claiming the right to recruit clerical staff in newspapers and a desire for institutional survival on the part of the NGA.

More significant, however, was that Sogat saw the implementation of new technology as potentially increasing its bargaining power and decreasing that of the NGA. It felt that the NGA was a declining influence in the industry. By collaborating with provincial newspaper employers Sogat felt it could quicken the NGA's decline and the advent of its own perceived enhanced bargaining power. It may have believed its interests were best served by standing on the side—lines watching the NGA being defeated by employers, and assisting in this process if necessary, and then picking up the pieces and using new—found bargaining power to improve the terms and conditions of its members.

The NGA sought to dissuade Sogat of these views by arguing that technology by itself would not bring enhanced bargaining power if it was not accompanied by 100 per cent organisation. In the advertising departments of newspapers, unionisation was low and the NGA contended that if the two unions did not have a common approach then the implementation of new technology would make it more difficult to gain organisation in the advertising departments. The NGA also told Sogat that it was naive to think newspaper employers would neuter the bargaining power of the NGA merely to give the NGA's former bargaining power to another group of workers or union. The NGA has been proved right in this analysis. By the late 1980s the print unions retreated significantly in the newspaper battle. The NUJ and Sogat were weaker in their areas than in the early 1980s and the NGA had seen reductions of staff in the composing room by a half to two—thirds of their previous size. However, technological developments in the general printing trade at the end of the 1980s were favourable to the NGA and threatening to Sogat. The background to the NGA/Sogat merger talks is today the reverse of the situation when they began over five years ago. This change in the balance of need for the amalgamation has been reflected in the tone of the merger talks since 1988.

One of the effects of the NGA–Sogat problems in the provincial newspaper industry was that the respective amalgamation panels did not meet for over twelve months. It was felt, given the state of the relationship between the two unions in 1985, that the prospects of achieving an amalgamation package were slim. In February 1986 merger talks were resumed in the light of the common problems suffered by the members of the two unions at News Internatinal, which in January 1986 dismissed some 6,000 Sogat and NGA members as it transferred production from Fleet Street to Wapping in East London (see Chapter 14). Although progress was slow, agreement was reached on a number of matters, including chapel structures, a regional structure, the size and basis of representation on the national executive, a biennial delegate meeting, the General Secretaryship and General Presidency, and a continuation of a political fund.

The financial and branch structures of the proposed union remained the major problem. To overcome these the NGA produced a document entitled *An NGA Response*, which proposed that existing branches and chapels of both unions should operate as now until a merger, and that national subscriptions should be gradually levelled until they became equal at £1.76 in five years' time, when all branches would receive a 75p rebate from the General Fund. Subsequent discussions with Sogat brought the prospect of amalgamation closer when Sogat agreed to accept the financial proposals of *An NGA Response*. Unfortunately, Sogat was unwilling to accept the NGA proposals with respect to the branch structure. At the end of August 1987 Sogat told the NGA that not only was it not prepared to accept its branch proposals, but it was now reconsidering its attitude towards the financial proposals as it believed these would bring into doubt the viability of the new union. Sogat insisted that a 'blueprint' of the branch structure should be produced by the merger panels, then notified to the branches through a process of consultation and finally included on the amalgamation ballot paper.

The NGA expressed serious reservations about the 'branch blueprint', arguing that it would be lengthy, impractical, delay the prospect of a national amalgamation, and act as a catalyst for the opponents of amalgamation. It was subsequently agreed that two working parties should be established to (a) reassess the viability of the proposed new union and (b) prepare a blueprint for the amalgamation of NGA and Sogat branches. The NGA favoured the achievement of a national amalgamation allowing NGA and Sogat branches to conduct their own merger negotiations over a time span of four years. At the end of the four—year period the National Council of the new union would have authority to bring proposals to a biennial delegate conference for authority to instruct branches to complete total amalgamation. In this way the respective memberships would gain all the benefits and protections of one union for the industry whilst the branches integrated within a set time period. In March 1989 Sogat agreed to take the branch blueprint off the table. In effect this meant that Sogat accepted that the only way to amalgamation between the two unions was from the top, by moving towards a ballot on terms of a national amalgamation, instead of waiting for the outcome of local branch merger talks. Although the blueprint had gone, Sogat had not gone all the way with the NGA. It was proposing that if branches disagreed with National Council recommendations on imposed branch mergers then they would have the right of appeal to the delegate meeting.

However, developments between the two unions had moved

considerably over the last few months of 1989 to such an extent that by March 1990 a final 'amalgamation package' was agreed by the two panels which was subsequently endorsed by the respective executives. The proposals will be placed before the delegate meetings of the two unions scheduled to take place in May and June of 1990. Providing the delegate meetings of Sogat and the NGA endorse 'the amalgamation package' then the whole set of proposals will be voted on by the total membership of the two unions in November/December of 1990.

In essence, the 'package' provided for a set of arrangements which both panels could agree with regards to the size and composition of the National Council; an interim arrangement for subs and finance; the regional structure; chapels; biennial delegate meeting; members' benefits; national officers; location of head office and the name of the union.

The proposed name of the new union is the GPMU (Graphical Paper and Media Union). Arrangements for the National Council will be to have 40 members elected on a regional basis. The first new council will hold office for an interim period of three years and three months, after which the term of office will be two years. During the 'interim' period, there will be guaranteed equality of representation on the council, with 20 members being elected by and from NGA members, and the same arrangements applying to Sogat. From 1994 onwards, there will be no guaranteed representation, and the principles of 'best person government' will apply.

The new union's regional structure will comprise nine regions acting as electoral constituencies for the National Council and other union delega—tions. Delegate meetings will continue to be held biennially in the new union. However, branches that have not merged within the three year period will be required to do so, although the right to appeal to the 1996 conference will be available to branches. The final decision will be made by delegates at that conference. Structure proposals will be submitted to the first conference of the new union by the National Council, and a three year period will be provided for branch mergers to take place.

Regarding the new unions officer structure, the GPMU will at first have five 'Senior Officers': General Secretary, Deputy General Secretary, General President, Vice—President and Assistant General Secretary. Tony Dubbins, the NGA's General Secretary, and Sogat's General Secretary, Brenda Dean, will stand for election as the new union's General Secretary with the runner up in the ballot automatically taking over duties as Deputy General Secretary, the second most senior position in the union. Similar arrangements have been agreed for deciding which of the existing two General Presidents will be the General President of the new union.

An independent arbitrator was agreed by the two unions to investigate both of the existing head office sites with a remit to make a decision as to which was the most suitable. The arbitrator, Moss Evans, former General Secretary of the Transport and General Workers' Union carried out a very detailed examination over a two week period after which he decided upon the Bedford office of the NGA.

NOTES

1. See *Print*, January 1974, vol. II, no. 1.

2. See *Report of the Delegate Meeting, 1976*, National Graphical Association, p. 33. The Scottish Graphical Association and Sogat amalgamated on 1 October 1975 to form the Society of Graphical and Allied Trades (1975). The craft section of the SGA voted by 1,913 votes to 1,857 for amalgamation and its auxiliary section voted by 689 votes to 338 in favour of amalgamation.

3. See *Report of the Delegate Meeting, 1969*, National Graphical Association, p. 35.

4. See *Report of the Delegate Meeting, 1972*, National Graphical Association, pp. 360–1.

5. See *Report of Inquiry into certain Trade Union Recruitment Activities*, Cmnd 7706, HMSO, London, September 1979.

6. See *Report of the Delegate Meeting, 1974*, National Graphical Association, p. 323.

7. The successful NGA Manchester branch resolution proposed: 'This Conference instructs the National Council to make a determined approach to other print unions to bring about one union for the industry.' See *Report of the Delegate Meeting, 1976*, National Graphical Association, pp. 347–53.

8. See *Report of the Delegate Meeting, 1976*, National Graphical Association, p. 32, para. 58.

9. See *Report of the Delegate Meeting, 1980*, National Graphical Association, p. 37, para. 46.

10. In 1975, at the suggestion of the NUJ, the NUJ/NGA Technological Developments Sub—Committee was set up. Many useful discussions took place in the committee and agreements were reached on the use of document facsimile equipment and confirmation was given that the origination of copy – including that of OCR – was the prerogative of NGA members. It also undertook investigations into develop—ments in facsimile transmission, direct input and various processes in the alternative technologies.

11. See *Report of the Delegate Meeting, 1978*, National Graphical Association, p. 187, and *Print*, vol. 15, no. 5, June 1978.

12. See *Report of the Delegate Meeting, 1984*, National Graphical Association, p. 72, para. 100.

13. See *Report of the Delegate Meeting, 1982*, National Graphical Association, p. 258.

14. See *Report of the Delegate Meeting, 1984*, National Graphical Association, p. 457. A detailed background to the breakdown of the merger talks was given in *Print*, vol. 20, no. 2, February 1983, pp. 6 and 7.

15. See 'Amalgamation Talks – What Went Wrong', *Print*, vol. 20, no. 2, February 1983, pp. 6 and 7.

16. See *Report of the Delegate Meeting, 1986*, National Graphical Association, p. 43, para. 41.

17. The NGA has the minority of print workers in Scotland, somewhere in the region of 7 per cent of the total print union members employed as opposed to approximately 93 per cent in Sogat. See *Report of the Delegate Meeting, 1988*, National Graphical Association, p. 28, para. 22.

18. See *Report of the Delegate Meeting, 1986*, National Graphical Association, p. 118.

PART II

CONSTITUTIONAL AND FINANCIAL STRUCTURE

CHAPTER 7

DECISION-MAKING STRUCTURE DEVELOPMENTS

MEMBERSHIP TRENDS

Table 7.1 shows the membership of the London Society of Compositors in the period 1947–54. Its total membership showed a slow but steady increase. Its working membership increased faster than its total membership. The bulk of its non-working membership was retired members.

Table 7.1

Membership of the London Society of Compositors, 1947–54

Date	Working membership	In the forces	Non-working membership	Total membership
1947	9,602	224	3,260	13,085
1948	9,851	170	3,281	13,302
1949	10,243	186	3,145	13,574
1950	10,349	221	3,046	13,616
1951	10,240	385	2,974	13,599
1952	10,306	429	2,874	13,609
1953	10,531	465	2,836	13,832
1954	10,556	577	2,857	13,990

Its membership was in two departments. The General and Periodical Department serviced all journeymen in offices producing bookwork, jobbing and weekly newspapers. The News Department contained all journeymen employed on daily and Sunday newspapers. The growth in use of miniature printing processes by the London printing industry and by employers outside the industry led the LSC in November 1951 to form a third department – the Allied Processes – to organise workers employed on these processes, but with little success.

Table 7.2 shows that London Typographical Society membership over the period 1955–62 remained static at 20,000. Its non-working membership increased mainly because of a rise in retired former PMMTS members. There were 3,500 journeymen in its Printing Machine Department, which catered for machine managers employed in the general trade and non-national newspapers. Its Composing Department contained some 12,000 journeymen employed in offices producing bookwork, jobbing and weekly newspapers. Its News Department contained 3,500 journeymen employed on daily and Sunday newspapers. Less than a third of LTS membership was employed in Fleet Street.

Table 7.2
Membership of the London Typographical Society, 1955–62

Date	Working membership	Reciprocity members	In the forces	Non-working membership	Total membership
1955	15,168	316	710	3,947	20,141
1956	15,173	299	584	3,965	20,021
1957	15,370	295	396	3,951	20,012
1958	15,359	291	276	4,056	19,982
1959	15,361	279	225	4,137	20,002
1960	15,470	248	154	4,165	20,037
1961	15,568	225	58	4,163	20,014
1962	15,618	207	9	4,217	20,051

Table 7.3 shows the working and total membership of the TA over the period 1948–62. To encourage apprentices to participate in the affairs of the TA, each branch had an apprentice committee. To assist this work, apprentices were formed into a 'Guild of Young Printers' whose activities were under the jurisdiction of the Executive Council. The main category of non-working membership was retired membership. Members over 65 years of age who had retired from the industry were entitled to funeral benefit and those with over twenty years' of membership were entitled to superannuation benefit.

Table 7.3
Membership of the Typographical Association, 1948–62

Date	Working membership	Reciprocity members	In the forces	Non-working membership	Total membership
1948	39,443	122	1,289	4,932	45,786
1949	40,733	–	1,094	4,927	46,754
1950	42,838	96	1,072	4,845	48,851
1951	43,850	91	1,739	4,739	50,419
1952	44,403	89	2,212	4,851	51,555
1953	44,740	68	2,543	4,949	52,300
1954	45,397	62	2,608	5,095	53,162
1955	46,412	87	2,632	5,291	54,422
1956	47,616	97	2,374	5,365	55,452
1957	48,970	–	1,881	5,648	56,499
1958	49,958	–	1,572	5,892	57,422
1959	50,138	–	1,307	6,108	57,553
1960	50,933	–	1,156	6,333	58,422
1961	52,727	–	674	6,538	59,939
1962	54,075	–	209	6,796	61,080

Table 7.4 shows that from 1964 to 1982 NGA membership was on a rising trend, with significant increases in 1969 and 1982 reflecting the mergers with the two main litho unions. Since 1982 membership has declined, reflecting increased unemployment in the industry stemming from the implementation of technological change, increasing inflation and increasing import penetration. However, overall the 1980s have seen NGA total membership stand up reasonably well. Since 1979 its total membership has fallen by less than 8 per cent compared with an average of 28 per cent for all the TUC affiliated unions.

However, technological change has caused the NGA to extend its membership into new areas. In 1972 it introduced the category of 'protective membership' for employees in newly organised firms, which allowed newly recruited members to pay only a fraction of the normal full member subscription but still receive the union's industrial benefits and free legal advice. A further assistance to the recruitment of new members in unrecognised offices of new areas, and to encourage transition to full membership, was accepted in 1988 when introductory membership was introduced. Individuals can remain in this category for two years from entry, or for a shorter (or longer) period if recommended by the branch and approved by the National Council.

Table 7.4
Membership of the National Graphical Association, 1964–88
(September each year)

Date	Working membership	Non-working membership	Total membership
1964	71,332	10,605	81,937
1965	74,744	10,867	85,551
1966	75,362	11,076	86,438
1967	74,679	12,265	86,944
1968	78,936	12,984	91,920
1969	92,800	14,585	107,385
1970	92,488	15,397	107,885
1971	92,129	16,587	108,716
1972	90,564	17,489	108,053
1973	90,230	18,066	108,296
1974	90,327	18,465	108,792
1975	89,188	19,488	108,676
1976	87,557	20,166	107,723
1977	88,686	20,752	109,438
1978	88,894	21,010	109,904
1979	90,438	21,103	111,541
1980	95,146	21,292	116,438
1981	92,404	21,501	113,905
1982	112,112	24,272	136,384
1983	109,772	24,177	133,949
1984	107,465	24,119	131,584
1985	107,154	24,568	131,721
1986	106,645	25,085	131,730
1987	105,351	25,641	130,992
1988	105,261	26,277	131,538

In the last twenty-five years the NGA membership has diversified from a craft to an industrial base. On its formation it was a union of hand and hot metal compositors, readers and letterpress machine managers. Today, in addition to those groups, it organises, *inter alia*, telegraphist operators and technicians, stereotypers and electrotypers, litho plate-makers, litho machine managers, litho artists, designers and engravers, camera operators, tele-ad operators, wage clerks, sales staff, supervisors, tin printers, silk screen printers, transport drivers and even gardeners. A feature of its diversifying membership is a growing number of female members. In 1972, according to TUC affiliation membership figures, the NGA had only 203 women members. By 1988 the same source showed it to have over 8,000 such members, the merger with the NUWDAT having brought in over 1,000 women. The changing membership of the NGA over the past twenty-five years is also reflected in the changing proportions of occupational trade groups within the total membership. In 1973, over 77 per cent of the membership was employed in the letterpress sector of the industry and only 17 per cent on the litho side. By 1989 the corresponding percentages were 55 per cent and 27 per cent.

A common misconception of the NGA is that it is predominantly a newspaper-based union. At the peak of its membership, only 10 per cent were employed in provincial newspapers and five in national newspapers; 85 per cent of its members were employed in the general, periodical trade, packaging, tin and books etc. The technical changes of the 1980s have significantly reduced the NGA members employed in newspapers. These are now an even smaller proportion of total membership.

ORGANISATIONAL PROBLEMS AND WIDENING THE MEMBERSHIP

The increasing diversification of NGA membership is not due entirely to mergers. It also reflects growth into new areas, such as small offset operators within and outside the industry, supervisor grades, art and advertising studios and clerical areas. The impact of technological change, by giving rise to alternative workforces to the NGA, has been a powerful incentive for it to extend its membership base. The inroads into traditional typesetting work have greatly increased in the late 1980s with the development of electronic publishing or desktop publishing systems. These alternative workforces are either unorganised or in membership of other unions and receive inferior employment conditions relative to traditional NGA members.

However, the need to safeguard against the emergence of an alternative cheaper workforce has always been a problem for the NGA and its constituent unions. The problem has become more widespread and difficult to control since the mid-1970s than previously was the case. It is often thought that the LSC exercised complete control in London, but, as Howe and Waite point out, the Society always faced an unorganised sector or employers wishing to undermine the conditions it had established.[1] Such an unorganised sector existed within the jurisdiction of the LSC over the period 1948–55. Its organiser spent much time attempting to bring non-union houses within the Society's control and on to its Fairs List. The firms added to the Fairs List in the period 1948–55 were a mixture of some which had been outside the union's control for many years, some which had become non-union and were being reorganised, and yet others which were new firms. As we have seen elsewhere, the organiser also attempted to bring into membership, though with little success, those operating miniature printing machines both within and outside the printing industry.

The LSC organiser was assisted in these activities by advisory committees which had been established at the turn of the century.[2] They had no official status within the decision-making machinery of the LSC but were 'recognised' in that their activities were subsidised from its funds. The number of members attending advisory committee monthly meetings was small. The Advisories were vigilant in 'watching the imprint' and where members found printed work which had been done in an unrecognised house the Advisory informed the organiser, who then attempted to bring the 'house' within the control of the LSC or persuade the publisher to have future work placed in an LSC house.

The organisational problems of the LTS were virtually the same as those of the LSC. An additional problem was firms where one or other of the composing or machine departments was non-union. The LTS organiser, assisted by advisory committees, attempted to bring these areas under LTS control. Although apathy towards participation in advisory committee activities remained amongst LTS members, the active committees continued to provide useful information for organising efforts.

The TA also faced competition from unorganised sectors and the growth of miniature printing machines within and outwith the industry. TA branches and groups engaged in organisation activities. The Executive Council could appoint special deputations to visit firms they thought it desirable to organise. The TA organisational efforts were spearheaded by four organisers – three for England and Wales and one for Ireland. The organisational problems included companies employing 'dilutees', companies exceeding apprenticeship quotas and firms paying wages below the national agreements. Like its London counterparts, the TA had little success in organising employees on miniature printing processes outside the industry. Within the industry it accepted in 1953, as we have seen, that these machines were the preserve of the ASLP.

The problem of organising a potential alternative workforce continued with the NGA, which therefore began in the early 1970s to widen its recruitment base. In doing this the NGA sought to avoid the problems experienced by Slade, which had built up an art section of 'conscripted' membership, and the problems it had itself faced with its Executive, Technical and Overseer Section (E, T & O). This was formed in 1969 to provide a service to NGA members who held managerial positions and whose employment conditions were not regulated by a national agreement. The section never developed in the way expected, although at the time of its incorporation into the NGA's ACTA Trade Group in 1979 its membership stood at 2,760, having been 1,500 in 1972. The section failed to provide a proper service to its members because a constitutional means of representing their interests within the NGA's structure could not be found that was acceptable to the traditional membership. A further problem in widening the NGA membership base was the lack of specialist officers acquainted with the problems of organising non-manual employees, since in the past the pre-entry closed shop had eliminated the need to 'sell' the union. Additionally, not only were NGA's subscription rates high relative to other unions but the workers it was hoping to recruit had no basic union backgrounds. There was also the problem that the decision to organise in new areas was not keenly welcomed by the whole NGA membership.[3]

The desire to widen its membership basis became a reality on the transfer of engagements in 1979 of NUWDAT. This enabled the NGA to establish a white-collar section serviced by professional and experienced officials with the responsibility of recruiting, organising and securing recognition and negotiating rights for salaried employees in the printing and allied industries. The NGA takes a step-by-step approach to recruitment. The first step is recruiting non-manual employees and then seeking recognition from the employer. The second step is to gain full negotiating rights and to attempt to negotiate improved terms and conditions for the new recruits. The final step seeks to establish a post-entry closed shop, but only when asked to do so by the members concerned. The problem of recruiting in competition with non-print unions such as Manufacturing Science and Finance (MSF) and APEX, which charge lower subscription rates, was tackled by using the NGA's protective membership rule, which allowed those recruited for the purpose of organisation or industrial control to be charged 30 per cent of the normal weekly subscription in return for restricted industrial protection. Only when the NGA achieved reasonable wage rates for protective members were they obliged to pay the full subscription rate. This policy was an important incentive to fulfil its promise to secure an acceptable pay rate for new members.

In the 1980s the NGA devoted increased resources to recruitment. Literature aimed at all categories of potential membership was produced.[4] Its regional officers were encouraged to spend more time on recruitment and organisation work and branches to give a higher priority to developing their own organising activities. Since the mid-1980s much thought has been given to subscription rates and the level and type of servicing required to attract new areas of membership. Important steps in this direction were made at the 1988 Delegate Meeting, which accepted an introductory membership category under which new members from unrecognised offices or areas are admitted for a subscription of £1 per week. Where such members are part-time employees the subscription is 50p per week. This category of membership is designed to attract employees involved in desktop publishing and in-plant printing and other areas which impinge on traditional print establishments and where such work is being transferred to publishers' own in-house origination operations.[5] The 1988 Delegate Meeting also agreed to offer NGA membership to young people on print-related Youth Training Schemes, and to offer to all members a 'Membership Services package' giving discount deals on holidays, cars, insurance, etc.

The NGA's attempts to recruit in new areas have not been without obstacles. Resistance has come from employers who argue that union membership is inappropriate to their staffs. There has also been opposition from other unions. In addition, the general industrial climate of the 1980s contributed to a general apathy towards union membership amongst white-collar workers in the communications industry. Despite these obstacles the NGA has had some success in that in the 1980s over 25 per cent of its new members have been recruited from non-union establishments.

NGA DECISION-MAKING MACHINERY, 1964–72

The NGA's original constitution took that of the TA as the basis. At the bottom of its organisational structure were members who were organised into chapels, which remain its basic unit of organisation. The chapels were grouped into branches, which in turn were organised into eleven geographical regions for National Council electoral purposes but had no decision-making powers. The final authority of the NGA is the whole membership by ballot where required. Between delegate meeting the governing body was the National Executive Council, which was accountable to the delegate meeting for its activities. The implementation of union policies, rules and agreements was the responsibility of the National Council and a team of national officers, the chief of which was the General Secretary elected by the whole membership (see Figure 7.1). The channel of communications in the NGA was chapel to branch to National Executive Council, and vice versa. Branches had direct access to the National Executive Council.

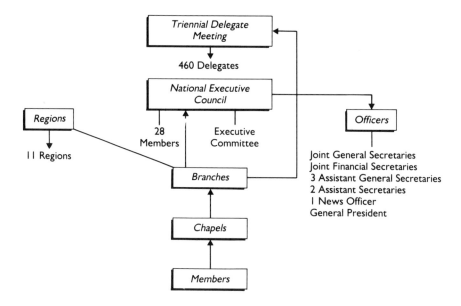

Figure 7.1   The organisational structure of the NGA on its formation

On its formation the NGA had 218 branches each with its own rules which had the approval of National Executive Council. The branches varied in size and only seventeen had full-time secretaries. The branch committee is still today elected by the membership. Most branches allow any member to attend meetings but only delegates from the chapels can vote at branch meetings. The branches retained financial autonomy and the salaries of full-time branch secretaries were met from branch funds and not those of the national union. Branch secretaries were and still are employees of the branch. Today the branches jealously guard this autonomy and the national union does not normally interfere in the management of branches, unless they are in breach of national rules or policies. The method of operation varied and remains so from branch to branch. Although retaining financial autonomy, branches had to operate within the constraints of national rules, policies and agreements. If a branch acted outside these limits the national union could withdraw all national benefits and services to the members of that branch until compliance with national policy was restored. This remains the position today.

The TA group system was the basis of the eleven regions in the original NGA decision-making structure. The regions established were:

    No.1   – London Region
    No.2   – Home Counties and South Eastern Region
    No.3   – North West Region
    No.4   – Midland Region
    No.5   – Yorkshire Region
    No.6   – South Western Region
    No.7   – Northern Region
    No.8   – North Wales and Border Counties Region
    No.9   – South Wales Region
    No.10 – North of Ireland Region
    No.11 – South of Ireland Region

Mergers with NUPT, ACP and NSES led in 1967 to the establishment of Region No. 12 – Scotland. These regions undertook organising and other work as advised by the National Executive Council, for which they produced periodical reports which *inter alia* highlighted particular problems in the region.

Although NGA regions held annual conferences, they had few decision-making powers. Like the TA group system, they were not integrated into the formal constitution. Regional committees and conferences considered motions but both branches and/or the National Executive Committee could bypass a region. However, regional annual conference provided a sounding board for opinion within the NGA to the National Executive Council.

The London Typographical Society became both a region and a branch of the NGA and ran its affairs similarly to that which it had done as an independent union. As a branch/region it had local autonomy subject to national rules, policies and agreements. It had its own head office, and continued to use the title 'London Typographical

Society' until 1966. The management of the region lay with a regional council which was accountable to the annual conference and to trade delegate meetings.

The London Region annual conference still today approves the regional council's report, the region's finances, appeals by members against discipline and alteration to its rules. It decided, and still does, policy on the basis of motions submitted by chapels, which send delegates to the conference.[6] The London Region trade executive committees, composed of lay members, answered, and continue to do so, all questions submitted by chapels and individuals. Initially there were two such committees. In response to amalgamations the number was extended to cover press telegraphists, readers, electrotypers and stereotypers and litho members. Today there are only four trade committees – origination, machine, news, and technical and telecommunications.

Quarterly trade delegate meetings held in February, May, August and November of each year were policy-making bodies within the LSC but in the LTS and the London Region their powers were limited to recommendations to the Regional Council. The delegate meetings continue to be the contact between the regional council and the membership. Initially, London Region officers, as was the practice in the LTS, were elected by the membership and then subjected to re-election every other annual conference. Today, London Region officials elected since 1970 are subject to re-election every three years. In the LSC and the LTS, the News Department, with its News Secretary, serviced members employed on national daily and Sunday newspapers. However, on the formation of the NGA, the London News Secretary became a national NGA official acting also for those in Manchester employed on NPA newspapers.

The original NGA National Executive Council (NEC) consisted of twenty-eight members elected by a ballot of the membership serving for three years and determining union policy between delegate meetings. The principle of representation on the Council was that, irrespective of where a member worked (e.g. a jobbing or news office), the membership should elect the individual who would best serve the membership in their constituent regions. An Executive Committee dealt with everyday matters, leaving the National Executive Council to deal with high policy. The NEC had consultative committees covering Jobbing Compositors, the Newspaper Society, Machine, Photogravure Periodical, Advertising Production Employers' Federation and the Newspaper Proprietors' Association. These related to the major employers' association with which the NGA had collective agreements. However, the National Executive Council had, and continues to have, no authority to sign any agreement involving alterations in wages and working conditions without first submitting the proposed agreement to a vote of the members concerned.

The delegate meeting, as in the TA, was the NGA's parliament. It met every three years with authority to change the Association's rules, to approve the Executive Council report and to determine policy. Representation at this meeting was related to the size of a branch, varying on the one hand from branches with up to 149 members having one delegate, to branches with 3,000 or more members sending eight delegates. London sent one delegate for each 149 members. Whilst broadly adhering to the representation formula of the former TA, the NGA introduced changes to the scale of representation in that branches with 3,000 members or more sent eight delegates and London delegates were elected on a group chapel basis.

The delegate meeting was not the ultimate authority on financial matters or changes to the objects of the union. Here final approval lay, and continues to do so, with the ballot vote of the membership. The NEC had, and still retains, authority not to implement delegate meeting decisions considered inimical to the best interests of the Association or incapable of administration. However, such NEC decisions required, as is the case today, confirmation in a ballot of the members.[7]

On its formation the NGA had eleven national officials. Fred Simmons, the TA General President – an office absent from the LTS or LSC – became the first General President of the NGA. The remaining ten national officerships were divided equally between former TA and former LTS officials. John Bonfield and Robert Willis became Joint General Secretaries. Harry Griffin (former LTS), Roy Hutchings and Joe Wade (both former TA) became Assistant General Secretaries, whilst John Clifford (former LTS) became NGA News Secretary. Arthur Matthews and Geoff Moore (former TA) became Joint Financial Secretaries, whilst John Jones (former TA) and Ron Stafford became Assistant Secretaries. Former LTS full-time officials Bill Booroff, Ernie Welham and Wally Potts became officials of the London Region, with Bill Booroff becoming its first regional secretary.

The LSC, the LTS and the TA made frequent use of membership referendums by secret workplace ballot on many issues, including the election of executive committees, officers, financial matters, wage agreements and delegates to represent the union at the TUC, the

International Graphical Federation, the Labour Party Conference and the Printing and Kindred Trades Federation. This practice remains today in the NGA. Mergers with the NUPT, the ACP, the NSES and the ASLP led to adjustments to the NGA's original structure. These were described in Chapter 3 and need not be repeated here.

THE 1969/1972 REFORMS

The growth in size of the NGA over the period 1964–9 in response to a changing economic and technological environment created a requirement for a comprehensive reorganisation of its constitutional and administrative structure. The 1969 Triennial Delegate Meeting considered such proposals, the basis of which was derived from several sources. First, the 1965 Rules Revision Conference had remitted to the NEC a motion calling for a modernisation of the NGA based on a regional system. The 1966 Delegate Meeting also called for the union to be reconstituted on a regional system. Second, the 1966 Delegate Meeting adopted the policy of branch amalgamations, although this in effect confirmed the existing national policy of encouraging small branches to form larger units and appoint full-time branch secretaries. Third, in the amalgamation discussions with the ASLP the question of trade representation arose, as a result of which special representation for lithographers became part of the NGA/ASLP amalgamation terms. It was recognised that for one trade to have separate representation and not others was inequitable. The time was right for an extension of this principle.

With the ASLP amalgamation accomplished, the NEC called a temporary halt to further mergers. The priority now was to reorganise the NGA structure to provide the necessary servicing for the members in the changing environment expected in the 1970s and 1980s. Each of the amalgamations between 1965 and 1969 had been a political act involving compromises in the NGA's constitutional and administrative procedures. Consequently, by 1969 its organisational structure was unwieldy, expensive and not always capable of responding rapidly to members' needs. However, some progress towards reorganisation at the national level had been made with the opening of a new head office (Graphic House) at Bedford in 1968, the creation of a new officer structure in 1969, the establishment of an economic and research department in 1968 and the introduction of computer-controlled branch accountancy in 1968.

In reforming the NGA's constitution the NEC gave the highest priority to the amalgamation of branches into larger units serviced by full-time secretaries. Approval for the immediate implementation of this policy was sought from the 1969 Delegate Meeting along with other proposed constitutional reforms involving a new regional structure, trade group boards, the National Council and the delegate meeting. The National Council sought approval in principle from the delegate meeting, after which it could conduct a consultative exercise with interested parties.

The 'Reorganisation' document[8] proposed a new branch structure based on larger geographical units with full-time branch secretaries. The 211 existing branches were to be reduced to sixty-seven. Given that the printing industry was not uniformly spread throughout the country, the number of members covered by the new larger branches would vary, but the aim was to provide administrative units of 1,500 full members within an area of 30 miles radius. The mergers of 1965–9, together with the increasingly complex technological changes introduced into the industry, imposed new burdens on a predominantly part-time branch structure such that the position of many branch secretaries had become impossible. The union was experiencing difficulty in securing volunteers to replace retiring part-time branch secretaries.

A major obstacle to branch amalgamation was finance, since larger branches with a full-time secretary would mean an increase in branch subscriptions. Although branch mergers would result in better servicing to members, increased subscriptions were a disincentive to amalgamation. A new administrative branch grant as an alternative to the existing branch administration grant and branch secretaries' allowance was to be introduced to reduce the costs of mergers. It would be available to existing full-time branches and those becoming full time via branch mergers. A further financial incentive to branch amalgamation was to be assistance from head office to help branches incurring capital expenditure in establishing a full-time secretariat. The approach was to be branch mergers on a voluntary basis assisted by the NGA nationally removing practical obstacles to such moves. Large branches outside existing centres of large membership pockets was a new concept for the NGA.

For many branches it would make attendance at branch meetings as of right difficult. Many reacted to this by introducing chapel delegates to branch meetings. Given the changing economic and technological environment and the widening base of membership of the union, a comprehensive training programme for branch officials was to be introduced, so that branch secretaries could do their jobs effectively. The establishment of larger branches would increase the importance of the role of the chapel and in recognition of this the National Council proposed to institute training courses for chapel officers.

The 1969 Delegate Meeting accepted these branch reforms. By 1972 the number of branches had fallen to 117, of which forty were full-time and serviced some 87 per cent of the members. By 1988 the NGA had eighty-five branches of which forty-two were full time, catering for some 90 per cent of the membership. The 1969 branch reforms were successful and transformed NGA branches into efficient administrative and industrial units staffed by well-trained officers. Part-time branches received considerable support from the regional officers. The NGA provides a level and quality of service to its chapels and members surpassing anything offered by any other trade union. Given the envisaged improved servicing of members from branch level, the National Council's restructuring document proposed a regional system less elaborate than envisaged by the 1965 Rules Revision Conference, although it accepted that future amalgamations could change this picture. The union was to be divided into six administrative regions – South West and South Wales, South East, Northern, Midland and North Wales, Ireland and Scotland. The London Region was to remain unchanged from its position as both a region and a branch of the NGA. The Scottish Region, on the grounds of size, was to have a part-time secretary, whilst four other regions were to have full-time secretaries. In Ireland, the Organiser and the Dublin branch secretary were to be joint regional secretaries.

The regions were to be governed by a regional council on which each full-time branch would have one representative together with one seat for part-time branch secretaries. Regional secretaries would be appointees of the National Council and attend National Council meetings as observers in order to be familiar with council policy. Although directly responsible to the National Council, regional secretaries would carry out their duties under the authority of the regional council but would ensure that the regions operated to national policy, supervise branch administration, and assist and support part-time branches.

Regions were to make their own arrangements for the protection of the interests of the various trade groups on the regional council and at the annual conference. To give a purpose to regional conferences, a major change was proposed in the relationship between the national delegate meeting and the annual regional conferences. The latter were to become effective constitutional assemblies. In 1969, motions passed at regional conferences could only be submitted for consideration by the National Council. It was now proposed that branches, instead of submitting motions directly to the national delegate meeting, would first submit them to the regional conference. Any motion carried there would appear on the national delegate meeting agenda in the name of the region and be moved on behalf of the region.

The 1969 reorganisation reforms proposed that consultative committees be replaced by trade group boards. The Litho Trade Group Board would remain and the principle of trade representation would be extended by the creation of two additional trade group boards. A Letterpress Trade Group Board of twenty members was to be elected on a national basis from amongst letterpress members, whilst a News Trade Group Board of the same size would be elected nationally from amongst national and provincial news members. Members of trade group boards would serve for three years and elect from amongst themselves representatives to the National Council. The trade group boards were to consider issues and problems within their area of jurisdiction, including claims to employers for improvements in wages and conditions. Their decisions would be forwarded as recommendations to the National Council. Any agreements with employers that the trade group board was prepared to sanction would go first to the National Council for approval and then to the membership concerned for endorsement.

The extension of trade representation was to have at least two advantages. First, the existing consultative committees made it impossible to formulate and implement consistent national policies for developments such as web-offset, computers, film-setting, machine and keyboard extras. Second, it was likely to ease future mergers:

> The prospect of a single union for the industry is, in the Council's view, at least several years ahead. But it is felt that in this scheme of NGA re-organisation, the opportunity should be taken to facilitate further amalgamation in due course and that the structure of trade group representation as is proposed from the NGA as at present constituted would provide a sound basis for future development when the time came for further amalgamations.[9]

It was also proposed that National Council representation be based on both regional and trade interests, but that regional representation should reflect proportional representation to a greater extent than at present. A National Council of thirty members was envisaged – eighteen would be elected from the regions and twelve from the trade group boards. The Council would meet quarterly and an Executive Committee at three-weekly intervals. These National Council proposals, when taken with the trade group board proposals, were designed to meet the principles of the widest and fairest representation of trade and regional interests but prompt and effective executive functioning.

The 1966 National Delegate Meeting had been attended by 480 delegates. The NGA regarded this as too many if the delegate meeting was to be a deliberative assembly. On the other hand, there were pressures for delegate meetings to be held more than once every three years. The National Council concluded that delegate meetings needed to be revised and it suggested an annual three-day meeting of some 170 delegates elected by regions, and not branches, on the basis of one delegate for 500 members, or part thereof, to consider the National Council's Report and resolutions submitted from annual regional conferences.

The 1969 Delegate Meeting accepted these restructuring proposals in principle and the National Council undertook consultations with a view to bringing appropriate rule changes to the 1972 Delegate Meeting. The National Council submitted a revised reorganisation of the NGA to the 1972 Delegate Meeting. The major changes relative to 1969 were that future regional secretary vacancies would be filled by election not appointment, there would be an additional seat on the National Council, there would be a five-day biennial delegate meeting with direct representation from the branches and the Litho, T&E, and E&S trade sections on the basis of one delegate per 300 members or part thereof, and that T&E news agency members would be represented on the News Trade Group Board.

The 1969 document had proposed giving regions constitutional authority at the expense of branches. Representation at the delegate meeting was to be on the basis of region, and not the branch, with the result that automatic branch representation at the delegate meeting would end. Motions debated at delegate meetings were previously submitted directly by the branch and moved by the branch but the 1969 proposals would have ended this. Branches were to submit motions to the regional annual conference and if carried there the region would forward them to the delegate meeting where they would be moved in the name of the region. The branches strongly resisted these proposed changes and the National Council conceded that branches should continue to be automatically represented at the delegate meeting and that motions and amendments considered there should continue to be submitted directly by the branches.[10] However the proposed regional committee structure, annual conference and officials was to be implemented despite the regions continuing to have no decision-making authority with the new structure of the union.

The original 1969 proposals, together with the above amendments, were accepted by the 1972 Delegate Meeting, which did, however, succeed in securing some further changes. The National Council proposal that it should meet quarterly was rejected in favour of meetings every six weeks, whilst regional secretaries were to be chosen from amongst the members of the region concerned. The main concern of those seeking to amend the National Council's restructuring proposals centred around fears that minority interests that had been protected in merger arrangements would now be swamped. The 1972 constitutional reforms were approved in a ballot of the membership.

From July 1973 the NGA organisational structure through which policy was decided, power exercised and the membership serviced consisted of chapels, branches, regions which had no constitutional authority, trade group boards, the National Council, a biennial delegate meeting and a team of national officers (see Figure 7.2). This structure provided an efficient organisation and a greater degree of membership participation than had existed previously in the union and was to remain intact until 1985 except for minor adjustments to accommodate the mergers with NUWDAT and Slade (see Chapter 6).

THE 1983 REFORMS

These proposals, which were complex and wide ranging, involved major reforms of the regional structure, the National Council and the trade group boards and an overhaul of the union's disciplinary procedures, in addition to changes to strengthen the finances of the union. The reforms were to provide a new organisational and financial structure to meet the needs of a printing industry in the throes of a technological revolution. The reforms sought to provide a more efficient and effective structure, both industrially and financially, capable of responding to the future requirements of the membership whilst maintaining a high level of

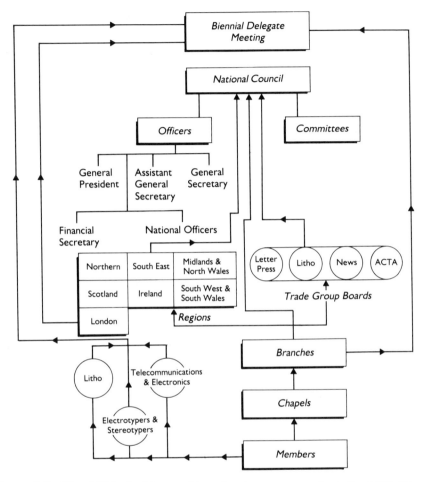

Figure 7.2 The NGA decision-making structure as agreed at the 1972 Biennial Delegate Meeting

membership participation, democratic control and accountability. The proposals were put to a special delegate meeting – the first in the history of the NGA – held at Blackpool in November 1983.

There were a number of factors behind the proposed changes. First, the parlous financial position of the NGA in 1983 demanded that the union be not only industrially effective but also cost effective. These financial pressures stemmed from the sharp increase in unemployment amongst NGA members in the early 1980s. Unrelenting high levels of unemployment and the consequent need to pay high levels of unemployment benefit gave rise to the prospect of severe financial problems which would detrimentally affect the industrial interests of the members and which were only avoided by the membership in May 1982 voting to pay a 75p per week levy to meet unemployment benefit claims.

Second, the regional system and the trade group board structure had in recent years come under criticism. Motions critical of the regional system and the trade group boards had frequently been passed at branch and regional meetings and forwarded to the National Council. Technological change called into question a trade basis of representation. If the NGA was to survive in this changing world, mergers with unions with different structures, financial organisation and administrative practices would be necessary. The existing organisational structure was inappropriate to achieve marriages with unions, which in 1972 were not thought of, to maintain the industrial effectiveness of the NGA.

Third, the NGA was committed by previous delegate meeting decisions to bring proposals to the 1984 Delegate Meeting concerning the regional system and the trade group board structure.[11] A special delegate meeting was imperative if the proposed changes were to come into effect on 1 January 1984. Time was not on the NGA's side. The General Secretary told delegates, 'to wait would have meant a two year delay to plans to scrap the Trade Group Boards and Regional Councils and to cut the size of the National Council delaying again restructure and costing our members more to administer than is necessary.'[12] The chapel would remain the basic unit of government, but chapel amalgamation would be encouraged by practical assistance so that at this level the union more accurately reflected changes taking place in the industry. The geographical branch structure would remain, but part-time branches would be encouraged to amalgamate with, or to form, full-time branches.

The regional structure was to be eliminated. The region had no industrial power, little authority over branches, and their delegate meetings were regarded as little more than social occasions. Many large branches did not use the facilities offered by regions, preferring to bypass them and contact head office direct for advice and assistance. The abolition of the regional structure would give shorter lines of communications and decision-making between chapels and head office. There would be major cost savings and the elimination of confusion over the role and functions of the regions. Regional officers were never sure if their accountability lay to their regional council or to the

National Council or to both, since substantial part of their work was allocated by head office rather than regional councils. Under the proposed changes, regional officers would be responsible to the National Council, reporting in the same way as national officers. They would be field officers, serving particular geographical areas, available to give industrial assistance to branches within their particular region. The present regional system provided the facade of power, democracy and accountability and as constituted they would remain 'expensive talking shops'. There was a desire amongst lay members to retain an annual regional forum in which to meet and discuss mutual problems and to exchange experiences. There was, therefore, to be a regional annual consultative conference to which branches would submit motions for consideration by the National Council, which in turn would use this forum to discuss developments within the industry and to test reactions to its policy.

The size of the National Council had increased as a result of mergers and was becoming unwieldy. Radical changes to both its size and structure were proposed which would produce substantial cost savings. To increase individual participation and more detailed debate, the National Council was to be reduced to thirty-one members, although interim arrangements providing for a thirty-two member National Council would operate until the end of 1986. Representation would be on a regional basis only. The principle of best-person government would apply and in future only lay members would serve on the National Council. This debarring of full-time branch secretaries was controversial, as branches had always claimed the right of self-determination as to their representatives on the National Council without interference from Association rules. Nevertheless, delegates to the special delegate meeting accepted this proposal.

The Council was to meet ten times a year and this increased frequency of its meetings was to be offset by ending the Executive Committee. Election to the National Council was open to all members on the same basis, but since it was only fifteen months after the Slade merger it was thought too soon to take this step immediately, so Slade was guaranteed five seats on the National Council until December 1986.

The trade group boards were replaced by National Council subcommittees. The relevance and value of the trade group boards had been severely questioned. The introduction of new technology had eroded the trade demarcation lines on which the trade group structure was based. They were considered no longer relevant to the needs of the union and its members. The trade group boards had little power and were regarded by branches as a hurdle to be overcome in the decision-making process. Branches were reluctant to allow the trade group boards to advise them on technical questions or house agreements. They saw little reason for them since they had no authority to give industrial assistance in branch dealings with employers.

Although the trade group boards were abolished, the National Council was anxious to receive specialist advice on sectional interests. This was essential if the full benefits of a council based on best-person government were to be achieved. The trade group boards were replaced by subcommittees that 'will be more responsive to the requirements of our members and be constructive and viable partners with the National Council'.[13] These subcommittees were to advise the National Council on sectional interests and covered provincial news, national news, origination, machine, and clerical and administrative. Representation on these subcommittees was equally divided between National Council and lay representatives, as this would remove tensions between the National Council and the subcommittees whose size was to be limited. If the National Council considered it necessary to have representation or specialist advice on particular issues which were not catered for by the subcommittees, co-option could take place.

The Council's standing committees were restructured. The Branch Rules and Disciplinary Committees were merged to form the Rules and Disciplinary Committee, whilst the Training and Education Committee amalgamated with the Health and Safety Committee to form the Training, Safety, Education and Research Committee. An Organisation Committee was formed by merging the existing Organisation and Agency and Studio Committees. In addition, the Women's Committee was to be formalised within the constitution as it was unlikely within the foreseeable future that there would be eight women members of the National Council. The Women's Committee was to be the only National Council committee with lay member involvement on the same basis as lay membership of the National Council subcommittees, namely 50 per cent of the committee elected by the lay membership.

It was also proposed to establish an Irish Industrial Council to ensure that the particular political, economic and industrial problems confronting the Irish membership received proper consideration by the National Council, as would the different trade union and industrial relations legislation applying in the Irish Republic. The Irish Industrial Council advises and makes recommendations to the National Council on matters relating specifically to Ireland. Although mainly consisting of lay representation from Ireland, the Council is chaired by the General President who is responsible to the National Council for Irish affairs.

Concern had been expressed from various quarters about the level of 'natural justice' in the Association's disciplinary and appeals procedure. In 1983 the National Council was responsible for making policy and for disciplining those who breached it. Under the disciplinary procedures it was possible for national councillors who served on their branch committee to be involved in imposing a penalty at branch level and then being a member on the National Council committee considering an appeal against the branch penalty. An Appeals Committee, composed of lay members elected separately from the National Council, was to be established to provide the right of appeal against National Council disciplinary decisions. The Appeals Committee members are precluded from involvement in disciplinary matters at any other level of the union. The Committee's decision is final and not subject to alteration or challenge by the National Council. The National Council has power to instruct branches to institute formal charges against members. Previous lack of such power sometimes left the National Council helpless to act even where it could demonstrate that a branch had allowed members to flout the union's constitution in the most disreputable ways. Now that the National Council's role in disciplinary matters had changed, to give it this power was now appropriate.

The final piece of the 1983 constitutional reforms was the elimination of separate representation at delegate meetings for electrotypers and stereotypers, telecommunications and electronic members and former NUWDAT members. Separate representation for former ASLP members had been ended by the 1980 Delegate Meeting on the grounds that the litho section was no longer, as had been the case in 1969, a small minority of the membership that needed the protection of guaranteed representation at delegate meetings. The 1970s saw litho membership expanding rapidly and a steady increase in letterpress to litho membership reclassification, and by 1980 40 per cent of the admission of youths into the union were to the litho section. So, twenty years after its formation, the NGA had a delegate meeting where representatives were NGA members first and compositors, machine managers and stereotypers, etc. second.

The National Council's proposals were accepted by the special delegate meeting and came into being on 1 January 1985. They are the basis of the present-day decision-making structure of the NGA (see

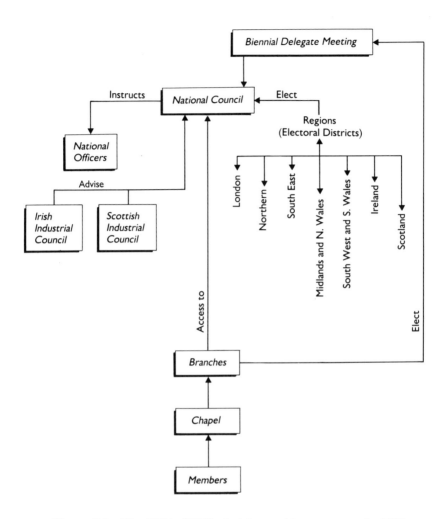

Figure 7.3   The NGA (1982) decision-making structure in 1989

Figure 7.3). The only changes since this date were the creation of the Scottish Industrial Council and the termination of the National Council subcommittees. The establishment in 1986 of a Scottish Industrial Council provided a forum for advising and making recommendations to the National Council on Scottish matters. In September 1985 the National Council decided not to replace the retiring Scottish regional officer, arguing that the union had only 2,000 members in Scotland and three full-time branches, and that to add a full-time regional officer would not be a prudent use of Association funds. However, the 1986

Delegate Meeting upheld an appeal from the Glasgow branch against this National Council decision. Following this, discussions took place between the National Council and the Scottish branches. The Council decided not to replace the Scottish regional officer but, in response to concerns about the level of representation in Scotland and the level of lay member input into the Scottish Industrial Council, it agreed to recommend to the 1988 Delegate Meeting that the Scottish Industrial Council be doubled in size. At the same time the National Council repeated previous assurances as to the availability of a national officer, and, in appropriate dispute situations, the secondment of a regional officer to assist in Scotland. This approach was finally accepted by the Scottish membership and approved by the 1988 Delegate Meeting.[14]

In 1988, after five years of operation, the delegate meeting terminated the National Council subcommittees, arguing that the now totally regionally based National Council had resulted in a council elected from a very wide variety of trade interests, e.g. former Slade members, former T&E members, litho printers, etc. Virtually every trade section in the NGA had gained representation on the National Council through the system of best-person government from regional, not trade, constituencies. Therefore the number of occasions when the National Council needed the specialist advice of its subcommittees had been few and far between. In addition, when necessary, the Council had talked directly with chapel representatives in particular sectors. Both these factors convinced the National Council that the days of the subcommittees and specialist trade representation could come to an end. The delegates agreed.

RANK AND FILE ATTEMPTS AT CONSTITUTIONAL CHANGES

The 1976 Delegate Meeting agreed that rule changes should be considered only at every other delegate meeting. In 1976, 1980, 1984 and 1988 the Liverpool branch sought to introduce annual, rather than biennial, delegate meetings without any reduction in the size and duration of the meeting. Their main argument was that the speed at which economic, political and technical developments were taking place both within and outside the industry required the union to constantly reassess and fomulate policies to meet changing situations. In this fast-changing world the NGA membership needed the opportunity to air their views more often if they were to have any influence on this situation.

However, the Liverpool attempts were unsuccessful and a number of counter-arguments always won the day. There was the question of costs, since a delegate meeting costs the union some £250,000, excluding the costs borne by the branches in sending their delegations. At the 1988 meeting Liverpool suggested that an annual conference's costs could be offset by ending regional consultative meetings, but the National Council was quick to point out that these cost only £13,000. Second, there were often difficulties in implementing policies decided every two years and it was feared that an annual conference changing policy every year would give the membership an inconsistent and fluid picture of the Association policy. Thirdly, it was argued that the increased cost of holding an annual delegate meeting would reduce the amount of money available to protect the members industrially. The members paid subscriptions for industrial protection. It was one thing to ask members to pay increased subscriptions for this but quite another to ask them to pay more to provide an annual conference. A further National Council argument was that they could always obtain a rapid response from the membership via regional consultative conferences, branch secretary consultative meetings, meetings of FOC, etc., and if there was something that the Council really could not handle there was the option of a special delegate meeting.

The 1980 and 1984 Delegate Meetings saw unsuccessful attempts by London and Bristol respectively to make the delegate meeting the supreme policy-making body of the association. Both motions argued that the status of decisions made at delegate meetings was not clearly stated in the rules, despite post-conference balloting safeguards on many issues, for example finance. The problem, it was argued, was that on all other motions the National Council could vary the policy in the light of the circumstances, thereby giving disproportionate authority to that body. The London and Bristol motions sought to make delegate meeting decisions, except those subject to a post-conference ballot of the membership, binding on the National Council. The main arguments used in defeating these motions were that they would remove from the National Council its power to make decisions and formulate policies, nullify the existing democratic control through the chapels, branches and the regions, and would hamper the National Council in its work between delegate meetings. It was feared that the Council would be in a straightjacket unable to vary policy in the light of new developments.

The Manchester branch objected strongly to both these motions, arguing that they conflicted with other rules and that the union's constitution was quite clear that the supreme policy-making body was the membership and that to accept these motions would give control of the union to conference activists. The balance of power between the National Council, the delegate meeting and the membership would be upset.[15]

The 1988 Delegate Meeting saw an unsuccessful attempt by the Liverpool branch to gain two 'reserved seats' for women on the National Council. They argued that the demand should be seen as a transitional step towards women being on the Council through their own merits. Reserved seats were to be the catalyst towards this longer-term objective, as it would give women members the confidence to stand for election and participate more fully in the union's affairs. A woman delegate argued that the structure of meetings at national level prohibited women, especially those with children, from participating as freely as men and there would never be a woman on the National Council unless positive action was taken. The National Council opposed the motion, arguing that the current system of election to the Council did not act against women wishing to stand for election and that it had not been tried and tested by them. In addition, it pointed out that 'reserved seats' would give only token representation, that the National Council's agenda was not made up of matters pertaining solely to male or female members, that working conditions in the NGA areas of the industry were the same for women as they were for men and that the Women's Committee existed to advise the National Council on the special requirements and employment needs of women. The delegates accepted the National Council recommendations that it should continue with its present system of election to the National Council, which is equal to all lay members irrespective of sex, race, colour or creed.[16]

THE NATIONAL OFFICERS

The principal officers of the NGA have always been the General President, the General Secretary, since 1969 the Assistant General Secretary, the Financial Secretary and as many other national officers as are considered necessary for the efficient running of its affairs and the servicing of the membership to protect and advance their interests. The national officers of the union, as was the case with the TA, the LSC and the LTS, have always come from the trade and have had to have been members of the union for at least five years. They are elected by a ballot of the membership, but do not have to stand for periodic re-election. They remain in office subject to giving to or receiving from the National Council three months' notice. If an officer is given notice, the decision must be endorsed by a membership ballot in which both the Council and the officer concerned state their respective cases. However, in the history of the NGA no national officer has ever been given notice of termination of employment. The national officers are not policy makers but policy implementors. In doing this, they work under the direction of the General Secretary who is the chief executive of the national officer team. The salaries of the officers are decided by the National Council and published in its report to the delegate meeting, which has the power, although it has never exercised it, to change officer salaries.

The TA required those nominated for any national officer vacancy to be subjected to a written examination conducted by the National Council and designed to ensure that those who aspired to national office had the basic qualifications and qualities for such a post. This practice was adopted by the NGA. The examination paper, set by the Establishments Committee of the National Council, was in two parts. First, there was a three-hour written examination containing questions on the rulebook, the union's collective agreements and its policies. To ensure secrecy, candidates entered a number instead of their name on the paper. Only those who reached the pass mark for the paper moved on to the second part, which was an appearance before the National Council to answer set questions. Only candidates deemed successful by the National Council in both parts of the examination system appeared on the ballot paper. Ballots for national officer posts were, until March 1982, decided on the first past the post electoral system which had been adopted in 1950 by the TA, which before that date used a system of preferential voting.

The examination system was always proudly presented as an essential safeguard in ensuring that TA and then NGA national officers had an all-round knowledge of the union and basic competencies. However, in 1976 the credibility of the examination system was badly dented. The London Region member was successful in the General Secretary examination of that year but failed the Assistant General Secretary examination later in the same year. The London Region was puzzled and at the 1976 Delegate Meeting unsuccessfully sought the end of the examination system on the grounds that it had unknown requirements, was carried out by unqualified examiners, was outdated and archaic and that although the rules provided that officers be elected by the membership they could in effect vote only for the names that the National Council allowed.[17] These were also criticisms of the system in the late 1970s in terms of its confidentiality as to the non-identifying of candidates and that no account was taken of a member's experience, known abilities and service to the Association.

The examination system was ended by the 1982 Delegate Meeting, with delegates arguing that the system had become unfair, inadequate and an 'insult to the intelligence of the members'. Since 1982 any member nominated for a national officer vacancy has automatically gone on to the ballot paper. The creation of NGA (1982) saw the ending of the first past the post system of deciding elections and its replacement by one based on the exhaustive principle, subject to a maximum of three ballots. The new procedure was first tested in the Assistant General Secretary election of 1985 when three ballots were required to find a successful candidate, namely the current Assistant General Secretary, John Ibbotson. Slade had insisted that the NGA first past the post system be replaced by one based primarily on the exhaustive principle. The irony is that it cost the former Assistant General Secretary of Slade the Assistant General Secretaryship of the NGA (1982). In the first ballot for this post he topped the poll and, had the NGA system continued into the NGA (1982), he would have been declared its Assistant General Secretary.

That NGA officials should be elected by the members is a jealously guarded principle and the National Council has been defeated at delegate meetings on each of the two occasions that it claimed authority under the rules to be able to appoint or re-deploy national officers. In 1967 the officer structure was examined in the light of amalgamations, the need to deploy officers in the most efficient ways and to give relief to the Joint General Secretary (John Bonfield), whose range of duties was increasing in size and complexity.

The National Council, *inter alia*, appointed an existing officer Mr Joe Wade to the post of Assistant General Secretary, although in future it would be an elected post. Nevertheless this led to a successful motion to the delegate meeting instructing the National Council to submit 'their nominee to the membership for endorsement'. Amalgamations had given the NGA a surplus of officers, but promises had been given to the unions involved that the officer corps would not increase. The National Council felt that putting an Assistant General Secretaryship up for election would imply a preparedness to accept another officer when promises had been given to the contrary. The General Secretary needed assistance and the Council felt it reasonable to appoint from existing officers, since it had powers, under rule, to delegate officers' duties. However, Joe Wade's nomination was subsequently approved in a membership ballot.

The second occasion arose in 1977 when John Jones, an existing national officer, was appointed Financial Secretary by the National Council. The 1978 Delegate Meeting annulled the Council's decision and instructed it to seek nominations for the position. The background to the Council's decision was that the then Financial Secretary, Mr Geoff Moore, was going to retire in 1978 and, given the specialised nature of the post, it was proposed to have a Financial Secretary elect who would be trained before his retirement. In April 1977 an examination had been held of candidates nominated for the position and three candidates had been successful. On 20 May, following Geoff Moore's untimely death, the candidates were told that Mr Jones had been appointed Financial Secretary and the ballot for Financial Secretary designate cancelled. The Delegate Meeting said that the fundamental tradition and practice of the NGA of electing national officers must be upheld and what had been done with the Financial Secretaryship could be done to other offices, for example the General Secretaryship.

The National Council strongly, but unsuccessfully, defended its action. It argued that the 1966 Delegate Meeting had ensured that it was in control of the duties of all national officers, including the Financial Secretary, by giving it powers to assign national officer duties. All it had done was to act in accordance with this authority. Accusations of undemocratic behaviour by the National Council were rejected on the grounds that it was merely carrying out the rules of Association, it was not seeking powers to appoint officers and it was, in the interests of the membership, recognising the special responsibilities of Financial Secretary in administering the funds of the union. It also stressed that, although the Financial Secretary's duties were set out in the rulebook, the post was not exempt from having duties assigned to it by the National Council, which had in fact done so by giving it responsibility for property, membership, investment, branch amalgamations and pensions.

The circumstances in which the National Council appointed a Financial Secretary were exceptional. Geoff Moore had died in May

1977 and it was felt impossible to proceed with the ballot for Financial Secretary designate, given that there was now no Financial Secretary. Given the specialist nature of the Financial Secretary's duties, the Council concluded that the interests of the membership would be best served by an existing national officer with a wide range of industrial experience, including the Finance Department, being allocated these duties. John Jones met both these criteria. However, following the delegate meeting decision, John Jones resigned his national officership and went to work outside the industry. In the subsequent election, Mr Colin James, the West Midlands branch secretary, was elected Financial Secretary.

The LSC officers were subject to re-election at its Annual General Meeting, whilst those of the LTS were subject to re-election every two years at its annual conference. TA national officers were not subject to periodic re-election and this system was adopted for NGA officers. However, over the period 1972–88, there were unsuccessful attempts at six delegate meetings (1972, 1974, 1976, 1980, 1984 and 1988) to introduce a system of periodic re-election of NGA national officers and an unsuccessful attempt at the 1982 Delegate Meeting to get a membership ballot on the principle of periodic re-election of full-time officers. The arguments used by both sides remained virtually the same. Supporters of re-election considered that national officers would become more responsible since they would be accountable to the membership, that a steady job and non-accountability tended to make them remote from the membership, that being a national officer was not a career and that if FOCs, branch committee members, branch officers and national councillors had to stand for re-election why should national officers be exempted.

The opponents of re-election always argued that the loosening of employment security that would result from re-election would dissuade good people from coming forward to be national officers, that officers would be forced to woo popularity rather than be prepared to say what they felt was best for the union, and that it would have adverse effects on the servicing of the membership in that officers would be tempted to concentrate on the problems of the large chapels where the votes were, at the expense of small chapels. However, the main argument presented against re-election was that the contention that it would improve democracy and accountability in the union was false. Within the NGA there is a clear line of accountability of national officers to the National Council and every two years of the National Council to the membership. Officers are obligated to execute the union's policies even though they have no vote in their determination and irrespective of whether they agree with them. Re-election would introduce a fundamental change in the relationship between national officers and the National Council. The latter is accountable through re-election every two years and it would be unreasonable to make officers accountable for policies they did not finally make. The national officers, if subject to re-election, would cease to be accountable to the National Council, as they would become directly accountable to the membership. If periodic re-election was introduced, the effect would be to put power in the hands of the officers and they, and not the councillors, would determine policy. The National Council would become an advisory rather than a governing body.

In both the TA and the NGA, the General President presides over National Council and national delegate meetings, exercises a general supervision over the affairs of the union and gives assistance or advice to the General Secretary and national officers between National Council meetings. The General President has always played an elder statesman role, but held himself available to take up industrial duties if and when necessary. The tradition in the TA, which was continued within the NGA, was that the General President looked after the industrial interests of the Irish membership.

The first General President of the NGA was Mr Fred Simmons, who held office until 1974. Including his period of office within the TA, Fred Simmons was the General President for seventeen years. He was highly regarded as a conference chairman and presided over five NGA delegate meetings with great efficiency and understanding. He developed a deep knowledge of incentive schemes based on work measurement. He was particularly concerned with apprentices and sought to further their industrial and educational interests. He believed apprentices should be properly trained and appropriately paid for the work they did. He gave attention to detail.

Les Dixon, who replaced Fred Simmons, remained in office until 1982 and brought a different style to the General Presidency. He became actively involved in industrial work and had an impressive personality. He is probably best remembered for his outstanding efforts and achievements on behalf of the members in the direct entry dispute with Times Newspapers Ltd in 1978/9. He undertook his General Presidency duties with energy, drive and commitment. He was a committed amalgamationist and, during his eight years as a General

President, significant steps were made towards the formation of one union for the industry, particularly by the formation of NGA (1982). Following Les Dixon's retirement, Bryn Griffiths was elected General President and remains in office today. He is continuing the established great traditions and high standards of NGA General Presidents. He has been particularly successful in raising the profile and influence of the NGA in the International Graphical Federation, and was instrumental in developing the European Graphical Federation. He has also earned considerable respect from all sections of the NGA's membership, not least those in Ireland, for his negotiating ability and experience, a good grounding having been received by spending many years as the NGA's Northern Region Secretary. He is also an excellent Council and Conference Chairman, combining firmness and fairness, with a mischievous sense of humour.

The General Secretary is the chief officer of the Association. From 1964 to 1969 John Bonfield and Bob Willis were Joint General Secretaries. Bob Willis, who had been General Secretary of the LTS and LSC, had a reputation as a formidable negotiator and was responsible with John Bonfield for achieving the TA/LTS amalgamation. He was active as a General Council member of the TUC but gave up his seat in 1965 when George Brown, the then Minister for Economic Affairs, asked him to become a full-time member of the National Board for Prices and Incomes. In 1967 he resigned over policy differences and returned to his Joint General Secretaryship, which he held until his retirement in 1969. John Bonfield continued as sole General Secretary until his death in 1976. His vision and determination proved an impetus not only for the formation of the NGA but for the marriages that were to follow in the NGA's early years. He also played an active part in building links with other print workers both at home and abroad. He was President of the P&KTF from 1961 until the Federation was wound up in 1974. He was for many years a member of the Executive Committee of the IGF, being elected its President in 1967 – a post he held until his death. He was respected for his statesmanship, wise council and charm as well as penetrating flashes of insights and wit.

Following John Bonfield's death in 1976, Joe Wade became the General Secretary, a post he held until his retirement at the end of 1984. Although he had been recognised as the heir apparent for some time, Wade brought a new style of General Secretaryship. During his years in office he instigated many changes. Apart from being an advocate of close international links with both the IGF and print unions in the socialist countries, he was for many years at the forefront of the campaign for amalgamation discussions and made many major contributions to the mergers that created and shaped the NGA into what it is today. Joe Wade was an advocate of greater internal democracy in the union and he was a major influence on the 1969 restructuring proposals. He created the NGA's Education and Research Departments and led the union through numerous difficult and challenging disputes, particularly the 1980 dispute with the BPIF and the Newspaper Society, which led to a 37½ hour week and the £80 minimum wage in the industry, in advance of the rest of British industry and the West European printing industry. He played an important role in rebuilding the NGA's relationship with the TUC, which had been damaged by its resignation in 1972.

Tony Dubbins replaced Mr Wade as General Secretary in 1985. He has been an innovator, and has forced the NGA members to come to terms with changes in the industry that would have been unthinkable to its founding fathers of twenty-five years ago. He is a skilled and respected negotiator, has done much to raise the profile of the NGA within the TUC and the Labour Party, and was the creator of the 1983 financial and organisational reforms initiating the separate Provident and Dispute Funds, and the implementation of the Introductory Membership category. He has great energy, drive and foresight. His prediction as to what would happen to the printing unions in newspapers if they could not agree a common approach has been proved to be true. He led on behalf of the NGA the merger discussions with Slade to achieve NGA'82, and has done much to work towards the amalgamation with Sogat and was the motivator behind the NGA's decision to attempt to finance, with the largest general printing employers and machinery manufacturers, a national training centre. It is his foresight and imagination that gives the NGA a significant influence in today's industry, in the Labour Party and in the TUC considerably in excess of what might be expected of a union with 125,000 members.

In addition to the General President, Bryn Griffiths, and General Secretary, Tony Dubbins, this is the current National Officer team of the Association, and their main areas of responsibility: John Ibbotson was elected Association's Assistant General Secretary in 1984. Since then his main task has been the co-ordination of the work of the Association's Industrial Officers, and the day to day implementation of industrial policy in the newspaper, general printing, tin printing, typesetting, and agency and studio areas of the Association's activity. John was previously the Association's officer dealing with provincial newspapers, and has been directly involved in many of the major disputes which the Association has had to contend with over the past few years. Recently John has also been deeply involved in developing organisational policy, utilising the Association's new Introductory Membership category. To assist with developing organisation he has also been the officer mainly responsible for the Association's 'Services Package' which was made available to the membership in 1989. As Assistant General Secretary, John also co-ordinates the activities of the Association's Regional Officers.

Alf Parish, the current NGA's National Secretary became an Officer of the Association as a result of the amalgamation with Slade, where he had been the Assistant General Secretary. His main responsibility is for the turbulent National News area, as well as servicing members working in Cunaud Metal Box. He also shares responsibility for providing a service to members working in the Litho House Agreement area of the industry, particularly with the larger groups such as Wace and Parkway.

Chris Harding, National Officer, services members working under the RAGA (Reproduction and Graphics Association), and Arts Studios & Agencies Agreement. He is also responsible for looking after the interests of NGA members working in a number of large groups, for example St. Ives, Hunterprint, Bowater etc., particularly in respect of problems associated with technological change in the press rooms. He is additionally responsible for the magazine publishing industry, and has been deeply involved in the development of the Association's policies on word processing, and new technology in the origination area.

George Jerrom, National Officer, is involved in the area of commercial printing where he has been responsible for the Association's industrial representation with a number of large groups of companies such as BPCC, DRG, HMSO, etc. In the recent past, the MPMA Agreement and the tin printing area has also been added to that list of responsibilities. To that extensive list has now been added the responsibility for dealing with the SMPS Agreement, and issues concerning our members in Scotland.

Eddie Martin, who became a National Officer of the NGA as a result of the amalgamation with Slade in 1982, has a shared responsibility for servicing those members who work under the 'Litho House Agreement' policy, as well as carrying out general industrial duties.

Recently, Eddie Martin has taken on board the unenviable responsibility for the provincial newspaper industry, and maintained a role in supporting NGA members in the news agency field.

Brenda Philbin became a National Officer of the Association as a result of the transfer of engagements of NUWDAT (National Union of Wallcoverings, Decorative and Allied Trades) in 1979. She is primarily responsible for developing organisation, and servicing the interests of NGA members working in the wallcoverings industry, and services the Women's Committee, as well as undertaking other general industrial duties.

Fred Tanner, National Officer, is now responsible for the administration of the head office of the union, and relations with its staff. In addition he is the officer responsible for the legal advice and services that are offered by the NGA, and takes on board the arrangements for the Association's Biennial Delegate Meeting.

John Willats, National Officer, is responsible for servicing the National Council, has overall responsibility for the Research, Training, and Education and Health & Safety Committee of the NGA, as well as being the officer preparing the day to day editorial work of the Association's journal *Print*. He is also deeply involved in maintaining and developing relationships with organisations such as Amnesty International, Chile Solidarity Campaign, and SACTU. He is Chairman of the Joint Training Council.

Brian Willoughby was elected National Officer in 1990 and will take over the full range of responsibilities currently undertaken by John Willats, who will retire in 1991.

Colin James, Financial Secretary, is directly responsible to the General Secretary and National Council for the Association's finances, administration, and membership records, and additionally co-ordinates investment and subscription policy, as well as maintaining a close liaison with the Association's branches.

THE JOURNAL

With the amalgamation of the LTS and the TA the two unions' journals (the *London Typographical Journal* and the *Typographical Circular*) were merged into the *Graphical Journal*, the main features of both journals being retained in the new publication. The General Secretary was the responsible editor and the journal was supplied free via the branches to every working member of the union. The journal is the only direct contact between the National Council and the members. It informs them of union policy and agreements and any alterations to these as well as of developments taking place within and outside the industry.

With the December 1967 issue the *Graphic Journal* ceased publication and was replaced by *Print*, printed in newspaper tabloid format as from January 1968. The most serious criticism of the *Graphic Journal* was that it lacked news and sufficient illustrations and was invariably late into the membership's hands. *Print* informs the membership, quickly and in a readable manner, of events which bear on their livelihoods.

Print, nevertheless, is not without its critics. There were complaints that its general appearance and presentation of material lack flair and originality, that it is delivered late, and that the quality of paper used is poor. In response to a 1986 Delegate Meeting calling for a new format for *Print*, a new style was launched in January 1988 designed to appeal to a wide spectrum of the membership. At the same time it was decided to publish a magazine entitled NGA *Focus* designed for the shopfloor activists and to expand on the wider, important issues facing the union. *Print* is published ten times a year and *Focus* quarterly.

NOTES

1. E. Howe and H.E. Waite, *The London Society of Compositors: A Centenary History*, Cassell, 1948, Part I, Ch. XI, and Part III, Ch. XVIII.

2. ibid., Part III, Ch. XX, pp. 332–3.

3. See *Report of the Delegate Meeting, 1980*, National Graphical Association, p. 82.

4. See John Gennard, 'The NGA and the Impact of New Technology', *New Technology, Work and Employment*, vol. 2, no. 2, Autumn 1987.

5. A motion to the 1988 Delegate Meeting seeking the establishment of a special recruitment department was defeated. The National Council argued that the union already had the ability, resources and commitment to a positive recruiting policy and that there had always been full support for branches which wanted help in organising new members.

6. The London Society of Compositors had an annual general meeting which was open to all Society members. However, only a small proportion of members ever attended this meeting. The two highest-attended meetings were those of 1950 and 1954 when there was an unsuccessful attempt at the former to remove both the Chairman and General Secretary from office and at the latter (attended by over 500 members) to remove the General Secretary. The officers of the LSC were subject to annual re-election at the annual conference.

7. The TA National Executive Council evoked this power with respect to a decision at the 1950 Delegate Meeting that the 50/50 agreements with Natsopa be abrogated,

and three decisions – the duties of readers, the publication to all members of *all* agreements reached between employers and the TA, and members in membership of a social club having a printing press on their premises committing a disciplinary offence – taken at the 1957 Delegate Meeting. In all cases the members voted to support the Executive Council action.

8. See *National Council Report on the Re-organisation of the NGA Structure, Triennial Delegate Meeting, 1969*.

9. ibid., p. 7.

10. See *Revised National Council Report on the Re-organisation of NGA Structure, Triennial Delegate Meeting, 1972*, p. 15.

11. The 1980 Delegate Meeting had discussed a National Council discussion paper on branch restructuring which considered two options – one devolving more power and decision-making functions to the regions and the other suggesting a number of alternatives which would modify the region's role and function. See NGA, Discussion Paper, *Regional Restructure*, Delegate Meeting, June 1980. A motion to the same delegate meeting calling for the abolition of the Litho and Letterpress Trade Group Boards and their replacement by four boards – origination, machine, news and ATLA – was remitted to the National Council.

12. See *Report of the Delegate Meeting, 1983*, National Graphical Association.

13. ibid., p. 23.

14. See *Report of the Delegate Meeting, 1988*, National Graphical Association, pp. 154–6.

15. See *Report of the Delegate Meeting, 1980*, National Graphical Association, pp. 183–9, and *Report of the Delegate Meeting, 1984*, National Graphical Association, pp. 210–17.

16. See *Report of the Delegate Meeting, 1988*, National Graphical Association, pp. 223–9.

17. See *Report of the Delegate Meeting, 1976*, National Graphical Association, pp. 256–64 and *Report of the Delegate Meeting, 1978*, National Graphical Association, pp. 292–6.

CHAPTER 8

THE FINANCIAL STRUCTURE
OF THE NGA

THE LSC/LTS STRUCTURE

The LSC

The members' subscriptions were allocated to the Society's two funds –
the Disputes and General Administration Account and the Provident
and Superannuation Account. A sum of 2½p per member per week was
allocated to the former fund and the balance to the latter. Changes to
this distribution required the approval of the membership. Following
the 1950 wage dispute between the Society and the LMPA, the
members voted by 7,282 votes to 518 that for a twenty-four-week period
the full subscription be allocated to the Disputes and General
Administration Account to replenish the £128,000 which had been paid
in strike allowances during the dispute.[1]

The Disputes and General Administration Account provided industrial protection to the membership. If the fund was inadequate,
particularly in the case of emergencies, the LSC could impose levies on
its members so long as a delegate meeting approved. During the 1950
wage dispute a 50p per week levy bringing in almost £11,000 was
sanctioned and paid by those members not involved in the dispute.
Strike benefit was paid at the rate of £3.60 per week for ten consecutive
weeks, but the period of payment could be extended by one week for
each six months' membership until a maximum of twenty-six weeks was
reached.

The Retiring Allowances for Officials and Staff Fund and the

Educational Trust Fund received their income via allocations from the Disputes and General Administration Account. The Educational Fund, established by the May 1953 Quarterly Delegate Meeting, provided educational facilities to the membership. Although the LSC was a strong industrial union, from an education standpoint it was in the background compared with other unions in the early 1950s. Many unions had their own education and training programmes whilst the LSC relied on courses offered by the WEA and the National Council of Labour Colleges. It was often difficult for members to take advantage of WEA and NCLC courses and scholarships since prior sanction of the costs was required from a delegate meeting and by the time this happened it was often too late for members to participate in courses. An equally important factor in the establishment of the Educational Trust Fund was the realisation that the post Second World War period created new training and education needs for trade unions and their members. Unions were playing a much larger part in the economic and social affairs of the union. Trade union officials were frequently consulted by government.

The August 1953 Delegate Meeting established retiring allowances for officials and staff at the level of one-third of their basic salary at the time of their retirement. The beneficiaries of the scheme contributed 2 per cent of their basic weekly salary to which was added annually by the union a sum equal to ½d per week per member.

The Provident and Superannuation Account provided unemployment, emigration, removal, funeral and superannuation allowances and some minor benefits to cover such things as loss of tools by fire. The rules of the LSC permitted, subject to approval by a special delegate meeting, suspension of all or any of these allowances and variations of their levels in emergencies or crisis. From 1948 until its merger with the PMMTS the LSC unemployment allowance remained at £1.50 per week. The emigration allowance was a lump sum benefit to help members with the costs of starting new lives overseas. The removal grant benefit assisted members wishing to leave London because they had secured jobs as compositors outside London. Funeral benefit was paid to dependants of a non-retired member at the rate of £2 per year for each year of service.

LSC paid superannuation allowances under three different schemes. Scheme No. 1, which started in 1877 and closed in 1922, applied to the oldest members of the Society; at the time of the PMMTS merger only two retired members were in this scheme. Scheme No. 3 existed for members who were over 40 when they entered the scheme, which began in July 1924. By the time the LSC's separate existence ended there were 154 retired members in the scheme. However, the majority of LSC retired members received benefit under Scheme No. 2, which had started in 1923.

Superannuation allowances were a regular topic at quarterly delegate meetings, at annual conferences and in the pages of the *London Typographical Journal*. There were, however, only two major changes to the allowance between 1948 and the merger with the PMMTS. First, in 1953 a delegate meeting accepted that members on superannuation allowance should receive the benefit for at least five years. If within five years of retirement a member died, then his widow or nearest dependant would receive the benefit until a full five years had elapsed since the member retired from work. Second, in February 1954 a delegate meeting agreed that the 25 per cent cut in superannuation allowance after ten years of receiving it should end. In future, members would draw their superannuation allowance without reduction until they died.

There were frequent attempts to increase the level of superannuation allowances on the grounds that the cost of living was rising rapidly, retired members were finding it difficult to make ends meet and the finances of the LSC were sufficiently healthy to fund such rises. The union leadership opposed these demands, arguing that the state should increase old age pensions, that although the union's funds were reasonably healthy a trade slump would reverse the financial situation and that there was a need to conserve union funds.[2] The main problem was convincing the members that an apparently healthy balance of funds could not be the basis of long-term increased financial commitments since such reserves could disappear with startling rapidity. Increased membership unemployment, for example, would increase the demands on the Provident and Superannuation Account. Ultimately, provident benefits could only be sustained by members voluntarily, via levies, agreeing to put more money into the account. There were limits to which members would dig into their own pockets to counteract any rapid depletion of the Society's funds through unforeseen events.[3]

The LSC attitude was clear. Although it would always stand by its superannuants, even to the extent of levying the membership, this did not mean that burdens would be imposed upon the working membership which they could not carry. The LSC's primary function was the maintaining and improving of its members' working conditions. It was not merely a friendly society having no other business than the payment of superannuation allowances. The benefits side of the activities were an addition to its industrial activities, although indicative of the care and concern which the working membership had for those members who had retired. The LSC leadership were never slow to point out that superannuation allowances existed, not because they were actually sound, but because of the past loyalty and sacrifices of the members.

During the period 1948–55, the balance of LSC funds showed a steady increase. The average amount of funds per member was £43 in 1948 but stood at £51 per head in February 1955. It was a period when the union spent little on unemployment allowances (see Table 8.1). The fear was that any return to long periods of unemployment amongst the membership would soon reduce these healthy balances to a deficit and cause concern for the functioning of the union.

The LTS

The members' subscriptions were allocated to two funds: 7½p per member each week was allocated to the Disputes and General Administration Account, which provided the industrial protection to the membership; the remainder was deposited in the Provident and Superannuation Account, which financed the Society's friendly society benefits. The 1956 and the 1959 wage disputes in the general printing industry had a destabilising effect on the Disputes and General Administration Account. The former dispute, which involved more than half the membership, cost the Society £257,000 in strike allowances, the hiring of halls and other related costs. To repair its finances a special conference held on 4 December 1956 agreed that the weekly subscription allocated to the Disputes and General Administration Account be raised from 7½p to 10p and £200,000 be moved into the account from the Provident and Superannuation Fund.

The 1959 dispute caused the LTS to spend some £265,000, less £53,000 recovered from a levy on the membership, on dispute benefit and other dispute-related costs. In addition, the union financed strike expenditure by a bank overdaft which reached £180,000. To replenish LTS funds a special conference held on 17 September 1959 accepted the allocation of £75,000 from the Provident and Superannuation Fund to the Disputes and General Administration Account, the imposition of a

Table 8.1

Expenditure on benefits by the London Society of Compositors, 1948–55

Date	Strike allowances £	Unemployment allowances £	Emigration allowances £	Removal grants £	Funeral allowances £	Superannuation allowances £
1948	335	308	358	73	7,843	166,946
1949	3	59	227	45	9,006	169,057
1950	127,567	160	184	31	8,524	160,598
1951	5,010	232	164	65	11,439	157,169
1952	114	260	210	50	9,186	155,842
1953	11,409	78	148	111	10,426	147,056
1954	1,418	19	208	108	8,476	161,596
1955	797	na	70	23	3,341	na

Source: London Society of Compositors, *Annual Reports.*

levy of 12.5p per week and a 2.5p per week increase in certain categories of membership. However, they were rejected in a ballot of the membership.

This meant a new set of proposals could not be put before the members until 1961, when the members accepted by 7,865 votes to 3,719 a financial package consisting of (i) a 5p per week increase in subscriptions; (ii) 5p per week per member to be allocated to the Reserve Fund; (iii) the imposition of a 25p per week dispute levy to be paid by members for, if necessary, a maximum period of five years; and (iv) the Executive Council to control the Reserve Fund and have authority to transfer monies from the fund, as and when required, to the Disputes and General Administration Account and/or the Provident and Superannuation Account. It was to deal with short-term problems in the Provident and Superannuation Account (for example, by a sharp rise in unemployment amongst the membership) and the Disputes and General Administration Account (for example, major disputes) without having to gain permission from the members to change the allocation of subscriptions between the two funds, or to borrow from one fund to replenish the other, or to transfer money between the two funds. Membership ballots took time to complete and ran the risk that the members might say no to the proposals. The union now had a fund from which to take money for purposes which would be indicated to the membership at the time.

Like the LSC, the LTS made allocations from the Disputes and General Administration Account to an Education Fund and to the Retiring Allowances for Officials and Staff Fund. In 1958 the Society introduced two-day schools for journeymen and a one-day school for senior apprentices. They were to deal with matters specific to the LTS rather than the wider range of subjects offered by schools organised by the wider labour movement. Journeymen and apprentices were given an insight into the work and administration of the LTS. In 1956 the Society endowed a scholarship at Ruskin College to enable a member to take that college's two-year full-time course in labour studies.

The payment of retirement allowances for officials and staff was inherited from the LSC. In 1958 the union extended pension arrangements to staff who had not been elected by the members. In the LSC, apart from about two members of staff, every employee was at least an elected assistant and a society member. With the merger, the PMMTS brought in clerical staff who were not former PMMTS members and were not entitled to superannuation benefit from the union. The 1959 LTS Annual Conference approved a pension scheme to cover officials, elected assistants and appointed members of staff. It was non-contributory and was started by the union paying a capital sum of £16,634 to the trustees of the scheme and thereafter an annual payment equal to 1d per week per head of working membership or such other sum as the actuaries advised.

The main source of income for the Provident and Superannuation Account was members' subscriptions plus interest and dividends from investments. From 1957 to 1962 the fund also received £2,000 per annum interest on a £50,000 loan made to the Disputes and General Administration Account to allow the Society to purchase a new head office. In 1960 the LTS made a major change in its investment policy. Prior to that date investments had almost exclusively been in government securities and local government loans. By 1959 the union was concerned about the erosion of its capital funds due to large gilt-edged security holdings. Its 1959 Annual Report remarked, 'These gilt-edged securities and undated stock that have been held for very many years have been an embarrassment, not only because of their low yield in interest but because they could only be sold at a very heavy loss.'[4]

The 1960 Annual Conference agreed, in the interests of improving the union's capital stock, that the executive and the trustees sell a certain proportion of these securities and reinvest the proceeds in trust stock to give a wider investment portfolio. The Society adopted a policy of selling undated Government stock and reinvesting the proceeds in short-term loans at high interest and in industrial equities through the Trade Union Unit Trust. All these moves assisted the LTS in re-establishing its financial stability.

The £50,000 loan made in 1957 to the Disputes and General Administration Account was repaid in 1962 by a payment from the Reserve Fund. The £2,000 annual interest payment was a source of disquiet to the LTS leadership, which considered it ludicrous that because of trade disputes the union was unable to repay a loan from one fund to another, whilst the Provident and Superannuation Account was run without any establishment expenses or staff salaries.

The main items of expenditure from the Provident and Superannuation Account were unemployment, emigration, superannuation, funeral and removal allowances. The amount of these benefits paid out by the LTS are shown in Table 8.2. The LTS also had a Benevolent Fund, which had been established in 1952 by the former LSC as the Ernest Barnes Distress Fund. Ernest Barnes was a compositor who when he died made provision in his will that, after his wife had also passed away, any monies that remained should go to the Society. His widow, however, made an immediate contribution to the LSC of £1,200. The executive created the Ernest Barnes Distress Fund to relieve acute cases of distress amongst the membership. From time to time, Mrs Barnes sent further donations. If any superannuated or other members left money to the Society in their will, that too went into the Ernest Barnes Distress Fund, which existed to give assistance in genuine cases of distress.

During its lifetime the balance of the LTS funds remained relatively static, although they were affected by the 1956 and 1959 wages disputes. In 1959 the balance of funds was £1.1 million but by the time of merger with the TA it stood at a little over £1 million. The balance of funds reached its lowest point in 1960, when it stood at £883,030. Put another way, at the time of its formation the LTS had assets equal to £55 per member, whilst at its marriage with the TA the figure was £53. However, in 1960 the figure stood at only £44. Following the 1959 dispute the LTS was faced with improving its financial position, particularly since 1962 would be another year for major wage negotiations in the general trade and the previous three negotiations – 1950, 1956 and 1959 – had involved the Society in large-scale disputes. The Society attempted to rescue its finances by changing its investment policies, by establishing a Reserve Fund, and by the imposition of a levy to operate, if necessary, for five years. It is unlikely that the LTS funds could have withstood a major wage dispute in 1962. Fortunately that year saw the first peacefully negotiated agreement in the general printing industry since the Second World War.

The stability of the LTS funds depended on the Society not becoming enbroiled in frequent long-running disputes involving a relative large proportion of the membership and on the membership not suffering unemployment on a large scale for any length of time. Both events would have adverse effects, in that subscription income would fall but expenditure would increase. Money could be transferred from one fund to the other or the relative allocation of members' subscriptions to the funds changed only after a ballot of the membership. If transfers between funds was not an option, then the funds and benefits could be maintained only by a levy on the working membership. If working members would not pay such levies, the funds would ultimately become exhausted and benefits suspended or ended. These potential threats to the longer-run viability of the funds caused the LTS leadership to urge

Table 8.2

Expenditure on benefits by the London Typographical Society, 1955–63

Date	Strike allowances £	Unemployment allowances £	Emigration allowances £	Removal grants £	Funeral allowances £	Superannuation allowances £
1955	–	nil	365	89	10,240	175,855
1956	252,939	24	417	68	13,605	234,808
1957	746	58	690	92	12,681	243,054
1958	947	55	327	69	12,534	255,184
1959	266,827	26	120	49	12,471	266,933
1960	672	18	264	59	11,166	277,515
1961	407	5	187	77	11,793	277,225
1962	595	73	283	75	12,436	280,039
1963	2,100	492	389	100	13,411	280,779

Source: London Typographical Society, *Annual Reports,* 1955–63.

caution on the members when they wished to spend accumulated surpluses on increased benefits or the reduction of subscriptions.

The LTS's financial difficulties of the late 1950s were the result of the large-scale disputes of 1956 and 1959. The 1959 dispute, however, brought home other problems in the union's finances. The union wished to finance the dispute by selling off investments. To do so would have resulted in a capital loss of some £800,000. After the members indicated that they would not allow the Disputes and General Administration Fund to borrow from the Provident and Superannuation Account, it was decided to finance the dispute by bank overdaft facilities. After the dispute, the members rejected proposals to replenish the 'fighting fund' by a transfer of monies from the Provident and Superannuation Account and by a levy.

The Provident and Superannuation Account suffered two particular problems. First, to sell its investment portfolio would have brought significant capital losses. This was tackled by adopting, after 1960, an investment policy of keeping good Government securities but also investing in industrial equities via the Trade Union Unit Trust and placing reserve money on short loan to local councils at high interest rates. Second, the effect of the LSC members' decision whereby superannuation allowance was paid to the widow or dependant if the superannuant member died before being on the fund for five years became a full burden on the fund. In addition, 1958 saw an abnormal number of members retiring at the maximum superannuation allowance of £2 per week. This was caused by the large number of entrants to the former LSC and the former PMMTS after the mass organisation of London offices immediately following the 1914–18 war. In 1959 the Provident and Superannuation Account entered a deficit.

The Reserve Fund proposal of 1961 was an imaginative way of isolating the impact of large-scale disputes, increased unemployment and an increased number of retired members on the union's two main funds. It also overcame the problem of asking the members to agree to transfers between the funds or to pay a levy to maintain them at sufficient levels. The Disputes and General Administration Account provided the industrial defence of the membership and the Reserve Fund now meant that unforeseen calls on the provision of friendly society benefits would not weaken the amount of money available for the industrial protection of the membership. The problems of links between industrial funds and friendly society benefit funds, as had happened to the LTS in 1959–61, were to face the NGA in the early 1980s.

THE TA STRUCTURE

The General Fund

Members' subscriptions were paid into the General Fund from which the costs of industrial servicing were met. Prior to a major change in the Association's finances in 1953, all benefits to members (out of work, funeral, rail fares, strike and legal) were paid from this fund. After 1953, however, only the last three benefits were the liability of the General Fund. There were also appropriations from this fund to the branch officials' guarantee fund, the triennial delegate meeting reserve fund and, after 1953, interest from investments.

The TA had a number of categories of membership, all of which paid a set weekly contribution. The main category was full subscriptions for members in employment in grade 1 and grade 2 towns plus additional subscriptions for each 25p in excess of the minimum grade rate of the branch obtained as a result of national or Association agreements. These so-called 'extra pennies' were a regular issue of debate at delegate meetings. Prior to a decision by the 1950 Delegate Meeting, members were required to pay 1d additional subscriptions for every 25p in excess of the minimum grade rate obtained in national, branch and chapels agreements. The 1950 meeting removed branch and chapel agreements from the 'extra pennies' subscriptions. The 1957 and 1960 Delegate Meetings rejected resolutions to end these additional contributions. However, the latter meeting accepted an EC motion which made 'extra pennies' payable not only on national or association agreements but also on agreements based upon them. This was to remove an anomaly which existed in the Manchester branch concerning two newspaper offices which negotiated their own agreements and were not parties to the TA–NPA agreements. Members in these offices were not paying the 'extra pennies' subs whilst others in the branch employed in NPA offices were. The agreements were invariably negotiated after the EC had reached agreement with the NPA and the rates were basically the same as those in the NPA agreement. Naturally the anomaly caused tension in the Manchester branch, as members

225

enjoying roughly the same conditions were treated differently with regards to subscriptions. Although these 'extra penny' subscriptions brought in some £20,000 of income to the TA, they were a source of irritation to members, branch officials and the Financial Secretary. Some felt that the rule was out of date and that the union had only one rate of benefit and therefore should have only one rate of subscription. Those favouring the 'extra pennies' considered that it was a trade union principle that the strong should help the weak and that those who were earning the money should help to pay for those who were not in the same financial position. However, the LTS did not extract 'extra pennies' and since a guiding principle in the LTS/TA marriage was that where there were variations the better should be chosen, the 'extra pennies' rule was not adopted by the NGA.

The 1959 strike in the general printing and provincial newspaper industry cost the TA over £900,000 in dispute benefit. The union's total assets had fallen by March 1960 to £0.9 million, compared with £1.4 million in March 1957. To restore the General Fund by August 1962 – when the hours and wages agreement made in 1959 expired – to the £1.5 million at which it stood before the dispute, the Association increased its weekly subscriptions by 4½p per week. The object was to prepare for eventualities when the 1959 agreement expired. To leave the union in a weak financial position would encourage the employers not only to resist any claims made in 1962 but to attack existing conditions. The 1959 dispute had cost the TA almost two-thirds of its General Fund, but by September 1962 the fund had been restored to within £220,000 of its 1959 level. At the time of the LTS merger, the TA's finances were sound and restored to their pre-1959 strike level.

Expenditure from the General Fund covered administration, appropriations and industrial benefits. The amount of money expended by the TA on rail fares, legal defence and strike benefit over the period March 1949 to September 1963 is shown in Table 8.3. The rail fares benefit assisted members in one branch gaining employment in another. Legal defence was available to members injured at work and members and their families involved in road accidents. In addition, free legal advice on any matter was also provided to a member and his family. Strike, lock-out and victimisation benefit was one-third the minimum jobbing rate, providing that more than 25 per cent of the working membership were on strike or locked out. If 25 per cent or less of the working membership were on strike or locked out, the benefit was one-half of the minimum jobbing rate. The benefit was available for fifteen

Table 8.3
Expenditure on benefits by the Typographical Association, 1949–63

Date	Out of work benefit £	Funeral benefit £	Rail fares £	Strike benefit £	Legal defence £
March 1949	2,627	6,969	7	14	200
Sept	833	5,070	11	44	400
March 1950	686	5,934	8	2	400
Sept	616	4,665	42	90	400
March 1951	1,630	9,816	18	232	400
Sept	708	7,824	17	27	400
March 1952	1.133	9,202	19	74	400
Sept	1,806	6,697	36	1,380	405
March 1953	2,455	10,001	33	66	400
Sept	1,199	7,073	96	54	400
March 1954	771	8,416	28	4,542	400
Sept	920	7,425	13	11,103	400
March 1955	588	10,054	5	403	414
Sept	404	7,158	14	3,330	405
March 1956	1,751	9,127	13	1,854	212
Sept	573	6,965	20	230	–
March 1957	1,078	7,953	19	169	–
Sept	1,185	7,640	21	48	–
March 1958	1,316	11,156	21	10	–
Sept	1,468	7,846	24	1,697	–
March 1959	2,828	10,062	26	148	–
Sept	2,161	6,467	35	923,369	1,003
March 1960	1,702	9,691	38	9,148	918
Sept	1,107	7,820	15	2,016	906
March 1961	1,330	13,289	23	1,069	900
Sept	790	10,781	7	454	911
March 1962	873	13,367	14	441	1,412
Sept	1,190	8,951	34	703	1,150
March 1963	1,806	15,579	15	181	450
Sept	1,638	9,225	5	125	1,250

Source: Typographical Association, *Half Year Reports*, 1949–63.

consecutive weeks. If an FOC, part-time branch secretary or branch president was victimised for carrying out these duties, they received a victimisation benefit equal to the rate of pay for the job they were doing when victimised.

The TA offered educational services to its members. By affiliating to the National Council of Labour Colleges, its members had access to classes, postal courses, day and weekend schools and special lectures organised by these bodies. In 1957 the delegate meeting accepted that over the next three years the EC should consider the provision of a comprehensive educational scheme for its members. 'A Report on Education and Research' was presented to the 1960 Delegate Meeting, which recommended that an education department wholly financed by the union was an impractical proposition, that the union should not duplicate the services available to the membership via the WEA and the NCLC, that there was a need for training courses for branch and chapel officials, that during the next three years a series of weekend schools be instituted covering industrial relations, wider trade union matters, and book-keeping, and that the cost of each school be £500. The union committed itself to an overall annual education expenditure over the next three years of £3,000. The report was accepted by the delegates and the first branch course held in March 1961 and a second in November 1961. However, events beyond their control, for example the sudden death of the Financial Secretary which meant the reorganisation of officers' duties, made it impossible for the EC to complete the pilot scheme in the envisaged three years.

The value of the General Fund rose steadily over the period 1949–63 but fell dramatically during the 1959 stoppage and only recovered its pre-dispute level in September 1963. In March 1949 the value of the fund per member was £13 but by the time of the amalgamation with the LTS it had risen to £34. The financial reforms of 1953 made a significant contribution to this.

The 1953 financial reforms

The 1950 Delegate Meeting passed the following resolution:

> . . . that clause 10 of rule 34 should be reviewed by the EC. Their findings shall be submitted to the membership not later than December 1951, for endorsement. In the meantime the

present rate of out of work benefit shall be increased by 33⅓ per cent.

In November 1951 the EC recommended that out of work benefit should remain at current rates but that the whole question of benefits and subscriptions should be referred to the next delegate meeting for review, having regard to changed money values, increased membership and total liabilities. The review of out of work benefit involved a searching investigation into the TA's finances as a whole. The December 1951 *Typographical Circular* warned that the absolute size of the General Fund had to be treated with caution. What appeared a lot of money on the surface had to be judged against all possible claims on it – out of work benefit, funeral benefit, strike and victimisation benefit, rail fares, administration costs, legal benefit, etc. When this was done, the 'huge absolute sums' in the General Fund amounted to £17.42½p per full member. A moderate recession, the article warned, would soon eat into this figure.

There had been a steady rise in the TA's costs since 1939, for which inadequate financial provision had been made. Funeral benefit in 1951 was 100 per cent above its 1939 level, whilst strike benefit had risen proportionally to rises in the rate of wages. The General Fund gains since 1948 had been due entirely to the almost complete absence of unemployment. In reality, the TA was not paying its way. The 1950 Delegate Meeting voted £3,838 additional half-yearly expenditure, but gave no consideration as to how the additional financial burden was to be met. The TA executive concluded that the whole question of finance in relation to the union's industrial and other needs required a radical review.

The new financial policy was based not on what it hoped would happen (for example, continued industrial peace and no unemployment), but on what it knew could happen. In presenting its comprehensive financial proposals to the 1953 Delegate Meeting the EC argued that in considering subscriptions and benefit it should be remembered that the primary reason for the existence of the TA was the desire to secure fair wages, good working conditions and reasonable hours. Having secured these, it wished to retain them. Other benefits were of comparatively minor importance compared with this basic objective. It stressed that past delegate meetings had a lamentable record of ignoring the principles of sound finance and the fundamentals of trade unionism. It argued that the financial soundness of the union could not be judged solely by the balance of the General Fund, but had to be seen against all the liabilities that could arise on the fund. It estimated that a capital reserve of at least three times the amount existing in 1953 (£750,000) was needed if the union was to have financial security.

The proposals were designed to safeguard the union's funds. The 1939 TA scale of contributions and benefits was brought into line with 1953 requirements. The subs of members working in grade 1 towns were increased from 7p to 9p per week and those working in grade 2 towns from 6p to 8p per week. Honorary membership subscriptions were raised from 1p to 2½p per week. Out of work benefit increased by 66⅔ per cent over the 1939 figure to give a low of 85p per week for members with less than five years' membership to a high of £1.25 for those with over fifteen years' membership. There was no change to the strike, lock-out and victimisation benefit, as this benefit, being a percentage of the jobbing rate, had increased pro rata with the wages increases secured since 1939. There was no increase in funeral benefit since alteration to this rule since 1939 had resulted in substantial increases payable on the death of a member.

The proposals underlined the interrelation between TA contribution income and its benefit expenditure. Their theme was that it was better in times of full employment and high wages to build up reserves against times when the situation was less happy and having to institute crisis measures. The financial reforms were accepted by the 1953 Delegate Meeting and subsequently by a substantial majority in a ballot of the membership. These reforms completely reversed the approach to financial matters which had characterised the TA for more than a century, often with disastrous results. They were a clear indication that the TA recognised that its finances were a vital instrument of industrial policy. The reforms were introduced at a time of industrial peace but it was in such circumstances in the past that proposals to put the union's finances on a secure footing had always been rejected.

The Provident Fund

This fund was established in 1953 following the delegate meeting of that year accepting a new rule 49, which read:

    1. All Income from investments, loans, bank interest and

interest from co-partnership firm loans, shall be hypothecated to provide such provident benefits as are provided for by the Association's Rules and as are written with the provision of Section 39(2) Income Tax Act, 1918.

2. This rule shall not be amenable to the provisions of Rule 44 (proposed Alterations of Fundamental Principles and Rules).

One of the basic principles of British income tax is that all investment income should be taxed at source, at the full rate of tax. The 1918 Act exempted registered unions from payment of income tax provided three basic principles were observed. First, the registered union had to pay provident benefits. The TA's funeral and out of work benefits fell into this category. Second, all investment income had to be hypothecated for provident benefits. The TA's rules did not provide for this, hence clause (1) of the new rule. Third, income on which tax had been exempted could not in any circumstances be used for any other purposes. The TA thus established a Provident Fund account. The Financial Secretary told the delegates, 'to bring it down to coppers, if this resolution is not passed, as and from this Delegate Meeting, 2½d per week of your subscriptions will go in income tax.'[5]

A unique feature of the TA's financial structure was that now none of its investment income could be used by the General Fund. Any reduction in the amount of capital in the General Fund brought with it a corresponding reduction in the income of the Provident Fund. The quid pro quo for the non-use of investment income for industrial purposes was exemption from the payment of income tax on investment income. However, the Inland Revenue insisted that the 'hypothecation rule' be unchangeable by the union. Hence clause (2) of the new rule. The rule was carried into the NGA and was to prevent the NGA in 1972 from complying with the TUC recommendation that affiliated unions should deregister under the Industrial Relations Act (1971) (see Chapter 10).

The TA wound up its Superannuation Fund in 1947.[6] So its two Provident Fund benefits were funeral benefit and out of work benefit. The amount paid out in funeral benefit by the TA in the period 1949–63 is shown in Table 8.3. Between 1949 and 1963 there were many attempts to improve the level of funeral benefit. The 1950 Delegate Meeting raised the maximum level from £20 to £30 but the 1957 meeting rejected an increase to £40. Those attempting to improve the level of benefit argued that its current level had remained unchanged for too long, that the cost of dying had increased, that the cost of the proposed new levels of benefit would be small, and that members' relatives should not have to worry about the cost of a funeral. The executive usually countered by arguing that the state now provided funeral benefits, that increases would whittle down reserves and that the amount of funeral benefit paid out by the union had increased almost three times since 1939. The out of work benefit varied with the length of membership and at the time of the merger with the LTS stood at a lowest rate of £1.25 per week and a highest of £2 per week.

THE NGA's FINANCIAL STRUCTURE ON ITS FORMATION

On its formation the NGA had two main funds – the General Fund and the Provident Fund – which had the same sources of income and liabilities as when they were TA funds. Discussions on the merging of the funds of the LTS and the TA centred on maintaining the LTS Superannuation Fund. To this end, £500,000 of the LTS assets were set aside to maintain the fund for the foreseeable future. Former LTS members continued to pay subscriptions to provide for superannuation allowance.

As we have seen, both the TA and the LTS argued at the formation of the NGA that their former members should not pay increased subscriptions. In respect of benefits, the guiding principle was that 'no one should suffer' by amalgamation and that where one of the unions had a better benefit than the other then the more favourable benefit would apply in the NGA. For example, former TA members with less than fifteen years' membership became entitled to £1.80 per week unemployment benefit instead of £1.25 for up to five years membership and £1.50 for from ten to fifteen years. Former LTS members whose maximum out of work benefit was £1.80 became eligible for £2 per week for a fifteen-year membership, as had been the case with the TA.

FINANCIAL CHANGES, 1964–72

One problem in the ACP/NGA merger was the higher unemployment benefit rate of the ACP. The NGA rejected this higher benefit but assured the ACP that within two years the NGA would present to a delegate meeting a review of its subscriptions and benefits. The same assurance had been given to the 1965 NGA Rules Revision Conference. The 1966 Delegate Meeting received the union's review of benefits and subscriptions and accepted important financial reforms.

The background to these reforms was a reducing annual surplus on the General Fund caused by increased expenditure against a fixed income. Reducing reserves risked weakening the NGA's industrial strength. Throughout their history the TA and the LTS were bedevilled by the fact that subscription rates were laid down in the rules and with inflation the same money income meant less real subscription income. To solve this problem the then Financial Secretary, Mr Geoff Moore, asked the delegate meeting that subscriptions payable by all members should be uniform and related to the basic minimum rate for members employed in grade 2 towns in the NGA/BFMP Agreement. Whilst this rate was below £15 per week the weekly subscription rate was to be 15p. Every 50p advance in the national minimum rate over £15 would automaically trigger a 1p per week increase in subscription. A weekly subscription of 15p was estimated to bring the NGA an additional £65,000 per annum in contribution income and every subsequent 1p increase would give an additional £40,000. By relating subscriptions to the basic rate the NGA erected a built-in provision to take account of rising costs and benefit.

In addition to a uniform subscription linked to the BFIP basic rate, the union also linked out of work benefits to this rate by setting it at one-third of the basic rate rounded to the nearest 50p. With an increase in subscriptions, consequent upon increases in basic rates, the out of work benefit would increase in the same proportion to retain the relationship of the benefit to one-third of the basic rate.

With an out of work benefit of this magnitude, a protective clause, limiting the period of entitlement to twenty-six weeks in any one year, was imposed. The out of work benefit budget was based on an assumption that unemployment amongst NGA members would never exceed 1 per cent. The linking of subscriptions and unemployment benefit to the basic rate in the general printing industry was revolutionary. It represented a change to the union's traditional attitudes towards its financial and administrative functions. It was a recognition that radical reforms were required if the union was to have relevance in the second half of the twentieth century.[7]

The 1966 Delegate Meeting also adopted a new financial policy designed to reverse the falling value of the NGA capital reserves by permitting investment in industrial equities, the purchase of properties for branches and regions and arranging for £250,000 presently on a short-term loan to be available at any time within seven days, so as to give protection against unforeseen emergencies. Half of its assets were to be in fixed-interest securities and the other half in the Trade Union Unit Trust and companies of not less than £1 million of share capital.

In 1965 the NGA engaged the services of professional investment managers to maintain its investments at the highest possible level whilst holding approximately £250,000, under its own direct control, on short-term mortgages to local councils for immediate use should the necessity arise. However, the authority of the investment managers was limited to making recommendations. The professional management of the union's investment portfolio was guided by the general policy that the capital growth of its investments should at least offset the effects of inflation.

The principle agreed at the 1966 Delegate Meeting of allocating a proportion of the union's investment portfolio to property had a two-fold objective. First, the property had to provide a viable investment proposition. Second, it would provide office accommodation for NGA branches on a scale which could not be obtained by other means. These property investments have given a very satisfactory return on the capital invested and have been an appreciating asset. Although office accommodation was only a by-product, it was nevertheless an important factor in the NGA's future development. Property investment has provided a financial base not subject to the same fluctuations as the stock market, as well as being a source of funds should money need to be raised at short notice. In 1988, the NGA received an income in excess of £300,000 per annum from the rent of property.[8]

The 1969 Delegate Meeting accepted further financial reforms based on proposals to reorganise the union's decision-making structure. The foundations for the establishment of a professional service at branch level were to be laid by the introduction of a branch administration alternative allowance as well as retaining the two existing branch allowances. Under one scheme, branch secretaries received, from national funds, a half-yearly allowance in proportion to the total branch membership. Under the other scheme, branches received a half-yearly grant related to the branch's numerical strength for carrying out duties assigned to them by the national union. The Financial Secretary, Geoff Moore, now proposed a third scheme providing for an alternative scale of allowances, payable at the rate of 62½p per full member. To qualify for the alternative allowances branches must already have or were to appoint a full-time secretary and agree to conform to five basic conditions.

First, the branch had to justify the services of a full-time officer. Second, the allowance was payable so long as the administration of the branch was maintained at a standard acceptable to the National Council. Third, candidates submitted to the branch membership for election as full-time secretary had to be examined by the National Council. Fourthly, the employment contract offered by the branch to the secretary had to receive National Council approval. Finally, the branch must appoint professional auditors. It was estimated that this new branch allowance would cost some £110,000 when the restructured proposals were fully implemented. It made a substantial contribution to branch finances and allowed some branches to reduce their subscriptions or hold them at their present rates.

The 1969 Delegate Meeting also accepted changes to the branch secretaries' allowances rule by agreeing that the allowance be a flat rate of 17½p per full member rather than related to a scale of membership size. This change represented an additional £17,500 per annum on this item of expenditure, which was predicted to rise to £32,500 if the reorganisation proposals were fully implemented. However, a new principle was embodied in this change and was deisgned to rectify an anomaly whereby over the years allowances had become weighted unfairly towards the very small and medium-sized branches to the detriment of the larger ones. This disparity was no longer justified as the larger branches were not being supported financially to the extent to which they were entitled. The allowance was therefore now to be based on the number of full members in the branch without any loading at the lower end of the scale.

The third leg of the 1969 financial proposals was the introduction of a half-yearly administration grant to branches of 20p per full member in place of the existing grant which was based on a scale of membership and was weighted towards the small branches. The adoption of this reform increased the cost of branch administration grants to national funds to some £35,000 as opposed to £21,000 prior to the change. This proposal, like the two outlined above, made a substantial contribution to branch administration costs.

The 1969 Delegate Meeting also saw comprehensive proposals as a tidying-up process based on the experience of the previous three years. The basic rate for subscription purposes was increased from £15 to £17 to take account of the assimilation of the cost-of-living bonus into the basic rate. The need to pay subscriptions while sick, irrespective of whether the employer paid wages during sickness, was ended. In anticipation of the introduction of decimal currency in 1971 the subscription was reduced from 3d to 1p, a reduction of 0.6 of an old penny per week. These changes simplified the union's accountancy procedures.

Further financial reforms were made by the 1972 Delegate Meeting. The financial Secretary, Geoff Moore, argued that the principle of linking subscriptions to the basic rates had worked well in building up reserves at the same time when the NGA, in common with other unions over the period 1969–72, had had to meet increased costs. In 1972 the union had sufficient reserves to sustain industrial action by 67,000 members at £10 per week for seven weeks. The National Council submitted proposals to the 1972 Delegate Meeting which both reduced subscriptions and enhanced allowances to the branches. The basic rate. on which subscriptions were to be charged was raised to £25, with subsequent increases of 1p for each complete £1 increase in the basic rate above £25. In percentage terms the union reduced the subscription income progression relative to the basic rate from 2.5 per cent to 1 per cent. By amending the base rate for subs, the union lowered contribution income by some £280,000 annually. At the same time, out of work benefit increased from £7.17 per week to £8.33. In addition, the anomalies which the progression of full subscriptions had brought to other categories of membership were tidied up by putting other categories on the same progression basis as the full member but at a percentage of the rate to take account of the benefits which each category of membership derived from their membership.

By 1972 it was clear that branch allowances could not be based solely on a per capita figure. The 1969 restructuring proposals had added significantly to the liabilities of branches and their funding could not be left to the chance of local ballots increasing contributions. The NGA now decided that the principle of automatic progression should be applied to branch allowances. The branch administration alternative allowance was to be 17 per cent of the potential national income of the branch. The allowance depends not on subscriptions actually paid but on potential subscriptions due. The aim was to keep increases in the allowances in line with rises in branch costs without the need for branches to ask their members for increased local contributions to meet every increased liability. The branch secretary's allowance and the grant to part-time branches was set at 5 per cent of the potential NGA

General Fund subscription income of the branch. These reforms were estimated to cost the national union £195,000. The Financial Secretary described the changes in subscriptions and the automatic progression of branch allowances as 'the biggest financial bonanza which any Financial Secretary has ever had the privilege to present to conference'.[9]

THE FINANCIAL PROBLEMS:
THE 1970s AND EARLY 1980s

The 1970s saw a continuing deterioration in the assets of the General Fund. Table 8.4 shows that up until 1972 the value of the fund increased steadily. In September 1972 the union put £530,000 into reserve, but from that date until 1981 the General Fund declined. In 1979 and 1980 the union had to eat into its reserves. The Financial Secretary consistently expressed his concern to delegate meetings and in the annual financial report at the failure of the union to generate sufficient surpluses on the General Fund. At the same time, regional conferences expressed concern about regional and branch finances and the 1978 Delegate Meeting instructed the National Council to investigate the financial problems of NGA branches and to report back.[10] The National Council decided that a discussion document on the union's financial structure should be submitted to the 1980 Delegate Meeting and then to place financial proposals before the 1982 Delegate Meeting. What had gone wrong?

One factor was that the costs of the implementation of the NGA's restructuring proposals of 1969 and 1972 caused steep increases in deputation and delegation expenses. The situation changed rapidly from one where the NGA was paying less than £1,000 per year for regional administration to a position whereby the regional structure was costing £230,000 per annum.[11] Phase One of the 1969–72 restructuring proposals centred on the branches and the provision of a new allowance from national funds to encourage the creation of full-time administered branches. The 1972 Delegate Meeting based these allowances on a percentage of 'potential' national income contribution, whilst the 1974 Delegate Meeting increased the percentage of national contribution retained by full-time branches to 20 per cent and the allowance paid to part-time branches to 7 per cent.

Restructuring costs were not the sole cause of declining General Fund surpluses in the 1970s. There were also alarming increases in overall administrative costs. In the year to September 1973, administrative

Table 8.4
The National Graphical Association General Fund, 1965–89,
September each year

Date	Balance of fund over expenditure £	Excess of income £
1965	2,576,425	+ 215,857
1966	2,768,200	+ 222,320
1967	3,012,448	+ 244,248
1968	3,384,754	+ 204,637
1969	3,884,206	+ 276,427
1970	4,148,755	+ 253,368
1971	4,434,583	+ 285,828
1972	4,964,583	+ 530,000
1973	5,302,732	+ 338,149
1974	5,519,258	+ 207,526
1975	5,611,795	+ 101,537
1976	5,947,436	+ 335,641
1977	6,216,208	+ 268,772
1978	6,412,234	+ 196,026
1979	6,293,782	− 118,452
1980	6,458,252	− 24,141
1981	7,050,653	+ 592,401
March 1982	7,305,399	+ 254,746
Sept 1982	8,446,559	+ 240,131
1983	8,885,806	+ 338,819
1984	8,235,726	− 650,104
1985	8,241,000	−1,619,535
1986	7,488,144	− 752,862
1987	6,734,527	+ 246,383
1988	7,847,289	+1,112,762
1989	5,859,009	+ 861,720

Source: NGA, *Annual Statement of Accounts*, 1965–89.

costs were £620,000, but by September 1977 the figure had increased to £1.4 million. In the same five-year period the Index of Retail Prices rose by 85 per cent. There were considerable increases in costs of printing, postage, telephone and stationery and the providing of branches with suitable accommodation. There were constant increases in general expenditure not only at head office but at various regional offices, and in addition, because of legislative and other requirements, there was the need to obtain professional advice. The 1970s were a period of increasing rates of inflation and the union was unable to gain increases in its income equal to, let alone above, these rates of price increases.

A third factor in the declining financial base of the NGA was that in the 1970s it assumed responsibility for additional items of expenditure against which there were no compensating increases in contribution income or decreases in spending elsewhere. From 1972 to 1977 the NGA's income suffered from the effects of various government incomes policies which involved wage freezes, flat additions to basic rates, and threshold payments related to changes in the Index of Retail Prices. The basic minimum rate to which the Association's subscription structure related remained unchanged, with the result that though members received increases in pay the union received no additional subscription income. To offset this incomes policy effect, an emergency motion was carried, and subsequently endorsed in a ballot of the membership, that the subscription rate should be related to the minimum sum receivable by a craftsman in the BPIF wage basis agreement. This was not a departure from the principle, agreed at the 1966 Delegate Meeting, of relating subscriptions to the basic rate but specified that subscriptions be related to minimum rates receivable under the national agreement. No real increase in the amount of subscriptions paid was sought since percentage wise to the basic rate the contributions remained unchanged. Although this rule change helped to sustain the union's finances, it could not make good the erosion to subscription income sustained in the period 1972–7.

The Provident Fund (see Table 8.5) is funded by investment income only. Any diminution of General Fund balances had an adverse effect on this fund. This 'knock-on' effect was to some extent offset in the 1970s by allocations when mergers took place, sound investment policies and high interest rates. In 1976 the Provident Fund expenditure exceeded its income by £279,000. The loss stemmed from two factors. First, the decision of the 1974 Delegate Meeting, against the advice of the platform, to increase the annual superannuation grant from £10 to £14 increased the liability of this benefit (see Table 8.6) to £179,000. This decision was doubly worrying in that by the mid to late 1970s the proportion of retired NGA members to working members was increasing by 1 per cent each year. The second, and by far the largest

Table 8.5
The National Graphical Association Provident Fund, 1965–89,
September each year

Date	Balance of fund £
1965	+ 261,599
1966	+ 311,747
1967	+ 373,230
1968	+ 460,283
1969	+ 608,783
1970	+ 775,708
1971	+ 893,009
1972	+1,023,308
1973	+1,329,772
1974	+1,573,486
1975	+1,698,716
1976	+1,431,130
1977	+1,453,197
1978	+1,662,637
1979	+1,903,951
1980	+2,032,302
1981	+1,646,049
March 1982	+1,444,663
Sept 1982	+ 875,113
1983	+ 646,152
1984	+4,677,702
1985	+2,850,811
1986	+4,096,972
1987	+4,059,562
1988	+4,200,095
1989	+7,761,026

Source: NGA, *Annual Statement of Accounts*, 1965–89.

factor, was the unprecedented level of unemployment, which at its peak involved 1,500 members and the union spending £463,200 on out of work benefit. The Financial Secretary warned delegates to the 1976 Delegate Meeting: 'If outgoings continue at the present rate, in three years the Provident Fund will cease to exist – a Provident Fund which has been built up over the past twenty years, and benefits will have to be paid out of the General Fund.[12] Since out of work benefit was linked to minimum earnings in the same way as contributions, the NGA

Table 8.6
Payment of benefits from the National Graphical Association
Provident Fund, 1965–89

Date	Funeral benefit £	Out of work benefit £	Superannuation benefit £	Other £	Total £
1965	35,668	1,715	36,845	–	74,228
1966	38,400	1,453	37,900	–	77,753
1967	34,589	18,247	37,880	–	90,716
1968	40,274	25,980	42,782	–	109,036
1969	42,147	19,036	43,339	251	104,773
1970	49,183	30,672	45,951	665	126,471
1971	53,606	90,414	57,706	1,778	203,504
1972	55,699	119,462	61,376	2,487	239,024
1973	54,483	31,542	64,401	587	151,013
1974	56,444	41,486	111,432	401	209,763
1975	55,545	172,935	169,148	568	398,196
1976	54,695	463,201	179,453	2,170	699,519
1977	61,075	210,406	187,640	2,474	461,595
1978	58,122	95,742	196,156	960	350,980
1979	56,476	72,151	201,098	224	329,949
1980	57,510	215,625	208,248	1,053	482,436
1981	58,231	1,846,417	214,808	5,275	2,124,731
March 1982	32,727	972,477	219,172	2,256	1,226,632
Sept 1982	28,000	1,131,290	413	3,031	1,162,734
1983	64,488	2,050,466	224,534	5,615	2,345,103
1984	63,498	1,782,466	30,872	3,112	1,879,948
1985	–	–	–	–	–
1986	62,158	1,755,636	241,928	5,827	2,065,549
1987	65,241	1,929,363	252,529	6,998	2,254,131
1988	58,965	1,668,482	261,332	2,376	2,591,155
1989	90,764	1,327,515	382,274	22,854	1,823,407

Source: NGA, *Annual Statement of Accounts*, 1965–89.

needed an ever-increasing investment income to meet this benefit liability. There was a constant need to at least maintain the balance of the General Fund.

The 1980 disputes in the general printing and provincial newspaper industry involved the NGA in £1,345,357 dispute expenditure, of which £1,024,242 was offset from a levy of £6.20 per week on full members not directly involved in the dispute. However, this was not the main concern for the NGA in 1980. By September 1979, 80 per cent of

Table 8.7
Payment of main benefits from the National Graphical Association General Fund, 1965–89

Date	Strike victimisation benefit £	Legal defence £	Rail fares £	All benefits total £
1965	6,319	1,836	36	8,191
1966	2,194	2,230	18	4,442
1967	1,799	2,100	31	3,930
1968	38,698	2,539	39	41,276
1969	37,647	5,225	54	42,926
1970	29,923	9,439	35	42,925
1971	63,668	3,675	164	67,507
1972	12,158	12,110	117	27,533
1973	61,006	6,288	96	67,390
1974	242,514	7,811	12	250,337
1975	133,241	26,986	22	160,249
1976	71,501	23,847	85	95,433
1977	103,169	23,652	70	126,891
1978	246,041	22,355	8	268,404
1979	611,164	72,416	64	688,644
1980	407,385	63,524	48	470,957
1981	103,189	55,468	258	158,915
March 1982	88,489	20,874	1,671	106,034
Sept 1982	55,025	26,925	82	82,032
1983	207,767	51,640	355	259,762
1984	248,082	51,200	110	299,392
1985	1,640,163	116,123	96	1,756,382
1986	2,202,074	77,733	98	2,279,905
1987	177,116	93,391	638	271,145
1988	12,989	70,344	323	83,656
1989	7,220	20,996	30	28,246

Source: NGA, *Annual Statement of Accounts*, 1965–89.

General Fund income was required to support the union's decision-making structures at both national and regional level, compared with 49 per cent in 1972. Only 20 per cent was available to deal with other situations and help achieve the surplus necessary to the future of the

Provident Fund. If membership continued to fall, so would income, with consequential proportionate increase in the percentage needed for support of the union's infrastructure. This situation could not continue and was a major factor in the constitutional proposals considered by the 1983 Special Delegate Meeting.

While all the prophecies made by Financial Secretaries were coming true with regards to the General Fund, the Provident Fund had to face up to the completely unexpected. In the early 1980s unemployment became a feature of British industry and the printing industry did not escape the scourge. Whilst there had been minimal numbers involved in unemployment since 1975, a sudden upsurge appeared in late 1980, with the result that 1,500 members were without jobs by the end of that year. The Provident Fund began to make losses and dispose of investments to support out of work benefit and a decline in the union's total assets.

In the light of increasing unemployment the National Council had no option but to ballot the membership on a £1 per week levy to enable the union to meet its commitments on out of work benefit. The ballot result was in favour and the levy commenced from 1 June 1981 but ended on 28 November 1981. Between October 1980 and the end of September 1981 the union paid out some £1.8 million in unemployment benefit.

However, it was becoming increasingly difficult for the union to maintain unemployment benefit linked to increases in the BPIF basic wages agreements. An unemployment benefit of £29 per week in any six-month period was costing £2.6 million. The time had come for the membership to accept that the union in the future was not going to be able, without severely undermining its industrial power, to maintain let alone increase unemployment benefits in the way that had been done in the past. The National Council and the delegate meeting needed flexibility to control the liabilities of the Provident Fund, or the membership would have to accept that benefits would severely jeopardise the NGA's ability to support its members industrially. If the Provident Fund became bankrupt then provident benefit would have to be met from the General Fund, causing a further deterioration in the resources to protect the membership industrially.

The National Council decided that now was the time for action and a resolution in two parts was put to the 1982 Delegate Meeting. The first part proposed to increase contributions from 1 January 1983 from 1p in every £1 above a minimum rate to 1p in every 50p. The second part sought to break the link between the level of out of work benefit and the minimum rate in the BPIF agreement by pegging unemployment benefit at its level prevailing on 1 January 1983 (£31) and giving the National Council the power, between Delegate Meetings, to vary out of work benefit upwards or downwards. Success in carrying the motion was seen as so important to the future of the NGA industrially and financially that it was moved by the General Secretary and not the Financial Secretary.[13] Despite this, the delegates, although willing to support the call for an increase in subscriptions, were not prepared to break the link between increases in wages and the level of out of work benefit. Further problems arose when the proposed subscription increase was rejected by a ballot of the membership.

THE SPECIAL DELEGATE MEETING: NOVEMBER 1983

The 1982 Delegate Meeting, however, required the National Council to prepare proposals for the 1984 Delegate Meeting which would establish a sound base from which the NGA could fulfil two objectives: first, to ensure that the General Fund was sufficient to support all necessary industrial activity and, second, to ensure that the continuing need to fund out of work benefit did not become a liability against the General Fund. Unrelenting high levels of unemployment from September 1980 onwards had reduced the value of the Provident Fund to such an extent that the prospect of supporting benefits from the General Fund loomed ever nearer. At the same time, the potential threat posed to the NGA's funds by the Employment Act (1982) placed a further strain on the situation. The interdependence between the General and Provident Fund was now a matter for increasing concern.

In the event, the rejection by the membership of the proposed subs increase, together with the publication of the September 1982 accounts, hastened the Council's considerations. The accounts confirmed not only that the Provident Fund would be exhausted by March 1983, but also that the decline in membership, which first began in 1980, was beginning to have a retarding effect on the balances of the General Fund. Unless steps were urgently taken to counteract the effects, there would be serious consequences. The Council decided on three courses: first, a levy to support the immediate payment of unemployment benefit; second, a major restructuring of the union designed to improve efficiency and to give greater cost effectiveness; third, the creation of a separate subscription-supported Provident Fund able to meet its own liabilities. In addition, the Council took the unprecedented step of calling a special delegate meeting to be held in November 1983, some eight months earlier than the 1984 Delegate Meeting, to allow decisions to become effective at a date earlier than otherwise would have been the case. A 75p per week levy to support the immediate payment of out of work benefit was approved by the membership and came into effect on 2 May 1982. The levy was to remain in force until no longer necessary, but was to be payable only by those who were eligible to receive the benefit.

The National Council presented the special delegate meeting with four motions. The first two dealt with the problems associated with the provision of provident benefits, particularly during periods of high unemployment. The first ensured that the liability for the Provident Fund could no longer become a charge against the General Fund. The second introduced subscription-supported benefits and was intended to replace the existing 75p levy arrangements. The proposals included provision for the National Council to review the state of the Provident Fund half-yearly and to reduce and/or increase contributions if they saw fit. The other two proposals were concerned with the revision of the levels of allowances retained by branches.

The delegates approved the setting up of a Provident Fund which would draw its income from interest on investments and a new Provident Fund weekly subscription. The Council was also given powers to switch money from the General Fund to supplement the Provident Fund, but was expected to do so only in extraordinary circumstances. The fund was to be sufficiently independent to meet its liabilities. The proposals directly linked the income of the fund to the number of members being paid out of work benefit and took care to build in the utmost flexibility for the National Council to make adjustments to ensure that benefits could be paid and that the members did not need to pay any more than necessary. Full members were to pay a basic Provident Fund weekly contribution of 25p plus an additional 4p for every 100 members in excess of 500 members receiving unemployment benefit. The Provident Fund would thus have its own income directly related to its needs, and the need to impose inflexible levies on the membership was eliminated. The balloting procedure necessary to introduce or to change levies to suit the needs of the Provident Fund was slow and expensive. In addition, top-ups for the fund from the General Fund reduced the ability of the union to protect its working members against the indiscriminate introduction of new technology and in any future industrial dispute involvement.

The special delegate meeting, amid accusations of being monetarist and adopting a 'Thatcherite approach', accepted the National Council's plan to break the link between unemployment benefit and national minimum pay rates. Out of work benefit was pegged at £33 per week. However, the Council's attempt to reduce the allowance to full-time branches from 20 per cent to 17.5 per cent of the branch's potential General Fund income was defeated. Instead, delegates agreed an amendment by the Kent branch reducing the allowance to 19 per cent. Delegates heavily defeated proposals to deduct General Fund arrears from the potential General Fund subscriptions before calculating branch allowances.[14]

The decisions of the special delegate meeting were approved in a ballot of the membership. The changes came into effect on 1 October 1984 and the separate Provident Fund subscription was set at 49p per week, replacing the 75p unemployment benefit levy. At the end of 1989 the Provident Fund subscription stood at 35p per week.

The measures quickly proved effective and, despite the continuing need to pay out unemployment benefit (for example, £2.4 million was paid between October 1983 and March 1985), the fund enjoyed some degree of stability and had a balance in excess of £4 million at the time of the 1988 Delegate Meeting. The amount of unemployment benefit paid over the period September 1980 to September 1987 totalled over £13 million. During mid-1987 the effect of the industrial situation in the news sector of the industry began to be reflected in the numbers in receipt of unemployment benefit. This was expected and the fund proved more than adequate to cope with it. The NGA had achieved its objective of establishing a sound Provident Fund to provide unemployment benefit, whilst the General Fund was safeguarded to provide the essential industrial support over the whole area of NGA affairs.

FINANCIAL CRISIS: MID-1980s

The Financial Secretary told the 1984 Delegate Meeting that the financial position of the union, despite the sequestration of its funds by the courts in November 1983 in connection with the dispute with the Messenger Group of Newspapers, had swung round; balances had improved and there was cause for optimism. However, within weeks of the 1984 Delegate Meeting, which had been held in November, the NGA was again plunged into a serious financial crisis. The main cause was the union's involvement in a number of disputes in newspapers over the implementation of direct entry origination systems. These disputes were considered vital to the survival of the union in newspaper production and therefore considerable sums of money were made available for dispute benefit. In addition to these industrial problems, the continuing decline in membership, the loss of subscription income and continuing demands for out of work benefit did not help.

The *Wolverhampton Express and Star* and *Kent Messenger* disputes in early 1985 were considered to have implications so far-reaching for the whole of the newspaper membership that a special dispute benefit of £160 per week was paid to those members involved. In January 1986, 923 members became involved in a dispute with News International when that company transferred the production of four of its newspaper titles from 'Fleet Street' to a new production plant at Wapping in East London.

The disputes at Wolverhampton and Kent cost the NGA over £50,000 per week in dispute benefit. By the time these disputes ended the union had expended over £2.3 million in dispute benefit and over £125,000 in unemployment benefit. By the time the News International dispute ended in January 1987 over £2.1 million had been spent on benefit in that dispute. The funding of these industrial disputes was a large drain on the General Fund, yet they involved a small proportion of the membership. Industrial disputes were affecting the ability of the union to provide adequate industrial protection to the bulk of its members. It was now faced with the challenge of funding industrial disputes. The first response was to initiate a voluntary dispute levy on the membership in August 1985. The levy commenced with high hopes and thoughts were abroad that some £30,000–£50,000 would be raised weekly, mostly from members working in news offices.[15] However, the response was disappointing and in nine months only £158,000 was raised. Given the likelihood of continued new technology disputes and the decline in membership the National Council decided that stronger measures to protect the General Fund were needed. First, a number of in-house economies were announced at regional consultative conferences in the spring of 1986. These economies included a review of secretarial assistance at regional offices, voluntary early retirement and a redundancy scheme for officers and staff, suspension of the chapel officials' and branch officers' courses for twelve months, and more extensive budgetary control at head office. Second, the Council proposed to ballot the membership on a 50p per week emergency dispute levy to allow the union to continue to meet its financial commitments and to support members involved in new technology disputes. The levy was to be a short-term measure whilst more detailed financial reforms were worked out for presentation to the 1986 Delegate Meeting. In May 1986 the members voted by 29,566 to 26,528 to support the emergency dispute levy, which commenced on 2 June 1986.

Permanent measures to prevent industrial disputes draining the General Fund were presented to the 1986 Delegate Meeting. A Dispute Fund was to be established, from which all payments of strike and lock-out benefit would be made. The fund was to be established by an appropriation from the General Fund of £2 million, but, should the National Council deem it appropriate, it could make appropriation from the General Fund to supplement the Dispute Fund. All full, apprentice, learner, juvenile, trainee and protective members and members over state retirement age, were to pay a weekly subscription of 20p to the fund. Every member for whom the NGA had a liability to pay dispute benefit would contribute to a fund set up to deal exclusively with that liability. The level of subscription could vary in the light of needs. If the fund fell below £2 million then the 20p subscription would increase. The National Council would assess the state of the fund every six months and have powers to decrease, as well as increase, the 20p subscription. Strike and lock-out benefit would be increased to £60 per week for the period of a dispute. A member holding the position of part-time branch secretary, branch secretary, branch president, father/mother or clerk of the chapel or safety representative when victimised in the course of their duties would receive a victimisation and compensation benefit at the rate of wages being received at the time of such victimisation, for such period as decided by the National Council. However, this benefit would be charged against the General Fund. A proposal to reduce the branch administration alternative allowance from 19 per cent to 17.5 per cent was defeated.

The use of levies to fund industrial disputes was now ended. The Council viewed levies as a less than ideal answer to financial problems. Generally speaking they had to be pitched at a higher level than was actually required. They did not have in-built flexibility which allowed an adjustment in the light of circumstances. A needs-related subscription arrangement, replacing the use of levies, was a considerable advance. In December 1986 the members voted by 40,349 to 15,910 to establish a Dispute Fund, which came into being on 1 January 1987.

During its first seven months, expenditure from the fund outstripped income by a significant amount. However, following the termination of the new technology disputes in newspapers, the fund quickly recovered lost ground and ended its first year with a balance of £1.94 million, only some £51,000 below the opening balance. Despite the initial heavy calls upon the fund, it has met its liability and is now earning considerable surpluses. The effect of the establishment of the Dispute Fund on the General Fund was quite dramatic and from April 1987 the NGA's financial position eased; by the spring of 1989 it had not only been consolidated but was gaining in strength. In a period of two years the financial fortunes had changed in an exceptional way. From the poor position of June 1986 when all the clouds were black and the NGA faced one problem after another the General Fund, as well as the new Provident and Dispute Funds were now growing and increasing in strength.

SERVICES TO MEMBERS

The NGA provides legal advice and assistance to members involved in accidents at work (compensation claims) as well as to members and their dependants involved in road accidents. Other legal benefits available to members include free legal advice and the drawing up of wills. These services have been and are appreciated by a steadily increasing proportion of the membership as are the excellent services provided by London solicitors Kershaw, Gassman and Matthews (now reorganised as Kershaws) and the legal department at the NGA head office. The NGA also provides educational services to its members. In the initial years of the NGA, facilities for members to undertake general educational studies fell broadly into three categories – residential schools (TUC summer schools and the long weekend schools organised by the P&KTF), the TUC Training College and two-year scholarships at Ruskin College. In addition, the union's members in Scotland received financial assistance to attend STUC schools and in the Republic of Ireland courses organised by the Irish Congress of Trade Unions. The NGA itself organised individual courses on particular issues.

In 1968 the National Council gave consideration to using Radlett House, Aspley Guise, its first headquarters, as an educational and training establishment. A motion by the London Region to this effect was referred by the 1969 Delegate Meeting to the National Council, which subsequently concluded that such a venture was not feasible. Considerable sums of money would have been required to convert the premises for residential accommodation, whilst its running costs would have been very high. However, following the 1969 Delegate Meeting a series of pilot training courses for branch and chapel officials were held at Graphic House. Two courses of two weeks' duration were provided for full-time branch officers and three one-week courses for chapel officials.

In the light of these pilot courses and the fact that resignation from the TUC meant exclusion from its educational programme, the union decided in 1972 to expand its education and training courses for chapel officials and branch officers. These presently consist of a postal course, a week-long residential course for chapel officials and a two-module training package for full- and part-time branch secretaries. In the chapel official's course, emphasis is placed on skill development, negotiating techniques, collective bargaining and communications. The NGA continues to provide scholarships and bursaries to its members wishing to take part in long-term residential education and TUC-organised national courses. It also provides financial assistance to those taking Open University courses.

NOTES

1. See *Annual Report, 1950*, The London Society of Compositors, p. 30.
2. For a full discussion see *London Typographical Journal*, April 1951, p. 2.
3. In the early days of the Second World War the Society's funds for the payment of benefit did practically disappear. Extremely heavy levies had to be paid by the members to counter this. The Secretary was always quick to use this example to warn delegates that large surpluses of funds could quickly disappear and the provision of benefit could only continue if the members were prepared to pay levies.
4. See *5th Annual Report*, London Typographical Society, 1959, p. 10.
5. See *Report of Triennial Delegate Meeting*, Typographical Association, 1953, p. 106.
6. For a full account of this see A.E. Musson, *The Typographical Association*, Oxford University Press, 1954.
7. See *Report of the Delegate Meeting, 1966*, National Graphical Association, pp. 261–5.
8. See *Report of the Delegate Meeting, 1988*, National Graphical Association, p. 50, para. 57.
9. See *Report of the Delegate Meeting, 1972*, National Graphical Association, p. 290.
10. See *Report of the Delegate Meeting, 1978*, National Graphical Association, pp. 226–31.
11. See Discussion Paper, *Financial Structure*, National Graphical Association, June 1980.
12. See *Report of the Delegate Meeting, 1976*, National Graphical Association, p. 170.
13. The General Secretary told delegates, 'In short we are about to decide today whether this union can survive in its present form during the next decade and issues of that magnitude are my responsibility, a responsibility which I accept.' See *Report of the Delegate Meeting, 1982*, National Graphical Association, p. 286.
14. The 1988 Delegate Meeting agreed that branch allowances under Rules 26, 27 and 28 should be calculated on the basis of actual income collected by the branch rather than 'potential' income.
15. See *Report of the Delegate Meeting, 1986*, National Graphical Association, p. 288.

PART III

THE WIDER TRADE UNION AND LABOUR MOVEMENT

CHAPTER 9

RELATIONSHIPS WITH WIDER PRINT UNION BODIES

The NGA and its founding unions were in membership of two wider print union organisations. These were the Printing and Kindred Trades Federation (P&KTF), which was founded in 1901 and disbanded in 1973, and the International Graphical Federation (IGF), which was formed in 1949.

THE PRINTING AND KINDRED TRADES FEDERATION

Structure

The P&KTF sought to secure unity of action amongst its affiliated unions, to obtain uniform customs and hours of work in different sectors of the industry, to prevent as far as possible the occurrence of strikes and, in their event, to encourage their settlement by peaceful means, to establish a central fund for mutual assistance and to conduct research and enquiry work. In 1948 seventeen unions with a total membership of 215,053 were affiliated to the P&KTF. By the time of its dissolution in 1973, there were seven unions with a total membership of 218,354.

The affiliated unions jealously guarded their autonomy and rule 6(a) of the Federation stated 'the Federation shall not interfere in the internal management of any union, nor its rules and customs'. However, it had been given powers in certain areas. Where a dispute between two or more affiliated unions over demarcation of work or organisation could not be settled by the unions concerned, the matter could be referred to a P&KTF Arbitration Board whose decision was

253

binding on the parties. The Federation negotiated agreements with employers on hours of work, holidays and the pay of apprentices. Throughout the period from 1948 to its dissolution it frequently sought to negotiate industry-wide agreements with the major printing employers' organisation on sick pay and compensation for redundancy. Wages, however, were always viewed as a matter of autonomous concern to the individual unions. When the print unions made a collective approach on wages to the employers, it was the unions acting together with the Federation as the coordinating body, for example by providing common facilities.

The policy-making machinery of the Federation consisted of membership ballots, an administrative council and an Executive Committee.[1] The administrative council was appointed annually. Each affiliated union had at least one representative on the council but was entitled to additional representatives in proportion to its size. The LSC had six representatives on the council, the LTS seven and the TA eleven. The NGA initially had thirteen representatives, but at the time of the Federation's dissolution it had seventeen.

The council appointed a President, a Vice President and twelve members (fifteen from 1965) from its own ranks to act as an Executive Committee to run the affairs of the Federation between administrative councils. At least one member of the executive had to be a woman. The General Secretary of the LSC and then subsequently the General Secretary of the LTS was a member of the Executive Committee over the period 1948–63. The TA was also represented on this Committee by its General Secretary, namely Harry Riding (1950–4), Cecil Blackburn (1955–6) and John Bonfield (1957–63). The NGA initially had one representative on the Executive Committee.

The major officers of the Federation were the General Secretary, who was also the Treasurer, the Assistant General Secretary and the Assistant Secretary. The General Secretary of the Federation in 1950 was Mr J. Fletcher who was a TA member. He was replaced in 1958 by Mr Granville Eastwood who was also a TA member. He reached retiring age during 1971 but he accepted the Federation executive's invitation to continue in office for a further period not exceeding two years. He finally retired from office in September 1973 after thirty years' service, divided equally between the office of the General Secretary and Assistant General Secretary. Miss Gloria Hart, Assistant Secretary, assumed the office of Acting General Secretary until the setting up of the Printing Trade Union Co-ordinating Bureau in January

1974 (see below) when she assumed the Secretaryship of that Bureau. John Bonfield, General Secretary of the NGA, became President of the Federation in 1961 and remained in that position until the Federation's dissolution in 1973.

LSC, LTS, TA and NGA at the administrative council

The NGA and its founding unions played an active part in the affairs of the Federation. As well as participating in debates at the annual administrative council, they also proposed and/or seconded motions there. The TA was particularly active in this regard. At the 1951 council it successfully proposed motions amending the BFMP/NS hours and holiday agreement to provide *inter alia* that the period for taking annual holidays should be from 30 April (instead of 31 March) to 30 September and one which sought an increase in the percentage of the journeymen rate received by apprentices. At the 1952 council the TA submitted a motion expressing appreciation of the stand taken by Natsopa and its members against the anti-union attitude of D. C. Thomson's of Dundee, of the response made by other print unions in support, of the assistance of the TUC, the STUC and unions outside the printing industry, and reaffirming the determination of print unions to resist the company's non-strike stance. The roots of the D. C. Thomson dispute went back to the General Strike when the company declared itself a non-union company. In 1951 at its Manchester establishment Thomson's dismissed a NUPB&PW member, who was also a Father of the Chapel, and fourteen Natsopa members. In April 1952 the company dismissed a Natsopa FOC in Glasgow as well and seventy-four other members came out on strike in support of their FOC. Despite pressure from the whole trade union movement, a Court of Inquiry[2] and intervention by the TUC and the Prime Minister, the print unions were unable to persuade this company to drop its policy of non-recognition of trade unions.

The TA was also active at the 1954 council meeting, proposing that the P&KTF and the BFMP investigate the practicability of an industry-wide sick scheme. The LSC supported this move on condition that the Federation was left to decide when to act on the matter. However, the debate ended when the STA successfully moved 'the previous question'. At the 1955 administrative council the TA succesfully proposed that the Federation, acting as an honest broker, initiate discussions to bring about mergers of unions with overlapping interests. The LTS opposed this on the grounds that the Federation was an inappropriate body for this purpose. The Federation delayed implementing the resolution because of the 1955/6 wages movements, but on two subsequent occasions considered the time inopportune to initiate merger talks between affiliated unions.

Despite the TA's high profile in the P&KTF, the 1957 Delegate Meeting debated an unsuccessful Newcastle branch motion that it withdraw from the Federation. It was argued that the Federation had been less than helpful to the TA in the 1955/6 wage negotiations and that the TA could do better on its own without having to resort to some higher authority. In opposing the motion, the TA General Secretary pointed out that the P&KTF was responsible for the hours and holidays agreements in both the general trade and provincial news, the apprenticeship wages agreement, health and safety, pension schemes and apprentice selection and training. These were all matters of common concern to the Federation affiliates and he doubted whether the TA could tackle all these issues on its own.

The NGA recognised that there were a wide range of activities on which it was desirable the print unions acted together and for which the coordinating function of the Federation was essential. It was therefore very participative in the affairs of the Federation. At the May 1971 administrative council the NGA successfully moved a motion confirming the Federation's opposition to the Conservative government's Industrial Relations Bill (subsequently Act) which *inter alia* sought to reduce the legal immunity of trade unions in industrial disputes, declare closed shops null and void, give greater control by full-time officials over workplace representatives, interfere in the internal affairs of trade unions and reform collective bargaining.

Co-ordinated wage claims

1947–51

The printing unions jealously guarded their autonomy with respect to wages. The immediate post Second World War period saw many 'leapfrogging' wage demands from print unions as they sought either to re-establish the 1919 relationships or to maintain their differential position following the 1920s wage cut. In an attempt to re-establish an agreed wage structure, the BFMP and the NS urged the unions, under the auspices of the P&KTF, to agree amongst themselves acceptable wage relativities.

Attempts to devise such a structure failed in 1947 when the employers found the unions' proposals unacceptable. Following this, individual unions entered into separate negotiations with employers and settlements for varying amounts of increases were achieved. However, the question of a wage structure again arose following a JIC Conciliation Committee held in September 1948 to hear the employers' complaints that the TA had taken unconstitutional steps to abrogate certain parts of their national agreement. The JIC concluded that the broad question as to whether it was desirable or practicable for some form of wage structure to be agreed for the industry should be put to the P&KTF, the BFMP and the NS for their consideration. In response, the Federation called a conference of the executives of affiliated unions for 17 November 1948 on the understanding (a) that it was an exploratory conference only as to the desirability and practicability of an agreed wage structure; (b) that no union was committed in any possible way by attendance; and (c) that no vote of any kind would be taken at the conference, so there could be no possibility of a union being outvoted.

The LSC and the TA attended the November meeting, at which there was a general acceptance that a wage structure was 'desirable' but no decision was taken as to whether such a structure was 'practicable'. The Federation established a subcommittee to examine these practical problems. This reported to a conference of union executives, held on 15 December 1948, at which was considered not only the subcommittee's report but a letter from the BFMP stating its basis for a stable wage structure. After debate the conference agreed to the employers' invitation for informal talks on the understanding that the talks were purely exploratory, that the subcommittee devise a voting system acceptable to both large and small unions in the Federation, and that a further conference of executives be convened to consider the outcome of the informal talks and the subcommittee's investigations into the problems of voting.

The subcommittee met on 5 January 1949 and reported that the employers had given no definite response to points raised by the unions, e.g. a reduction in the number of geographical grades of pay and that payment systems designed to increase productivity should not be a feature of the wage structure. They had, however, suggested the establishment of a small joint committee to explore further an agreed wage structure. Another conference of union executives was held on 27 January 1949. The initial contributions, including that from the TA, considered the voting problems to be of secondary importance and that the unions should proceed immediately with devising a wage structure. It was proposed that each union should declare whether it would participate in further efforts to agree a wages structure so that like-minded unions might proceed with their own scheme. The LSC argued that this introduced a new principle and sucessfully moved an adjournment of the conference so that each union could consider its position towards this new development.

Following the adjournment the LSC argued that the voting system was important, that it was not prepared to surrender wage autonomy without some assurances as to the practicability of any proposals, that the basis of a new wage structure must be give and take and that the employers should settle outstanding wage claims prior to drafting a pay structure.[3] Only three unions supported an approach to the employers to devise a wage structure. The conference agreed three things. First, each union should inform the Federation whether it was prepared to continue the consideration of a wages structure and meet with the employers for negotiations. Second, that each union should submit its views as to the form a wages structure might take. Third, that when the Federation had considered these replies it would determine future action.

When the replies were considered at a meeting held on 29 February 1949 the Federation found that two unions did not wish to be associated with further discussions. Whilst the remainder were in favour of such discussions proceeding, the agreement of some unions, including that of the LSC, was conditional on assurances being given on a number of points or principles, e.g. a voting system satisfactory to both large and small unions. Whilst some unions considered the employers should be approached without delay, others felt that further consideration should be given to the practical problems of a wage structure, for example all outstanding claims be settled. After further consideration, on 3 March 1949 the Federation executive passed the following resolution:

Owing to the inability of the P&KTF Federation to secure harmony in the views of the individual unions regarding a wages structure we inform the employers and the unions that the Federation is unable to proceed with the movement for a wages structure for the industry.[4]

Why had the attempt to agree a wages structure for the printing industry failed? The TA was committed to facilitating a wage structure which would reduce the number of geographical rates of pay and deal with the inter-provincial and London/provincial craft differential. It blamed the failure to gain agreement on the parochial outlook of unions, like the LSC, who felt their autonomy was jeopardised and who concentrated too much on the voting system applicable at meetings of the executives of affiliated unions. As the 200th Half Yearly Report of the TA described it, the meetings of the executives of affiliated unions to discuss the establishment of a new wage structure, 'after consuming time and patience alike, proved entirely abortive'.

The LSC, however, claimed that the causes of the failure had been present at every conference of the unions' executives. It saw two main problems – first, the wisdom as to surrendering its autonomy in wage matters, and, second, the fear that the wage policy would be determined by the larger unions on the basis of numbers regardless of craft interests. In May 1948 the Federation had introduced a new system of voting in proportion to the size of affiliated unions. Previously policy was decided on the basis of one union, one vote regardless of size. This was disliked by the large non-craft unions, particularly the NUPB&PW, which were not prepared to allow small craft unions to determine the wages of their members.[5] The LSC regarded the new voting system as one of domination by large unions on the basis of sheer numbers and complained,

> It is essential, therefore, that any proposals for a wage structure must be of such a character as to remove any suspicion that the industry as a whole will be tied on what may be an attractive offer to lower paid groups but would only serve to exasperate the more highly skilled sections of the industry.[6]

As a condition of supporting a stable wage structure, the LSC was looking for a readiness on the part of other unions to consider various methods of representation and voting, since under the proportionate voting system three unions (the TA, Natsopa and NUPB&PW) could collectively outvote the other fourteen unions of the Federation. Two of these unions' members were largely concerned with unskilled employees.

The LSC was not prepared to surrender its independence on wages matters unless it could be assured it would not be 'sacrificing' substance for shadow. It had on two previous occasions offered to restrain its autonomy on wages matters in order that a fair and equitable wage structure could be established, but on both occasions it claimed that its initiative had been rebuffed. These initiatives, made at conferences of union executives held in February 1948 and January 1949, involved an offer to the employers not to press for traditional differentials provided the outstanding claims of other unions were met. This would enable any wage structure to be founded upon an equitable basis and would have the additional advantage of ending the procrastination of the employers over the settlement of outstanding claims.

The LSC, like the TA, was desirous of participating in the devising of a wage structure. However, unlike the TA, it was disappointed at the attitude of some of the unions, which it viewed as not only refusing to consider suggestions made by the LSC but also refusing to compromise on any point of view held. The LSC strategy was to seek agreement on the method of voting, the London/provincial craft differential and that all outstanding wage claims be settled as prerequisites for evolving an agreed wages structure for the industry. It told its members in its monthly journal,

> It has to be recognised that if the union enters into such an arrangement much of its autonomy and rights would have to be sacrificed. It is for that reason that we are very naturally concerned at ensuring that all those difficulties and differences that could well break-up not only a wage structure but the Federation itself, should be solved so far as that is possible, before entering upon more ambitious ventures.[7]

This was the third occasion since the end of the Second World War on which attempts to evolve an agreed wage structure under the auspices of the P&KTF had failed. The first attempt was made in 1947 after thirteen unions had presented uncoordinated claims to the BFMP and the NS, which both feared that the granting of one claim would disturb the differentials and precipitate avalanches of new claims for restoration of relativities. The employers' organisations saw it as undesirable to deal with each claim separately, as individual settlements would merely lead to further sectional disputes. In November 1947 the BFMP, the NS and the Federation held an exploratory conference to hear the employers' views, without prejudice to any of the unions' claims. The employers stressed the difficulties and delays if the claims were pressed separately and threw back to the unions the responsibility for resolving their differences and stated categorically 'that the procedure of separate negotiations on the major question of wages in an industry such as ours is archaic and outmoded.'[8] The employers proposed parity of provincial craft rates and a London differential of 45p. Following a meeting of affiliated unions the P&KTF reported that a collective approach could not be agreed and the unions would pursue their claims individually.

The second attempt to get the print unions to agree a wage structure occurred shortly after a NAT Award (January 1948), which gave the LSC an increase on the basis that the London/provincial compositor differential had narrowed in recent years. A joint union-employer conference followed at which the print unions proposed a uniform rate of £7.00 for craftsmen in London and £6.50 for craftsmen in grade 1 towns in the provinces and that the existing craft/non-craft differentials be maintained. To facilitate agreement the LSC agreed to waiver its claim to maintain the NAT-awarded London/provincial differential. Influenced by the government's White Paper, *Personal Incomes, Costs and Prices*, the employers rejected these proposals and suggested that agreement should be reached with the various unions on outstanding claims, based on the NAT award and the January 1948 TA agreement, with appropriate increases for non-craft workers. When the unions rejected these proposals, joint discussion ended.

Following the inability of the unions to reach agreement on a wage structure, four unions – the TA, NUPB&PW, ASLP and Natsopa – put forward proposals for such a structure to the BFMP in March 1949. The employers in the meantime had devised their own proposals, which they presented in July 1949 not only to the four unions but to all other unions. In August 1949 the Federation informed the employers that its affiliated unions were unable to accept the employers' proposals and that the main obstacle was the reluctance of the unions to surrender autonomy on wage matters.

Three unions – the TA, NUPB&PW and Natsopa – then negotiated wage settlements with the employers in November 1949. The ASLP claim was referred to the NAT, which in March 1950 gave an award which, like the three unions' negotiated settlements, was in line with the employers' wage structure proposals of July 1949. The TA settlement disturbed the London/provincial craft differential and the LSC claim for restoration of this led to the 1950 wage disputes between the LSC and the LMPA. This was resolved, following a Court of Inquiry, in November 1950. Early in 1951, in the light of the London settlement, the November 1949 agreements were readjusted and the industry had stumbled to a wage structure which was to remain stabilised for at least five years.

1955–74

In anticipation of the termination of the 1950/1 stabilisation agreements, the Federation held a meeting of affiliated unions to see if a common approach could be agreed for the renegotiation of these agreements. The meeting was held in March 1955 and attended by eleven unions. The TA attended but the LTS was not interested in a collective approach. Eventually six unions, including the TA, decided to proceed on a collective basis and met with the BFMP and NS in July 1955. However in November the TA withdrew to negotiate separately with the employers.

The separate negotiations between the employers and the LTS and the employers and the TA broke down and the unions took industrial action. Courts of Inquiry were established, but during the early stages of the TA inquiry the employers and the TA announced that they had agreed to resume negotiations under the chairmanship of a Ministry of Labour conciliation officer immediately following the report of the Court of Inquiry into the London dispute. The Court's report urged, *inter alia*, that further efforts be made to establish comprehensive national machinery on a two-tier basis (one for craft unions and one for non-craft) for the negotiation of wages and conditions in the industry.

The lack of unity amongst the print unions during the 1955/6 wage negotiations led the NUPB&PW to submit the following motion to the 1956 P&KTF Administrative Council:

> That, in the opinion of this Conference, recent events have demonstrated a serious lack of unity between the unions affiliated to our Federation. As a means towards restoring this unity this Conference instructs the General Secretary to call a meeting of two or three representatives from each union in the Federation, such meeting to endeavour to devise a basic wage structure for the industry.[9]

The Paperworkers argued that there was an atmosphere between craft and non-craft employees in the industry but that bitterness and bad feelings should be forgotten and the two groups should sit down together and solve the problem. The LTS moved, and the TA seconded, an amendment to the NUPB&PW's motion, which proposed:

> Conference accepts the recommendations of the Court of Inquiry for a two tier wage structure for the industry. In order that this can be achieved the Conference requests the Federation officers to act as convenors for calling together the affiliated unions at two meetings; one for craft workers and the other for non craft.[10]

Both the Paperworkers' resolution and the LTS amendment were designed to secure the unity of purpose in finding some machinery for wage negotiations and which would prevent the problems of the past. The LTS envisaged that if there was one tier for craftsmen and one for non-craft, then those 'non-craft' unions with craft members would put their case for those members at the craft group conference. Unions with both craft and non-craft members would put the case of their members to both sections. The LTS and the TA believed a two-tier structure was the only practicable way of solving the craft/non-craft differential problem. The LTS amendment was defeated by 46 votes to 25, whilst the NUPB&PW motion carried by 47 votes to 25.

In February 1957 the Federation called a meeting of two representatives from each affiliated union during which two sets of proposals emerged. The first included that there be a basis of agreement between all the unions, craft and non-craft alike, for a period of five or ten years; that that basis include agreement at a preliminary union conference on what the unions would claim and the percentage craft/non-craft differential, and that all craft and non-craft would negotiate as one body; that as the unions would not have individual autonomy, as in the past, there be acceptance that a union could withdraw from a united movement; and that a small subcommittee deal with the question of percentage differentials and present a report. The second set of proposals were largely the work of the LTS, and contained four elements. First, there should be an initial conference of all craft unions to discuss the craft demands. At the same time there should be a conference of non-craft unions for the same purpose. The second element would be a conference of all unions to agree the percentage craft differential. Third, the negotiations with the employers and the craft and non-craft union would then proceed, not joinly, but side by side. The fourth element envisaged consultation via the P&KTF, a joint conference and report on the progress being made by both sections.

Both sets of proposals were fully discussed at a further conference of affiliated unions and the second set outlined above were approved. It was firmly believed that these proposals would unite the Federation and the unions within it, and avoid the problems of previous wage negotiations. The unions were now to divide into craft and non-craft interests and those unions which had both craft and non-craft members would participate in negotiations and consultations when both craft and non-craft interests were being considered.

In April 1958 the Federation initiated discussions to devise a basic wage structure in readiness for the negotiations to be conducted prior to the termination, in April 1959, of the three-year wages stabilisation agreements. A meeting of the craft subcommittee took place on 17 June 1958 to which Natsopa sent a delegation. The craft unions objected to its presence and it was apparent that, if Natsopa remained, some of the craft unions would withdraw from the attempts to devise a wage structure. The LTS General Secretary suggested that Natsopa belonged to the second tier of negotiations – non-craft – and it should leave the meeting. This it did with a certain amount of ill-grace, claiming that its exclusion was unconstitutional and an insult. Getting no satisfaction from the P&KTF to their complaint, Natsopa gave notice in August 1958 to disaffiliate from the Federation. In January 1959 it departed, stating that re-affiliation would not be sought until there was a change in attitude on the part of the P&KTF.

Following the acceptance of the principle of a two-tier wages structure, discussions on the details of claims proceeded at separate meetings of craft unions and those unions with non-craft and women members. There was full consultation between the two groups, and agreement was reached between them as to the claims to be presented to the BFMP and NS to replace the wage agreements due to terminate on 20 April 1959. Although the 1959 wages and hours movement was a collective one, it was not a Federation movement. It was a collective approach by two groups of unions in which the Federation acted as liaison and its General Secretary was closely associated with negotiations. As the hours and holiday agreement was between the Federation and the BFMP and the NS, the hour claim was a Federation movement and the case presented by the Federation's General Secretary. The wages and hours agreement made following the 1959 dispute was to operate to 6 August 1962, but in 1961 consideration would be given as to whether further reductions in hours and/or an increase in basic wages were justified (see Chapter 12).

In January 1962 the Federation was requested to arrange a preliminary meeting of the unions that took part in the 1959 collective hours and wages movement to ascertain whether there was a general desire to renegotiate, on a collective basis, the wage agreements due to terminate on 6 August 1962. Eight (including the TA and the LTS) of the ten unions involved favoured a collective approach to the BFMP and the Newspaper Society. As in 1959, the collective wages claim was not a Federation movement but a group of unions acting collectively. However, the 1962 claim included a demand for three weeks' paid holiday and a change to the apprentices' wage agreements. Since these were Federation agreements these parts of the claim were a Federation movement. The wages agreements negotiated in 1962 were stabilised until 31 March 1965.

In December 1964 nine unions, including the NGA, met to formulate a collective claim for new wages agreements with the BFMP and the Newspaper Society. Eventually unanimity was reached between the unions as to the claim to be submitted. The claim was confined to wages and was one of unions acting together, not a Federation movement. However, the P&KTF General Secretary was closely associated with the negotiations. The 1965 agreements became operative from May 1965 and were to terminate in December 1966.

In July 1966 six unions, including the NGA, met to consider a claim to replace the national wage agreements expiring at the end of 1966. A collective approach to the employers was readily agreed. However, negotiations with the employers were opened only in December 1966 because of delays in reaching agreement amongst the six unions about the nature and scope of the claims to be submitted and the difficulty of obtaining agreement to drop all 'domestic' claims so as to concentrate on an increase in the basis rate. In the event a settlement to operate to 30 October 1969 was not reached with the BFMP and the NS until October 1967 and only then after the imposition of an overtime ban in provincial daily newspaper offices.

The NGA refused to be involved in a collective wages movement to replace these arrangements. This action was announced by the General Secretary to the 1969 Delegate Meeting when he moved a National

Council emergency motion on proposals for new wage agreements with the BFMP and the NS. He told the delegates,

> Delays in reaching settlements in recent years had been due not to the employers but wholly to lack of agreement among the unions – first on what the claims should be, and then by lack of unity during the negotiations. The National Council, therefore, have decided that this time the NGA will negotiate on its own.[12]

The NGA took the opportunity presented by unilateral negotiations to remove the anomaly of justified claims for increases in various extras being consistently 'swept under the carpet' in collective movements. In all subsequent wage negotiations prior to the dissolution of the P&KTF, the NGA negotiated unilaterally with the BFMP and the NS.

Hours of work

The 1937 hours and holiday agreement between the P&KTF and the BFMP and the NS established a 45 hour working week, the continuation of one week's paid annual holiday (granted in 1919) and provided for three years' stabilisation. In 1940 the country was at war and the Federation postponed reopening negotiations on hours. However, an important element in the print unions' post-war programme was a further reduction in hours. In March 1946 the P&KTF submitted a claim to the BFMP and the NS for a 40 hour working week and a fortnight's paid annual holiday. The employers rejected the claim, arguing that a labour shortage and the growing competition from office printing machines militated against any increase in printing costs. A dispute developed and an overtime ban was imposed in August 1946. A separate agreement was reached with the NS giving print employees a fortnight's annual paid holiday and a 43½ hour working week from October 1946. In August 1946 the Minister of Labour established a Court of Inquiry into the dispute and, following its report, negotiations were resumed and a settlement reached which provided, *inter alia*, for a 43½ hour working week and two weeks' paid annual holiday. Both parties, however, accepted the principle of the 42½ hour week and agreed to work towards it when the industry's labour shortage had been overcome.[13]

At the 1953 P&KTF Administrative Council, Slade moved a resolution calling for a basic working week of 42½ hours, but after much discussion it was referred back to the Federation executive. The LSC opposed the motion on the grounds that the industry was not yet ready for a further reduction in hours of work. The TA's attitude was that it would be tactically wrong to defeat the motion, but Slade had to recognise that the employers would strongly reject the claim. When the Federation considered the Slade motion, it decided against an approach to the BFMP and the NS during the current wage agreements or until the employment situation in the industry justified such an approach.

Both the LTS and the TA supported the Natsopa motion to the 1958 administrative council that 'this Society urges the P&KTF to press on with collective representation for the establishment of a forty hour week in the general printing trade'. Natsopa argued that print employees wanted a 40 hour week, that greater leisure was part of social advance, that productivity per head in the British printing industry had increased by 25 per cent and that the industry's labour shortage had now been overcome. The three-year wage agreements with the BFMP and the NS signed in 1956 were due to terminate in April 1959 and the unions were aware that the 40 hour working week would now have to be included in the 'shopping list'.

On 1 December 1958 the nine unions submitted their claims to the employers, including that the hours and holiday agreement (1946) be amended to provide a working week of 40 hours. The employers rejected the claim and in June 1959 work ceased by the members of nine unions and they did not return until 6 August 1959. The return to work formula included that the standard working week for day workers should be 42 hours. The 1959 hours and holiday agreement was to operate for three years, but contained a clause that consideration could be given in 1961 to whether there was a case for a reduction of hours and/or an increase in basic wages to operate from September 1961.

In December 1960 the nine unions presented the balance of their 1959 claims to the employers to be granted in 1961. The employers responded by saying that, provided the industry could get the labour it needed, they were prepared to negotiate an agreement which would give the unions by stages a 40 hour week and the balance of the 10 per cent wages claim. The unions said that if they granted the claims on hours and wages without delay then they would talk about the labour supply situation, including apprenticeship quotas. Eventually, on 30 June 1961 an hours, wages and labour supply agreement was signed between the BFMP and the Newspaper Society on the one hand and the printing unions, including the LTS and TA, on the other. From the hours of work perspective, the main feature of the agreement was that the standard working week was to be reduced as from September 1961 to 41 hours and from September 1962 to 40 hours. The printing unions thus became the first group of manual workers on an industry-wide basis in Britain to achieve the 40 hour working week. The P&KTF President told the 1962 administrative council Annual Conference,

> But it is, manifestly, the 40 hour week that makes the greatest impact on the imagination. For this has been the aim not only of the printing unions but the whole British trade union movement for more years than one cares to remember. As in so many other fields of industrial endeavour, the honour of effecting the final breakthrough to this desirable objective has fallen to the printing unions. But, as we now recall this achievement, we shall remember that it – and the wage increase to which I referred – flowed directly from a 6 week stoppage of the industry and the longest set of continuous negotiations in the history of industrial relations in this country.[14]

Holidays

The hours and holiday agreement (1946) provided for two weeks' annual holiday with pay. The print workers were the first group of manual employees in the UK to achieve this. At the 1953 administrative council a Slade call for three weeks' paid holiday was defeated. The LSC played a leading part in this, arguing that the industry could not afford a further increase in holidays. In 1957 the Federation adopted an Executive Committee report that when circumstances were opportune an approach be made to the BFMP and the NS, with the first priority being a shorter working week and the second a third week's annual holiday. Following the achievement of the 40 hour working week in 1962, the P&KTF turned its attention to a third week's annual holiday.

This was included in the union's claim for the 1962 wages negotiations, but was totally rejected by the employers. However the 1962–5 wages stabilisation agreement contained a clause that, if at some time during the life of the agreement the unions felt circumstances warranted, the employers would make an objective assessment of the position with them and consider if there was justification for an additional week of holiday or some lesser period. In October 1963 the Federation made an application for the third week's paid holiday. In March 1964 the employers replied that they did not consider there was any justification at that time for a further week's holiday but they were prepared to discuss some improvement if ways could be found of maintaining production and avoiding increases in costs. The Federation rejected the contention that any additional holidays must be self-funded. Months of bargaining followed in which the employers argued that, if extra holidays were granted, 'extra labour' must be introduced at once in view of the shortage of craftsmen. The Federation on the other hand contended that manpower should be removed from the discussions and dealt with separately by a joint committee representing both sides of the industry. Eventually, the Federation negotiators obtained an agreement, ratified in January 1965, for the introduction of a third week's annual holiday. However, the unions accepted certan conditions in return, including the setting up of a Joint Committee on Manpower and an amendment to the Retraining and Transfer of Membership Agreement covering letterpress and litho machine departments.

The Joint Committee on Manpower was to make a careful study of the present and future manpower needs of the industry. Following discussions in the committee, the NGA said that as part of the settlement for three weeks' annual holiday they would accept an immediate allocation of 300 bonus apprentices, some extension of the duties of auxiliary workers, and a revision of the provincial apprentice quota. Subsequently a crash programme for training keyboard operators and readers was agreed to deal with shortages of labour in these areas.

However, during 1966 it became apparent that the committee was not functioning as intended. First, it had confined itself to dealing with short-term manpower problems raised by the employers and no attention had been given to the industry's long-term manpower requirements. Through Mr Richard O'Brien, who had been appointed independent chairman of the committee following recommendation of such an appointment by the National Board for Prices and Incomes in their report on the 1965 general printing and provincial newspaper industry wage settlement, the Ministry of Labour agreed to conduct a survey of the industry's long-term manpower needs in the light of economic and technological trends. Second, not all unions were accepting their obligations and the employers seemed intent on widening the terms of reference to include matters the unions felt should be the subject of negotiation. Finally, Mr O'Brien and the employers insisted that the Report of the Cameron Court of Inquiry should be considered by the committee. The NGA viewed this as extending the committee's terms of reference far beyond what had originally been envisaged. At this point the NGA – having fully filled its obligations under the terms of the third week's holiday agreement, if not more – withdrew from the committee, and the other unions (ASLP, Sogat and Slade) followed suit. In 1967 the Joint Manpower Committee ceased to function.

Print workers were the first group of manual workers in the UK to gain three weeks' paid holiday. In 1971 the Federation opened negotiations with the BFMP and the NS for a revision of the hours and holiday agreement to provide for a fourth week's annual holiday to be taken during the summer period. It argued that the claim would bring the British printing industry into line with the industry in other countries, would bring provincial newspapers into line with national newspapers, and would provide more leisure time, which was necessary given the pace of modern industry. Although initially the BFMP and the NS rejected the claim, agreement was reached in 1972 for the staged introduction of a fourth week's annual holiday from 1974. Print manual workers were again the leaders in obtaining four weeks' paid holiday.

However, the Federation not only sought an increase in holidays but for a long time it campaigned for holiday pay based on average earnings rather than basic rates. The Federation became committed in 1951 to a policy of holiday payment on the basis of average earnings, but the employers rejected this demand in 1952 and 1953. Although disappointed at this attitude, the Federation decided not to press the matter further until a more appropriate time in the future. In 1958 the Federation confirmed its policy of holiday pay on the basis of average earnings, but delayed a renewed approach pending the 1959 wage negotiations in which priority was given to the 40 hour week and a 10 per cent wage increase. Following a resolution passed at the 1971 Federation Annual Conference, the employers were approached with a claim for average earnings holiday pay. The unions argued that it was a denial of the principle of 'holidays with pay' to give workers who went on holiday less than the amount they would have received during the same period had they been at work and that workers need more, not

less, money when they go on holiday. In rejecting the claim, the BFMP
and the NS stated that to concede it would increase the annual wage bill
by some 2 per cent. By the time of its dissolution, the Federation had
still not achieved holiday pay on the basis of average earnings.

Sick Pay, Pensions and Other Matters

A TA resolution to the 1954 Federation administrative council
proposing an investigation into the practicability of an industry-wide
sick pay scheme was defeated. However, four years later a similar STA
motion was remitted to the Federation executive, which conducted an
enquiry into the extent and nature of sick pay schemes then in
operation. On the basis of the results they decided that a sick pay
scheme 'should be deferred until a more appropriate time in view of the
circumstances prevailing in the industry'. Although an industry-wide
sick pay scheme was raised on subsequent occasions when claims were
being formulated by affiliated unions, the priorities were such that it
was never decided to include such a request in the claim.

Efforts by the P&KTF to persuade the BFMP to adopt an industrial
pension scheme completely failed. The first post Second World War
approach was made in 1953. The difference between the two sides was
clear. The Federation wanted a scheme in which there would be a
uniform subscription and benefit and which accepted the principle of
transfer of pension rights for workers changing jobs. The BFMP,
however, consistently argued that a pension should be a reward for
service to the firm, but indicated a readiness to cooperate with the
unions in efforts to persuade member firms to introduce 'house'
schemes.

This remained the situation until August 1965 when the National
Board for Prices and Incomes in its report on the industry's wages
settlement recommended 'as a means of overcoming the fear of
redundancy the introduction of an industrial pension scheme'. This was
welcomed in principle by the Federation, and the employers agreed to
discussions on the subject. However, before approaching the employers
the Federation conducted a survey of the extent to which pension
schemes already existed. The survey showed that 73 per cent of men
and 42 per cent of women in the industry were covered by house
pension schemes. This compared with a figure of 60 per cent provided
by the BFMP in February 1967.[15] The Federation told its affiliates they
would have to decide where an industrial pension scheme stood in their

list of negotiating priorities. To bring the matter to a head it recommended that when the current wages negotiations with the BFMP and the Newspaper Society were concluded the unions consider the possibility that in the next round of negotiations the main claim should be a request for an industrial pension scheme rather than an increase in wages. This did not find favour with its affiliates.

Given that so many workers in the general and provincial newspaper trade were already covered by house pension schemes, it was unlikely that a national movement to secure an industrial pension scheme would receive the universal support of union members. There was increasing realisation that members already in house pension schemes would not support, by vigorous action, efforts to obtain pensions for workers not already covered. The Federation concluded that affiliated unions should be asked frankly if they were prepared to agree a collective approach to the BFMP and the NS on behalf of members not at present covered by schemes. The NGA and Slade considered such an approach should be made, but Sogat was not attracted to the idea. Following further discussions with affiliated unions, the Federation concluded in 1970 that an approach to the BFMP and the NS for an industry-wide pension scheme should be deferred indefinitely.

The 1958 P&KTF Conference considered a report on problems in the newspaper industry which identified the need for an agreement between the unions on policy for compensation for redundancy when newspapers closed. The NPA, NS and the Scottish Daily Newspaper Society were approached for agreements to provide for compensation for redundancy on the basis of one month's salary for each year of service. As a first step the Federation decided that claims should be made to the newspaper employers and that the BFMP should be approached only when precedents had been established elsewhere. A claim was accordingly made to the NPA in 1958 for compensation on the basis of one month's wages for each year of service. This was rejected but eventually the employers offered an agreement providing for minimum compensation of one week's wages for each year of service to be increased in accordance with the individual circumstances of closures. However, negotiations were interrupted by the NPA issuing, in 1963, their memorandum 'Efficiency and Production' which dealt *inter alia*, with compensation for redundancy (see Chapter 15).

After a conference in 1959 the Scottish Daily Newspaper Society said it considered a collective agreement on behalf of its member firms impracticable. The Newspaper Society told the Federation that, though the time was inappropriate for a redundancy compensation agreement, it was prepared to discuss the issue. However, in 1960 the NS notified the Federation that it had rejected the claim for a redundancy compensation agreement.

The 1963 Federation administrative council Annual Conference agreed a new policy with respect to claims for compensation for redundancy. Compensation was to be sought in accordance with the following scale:

Less than 5 years' service – 1½ weeks' wages for each year of service
5 years and less than 15 years' service – 2 weeks' wages for each year of service
15 years' service and over – 3 weeks' wages for each year of service

This formula had been devised in the light of the varied experience in attempting to base compensation on one month's pay for each year of service. One of the problems had been the widely varying circumstances in which firms had had to close down. In pressing compensation claims, the Federation and the unions had been forced to take into account the financial resources available in each particular case. Varying amounts of compensation had been secured. The Federation policy was not to agree to compensation at the rate of less than one week's wages for each year of service. If this fall-back position could not be achieved, it was left to individual chapels to decide whether or not lesser amounts were acceptable.

Notwithstanding the Redundancy Payments Act (1965), Federation policy remained as agreed in 1963. Each affiliated union when faced with redundancy endeavoured to secure compensation terms not less favourable than Federation policy. In 1967 the Federation again approached the BFMP and the NS for a compensation for redundancy agreement, but was told by the employers they did not consider the proposals formed a basis for an agreement or understanding covering the whole industry and that it was impractical to make a national agreement on redundancy compensation. Although the Federation was unable to achieve such an agreement, it continued its policy of reaching agreements on compensation for redundancy with individual and groups of companies. In 1968 it produced a model compensaation for redundancy scheme which was accepted by all its affiliated unions. The main objective of the 'model agreement' was to provide redundancy pay based on two weeks' wages for each year of service between the ages of 18 and 65 with no limit. In practice, in the majority of instances where NGA members were unfortunate enough to become redundant, either through closure or part closures, the employers accepted the Federation scale of redundancy pay, even though in some cases the NGA did not have an agreement with them.[16]

The Dissolution of the Federation

By the late 1960s the future of the P&KTF was questioned in the light of union mergers over the period 1964–9 and the prospect of future mergers. At the 1969 administrative council, Sogat proposed that the P&KTF be wound up, its assets be distributed amongst affiliated unions, and affiliates each appoint a national officer for liaison purposes and to arrange meetings from time to time on instructions from their respective Executive Councils when matters of mutual interest occasioned such meetings.

Sogat's case was simple. The industry was down to two major unions – the NGA and Sogat – and the time was ripe to wind up the Federation as its days were numbered. Bob Willis of the NGA, speaking on behalf of the Federation executive, opposed the motion, arguing that Sogat's case was based on the desirability of one union and the need for amalgamation and no case had been made for the dissolution of the Federation. He advised delegates that the P&KTF should be left as it was for as long as there were a number of affiliated unions. When put to the vote the Sogat motion was defeated by 37 votes to 26. The Sogat delegates voted in favour but the NUJ, STA, NGA, Slade, Wallpaper Workers' Union and the Sign and Display Union voted against.

In 1970 the Federation executive consulted unions as to the future of the Federation. Affiliates were asked if the Federation should continue with an unaltered constitution or if, in the light of experience and developments in printing trade union structure, consideration should be given to amending the constitution. Unions were also asked, should neither of these courses be acceptable, if they wished the dissolution of the Federation and the setting up of a TUC industry committee. Two unions (Natsopa and Sogat) were in favour of the Federation being dissolved. The rest, including the NGA, expressed the desire that it should continue. Four of these unions, however, felt that the Federation constitution should be amended.

However, Sogat proposed in 1972 'that steps be taken to wind up the Printing and Kindred Trades Federation at the earliest suitable date and under suitable conditions, having regard to the rights and claims of employees of the Federation'.[17] The motion, seconded by Natsopa, was defeated by 40 votes to 34 after a lengthy debate. The President (John Bonfield) said the Federation executive would take note of a point emphasised in the debate that the Federation constitution needed streamlining in the light of modern conditions. He also stressed the hope that the unions that had voted to wind up the Federation would nevertheless 'support the Federation both in the work of streamlining its constitution and the industrial problems they faced'. In the event, Sogat indicated its withdrawal from the Federation by allowing its affiliation fees to lapse. In January 1973, because of arrears of contributions, Sogat ceased its connection with the Federation.

The Federation executive set up a special subcommittee to examine how the Federation constitution might be modified. The committee eventually recommended that the Federation be transformed into a purely coordinating body, as the function of coordinating affiliated unions' activities was one that even the fiercest critics of the Federation had always admitted was necessary. It proposed the setting up of a printing trade union co-ordinating bureau, whose function would be confined to coordinating union activities whenever the unions felt this was necessary or desirable. The executive considered that the bureau would cater for all foreseeable contingencies. If one union for the industry was established the bureau could be disbanded at any time. On the other hand, if it were felt at some time in the future that something on the lines of the Federation was required, the nucleus of machinery, staff and premises would be available on which to build. It was proposed the bureau begin its operations on 1 October 1973.

The constitution for the bureau was unanimously approved by the 1973 Annual Conference. It was then, as required under the Federation rules, put for endorsement by each of the affiliated unions. Six of the seven unions subsequently signified their acceptance, but Natsopa declined to do so unless arrangements were agreed, prior to the establishment of the bureau, as to how the Federation funds would be distributed among the affiliated unions. The Executive Committee pointed out to Natsopa that the setting up of the bureau was not a device for winding up the Federation and distributing its funds but a genuine attempt to provide machinery for coordination of union activities, and only in the event of the bureau failing to fulfil this function satisfactorily would the question of its dissolution and the distribution of funds arise. The reaction of Natsopa was, on 4 July 1973, to give six months' notice of its intention to disaffiliate from the Federation or the bureau 'as the case may be'. This amounted to notice to withdraw from the Federation, which was the only body at that time in existence until the notice had expired.

In the circumstances the executive recognised that it had no alternative but to defer the setting up of the bureau from 1 October 1973 until 1 February 1974, by which date Natsopa would have left the Federation and the acceptance of the remaining affiliated unions would enable the new body to become operative from that date. Over several months during 1973 both formal and informal efforts were made by the Federation to persuade Sogat to re-affiliate and both Sogat and Natsopa to accept membership of the bureau, but without success. In September 1973 the P&KTF President wrote formally to the President of Sogat inviting his union to re-affiliate, but the reply indicated that Sogat did not wish to do so. In October 1973 the executive recognised that in the absence of Sogat and Natsopa the proposed printing trade unions co-ordinating bureau could not be as effective as originally envisaged. In November the executive decided that immediate plans should be made for a special conference of the administrative council to which a resolution dissolving the Federation and abandoning the bureau project would be submitted. The special conference was held on 17 December 1973 and unanimously agreed to dissolve the Federation, to refund all affiliation fees paid by unions since 26 April 1972, to distribute the remaining assets of the Federation among the affiliated unions, and to abandon the bureau project.[18]

THE INTERNATIONAL GRAPHICAL FEDERATION

In 1889 the first graphical trades International was founded when the typographers meeting in Paris decided to join together internationally. Seven years later, in 1896, the Lithographers International was born and after a further eleven years the bookbinders followed by setting up their international union in Nuremberg. In 1939 these three separate international organisations came together with the intention of creating a new all-embracing International. However it was not until 1946, on the initiative of the P&KTF, that a coordinating committee to draft a constitution for the new body was established. The inaugural conference of the IGF met in Stockholm in May 1949. The IGF came into being to protect and further the occupational, economic and industrial interests of printing workers. It is a non-political body and coordinates activities on technical matters, for example coordinating union responses to technological change in the various sections of the industry. In addition, it provides information on terms and conditions of employment in the printing industry in the countries of member unions, on health, safety and welfare matters, and informs affiliated unions of disputes that member unions have with employers.

The LSC, LTS and TA participated actively in the affairs of the IGF and sent delegates to its triennial conference. In its 1950 wage dispute with the LMPA the LSC received assistance from the IGF in the form of it notifying member unions of the London dispute and asking them to take appropriate action, including the refusal to handle work diverted from London to their own countries.[19] The LTS received support from the IGF during the 1956 and 1959 wages disputes with the major printing employers' organisations. On 3 April 1959 the P&KTF asked the IGF to send circulars to all affiliated unions asking them not to carry out work being placed abroad as a result of the dispute. The IGF passed on thirty-three cases of information to continental unions concerning British printing orders to be investigated and stopped, and in most cases this happened. Print unions in Denmark and the Federal Republic of Germany were in fact sued and ordered to pay compensation to print employers in their countries for refusing to print work diverted from Britain.

The IGF faces problems in applying its procedures for calling on the solidarity of member unions to support others in dispute with their employers. It provides financial support and a decision on this rests with the Executive Committee, which can recommend that a collection be made for members of affiliated unions involved in a strike or lock-out. The affiliated unions involved in such a dispute must keep the IGF Secretariat informed on the course of the dispute. Unions involved in a dispute usually request the IGF to inform other unions of this and to ask them to ensure that work that is usually carried out in the country where the conflict is happening or proceeding is 'blacked' if the work is transferred to other countries. It is, however, difficult for IGF affiliates to act in this way because of the potential consequences for the workers of an individual firm and their unions. Difficulties arise depending on existing legislation (e.g. the law on sympathy strikes), the provision of collective bargaining (both of which can lead to court cases and claims for damages), the vague and inaccurate information given to the IGF by unions in disputes, deciding what is legitimate work and what is not, and the transfer of work in anticipation of a dispute on the termination of agreements.

The NGA also received support from the IGF in its major industrial disputes. When it was in dispute with IPC over the web-offset at Southwark Offset in 1966 the NGA received the cooperation of Dutch and German printing unions in stopping a number of publications that had been diverted to the continent. This action helped the NGA secure a satisfactory settlement to the dispute.

The 1979 IGF Congress approved the establishment of an International Solidarity Fund. The fund's basic capital was provided by a donation from the Scandinavian unions. The fund provides support for graphical unions involved in industrial disputes and aids the development of national unions, principally in countries where trade union organisation is obstructed for political reasons. The NGA gave full support to the establishment of the fund, particularly as the IGF unions had not only provided practical assistance in the 1978/9 dispute with Times Newspapers Limited by prevening the production of *The Times* in Europe, but had also offered financial assistance.[20]

The IGF gave full support to the NGA in its dispute in 1983 with the Messenger Newspaper Group by issuing communiqués condemning the actions of the Messenger Group management in failing to reinstate the 'Stockport Six', in breaking agreements made with the Association, and in invoking anti-union legislation. In addition, the IGF contributed £8,000 to NGA funds from the IGF Solidarity Fund, and the West German Printing and Paper Union contributed £10,000. The French printing union (FFTL) donated £800 and the Nordisk Graphical Union £42,000. The NGA dispute with News International, which began in January 1986, again proved the value of its continued membership of the IGF. During the dispute both the President and General Secretary of the IGF addressed a special news conference at the TUC to express their support and solidarity with the NGA, Sogat, the NUJ and the AEU. In addition a total of £178,400 was received in financial support from members of IGF affiliates.

In 1976 the NGA together with the other British affiliates – Sogat, Slade and NUWDAT – submitted proposals to the triennial congress of that year for a fundamental change in the IGF rules.[21] These provided for the abolition of the three trade group boards and the Bureau, which consisted entirely of Swiss representatives, and the transfer of their responsibilities to the Executive Committee, which was to be more widely representative. The proposals also envisaged the transfer of the IGF headquarters from Berne in Switzerland to Brussels. In the event the proposals were rejected by congress, as was a compromise formula worked out during congress. During a heated debate when it was felt by many British delegates that constitutional procedures had not been observed, the British unions' delegations spontaneously withdrew from the congress and subsequently the three delegations decided to recommend to their representative executives that they withdraw from the IGF.

This recommendation was considered by the NGA National Council immediately following the congress, by which time the federation of Scandinavian unions had proposed that discussions should take place between their federation and the British unions to ascertain if it was possible to effect reconciliation. The National Council therefore deferred a decision about disaffiliation pending the outcome of discussions with the federation of Scandinavian unions. Although Sogat was represented at the initial meetings between the two groups of unions, it subsequently declined to attend any further meetings and formally withdrew from the IGF. The NGA, Slade and NUWDAT continued with discussions and eventually agreed that efforts should be made through the constitutional machinery of the IGF to achieve compromise proposals which would meet with general approval at the 1979 IGF Congress. In the meantime, in addition to the Scandinavian federation, the German and French printing unions indicated that if a compromise solution proved impossible they would support the British proposals put to the 1976 Congress at the 1979 Congress. In the light of these developments, the NGA and the other British unions informed the IGF of their intention to remain affiliated.

Although the British proposals of 1976 had been rejected, a number of changes were accepted at that time, principally the establishment of a Management Committee representing the three trade groups – typographical, bookbinding and lithographic – and the different language groups in place of the Bureau. At the 1979 Congress further changes were unanimously approved. The main change was the abolition of the trade group boards and their replacement by special working parties. Instead of dealing solely with trade matters, the working parties were to deal with wider aspects of IGF activities, including the IGF's involvement in the European Economic Community in respect of wages and working conditions, the IGF's relationship with the Permanent Committee of Graphical Unions (the East European equivalent of the IGF) and with the International Federation of Journalists. Previously the trade group boards operated on a virtually autonomous basis, having their own funds, the right to determine their own work programme and even submitting motions for congress agendas. The working groups were to operate under the control of the IGF's most widely representative bodies, the Executive Committee and the Management Committee, thereby ensuring a greater measure of control and continuity as well as a higher degree of participation in the decision-making process at every level by affiliated unions. Although the trade group boards were abolished, the trade groups continue and trade interests are catered for through the special working parties. However, the structure of these groups was changed to take account of technological changes in the industry.

The NGA played a leading role in the expulsion of the South African Typographical Union from the IGF at the 1985 Congress, where it successfully moved a motion to this effect. These moves began when the 1982 Delegate Meeting referred to the National Council a resolution from the London Region calling for a campaign for the expulsion of the South African Typographical Union from the IGF until such time as work in the South African printing industry and membership of the appropriate union were not defined by colour or race. In response to this and complaints by Scandinavian unions about the role of the South African Typographical Union as part of the apartheid system in South Africa, the IGF visited South Africa on a fact finding tour. The visit indicated that the South African Typographical Union had traditionally been part of the segregation of races in South Africa, though the situation was developing and changing. The NGA, however, remained convinced that the union was part of the apartheid system and successfully moved a resolution for its expulsion from the IGF.

NGA officials have occupied important positions in the IGF. At the 1967 Congress, John Bonfield, NGA Joint General Secretary, was elected President of the Federation and held this position at the time of his death in 1976. Joe Wade, who became General Secretary in 1976, was elected in the same year as one of the IGF's three Vice Presidents and he held this position until October 1985. The National Council in 1984 nominated the General President, Bryn Griffiths, to replace Mr Wade as one of the three IGF Vice Presidents and the General Secretary Elect, Tony Dubbins, to serve on the Federation's Executive Committee. These two individuals still hold these positions in 1989. The NGA's increasing role and influence within the IGF in the 1980s culminated in one of its officers, Mr Bob Tomlins, becoming General Secretary of the IGF on 2 January 1990.

Important changes are taking place in the European graphical industry related to the creation of the Single European Market in 1992. The European Graphical Federation set up by the IGF in 1988 now has recognition from the ETUC and will play an increasingly important role in co-ordinating the health and safety, industrial and economic policies of European graphical unions. A second officer to concentrate primarily on these developments has been appointed as IGF/EGF Deputy General Secretary. The NGA at first adopted a cautious attitude towards the IGF but this gradually changed to one of positive affirmation and readiness to give the Federation its full and active support. From the mid-1970s it played a leading role in the business of the IGF and is firmly committed to maintaining, and extending, close working relationships with IGF affiliates. It is equally committed to developing relationships with the affiliates of the Permanent Committee of Graphical Unions, believing that in this way the NGA can play a small part in improving international relationships and thereby increase the possibility of detente and disarmament. The NGA regards the IGF as a necessary pillar of strength in the international trade union movement.[22]

NOTES

1. In places where two or more branches of affiliated unions existed, such unions were obliged to instruct their branches to cooperate and form a local federation. All unions affiliated to the P&KTF were responsible for their branches becoming members of local federations.

2. See *Report of a Court of Inquiry*, 7 July 1952, HMSO.

3. See the *London Typographical Journal*, March 1949, pp. 11–12.

4. See *Annual Report, 1948 and Report of Administrative Council, May 1949*, Printing and Kindred Trades Federation, 1949.

5. See *The Paperworker*, January 1949.

6. See the *London Typographical Journal*, February 1949, p. 11.

7. See the *London Typographical Journal*, March 1949, p. 12.

8. See J. Child, *Industrial Relations in the British Printing Industry*, Allen & Unwin, 1967, Part IV, p. 312.

9. See *Annual Report 1955, and Report of Administrative Council, May 1956*, Printing and Kindred Trades Federation, 1949, pp. 36–41.

10. ibid., p. 37.

11. Natsopa re-affiliated in 1960. See also J. Moran, *Natsopa: Seventy-five Years*, Heinemann, London, 1964, Ch. 15, p. 118.

12. See *Print*, vol. 6, no. 7, July 1969, pp. 1–3 inclusive.

13. For a fuller discussion of this dispute, see A.E. Musson, *The Typographical Association*, Oxford University Press, 1984, Ch. XXIV, pp. 493–7, and John Child, *Industrial Relations in the British Printing Industry*, Allen & Unwin, 1967, Part V, Ch. XVII, pp. 299–303.

14. See *Annual Report, 1961/62*, Printing and Kindred Trades Federation, p. 65.

15. See *Annual Report, 1967/68*, Printing and Kindred Trades Federation, p. 14.

16. See *Report of the Delegate Meeting, 1972*, National Graphical Association, p. 39.

17. For the debate on this motion, see *Annual Report, 1971/72*, Printing and Kindred Trades Federation, p. 59–70.

18. See *Final Report, 1973–74*, Printing and Kindred Trades Federation.

19. See *Annual Report, 1950/51*, Printing and Kindred Trades Federation, p. 28.

20. The NGA set up a special fund by investing £10,000, the interest from which is paid annually into the Solidarity Fund.

21. See *Report of the Delegate Meeting, 1978*, National Graphical Association, p. 68.

22. See *Report of the Delegate Meeting, 1988*, National Graphical Association, p. 10.

CHAPTER 10

RELATIONS WITH THE TRADES UNION CONGRESS

THE LOW-PROFILE YEARS, 1948–72

From 1948 to 1976 the TA, LSC, LTS and the NGA did not have a high profile within the TUC. A full delegation was always sent to the Annual Congress and invariably loyal support was given to TUC and General Council policy. However, from 1947 to 1965 Bob Willis was a member of the General Council and during 1958/9 President of the TUC. He resigned in 1965 to become a member of the National Board for Prices and Incomes. The NGA did not regain membership of the General Council until 1983 when representation became automatic for unions with memberships of 100,000 or more.

Participation in Congress Affairs

The LSC always sent three delegates, its full entitlement, to Congress whilst the LTS sent five delegates. The TA sent six delegates elected by the members on a regional basis, plus two delegates who were members of the EC. When subsequently the number of TA delegates was increased to ten, the additional two delegates also came from the Executive Committee. The TA vote at the TUC on any question was initially cast in accordance with a majority decision of the Association's delegates attending the Congress. However, the 1953 Delegate Meeting changed this to one where 'the policy of the Association on any question to be considered at these conferences shall be defined by the Executive Council who shall instruct the TA delegates to conferences to vote in accordance with the policy defined by the Executive Council'.

283

The low profile of the NGA and its founding unions was seen in a number of ways. First, between 1948 and 1978 there was only one motion proposed to Congress. This was in 1951, when the TA proposed 'That we call upon the General Council to issue an appeal to all trade unions to give all possible support to the printing trade unions in their campaign to secure for the employees of Messrs D.C. Thomson of Dundee, Manchester and Glasgow the right to belong to their appropriate trade union'. Following the General Strike of 1926, the company required its employees as a condition of returning to work to sign a 'document' in which they renounced trade unionism. Despite the 'document' the print unions had some success in organising D.C. Thomson employees, but believed that if the 'document' could be scrapped the majority of the company's employees would join the appropriate union. The purpose of the motion was to solicit the sympathy and support of other trade unionists throughout industry so that organising activities could be successful and the company remove 'the document'. Other than this motion, the LSC, the LTS, the TA and the NGA pre-1978 did not move or second any motions debated at Congress.

Second, pre-1978 the NGA and its founding unions contributed little to Congress debates other than on issues of direct industrial interest to themselves. At the 1950 Congress the LSC supported an unsuccessful motion moved by the NUR, which stated 'That this Congress urges the Government to discontinue immediately the Conditions of Employment and National Arbitration Order No. 1305'. Speaking for the motion, the LSC General Secretary illustrated how the Order had worked against the industrial interests of his union in its 1950 dispute with LMPA and said that it tended to consider cases against the national background rather than their own merits.

Third, the NGA and its founding unions rarely found themselves in conflict with affiliated unions outside the printing industry. Inter-union problems between printing unions were either settled voluntarily between the unions involved or referred to the P&KTF. An exception to this occurred in 1949 when the LSC was involved in a membership dispute with the NUR over the printing of railway timetables, which despite TUC intervention could not be settled and NUR members continued to print railway timetables on railway premises.

Although the TA, the LSC, the LTS and the NGA played little active part in the Congress, they invariably loyally supported TUC policy. Both the LSC and the TA supported TUC efforts to neutralise the effects of communism in trade unions. At the 1949 Congress, they both supported the General Council policy of withdrawing from the World Federation of Trade Unions on the grounds that to remain in that body, which was under communist domination, was a travesty of justice. They fully backed TUC participation in the formation of the International Confederation of Free Trade Unions (ICFTU), open only to trade unions in free democratic countries.

In 1957 the TUC supported the ICFTU International Solidarity Fund and adopted as a target for the British trade union movement the sum of £500,000 to be raised on the basis of voluntary contributions over three years. The fund was to provide practical projects aimed at achieving wider trade union solidarity and organisation but was also to give speedy aid to victims of totalitarian oppression.[1] The TA agreed to contribute £4,157 over the three-year period but by March 1961 the amount forwarded to the TUC had reached only £1,036. The response of its members fell short of expectations because of difficult financial and industrial times, particularly during and following the 1959 dispute. Although the 1958 LTS Annual Conference agreed to the imposition of a voluntary levy of 2½p per member per quarter, the money did not materialise. At the end of the time period allocated for voluntary contributions, only £501 had been raised against an expected £1,050. By March 1960 this had increased to £644 and the union warned,

> One point that troubles the Executive Council is the fact that we cannot permit a union of our standing to default on an obligation entered into by the trade union movement as a whole. It would be tragic in the extreme should the Executive Council have to go to the members and ballot them for money from the General Fund in order to meet the amount allocated to our society.[2]

By the time the TUC's three-year period ended, the LTS had still not met its target, so the 1960 Annual Conference agreed to forward to the TUC International Solidarity Fund £400 to make up the LTS's contribution. Both the TA and LTS leaderships backed the fund, as they considered its work essential for assisting in maintaining standards in the Western democracies where trade unionism was firmly established.

The 1960 TUC Congress was dominated by the issue of defence and the H-bomb. A TUC–Labour Party statement on this question was debated. The TA voted in favour of the statement but the LTS backed a Transport and General Workers' Union motion, which argued that the defence and foreign policy of a future Labour government should be based on the rejection of the threat of the use of nuclear weapons, the permanent cessation of the manufacture or testing of nuclear weapons, the end of patrols of aircraft from British bases carrying nuclear weapons, continued opposition to missile bases in Britain, the strengthening of the United Nations and the re-opening of talks between nations to achieve world disarmament and peaceful coexistence. However, because of mistakes in voting by the AEU delegation, both the T&GWU motion and the TUC–Labour Party statement were carried.

The 1961 Congress again debated a joint General Council–Labour Party statement favouring multilateral nuclear disarmament. Again the LTS opposed the statement but the TA, armed with a ballot result of its members, supported it. In May 1961 the TA had balloted its members on the defence policy issue, believing that to do so would strengthen the hands of its delegates at the 1961 Congress (see Chapter 11). After a long debate the Congress accepted the joint TUC–Labour Party statement by 5.8 million votes to 2 million.[3]

The TUC gave qualified support to the government opening negotiations in 1961 for Britain's entry into the Common Market. TA delegates to the 1961 Congress endorsed the common sense approach of the TUC to discover what the conditions of entry would be, and what safeguards could be secured for Britain's special interests before a final decision was made on whether to join the Market or not. The LTS, on the other hand, was opposed to entry regardless of the terms, arguing that the alleged economic benefits of membership could be achieved by increased trade with Commonwealth and developing countries, and that the Common Market was merely an extension of NATO in Europe and would increase the existing tension in Europe. Subsequently the TUC General Council formed the view that Common Market entry was not in the best interests of working people.

Incomes Policy

In February 1948 the government introduced a wage freeze, which received support from the 1949 Congress. In January 1950 the TUC held a conference of union executives to consider the General Council statement, *Trade Union Wages Policy*, which argued that the freeze policy should continue despite the likely inflationary consequences of the government having devalued the pound in 1949. The statement was accepted by 4.3 million votes to 3.6 million. The LSC voted in favour of the statement but on the condition that all other affiliated unions, particularly printing ones, kept to the policy. The TA did not register a vote at the conference. At the time, a wage claim by the ASLP related to a recent TA settlement had not been resolved. The TA understood the case for continuation of a wage freeze, but felt unable to support a policy that would deny the ASLP what had been conceded to it. In 1950 the government's wages freeze collapsed as prices increased faster than wages as a result of rising import prices caused by the 1949 devaluation and the outbreak of the Korean war. At the 1950 Congress the LSC and the TA supported an unsuccessful ETU motion that support for wage restraint should end because of falling living standards and declining craft differentials.

A Conservative government turned to a formal incomes policy in 1961 when it introduced a 'Pay Pause' whilst the details of a policy acceptable to the unions, employers and the government could be worked out. In 1963 the government proposed, as part of its policy, that a National Incomes Commission be established on which would be trade union representatives. The TUC decided not to participate in this body, arguing that expansionist economic policies were required and not wage restraint in another form. Both the TA and LTS supported this stance, particularly in the absence of restraint of other forms of incomes.

The October 1964 general election returned a Labour government committed to expansionist economic policies and a voluntary productivity, prices and incomes policy. In December 1964 the government announced the agreement of the TUC and the main employers' central bodies to a Declaration of Intent as to the policy, and in February 1965 the government announced its criteria for the movement in prices and incomes, including the establishment of a National Board for Prices and Incomes to which Bob Willis, the Joint General Secretary of the NGA was appointed. In the latter half of 1965 the voluntary productivity, prices and incomes policy began to experience difficulties. To head off government intentions to tighten the policy, in November 1965 the TUC proposed the introduction of an early warning procedure under which affiliated unions would give prior notification to the TUC of any impending claims regarding wages and working conditions and unions would refrain from pursuing any such claims until they had been examined by a TUC Incomes Policy Committee. The NGA was sympathetic to this idea, having voted at the 1965 Congress against a motion rejecting a prices and incomes policy but having supported one acknowledging that an incomes and prices policy was essential but calling the government's attention to the plight of the lower paid.

However, the voluntary productivity, prices and incomes policy continued to experience difficulties and in July 1966 the government introduced a statutory policy under which there was to be a freeze on income increases for the next six months to be followed by a further six months of severe restraint. Under the Prices and Incomes Act (1966) a union and employer were to submit claims to the minister within seven days of their notification or be subject to a fine of £50. When a settlement was reached, the employer, on the payment of a fine, was obliged to report this to the minister. Once the settlement had been notified, there was to be a thirty-day standstill on its implementation. If during those thirty days the minister decided to refer the matter to the National Board for Prices and Incomes there was to be a further three months' standstill on the settlement of any claim that was outstanding and during that standstill period it would not be permisssible for either the employer or the union or anyone associated with the union to attempt to influence the settlement of the claim. They were to be subjected to fines – as far as the employer was concerned to an unlimited amount or, as far as the union or members of the unions were concerned, to a maximum sum of £500.

The 1966 NGA Delegate Meeting rejected this policy and over-whelmingly supported an emergency motion: 'whilst supporting the underlying principles of a Prices, Incomes and Productivity Policy, the NGA Triennial Delegate Meeting is opposed to the introduction of legislation which will impose penalties upon trade unions that fail to notify claims or settlements to governmental authorities.'[4] At the 1966 Congress the NGA again supported the principle of a voluntary prices, incomes and productivity policy, even to the extent of on occasion acquiescing in a freeze, but voted against any form of legislative compulsion. It argued that the corollary of voting against legislative compulsion was the acceptance of a voluntary policy, for the only other alternative was to reject economic planning altogether. The NGA was prepared to recognise and accept that the 'freeze and severe restraint' policy of the government was essential to deal with the immediate economic crisis. Nevertheless, it viewed the powers the government had secured to enforce the policy a most serious threat to the principles of free collective bargaining and should be revoked as soon as the immediate economic crisis was over.

In November 1966 the TUC General Council issued a statement concerning a long-term incomes policy. Its main proposal was that each year the General Council should produce a review of economic prospects, indicating what general level of pay increase would be appropriate in the following year and the circumstances in which deviations from that figure would be justified. Following the publication of an economic review, a conference of affiliated unions should be convened to consider the TUC's incomes policy proposals. A conference was held in March 1967 and overwhelmingly endorsed the TUC proposals. The NGA, however, voted against the TUC's own incomes policy mechanisms, arguing that it saw the exercise as no more than a facade of TUC independence behind which the reality was government compulsion. This was consistent with NGA policy of supporting a prices and incomes policy but opposing government powers of compulsion.

The first of the TUC's economic reviews was published towards the end of 1967 and recommended that for the period mid-1968 to mid-1969 national wage settlements should not exceed 3.5 per cent with another 1.5 per cent allowed for wages drift. In February 1968 the NGA considered favourably the TUC's economic review, recognising it as a realistic attempt to deal with the current economic situation. However, for the NGA success would depend to a large extent on the TUC's ability to persuade the government to adopt the measures it was proposing. Moreover, the NGA was prepared to back TUC policy only with reservations. The first was that the government should accept the TUC's proposals for vetting wage claims. A second that the TUC should recognise the legitimate claims of craftsmen on the question of differentials and not seek to reject claims from craft unions on the grounds that they would militate against the interests of lower-paid workers. A third reservation was that the TUC should accept the necessity for more flexibility with regards to the proposed permitted percentage increase in weekly pay. A fourth NGA reservation was that the government should act with more resolution to restrict increases in prices and dividends and that the TUC should press the government more vigorously than in the past to ensure that such action was taken. The NGA forcibly argued these points to a conference of union executives held in February 1968 and, although the economic review was accepted, it was by such a small majority that the TUC's voluntary prices and incomes policy was really no longer credible.

In February 1969 the NGA again decided to back the TUC voluntary prices and incomes guidelines in the light of the TUC's economic review for 1969/70 but with the same reservations as in 1968. However, the NGA decided to continue its policy that until the government withdrew its statutory regulation it was not prepared to cooperate with the system of clearing wage claims with the TUC and then the final settlement with the government. The introduction by a Labour government of a compulsory productivity, prices and incomes policy had led Bob Willis in 1967 to resign from the National Board for Prices and Incomes and return to the Joint General Secretaryship of the NGA. In the June 1970 general election the Labour government lost office and the incoming Conservative government rejected a prices and incomes policy as an instrument of managing the economy.

Industrial Relations Legislation

The NGA also gave loyal support to the TUC in its opposition to attempts by the Labour government in 1969 and the Conservative government in 1970/1 to change the legal framework in which trade unions operated. In 1965 the Labour government established a Royal Commission to examine the UK industrial relations system.[5] The Commission (generally referred to as the Donovan Commission) reported in 1968 and advocated few major changes to the existing industrial relations legal framework. In January 1969 the Labour government issued a White Paper entitled *In Place of Strife* setting out proposals based largely on the Donovan Report for an industrial relations Act.

The TUC accepted that many of the government's proposals would strengthen collective bargaining and promote trade union objectives. However, there were four proposals to which the TUC, and the NGA, took particular exception. These were those that: would empower a minister to impose a twenty-eight-day 'conciliation pause' when in his opinion this was required and to enforce it by the Industrial Board imposing fines on workpeople who did not comply with an Order to return to work; would give a minister the right to force a union, under the threat of financial penalties, to conduct a ballot on the basis of a question decided not by the union but by the minister; would give an outside agency (the Industrial Board) acting under a Ministerial Order the power to impose financial penalties on a union which refused to comply with a recommendation that it should, in the case of an inter-union dispute over recognition, be excluded from recognition; and would, under threat of a financial penalty, compel trade unions to register their rules and to include in those rules provisions that would require approval of an outside agency. In March 1969 the government introduced a Bill to Parliament to give effect to the 'penal provisions' outlined above. This was met by a storm of protest from the whole trade union movement, including the NGA.

The NGA General Secretary spelt out the union's opposition to the government's proposed legislation to the 1969 Delegate Meeting. He made it clear that the NGA opposed the legislation not because it wished to curb unofficial/unconstitutional strike action, which the NGA accepted as harmful to the economy and trade unions, but because the NGA believed that if trade union reforms were needed the movement should be allowed to put its house in order first before the government intervened with legislative measures. The NGA also opposed the government's action on the principle that imposing legal sanctions on trade unions and their members, no matter how mild initially, could be the thin end of the wedge in the future to much wider and more stringent control of trade union activity. The NGA committed itself to a policy that any attempt by the government to impose legal sanctions on its members would be met by a reaction from the shop floor.

The government agreed to reconsider its proposals if the TUC could present viable alternatives. In response to this challenge the TUC issued a document entitled *Programme for Action*, which proposed increased powers for the TUC over its affiliates with respect to unofficial, unconstitutional and inter-union disputes. The TUC was to be notified of any dispute which involved large numbers of workers. Where only small numbers would be involved the unions concerned were still to inform the TUC unless they were confident the dispute could be settled without wider repercussions. There were to be no official strikes about inter-union disputes until the TUC had carried out an investigation and unofficial strikers in such disputes were to be instructed to return to work. Where a TUC enquiry into a dispute was necessary, a TUC committee would make recommendations for settling the dispute, or if there was an inter-union issue it would give a ruling which the union concerned could ignore only at the risk of being expelled from Congress. These proposals, with the NGA voting in favour, were accepted by a special TUC Congress held on 5 June 1969. On 18 June the government decided to withdraw its 'penal' legislation following the TUC General Council giving a 'solemn and binding undertaking' that it would deliver the proposals contained in *Programme for Action*. However, the Labour government was defeated in the June 1970 general election and replaced by a Conservative government pledged to introduce radical changes to the legal framework of the UK industrial relations system.

The new government presented its proposed industrial relations legislation, which subsequently became the Industrial Relations Act (1971), in December 1970. From the outset the TUC expressed opposition to the proposals and began a campaign of education and protest. This culminated in a massive demonstration held in London, in which the NGA was well represented, when thousands of trade union members marched in protest. The TUC held a special Congress on 18 March 1971 at which it put forward seven recommendations to neutralise the possible industrial impact of the government's proposals. These were: a requirement to deregister; seeking an assurance from the Labour Party on the repeal of the Act by a future Labour government; all collective agreements should embody a non-legally binding clause; strict observance of the Bridlington principles; non-cooperation with statutory bodies set up under the Act – for example, the National Industrial Relations Court and the Commission on Industrial Relations; assistance to unions by the TUC General Council to meet the costs of actions brought against unions for contravention of the Industrial Relations Act; and united action by affiliated unions to support these recommendations. The NGA supported all these recommendations except the last. Its own suggestion for a 'day of protest' against the Act was rejected by the special Congress.

The NGA acted to conform with the TUC policy. The NGA viewed the Act as a piece of deliberately calculated legislation designed to weaken the unions in relation to the employers and commercial interests generally. The NGA adopted the policy that, if any employers, employers' organisations, or the government invoked any of the provisions of the 1971 Act to the detriment of NGA members, steps would be taken to protect them, including the union being in technical breach of the law.[6]

The NGA found itself in a unique and difficult position, because of the need to change an 'unalterable' rule in the NGA Rule Book referring to the 'hypothecation' of investment income, when it sought to comply with the TUC's advice that affiliated unions should deregister under the Act. Legal opinion, submitted through the TUC's legal advisers, told the NGA that it had no alternative but to remain a registered union. A second opinion confirmed this view. In 1972 the NGA saw no option but to resign from the TUC, as it could not comply with the TUC's policy on registration. It was not to return until 1976. In resigning, the NGA assured the TUC that its opposition to the Industrial Relations Act remained unabated and it would not use its continued registration to the detriment of any other union. In return, the NGA expected that no other union would act to the detriment of the NGA by its continued registration.

Why did the NGA and its founding unions project a low profile in the TUC over the period 1948 to 1976? First, the NGA was successfully able to protect the industrial interests of its members without the need for support from wider movement. Its members controlled the 'key points' in the production process. Through the operation of the pre-entry closed shop, the union was able to balance the numbers of individuals who could gain access to training to acquire the skills required for these 'key' jobs in the production process. It was almost impossible for employers to recruit an alternative workforce. The NGA and its predecessors had considerable bargaining power and were capable of 'winning' industrial battles on their own. There was little industrial pressure to develop industrial relationships with unions outside the industry.

Second, over the period 1948 to 1976 NGA was usually able to accommodate inter-union problems stemming from the impact of the introduction of new technology on a voluntary agreed basis. Accommodation between the craft unions in the industry was met by closer working agreements, agreed demarcation formulas and mergers. Usually the print unions resolved their differences themselves or via the P&KTF without the need for assistance from the TUC.

Third, the demarcation lines between the printing industry and those of other industries remained fairly clear over the period 1948 to 1976. Although the lines were gradually becoming less clear, the boundaries remained relatively distinct. As a result the print unions had little day-to-day contact with non-print unions. This mitigated against the development of relationships with the wider trade union movement.

In short, over the period to 1976 the NGA and its founding unions operated successfully in the industrial arena in relative isolation from other TUC affiliates. Nevertheless the need to be part of a wider trade union movement was accepted, as the union could not at the end of the day isolate itself completely from the wider union perspective. After all, the TUC was consulted by government and if the NGA was not part of the TUC then the NGA view of the industry would not figure in the trade union movement's collective response to any government calls for a union view on the printing industry, or industry generally.

RESIGNATION FROM AND RE-AFFILIATION TO THE TUC, 1972–6

The TUC recommendation to affiliated unions not to register under the Industrial Relations Act (1971) also asked unions, before they decided to apply for registration or took steps to remain registered, to inform the General Council of its reasons for doing so. In considering this recommendation the NGA was conscious that at the March 1971 Special Congress there were differences on the issue in that some unions had declared their intention to register. The NGA also took into account that deregistration meant that in any industrial action it exposed itself to the unlimited penalties under the law and precluded itself from seeking agency shops under which all employees, except under very limited circumstances, would have to pay a contribution to the union or a charity regardless of whether they were a union member or not. There were also financial considerations, for a non-registered union would lose the protection of the Income Tax and Corporation Tax Act (1970) under which the NGA had hypothecated the Provident Fund and thereby received tax advantages.

The National Council decided on a membership ballot on the question of registration. However, before this could be done the NGA was hit in September 1971 by what was described as a legal 'bombshell' in the shape of the opinion from Professor Wedderburn, handed to the NGA via the TUC, that it could not deregister anyway because the rule hypothecating income for provident benefits and tax relief on that income was unchangeable.[7]

The NGA's own counsel confirmed the TUC view. If the NGA sought deregistration it would be acting unlawfully, not under the 1971 Act, but at common law. Counsel advised the NGA that in considering its attitude to registration it must bear in mind certain basic principles. First, the NGA could act only according to its rules. Second, its funds were held in broad terms in trust for the existing members in accordance with existing rules. Third, the NGA rules could be amended only in accordance with rules.

In legal terms the NGA held a special, if not unique, position in the trade union movement, in that since 1953 all investment income had been hypothecated to provide benefits, whether or not the income was spent in the current year or carried forward for use in future years. As a result all investment income had enjoyed tax relief. To ensure that income that had been exempted from tax could not (by change of rule) be used in later years for non-provident benefit purposes the Inland Revenue had required that the appropriate rule should be made unalterable. The NGA was further advised that this tax exemption could continue only if it remained a trade union registered under the Industrial Relations Act (1971), that members were entitled under the rules to provident benefit, and that any application to deregister would amount to a breach of trust. The NGA counsel's advice concluded,

> In short, as the rules stand today in the opinion of leading counsel, junior counsel and in my own opinion, the Association would not be acting lawfully if application was made for deregistration and it would be open to the trustees and any member entitled to provident benefits to take steps to prevent such an application being made.

Deregistration would have given rise not only to legal problems but to a serious financial situation. The NGA was advised that on deregistration it would have to put aside funds for the funeral benefit and superannuation grant. In the case of funeral benefit this sum was estimated to be about £2 million and in the case of superannuation about £1.5 million plus a further £1 million to meet obligations under the electrotypers and the litho printers' superannuation funds. The effect would have been the virtual disappearance of all the NGA's financial reserves of £5 million.

The NGA considered possible escape routes from its position (of rule 53) but concluded that none were practical. Attention was given to dissolving the union which required the assent in writing of five-sixths of the members on a particular day in the year. With the Industrial Relations Act in existence, if the union was dissolved there was the possibility that some members might not join the new union, since the Act gave employees the statutory right to be a union member or a non-unionist. In addition to this danger, there were all the complications of actually dissolving the union, for example the temporary disposition of assets. A further escape route considered was an uncertainty in the Act. On the one hand it was unlikely that the Registrar would feel able to deregister the NGA, for the reasons outlined above. On the other hand, the Act provided that the Registrar 'shall de-register a union if he is requested to do so'. Some argued that the Registrar might agree to a deregistration request and leave the situation open to any NGA member to challenge it at law. However, others considered that equally the Registrar might refuse deregistration or at best, noting the legal conflict in the Act with respect to registration, refer the matter to the High Court for judgment. Whichever course the Registrar decided upon, once started the process could not be stopped. It was too risky to rely on the Registrar accepting the NGA request for deregistration, and leaving it to members to challenge the decision.

Whilst all this was going on the TUC was badgering the NGA to tell it what it intended to do about registration. The NGA feared that the TUC did not understand its difficulties, and decided to ask the General Council its view on the deregistration 'bombshell', particularly in view of the decision taken at the 1971 Congress that unions should be instructed to deregister instead of being 'strongly advised'. However, despite the 1972 Delegate Meeting voting in favour of deregistration subject to confirmation by a ballot of the membership, the NGA was suspended from Congress in the summer of 1972 because of its failure to apply for deregistration. The NGA, supported by a delegate meeting decision, was recommending to members that the union should deregister. When no reply to the protest had been received by August 1972, the NGA boycotted the 1972 Congress. The General Secretary told the delegates,

We are not a union that normally allows anyone to push us around. We have put up with a lot from the TUC over deregistration because of our traditional loyalty to the wider trade union movement which the TUC are supposed to represent. But enough is enough – and that is why we are boycotting Congress this year. The issue of de-registration will now be decided by our members – the only people who have the ultimate right to do. Anyway the TUC, like the rest of us, will now have to await their decision.[8]

The complicated financial and legal matters surrounding the deregistration issue had taxed the National Council for over twelve months, but eventually they submitted an emergency motion to the 1972 Delegate Meeting recommending deregistration.[9] However, the delegates refused to accept the National Council motion as an emergency on the grounds that there were already three motions on the agenda dealing with the question of deregistration and that an emergency did not exist simply because the National Council had only recently come to a decision on deregistration. The 1972 Delegate Meeting overwhelmingly carried a composite motion moved by London and seconded by the Kent branch which instructed the National Council to continue its support of TUC policy on the Industrial Relations Act. The National Council supported the composite motion on two conditions: first, a ballot vote of the members should be held and, second, in that ballot all aspects of the deregistration issue and all the information available should be put to the members. The Council stressed that its support for deregistration was not legal and financial but that the union should ally itself with TUC policy as part of its opposition to the Act. To ignore the TUC instruction would result in the NGA's expulsion from that body and lay it open to the charge of disloyalty to the UK trade union movement. The NGA was also conscious that Sogat, Natsopa and Slade had all deregistered and it wished to be in line with the other printing unions. The case against deregistration rested on the possible financial consequences of such action and the impact that this would have on the industrial effectiveness of the NGA. However, the National Council considered that these financial considerations should not take priority. The General Secretary told delegates,

> What is more the Council are confident that in the final analysis, if the financial consequences predicted by the best advice were to happen we are sure our members will not hesitate to put their hands in their pockets – and put them in deep – to repair the position because of their detestation of this Act and those who were responsible for its introduction.[19]

Following the 1972 Delegate Meeting the ballot of members was held on the question of deregistration. In spite of recommendations for deregistration from the National Council and the delegate meeting, 32,770 members voted against the recommendation and 30,630 for – a majority of 2,140. The National Council had no alternative but to accept the decision of the membership and remain a registered trade union. The ballot result left the NGA with the choice of awaiting expulsion from the TUC or tendering its resignation. The NGA decided that the only honourable course of action was to resign. Subsequently a similar situation arose with the STUC, and the NGA resignation was also tendered to that body.

The Labour government taking office in March 1974 pledged to repeal the Industrial Relations Act. Once this was known, in May 1974 the NGA applied to re-affiliate to the TUC. It had been outside the TUC for eighteen months, during which time it functioned well. But the NGA considered this an unimportant point. However, the deregistration issue had remained an extremely divisive and disruptive issue inside the NGA's National Council and throughout the active membership, assuming a greater importance than any other during this difficult period. It was a matter of principle that the NGA be affiliated to the TUC. The NGA was confident that its application for re-affiliation would be accepted because, registration apart, it had taken a tougher line in practical opposition to the Industrial Relations Act than most other unions. It had refused to attend the National Industrial Relations Court on three occasions and Industrial Tribunals numerous times and had rebutted approaches from the Registrar about changes to its rules required as a registered union, insisting that only members could determine NGA rules. The NGA's record of opposition to the 1971 Act compared favourably with that of other unions.

However, the application for re-affiliation made remarkably slow progress. The NGA was told on a number of occasions that 'the matter is under active consideration by the General Council who are in touch with the affiliated unions in the printing industry'. Although the NUJ, the Wallpaper Workers' Union, Slade, the Scottish Graphical Association, Natsopa and the EETPU supported the NGA re-affiliation, Sogat expressed opposition. Sogat was influenced by its inter-union conflicts with the NGA. In the middle of 1974, at the suggestion of the Secretary of State for Employment, the NGA and Sogat agreed to talks under the auspices of ACAS to resolve their outstanding difficulties, particularly in London, over photocomposition and the manning of litho machines. However, the first meeting did not take place until early 1975, when Sogat indicated that it would no longer respect traditional union demarcation lines. The NGA told Sogat that any accommodation it was prepared to make to protect Sogat interests had to be in the context of Sogat assurances that it would cease to challenge the NGA's jurisdictional position. In the absence of such assurances, the NGA questioned the value of the ACAS talks. The NGA then received a letter from the TUC in which it was told that, if, like Sogat, it would undertake in advance to accept any ACAS decision, this would carry 'considerable weight with the TUC General Council in processing the

NGA's application for re-affiliation'. For the NGA, its difficulties with Sogat were irrelevant to the question of re-affiliation, and under no circumstances would it engage in 'horse-trading' over union demarcation lines as the price for re-affiliation.

The NGA found the long delay in securing a reply to its re-affiliation application increasingly intolerable. In July 1975 the General Secretary wrote to the TUC stating that, if the NGA had not received a definitive reply by the time of the August 1975 National Council meeting, he would have no alternative but to recommend that the union notify the TUC that its re-affiliation application would be withdrawn. The NGA was called to a meeting on 21 July 1975 at which Sogat and TUC representatives were present, but at which the NGA was not required to discuss its re-affiliation in the presence of Sogat and at which NGA–Sogat differences would not be discussed. Immediately following the meeting the TUC offered the NGA re-affiliation on two conditions: first, that the NGA accept that any complaints by another affiliate against its behaviour whilst outside the TUC should be dealt with through the TUC Disputes Principles and Procedures; second, that the NGA should pay to the TUC the equivalent of the affiliation fees it would have paid had it not resigned from the TUC. This sum was estimated to be some £35,000.

Complying with the first condition gave no problems to the NGA, but it balked at the second, which it considered unfair as it was being asked to pay 'affiliation fees' for a period during which its re-affiliation was being blocked by other printing trade unions for their own reasons. The NGA also noted that the TUC, after much delay, had made a decisive decision on its re-affiliation when if the NGA were to return it would be too late to attend the 1975 Congress or to nominate for a place on the TUC General Council, given that Richard Briginshaw, who represented the printing unions on the General Council, was due to retire. The NGA was angered by the £35,000 price tag, which it considered was less favourable treatment than that given to those unions that had been expelled from the TUC, having made clear their intention to remain on the Register to take advantage of the Industrial Relations Act (1971), and that had immediately been accepted back into Congress in 1974. The NGA, in contrast had opposed the Act as forcefully as any other union, including other print unions. Following further discussions between the NGA and the TUC, the NGA was re-admitted in December 1975 on the payment of £42,000. Having rejoined the TUC, the NGA realised that with the faster introduction of new techniques it could no longer remain isolationist. It was determined not only to repair relationships but to play a more active role in the TUC.

THE YEARS OF HIGH PROFILE, 1976–89

Participation in Congress affairs

By 1989 the NGA was exercising an important influence on the evolution and development of TUC policy and strategy in many crucial areas, such as industrial training and the repeal of the employment legislation established by the Conservative governments in the 1980s. The period 1976–89, however, was also one in which relationships between the NGA and the TUC were at times severely strained. Particularly severe tensions were experienced over the TUC's attitude towards the NGA in the Messenger Newspaper Group dispute of 1983 and over the TUC's perceived tolerance towards the EETPU given that union's collaboration with News International in the Wapping dispute of 1986–7 (see Chapter 14).

The NGA's higher profile in the TUC has been seen in a number of ways. First, it has actively participated at the annual Congress in moving and seconding motions, contributing to the debates and questioning the General Council's report to Congress. Second, it gained representation on the General Council under reforms to membership of that body introduced in 1983, and its present General Secretary has participated in the work of its major standing committees. Third, the Association played a prominent role in the affairs of the TUC Printing Industries Committee and attempted to use the committee to ensure that a coordinated and unified approach was made to the problems confronting the printing industry. Fourth, it played a leading role in shaping the TUC's policy of practical opposition to the Conservative government's Employment Acts of 1980, 1982 and 1988 and the Trade Union Act (1984) and to the formulation of the industrial relations legal framework to replace these Acts when they are repealed by a future Labour government. Fifth, it campaigned vigorously to ensure that the TUC policy of opposition to the 1980s' Employment Acts agreed by a conference of executives of affiliated unions, held at Wembley in April 1982, was upheld. This stemmed from the NGA finding itself in 1983 to be the first TUC-affiliated union involved in a major confrontation with an employer using the Employment Act

(1982) against a union. Sixth, between 1986 and 1988 it played a leading role, along with Sogat (82), in attempting to ensure that the TUC enforced its rules over an affiliate – EETPU – whose behaviour in the News International dispute of 1986–7 the NGA considered to be totally unacceptable, detrimental to the good standing of trade unionism in that it had led to some 6,000 print workers being dismissed by the company. Seventh, over the period 1976–9 the NGA played a leading role in opposing certain aspects of the 'Social Contract' agreed between the TUC and the then Labour government. In this regard, relationships between the TUC and the NGA became particularly strained in 1977 when the NGA launched a campaign to improve the position of its lower-paid members. Eighth, the NGA played a prominent part in trying to reform the TUC Disputes Procedures and Principles on the grounds that these did not recognise any particular work or occupation as the prerogative of any one union but operated on the basis that any affiliated union was appropriate so long as it obtained the membership and the negotiating rights.

The NGA had not had an official of its own on the General Council since Bob Willis. After his resignation from the General Council on his appointment to the National Board for Prices and Incomes, the print unions were represented on the General Council by the Natsopa General Secretary, Richard Briginshaw. Following its re-admission to the TUC, the NGA was determined to regain a direct voice on the General Council. To this end it supported a Post Office Engineering Union motion to the 1981 Congress proposing automatic representation on the General Council based on a union's affiliated membership to the TUC. A union with 100,000–500,000 members was automatically to get one representative on to the General Council progressing up to unions with 1½ million members having five. The POEU motion was approved by a majority of nearly 1.3 million. Detailed proposals to implement this reform of the General Council were approved by the 1982 Congress and in 1983 the then NGA General Secretary, Joe Wade, automatically became a member of the General Council. Since the 1984 Congress, the current NGA General Secretary, Tony Dubbins, has played an active part in the work of the General Council and currently serves on its Economic, Education, Employment Policy and Organisation, and Education and Training committees. He is also a member of the General Council's Finance and General Purpose Committee. The 1981 General Council reforms also increased the number of seats reserved for women and the NGA sought in 1985 to increase its influence on the

General Council by nominating Brenda Philbin, one of its national officers, to one of these seats. The move proved unsuccessful and has not subsequently been attempted.

The NGA participated in the work of the TUC Printing Industries Committee which comprised twenty members plus two General Council representatives. Of the twenty members, six are representatives of the NGA. The NGA was prominent in the committee's work, which highlighted the industrial, structural and economic problems affecting the printing industry. One of the more important issues facing the PIC in the early 1980s was the industry's economic difficulties stemming from the government's economic policies. In 1981 the committee produced a document entitled *Prospects for Print: Difficulties Facing the Printing Industry*, which considered the serious problems facing the industry, particularly with regard to exchange and interest rates, energy policies, unfair international competition, employment and investment.

The PIC had a Health and Safety Sub-Committee which met regularly and, in conjunction with the TUC guidelines for the training of safety representatives, developed guidelines specifically for the printing industry. In the mid-1980s it expressed grave concern at government cutbacks in the role of the Health and Safety Executive and the detrimental effects this would have for the government's Inspectorate in monitoring workplace health and safety standards.

The committee investigated the development of free newspapers and their effect upon unionised members working for paid-for newspapers. A meeting between PIC representatives and the Association of Free Newspapers took place in 1985 at which the latter supplied factual information about 'free' newspapers. The Association is not an employers' association and as such it felt unable to participate in industrial relations discussions. However, informal contracts are maintained between the committee and the Association so as to keep each other up to date with developments in this particular sector of the industry.

The NGA sought to encourage a common PIC attitude towards the organisation of print union workers employed on printing work in various establishments, including banks, universities and local authorities. Although the PIC coordinated joint action by the printing unions to achieve recognition at T. Bailey Foreman of Nottingham and D. C. Thomson of Dundee, the unions were unable to normalise organisation in these establishments. In 1985 a new daily national newspaper, *Today*, was launched by News (UK) Ltd, which had offered a 'single-union

NGA 1982: J. Wade – General Secretary
A. D. Dubbins – Joint Assistant General Secretary
J. Jackson – Joint Assistant General Secretary
(former General Secretary of SLADE)

J. M. Bonfield   Joint General Secretary (1964–69)
General Secretary (1969–76)

R. Willis   Joint General Secretary (1964–69)

J. F. Wade   General Secretary (1976–82)

F. Simmons   General President (1964–76)

L. S. Dixon   General President (1976–82)

J. B. Griffiths   General President (1982 to present)

J. A. Ibbotson   Assistant General Secretary
(1985 to present)

C. James   Financial Secretary (1979 to present)

A. Parish   National Secretary (1982 to present)

Current National Officials:

G. Colling

C. W. Harding

G. Jerrom

E. Martin

Ms. B. Philbin

F. G. Tanner

J. Willats

B. Willoughby

Current Regional Officials:

D. L. Walker   Northern Regional Officer

T. Burke Northern Regional Officer (elect)

P. Ellis   South-Eastern Regional Officer

T. W. Stalker   South-Eastern
Assistant Regional Officer

D. A. Install   Midland and North Wales
Regional Officer

M. P. Martill   Midland and North Wales
Assistant Regional Officer

F. H. Golledge   South-Western and South Wales
Regional Officer

P. J. Harris   South-Western and South Wales
Assistant Regional Officer

N. S. Broughall   Irish Regional Officer

N. F. Robbins   London Regional Officer

Current National Council:

J. Anderson

M. Appleby

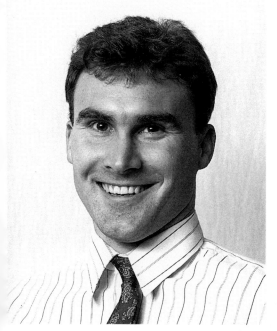

S. Attwill

W. G. Bailey

D. Baker

J. Beck

H. Capel

A. Carr

R. G. Chizlett

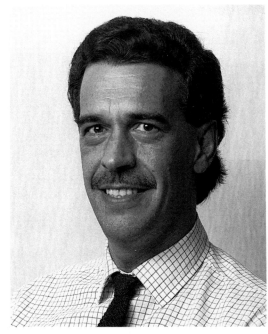

J. C. Clifford

D. Douglas

M. A. Duncalfe

K. Gardner

M. K. Griffiths

D. Hargreaves

M. J. Holland

T. Howley

R. Hughes

R. P. Hutchison

A. Kavanagh

T. Lyons

D. Marsh

J. McHugh

T. Pilling

K. Price

R. Pritchard.

E. Saltmarsh

E. G. Smith

A. Speed

M. Talbot

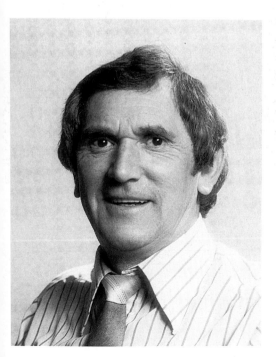

P. Taylor

agreement' with the EETPU. The PIC attempted to achieve a united approach to this situation, as the single-union agreement challenged the traditional position of the closed shop for production workers in the industry and had implications for trade union rights and employment conditions in the industry. It was hoped that the EETPU would reconsider the News (UK) Ltd agreement and join a common union approach to the company on union recognition and negotiating rights. The EETPU indicated that, although it favoured a joint approach, there had been little effort to achieve such approaches in the past, a situation they claimed was due mainly to the attitude of the NGA. However, over this particular issue the electricians said they were not prepared for a joint approach. The *Today* newspaper was not successful and was subsequently bought by News International; the union organisation on the paper is presently far from clear.

In the late 1980s the PIC met infrequently, not least because of strained relationships between the printing unions as the newspaper employers implemented new technology. But also, following the merger of Natsopa with Sogat, and Slade with the NGA, the number of production unions was reduced to two. On the occasions it did meet, much time was spent considering the committee's future. A number of unions expressed reservations about the need still existing for such a committee. The NGA thought the committee was not really addressing the issues confronting the industry in the late 1980s and early 1990s. The committee now meets quarterly, but remains relatively inactive. However, an area of activity in recent years has been the coordination of the industry's campaign against government threats to impose VAT on books, periodicals and newspapers.

At the 1978 Congress the NGA played a major role in getting Congress to review its procedures for settling inter-union disputes. The background to this was the growth of alternative sources of print origination work, particularly the rise of in-plant printing houses,[11] and foreign companies establishing new enterprises in the UK and giving sole bargaining rights to another union in spite of a national agreement defining certain areas of the operation to the NGA. The NGA policy towards membership rights in these alternative sources of print origination was to avoid falling foul of the TUC Bridlington principles for determining membership rights. These provide no union with sole rights to organise staff in a particular industry or trade category, or to claim sole rights to particular areas of work. They permit any union to organise in any industry or trade category where there is the prospect of that union recruiting non-union workers and obtaining sole negotiating rights. It was possible under Bridlington to have, for example, USDAW organising printing workers and the NGA organising shop workers.

In the NGA's view, the Bridlington rules were outdated and incapable of taking into account the major changes which had occurred in various industries through changing production methods. New technology was bringing dramatic changes to the printing industry (two of which were a movement of work into a 'new alternative' printing industry and the blurring of boundaries between the printing industry and other industries). The NGA argued, along with other printing unions, that a policy of 'prescribing the rights of members of particular unions to particular work' would be a better basis for the TUC to deal with inter-union disputes and problems stemming from the introduction of new technology. To this end it submitted to the 1978 Congress a successful resolution calling for a review of the Bridlington principles and for a report to be made to the 1979 Congress by the General Council with recommendations for improving the resolution of inter-union disputes. The NGA stressed that, in inter-union disputes, the TUC should look at the problems faced by unions, particularly single-industry ones, through the implementation of new technology. In submitting revised Bridlington principles to the 1979 Congress, the General Council argued that technological change made it difficult for the TUC to contemplate 'prescriptive rights to particular work'. Although some amendments were introduced to the Bridlington principles, e.g. with respect to sole negotiating rights and union membership agreements, they did not take on board the principle of prescriptive rights for particular work and fell short of what the NGA sought to achieve.

The NGA also played a prominent role at the 1985 Congress in seeking amendments to the Bridlington rules when it seconded a successful motion instructing the General Council to amend its inter-union disputes procedures to debar single-union agreements that exclude other unions which have existing recognition and negotiation rights. In doing this the NGA was influenced by the single-union agreement signed by the EETPU with News (UK) Ltd and described above. The NGA argued that single-union agreements stood trade union principles on their head, since under such agreements it was not the workers who decided who represented them but the employers. It also opposed such agreements on the grounds that they frequently involved unions in bidding against each other for recognition, often with adverse consequences for employment conditions not only for the workers covered by such agreements but for other members of the union employed elsewhere. Following the Congress, the Bridlington rules were amended to require that no union should enter into a sole negotiating agreement or any other form of agreement in any circumstances where other unions would be deprived of their existing rights of recognition or negotiation, except by prior consultation and agreement of the other unions concerned.

Nevertheless, there were occasions in the 1980s when the NGA protected its membership and negotiating rights through the Bridlington machinery. A notable such case occurred in 1982 when a TUC Disputes Committee ruled in favour of the NGA in a disagreement with Sogat over the negotiating rights and union membership of lithographers at the Glasgow establishment of Holmes McDougall. When a long-running dispute led the company to threaten closure, the TUC became involved. The NGA argued that, under the 1976 Perth Agreement, four machines and their operators should be the preserve of the NGA, and this was accepted by the TUC, which ruled that Sogat (82) should facilitate the transfer of membership to NGA of any of the four workers involved.[12]

Incomes Policy

In July 1975 the TUC entered into a voluntary wage restraint policy with a Labour government under which a universal pay rise limit of £6 per week was to operate from 1 August 1975 and under which a twelve-month interval between major pay increases would operate. The NGA was outside the TUC when this agreement was made but it had been re-admitted by the time the TUC needed to consider whether it should cooperate in a second phase of voluntary wages restraint. In 1976 the TUC and the government agreed that for the period 1 August 1976 to 31 July 1977 pay increases should be restricted to 5 per cent per annum with a minimum of £2.50 and a maximum of £4 per week increases, and that the twelve-month interval between pay increases should continue. A TUC special conference held in June 1976 approved this policy by 9.3 million to 0.5 million. The NGA representatives voted to support the policy but only after a very close vote in the pay policy debate at the June 1976 Delegate Meeting. By just three votes – 177 to 174 – an emergency motion in the name of the National Council on pay guidelines for 1976–7 had been defeated. The motion accepted the principle of a second phase of pay restraint, believing this to be essential if the rate of inflation were to be brought under control. However, it rejected the proposals agreed between the TUC and the government, which were to be considered by a special Congress set for 16 June 1975. The NGA's representatives to this Congress were instructed to seek changes to the TUC–government agreement which would provide some consolidation of the £6 paid under the first stage of the agreement, some move towards a restoration of differentials for skill and responsibility and provision for higher pay for higher productivity. The National Council motion was opposed by delegates who wanted total support for the agreed TUC–government policy and those who wanted a return to free collective bargaining. A further emergency motion, moved by London and seconded by the Liverpool branch, was rejected by 222 votes to 134. This called for a rejection of the pay policy guidelines reached between the TUC and the government and instructed NGA delegates to the June 1976 special Congress and all subsequent congresses held before the next NGA meeting to vote against such policies and in favour of all policies which gave recognition to responsibility, skills, productivity and the restoration of free collective bargaining. Although the rejection of these two emergency motions meant that there was no positive policy decision, the General Secretary, Joe Wade, told delegates that their decision could be construed in no other way than that the NGA should support the TUC General Council at the special Congress. The view was then endorsed overwhelmingly by delegates by a show of hands.[13]

In 1977, the government sought a third stage of pay restraint. The 1977 congress supported the twelve-month interval between major wage awards but rejected a government suggestion that pay movements over the period 1 August 1977 to 31 July 1978 be restricted to a 10 per cent increase on annual earnings. However, prior to the Congress the NGA had declared against the twelve-month interval and the 10 per cent limit on increases in earnings. The NGA appreciated the TUC view that the twelve-month 'rule' would help to ensure an orderly return to free collective bargaining and to avoid a pay explosion, but nevertheless felt that steps had to be taken quickly to alleviate the position of its lower-paid members (see below). The 10 per cent increase in earnings limit was opposed because it meant basic rate settlements of around 4–6 per cent.

Although the TUC was committed to opposing the continuation of the government pay policy over the period 1 August 1977 to 31 July 1978, the situation which developed during that period led some to believe that there was a tacit acceptance by the TUC leadership of the government's guidelines. In reality, the NGA, along with almost every other affiliated union, had to accept the 10 per cent guidelines in spite of its intention to have nothing more to do with pay policy after 31 July 1977. The government sought to extend its control over wage movements beyond 1 August 1978 by seeking to impose a 5 per cent pay increase limit at a time when inflation was at 8 per cent and rising. The trade union movement rejected support for this policy, which collapsed in the face of a number of low-paid worker strikes in the winter of 1978/9. By 1978 the NGA concluded that the time had come for the TUC to stop playing the role of policeman, either overtly or tacitly, over its affiliated unions in respect of incomes policy, and that any further government interference in wage bargaining should not be tolerated.

At the 1977 TUC Congress the NGA argued that one of the worst anomalies of the pay restraint policies operating between 1 August 1975 and 31 July 1977 was that they had widened the gap between the high- and the low-paid worker. The NGA even went so far as to suggest that it might well have found it possible to support the continuation of the twelve-month rule if some provision had been made for the lower-paid worker. Although the NGA was greatly concerned with the restoration of differentials and real monetary incentives to increase productivity, its immediate concern was for its lower-paid members. To this end the NGA in September 1977 launched a campaign in a restricted arena to improve the lot of its members receiving less than £55 per week gross pay. Despite a considerable amount of scepticism expressed by branches, the NGA pressed ahead with its campaign with enthusiasm. The NGA was not seeking a confrontation with either the TUC or the government, but was looking for improvements for its lower-paid members, who formed a small percentage of its total membership. The success of the campaign could be judged by the fact that, when it was suspended in February 1978, 2,400 members in fifty-nine branches, covering 395 firms, had received increases of up to, and in some cases more than, 7 per cent. Its success could also be judged in that the NGA came under heavy pressure to end the campaign not only from the BPIF but also from the TUC in respect of the twelve-month rule, and from the government. It was in response to these pressures that the NGA suspended its low-paid campaign.

The NGA resented these pressures. It had loyally supported phases 1 and 2 of the wage restraint policy and in 1977 accepted the continuation of the twelve-month rule for the great majority of its members, although it had voted against the rule at the 1977 Congress. In 1977 it had made a moderate settlement with the BPIF and the Newspaper Society and all other employers' organisations with which it held agreements. By early 1978 the government had persuaded the miners to settle within the 10 per cent guidelines and to accept the twelve-month rule. Given that the miners – a union with the industrial muscle to breach the guidelines – were prepared to stay within the pay policy, the NGA feared it could isolate itself from the TUC. In addition, the time was approaching for the renegotiation of the BPIF and the Newspaper Society national agreement, which covered the majority of its members who had not had a rise for a period of twelve months. The 1978 BPIF/Newspaper Society–NGA wage basis agreement contained provision for a series of talks on a number of issues between the parties, which were to be completed during the lifetime of the agreement. Amongst these was the question of removing low pay from the industry on a permanent basis. In suspending the lower-paid wages campaign the NGA had advised the employers that its reintroduction would depend almost entirely upon whether or not it would be possible to enter into constructive negotiation during the period of a new wage basis agreement and which would provide a comprehensive and permanent solution to the problem of NGA lower-paid members. This had been achieved and was a major reason for delegates to the 1978 Delegate Meeting rejecting an emergency motion from Liverpool branch deploring the suspension of the lower-paid campaign following pressure from the Department of Employment and the TUC and calling for it to recommence, with a £65 basic wage being the objective.

Industrial Relations Legislation

In 1979 a Conservative government was elected that was committed to introduce legislation to curb the alleged abuse of industrial power by trade unions against employers and individual workers. It outlined a 'step-by-step' approach by which the government would 'gradually' reform trade union law. The Employment Act (1980) limited the lawful ability of unions to mount industrial action, including picketing, placed restrictions on the operation of the closed shop, diluted, and in some cases withdrew, important rights hitherto enjoyed by individual employees, and removed provisions designed to support collective bargaining.

The TUC vigorously opposed this legislation and at the 1979 TUC Congress the NGA had moved a motion committing the TUC *inter alia* to mount a campaign of opposition to the Conservative government's proposed employment laws. The 1980 Congress reasserted the movement's opposition to the government's legislation, but also endorsed the General Council's plans designed to neutralise the 1980 Employment Act. These plans included developing the TUC guidance to affiliated unions on the importance of maintaining existing agreements and arrangements with employers and on the need to compensate, as far as possible, through collective bargaining for the Act's reduction of employee's employment rights.

The NGA's attitude to the Employment Act (1980) was determined at its 1980 Delegate Meeting.[14] It confirmed the union's opposition to the legislation and instructed the National Council to resist any attempt by the courts to impose the Act against the NGA. The delegate meeting rejected the government's attempts to weaken or eliminate trade union immunity in trade disputes and endorsed the National Council's policy of maintaining the closed shop, of continuing to refuse to accept work from non-union sources and of maintaining the Fairs List. In addition, the NGA General Secretary, Joe Wade, spelt out to the delegates the necessary ingredients for a successful TUC policy against the Employment Act (1980). He saw such a policy being based on the principle that an attack on any one union was an attack on the whole movement and that the full resources of the movement would need to assist and support any union under attack under this legislation. It was the NGA's firm belief that no one union, however big, however strong, however loyal and determined its members may be, would be able to defend itself adequately in isolation against existing and any future legislation of the Conservative government.

On 23 November 1981 the Employment Secretary issued a consultative document setting out proposals for further restrictive trade union legislation, which covered unions' immunities during industrial action, the closed shop and dismissals during strikes. The government proposed to expose union funds to claims for damages as a result of 'unlawful' industrial action and severely to restrict the type of dispute which would be legitimate. The government proposed that non-unionists 'unfairly' dismissed as a result of enforcement of the closed shop should receive substantially increased financial compensation at the union's expense and to make the 'fairness' of any closed shop dismissal dependent on obtaining 'overwhelming' support from the employees concerned in periodic secret ballots. In addition to outlawing any arrangement or action to ensure that contract work was done only by unionised labour, the government proposed to reduce the statutory protection against selective dismissals during strikes. When the government published its Employment Bill in January 1982, its provisions closely followed the November 1981 consultative document.[15]

The goverment's proposals raised such serious implications for unions that the TUC thought it essential that the movement should as speedily as possible examine how practical expression could be given to opposition to the legislation and how the adverse effects of the proposed laws might be countered. It therefore convened a special conference of executives of affiliated unions at the Wembley Conference Centre on 5 April 1982 at which eight recommendations for practical opposition to the Employment Act (1980) and the 1982 Employment Bill (subsequently Act) were accepted. Under the first recommendation affiliated unions were to commit themselves to campaign among their members to highlight the dangers in the Employment Bill and to support the TUC's campaign against the proposed legislation. Under the second, affiliated unions were recommended not to hold or to participate in secret ballots on closed shops, whilst the third recommended that unions observe Congress policy and not seek or accept public funds for union ballots under the Employment Act (1980) ballot fund schemes. The fourth recommended that affiliated unions, when in dispute with an employer, should consult closely with other unions whose support might be necessary to make industrial action effective or whose interests might be affected by the action.

The fifth recommendation related to support from the trade union movement for an affiliated union faced by or experiencing legal action by an employer. Where the General Council received a request to assist a union in such situations, and it was satisfied that assistance from the movement was justified, it was empowered (1) to coordinate action by other affiliated unions in support of the union in difficulties, including, if necessary, calling for industrial action against the employer concerned or more widely; (2) to provide financial assistance to a union which experienced severe financial problems as a result of damaging actions. However the General Council stressed that this recommendation did not mean that a union encountering legal difficulties would automatically receive support from the TUC and other unions irrespective of the circumstances. First, support would only be given if requested and then the General Council would need to be satisfied that the union was justified in the action it was taking and it would expect the union to take full account of views it might express about the form and continuation of the action which was giving rise to the legal case. In addition, the General Council would need assurance as to the response from other parts of the union to the group of members whose action had given rise to the legal case, as it would be unreasonable for a union in difficulties to seek TUC help unless it had mobilised its own members and resources and had the support of other unions in the workplace affected.[16]

The sixth recommendation was that affiliated unions should continue to observe the requirements of the TUC Disputes Principles and Procedures, whilst the seventh recommendation was that no trade union member of an industrial tribunal should serve on cases arising from the application of a union membership agreement or arrangement. The final recommendation empowered the General Council to impose on all affiliated unions a levy of 10p per member to establish a Campaign and Defence Fund to meet financial commitments arising from the proposed legislation. The Council was also given authority to impose a further levy or levies if, in their view, this became necessary.

The NGA was particularly interested in the TUC policy of opposition since, although the Employment Acts would affect all unions, they would impinge on the NGA in particular. The 1980 and 1982 legislation, with its central provisions covering the closed shop, secondary action and refusal to handle work received from or going to non-unionists, went to the very heart of the industrial practices whereby the NGA had traditionally maintained and improved the pay and employment conditions of its members. At the Wembley conference the NGA had made it clear that it would wholeheartedly support the TUC campaign. It had some reservations about whether this went far enough and had some doubts about the interpretation which might be placed on the policy. The NGA advocated that the TUC use the Campaign and Defence Fund to assist unions that had their funds or property sequestered and/or that needed assistance from the movement to continue their organisation and not to fight the legislation in the courts. Despite these reservations, the NGA thought it essential that unions should act in unity and that strong leadership was forthcoming from the TUC. The 1982 NGA Delegate Meeting reaffirmed its opposition to the government legislation and reaffirmed the union's policy that it would respond industrially to any use of the law against the Association and its members.

The first real test of the trade union movement's practical opposition to the Employment Acts came with the NGA's dispute with the Messenger Newspaper Group, owned by Mr Eddie Shah, which began on 4 July 1983 when six NGA members withdrew their labour and were dismissed by the company.[17] The events surrounding the dispute are fully described in Chapter 14. In an attempt to bring the dispute to a successful conclusion the NGA in December 1983 called upon its members to undertake a twenty-four-hour stoppage throughout the printing industry on 14 December. The NGA which had kept the TUC fully apprised of the developing situation regarding the Messenger Dispute, called for a 'Statement of Support' for its proposed action in line with policy decided at the 1982 Wembley Conference.

The General Council's Employment Policy and Organisation Committee (EPOC) pledged its support. However the TUC General Secretary immediately announced to the national press and on television, that the EPOC decision did not mean that the TUC endorsed the NGA's proposed action, since subcommittees could not determine General Council policy. The endorsement of the NGA's action would be a matter for the General Council. He added that he would do all he could to overturn the EPOC recommendation when it was considered by the full TUC General Council. On 14 December 1983 the General Council referred back EPOC's recommendation that a 'sympathetic and supportive attitude' should be taken towards the NGA's proposed strike action, expressed concern about the development of the dispute and pledged financial support to the NGA. In the ensuing confusion the NGA called off the proposed twenty-four-hour stoppage, as in its view the General Council decision was a 'green light' to the employers to attack an NGA now isolated by the TUC. Although on 6 January 1984 the TUC granted the NGA £420,000 out of the Campaign and Defence Fund to pay its provident benefits, the Association reacted angrily as it considered this to be a 'gesture' of little value in pursuing the dispute. On 18 January 1984 the NGA reluctantly agreed to purge its contempt and abide by the injunctions that had been imposed on it by the courts. This action was taken reluctantly, but was considered necessary if the NGA was to maintain its essential work and to protect the interests of its membership as a whole.

In February 1984 the NGA had begun a campaign to reverse the General Council decision not to support its proposed one-day strike throughout the printing industry. It submitted a motion to the Scottish TUC held in April 1984 calling for a return to 'the principles' of the

Wembley conference. The STUC approved the motion, which also 'regretted decisions to give the NGA support to continue only to pursue "lawful activities" and considered this completely contrary to the policy adopted at Wembley in 1982, particularly Clause 5'. The 1984 TUC Congress also backed the NGA stand in the Messenger dispute, reaffirmed the Wembley conference decisions, and rejected the General Council's decision not to issue a statement of support for the NGA's proposed one-day stoppage. At the same time, Congress also passed by a small majority an amendment rejecting automatic support for unions forced to break the law to defend themselves and retaining flexibility for the General Council to decide the circumstances in which such support would be given. The NGA was concerned that Congress had not gone as far as it would have wished and that the TUC had failed to deliver at the first challenge to its policy of practical opposition to the Employment Acts of 1980 and 1982. It was little practical comfort to the NGA that Congress had criticised the General Council for its failure to give support to its proposed one-day printing industry strike. Nevertheless it had made and proved its point.

The NGA was convinced of its entitlement to support under the Wembley conference decisions, as the whole purpose of that conference had been to assure support and assistance to unions attacked by employers using the Employment Acts. The NGA did not deliberately set out to break the law. This had been thrust upon it by the new legislation making unlawful virtually every effective industrial action in which trade unions could engage. The TUC had been approached for two reasons. First, by late November 1983 the NGA realised it could not win the dispute without the wider trade union movement declaring its support, and, second, the 1982 Wembley conference decisions gave a forum in which to seek a clear statement of support from the TUC for the principles involved in the dispute and for its one-day stoppage. It was not asking for strikes by other affiliated unions but hoped that, by extending the dispute, printing employers would pressurise the Messenger Group to accommodate the NGA. However, with the issue of writs against the NGA by provincial newspapers and several general printing trade employers, the union wanted the backing of the TUC as notification to those employers that it was not acting in isolation from the trade union movement. Although NGA members would have answered the strike instruction without TUC support, they considered they were entitled to such a statement of support since in their eyes the strike was designed to force other employers to put pressure on the Messenger Group. If the strategy of coercing other employers to pressurise Messenger into making a settlement had been unsuccessful, the NGA would have had to review their tactics. It was felt that, even if the one-day strike failed, the disruption caused to the printing industry might be a sufficient deterrent for many employers to decide not to repeat the Messenger Group's action. The NGA accepted that unions could not receive automatic support under the Wembley decisions and it had not accepted the TUC's advice on mass picketing, but the TUC never advocated either of these issues as reasons for not supporting the NGA. The NGA still considered TUC support was warranted since it had been fined £675,000, its funds had been sequestrated, it had been punished for protecting fundamental trade union principles and had been fined for protecting its members' conditions. Tony Dubbins, the NGA General Secretary Elect, told the 1984 Congress, 'We're proud of our stand. We actually thought the movement would also have been proud to give support to a union carrying out Congress policy.'

Why then did the TUC General Council not respond positively to the NGA's request for a statement of support for its proposed one-day stoppage in the printing industry? There were those amongst the majority view on the General Council who felt the NGA could not win the dispute and did not merit support since there was no point in backing illegal, and potentially very costly, action which would not achieve its industrial objective. There were those who also argued that the closed shop was not *the* issue on which a stand against the Employment Acts should be made. However, the overriding reason was put by those who argued that to support the NGA would bring the TUC itself into contempt of court, and possible legal action from employers or even the Attorney General, and would severely embarrass the TUC by committing it to support 'unlawful' action, and may tempt the government to bring in legislation to restrict, limit, or interfere with the activities of the TUC itself. The opponents of the NGA's proposed action also argued that support under the Wembley decisions was conditional and that events had moved on since then. The decisions taken in April 1982 carried the strong hope that at the next election a Labour government, committed to repeal the Employment Acts, would take office. The re-election in June 1983 of a Conservative government pledged to further legislation against unions had frustrated this hope. The 1983 Congress had taken a policy decision which prescribed a policy of negotiations with the government with less emphasis on confrontation.

The General Council members who supported the NGA fell into two groups. There were those who gave the NGA support because the NGA merely required a statement of support. The second group interpreted the NGA's request to mean that eventually some industrial action by their own unions might be necessary and they were prepared to give support even though their unions might run foul of the law for doing so. The 1984 NGA Delegate Meeting, which was postponed to November because of the Messenger dispute, rejected, after a highly charged and dramatic debate, a motion from the Liverpool branch criticising the National Council for calling off its planned one-day strike after the TUC refused to give its support. A Liverpool delegate described the TUC behaviour as 'treachery' and argued that the NGA membership was ready and willing to heed the call but 'the call never came'. In a powerful defence of the National Council, the General Secretary Elect, Tony Dubbins, said that to have pressed ahead with the action would have been asking the membership to commit suicide, as they would have been left isolated.

The Delegate Meeting also criticised the behaviour of the TUC leadership for what many delegates clearly regarded as the betrayal of the Association. Two motions from the Liverpool branch – one condemning the 'treacherous outburst' from Len Murray, the TUC General Secretary, when he 'denounced' the TUC EPOC Committee decision to support the NGA, and the other criticising the majority of the General Council who voted to 'abandon' the NGA at a crucial juncture in the dispute – won support from the National Council and delegates. However, after an intervention by the General Secretary Elect, Tony Dubbins, the Liverpool branch agreed to remit its first motion, the final part of which called for the TUC to be immediately reconvened. The General Secretary Elect argued that, since the 1984 TUC Congress had given support to the NGA, it would be counter-productive to reconvene it.

The News International Dispute

Relationships between the NGA and the TUC again became highly strained during the News International dispute. The events surrounding this dispute are described in Chapter 14. Complaints tabled by the NGA, Sogat, NUJ and the AUEW against the EETPU behaviour in the events leading up to the dispute were considered by the TUC.[18] The two main complaints were first that the EETPU had not fully complied with the 'considered opinion and advice' of the TUC General

Secretary. Second, its actions were 'detrimental to the interests of the trade union movement' in that they imperilled the employment conditions of members of the four other unions involved, and it had collaborated with News International with the purpose of reaching an agreement which excluded the four other unions from the Wapping and Glasgow establishments and that they already had such an 'arrangement'. Arising from its investigation of these complaints, the TUC issued seven directives to the EETPU on 5 February 1986. The General Council judged the EEPTU activities in relation to News International to be detrimental to the interests of the trade union movement in that they had jeopardised the prospects of negotiations resulting in an agreement acceptable to the other unions.

Further, the General Council directed the EETPU to do six things – not to facilitate or assist further in recruitment of staff for News International; not to recruit into membership any persons employed by News International at Wapping or Glasgow who either were not members of a trade union or were, or had been, members of any other trade union; to inform its members at Wapping and Glasgow that they were engaged in work normally done by print unions and that those normally involved in this work were currently in official dispute with News International and had been sacked without notice and compensation; not to enter into any agreement or continue any non-contractual arrangements with News International without the agreement of the other four unions or, in the absence of this, without adjudication by the TUC; not to enter any unilateral negotiations with News International, and in conjunction with the TUC to use its best endeavours to bring about fresh negotiations between News International on the one hand and the four unions and to join in any negotiations which might take place and to keep the TUC General Secretary informed; and not to enter into a sole negotiating agreement, union membership agreement or any other form of agreement in any circumstances where another union would be deprived of its existing recognition and/or negotiation rights except with the agreement of the other unions concerned. The EETPU was required to give an undertaking by 12 February 1986 that it would accept and act on these directions, otherwise the General Council would suspend the EETPU from Congress until the 1986 Annual Congress. On 11 February 1986 the EETPU accepted all the TUC's directions without qualification.

The NGA was far from happy with the General Council decision, and its 1986 Delegate Meeting unanimously passed a motion on the News

International Dispute which, *inter alia*, 'condemns the anti-union collusion of the EETPU with News International which led to the dispute and instructs the National Council that if the dispute has not been brought to a satisfactory conclusion a motion must be submitted to the 1986 Trades Union Congress seeking the immediate expulsion of the EETPU'.[19] As the dispute remained unresolved the NGA moved a motion at the 1986 Congress calling for negotiation on recognition in Wapping and Kinning Park, coupled with employment opportunities and retraining of NGA members, coupled with adequate compensation for those who would retire. The resolution also asked Congress to reject the decision of the General Council not to issue directives to the EETPU aimed at stopping its members from doing work normally undertaken by members of printing unions at Wapping. At the beginning of August 1986 the NGA put down an amendment to the motion calling for the EETPU's suspension from the TUC, as members of that union continued to cross NGA and Sogat picket lines at Wapping. The TUC's Finance and General Purposes Committee ruled the NGA amendment out of order. This was unacceptable to the NGA, which announced that it would challenge the decision at the Congress. The NGA's annoyance was summed up by its General President, Bryn Griffiths,

> The TUC does a first class job in supporting oppressed people who are denied their rights in South Africa, Nicaragua and elsewhere. It is a pity the TUC does not do anything like as much in pursuing the dispute with News International on behalf of the sacked five and a half thousand unionists. If the TUC continues to condone print workers being robbed of their jobs and official picket lines being broken by the EETPU, the TUC may possibly have to make a choice about whether or not they want the EETPU or the NGA as affiliates.[20]

The 1986 TUC Congress voted by 5.8 million to 1.3 million to demand more support for the printworkers dismissed by News International. The NGA General Secretary, Tony Dubbins, moved the successful resolution, which also condemned the Tory anti-union laws 'which had been instrumental in asisting Rupert Murdoch to dismiss 5,500 British workers in order to increase profits to fund his media empire in the USA', backed a call for jobs and union recognition at Wapping and Kinning Park, and for retraining and adequate compensation to be negotiated with News International. The motion also instructed the TUC to mobilise more support for demonstrations and for the boycott campaign of the *Sun*, *The Times*, *News of the World* and *Sunday Times*. There is little doubt that the Congress decisions would have been little short of unanimous had it not been for the condemnation in the motion of the General Council for not instructing the EEPTU to tell its members to stop crossing the Wapping picket lines and doing the work of the dismissed printers. When the General Council's opposition to this part of the NGA motion was rejected, the NGA insisted that the General Council must issue such an instruction to the EEPTU if the negotiations with News International then proceeding did not produce a satisfactory settlement to the dispute.

Following the rejection of News International's final offer of September 1986, the NGA applied further pressure to the TUC, demanding action and support from the movement as a whole for their union members dismissed by News International. There followed a lobby of the TUC Finance and General Purposes Committee in support of the demand that it act against the EEPTU in line with the 1986 Congress resolution, but the committee voted to do nothing. However, on 6 February 1987 the NGA National Council were compelled to end the dispute and accepted a settlement based on the 'final offer' of September 1986. This traumatic decision was taken against the background of possible sequestration of its funds and of the decision on 5 February 1987 by Sogat, whose members formed 80 per cent of the dismissed former News International employees, to end the dispute. It had always been the NGA's view that it could not sustain the dispute in isolation and that position now prevailed.

Another reason for ending the dispute was what Tony Dubbins, the NGA General Secretary, described as 'the way the TUC let down the print unions, and certainly the NGA, and was quite unwilling to uphold trade union principles and trade union solidarity and take the action which we believe we were entitled to expect them to take against the EEPTU'.[21] For the NGA the action of the EEPTU in the dispute was crucial to its outcome, in that, in conjunction with the company, it actually got the Wapping plant operational. The EEPTU had throughout colluded with the News International 'to steal' printworkers' jobs. Tony Dubbins summed up the NGA's attitude to the TUC's role in the dispute in an editorial in the NGA's monthly journal,

It is necessary to make it quite clear that the role of the TUC in the dispute has been questionable. Twelve months ago the

General Council refused to tell the EETPU to instruct its members to stop doing print workers' jobs. They built on this cop-out when they did nothing to take the EETPU to task when new evidence came to light a few months ago. They hid behind pseudo judicial excuses and dubious interpretations of their rule book. I say to the TUC General Council that this is an issue which will not go away until we receive satisfaction for the treacherous way in which our members have been treated by the EETPU leadership in actively conniving and colluding with News International to take over and steal print workers' jobs.[22]

Even after the ending of the Wapping dispute the NGA, and the other print unions, continued to pursue their complaints to the TUC against the EETPU. The 1987 Congress, for the second year running, told the TUC to take action against the electricians' union when it referred back the General Council's report on the Wapping dispute. As far as the NGA was concerned, the penalty imposed by the TUC on the EETPU was no more than a slap on the wrist and did nothing to take back its gains. The motion to 'refer back' the General Council's report, seconded by the NGA, asked Congress to take this course because of the wider implications of the dispute for the credibility, democracy and future of the TUC. The NGA reminded delegates that the 1986 Congress had agreed that, if negotiations then proceeding between the print unions and News International failed, the General Council should be required to tell the electricians to 'instruct their members to stop doing the work of printers at Wapping'. But by twenty-three votes to twenty-one the General Council had decided not to carry out this decision. The NGA believed that, unless the TUC demonstrated the will to protect its existing affiliates and their members, to uphold trade union values and principles and to safeguard loyal trade unionists from attacks from within the movement, the credibility of the TUC would be in jeopardy.

On 4 September 1987 the TUC General Secretary, Mr Norman Willis, informed the General Council that a report in the *Guardian* newspaper that day contained allegations that the EETPU had acted in breach of the directives issued to it by the General Council in February 1986. The electricians established an internal Committee of Inquiry to investigate these allegations, which had come to light from disaffected EETPU members employed at Wapping. The inquiry revealed that there had been a technical breach of the February 1986 directives.

The NGA was far from satisfied with the EETPU internal inquiry, being concerned that only three Wapping witnesses, who had contradictory stories, had been interviewed. It pressed the TUC to conduct its own inquiry, stressing that the General Council was the custodian of its own directives and rules and not the EETPU. In June 1988 the TUC considered the EETPU breach of the February 1986 directives but decided only to censure the electricians, as it was satisfied that the EETPU had corrected the breach, had apologised for it and had derived no benefit from it. Some General Council members felt that to suspend the electricians over 'the breach' issue would look like revenge rather than justice. For the NGA, however, the TUC's behaviour was an example of the TUC bowing to implied legal threats of the EETPU and a total abdication of its responsibility as the custodian of the TUC constitution.

Although over the period 1983–8 TUC–NGA relationships were strained, there were no serious moves by the leadership or pressures from members for the NGA to disaffiliate. However, by the end of 1989 there were some who were beginning to question whether a high profile within the TUC since the mid-1970s had been of any positive benefit to the union and to express doubt about the continuation of such a stance.

There were a number of reasons why the NGA adopted a high profile within the TUC over the period 1976–89. It had been taken aback at the difficulties it had encountered in returning to the TUC. The NGA felt the wider trade union movement never really understood its technical difficulties over deregistration, feeling that other unions saw it as a cover for support for the Act. Its low profile role in the TUC had fostered an attitude amongst TUC affiliates of 'The NGA, who's that? One of those print unions'. It was perceived as a union of national newspaper workers who were exceptionally well paid and were able to operate working practices the like of which other workers could only dream of. The NGA realised that if it was to be understood by TUC affiliates it would have to play a more positive role in TUC affairs. Then its culture, problems and the nature of its membership would become known and understood. The policy of 'splendid isolation' at the TUC could not continue.

Second, the new General Secretary, Joe Wade, and the new Assistant General Secretary, Tony Dubbins, both elected in 1976, had different perceptions of a role for the NGA in the TUC than the previous General Secretary, John Bonfield. Both felt the NGA had had experiences that could be useful to other unions and that the NGA in turn could learn from the experiences of other affiliated unions. They wanted to make the NGA a much more influential force within the TUC. John Bonfield saw the NGA's role in the TUC as a passive one in which the union never submitted motions on wider union issues, its delegation never contributed to debates, and indeed were never encouraged to do so, and the delegation was never really briefed on issues. Wade and Dubbins deliberately set out to change this and, since 1976, at each Congress the NGA has moved some of the most fundamental, and far-reaching, motions on the TUC Congress agenda. Officials and other members of the delegation attending Congress have been encouraged to play a positive role in its debates. Whereas before 1976 unions affiliated to the TUC might have said 'The NGA, who's that?' today they know who the NGA is, of what it is capable, and its excellent reputation for representing and protecting the interests of its members.

Third, the technological developments within the printing industry and industry generally meant that the NGA could no longer solve its industrial problems in isolation from the rest of the trade union movement. The blurring of demarcation lines between the printing industry and other industries meant that the NGA clashed with non-printing unions over membership and negotiating rights on a much more significant scale than before 1976. Hence the NGA's efforts to get the TUC to write 'prescriptive rights' into its Disputes Principles and Procedures. Technological developments also threatened the NGA's ability to control the industry through control of entry of labour into the composing area. The growth of computer-based typesetting techniques made it possible for employers to produce print origination material without the help of skilled labour. To win its industrial battles today the NGA, unlike pre-1976, is more likely to require the help of other trade unions. For example, the outcome of the News International dispute might have been very different if the distribution of that company's four main newspaper titles could have been stopped. Despite the extensive efforts of the leadership of the T&GWU the required support of the T&GWU road haulage members, for example, was not forthcoming. Given that the NGA was now more likely to require the help of other unions to win its industrial battles, 'splendid isolation' from the wider trade union movement was no longer feasible.

The 1970s saw a Labour government introducing legislation suppor-tive towards trade unions and collective bargaining. If the NGA was to influence TUC thinking in suggesting appropriate legislation, then it needed to be a visible union within Congress. The 1980s saw a

Conservative government introducing legislation with an opposite design, much of which was directed at the industrial practices of the NGA. Only a future Labour government was likely to change this situation. If the NGA was to influence future Labour government legislation and its priorities in bringing that legislation forward, then a continued passive role within the TUC was not possible. The same was also true of government economic policies in the 1980s. The NGA's higher profile within the TUC was the result of technological, economic and political developments relative to pre-1976. However, these factors, although necessary, were insufficient in themselves. It also required the genuine change of philosophy in the NGA to its role in the TUC provided by Wade and Dubbins.

OTHER WIDER TRADE UNION BODIES

The London Trades Council

The LSC played an active part in the activities of the Council by sending delegates to its monthly meetings who then reported back to the membership via quarterly delegate meetings and by an annual report to the Society's annual general meeting. The London Trades Council undertook a number of tasks, including lobbying and writing to ministers on matters affecting workers' interests in London, lobbying and pressuring the London County Council, organising an annual May Day demonstration, and giving assistance in the form of moral, and sometimes financial, support when requested by affiliated unions involved in official disputes.

In 1949 the LSC became concerned that the London Trades Council was under the control of the Communist Party. The Society's London Trades Council delegation report to the February 1950 Quarterly Delegate Meeting contained criticisms of the political activities of the Council's secretary. The LSC's executive and delegate meeting accepted these criticisms and wrote a letter of protest to the TUC, which in turn expressed to the London Trades Council its concerns over disruptive bodies manipulating its affairs. The TUC warned the Council that its registration would not be renewed for 1951 unless positive proof of its willingness and ability to support TUC policy could be provided.

The London Trades Council investigated the TUC complaints and found the charges unfounded. However, in 1952 the LSC, along with seven other unions, disaffiliated from the Trades Council on the

322

grounds that its communist activities and propaganda alienated their members to such an extent they could no longer associate with it. In May 1952, following these disaffiliations, the TUC refused to continue the London Trades Council's registration. This decision was confirmed by the 1952 Congress.

In October 1952 the TUC invited affiliated unions with London membership to a consultative conference to consider whether a new London Trades Council should be formed. The conference decided that a new Council should be formed and an eight-man committee, including Bob Willis, General Secretary of the LSC, was elected to draft a constitution. In January 1953 a constitution was adopted, but letters were received from solicitors warning that if any attempt was made to use the name 'London Trades Council' injunctions would be sought in the High Court. It was then decided to call the new Council the London Trades Council (1952); its constitution was subsequently approved by the TUC General Council. The LSC General Secretary told its February 1953 Delegate Meeting, 'your Executive Committee rightly assume that this Society which played a leading part in the walk out from the old Trades Council will wish to take its full share in the building up of the new organisation.'[23]

The new Council held its first meeting in March 1953 and Bob Willis was elected chairman. As a TUC-recognised Trades Council the London Trades Council (1952) put its members in touch with educational facilities, assisted in recruiting and strengthening trade union organisation, nominated union representatives to a wide range of committees and tribunals and made more widely known the national policy of the TUC. Like the old Trades Council, the new one dealt with matters affecting all workers in London, for example proposed fare increases by the London Transport Executive, but on occasions covered wider issues, for example campaigns for increases in old age pensions. It was also frequently involved in lobbying Parliament, ministers and the London County Council. Bob Willis continued as its chairman until 1959, when the weight of his TUC duties prevented him from continuing in this position.

The London Region of the NGA also participated fully in the affairs of the London Trades Council, but in September 1972 it withdrew following its resignation from the TUC. This decision came under successful criticism at the London Region's 1972 Annual Conference, where some delegates complained that the Trades Council might have been more sympathetic to the reasons why the NGA could not deregister than the TUC, and that the attitude of the London Trades Council should have been sought before the NGA took the step of dissociating itself from the London Trades Council.[24] The NGA never returned to the London Trades Council, which in 1977 went out of existence, reflecting the decline of London as an industrial centre over the previous twenty years with the continued relocation of industry outside London.

The Irish Congress of Trade Unions

Prior to 1959 the Irish trade union movement was divided into two sections – the Irish Trade Union Congress (ITUC), comprising both unions with headquarters in Ireland and others with head offices in Britain, and the Congress of Irish Unions (CIU), composed of unions with head offices solely in Ireland. In 1954 the two organisations issued a joint memorandum agreeing that the Irish trade union movement should be wholly Irish based and controlled and that the existing disunity prevented the coordination of union action in almost every sphere. However ITUC and CIU could not agree on the practical application of the principle. The latter favoured immediate unification, believing that Irish-based and controlled unions should take place before unification. To resolve this difference the two bodies proposed that the views of Irish trade unionists should be secured by means of an inquiry or ballot. They recognised that the consent of unions with head offices in Britain would be necessary for the conduct of any such inquiry, and it was suggested that the TUC convene a conference of executives of interested British unions to discuss these proposals with representatives of the ITUC and the CIU.

However, it was not until 1959 that the two organisations merged to form the Irish Congress of Trade Unions, thereby ending the split in the Irish trade union movement which had existed since 1945 when certain Irish unions seceded from the ITUC over affiliation to the World Federation of Trade Unions. At the conference establishing the ICTU, the TA abstained from voting. Three things worried the TA. First, the constitution proposed that, on its executive, representatives of Irish-based unions would always be in a majority. Second, it was proposed that anyone who was not resident in Ireland would be excluded from being a Congress delegate and from holding office. Third, and the most important as far as the TA was concerned, the proposed constitution vested ultimate authority for the policy of affiliated unions' policy in

Ireland in a conference or committee of Irish members of that union. The TA considered the first two provisions unnecessarily exclusive, considering that trade unionism in Ireland had always sought to bridge geographical and national barriers in the interests of the widest possible unity. The third provision, however, cut right across the final authority in all matters of TA policy, namely the TA Executive Council. The TA had been assured by the Provisional United Trade Union Organisation on the Constitution for a United Trade Union Centre that the TA set-up in Ireland – North of Ireland and South of Ireland geographical, not political, groups plus the annual All-Ireland Conference – would satisfy the new Congress constitution. The TA delegation was thus in a difficult dilemma of voting for the constitution on the basis of what it said or on the basis of how the Provisional Organisation and the conference platform interpreted it. In these circumstances the TA delegation decided to take the unusual step of abstaining from voting.

The TA affiliated to the Irish Congress of Trade Unions but was not prepared to change its own decision-making structure to suit that of the ICTU. The TA's application was accepted and for the purpose of representation at the annual meeting of the ICTU the TA delegation consisted of one member from the TA North of Ireland Group, one from the TA South of Ireland Group and two appointed from the Executive Council.

An event of some significance to the NGA occurred at the 1975 Annual Conference, when its Irish Regional Secretary, Bill Trulock, was elected to the ICTU Executive. However, at the 1977 Annual Conference Bill Trulock lost his seat. The NGA believed this to be due to the lack of support from the General Workers' Union for condemning their encroachment onto printing work by members of non-recognised printing unions.[25] The NGA regained representation on the ICTU Executive Council in 1989 when its Irish regional officer, Nick Broughall, was so elected.

In March 1967 the assistance of the Irish Congress Arbitration Tribunal was sought by the Irish Transport and General Workers' Union over a dispute between itself and the NGA in respect of a Registascope which had been introduced into a printing office in Cork. At this particular establishment the production of rubber stereos had for many years been the responsibility of IT&GWU members. This was the first time that the NGA had been called to account by the Irish Congress and the Association was relieved that its claim to the work was upheld. The NGA relationship with other affiliates also came up at the 1977 Annual Conference when the NGA proposed a motion condemning the encroachment on printing work by members of non-recognised printing unions and called for the support of the ICTU in re-establishing the control of printing work by printing trade union workers. The motion was seconded by the Irish Graphical Society and supported by almost all other affiliated craft unions. Regrettably, the General Workers' Union and those unions catering for white-collar workers opposed the motion, which was defeated by only 13 votes.

As in the United Kingdom so in the Republic of Ireland the NGA played an up-front role in health and safety matters. The Association played a significant part in the development of health and safety legislation in the Republic and in particular the Irish Safety in Industry Act. The NGA has established firm links with the ICTU on health and safety matters and health and safety weekend schools for NGA Irish members are held.

In Northern Ireland the NGA always opposed victimisation, sectarianism and discrimination. It was fully supportive of an ICTU campaign, launched in 1986, against such behaviour. The NGA has long held the view that everyone, regardless of religion, race or creed, has a right to security of employment and to live free from violence, intimidation, sectarianism and discrimination.

In the Irish Republic the NGA consistently opposed incomes policies. The end of the 1970s saw an agreement between the government, the employers and trade unions which established a voluntary incomes policy. It represented a compromise, against the government's threats that it would introduce a statutory policy. However the conference called to give approval to the agreement was done with little warning. In fact many delegates were unaware the subject was to be discussed. This state of affairs led the NGA to protest to the ICTU, which defended its action on the grounds that an immediate special Congress was necessary if the ICTU was to intervene successfully with the Irish government.

At both the 1976 and 1977 ICTU annual conferences the NGA continued to oppose further national wage agreements. In spite of criticism against participation in further discussions on future national agreements, the 1978 Congress voted to permit the ICTU to negotiate a new agreement for 1978. On 21 May 1980 the ICTU called a meeting to authorise the Executive Council to enter discussions with the Irish government and the employers for an integrated national understanding, to come into effect on the termination of the current pay policy. At this conference the NGA voted against giving the executive such authority. Although the motion was carried by a substantial majority, the NGA continued its stand against the national understandings. It has always found itself in a minority position on incomes policy in Ireland because of the support given to such 'understandings' by the General Workers' Union. In 1983 the 'national understanding' came to an end, much to the satisfaction of the NGA.

At the 1988 ICTU Annual Conference the NGA supported an amendment in a debate on the Republic of Ireland's Programme for National Recovery which, *inter alia*, provided for a three-year pay agreement. The amendment called for a special conference to be convened to consider the trade unions' withdrawal from the programme if its targets, particularly those on job creation, were not fulfilled. However, the amendment was defeated after supporters of the Recovery Plan stressed the need for the ICTU to remain in a position to influence the formulation of the Irish government's economic and social policy.

The Scottish Trades Union Congress

Following the transfer of engagements of the NSES in 1967, the NGA gave consideration to continuing NSES affiliation to the STUC. The NGA decided to affiliate all its members in Scotland, which meant that former NUPT members in Scotland became affiliated for the first time. An amendment to the STUC constitution in 1967 brought printers' representation on the STUC General Council, but Mr George Lambie of the then Sogat (Division 1) was elected to represent them.

In 1972 the NGA resigned from the STUC over deregistration under the Indusrial Relations Act (1971). At the same time that the NGA returned to the TUC it also re-affiliated to the STUC.

The NGA always sent its full delegation to the STUC Annual Congress and participated in debates, and when its industrial interests needed to be protected it moved or seconded motions. However, in the wider Scottish trade union movement the NGA has always taken a back seat to Sogat which has by far the majority of organised print workers in Scotland.

NOTES

1. For a detailed account of the Fund, see 'International Solidarity Fund', Appendix A in the *Trades Union Congress Report, 1957*, pp. 486–8.

2. See 'They need your help', *London Typographical Journal*, February 1959, pp. 7–8.

3. See 'The 92nd Trades Union Congress', *London Typographical Journal*, October 1961, pp. 16–17.

4. See *Report of the Delegate Meeting, 1966*, National Graphical Association, pp. 334–6.

5. This Royal Commission was chaired by Lord Donovan and reported in June 1968. The NGA declined to give evidence to the Commission on the grounds that it considered that the government's intention in establishing the Commission was not to assist unions but to provide an eventual means of curbing trade union activities.

6. See *Report of the Delegate Meeting, 1972*, National Graphical Association, pp. 218–22.

7. See *Print*, October 1971, pp. 1 and 20.

8. See *Print*, September 1972, p. 1.

9. See *Report of the Delegate Meeting, 1972*, National Graphical Association, p. 96.

10. ibid., p. 222.

11. The NGA Assistant General Secretary, Mr Tony Dubbins, told the 1978 Congress that the latest figures for investment in the printing machinery showed that the suppliers expected 35 per cent of all equipment to be installed not in the printing industry, but in in-plant and similar situations, which could put the jobs of thousands of print workers at risk.

12. See *Print*, December 1982, p. 1.

13. See *Report of the Delegate Meeting, 1976*, National Graphical Association, pp. 97–117, and *Print*, July 1976, p. 6.

14. See *Report of the Delegate Meeting, 1980*, National Graphical Association, p. 140–2.

15. The main departure from the proposals was the inclusion of a retrospective compensation scheme for employees dismissed between 1974 and 1980 as a result of union membership agreements during the currency of the relevant provisions of the 1974 Trade Union and Labour Relations Act.

16. *Industrial Relations Legislation: The Employment Act 1980 and Employment Bill, 1982*, Report by the TUC General Council, April 1982, p. 17, paras 69 and 70.

17. For a full account of this dispute and its wider implications, see John Gennard, 'The implications of the Messenger Newspaper Group dispute', *Industrial Relations Journal*, vol. 15, no. 3, Autumn 1984, pp. 7–20, and M. Dickinson, *To Break a Union: The Messenger, the State and the NGA*, Booklist Ltd, 1984.

18 These were that: (a) the EETPU had jeopardised the possibility of an agreement acceptable to all five unions involved; (2) by assisting in the production of *The Times*, *Sunday Times*, *Sun* and *News of the World*, the EETPU had imperilled the jobs and conditions of employment of members of the print unions who had been employed at the plants at Gray's Inn Road and Bouverie Street; (3) it had assisted a recruitment agency in recruiting staff on behalf on News International for the purpose of being trained upon, and subsequently, operating equipment and processes at News International's establishments at Glasgow and Wapping, which are normally operated by members of the print unions and the AUEW; (4) it had

cooperated in producing at Wapping a twenty-four-page supplement for the issue of the *Sunday Times* dated 9 January 1986 in breach of agreements held with News International with respect to Gray's Inn Road and Bouverie Street; and (5) it had entered into and/or continued an agreement or arrangement with News International covering all or part of the operation of groups of employees at Wapping without the consent of the other unions concerned and in contravention of advice received from the TUC General Secretary.

19. See *Report of the Delegate Meeting, 1986*, National Graphical Association, pp. 259–69.

20. See *Print*, September 1986, p. 1.

21. See *Print*, March 1987, p. 1.

22. ibid., p. 4.

23. See *London Typographical Journal*, March 1953, p. 2.

24. See *1972 Regional Annual Conference Report*, London Region, National Graphical Association, 1972, pp. 38–42.

25. See *Report of the Delegate Meeting, 1978*, National Graphical Association, p. 30.

CHAPTER 11

RELATIONSHIP WITH THE LABOUR PARTY

For the NGA and its founding societies their relationships with the Labour Party were an extension of their industrial activities. The industrial protection of their members could not be provided solely by industrial means since their members' employment relationship can be regulated adversely or favourably by Parliament. The need to influence Parliament and the policies of political parties was well recognised. Radical change to the existing order of society was not a major factor in its approach to politics and the Labour Party.

THE POLITICAL FUND

The LSC
In 1902 the LSC members voted to pay a compulsory levy of 5p per year to secure the return of members to Parliament. Following the 1910 Osborne judgment, the levy became voluntary. In 1916 the LSC successfully balloted its members for approval of 'the furtherance of political objects within the meaning of the Trade Union Act (1913) as an object of the Society'. The 1927 Trades Disputes and Trade Union Act, which introduced a system of 'contracting in' to a union political fund, did not prevent the majority of LSC members continuing to pay the political levy. Howe and Waite report that, in 1928, of a total journeyman membership of 12,098 some 9,947 were 'contracted in'.[1]

Table 11.1 shows the Political Fund income for the LSC over the period 1948–54. It also shows that, in both absolute and relative terms, LSC members paying the political levy fell. This downward trend was the result of two events. First, the 1950 general election saw the LSC lose all representation in the House of Commons. Some members were

330

Table 11.1
The LSC Political Fund income, 1948–54

	CONTRIBUTIONS (£)			No. of members contributing to Fund	Contributing members as % of total membership
Date	From members	From other sources	Total		
1948	1,005	18	1,023	10,050	76
1949	928	38	966	9,280	68
1950	898	46	944	8,980	66
1951	900	37	937	9,000	66
1952	869	41	910	8,690	64
1953	858	42	900	8,580	62
1954	850	42	892	8,500	61

Source: London Society of Compositors, *Annual Reports*, 1945–54.

willing to pay the political levy whilst the Society had members in the House, as they could be confident that their industrial interests were being directly represented in Parliament. Without this direct payment/service link these members saw little point in continuing to pay the political levy. The second event was the Labour government's treatment of the Society in relation to Order 1305 during the 1950 wage dispute with the LMPA. The union was disappointed that the Attorney General failed to prosecute the Master Printers for locking out its members. The Society regarded the lock-out to be an infringement of Order 1305, which had been passed as a Defence Regulation by Parliament in 1940 and which outlawed strikes and lock-outs. Following the end of the dispute, the Society thought no more about the matter until the Attorney General, speaking in the House of Commons on unofficial strikes, indicated that in his view both sides in the 1950 printing dispute had acted illegally but the initial illegality was that of the union.

The LSC protested to the Attorney General in the strongest terms. His reply that his statement in the House was correct naturally angered the LSC. Its General Secretary, Bob Willis, told the 1951 Annual Meeting of its Political Section

This action of the Government had not had, obviously, very

331

encouraging effects so far as the membership were concerned and indeed there has been talk of withdrawing from the Labour Party as a means of showing strong disapproval. Whilst that would not, of course, serve any useful purpose it was necessary to express disappointment at the attitude of the Government and of the Labour Party, and to say as we have said before, that it would seem that the only time that the Labour movement begins to take an interest in the unions is when they are wanting money for elections or other purposes.[2]

Although about two-thirds of LSC members paid the political levy, attendance at its Political annual general meeting was usually low. The 1950 meeting was attended by fewer than 10 per cent of the Society's political levy payers, whilst its 1954 meeting was attended by fewer than 40 members inclusive of officers.[3] The LSC membership were not political activists and their interest in political methods to achieve their industrial objectives ceased with their political levy payment.

The LTS

The total amount of income received each year by the LTS Political Fund and the proportion of its membership paying the political levy are shown in Table 11.2. Approximately three-fifths of LTS members paid the political levy. Apart from 1958 and 1959 (a general election year), the balance of the fund remained in surplus. In January 1958 the political levy contribution was increased due to the small balance of the Fund and a fear that proposed increased affiliation fees to the Labour Party would put the Fund in deficit, that the fund was too small to finance a parliamentary candidate and to give adequate grants towards the election expenses of members fighting municipal elections.

The TA

In 1900 the TA members voted by 3,097 votes to 1,077 to affiliate to the Labour Representation Committee (LRC). Following the Taff Vale decision, the TA considered labour representation in Parliament and on local councils an urgent necessity. In 1903 it decided to establish a Labour Representation Fund into which members would contribute 1d per month. Those who failed to pay the contribution were excluded from benefit and ultimately expelled.

However, following the Osborne judgment, two TA members instituted legal proceedings on behalf of all TA members who objected

Table 11.2
The LTS Political Fund income, 1955–63

Date	CONTRIBUTIONS (£) From members	From other sources	Total income of the Fund (£)	Balance of Fund (£)	No. of members contributing to Fund	Contributing members as % of total membership
1955	829	16	845	+430	8,290	41
1956	1,094	30	1,124	+320	10,940	55
1957	1,287	37	1,324	+247	12,870	64
1958	1,171	44	1,215	−213	7,807	−
1959	1,903	37	1,940	−759	12,687	63
1960	1,656	33	1,689	+558	11,040	55
1961	1,651	201	1,852	+521	11,007	55
1962	1,621	247	1,868	+360	10,807	54
1963	1,680	285	1,965	+ 96	11,200	56

Source: London Typographical Society: *Annual Reports*, 1955–63.

to contributing to the Labour Representation Fund. The case was heard in 1910 and the court ruled that the non-registration status of the TA did not affect the position and the union was bound by the Osborne judgment. The TA executive then introduced voluntary contributions to maintain its Labour Representation Fund.

The Trade Union Act (1913) allowed trade unions to expend money on political purposes on certain conditions. A ballot of TA members held in May 1914 voted by 6,609 to 3,793 to establish a TA Labour Representation Fund to operate from January 1915. Following the 1927 Trades Disputes and Trade Union Act the majority of TA members accepted the union's advice that they should 'contract in' to the LRF. The annual income of the fund, which had averaged £1,680 in the years 1915–24 fell to only £1,420 in the period 1928–34. The income, expenditure, and balance of the TA Labour Representation Fund for the period March 1949 to September 1963 are shown in Table 11.3.

By March 1950 the state of the Labour Representation Fund was giving cause for concern. In the previous twelve months the fund had overspent by some £2,498 and its accumulated balance had been reduced from £4,020 in March 1949 to £1,521 in March 1950. An important factor in this declining financial position was the TA's £1,192

Table 11.3
The Typographical Association: the Labour Representation Fund, 1949–63
(September each year)

Date	Income (£)	Expenditure (£)	Balance of Fund (£)
1949	766	1,684	3,101
1950	801	315	2,008
1951	774	283	2,257
1952	780	333	1,682
1953	785	370	1,842
1954	778	236	2,035
1955	799	896	1,519
1956	1,678	1,454	1,743
1957	1,690	1,489	1,944
1958	2,903	1,936	2,911
1959	1,404	1,236	4,409
1960	1,657	304	5,256
1961	1,775	651	6,570
1962	1,767	947	7,738
1963	1,774	3,711	5,970

Source: Typographical Association, *Half Year Reports*, 1949–63.

contribution to the Labour Party's General Election Fund for the February 1950 general election. To improve the fund the EC proposed to the 1950 Delegate Meeting that branches should retain only a quarter, and not a half, of the political levy they collected. This remained the case until the 1969 NGA Delegate Meeting agreed that branches could retain 40 per cent. The motion was defeated despite strong pleas from the EC that an increase in the fund's income was necessary if the TA was to continue to sustain representation in the House of Commons and that if branches had members contesting seats on the local council they should support them from voluntary contributions. The opponents of the motion argued that supporting members as parliamentary candidates in unwinnable seats, for example Seymour Hills fighting Winston Churchill in Woodford, was wasteful expenditure and that since local government was a breeding ground for future MPs support should be given to TA members on local councils and to their local Labour parties.

The fund continued to decline and the 1953 Delegate Meeting was warned by the General President:

> No reference to the political field would be complete without drawing your attention to the parlous state of the Labour Representation Fund. It will be remembered that after the 1950 Election we had to drop the second Parliamentary candidate because the Fund could not stand the expense and with Labour Party affiliation fees and by election guarantees taking more than half of the contribution received it cannot be long before our slender assets will disappear.[4]

Although the meeting carried a resolution from the Stroud branch increasing the political levy to 1d per week to enable the Association to increase its parliamentary representation without sacrificing its contributions to local Labour parties, the proposed increase was rejected in a membership ballot.

By the time of the 1957 Delegate Meeting the balance of the LRF had fallen to just over £1,000 and the TA auditors had, on at least one occasion since 1953, indicated that this fund might not be able much longer to meet all its commitments. The 1957 Delegate Meeting accepted an EC resolution to increase the political levy from ½d to 1d per week. The EC pointed out that, first, the fund would have been in an even worse state if the TA's parliamentary representative had claimed the grant to which he was entitled under rule[5] and, second, the fund was bankrupt. Third, the EC also argued that the Hastings Agreement, which regulates the relationships between the Labour Party and trade unions over the political financing of trade union sponsored candidates, had been revised so that now, instead of paying £250 to the constituency of its parliamentary representatives, the TA would have to pay £325 per annum.[6] In addition, the Labour Party had recently increased its affiliation fees from 2½p to 4p and as a result the TA, for the first time in its history, was affiliating to the Labour Party not on its full LRF membership.[7] It was affiliating only 25,000 LRF payers because to affiliate on the full membership would reduce the fund by a further £257 per year. However, the size of affiliated membership enabled the TA to send five delegates, as required by rule, to the Labour Party Conference. In reality it was no longer honouring its full financial obligations to the Party.

Table 11.4
The Typographical Association: Labour Representation Fund
contributors, 1949–63 (September each year)

Date	Total membership	Numbers contributing to Labour Representation Fund	% of membership contributing to Labour Representation Fund
1949	46,754	29,035	62
1950	48,755	29,181	60
1951	50,328	29,511	59
1952	51,466	29,564	57
1953	52,232	30,095	58
1954	53,129	29,970	56
1955	54,335	30,774	57
1956	54,721	30,822	56
1957	56,449	32,267	57
1958	57,422	31,442	55
1959	57,553	30,648	53
1960	58,422	30,809	53
1961	59,879	31,436	52
1962	61,080	32,000	52
1963	62,601	32,710	52

Source: Typographical Association, *Half Year Reports*, 1948–63.

The Executive Council was in an invidious position. Disaffiliation from the Labour Party was inconceivable, but the question had to be faced that if increased income was not forthcoming the TA would have to reconsider its continuing support for its one remaining parliamentary representative. The TA was also bound by rule to remain affiliated to the Labour Party. If it wished to send its full delegation to the Party Conference an affiliation of no fewer than 25,000 members was necessary. If affiliation and its consequences were to take up the bulk of a stagnant/declining fund the TA would have insufficient funds to meet its responsibilities to any Labour constituency that migh adopt a TA parliamentary representative as its prospective candidate. A members' ballot approved the 1957 Delegate Meeting decision to increase the contributions to the LRF by 14,335 votes to 9,760; the balance of the fund improved and the TA continued its support of its parliamentary representative, Mr W.A. Wilkins, MP for Bristol South. By May 1961 the fund had recovered to such an extent that the EC decided to invite nominations for a second parliamentary representative as the first step towards the TA again having two of its members in the House of Commons (see below).

The NGA

Table 11.5 shows the income and expenditure of the NGA, and subsequently the NGA(82), Political Fund. By 1970 the fund was in difficulties. The decline in the fund was largely due to increased Labour Party affiliation fees, a diminishing income and an increase in the number of members contracting out of the political levy particularly in protest over the Labour government's 'In Place of Strife' proposals of January 1969. The NGA's commitments to constituency parties had ceased since the 1970 general election had left it with no member in the House of Commons. However, if the Association were to sponsor candidates in the future the fund would have to be built up. To this end in 1970 the Political Executive introduced a number of short-term economy measures, including the suspension of political expenditure in the constituencies, a reduction in the number of members on which affiliation fees to the Labour Party were paid and a decrease in NGA representation at the Party's Annual Conference. A 1972 Delegate Meeting decision to increase the weekly Political Fund contribution from 1d to 1p was accepted in a ballot of the membership. The effect of all measures when taken together was that by September 1973 the fund had a surplus of £4,600 and a balance of just under £11,000.

Given the policies adopted by the Heath Conservative government in the early 1970s, particularly those in relation to the Industrial Relations Act (1971), wage restraint and Common Market entry, it was hoped that NGA members would become politically aware and, more, start to pay, or re-start to pay, the political levy. However, the period of the Heath government still saw the union being bombarded with requests for contracting-out forms, particularly from apprentice members. Nevertheless, in the February and October general elections of 1974 the NGA met its financial commitments to the Basildon Constituency Labour Party in connection with the election of Eric Moonman, its parliamentary representative, and donated £5,000 to the Labour Party General Election Appeal. The Political Fund had a small deficit by the end of 1974 but recovered during 1975 to show a gain on the previous twelve months of some £6,000, due mainly to a financial appeal to

Table 11.5
The NGA/NGA (1982) political fund
1964–89 (September each year)

Date	Income (£)	Expenditure (£)	Balance of the Fund (£)	No. of Political Fund payers	% of membership contributing to Political Fund
1964	4,445	1,991	8,396	42,646	52
1965	4,686	4,272	8,976	44,481	52
1966	6,200	7,068	8,108	44,083	51
1967	4,826	4,413	7,694	43,456	50
1968	4,534	4,158	8,479	48,404	53
1969	4,340	4,579	8,222	43,765	41
1970	4,814	8,461	4,575	45,022	42
1971	5,099	5,577	4,097	43,987	41
1972	5,551	3,474	6,174	43,874	41
1973	8,687	4,036	10,825	43,906	41
1974	12,307	12,467	10,665	50,653	47
1975	13,466	7,314	16,817	49,803	46
1976	11,466	8,137	20,146	49,303	46
1977	11,193	10,870	20,469	48,724	45
1978	11,384	10,389	21,464	49,188	45
1979	11,519	17,706	15,277	50,949	46
1980	13,054	11,984	18,764	54,659	47
1981	20,983	12,948	26,799	50,032	44
1982	25,285	8,202	69,141	55,741	41
1983	51,550	66,058	54,633	59,457	44
1984	50,555	26,008	79,180	57,725	44
1985	67,870	32,685	114,365	57,753	44
1986	82,088	34,679	161,774	58,518	44
1987	88,327	140,701	109,400	59,400	45
1988	101,139	54,889	155,650	60,949	46
1989	121,200	65,236	211,614	62,588	47

Source: NGA, Annual Reports and Statement of Accounts.

branches and members which brought in £1,929 from some seventy branches and chapels.

A problem for the Political Fund was that its income was less than it should have been given the number of registered contributors. In 1975 there were some 50,000 registered contributors to the fund, which should have given an income of £15,000, when in fact the fund received some £3,000 less. This meant that some 10,000 members on the political register were not contributing. By the 1978 Delegate Meeting the fund was in a far more healthy state with a balance of nearly £21,500, but there was still need for improvement if the NGA was to play a full part in influencing government policy and to express, through its parliamentary representatives, its attitude to any political situation. The problem remained one of how to get more members to subscribe to the Political Fund so as to gain the necessary extra income to sponsor two parliamentary candidates and send full representation to the Labour Party Conference.

By 1980 the NGA remained concerned that its Political Fund was adequate only to meet its liabilities. The election of a Conservative government in 1979 committed to trade union reform in areas directly relevant to the NGA created a need to expand the Association's political activities. If, however, this was to be a reality the Political Fund income would need to increase. The NGA began this task at the 1980 Delegate Meeting when a National Council motion relating changes in the Political Fund contribution to increases in basic rates of pay of the member was carried. For every £10 advance above £60 in the minimum rate of pay received by the members under national agreements the political contribution would increase automatically by 1p per week. This decision was subsequently confirmed by a ballot of the members and the new contributions formula came into effect at the end of March 1981. Armed with this increased income the NGA set about developing an organisational structure to expand its political activities and develop a higher profile in the Labour Party.

The 1984 Trade Union Act requires unions *inter alia* to hold, at least once every ten years, secret ballots of their members to ascertain whether they wish their union to retain a political fund. The NGA quickly decided that if it failed to comply with this legislation then after 31 March 1986 expenditure on political objects would automatically become illegal and open to challenge from the members. The loss of the Political Fund would adversely affect the NGA's ability to protect and advance its members' interests against, or by, legislative intervention.

The NGA decided to prepare the ground thoroughly before balloting its members. Its campaign concentrated on the need to retain a Political Fund if members' industrial interests were to be protected. Its campaign stressed three themes. First, that Parliament takes decisions that affect

NGA members in their jobs, for example health and safety and taxes on printed products. Second, that if the union lost its Political Fund it would be unable to have parliamentary representatives and when Parliament was considering matters of direct relevance to the printing industry the only voice to be heard in the House would be that of the employers.[8] The third theme stressed that a 'yes vote' would enable two sets of individual rights to be accommodated, namely the right to contribute and the right not to contribute. By voting 'no', those who did not wish to contribute to the Political Fund were in danger of removing the rights of those who did. The NGA stressed also that the ballot was about the union's freedom to have a Political Fund, parliamentary representatives and to conduct political campaigns. It was not about how it was spent, since such decisions could only be taken by those contributing to the fund.

The procedure for balloting members on the continuation of political funds required under the 1984 Act clashed with that of taking a ballot of the membership set out in the NGA rulebook. First, the Association's retired members, honorary members and juvenile members were excluded from all membership ballots by the union's rules, but the 1984 Act said they must be included in Political Fund retention ballots. Second, retired members and certain other groups, for example unemployed members, were required to vote by secret postal ballot, whilst the Association's rules permitted only secret workplace ballots. Third, the NGA is required by rule to publish the results of membership ballots on a branch by branch basis. This is possible because members, after casting their votes, are required to sign the envelope in which they have put the ballot paper and add the name of the branch. The votes are then counted in the branch and the result forwarded to head office. This procedure breached the Act's test of secrecy, so for the ballot the NGA was obliged to operate a system of blank envelopes with the branches forwarding them to head office for counting. The type of ballot paper and the procedure used were resented by many members. In December 1985 it was announced that in a 72 per cent poll NGA members had voted by 68,559 votes to 18,931 in favour of the retention of a Political Fund.

The NGA was determined to build upon the Political Fund campaign and the raised interest in political affairs this had caused amongst its members. It was involved in the establishment and development of Trades Unionists for Labour (TUFL), an organisation made up of union General Secretaries, including NGA General Secretary, Tony Dubbins, Gordon Colling, an NGA national officer, acts as substitute representative as well as being a trustee of TUFL. In July 1986 the NGA established 'NGA for Labour' as a campaigning organisation for the return of a Labour government. It was to achieve an increased interest in Labour Party affairs and its policies amongst NGA members by increasing the number of NGA Political Fund contributors, the number of members being individual members of the Labour Party and the number of branches affiliating to constituency Labour parties. 'NGA for Labour' continues to flourish and has helped increase the number of NGA Political Fund contributors and the number of members becoming individual members of the Labour Party.

PARLIAMENTARY CANDIDATES

The LSC
In 1948 the LSC had two members in the House of Commons, Mr T.E. Naylor, Labour member for South East Southwark had been first elected to the House in 1921. The other member, Mr W.G. Cluse, Labour MP for South Islington, had been in the House since 1923. However in 1950, under a redistribution of parliamentary seat boundaries, the constituencies of South East Southwark and South Islington disappeared. Every effort was made by the LSC to secure the selection of Naylor and Cluse by other London constituencies but the 1950 general election found the LSC without any members in the election. Given that Mr C.W. Bowerman, the Society's Assistant Secretary, had been elected to Parliament in 1906 and retained his seat until his retirement in 1931, for the first time since 1906 the LSC found itself with no member in the House of Commons. In view of the considerable amount of printed material issued by the government, the LSC viewed this absence with concern and its reversal a matter of urgent priority.

The LSC made many efforts to have one of its four approved parliamentary candidates adopted by London constituency Labour parties. These efforts included talks between Bob Willis, LSC General Secretary, and the National Agent of the Labour Party at which various suggestions were made,[9] the LSC affiliating on a nominal figure to every local party in London so that it could submit nominations when vacancies occurred, encouraging members to gain election to the County Council as this could be a good training ground for potential parliamentary candidates, and LSC members seeking seats in the North of England and not just in London and its periphery. However, this last suggestion was never really pursued as an option. The 1954 Political Annual General Meeting was told by a member that it was necessary to push a national figure as a candidate and moved unsuccessfully 'that this meeting ask the delegates to request the Secretary [i.e. the General Secretary] to reconsider his promise that he would not stand for Parliament, as there is a need for more printing representatives in Parliament'.[10]

Some delegates thought it inadvisable for the General Secretary to take on additional responsibilities. The General Secretary refused to go back on his promise, made to the membership at the time of his election, about not standing for Parliament unless approached by the whole membership.[11] The LSC's concern about the lack of representatives in Parliament was also the case with the similar situation with the London County Council. For many years the Society had had two members sitting on the LCC, but by 1950 both seats had been lost. Non-representation on the LCC was also a concern because of the large amount of print work required by the Council. However, it was difficult to get members to stand as candidates, since the loss of pay involved in being a councillor on such a large authority was great as it involved two or three days a week absence from work if the job was to be done effectively.

The LTS
The LTS failed to get any of its members elected to the House of Commons. Its 1956 AGM discussed how the chances of achieving parliamentary representation might be improved and two views emerged. There were those who argued that the LTS should institute a panel of parliamentary candidates whose names could be submitted to the Labour Party and through that body to the various constituencies. Others, amongst whom was the General Secretary, argued that this approach had been unsuccessful for the former LSC and that the way forward lay in backing a member who had the support of a constituency and to whom every assistance could be given.

The LTS's lack of success in gaining representation in the House of Commons was related to the relative inactivity of its members in their Labour Party wards and constituencies.[12] The Society was the poorer for its lack of parliamentary representation but the thousands of its members who paid the political levy appeared to consider that such was all that was expected of them as far as the political side of the Society's activities was concerned. Although a panel of members available to be adopted by constituencies existed, little success was achieved in adoption due to a lack of interest on the part of LTS members in London constituencies. At this level many LSC members were inactive, apathetic and uninterested. The LTS was unable, despite constant messages, to convince its members that a much greater interest was required if LTS representation in the House of Commons was to be achieved.

The LTS was also concerned about its lack of representation on the London County Council. Many London local authorities had taken decisions to introduce office printing machines without any guarantee that these methods would be cheaper, or more reliable. The LTS had little doubt that, had it had representation on local authorities when the decision to switch to office printing processes had been made, a different view would have prevailed. The union estimated that thousands of pounds worth of print had been lost to London printing houses because nobody had been present to speak against the growing tendency of local councils to undertake their own printing.[13]

Although the LSC and LTS had no representatives in the House of Commons, they contributed to the Labour Party's General Election Fund. The LSC contributed £350 to the 1951 General Election Fund, whilst the LTS gave £1,903 to the 1959 General Election Fund. In addition, they recommended at the 1950, 1951, 1955 and 1959 general elections that members should vote Labour, and not Conservative, if their industrial interests were to be best protected.

The TA
The first priority on expenditure from the TA Labour Representation Fund was the maintenance of at least one of its members in the House of Commons. Although under Association rules two parliamentary representatives were permissible, the state of the Political Fund over the period 1950–63 meant that only one parliamentary representative could be financed. Each TA branch could nominate a member to be a parliamentary representative, and if the Political Section considered the nominees satisfactory they were subject to a ballot of the membership and the successful candidate became the Association's parliamentary representative. They then sought adoption as a prospective Labour Party candidate in a parliamentary constituency.[14]

In 1950 the TA had two parliamentary representatives – Mr W.A. Wilkins, Labour member for Bristol South, and Mr Harry Walker, Labour member for Rossendale. Prior to the 1950 general election,

Mr Walker announced his retirement from the House and Mr Seymour Hills was elected as a parliamentary representative. In the February 1950 general election, of the two TA-sponsored members, only Wil Wilkins, with a majority of 10,983, was elected.[15] Following the general election, the EC reluctantly decided, after careful consideration, that the parlous state of the LRF made it impossible to proceed with an election for a second parliamentary representative. It was not until 1961 that the TA decided that the LRF was sufficiently strong to support a second parliamentary candidate, and in the subsequent ballot Mr D.F. Lindsay from the Watford branch was elected as the second parliamentary representative.

Although the Labour government lost office at the October 1951 general election, Wilkins retained his seat in Bristol South with a majority of 10,283. The Conservatives were re-elected to government at the May 1955 general election, but Wilkins retained his seat with an increased majority. The Tories won their third successive general election in October 1959, but Wil Wilkins retained his Bristol seat with a reduced majority. The invaluable service which Mr Wilkins gave the TA in representing its interests in Parliament on all questions was underlined in the period 1959–62 by the contributions he made in the House on such vital matters to the TA as the 1959 wage dispute, the closure of the *News Chronicle* and the Printers Imprint Bill. Through Wil Wilkins the TA had speedy access to ministers, MPs and leading Labour Party politicians.

However, in reality the TA never really developed formal liaison procedures with Mr Wilkins. The relationship was a personal one, in that Wil Wilkins had personal friendships with a number of TA senior national officers. The relationship was not on the basis of a need of the TA to express itself at Westminster or indeed of the need for an MP with a base in the industry. Little attention was paid to what way Mr Wilkins voted in the House of Commons or what he did there. The TA traditional view was that its parliamentary representative be regarded as a contribution to the Parliamentary Labour Party.[16] This attitude, which also continued in the early days of the NGA, reflected an 'arms-length, hands-off' relationship between the TA and its parliamentary representative, reflecting the attitude that the TA could best protect and advance the interests of its members through industrial devices and had no need in reality to pay much attention to political affairs.

In 1959 the issue of printing trade union representation in Parliament was raised at the P&KTF, which had received a letter from the TA General Secretary. The letter noted that since the retirement of Mr George Isaacs, a former Natsopa General Secretary, from the House of Commons the only voice of the printing unions in Parliament was Wil Wilkins. It enquired if the smaller printing unions could do something collectively to enhance parliamentary representation. As a first step the Federation sought the views of its affiliated unions, following which it investigated the financial obligations of sponsoring and supporting a parliamentary candidate in the House.

A meeting of P&KTF-affiliated unions with political funds, held in December 1960, agreed that there were occasions (e.g. the 1959 dispute, debates on the press and the Imprints Bill) when it was essential that the MP speaking on the print unions' behalf should have direct responsibility to the printing trade union movement. The Speaker and the House invariably recognised the interests of a sponsored member when matters affecting the industry with which that member was connected were under discussion. Some unions said they were willing themselves to support financially and sponsor a candidate, whilst others expressed willingness to contribute towards the expenses of candidates. Although the unions had suitable members that they could sponsor, the main difficulty would be gaining adoption by a constituency party. It was agreed that when suitable candidates had been found informal approaches would be made to the Labour Party by the Federation to discuss adoption by a constituency.

Following the meeting, the Federation's General Secretary wrote to unions requesting that they seek a suitable candidate without delay. Those unions unable to sponsor a candidate individually were recommended to give financial support to a printing union sponsored candidate and to indicate the extent of any support. Slade offered to pay £100 a year in any collective scheme, whilst the TA, LTS and Natsopa each indicated a desire to finance a candidate individually. By the time the TA merged with the LTS no further progress had been made towards increasing print trade union representation via the P&KTF in the House of Commons.

The TA always contributed to the Labour Party's General Election Fund. It contributed £1,192 to the February 1950 General Election Fund, £673 to the October 1951 General Election Fund, £675 to the May 1955 General Election Fund and £901 to the 1959 General Election Fund. In all the general elections between 1950 and 1962 the TA urged its members, in their best industrial interests, to vote Labour.

The NGA

On the formation of the NGA Wil Wilkins was still in the House of Commons. In the October 1964 general election he retained his seat with a majority of 11,289. In 1965 the NGA Political Executive began the steps to elect a second parliamentary candidate. Seven nominations were received but only two (G.H. Gunn and E. Moonman) went forward to the ballot paper. Subsequently Mr Gunn withdrew and Mr Moonman, who had been adopted as prospective Labour candidate for Billericay, a marginal seat, became the second parliamentary representative. In the March 1966 general election Wil Wilkins was returned to Parliament for the seventh consecutive time with a majority of 13,554. Eric Moonman became the NGA's second Member of Parliament when he won the Billericay seat by a majority of 1,642.

In 1969 Wil Wilkins announced his retirement. Mr Geoffrey Gunn was elected second parliamentary representative, but he was unable to secure adoption as a parliamentary candidate before the 1970 general election was called. In that general election Eric Moonman lost his seat at Billericay, which, with the retirement of Wil Wilkins, meant that the NGA was without a parliamentary representative for the first time. Although in 1972 Eric Moonman was adopted parliamentary candidate for the new constituency of Basildon, by the time the February 1974 general election was called Mr Geoffrey Gunn had still to find a constituency. In the February 1974 general election, Eric Moonman was elected member for Basildon and retained the seat in the October 1974 general election.[17]

In the 1974–9 Parliament, Eric Moonman developed close cooperation with the NGA and was instrumental in contacting ministers on problems involving the NGA. However, in the May 1979 general election Eric Moonman lost his Basildon seat and, at the time of the election of a Conservative government committed 'to curb' trade union power, the NGA found itself without representation in the House. In these circumstances the Association could not afford to be without representation in the House. Arrangements were to be made for a Labour MP to represent NGA interests in the House until one of its parliamentary representatives was elected to the House. Mr Christopher Price, MP for West Lewisham, who as an NUJ member had an association with and understanding of the industry, was approached. Discussions with Mr Price and his constituency were abandoned when the Labour Party insisted that any arrangements should be under the Hastings Agreement. The NGA could not accept this as it was contrary to its political rules that it must support one of its own parliamentary representatives. Eventually these obstacles were removed and arrangements were agreed in July 1981 for Chris Price to represent the NGA in the House in return for the NGA paying £250 per quarter to the West Lewisham Constituency Labour Party.

Just before the 1980 Delegate Meeting, Mr Ray Allen was elected the Association's parliamentary candidate and was later joined by Eric Moonman, who had been successful in a ballot of members. In 1982 Ray Allen was adopted as prospective Labour parliamentary candidate at Colchester. At the time of its merger with NGA, Slade had two sponsored MPs under Hastings arrangements – Arthur Davidson, Labour member for Accrington, and Martin O'Neill, Labour member for Clackmannan. These arrangements continued in the NGA(1982).

The June 1983 general election saw the re-election of the Conservative government with an increased majority. Ray Allen came third behind the Tory and Alliance candidates. Eric Moonman had failed to secure adoption as a parliamentary candidate. Of the NGA(1982)-sponsored MPs, only Martin O'Neill was re-elected. Chris Price was also defeated, while Arthur Davidson lost by 21 votes at Hydnburn, Lancashire.

In the 1983–7 Parliament, the NGA established closer liaison with Martin O'Neill, who facilitated frequent meetings between the NGA leadership and the Party leadership and Shadow Front Bench spokesmen for Employment and Industry. At these meetings the NGA provided detailed information to Shadow Cabinet members on a whole range of issues including the likely impact on employment prospects in the industry of the government's proposed imposition of VAT on newspapers and magazines, on the proposed deregularisation of small businesses, on Fleet Street industrial relations, and on union ballots. Martin O'Neill also ensured that the NGA had direct access to the Labour Party leadership. The policy of developing formal links between the NGA(1982) and its parliamentary representatives and between NGA(1982) leadership and Labour Party leadership was in sharp contrast to the 'arms-length, hands-off relationship' which existed with the TA and the NGA pre-1980. The change of approach reflected the NGA's realisation that the technological revolution implemented in the printing industry from the mid-1970s meant it could no longer live in an industrial world completely separate from politics, particularly with a government in office introducing legislation designed to curb the main industrial practices by which the NGA protected and advanced the industrial interests of its members. If the NGA was to have a major influence on what should replace such legislation it required to be at the 'heart beat' of Labour Party policy-making.

In 1985 the Political Executive approved the selection of two NGA parliamentary representative candidates. Ray Allen was re-elected in 1985, but by the time the 1987 general election was called he had not gained adoption as a parliamentary candidate. It was decided not to seek the election of a second parliamentary representative candidate until the result of the Political Fund ballot, required under the 1984 Trade Union Act, was known. Although there was a positive result, the majority of the Labour Party's targeted and winnable seats had by early 1986 already concluded their selection of candidates. Furthermore, where opportunities arose, the NGA gave priority to nominating Ray Allen, particularly given his long service as parliamentary representative candidate. However, in October 1986, to increase the NGA's influence in the House, the union sponsored Tony Lloyd, Labour MP for Stretford in Manchester, who came from a family of litho printers.

The difficulties experienced in attempting to get Ray Allen adopted as a parliamentary candidate led the NGA to conduct a survey of its branches regarding their affiliation to constituency Labour parties. The results revealed a mixed situation, but in the main the level of constituency Labour party affiliation by branches was unsatisfactory. This reinforced the view that if NGA parliamentary representation was increased it would have to raise its political profile, not in terms of campaigning about the major political issues of the day, but in terms of building networks of contacts with influence at the appropriate level in the Labour Party organisation. Affiliation to constituency parties was essential so that, if parliamentary candidate vacancies came up, the NGA would be in a position to nominate one of its parliamentary representatives. For these reasons the important function of 'NGA for Labour' was to erect an organisational structure to encourage more branches to affiliate to local constituency Labour parties.

The general election of June 1987 saw a Conservative government elected for the third consecutive time. Tony Lloyd and Martin O'Neill were both returned to the House and have continued to liaise between the NGA leadership and Labour leadership and the parliamentary Shadow Front Bench on many issues. In July 1989 the NGA increased its representation in the House of Commons when Jim Marshall, a Labour front bench spokesman on Northern Ireland and member for Leicester South, became the NGA(1982)'s third sponsored MP. In terms of sponsored MPs, the 1980s saw a pragmatic response by the NGA. The need for an NGA voice in the House of Commons was so strong in the 1980s that it was prepared to support Labour MPs already in the House, even though they were not involved directly in the NGA or the industry. For the LSC/LTS/TA/NGA to have had anybody other than a member representing the union's interest in the House would have been inconceivable.

Even before the 1987 general election, the NGA had been examining how it might in future be represented in Parliament. A consultative document on Association parliamentary representative candidates was discussed at the 1987 regional consultative conferences. The document spelt out that under its existing system the NGA had only once since the 1979 general election succeeded in having a candidate adopted, namely Ray Allen at Colchester North in 1983. It proposed that one option open to the NGA was to sponsor MPs as required and another might be to have no restrictions on the numbers of members that could be nominated, thus dispensing with the need to elect the required number of members by membership ballot. However, it was recognised that this might have to be balanced by nominees having to satisfy the union as to their experience and credentials to represent the union in Parliament. A third option proposed was that there should be provision both for getting members onto the Labour Party's 'A' list of candidates and also for sponsoring sitting MPs.

The intention of the NGA parliamentary representation system was to get NGA members into the House. However, although it was a highly democratic selection procedure, the NGA was not a parliamentary constituency. Although NGA Political Fund contributors could elect a parliamentary representative, it did not mean that they would actually end up in Parliament. In short, the policy did not necessarily achieve its objective. To overcome the problem, the Kent branch submitted proposals to the 1988 Delegate Meeting suggesting that, instead of concentrating efforts on getting one or two members adopted as prospective parliamentary candidates, there should be a panel of NGA candidates spread across the country so that at the appropriate time the NGA locally would attempt to get the appropriate member selected as the Labour Party parliamentary candidate in the constituency. When this had been achieved the NGA would give financial support. The proposals also envisaged nominees for parliamentary representatives from branches being examined by the Political Executive and the names of successful nominees being published in *Print*.

Candidates approved by the Political Executive would be placed on the 'A' List of candidates of the Labour Party. The NGA's list of candidates would be endorsed at the delegate meeting, and after each general election the list of candidates would be reviewed by the Political Executive. The Kent branch proposals also advocated the sponsoring of sitting Labour MPs to represent the NGA's interests in Parliament if there were no NGA members in the House. Political Fund contributors at the 1988 Delegate Meeting approved these proposals, which became operative on 1 January 1989.

The NGA always contributed to the Labour Party's General Election Fund. For example, £3,000 was given for the October 1974 General Election Fund and £25,000 to the 1983 General Election Fund. The NGA saw a Labour victory at the 1987 general election as being of the highest priority if the industrial interests of the members were to be advanced. This was the only chance that the legislative restriction on its traditional industrial practices imposed in the 1980s would be repealed. It therefore spent much money and time in assisting the Labour Party in that general election campaign. It mounted a major campaign in support of the Labour Party. A financial appeal for a day's pay from full-time officers and one hour's pay from individual members raised £6,771.65 for the Labour Victory Fund, whilst £35,240.22 (being 87p per affiliated member requested by Trade Unionists for Labour) was paid from the Political Fund. In response to a further appeal for finance in the closing days of the election, the NGA donated a further £30,000 from the Political Fund. In addition, the NGA campaigned amongst the membership in those branches having within them Labour Party target and marginal seats. The NGA national and regional officers were made available to visit plants and attend meetings to put the NGA's case for supporting the Labour Party, and the General Secretary undertook an intensive and arduous campaign in many parts of the country. This involvement in a Labour Party general election campaign was in marked contrast to its attitude towards previous general election campaigns.

THE LABOUR PARTY

The annual conference

The LSC and LTS always sent their full delegation of two to the annual conference but they never proposed or seconded a motion at any Labour Party conference between 1950 and 1954 inclusive. However, the LTS delegation via the General Secretary contributed to conference debates. For example, at the 1960 and 1961 conferences, Bob Willis, the LTS General Secretary, spoke in favour of unilateral disarmament.

The TA sent five delegates to the Party conference, one of whom was a member of the Executive Council and another the union's parliamentary representative. The other three delegates were elected on a regional basis by the LRF payers. Prior to 1953 the TA vote at the Party conference was in accordance with a majority decision of the TA's delegates attending the conference. However, from May 1953 it was on the basis of National Executive Council decision. During the period 1948–63 the TA never proposed or seconded a motion at a Labour Party conference. However, its delegates did on occasions make contributions to debates. For example, at the 1953 Annual Conference, Wil Wilkins, MP, speaking as a TA delegate, supported an unsuccessful proposal to bring the armaments industry under public control.

The NGA sent five delegates to the annual conference, but it was not until 1976 that it really began to take an active part in its business in terms of moving motions, seconding motions, contributing to debates and asking questions on the NEC report. An exception to this was the 1971 and 1972 conferences. At the latter the NGA spoke in favour of a resolution from the T&GWU calling for the immediate repeal of the 1971 Industrial Relations Act when Labour returned to office which was carried unanimously. Although the NGA had resigned from the TUC over the deregistration issue, it remained in membership of the Labour Party and at the 1972 conference seconded a motion which deplored the inadequate provision of training and retraining facilities for groups such as women, older workers and handicapped workers.

The NGA, as with the TUC, adopted a high profile within the Labour Party from this date. The reasons for this were the same as those for adopting such a profile within the TUC (see Chapter 10). The higher profile not only associated the NGA more openly with the wider issues facing the Labour Party but was a deliberate attempt to directly influence Labour Party policy-making from the inside by if possible gaining representation on the Party's NEC. The contributions at the 1971 and 1972 annual conferences related to bread and butter industrial issues, not to such issues as nuclear disarmament and membership of the Common Market.

Since 1976 the small NGA delegation has played a role in the conference out of proportion to its size. At the 1977 conference the NGA persuaded the Party to include in a successful composite motion on taxation that trade union members be allowed to claim a tax allowance on their union subscriptions. The 1979 conference saw the NGA successfully move a major motion criticising the Conservative government's proposed trade union reforms and attacks upon the trade unions from the judiciary. The NGA had an outstanding success at the 1985 conference in that it moved one of only two major resolutions on the Labour Party's Jobs and Industry campaign, which was one of the Party's most successful policy initiatives of the 1980s. It also amended a T&GWU motion on the economy to include a reference to opposition to the deregularisation of small businesses. In the following year, influenced by the News International dispute, the Association success-fully moved a motion calling for restrictions on the ownership of the British newspapers. At the 1988 Labour conference an NGA amend-ment was included in a successful composite on the Single European Market, which called for the European Community to implement 'social provisions' and a complementary Social Programme to ensure that the benefits of the single market were shared by all in the EEC and not just the business community.

The National Executive Committee

At the 1968 Labour Party Conference the NGA unsuccessfully proposed its General President, Fred Simmons, for membership of the NEC via the Trade Union Section. It was not until 1980 that the NGA again nominated one of its members for membership of the NEC. In that year and the following one it unsuccessfully nominated Gordon Colling. However, the size of his vote on both occasions was sufficient to give hope for eventual success. In 1985 the NGA succeeded in gaining a representative on the Labour Party NEC when Gordon Colling received 3.2 million votes in the Trade Union Section ballot. This was the first time in the history of the NGA and its constituent societies that direct representation on the NEC had been achieved. It was also the first time that such a 'small union' in relation to total UK trade union membership had gained such a position.

In subsequent years Gordon Colling was re-elected to the Labour Party NEC with increased majorities and played an active part on many NEC subcommittees and in the Policy Reviews Group.[18] Whilst the NGA was responsible for his nomination to the NEC, he was not a representative of just the NGA on that body. His election required the support of other unions, and the constituents to whom he is accountable as a member of the NEC are all unions affiliated to the Labour Party. The achievement of a representative on the Labour Party NEC was the 'jewel in the crown' of the NGA's policy of a high profile within the Labour Party. Although this higher profile, together with that developed by the General Secretary, Tony Dubbins, within the TUC, has been maintained, there still remains the need for the NGA to translate this higher national profile into relationships at local Labour Party level.

The Constitutional Reforms: the 1980s

The late 1970s saw the development of pressures for greater democracy within the Labour Party, centring around the reselection of Labour MPs, the election of the leader and deputy leader of the Party and that the NEC, not the Parliamentary Labour Party, should have control of the Party's general election manifesto. At the 1980 Labour Party conference the NGA delegation, in line with a decision of the 1978 Delegate Meeting, voted for the compulsory reselection of MPs, and for the re-establishment of a three-year rule with respect of changes to the Party's constitution. The NGA delegation voted against the Labour Party National Executive having sole control of the general election manifesto, and the adoption of an electoral college method of electing the leader and deputy leader of the Party. However, the 1986 Delegate Meeting voted to pursue the adoption by the Labour Party of the 'one member, one vote' principle in respect of the reselection of MPs. This has not been achieved within the Party, although the NGA voted in favour of it at the 1988 Labour Party conference.

In January 1981 a special Labour Party conference met at Wembley to consider the mechanics of an electoral college for electing the leader and deputy leader. The NGA delegation supported the principle of 'one man, one vote' for these elections on the grounds that such a system came closest to the NGA's own methods of consulting its membership and was the most direct way of widening the franchise for electing the Party leader. When this was heavily defeated, the delegation supported an electoral college in which 50 per cent of the votes would be held by Labour MPs and the other half divided equally between the trade unions and the constituency parties. The NGA supported the Parliamentary Labour Party having the biggest say in the electoral college, as Labour MPs had to have a leader of the Party with whom they could work. When this compromise was rejected, the NGA delegation voted for the 40/30/30 formula proposed by USDAW. Under this formula, which was accepted by the special conference, 40 per cent of the votes in the electoral college would go to the trade unions, 30 per cent to Labour MPs and 30 per cent to the constituency parties.

In 1981 there was a deputy leader election contest between Mr Tony Benn and Mr Denis Healey, the existing deputy leader, which was narrowly won by the latter. The NGA delegation voted for Denis Healey in accordance with a decision taken by its Political Executive at its September 1981 meeting. Despite this, the 1982 Delegate Meeting censured the NGA delegation for voting for Denis Healey. They rejected the view that Healey supported policies closest to the wishes of the NGA membership. They pointed out that Mr Healey supported wage restraint, Common Market membership and cuts in public expenditure and opposed greater accountability of elected representatives of the Labour Party. These were all policies to which the NGA by delegate meeting decision was opposed. The National Council opposed this censure on a number of grounds. First, that the time between the official announcement of the candidates and the Labour Party conference was barely adequate for the members' views, in a period heavily affected by holidays, to be taken. Second, the Political Fund could not bear the cost of a ballot of the members on the issue. Third, the Political Executive had the ultimate responsibility of instructing the NGA Labour Party delegation on how to vote on issues in the absence of a ballot of the members. Four, other than Common Market entry, the whole Political Fund membership had never voted against the other issues.

Michael Foot resigned as the leader of the Labour Party following the 1983 general election defeat. In the ensuing leadership ballot at the 1983 annual conference the NGA voted for Neil Kinnock for Labour Party leader and Roy Hattersley as deputy leader. Following Labour's defeat in the 1987 general election, the Kinnock–Hattersley leadership was challenged by Tony Benn (for leadership) and Eric Heffer (for deputy leadership). Following a ballot of its Political Fund paying members the NGA backed the successful re-election of Neil Kinnock as leader and Roy Hattersley as his deputy at the 1987 annual conference. In 1988, John Prescott challenged Roy Hattersley for the deputy leadership of the Party but the NGA again after a ballot of its Political Fund membership, supported the successful re-election of Roy Hattersley.

ATTITUDES TOWARDS MAJOR POLITICAL ISSUES

Disarmament

The LTS was strongly in favour of unilateral disarmament of nuclear weapons. Its 1960 annual conference debated and carried, with only four votes against, the following resolution moved by the Executive Council:

> That this Conference, conscious of the annihilating effects which the use of nuclear weapons would entail on industry and the possible destruction of humanity places on records its abhorrence and revulsion that Britain should possess and consider the use of such weapons. It urges that Britain should take the initiative in moves designed to ban the use of nuclear weapons, and in pursuit of such policy unilaterally to ban the manufacture or operation of those weapons from bases in this country.
>
> Conference further notes with regret the breakdown of the Summit Talks and expresses the hope that all possible steps will be taken to resuscitate talks of this nature between Heads of Governments in order to maintain and preserve the peaceful relationships which are essential to industrial progress and improvement of our standard of living.

The Executive Council felt it was important that guidance to the LTS delegations to the TUC Congress and the Labour Party conference of 1960 as to how they should vote on the issue should come from the annual conference rather than the General Secretary or from any of the delegations endeavouring to interpret what they considered to be the policy of the Society. The LTS opposition to nuclear weapons was based on three factors. First, if they were used it could result in the complete annihilation of human race. Second, that even if war never came and nuclear weapons were never used the very testing of them and the manufacture of them would slowly but methodically destroy the health of thousands and thousands of people. Third, that the radioactivity of such weapons would create new diseases for mankind and mean future generations of children being born malformed mentally and physically.[19]

The 1960 Labour Party conference voted in favour of unilateral nuclear disarmament but the Party leadership pledged 'to fight, fight and fight again' to reverse the policy. In the interests of restoring unity to the Labour Party, a statement entitled 'This Way to Peace' was sponsored by unilateralists. This statement was adopted by the January 1962 meeting of the LTS Political Section. The main thrusts of the statement were that the UN should become the cornerstone of British foreign policy, that regional pacts such as NATO, the Warsaw Treaty, CENTO and SEATO should be wound up and replaced, where necessary, by broader agreements, that nuclear weapons should be withheld from all forces in Western and Eastern Germany, that Britain would not resume nuclear testing, that no Polaris or Thor bases should be allowed to remain in Britain, and that there should be no more patrol flights by British aircraft carrying H-bombs and based on airfields in Britain.[20]

The TA, on the other hand, favoured nuclear disarmament on a multilateral basis. At the 1958 Labour Party conference it supported a joint TUC/Labour Party NEC statement on disarmament and nuclear weapons which favoured multilateralism. The statement, *inter alia*, urged the British government to make serious efforts to bring about Summit Talks in the near future, and to press for a general agreement to end all tests, hydrogen and atomic, if necessary as a separate measure, that test suspension by itself was not enough and agreement on tests must lead, within a reasonable period, to real progress on the basic problem of general disarmament, that general disarmament agreement should include a declaration banning the use of all nuclear weapons and that no physical steps should be taken to set up missile bases in Britain before a fresh attempt had been made to negotiate with Russia.

In May 1961 the EC decided to conduct a ballot of members on defence policy, as it believed that in this way the hands of the TA delegations to the TUC Congress and the Labour Party conferences of that year would be strengthened on a vital issue. The issue had been aired so widely that there was no reason to await the TUC agenda to know precisely what the issue was. In the ballot, members were asked to vote either for or against the TUC/Labour Party joint statement on a multilateralist defence and disarmament policy. The TA EC was confident that the membership would endorse the Council's support for this statement, although it was to be a 'free ballot' without recommendation as to how the members should vote. The TA favoured a ballot because of suspicion in the public mind that not all views expressed on behalf of unions on defence policy at the TUC and the

356

Labour Party conference reflected those of their ordinary members. The TA felt that, so long as this suspicion remained, the whole policy-making machinery of the trade union movement would be held in disrepute.

The ballot of the members on the TUC/Labour Party defence policy was 17,869 in favour, 6,115 votes against. At the time of the ballot decision, the question of whether to ballot the LRF members prior to the 1961 Labour Party conference had not been taken. The TA decided that the ballot result of all members meant that the question no longer arose. The TA delegates to the TUC Congress and Labour Party conferences of 1961 were instructed to support the multilateralist defence policy statement of the TUC and the Labour Party NEC.

The NGA 1982 Delegate Meeting referred to the National Council a pro nuclear disarmament motion which included a proposal that the NGA should affiliate to the Campaign for Nuclear Disarmament (CND). After considering the motion, the National Council affiliated to CND. In 1983, at the request of its branches, the NGA urged the Labour Party NEC to ensure the inclusion of unilateral nuclear disarmament in the Labour Party's 1983 general election manifesto.[21] The 1988 Delegate Meeting approved a Chiltern and Thames Valley branch motion which urged the Labour Party to maintain a totally unilateralist position on nuclear weapons. However, following its 1987 general election defeat the Labour Party decided to undertake a review of its existing policies. In 1989 a defence policy review statement entitled *A Power for Good: Britain in the World* proposed that, in the changed pattern of world power relationships following the Gorbachev–Reagan initiatives, Britain should pursue nuclear disarmament through negotiation rather than unilaterally. In September 1989 the NGA balloted its Political Fund paying members, recommending that they accept the Labour Party change of defence policy. The ballot resulted in overwhelming support for this recommendation.

The Common Market

In 1961 the British government applied to join the European Economic Community (EEC), a move that was opposed by the Labour Party. The TUC, however, gave qualified support to the government's action, as did the TA, which rejected the view that the EEC was nineteenth-century capitalism. It argued that it was better described as capitalist planning in which there was an acceptance of social obligations. It also considered that the argument that EEC entry would mean a loss of UK political sovereignty was more apparent than real given the polarised state of the world between the USA and Russia.

The General Secretary of the LTS, Mr Robert Willis on the other hand, was firmly opposed to Common Market entry. In an editorial in the Society's monthly journal he argued that assessment of the impact of EEC entry had to be wider than just economic considerations, where even here weight had to be given to whether the gains in potential customers would exceed possible losses from Commonwealth country customers. On the political aspects the General Secretary argued that, in the ultimate, entry into Europe meant participating in a virtual United States of Europe and the surrender, under the Treaty of Rome, of a considerable amount of national sovereignty. On the social side he pointed out that the provisions of the Treaty of Rome allowed the free transfer of capital, free transfer of labour and for the harmonisation of working conditions, but if that there were a flight of capital from the UK the British government would not be able to introduce controls to deal with such situations without the approval of the EEC authorities. The LTS General Secretary considered on balance that entry into the EEC was not to be welcomed by the British people.

However, Britain's attempts to gain entry into the EEC ended when they were vetoed by the French government. An attempt by the Labour government of 1966–70, under the premiership of Harold Wilson, to negotiate entry into the EEC was also unsuccessful. However, a Conservative government led by Edward Heath successfully negotiated terms of entry and Britain joined the EEC in January 1973. The Labour Party remained opposed to entry and became committed to withdrawal from the EEC, a policy stance that did not change until the late 1980s.

In July 1971 the NGA National Council decided to oppose Britain's entry into the EEC on the grounds that the onus of proof that entry would have net benefits rested with the pro-marketeers and that to date no conclusive case had been made out for entry. Bearing this in mind the NGA delegation to a special Labour Party conference on the EEC held on 17 July 1971 supported the view that the NEC should, in the light of the debate at the conference, formulate a definitive motion on the EEC for presentation and debate at the October 1971 annual conference. A resolution demanding an immediate commitment to stay out of the EEC was defeated by 3.2 million votes to 2.6 million. Given the importance of the Common Market debate, the NGA decided to ballot its Political Fund payers on the matter so that its delegation to the 1971 annual conference would have no doubt as to how to cast its vote. The result of the ballot, announced in September 1971, was 26,119 votes against Britain joining the Common Market and 18,908 in favour of joining. Only nine branches, including Birmingham and Bristol, voted in favour of entry.

In 1975 the Labour government held a referendum on whether Britain should remain in the EEC. Although the British electorate voted overwhelmingly in favour of continued membership, the NGA remained in favour of withdrawal. Its 1982 Delegate Meeting carried a motion from the Oxon and Berks branch which stated, 'This BDM supports TUC policy of withdrawal from the Common Market'.[22]

NOTES

1. See E. Howe and H.E. Waite, *The London Society of Compositors*, Cassell, 1948, Ch. XX, p. 324.

2. See 'Political Section', *London Typographical Journal*, April 1951, p. 10.

3. See *London Typographical Journal*, June 1950, p. 2; and *London Typographical Journal*, April 1954, p. 20.

4. See *Report of Triennial Delegate Meeting, 1953*, Typographical Association, pp. 15–16.

5. The TA's parliamentary representative claimed a grant of £50 as against the £150 allowed under rule.

6. In addition, under the Hastings Agreement the TA was responsible for 80 per cent of the expenses of the cost of the election in the constituency of its parliamentary representative. This involved the TA in an average expenditure of £100 when Parliament ran its full course but more when elections were more frequent. The Hastings Agreement also committed the TA to make an annual contribution of £110 to the Labour Party's By-Election Guarantee Fund.

7. The increase in affiliation fees from 2½p to 4p per member involved, on the 1957 contributing membership to the LRF, an annual payment by the TA of £1,194. The level of the LRF in 1957 could not afford this sum.

8. For example, in the 1983–7 Parliament there were sixteen Conservative MPs who represented paper, printing and publishing interests through direct consultancy appointments or business interests.

9. The difficulty facing the LSC was not so much that of a constituency but of securing names of members who had a national standing, for without that they were advised little opportunity for selection existed.

10. See 'Political Section', *London Typographical Journal*, April 1954, p. 20.

11. He remarked, 'I have made a promise to the membership. It is for them alone to release me if they so desire', see *London Typographical Journal*, April 1954, p. 20.

12. See 'This Apathy Concerns You', *London Typographical Journal*, September 1956, p. 7.

13. ibid.

14. Any member nominated as parliamentary candidate or by any branch as a candidate for any local public body had to sign an agreement to the effect that they would stand as a Labour candidate and not allow themselves to be nominated by any other party.

15. Mr Seymour Hills contested the Woodford Division, his principal opponent being Winston Churchill, who retained the seat. This defeat meant that Hills automatically relinquished his position as parliamentary representative.

16. See 'A Rarity: A Politician who cares about ethics – and people', *Print*, April 1969, p. 2.

14. In the 1974 general elections, Ivor Clementson, a head ofice research assistant, also won the Luton East Constituency. Unfortunately, another member of the head office staff at that time, Mr Gordon Colling, was not successful in his attempts to win the Bedford constituency for Labour.

18. For example, Gordon Colling was criticised directly in a Liverpool motion to the 1988 Delegate Meeting for leading negotiations on behalf of the NEC to close three Labour Party publications. A part of the motion stated, 'The BDM also deplores the spectacle of a national officer leading negotiations to secure redundancy of print and publishing workers who are employed by the Labour Party. The BDM believes that an NGA official should be in the forefront of the fight to defend jobs and to expand printing and publishing facilities.' The General Secretary, Tony Dubbins, defended Gordon Colling's behaviour on the grounds that 'he is, very clearly, obliged to carry out his responsibilities to decisions to the National Executive Committee of the Party'. He was faced with such responsibilities after the NEC made the decision to close *Labour Weekly*, *Socialist Youth* and *the New Socialist*. This Liverpool motion was defeated. See *Report of the Delegate Meeting, 1988*, National Graphical Association, pp. 404–9.

19. See 'The H-Bombs and the Future of Humanity', *London Typographical Journal*, July 1960, pp. 7–9.

20. See 'This Way to Peace', *London Typographical Journal*, January 1962, p. 9.

21. See *Report of the Delegate Meeting, 1984*, National Graphical Association, p. 82.

22. See *Report of the Delegate Meeting, 1982*, National Graphical Association, pp. 386–8.

PART IV

RELATIONSHIPS WITH EMPLOYERS

CHAPTER 12

THE GENERAL PRINTING TRADE AND PROVINCIAL NEWSPAPER EMPLOYERS: (I) WAGES AND HOURS MOVEMENTS, 1948–89

The main employers' organisation in the general printing trade in the UK is the British Printing Industries Federation (BPIF), which until 1974 was known as the British Federation of Master Printers (BFMP) which had been formed in 1901. Up to, and including, the 1980 wage negotiations the Master Printers negotiated with the print unions jointly with the Newspaper Society (NS), formed in 1920, which represents firms engaged in the production of provincial daily and weekly (including London suburban) newspapers. In the early 1960s the TA unsuccessfully tried to persuade the Newspaper Society to negotiate unilaterally. The Society argued that a separate daily newspaper agreement granted to one union would merely be an invitation to others to make the same request and that separate agreements for weekly and daily newspapers would greatly complicate the conduct of its affairs. The TA wanted a separate agreement because the greater profitability of daily provincial newspapers relative to other provincial papers and the general printing trade offered the opportunity to gain enhanced terms and conditions for its members employed in daily provincial newspapers.

THE JOINT INDUSTRIAL COUNCIL

From 1919 to 1966 there was a Joint Industrial Council for the Printing Industry, consisting on the employers' side of BFMP and NS representatives and on the employees' side of representatives from unions affiliated to the P&KTF. The Council had no authority to negotiate wage agreements but did operate conciliation machinery for dealing with industrial disputes, an apprenticeship panel to regulate apprentice matters and a Health Committee.

The 1959 Annual Meeting of the Council, in the light of the failure of its conciliation machinery in the 1959 dispute,[1] established a sub-committee 'to consider the position and examine the present JIC Constitution and Rules, and to report to the Council within 6 months with recommendations for a considerably revised constitution'. The failure of the conciliation machinery brought to the fore for both sides of the industry their concerns about the JIC's ability to regulate the industry. In January 1960 the employers submitted their detailed proposals for a revised constitution. The most important were that the JIC object 'to secure complete organisation of employers and employees throughout the trade' be deleted (Clause 2), that the size of the Council be reduced from eighty to sixty-eight, that the Council meet annually instead of quarterly, that the JIC 'shall not concern itself with disputes arising as to the meaning, operation, or construction' of agreements, and that if a dispute of a 'local character' were not settled by a JIC conciliation committee it be referred to an independent chairman whose decision would be binding.

The unions expressed concern at these suggestions and in June 1960 published counter-proposals: Clause 2 should remain, the Council should meet at least twice a year, disputes arising from claims for revision of national agreements should be outside the scope of the JIC, and local disputes procedures should remain unchanged. The employers accepted the unions' proposals, with one important exception. They were not prepared to accept the retention of Clause 2 of the constitution. It had been a source of bad feeling over many years because of the unions' support for Natsopa's attempts to invoke the clause in their desire to organise clerical workers, a purpose for which the clause had never been intended.

For the unions much more was involved than the organisation of clerical workers.[2] The aspiration of complete organisation of employers and workers in the industry was a central pillar of the constitution of the JIC. Its deletion would be interpreted as a significant departure from the principles on which the JIC had been founded. For the unions, the employers' desire to delete Clause 2 was an attempt to undermine union organisation and possibly to introduce an 'open house' policy. A measure of the strength of TA and LTS feelings was that they preferred to see the end of the JIC rather than the deletion of Clause 2. The full JIC referred the deadlock back to the constitutional subcommittee for further consideration.

The deadlock was not broken until January 1962 when both sides of the Joint Industrial Council accepted the insertion of a footnote to Clause 2 to the effect that the JIC had no powers to secure organisation of either side of the industry and that that responsibility lay with the parties. In October 1963 the first full meeting of the JIC for three years[3] approved a revised constitution, the main features of which included that the number of full JIC meetings should be reduced to two, the number of standing committees should be reduced to four, and disputes arising from the establishment or revision of agreements should be outside the scope of conciliation by the Council. The meeting then elected Mr Bob Willis, General Secretary of the LTS, as Vice-Chairman of the JIC, and in October 1964, after a gap of five years, the JIC annual convention was resumed.

However, in April 1966 the JIC dissolved itself because of continuing problems over the operation of the disputes procedures. The dissolution decision was deferred to allow time for arrangements to be made for the establishment of alternative joint machinery to deal with apprentice and health matters. Nevertheless, by May 1968 the NGA accepted that health and safety measures should continue to be dealt with by joint action through the offices of the P&KTF, the BFMP and the Newspaper Society. The Printing and Publishing Industry Training Board (ITB) was to absorb the JIC's training responsibilities.

WAGE MOVEMENTS, 1947–55

The 1948/9 Negotiations

In January 1946 the print unions received pay increases which were stabilised until 30 June 1947 provided the cost of living did not materially alter. The 1947 TA Delegate Meeting adopted a wage policy of 'nine bob or bust' designed to restore provincial craft parity and the London/provincial craft differential as established by the 1919 National Wage Basis Agreement. We saw in Chapters 2 and 9 that these relativities had been disturbed by the 1921–3 wage cuts.[4]

Immediately following the 1947 Delegate Meeting, the TA submitted a claim to the BFMP and the NS for a 45p per week increase to restore parity with the basic rate of other comparable craftsmen. A rider was added to the claim that any increase conceded by the employers to those already enjoying better rates than the TA would be the basis for a further TA claim. At the same time, wage claims were made by other unions, including the LSC, and the employers saw it would be impractical to deal with them separately. However, the unions could not agree a coordinated approach, so each union prosecuted its own negotiations. In December 1947 the BFMP and the NS reached an agreement with the TA, to operate from 1 January 1948, for an increase of 45p (9/-) per week in return for the TA making concessions on apprenticeship ratios and agreeing to a Joint Committee to consider the introduction of incentive payments in TA departments.

The LSC claimed a weekly increase of £1.10 and its members voted by 6,485 votes to 957 to stop work in support of it. An overtime embargo was imposed but, after several fruitless appearances before the JIC Conciliation Committee, strike notice was given. The employers reported the matter to the Minister of Labour, who referred the case to the National Arbitration Tribunal (NAT), which, on 14 January 1948, awarded the LSC an increase of 75p (15/-) per week, thereby raising the London craft minimum to £7 per week. The Tribunal findings had regard to the fact that in recent years the traditional wage differential between London and provincial compositors expressed in percentage terms had progressively declined. The NSES also received an increase in basic rates of 42½p (8/6d), so by March 1948 the TA's relative position had deteriorated once again.

In April 1948 the TA claimed an increase of 42½p per week to restore the relative position established by its January 1948 agreement. The BFMP and the NS received the claim with dismay, but the TA stressed that its members were not prepared to accept basic rates lower than those paid to comparable craftsmen in the industry. When in July the employers rejected the claim, the TA gave notice of termination of the provisions of the 1948 agreement covering incentive schemes and the apprenticeship ratio. Although the JIC considered the dispute, it realised that the TA's claim was part of the industry's wider difficulty of lacking an agreed wage structure. It recommended that both sides of the industry should meet to consider the advisability and practicability of a wage structure for the industry. However, the unions could not agree such a structure.

Following the breakdown of wage structure talks, the TA balloted its membership on termination of its national agreements, on withdrawal from the JIC and on branches taking local action to secure rates of wages not less favourable than those for stereotypers. The Ministry of Labour intervened and eventually enabled the two sides to get together and negotiate a new and comprehensive national agreement to operate from 1 November 1949. Under this, the number of wage grades remained at four but there was a considerable amount of upgrading,[5] the whole question of which was to be investigated by a Joint Committee. Basic rates were increased by amounts varying between 35p per week and 50p per week to give new rates of grade 1: £6.55, grade 2: £6.22½, grade 3: £6.17½ and grade 4: £6.10. The hourly rates for jobbing shifts were to be 25 per cent above the basic hourly rate, and 20 per cent for double day shifts. In return for these pay improvements the TA accepted a bonus of an additional 200 apprentices to meet an acute labour shortage, cooperation with the introduction of 'payment by results' systems, working reasonable overtime to meet the production requirements of the industry, and to give six months' notice to end the agreement. TA members ratified this deal of trading manpower concessions for increased pay and conditions by 21,283 votes to 10,859.

The agreement provided parity with the stereotypers, a fair measure of regrading and provision for further consideration of grading anomalies and an advancement on shift rates. On the other hand, the differential between the compositor and the machine typesetter was reduced and the need for incentive schemes stressed. However, the agreement was not without its critics, who made their feeling known in motions to the TA 1950 Delegate Meeting. The main complaints were that branches had not been consulted over incentive schemes, that individual incentive payments were inappropriate for craftsmen, that overtime had to be worked to complete work, that insufficient had been achieved on grading and that six months' notice was required to terminate the agreement.

The 1949/51 Negotiations

In November 1949 the LSC told the employers that the TA agreement had reduced the London/provincial craft differential below that established in the 1948 NAT Award and a weekly increase of 49½p (9/9) was necessary to restore this. Given the economic difficulties facing the country the LSC decided not to press its claim. However, in April 1950 it formally submitted a claim for an increase of 49½p and in addition it was prepared to trade further pay increases against concessions on labour supply issues. The London employers offered an increase of 12½p per week conditional on the LSC accepting an increase in the ratio of apprentices to journeyman. This was rejected and the May 1950 LSC Delegate Meeting voted to withdraw from the JIC, to strictly apply the Society's rules on working practices, to give notice to the employers that all overtime would be stopped from 18 May 1950, to refuse to accept new members for employment, and to withdraw its claim for the maintenance of differentials as awarded in the 1948 NAT decision.

On 5 May 1950 the employers reported the dispute to the Ministry of Labour, which referred the matter to the NAT, which was asked to determine an appropriate minimum wage rate and an adequate increased recruitment of labour into the composing room. A special LSC conference held on 25 May agreed that the executive should appear before the Tribunal, although it now considered that, having withdrawn its London/provincial craft differential claim, the Tribunal had no case to hear. The conference refused to lift the overtime ban unless 'the LMPA would recognise the LSC as the union authorised to speak for compositors in London and cease basing their negotiations on agreements reached with non craft unions'.[6]

On 20 June 1950 the Tribunal awarded the LSC a weekly increase of 17½p in the minimum rate and recommended that the two parties enter negotiation on the question of recruitment of labour into the industry and that if an agreement were not reached within three months it be open to either party to return to the Tribunal. On 6 July the reconvened special LSC conference voted to maintain the overtime ban unless the proposed negotiations were independent of any proposed wage structure for the industry, were based on the merits of the case and were not conditioned by threats emanating from other trade unions. Compensatory payments, at a level to be decided by the executive, were to be made to members involved in the overtime ban and members employed in non-federated firms and national newspapers were to pay a levy of 5p per hour on all overtime they worked so long as the overtime ban continued. The level of compensatory payment for lost overtime earnings was set at 50p per week payable from the 22 July 1950.

Informal talks between the LSC and the LMPA proved unsuccessful. On 23 August the Society instructed its members in LMPA firms to impose restrictions on customary working arrrangements immediately. The employers responded by recommending their members to warn

LSC members that unless they gave assurance by 30 August that they would work normally they would be individually dismissed for breach of contract. Not one LSC member gave such an assurance and, on 30 August 1950, 3,700 compositors were dismissed. The day before, the Minister of Labour had established a Court of Inquiry to inquire into the causes and circumstances of the dispute. Following an intervention by the P&KTF, the LSC and the LMPA agreed on 11 September to withdraw their respective sanctions against each other and to seek an adjournment of the Court of Inquiry, to which the Court consented.

The LSC suggested an agreement should be reached around five issues. First, a minimum rate of £8 per week stabilised for two, three or more years and accompanied by a cost-of-living bonus. Second, that the ratio of apprentices to journeymen should be regulated by a sliding scale but the ratio should be fixed annually for the following twelve months in the light of unemployment for the preceding twelve months. Third, a revision of the payment for night work. Fourth, acceptance that certain types of machines should be operated by compositors. Fifth, an automatic reduction in working hours and any manpower concessions made by the union when unemployment in the industry reached a given level. In addition, the LSC suggested that production in London could be increased significantly by overtime extensions, acceptance of printed matter from the provinces, dual working and incentive schemes. The employers said that a minimum rate of £8 was unjustified but they were prepared to recognise the special skills required of certain compositors by paying them 17½p per week above the rate awarded by the NAT. The LMPA considered the suggestions of stabilisation and a cost-of-living bonus impracticable unless acceptable to all other printing unions. The employers were prepared to consider a sliding scale ratio for apprentices but considered that more immediate measures, for example a block of additional apprentices and/or the recruitment of trainees, were necessary to deal with the industry's acute labour supply problems.

When the two sides could not find a way forward the LSC reimposed its overtime ban and the strict adherence to working practices and announced that it would seek separate agreements with individual employers. On 28 September the LMPA recommended its members to dismiss LSC members who would not give assurances to work normally. LSC members who, by 4 pm on 29 September, had not given this assurance were dismissed. The Court of Inquiry had recommenced its hearings the previous day. The employers' case to the Court rested on five arguments. First, it was impossible to consider the LSC claim in isolation from those of other printing unions. If a higher minimum rate were granted, other unions would merely submit fresh claims. Second, the January 1948 award had accepted that where workers were receiving merit payments the increase awarded should be reduced by half the amount of the merit payment. The employers had found that to retain their employees they had been obliged to continue payment of the whole merit money in addition to the basic increase. They were convinced that this experience would be repeated if a new minimum rate were granted. Third, there was an acute shortage of labour which was causing delays in completing orders, work to be sent abroad and firms to undertake their own printing. The employers felt that measures such as the admission into the LSC of provincial compositors, the importation of matter from the provinces, dual working and unlimited overtime would do little to alleviate the acute manpower shortage. Fourth, a sliding scale of apprentices would make no contribution towards solving short-term manpower problems. Trainees needed to be admitted into the industry. Fifth, the LSC was deliberately placing its own self-interest above that of the industry as a whole.

The LSC told the Court that it objected to the employers' attempts to force it to accept individually proposals that were part of a wage structure which the printing unions collectively had rejected. It also told the Court that the cost of the employers conceding their £8 claim would be small since, of its 7,350 members engaged in general printing, only 2,115 earned less than £8 per week. The LSC agreed that there was a shortage of labour in the industry but it was overstated by employers and under no circumstances would it admit trainees. It took individuals into membership for life and was hesitant about admitting extra men because they became liable for superannuation and unemployment benefit, both of which were costly to finance. It told Court that the fear of unemployment guided its policy on manpower but it was prepared to accept apprenticeship ratios fixed at an annual joint meeting and related to the employment situation in the industry in the preceding twelve months and to make other manpower concessions which would reduce the demand for labour, for example unlimited overtime.

The Court of Inquiry published its findings on 21 October 1950.[7] It recommended that negotiations between the two parties begin forthwith to reach an agreement covering both wages and manpower. On manpower issues the Court suggested the admission of a reasonable number of late entrants to be trained as compositors, the reduction within reasonable limits of the length of the standard working week if unemployment amongst compositors in London reached a given level, the periodical adjustment of the ratio of apprentices to journeymen in the light of the employment situation, a reduction of the period of apprenticeship from seven years to six and the consideration of proposals, such as the extension of overtime working and the introduction of incentive schemes, to overcome the labour shortage. The Court rejected the LSC view that the basis of entry to the industry should be that its finances would not be endangered:

> We cannot accept the argument that because the Society has undertaken superannuation and other benefit obligations towards its members which apparently exceed those of any other union it is entitled to restrict the number of compositors and apprentices working in London to a figure which will ensure that the union's finances will never be endangered by even a small amount of temporary unemployment. Important as that consideration is, it is not reasonable that it should be the sole criterion by which numbers in the trade are to be fixed.[8]

On wages the Court made five recommendations. First, the LSC should rejoin the JIC. Second, a wage structure for the industry should be established and to this end separate wage committees of the JIC should be set up – one for craftsmen only and the other for semi-skilled and unskilled workers – and their decisions should not be subject to review by the Council as a whole. Third, the parties should come to an agreement providing for a basic minimum London craft rate of £7.75 per week but where workers were already receiving (via house rates or merit money) weekly earnings in excess of £7 the employers should be free to reduce house and merit rates by the extent of the increase in the basic rate. Fourth, the Court saw merit in the LSC suggestion that any agreement should include provision for a cost-of-living bonus. Finally, the Court recommended that any agreement reached should remain in force for a fixed period of years.

Following the Court's report, LSC members resumed work on 1 November 1950 and negotiations for a settlement began on 3 November. Agreement, to operate for five years from 20 November 1950, was reached on 16 November. Employers were to consolidate merit money and house payments up to the size of increase in the basic minimum rate, which was to be now £7.75 per week. This minimum rate, however, was to increase by 5p per week for each point rise in the official Index of Retail Prices as at May and November and to be paid in the following June and January, respectively.

In return for these increases in pay, the LSC traded concessions on the supply of labour. It accepted that, whilst labour was short, unlimited overtime could be worked, that both parties would cooperate in practical steps to achieve greater efficiency, including the introduction of incentive schemes, and that, subject to the LSC being unable to supply labour, its members would handle type matter set outside London by members of the appropriate union. The Society also accepted a limited block intake of apprentices and that the length of their apprenticeship should be six years. However, its major manpower concession was the acceptance of a revised apprenticeship ratio and a reduction in the length of the apprenticeship from seven years to six. The proportion of apprentices was to be one to three journeymen up to thirteen apprentices and thirty-nine journeymen. In offices where forty or more journeymen were employed, one additional apprenticeship was to be allowed for each further seven journeymen employed. The ratios, however, were to be subject to an annual review by a joint committee of the LMPA and the LSC. The ratios were to be adjusted if unemployment amongst LSC members exceeded 2 per cent of the total journeymen working population. If unemployment reached 4 per cent, special steps would be taken to reduce the labour supply, for example a reduction in the normal working week, and encouragement of men over 65 years to retire. If unemployment reached 5 per cent, then there was to be a total cessation of intakes of apprentices.

The LSC settlement could not remain in isolation. The BFMP invited the P&KTF to a conference at which it suggested a settlement with the other print unions along the lines of that made with the LSC. In April 1951 the TA and the BFMP and the NS signed a new national agreement to operate from June 1951. The basic minimum rate was increased by 62½p per week but the employers could absorb merit money and house rates to this amount. However, absorption was permissible but not obligatory as in the London agreement. The TA's demand for the number of wages grades to be reduced was to go to arbitration. The cost-of-living bonus was 5p per week per point increase in the Index of Retail Prices and the agreement was to be stabilised until 20 November 1950. This, as with the London agreement, meant that any demands for changes in the national agreement were ruled out until its expiry. In return for these wage increases, the TA accepted a bonus of 300 apprentices additional to the normal quota and that payment by results systems could be introduced. However, the whole principle of the working of incentive schemes was to be kept under review by a subcommittee of the two employers' associations and the TA. TA members accepted the 1951 agreement in a ballot by 23,280 votes to 12,878.

From the 1950 London agreement a new wage structure for the industry had emerged, but there was no guarantee that the unions would consolidate this by acting collectively in the future. The 1950/1 settlements had not been the result of collective discussion and acceptance by the unions. However, a provincial craftsmen rate of 93 per cent of the basic minimum London craft rate, with a monetary differential of 57½p, had been established. Non-craft workers were receiving 80 per cent of the provincial craft rate. There were also moves towards the elimination of wage grades in the provinces.

The 1919 national agreement had established six grades of pay in the provinces, which were reduced to four in 1943. The 1950 TA Delegate Meeting carried a Shrewsbury motion that the time had arrived to make moves to achieve one wage grade for all areas of the TA. It was argued that the cost of housing, food, clothing, beer and tobacco was much the same in all cities, towns and villages and that the standard of craftsmanship demanded in the lower-grade towns was as high as in higher-grade towns. In October 1950 the employers conceded that the four grades be reduced to three by absorbing the grade 4 towns into grade 3, that a number of other towns be regraded and that the new grade schedule should be based on a formula of town population plus the number of TA journeymen employed. In January 1951 the TA told the BFMP and the NS that it would not consider any proposed wage offer in the light of the November London settlement until the grading question was settled. It feared that to enter negotiations on a wider offer would imply the acceptance of a three-tier grading structure for the next five years. The employers readily agreed that the grading issue be settled by the NAT.

The Tribunal awarded that there should be two grades only in the provinces and accepted a formula put forward by the employers on 30 September 1950 as to the means of determining in which grade a town would be. The formula produced an index figure for each town by adding the number of TA journeymen employed there to the number of thousands in the town's population. Towns with an index figure higher than 450 were to be grade 1 and those with a figure of 450 or less were to be in grade 2. Where a town was presently in a higher grade than warranted by the formula, it remained in the higher grade. The effects of the award were that thirteen towns were upgraded to grade 1 to give a total of twenty-four in that grade, the wage differential between the two grades remained unchanged, and the division of the total TA working membership between the two grades became grade 1, 47 per cent and grade 2, 53 per cent. It was not until January 1952 that the two grades were finally and completely established.[9]

The TA and the LTS had made solid gains from the 1950/1 negotiations. The introduction of the cost-of-living bonus was useful in that without it the two unions would undoubtedly have been involved in perpetual wage claims, with little hope of success if trade fell off. The stabilisation period enabled the industry to move away from the constant labour troubles of the immediate post-war period and concentrate on increasing production and improving the service offered to customers. The number of provincial wage grades had been reduced from four to two. However, the flat-rate cost-of-living bonus carried the danger that inflation during stabilisation would reduce the percentage craft and non-craft workers differential. In accepting this bonus the TA and the LSC did not expect the Index of Retail Prices to increase as rapidly as it did. During the period of the agreements the Index of Retail Prices rose by 33 points, so that by then print workers were receiving £1.65 a week in addition to their basic minimum rate. One effect of this was to reduce the skill/non-skill differential by 4 percentage points and the London/provincial craft differential by 1.2 percentage points. At the end of the stabilisation period, the TA and the LTS were determined to re-establish skill differentials.

WAGE MOVEMENTS, 1956–65

The 1956 Negotiations

In the spring of 1955 the LTS and the TA gave six months' notice to terminate the 1951 agreements. They expected hard negotiation with the employers. If anything was certain about the forthcoming negotiations it was that the employers would wish to retain this structure and prevent the London craft unions from setting the level to which other unions' pay would be adjusted.

The P&KTF called a conference of unions to explore the possibility of a collective approach. The LTS refused to be part of any collective approach, but six unions, including the TA, decided to approach the BFMP and the NS on a collective basis. The LTS claimed a £12 weekly basic rate in return for which it would accept manpower and production concessions, a continuation of a cost-of-living bonus, stabilisation for three years and apprenticeships for readers. In September 1955 the LMPA rejected the £12 per week claim and any continuation of a cost-of-living bonus but offered a basic rate of £10 per week, conditional on the introduction of 200 additional compositor apprentices and 75 in the machine department, the intake being spread over two or three years and recruited from men having completed their National Service. In December, the employers made a 'final' offer of a basic rate of £10.32½p. Although the LMPA was negotiating separately with the LTS, the offer was no different from that offered by the BFMP and the NS to the craftsmen in the collective negotiations. In January 1956 the LTS decided to bring immediate pressure to bear on the employers by issuing an instruction to 'work to rule'. The employers reacted by instructing their members to tell LTS members that unless they agreed to work normally they would be summarily dismissed at 4.00 pm on Wednesday 15 February 1955. By Friday the 17th, 6,500 members in LMPA offices had been locked out. In these circumstances on 25 February 1955 a Court of Inquiry established by the Minister of Labour opened its proceedings under the chairmanship of Sir John Foster.

The employers told the Court that their offer was the most the industry could afford if its printing products were not to be priced out of the market, and that on a £10.32½ minimum rate LTS members would be at no disadvantage to skilled craftsmen in other industries in the London area. The Court was also told that 'extras' could not be absorbed in the new rate since other print unions had refused to negotiate on that basis, that there was an artificially created manpower shortage in the London printing industry and that there was a need for a wage structure for the industry as a whole. The employers stressed there could be no stability while key unions like the LTS and the TA insisted on being considered in complete isolation from the rest.

The LTS argued to the Court that the value of the craftsmen had been devalued as a result of flat-rate increases, of scarcity payments and other means of providing wages other than laid down in the agreement. It asked the Court to set a cash value in terms of the basic rate on the concessions it was prepared to make on manpower – namely, a block

375

intake of 200 apprentices, the admission of apprentices on a ratio of 1:3 journeymen, the introduction of apprentice readers, unlimited over-time, the admission of semi-skilled assistants to the composing room, and cooperation in the introduction of incentive schemes. In addition LTS contended that given its high unemployment and superannuation benefits it had an apprehensive view of any possible recurrence of unemployment, that its £12 basic weekly rate claim was justified by the January 1948 NAT award and was a recognition of the actual wages being paid in the London printing industry. The LTS was adamant that it would not enter into negotiations in which its own interests as a craft union would be negated by the greater voting strength of the non-craft unions. Since 1947 it had negotiated separately and found the policy rewarding. It objected to other unions coming in on its success and claiming the benefits of th LTS's efforts.

The Court published its report in March 1956[10] and concentrated on three problems – manpower shortages, wages and the wage structure, and the establishment of joint negotiating machinery. It rejected the LTS view that its superannuation and other benefits obligations to its members entitled it to restrict the number of compositors working in London. The Court concluded that there was a substantial manpower shortage, which could be overcome by the LTS accepting the entry of junior and adult apprentices into the London printing industry. On the issue of joint negotiating machinery, the Court repeated the suggestion of the 1950 Court of Inquiry. On wages and a wage structure, the Court rejected the LTS view that manpower 'concessions' justified an increase over and above an appropriate basic rate and that the Lon-don/provincial craft rate differential had a traditional basis. It had varied from 42.5 per cent in 1920 to 17.5 per cent in 1955 and in money terms from 12½p to 87½p per week and had stood at 57½p during the period of the 1950/1 agreements. It also questioned the Society's view that printing craft wages compared unfavourably with those of other craftsmen in London.

As a possible basis for agreement the Court suggested that additional apprentices should be allowed, that merit payments should be absorbed into a new basic rate of £10.77, which was to include the consolidation of the £1.65 per week cost-of-living bonus, and that a new cost-of-living bonus of 5p per point rise in the Index of Retail Prices above an agreed threshold figure should be introduced. The Court also recommended that any settlement reached should be stabilised for a minimum period of three years and that comprehensive national machinery on a two-tier basis for the negotiation of wages and conditions in the industry should be established.

Little progress was made immediately after the Court's report. The LMPA considered the recommendations as its findings but the LTS saw them as a basis for renewed negotiation. Against this background the LTS and three other craft unions – the TA, the ASLP and the ACP – met, following which LTS members returned to work on 27 March 1956 on the understanding that negotiations began between the employers and the four unions. In May 1956 the four unions and the employers reached agreement. Before recording the details of this, one must show how the TA, which had originally been part of a collective approach to the employers, finished up negotiating a settlement alongside the LTS.

The six unions involved in the collective approach to the employers claimed the incorporation of the cost-of-living bonus into basic wages, one wage grade for all employees in the provinces, changes to the formula for calculating shift rates and a basic provincial craft rate of £10.50 per week, with a London craft rate of £11.07½. Semi-skilled were to receive 87.5 per cent of these rates, assistants 85 per cent and women 75 per cent. The unions claimed that the then value of the pound was about one-third of that of 1939 and that the industry was in a prosperous state. In October 1955 the employers offered to consolidate the £1.65 cost-of-living bonus but rejected one provincial grade and an amendment of the formula for calculating shift rates. The employers indicated that they were not opposed to a reasonable pay increase, providing the unions helped overcome the 'acute and dangerous' manpower shortage by adjustment to the apprenticeship ratio, acceptance of bonus apprentices and the easing of demarcation lines. They also indicated that they did not want any agreement subject to stabilisation.

In November 1955 the BFMP and the NS made an improved offer. The basic wage increase was raised to 85p per week but was to be accompanied by a new cost-of-living bonus and a two-year stabilisation period. This improved offer was conditional on the unions' recommending acceptance of the offer, meeting the employers' claims for additional labour, dropping their proposals on grading and accepting absorption of 'extras'. Although the unions expected that the employers would increase the basic rate offer further, the TA saw the grading issue as fundamental, the question of 'absorbing' of 'extras' to be entirely for the individual member and the firm, and a basic rate offer of £9.75 as too low to be recommended to the members. Nevertheless, for the sake of unity, the TA participated in a further meeting held on 17 November with the employers, who raised their pay offer to 92½p per week to give a basic weekly London craft rate of £10.32½ and a grade 1 provincial craft rate of £9.75. However, the manpower conditions remained and the employers stated that they had reached the limit as to how far they were prepared to go. At this point the TA left the collective wage movement, but the other five unions accepted the employers' terms.

On 21 November, to facilitate a settlement of the wages issue, the BFMP and the NS agreed that the grading question go to arbitration at a later date. In return, the TA agreed to place before its members the employers' offer on basic wages and their claims for additional labour. When the negotiations failed, the TA sought its members' views as to whether it should reject the employers' offer or seek fresh negotiations. The members voted by 33,828 votes to 1,954 to reject the wage offer. The result of the ballot on future action was 16,450 votes in favour of starting new negotiations and 19,333 in support of total rejection of the employers' offer. In January 1956 the TA issued a circular to members entitled 'Wages Negotiations – A Call to Action', which set out the sanctions to be imposed by members in all jobbing and news offices in England and Wales from 18 January. The sanctions included banning overtime, the withdrawal of recognition cards from dilutees and termination of incentive schemes. The members responded whole-heartedly, whilst the employers invoked the JIC conciliation machinery. The TA considered the JIC unfitted to resolve the dispute. Half the Committee would be composed of employers with whom the union was in dispute and the other half of representatives of unions that were either themselves in dispute or had settled their differences with the employers on the issues that were the cause of the TA's dispute. The employers insisted that before a conciliation meeting was called the TA must end its sanctions.

The employers now sought the assistance of the Ministry of Labour, which established a Court of Inquiry to examine the causes and circumstances of the London and provincial printing disputes. Following discussions between the TA and the BFMP and the NS and then subsequently with the chairman of the Court, it was accepted that negotiations to resolve the provincial dispute would resume under the chairmanship of the Chief Conciliation Officer of the Ministry of Labour as soon as the Report of the Court of Inquiry on the London dispute was published. In return, the TA lifted all its sanctions with effect from 27 February 1956. If these anticipated conciliation moves were to fail, the Court of Inquiry into the provincial dispute would be reconstituted.

Following the report of the Court of Inquiry into the London dispute, the LTS, TA, ACP and ASLP met with the employers, claiming a basic rate of £11.50 in London, £10.92½ in the provinces, one provincial grade and a cost-of-living bonus.[11] In April 1956 the four unions and the BFMP and the NS reached agreements which were to become operative on 1 May 1956. There was to be a London craft rate of £10.85, a provincial grade 1 rate of £10.27½ and a grade 2 rate of £10.00. There was to be a cost-of-living bonus of 5p per week per point rise in the Index of Retail Prices from a base of 155 as at March 1955. The new agreement would operate until 20 April 1959, but six months' notice was required to terminate it. The existing wage grading system was to operate until 20 April 1959, after which any towns not already in grade 1 but having a population of more than 100,000 or more than 125 journeymen TA members in employment would be moved into grade 1. The minimum grade 2 rate was to increase to £10.07½ from 20 April 1957 and to £10.15 as from 20 April 1958. The effect of this was the virtual elimination of the provincial grading system.

Both the TA and the LTS made manpower concessions in return for these wages improvements. The TA accepted 545 additional apprentices, whilst the LTS agreed to a block of 275 additional apprentices, to give favourable consideration to handling imported print matter from the provinces and to the introduction of experimental incentive schemes. The 1956 London settlement provided for an apprentice scheme for readers with effect from 1 November 1957. This meant that, for the first time, readers could now enter the industry through an apprenticeship. The LTS members accepted the May 1956 settlement by 11,214 votes to 901, whilst TA members voted in favour of acceptance by 33,984 votes to 3,043.

Peace had now been restored in the industry. The dispute had shown the conflict of purpose, the waste of time, the unnecessary duplication of negotiating skill and power, and the inherent possibilities for bad feeling between union and union. The LTS and TA 'battles' over wage differentials would only end when the unions accepted an agreed basis of relativities. However, during the 1956–9 stabilisation period the unions did devise machinery for a collective approach to the employers. This operated for the first time with the formulation of the 1959 wages and hours claims.

The 1958/9 Negotiations

These negotiations differed from those of the past in that there was a united approach by nine print unions, under the auspices of the P&KTF, to the BFMP and the NS, and that the claim embraced hours of work as well as wages. A key demand was for a 40 hour working week, which meant that unlike the 1950 and 1956 disputes the implications of the outcome of these negotiations would range wider than the confines of the printing industry. The negotiations were carefully watched by the government and the British Employers' Confederation, both of which saw that any reductions in hours of work granted in the printing industry would spread to the whole of the British industry.

The collective approach in the 1958/9 negotiations was an important point of comparison for the LTS relative to the 1948, 1950 and 1955/6 sets of negotiations. The 1948 dispute, which was settled by the NAT, was pursued unilaterally by the LSC, although other unions in the industry benefited from the award. The 1950 dispute again involved the LSC on its own against one section of the employers (LMPA) and a Court of Inquiry which recommended increased wages above the final offer of the employer, the benefits of which were again passed to other unions in the industry. In the 1955/6 negotiations, the LTS negotiated unilaterally with the employers, but following a Court of Inquiry negotiated an agreement with three other unions. Again, these gains from London's action were passed on to other unions.

In 1958, nine unions negotiated collectively with the BFMP and the Newspaper Society. Procedurally the 1958/9 negotiations were complex. The claim covered both wages and hours. The Hours of Work Agreement was between the P&KTF and the BFMP and the NS, and the claim was conducted by the P&KTF General Secretary. Following the 1956 dispute the unions agreed a two-tier wage structure – one for craft and one for non-craft. The craft and non-craft union claims on wages proceeded side by side and not together. However, the chairman of the craft group – Bill Morrison of the NUPB&PW – was also chairman of the non-craft group, so there was one spokesman for the two separate groups of workers.

In the summer of 1958 the employers suggested that the agreements due to terminate in April 1959 should continue for a further twelve months. When this was rejected, they indicated a readiness to negotiate but that they had in mind agreements without stabilisation or a cost-of-living bonus. On 1 December 1958 the nine unions submitted their claim for a 40 hour working week, a 10 per cent increase in the London craft rate, a reduction in the London/provincial craft differential, the continuation of the cost-of-living bonus, a three-year stabilisation period, the abolition of the provincial wage grade 2, and semi-skilled workers to receive 82.5 per cent of the craft rate, general assistants 85 per cent and women 66⅔ per cent. In February, the employers totally rejected the unions' claim, whilst on 23 March the unions consulted their members on steps to be taken in view of the attitude of the employers. In April a ban was placed on excessive overtime working, but firms which from 20 April were prepared to operate a 40 hour week and observe the final settlement on hours and wages were excluded from the dispute. The BFMP and the NS wished to take the deadlock to the JIC or to conciliation or arbitration. The unions saw nothing being achieved by either of these courses as the employers were simply refusing to negotiate.

In May the unions announced the result of the ballot on a series of measures to be introduced to break the deadlock. The measures were to be a ban on overtime, a ban on the extension of shift working, a policy of non-cooperation in the workshop, the withdrawal of participation in incentive schemes, and the tendering of strike notices if subsequently considered necessary: 80 per cent of the votes cast supported the recommended policy, the actual figures being 108,116 in favour and 25,926 against. Armed with this support for a progressive build-up of industrial sanctions, the unions again met the employers, who put to them a document containing a 'tentative list of 22 points or suggestions' dealing with labour supply, productivity improvement, new processes and method study. The unions said the document should be withdrawn as it was too revolutionary.

On 21 May the employers offered a reduction of hours from 43½ to 42½, a wage increase of 2.5 per cent, stabilisation, and continuation of the cost-of-living bonus providing the unions agreed to 'practically all' the twenty-two points presented at the previous meeting. The union rejected the offer as 'totally inadequate' but at a further meeting suggested that the hours claim might be met by a phased reduction to 40 hours spread over three years and the 10 per cent wage increase be met by granting 5 per cent immediately, a further 2.5 per cent in a year's time and a further 2.5 per cent a year after that. In return, the unions would discuss efficiency questions. The employers, however, insisted that their offer was dependent upon the unions agreeing in advance to methods of improving efficiency. Negotiations now reached deadlock and on 3 June 1959 the industrial sanctions authorised in the membership ballot became effective. The employers issued 'protective notices' and by 20 June the 120,000 members of the nine unions involved ceased work.[12]

The British Employers' Federation spoke scornfully of the print unions' claim, whilst the BFMP claimed that to grant the unions' request would set a pattern for a general reduction of hours all across the industry.[13] In early July informal talks between the unions and the employers under the auspices of the Ministry of Labour considered formulas designed to bring about a resumption of negotiations. The unions pressed for the restart of negotiations under an independent chairman who might guide and assist during the negotiations but who should not have the powers of an arbitrator. The employers wanted an independent chairman with authority to give decisions on issues on which the two sides could not agree and that both sides must accept the decision. The talks made little progress but, following further intervention by the Ministry of Labour and after over eleven hours of talks, the two sides agreed to the resumption of negotiations under an independent chairman. The Ministry of Labour was to appoint an independent chairman who would preside at joint meetings of the parties and assist them towards a settlement of the dispute. The chairman would advise, guide and control the discussions to achieve a negotiated settlement. If the parties failed to reach agreement on any point or points, they would submit the recommendation of the independent chairman on such points to their constituents as part of the final settlement and for acceptance or refusal by those constituents. Any settlement was to cover hours, wages, domestic claims, manpower problems and improved efficiency.

With the agreement of both sides, Lord Birkett was appointed independent chairman and joint discussions began on 14 July 1959. Seven days later the employers increased their offer on basic wages from 2.5 per cent to 3.5 per cent, that the standard working week should be reduced to 42 hours, that there should be three years' stabilisation and the acceptance by the unions of conditions covering labour demarcation, work study and new processes. The Newspaper Society made an additional offer of an enhanced payment of 25p per week to employees on provincial morning and evening newspapers who were already working 40 hours or less per week. This revised offer was unsatisfactory to the unions in that it had to be 'earned' by acceptance of conditions when the contributions made by the workers in the industry since 1945 were in themselves worthy of reductions in hours and increases in wages. The unions suggested that the 40 hour week be introduced gradually but no later than by January 1962. Whilst the negotiations went on, day after day well over 120,000 men and women remained on strike; 4,000 firms and nearly 1,000 provincial newspapers were affected by the stoppage.

The negotiations continued but no progress was really made until Lord Birkett put forward four suggestions. First, that the two sides should settle between themselves the 'basic requirements' provisions for greater productivity. Second, that the unions' 'domestic claims' should be cleared up along with the basic requirement provisions. Third, that a 42 hour week should be fixed for at least two years with provision for a judicial inquiry, binding on both sides, if there was disagreement about any further reductions in hours. Fourth, that the basic wage increase should be 4.5 per cent stabilised for two years and if there was a claim for further increases at the end of the period it should be referred to the judicial inquiry if there was a failure to agree. On 29 July the BFMP and the NS accepted this proposed settlement, even though they considered a 4.5 per cent increase in basic wages was too high. Despite initial difficulties, a return-to-work formula was agreed by both sides on 31 July. Work resumed on Thursday 6 August 1959. The return-to-work formula contained provision for no victimisation and both parties committed themselves to see it was scrupulously observed.

On 2 September it was announced that nine of the ten unions[14] in the collective hours and wages movement had accepted the proposed agreement in ballots: 108,582 votes were cast in favour of acceptance of the agreement and 34,901 against. TA members voted by 30,594 votes to 8,307 to accept the agreement and LTS members by 9,628 to 2,268. The cost of the dispute to the TA was some £905,000, which represented two-thirds of the value of its General Fund, whilst the LTS spent some £265,000 in dispute and related payments. One union – the NSES – voted by a majority of 507 against acceptance of the agreement.[15] Under the terms of the settlement the standard working week was reduced to 42 hours, the basic minimum grade rates were increased by 4.5 per cent with agreed 'extras' for readers and keyboard operators, stabilisation was agreed for three years, the cost-of-living bonus continued and all unions made manpower concessions. Although the agreement was to operate for three years, consideration was to be given in 1961 as to whether there was justification for a further reduction of hours and/or an increase in basic wages to operate from the first week in September 1961. If it was not possible to negotiate a settlement by 30 June 1961, then the application was to be referred to a judicial inquiry whose decision would be binding on both parties. The form of the judicial inquiry would be decided by Lord Birkett.

 General manpower concessions were made by all unions. Craftsmen were to be used to the maximum effect in the composing room, semi-skilled auxiliary workers were to be assistants to block and type storemen, double day shift or night shift working was to be encouraged, as was method study, and there was to be consultation and full cooperation between employers and unions in the adoption and development of new processes. In addition, where apprentice vacancies under the agreed ratio were not filled, mutual arrangements were to be made for those vacancies to be transferred to other establishments and the amount of time, up to a maximum of twelve months, that a boy remained at school beyond the age of 15 could be deducted from the six-year apprenticeship.

In addition to these general manpower concessions, the LTS and the TA made specific concessions. The LTS accepted that adult apprentices could be included in the normal apprentice quota and that there could be transferability of apprentice vacancies and withdrew its negative attitude towards apprenticeships in advertisement typesetting houses. The TA accepted adult apprentices, that apprentices could be trained in both composing and monotype casting operations, and the interchange of craftsmen between these two departments.

On the whole, the return-to-work agreement went smoothly and with little incident. However some employers, particularly the *Leicester Mercury*, *Leicester Evening Mail* and the *Shrewsbury Chronicle*, proved difficult. The two Leicester firms, both part of the Northcliffe Group, refused to take back 102 TA members and 15 NSES members. Both firms demanded that the TA take no punitive action against employees who had stayed at work during the dispute. The companies said they would view as punitive such action as fines, the withholding of cards, re-entrance into the union with loss of benefit rights and the charging of re-entrance fees. The TA regarded the companies' attitude as not only a breach of the return-to-work agreement but an attempt to interfere in its internal affairs. It also regarded this stance to be against the return-to-work agreement because in negotiating that agreement the employers and Lord Birkett accepted that the 'non-victimisation' clause did not preclude the unions from applying their rules against those members who had been expelled. The matter was resolved when it was agreed that the expulsions would stand, that the members concerned would be re-admitted to membership as from 5 October 1959 at an entrance fee of £20 each and, provided they were not guilty of further infringements of TA rules in the meantime, their previous years of membership would be restored on 31 December 1959. In return the two companies restored the full pension rights of the TA members involved and removed from TA areas those employees who had worked during the dispute.

The position was different at the *Shrewsbury Chronicle*, which had resigned from the NS in advance of the return-to-work agreement. It insisted that in future 60 per cent of its staff would be non-union and only 40 per cent unionised. It refused to discuss this policy change with the TA. On 23 October 1959, eleven TA members at the Welshpool and Newport offices of the paper withdrew their labour.[16] On 3 November the Welshpool office was sold to Wheatlands Journals Ltd, a firm of periodical publishers, which accorded full recognition rights to the TA and withdrew from the office former TA members expelled for disobeying the industrial action instruction. The TA members at Welshpool thereupon returned to work. At the request of the P&KTF the Ministry of Labour intervened in the dispute at the other office but to no avail. The TA saw no alternative but to advise its members to seek employment elsewhere, to assist them to do so, and to remove the *Shrewsbury Chronicle* and its associated companies from the Fairs List.

Neither the TA nor the LTS was fully satisfied with the 1959 agreement. Both accepted that the agreement was not the end of the matter but merely an interim settlement awaiting final settlement in 1961, through a judicial inquiry should the employers again prove difficult. The settlement provided a two-year pause in the negotiations. Efforts could now be made to increase productivity and to provide the conditions which would justify a further reduction in hours and an increase in wages in 1961.

The 1959 strike had been a traumatic experience for both sides. There was a feeling that the situation should not be allowed to arise again. Many on both sides thought, in retrospect, that the dispute had been a self-inflicted wound since in the final analysis both sides had had to settle their differences round the table. The employers had annoyed the unions with their stubborn and rigid attitude in the early stages of negotiations, whilst the unions had upset the employers by their refusal to use the industry's conciliation machinery or to submit their claim to independent arbitration. There had been little effort to close the gap between the two sides and tempers at times were high. Both the unions and employers realised that, now the dispute was over, they must continue to live together and there was little purpose in laying the blame for what had gone before. A fresh start was needed. This was reflected in the way the two sides approached the negotiations for the balance of the 1959 claim. The unions entered into negotiations with the employers in an endeavour to reach a settlement by direct negotiations. The employers hoped that, through negotiations, agreement would be reached within the industry without the need for external assistance.

The 1961 Negotiations

In September 1960 the BFMP and the NS and the ten print unions met to discuss the form that a judicial inquiry might take, should one prove necessary, to settle the balance of the 1959 claim. If any judicial enquiry were required, the unions preferred it to be conducted by Lord Birkett. The employers said that, in asking that the form of any possible judicial enquiry be settled now, they did not have in mind that it would necessarily be used. They thought it best if a settlement could be reached by negotiation. However, if this proved impossible they preferred Lord Birkett to act as single chairman for any inquiry. Birkett accepted the joint invitation to act as a single chairman should a judicial inquiry become necessary.

In December 1960 the ten unions presented their claim for the balance of the 1959 claim to be met in full. At the first meeting, held in January 1961, the employers argued that the shortage of skilled labour in the industry was more acute now than in 1959, that the reduction of hours in 1959 had not led to greater leisure for the unions' members and that, given the 'scarce' labour supply to the industry, further reductions in hours were unrealistic. However, they suggested further reductions in hours might be possible if additional labour could be introduced into the industry, although the amounts required from each union to provide an adequate and balanced labour force would vary, as would the methods of achieving this balance. As to wage increases, the employers sought to avoid further impetus to competing sources of print, for example miniature printing and work going abroad. For the unions, the only thing that had changed since the original claim was an improved economic position for the industry. The employers were prepared to meet the unions individually, not as a negotiating exercise but as a 'fact finding exercise', so that they could agree what the actual labour needs were. It was stressed to the unions that, if they were prepared to move on the labour situation, then the employers were prepared to trade hours and wages.

In March 1961 the employers announced that if the labour shortage was to be overcome then the industry required 3,084 additional craftsmen, 1,200 extra non-craft employees and some 1,800 extra women. Providing the industry could get the labour it needed, the employers proposed an agreement which would give the unions a 40 hour week by stages and the balance of the 10 per cent wage claim. The unions opposed the suggestion and asked that the balance of the 1959 claim be implemented by September 1961 subject to mutual agreement on labour requirements. On 8 May the unions told the employers that they would agree to a settlement by August 1962 under which the reduced working week and increased wages would be staged. A 5.5 per cent wage increase and one hour's reduction would be granted from September 1961 and the second hour's reduction from March 1962, and both would be conditional on a mutually agreed settlement on manpower questions.

Talks between the employers' organisations and individual unions on the labour supply were to begin immediately, starting with the LTS and the TA. These talks were held over a two-day period, after which joint negotiations were to resume on 11 May 1961. The employers estimated the labour shortage in TA areas to be 1,823, of which 1,166 were in the composing and reading rooms. The TA challenged these figures, claiming that they ignored the union's steadily increasing membership, that 1,000 of its members were presently on National Service and would return to the industry within the next two years, and the industry's rising productivity. The TA eventually agreed that, in addition to the normal provision for recruitment, firms were entitled to extra apprentices in the composing and machine room areas on the following scale: in the first year, all departments having thirteen journeymen and over – one apprentice; in the second year, all departments having thirty journeymen and over – a second apprentice; in the third year, all departments having fifty journeymen and over – a third apprentice. In addition, there was to be a general bonus of forty-five additional boys. Both sides estimated these measures would increase the labour supply by some 800. The new apprentice quota met the employers' objective of an automatic intake and that of the TA that the arrangement should be permanent but that the allocation bonus should be revised in 1962 and 1963 should circumstances have changed in either or both those years.

The LTS accepted an allocation of 230 compositor apprentices additional to the normal quota and that these should be allocated within twelve months of the date of the acceptance of the agreement, but that any not allocated within that period should be placed as soon as practicable afterwards. It also agreed an amended apprenticeship quota on the following scale: one to three journeymen – one apprentice; four to six journeymen – two apprentices; seven to nine journeymen and so on up to forty-nine – three apprentices; forty-nine to fifty-one journeymen and thereafter – seventeen apprentices; and for each one to five extra journeymen – one extra apprentice. In the machine area, the additional apprentices were to be allocated on a quota basis agreed between the LMPA and the LTS.

When the two sides' full negotiating teams met on 11 May, every union, except for the ASLP, had reached agreement with the employers on the labour situation. The employers proposed as the final settlement that the standard working week should be reduced to 41 hours from the first pay week in September 1961 and to 40 hours from the first pay week in September 1962. In addition, the maximum number of hours of overtime normally permitted under existing agreements was to be increased by one hour per week in September 1961 and by a further hour in September 1962. On wages, the employers offered to increase the basic minimum grade rate from September 1961 by 5.5 per cent on the rates operating prior to 3 September 1959. Following further discussions the unions decided to recommend acceptance of these proposals to their members. Both TA and LTS members voted to accept the agreement.

The major achievement of the 1959–61 negotiations on the longer view was the introduction from September 1962 of the 40 hour week. This had been amongst the foremost aims of British trade unions for many years. The printing industry was the first to achieve a universal 40 hour standard working week. Many sectors of other industries had a 40 hour working week, and some even less, but none had a universal working week of 40 hours. Following the printing unions' breakthrough to a 40 hour week, other industries were quick to follow. These included electrical contracting, heat, ventilating and domestic engineering, furniture manufacturing, docks, shipbuilding and ship repairing and the motor car assembly industry.

The settlement had also not been bad on the wages questions. Although the unions had had to trade manpower concessions for these advances, the employers had had to accept a lower number of additional apprentices from the TA and the LTS than they wanted. In addition, the extra apprentices were to be supplied on a one-off basis and not as the employers wanted, namely automatically and quota-based.

The 1961 negotiations had been conducted in a different atmosphere from that of any other wages and hours claims by the print unions since the end of the Second World War. These were the first post-1945 negotiations in which a settlement had been reached without reference to an outside body. The measure of goodwill now established between the employers and the unions had come after fifteen years during which there had been a series of strikes, overtime bans, references to Courts of Inquiry, the Ministry of Labour, Committees of Investigation and, in 1959, eighteen intensive days of negotiation under the guidance of Lord Birkett. Both sides felt the 1961 agreement was fair and reasonable. The TA and the LTS saw the new atmosphere auguring well for their policies of advancing the living standards of their members in every way open to them, whilst cooperating with employer measures to improve the industry's efficiency.

The 1962 Negotiations

In March 1962 the TA and the LTS gave notice to the BFMP and the NS to terminate their basis wage agreements. Both unions agreed to join other unions in a collective approach, but it was stressed that this was not a P&KTF movement but a group of unions acting collectively. The unions were seeking a third week's holiday, a three-year agreement, consolidation of the cost-of-living bonus into basic rates, an increase of £1.25 per week in the consolidated craft rate, a new cost-of-living bonus, the establishment of one wage grade for the provinces, increases in the provincial 'extras', an increase in apprentices' wage rates, and provisions for safeguards against redundancy arising from the implementation of new techniques. In addition to these general items, each of the ten unions had domestic claims of their own.

The employers' initial response was that the unions should reconsider their claims, as increasing competition and falling profits made it impossible for them to be met. Nevertheless, they offered to consolidate one-third of the current cost-of-living bonus, leaving the balance as a flat-rate additional payment, and to increase the first, second- and third-year apprentice wage rates. The employers argued that cost-of-living bonus payments were an unsatisfactory way of adjusting wages and that they wished to end them, whilst they

389

recognised that wage stabilisation would also have to go. The unions considered this response unacceptable. The proposals to abolish the cost-of-living bonus and stabilisation were considered irresponsible and provocative; for the unions, as they saw stabilisation over the next two years was fundamental. They believed that the expected onrush of technical developments and the possibility of Britain's entry into the Common Market required the industry to devote its energies to these problems, as well as others that might arise from national negotiations. The employers argued that union members regarded cost-of-living bonus payments as automatic entitlements that had little to do with wages, whereas in reality they were increases in wage costs which were difficult to recover from customers.

The employers continued to argue that the industry could not afford the claim because of increased competition, falling profits and substantial increases in wage costs over the period 1959–61, and that provincial newspapers were experiencing declining advertising revenue which had necessitated price increases that could not be repeated. Nevertheless, they indicated that they might be able to meet the unions' fear over threats of redundancy arising from the introduction of new techniques through measures such as retraining for workers affected, improved utilisation of labour and improved procedures for determining manning and rating levels on new machinery. Negotiations continued and in August 1962 the two sides reached an agreement, to operate from 3 September 1962 until 31 March 1965, and thereafter unless either side gave six months' notice to terminate the agreement. The new agreement provided for a staged consolidation over the three years of £1.05 of the cost-of-living bonus together with a 75p per week increase in the basic minimum rate to be paid in three stages – 30p in January 1963, 30p in January 1964 and 15p in January 1965. In addition, the cost-of-living bonus was to be adjusted annually in January instead of every six months as previously., For their part the unions agreed to a periodical review of the labour supply position and to explore methods of dealing with this, for example adjustments in labour intake and overtime limits. Apprentice wage rates were to increase during the period of the agreement by 5 per cent for the first, second and third years of apprenticeship. The unions' demand for three weeks' holiday could be raised during the period of the agreement and, if they exercised this option, the employers would make 'an objective assessment of the position' with them. There were also a number of separate agreements between the employers and individual unions covering a more efficient use of labour. The TA agreed to relax its prohibition on 'twicing' and accepted that in small firms compositors could help run machines and that machinemen could help with make-up and imposition. Compositors could in future be retrained as minders and vice versa.

The most difficult issues in the negotiations for the unions were the employers' resistance to continued stabilisation and a cost-of-living bonus. The unions found the attitude of the employers in resisting stabilisation puzzling, since 'one would have thought to anyone desiring peace in industry and the ability to plan on a forward basis, stabilisation would prove an important factor'.[17] The BFMP and the NS had first attempted to terminate the cost-of-living bonus in the 1958/9 negotiations and since that time both the government and the British Employers' Federation had called for the ending of agreements which provided for automatic wage increases according to movements in the Index of Retail Prices. In seeking to end the cost-of-living bonus in 1962 the employers were motivated by a number of factors. First, by mid-1962 the cost-of-living bonus in that year had already increased by 50p (or 4 per cent of wages) and this in itself was a bigger wage advance than that secured in most other industries. Second, when the 1962 bonus rise (4 per cent) was added to the September 1961 basic wages increase (5.5. per cent), the hour's reduction at that time (2.5 per cent) and a further hour's reduction due to September 1961 (another 2.5 per cent), a total advance in wages and conditions of some 14.5 per cent had been achieved by the printing unions. Third, the employers believed that the industry could not afford cost-of-living payments, increases in basic wages, shorter hours and longer holidays. The attitude of the TA and the LTS, however, was that wage stabilisation and cost-of-living bonuses since 1951 had given the industry a stability which was the envy of other industries and which for that reason should continue.

WAGE MOVEMENTS, 1966–79
(THE INCOMES POLICY YEARS)

The 1965 Negotiations

In December 1964, nine unions, including the NGA, met to formulate a collective claim for a new wage agreement with the BFMP and the NS. Following further meetings, unanimity between the unions was reached on the claim, submitted to the employers on 25 January 1965. The unions were seeking, *inter alia*, consolidation of 50p of the cost-of-living bonus, an increase in the London basic craft rate (after consolidation) of 5 per cent per year for the three years, expressed in terms of 75p per year, an increase in provincial grade rates of 87½p to reduce the London/provincial differential by 37½p during the life of the agreement,[18] semi-skilled rates to be 87.5 per cent, unskilled rates to be 85 per cent, and women's rates to be 66⅔ per cent of the new craft rate, proportionate increases in the provincial newspapers extras, continuation of the cost-of-living bonus scheme, with half-yearly rather than the present annual adjustments, and three years' stabilisation. In addition, individual unions put forward 'domestic' claims.

The employers considered three years' stabilisation was too long given the state of the British economy and suggested twenty-one months – March 1965 to 31 December 1966. During the early stages of the negotiations the employers referred to the Labour government's policy on prices and incomes and that they would have to keep within the 'norm' laid down by the Department of Economic Affairs. The unions replied that their claim did not contravene government policy. The employers' original offer was 20p immediately and 30p in 1966. After months of difficult negotiations the offer was increased to 75p, to be paid in two instalments – 45p immediately and 30p in 1966 – and the employers stressed that this was as far as they could go. Deadlock appeared likely but, following informal talks, the employers indicated that they were ready to offer an increase of 52½p immediately with a further 60p in January 1966. In return, the unions gave up payment for the first 3 points' rise above the 108 threshold figure for the cost-of-living bonus. Of the current bonus the employers agreed to consolidate 35p immediately and a further 35p in January 1966.

The difficulties in the negotiations centred around the unions' domestic claims and attempts to persuade the employers to revert to six-monthly adjustment of the cost-of-living bonus. The employers stood firm and refused to change the existing period of payment of the bonus. They considered the cost of the unions' domestic claims to be high. The unions had given a restricted list of domestic claims, which eventually were substantially accepted by the employers. In May 1965 the unions recommended their members to accept an agreement from 17 May 1965 providing an increase of 52½p on basic weekly rates for craftsmen, a further 60p increase from 1 January 1966, improvements in the cost-of-living bonus scheme, and stabilisation until 31 December

1966. The NGA members accepted this agreement, thus giving a new grade 1 basic rate of £13.97½p and of £14.77½p in London, leaving a 60p cost-of-living bonus. From 1 January 1966, 35p of that cost-of-living bonus would be consolidated, along with a further wage increase of 60p, making a new grade 1 basic rate of £14.92½p and a rate of £15.72½ in London.

In May 1965 the Minister of Economic Affairs, Mr George Brown, referred the settlement to the newly created National Board for Prices and Incomes on the grounds that the proposed settlement appeared incompatible with the government's policy on prices and incomes.[19] Strong exception was taken by the unions to the minister's action, especially as the terms of reference to the Prices and Incomes Board required it to consider the last 15p of the wage increases and a 36p cost-of-living bonus negotiated in 1962, both payable from 1 January 1965, and the effects of the award of the third week's holiday agreed in January 1965. Neither the unions nor the BFMP and NS could refuse to appear before the Board, although it had no power to enforce its decisions. The employers said they would pay the increases irrespective of the reference to the Board, whilst the unions proceeded to ballot their members on the proposed wage settlement. When the unions' members voted to accept the agreement, the employers implemented it from 17 May 1965.

The National Board for Prices and Incomes issued its report in August 1965.[20] It concluded that the increases from 17 May 1965 of at least 3.5 per cent on the basic rate were consistent with the White Paper on Prices and Incomes. However, since this was to be followed in less than a year by a further increase, the basic rate changes in the agreement would be higher than allowed in the White Paper. It concluded that the proposed agreement could be consistent with existing guidelines for movement in pay only if there took place in the industry a 'major change in working practices' making a direct contribution towards increasing productivity. The Board also concluded that the scope for improvement in efficiency in the industry was such that price increases as a result of the wage settlement would be out of line with the criteria for price movements set out in the White Paper. The Report recommended that the cost-of-living bonus in the industry be eliminated when the next national wage settlement was made; that the Joint Manpower Committee's terms of reference be widened to include the efficient use of manpower; that the Committee be headed by an independent chairman whose function would be to assist in securing major changes in working practices, that both sides consider, as a means of overcoming the fear of redundancy, the introduction of an industrial pension scheme; and that the printing unions continue as quickly as possible the process of mergers with a view to forming one union for the industry. The key to the Board's recommendations lay in securing a 'major change in working practices'. The Minister of Economic Affairs met separately with the unions and the employers' organisations on 17 September 1965 and urged them to cooperate with each other in implementing the Board's recommendations.

At the Joint Committee on Manpower's meeting of 20 September 1965 the employers wanted to discuss the National Board for Prices and Incomes' conclusions and recommendations dealing with the Committee's terms of reference, the appointment of an independent chairman, a regular review of performance of the industry, and the registration of increases negotiated in individual houses. The unions, however, pointed out that the Board's report was not limited to these subjects and included others such as the introduction of an industrial pension scheme, and that the report could only be discussed as a whole. In January 1966 the unions accepted the employers' view that the efficient use of manpower should be part of the Committee's function. As for the independent chairman proposal, the employers were told that the unions had no objection but they considered that such an appointment should be accompanied by a widening of the Committee's terms of reference to include an industrial pension scheme in addition to manpower. The employers proposed that an independent chairman should be appointed, the scope of the Committee should be limited to labour questions, and all matters not concerned with manpower should be discussed separately outside the Committee. The unions accepted that pensions should not be dealt with by the Committee after the employers had assured them that the issue could be raised at any time. The way was now clear for the unions to accept an independent chairman. After consultation, the two sides invited Mr Richard O'Brien, who had been seconded to the Department of Economic Affairs from the British Motor Corporation, to accept this position. He accepted and presided over the Committee for the first time at its 21 June 1961 meeting.

Subsequently the NGA became less enthusiastic about the Committee's work. It was concerned that its activities were restricted to immediate manpower problems when there was a need for a long-term survey of the future manpower needs of the industry. In response to this, the Committee agreed to a survey of the industry's longer-term manpower needs being conducted by the Manpower Research Unit of the Ministry of Labour. A severe difficulty, however, arose when the employers insisted that the Cameron Report, published in mid-January 1967, into the problems caused by the introduction of web-offset machines in the printing industry should be discussed by the Manpower Committee. Because of the attitude of the employers' organisations and that some unions had not been as cooperative as they might have been, the NGA decided to withdraw from the Committee. Sogat followed later. For all practical purposes the Joint Manpower Committee ceased to exist.

The 1966/7 Negotiations

Negotiations between six unions, including the NGA, and the BFMP and the NS for a new wage agreement opened in December 1966. This followed considerable delay in reaching agreement among the six unions about the claims to be submitted and the difficulty about agreement to drop all 'domestic' claims to concentrate on an increrase in the basic rate. The unions' claim centred around four issues. First, any new agreement should run from 1 January 1967 to 31 December 1968. Second, the current cost-of-living bonus should continue, but with 10p per point for all adult males and females and adjustments at six-monthly intervals from 1 January 1967. Third, the unions sought the abolition of provincial wage grade 2 and, fourth, increases in the basic craft rates of £1.75 in two stages of 87½p on 1 January 1967 and 1 January 1968, together with maintenance of present male basic wage differentials but an increase in the women's rate to 75 per cent of the craft rates.

The negotiations took place against the background of government White Papers on prices and incomes policy. In July 1966 the government had imposed a wage freeze for the period 20 July 1966 to 31 December 1966, to be followed by a further six-month period of severe restraint. In addition, the TUC had established a procedure for the notification of wage claims before they were submitted to employers. The TUC Incomes Policy Committee advised whether the proposed claim was compatible with the prices and incomes policy. On receipt of the claim, the BFMP and NS said there was little point in the two sides meeting until the criteria for wage movements in the period of 'severe restraint' were known. Although the unions continued to press for a meeting with the employers, it proved impossible to do so until December 1966, by which time two important things had happened.

First, the TUC had written to the P&KTF stating that 'they had given careful consideration to the claim on the basis of the information provided, and in view of the General Council's Incomes Policy Committee, it was not compatible with the requirements of the period of severe restraint and in the existing circumstances should not be pursued'. Second, the government had published its White Paper *Prices and Incomes Standstill: Period of Severe Restraint* setting out criteria for movements in prices and incomes during this period. The major criterion for wage increases during the period was that the employees concerned should make a direct contribution towards increasing productivity. Pay increases on this basis, however, were not to be made 'on account'. Another criterion for an increase in pay was genuine low pay, and increases granted on this basis were not to be passed on to other workers.

Against this background the two sides met in December 1966. The employers took the unusual course of replying immediately to the unions' presentation. They did not see any grounds upon which an increase in basic wages could be justified and proposed that the existing agreements continue for a further six months to allow discussions on schemes which would increase productivity and efficiency. The employers were opposed to any continuation of the cost-of-living bonus and emphasised that they would not be prepared to accept its continuation in any new agreement. They again stressed the possibility for the unions' members to earn more by effective productivity schemes, and that they were prepared to pursue the matter in negotiations.

The employers rejected the unions' offer to accept a six-month standstill provided the 40p cost-of-living bonus due on 1 January 1967 was paid. On 31 January 1967 the employers said an increase could not be justified in the light of the industry's economic position and would, in any event, be a breach of the government's criteria for the period of severe restraint. The unions attached importance to the retention of the cost-of-living bonus. Its retention, however, was just as vigorously resisted by the employers, who repeatedly quoted the recommendations of the National Board for Prices and Incomes that the 'cost of living bonus in the printing industry should be eliminated when the next national wage agreement is made'. Whilst continuing to feel strongly that it should be retained, the unions decided, in order to make progress, not to press the issue until a later stage. The employers made it clear that, so far as they were concerned, the cost-of-living bonus scheme was at an end.

In an effort to make progress, the unions proposed that there should be an immediate increase of 50p 'to remedy the injustice members had suffered by the reduction in their real wages' since the last cost-of-living bonus adjustment had been made. The BFMP/NS were not prepared to agree to any wages adjustment whatsoever that did not provide measures for greater productivity. The measures for which the employers were looking included flexibility of labour, a disputes procedure, assessment of manning and rating of equipment, measurement of individual output, the use of women on typewriters producing work for reproduction, and the use of the employees on more than one job in newspaper houses. In August 1967 the employers were prepared to settle on the basis of consolidation of the current cost-of-living bonus (45p for men) and wage increases of 62½p per week for craftsmen, 55–95p for non-craft men and 40p for women, provided their productivity proposals were met. The employers were told that unless they substantially improved their wages offer the unions would have no alternative but to embark on industrial action. When the employers refused to improve their offer, the negotiations broke down.

The unions now decided to approach individual groups of firms for separate agreements to provide flat-rate increases of 75p per week for craft workers and appropriate increases for other workers.[21] September saw informal contracts between the two sides followed by a formal meeting at which the employers made a revised offer of 80p conditional on the unions' accepting productivity proposals. The offer was rejected, as the unions wanted satisfaction not only on the productivity proposals but also on the proposed abolition of the cost-of-living bonus, a loss for which it was felt the unions' members must be adequately compensated.

The unions imposed an overtime ban in all provincial daily newspaper offices from midnight on 16 October 1967 and one week later recommended that two weeks' notice be given to extend the ban to all firms in membership of the BFMP and the NS. However, on 24 October the two sides reached a basis for agreement which would become operative on 30 October 1967. The agreement was to run until 30 October 1969, the remaining cost-of-living bonus (45p) was to be consolidated into basic rates, the cost-of-living bonus was discontinued, and wage increases of 80p were to be paid from 30 October 1967, with a further increase of 70p per week from 30 October 1968. There were increases in the newspaper extras. In return, the unions accepted flexibility in the use of labour and interchangeability, retraining and transfer of craftsmen. The agreement also provided a procedure for the assessment of manning and rating of machines and equipment and a new disputes procedure, which permitted 'acceptance of recourse to an impartial outside body or individual for a definite and final settlement'. Additional productivity arrangements agreed between the NGA and the Newspaper Society included the handling of additional publications in daily newspaper offices without extra pay, and the establishment of a Newspaper Society/NGA joint committee. This committee was to encourage productivity agreements in individual plants, to undertake manpower planning for the future needs of the provincial newspaper industry having regard to the introduction of new techniques, to help plan for the avoidance of redundancy through measures such as bans on recruitment, retirement and natural wastage, and to devise standards of output and the selection and proper training and retraining of NGA members.

The negotiations had been long and difficult but there was now a breathing space in which to take stock of the immense economic and technological changes that were beginning to impact on the industry. Prior to the 1966/7 negotiations, wage agreements had been basically improvements in wages and conditions in return for the unions' granting manpower concessions, with a cost-of-living bonus to protect real wages during the life of the agreement. The conduct of negotiations was becoming more complex, not only because of the government's prices and incomes policy but also because of the introduction of new techniques and the demand for interchangeability and flexibility in the deployment of labour. There was the additional problem of negotiating agreements with employers' organisations representing on the one hand the large groups and on the other hand the small jobbing printers employing only a few NGA members. In 1967 there were those in the NGA who were beginning to think the pattern of negotiations for the future would have to change as the industry changed.

The 1969 and 1970 Negotiations

In 1969 the NGA decided not to enter into a collective movement for the negotiation of a new agreement. Delays in reaching wage settlements in past negotiations had been, the NGA considered, due not to employers but wholly to lack of agreement among the unions on what the claims should be and to lack of unity during the negotiations.

To loud cheers from delegates at the 1969 Delegate Meeting, the General Secretary, John Bonfield, announced that the NGA would negotiate unilaterally for a new agreement to replace that due to expire on 30 October 1969.

Negotiations opened with BFMP and the NS on 31 July 1969. These were based on an emergency resolution on wages carried at the 1969 Delegate Meeting. The claim comprised a new basic craft rate of £20 in London and £19.20 in provincial grade 1 towns and £19.07½ in grade 2, together with the same percentage increase in provincial morning and evening papers' extras. The claim also included a new provincial shift-working agreement comprising a double day rate of 30 per cent and a night rate of 40 per cent. A new keyboard rate for London and the provinces was demanded – 10 per cent above basic – with a new rate for readers also to be 10 per cent over basic. Supplementary payments' demands were made for film-setting work of £5 for operators of linotron and similar machines, £3 for monophoto operators and those engaged on planning, page make-up, corrections and proofing, and £1.50 for operators of diatype and similar machines. The claim also called for restoration of the 1959 percentage values of London machine extras, with a comprehensive machine classification (letterpress and litho) to cover London and the provinces giving parity of extras. The claim recognised that, in the economic circumstances of 1969, wage increases had to be the first priority, and that from the question of practicability the membership had to face the fact the cost-of-living bonus had gone. To seek its restoration would be impossible. The employers had sought for ten years to end the bonus and having done so they were not going to return it. In addition, the government's prices and incomes policy, although considerably dented by 1969, saw no place for such a bonus.

The NGA was determined to use the opportunity presented by unilateral negotiations to prevent claims for increases in 'extras' being 'swept under the carpet'. However, they were aware that the claims for increases in extras would complicate efforts to secure a realistic improvement in the basic rate, which was the main objective. Indeed, it was the NGA's insistence that the claim in respect of the extras be met that at one stage in the negotiations almost brought about deadlock. Agreement was finally made. Although the amounts involved in the 'extras' increases were not substantial, the members recognised the significance of the fact that the employers had been persuaded to carry out a revision of the machine classification agreement (see Chapter 13).

NGA members accepted the offer by 38,102 votes to 21,809. The new agreement became effective on 1 November 1969 and ended on 30 October 1971. It provided increases in the basic craft rate of £2, staged as £1 from November 1969 and a further £1 from November 1970, increases for auxiliary worker members, qualified plate preparers and qualified members in the Small Offset Section of 87½p, and an increase for adult women of 72½p. In addition, there was an increase in the evening newspaper 'extra' of 12½p and in the morning newspaper 'extra' of 21p as from 1 November 1969 and a further increase of similar amounts from 1 November 1970. The agreement also provided an increase in keyboard extras and the readers' rate in London and the provinces of 12½p from 1 November 1969 and a further 12½p twelve months later, which was absorbable from merit money or from house payments. A treble shift agreement for the provinces was introduced and provided a rate of 33⅓ per cent above the basic day rate for each of the three shifts and a paid meal break of half an hour.

In return for these improvements the NGA accepted the employers could recruit extra labour under the supervision of a joint subcommittee. Although a clause covering the handling of magnetic tape was inserted into the agreement, it was accepted that due to the complex nature of film-setting payments these should be excluded from the settlement and be the subject of independent negotiations and agreement. The previous agreements were also amended in respect of productivity and disputes procedures to codify existing practices.

The increases in the basic rates amounted to some 6 per cent in each case and compared favourably with settlements at the time in other industries and other parts of the industry. In total, the offer fell only 32½p below the amount claimed, although the increase was to be staged over a two-year period. Although the BFMP and the NS would not accept the principle of equal pay for equal work for Small Offset Section members, they were prepared to offer improvements to those NGA members in this section who had three years' experience.

The collapse of the Labour government's prices and incomes policy in the autumn of 1969 and the winter of 1969/70 set in train a 'wages explosion'. Wage settlements statistics clearly showed that the October 1969 settlement was rapidly being overtaken by events. A special meeting of the National Council, held on 18 March 1970, decided on an immediate approach to the BFMP and the NS for 'a substantial increase in members' basic wage rates' in view of increases secured or being sought in other industries and services since the wages settlement of October 1969. The 'wages explosion' had depressed NGA members' relative position in the wages league table. The NGA was particularly concerned about those of its members in provincial grade 2 towns receiving £17.75 per week. The Association was not seeking to terminate or repudiate the current wage agreement but merely to amend its basic rate provisions, which were fast becoming overtaken by events over which neither the NGA nor the employers had any control.

A claim was submitted for increases in the London and provincial grade 1 craft basic rates of £5.32½ and for the abolition of the grade 2 rate. The object was to secure a London basic rate of £24, which, with the increase of £1 due in November 1970 under the 1969 settlement would ultimately give a basic London rate of £25. Negotiations on this claim – which were unique in that they were made during the lifetime of an existing agreement – continued until early July 1970, when a settlement was recommended to the members. Although the employers expressed sympathy with the plight of the lowest-paid NGA members, they rejected the claim for a weekly increase of £5.32½ for them as unrealistic. Many firms were already paying in excess of the NGA claim and the employers sought to absorb house rates and merit money into any increases granted. Mindful of the members' objections to absorption expressed at the 1969 Delegate Meeting, the NGA rejected absorption out of hand. It also rejected 'banded' increases, with the larger going to lower-paid members and correspondingly smaller amounts for the higher paid, as the NGA viewed this as graduated absorption.

After extremely hard bargaining, with no accepted offer being made by the employers, deadlock was reached. NGA branches were asked to show their disappointment at the employers' delaying tactics by embarking on a policy of non-cooperation on the shop floor. When the chapels responded positively, an improved offer was made from the employers. Although the amount offered and the accompanying conditions proved unacceptable, negotiations did continue and a settlement was reached. The new agreement, which NGA members approved by a substantial majority, came into effect on 5 August 1970.[22] It provided increases to craftsmen of £2.50 at 5 August 1970, with a further increase of £1.50 at 1 August 1971. Auxiliary workers, plate preparers and small offset operators were to receive an increase of £2.20 on 5 August 1970 and £1.30 on 1 August 1971. These increases incorporated the basic rate increases due on 1 November 1970 under the 1969 agreement. In addition, the increases in provincial news 'extras' due in November 1970 were brought forward to 5 August 1970. The

1969 agreement was extended until 31 January 1972, but it was agreed that, if during the period of the agreement there was an exceptional fall in the internal purchasing power of the pound, the NGA could request amendments to the agreement. Otherwise there was to be no change in the wages and conditions, either nationally or in individual firms, during the period of the agreement, although chapel claims based on 'special circumstances', and productivity bargaining were not precluded.

The 1971/2 Negotiations

Negotiations for an agreement to replace that due to expire on 31 January 1972 began in November, when the NGA informed the BFMP and the NS that its main concern in the negotiations would be with basic wages, and particularly those of its lowest-paid members. The NGA claimed increases in the London basic wage rate from £22.68 to £30 per week and one provincial rate of £29.25, thereby establishing a London/provincial differential of 75p, and abolition of the grade 2 rate. It also claimed proportional increases in the provincial newspaper 'extras' and in the rates for auxiliary workers, small offset machine operators and plate preparers. To facilitate these claims being met in full the NGA proposed that 50 per cent of the increase could be absorbed into merit money and locally agreed house rates. The claim also included increases in the apprentices' wage scale and in the provincial night and double day shift rates and overtime payments at time and a half for the first four hours of overtime and double time for all subsequent overtime. The NGA wanted an open-ended agreement, as its members feared stabilisation in a period of rapidly rising inflation and the absence of a cost-of-living bonus.

In December 1971 the BFMP and the NS made wage proposals which they described as 'the most their members could afford'. They offered to increase the craft worker rate by £1.32 per week as from 1 May 1972, with proportional increases for auxiliary workers, small offset machine operators, plate preparers and learners, together with increases in the evening news 'extra' of 15p per week and the morning news 'extra' of 20p. In addition, the employers offered one extra day of annual leave and proposed that this should take effect in the twelve months' qualifying period up to 30 June 1972. They rejected the claim for increased shift rates and overtime payments, but said they would consider improvements in apprentices' wages in the context of a complete revision of apprenticeship training and providing there were no substantial cost increases. The whole offer was conditional on six months' notice of termination, which could not be given earlier than 31 December 1972.

On 18 January 1972 the NGA, along with representatives of Natsopa, Sogat and Slade, received the employers' latest offer, which turned out to be 30p per week more than previously offered. This new offer of £1.62 represented some 7.4 per cent increase on basic rates but the employers insisted that if their offer was accepted it could not be paid until May 1972 and that the agreement would have to run until at least mid-1973. They also rejected the NGA's offer of part absorption of the basic rate increase into house rates and merit money. This offer was totally unacceptable to the NGA. In the following month the employers offered an increase in the craft rate of £1.82 per week for a fifteen-month agreement from April, but indicated informally that the offer would be raised to £2 if the four unions – NGA, Slade, Natsopa and Sogat – recommended it in a ballot vote. The NGA rejected this because the main bargaining objective was significantly to help its lower-paid members, but to date none of the BFMP and the NS offers had done this. Industrial action now seemed likely but did not materialise.

The employers progressively increased their offer to £2.50 and in May 1972 NGA members voted by 47,879 to 13,107 to accept the new agreement, which was to operate for two years from 24 April 1972. The agreement abolished the provincial grade 2 rate. After 53 years, wage grading in the provinces had finally ended. Craft minimum rates were increased by £2.50 per week from 24 April 1972, with a further £2 thirteen months later, by which time the minimum rate would be £26.38 in the provinces and £27.18 in London. At each implementation stage of the agreement, news 'extras' were increased by 30p and 20p per week respectively. Rates for the last two years of apprenticeship were increased to 70 per cent and 80 per cent of the craft rate. The agreement also provided for four weeks' paid holiday by 1974. The NGA had originally wanted an open-ended agreement. During the negotiations it sought a fixed-term agreement, as it was clear by early 1972 that the Conservative government was highly likely either to devalue the pound or introduce wage restraint or even a wage freeze. A fixed-term agreement offered protection against both these eventualities. Indeed, in November 1972 the government imposed a six-month wage freeze. The NGA insisted on retaining in the agreement the clause enabling the re-opening of negotiations in the event of any serious change in the value of the pound through devaluation, the imposition of VAT or entry into the Common Market.

The 1974–9 Negotiations

In January 1974 the NGA presented claims for a new basic craft rate of £34 per week in the provinces and £34.80 per week in London, for the first five hours of overtime to be paid at time and a half and double-time rate thereafter, for the abolition of late-night working in weekly newspaper offices, for increases of certain newspaper colour 'extras', and for discussions on a 35 hour week after settlement of the claims. In addition, the NGA proposed termination of the current agreement before 23 April 1974, on the grounds there had been 'an exceptional fall in the internal purchasing power of the pound' following the large increase in oil prices in the 1973/4 winter.

The NGA put priority on securing an increase in basic wage rates because of the large increase in the cost of living since the last settlement. It sought to re-establish the value of its members' wages to the level prevailing at the time of the 1972 settlement, with some insurance against future erosion by inflation. In commenting on the claim, John Bonfield, the General Secretary, remarked:

> Too many people think that all printers are highly paid. This is not so as the present provincial minimum basic rate of £26.38 shows. This figure is not much above the £25 national minimum wage the TUC are asking the Government to agree to. We recognise that this claim ignores the Government Phase 3 but it is the policy of the NGA to oppose all legislative interference in the collective bargaining processes.[23]

The BFMP and the NS rejected the NGA claim, but proposed 'threshold agreements' whereby there would be a flat-rate cost-of-living payment when the Index of Retail Prices reached 7 points above its level for October 1973. In the light of the employers' attitude, the NGA revised its claim to an increase of £5 per week on basic rates and a six months' extension of current agreements instead of a 'threshold arrangement'. Subsequently the employers offered an increase of £2.65 per week plus 'threshold arrangements'. The NGA rejected this and imposed a ban on overtime and on incentive schemes. Following an intervention in the dispute by the Secretary of State for Employment,

Mr Michael Foot, a settlement was reached and accepted by NGA members in a ballot in May 1974.

The agreement was to operate from 24 April 1974 to 23 April 1975. The basic minimum craft rate became £30.23 per week in London and £29.43 in the provinces. In addition, there was a 'threshold' cost-of-living arrangement under which a further 40p per week would be paid when the Index of Retail Prices rose by 7 points above the October 1973 figure of 185.4. A further 40p per week became payable for every subsequent 1 point rise in the Index. These 'cost-of-living payments' were additions to the basic rate and not included in it for overtime, shift or incentive bonus payments calculations. The provincial evening news rate and the morning news rate were increased by 39p and 56p respectively.

Last-minute difficulties about paying the increases arose when the Pay Board did not approve the agreement. The NGA advised its members that, if employers refused to implement the agreement, chapels should cease work and 'sit in' until management agreed to pay the new rates. However, before too much disruption took place the Pay Board approved the agreement, whereupon the NGA withdrew its instructions.

The 1974 negotiations had taken place against a background of a change from a government operating an incomes policy to one committed to ending such a policy. By the time the NGA presented its 1975 demands to the BPIF and the NS, agreement had been reached between the Labour government and the TUC that there be no return in the near future to the traditional collective bargaining system. In February 1975 the NGA presented a claim for a London basic craft rate of £45 and a provincial rate of £44.20, a twelve-month agreement, a 35 hour working week, time and a half for the first five hours of overtime, payment of average earnings for annual holidays, an increase in the provincial news 'extra's. The new basic rates were to include full consolidation of the existing £4.40 'threshold' cost-of-living payments. The NGA did not support further 'threshold' arrangements because further flat-rate payments would merely erode skill differentials further.

In April 1975 the employers made what they described as their 'final offer'. They proposed a £39.00 per week provincial basic craft rate and a £39.84 rate in London. After consolidation of the existing £4.40 threshold payments, this would have given £4.36 new money. Of this, 81p in the provinces and 85p in London was to be subjected to absorption into house rates and merit money. The employers were, however, prepared to grant a further £2 of new money in November 1975, to give a basic rate of £41 in the provinces and £41.84 in London. Other elements of the employers' final offer included an evening newspaper 'extra' of £4.40, with a £6.80 'extra' for morning newspaper workers, from July 1975 the abolition of time and quarter overtime payments and replacement by time and half, average earnings for all annual holidays, and the introduction of equal pay for women operators of small offset machines from August 1975. The employers were insistent that until 19 April 1976 the £4.40 threshold payment, even though consolidated into basic rates, should not count for incentive bonus calculations. Another condition the BPIF and NS attached to their 'final offer' was that any member losing time on his own account would, if required to work overtime the same day, make up his lost time before receiving overtime rates.

The NGA rejected the 'final offer' and imposed industrial sanctions from 5 May 1975. Following seven weeks of this action a new agreement with the BIPF and the NS came into effect from 23 June 1975, to operate until 24 April 1976. The agreement was accepted following a ballot vote in which the NGA recommendation to reject the employers' 'final offer' and escalate industrial action was defeated by 3,591 votes in a poll of more than 90 per cent. The NGA was left with no alternative but to accept the employers' 'final offer'. Efforts to obtain full retrospective payment proved abortive, but the settlement gave each craft member a flat payment of £15.

Discussions between the NGA and the employers' organisations over the implementation of the second stage of the 1975 agreement were necessary because of the government's counter-inflationary policy. Whilst it conformed with the policy for the £2 increase to be paid in full, the effects of this on individual earnings had to be offset against the £6 pay limit, which was to operate for twelve months from 1 August 1975. This increase in the basic rate during the period of the £6 pay limit made negotiations for a new agreement to operate from 26 April 1976 complicated. However, a settlement was reached which provided that minimum grade rates upon which the calculation of overtime, shift premiums, incentive bonus schemes and any other extras were based would revert to those applicable immediately prior to 3 November 1975. In addition, members would receive a flat-rate payment of £6 per week to give minimum earnings for craftsmen of £45.

The question of an adjustment to the incentive bonus calculator was also raised during the 1976 negotiations. Although the employers accepted that they were obliged to discuss the matter under the 1975 agreement, there was nothing they could do at that time since any adjustment would be outside the pay policy. In the event, the most the NGA achieved was to persuade the employers to agree to discuss the elimination of the bonus calculator rate as soon as the pay policy allowed.

A new agreement, which came into operation on 24 April 1977, provided for the maximum increase that could be obtained under stage 2 of the pay policy. The minimum grade rates upon which the calculation of overtime, etc. was based remained at their existing figures, as did the £6 flat-rate weekly supplement. In addition to these payments, a weekly individual earnings supplement was to be paid and was to be calculated each week by taking 5 per cent of the individual's total earnings for all hours worked. The employers were pressed to introduce an industry-wide sick pay scheme to cover all workers and to give average earnings for sickness periods of up to six months and then half average earnings for sickness periods lasting another six months.

In July 1977, formal agreement between the government and the TUC on incomes policy came to an end. However, the government issued pay guidelines which required that wage settlements should not exceed 10 per cent of present earnings during the period 1 July 1977 to 30 June 1978, whilst the 1977 Trade Union Congress decided to maintain the twelve-month interval between wage settlements. In the autumn of 1977 the NGA refused to participate in a joint approach with other print unions to the employers for an immediate increase in wages, as it was convinced that the BPIF and the NS would not concede any extra money since to do so would be a breach of the twelve-month rule.

However, the NGA decided it would no longer tolerate a position whereby some of its members were taking home less than £40 per week. Against this background, the Association launched a campaign in November 1977 to raise the wages of its lower-paid members. A general pay claim for the rest of the membership was to be left until April 1978, in line with the TUC's twelve-month rule (see Chapter 10). The campaign sought to secure rises for members receiving less than £55 gross a week (£57.70 in London) for a standard working week, excluding overtime. The NGA came under severe pressure from the government and the TUC to withdraw the campaign. In February 1978 the campaign was suspended, by which time 2,400 members in fifty-nine branches, covering 395 firms, had received increases of up to £7 a week.

In anticipation of the termination of the wage agreement in April

1978, the NGA in January of that year proposed to tbe BPIF and the NS a further 10 per cent supplement on individual total earnings, that machinery be established for the negotiation of the introduction of a 35 hour week, the restoration of the differentials, the consolidation of the phase I supplement of £6 and the phase II supplement of 5 per cent, improvements in the bonus calculator rate and the introduction of a national sick pay scheme. In addition, the NGA expected constructive negotiations during the term of the proposed agreement to find a permanent solution to the wages position of lower-paid members. In the ensuing negotiations an agreement was reached, to operate from 24 April 1978. The agreement provided for minimum grade rates for craftsmen to be increased by 10 per cent to £42.90 in the provinces and £43.82 in London, with appropriate increases for apprentices and learners. The phase I supplement of £6 and the phase II supplement of 5 per cent were replaced by a new flat supplementary payment of £10.82. These increases provided a minimum full-time earnings level for craftsmen of £53.72 in the provinces and of £54.64 in London. All machine and other 'extra' payments provided in the national agreements were increased by 10 per cent, but the bonus calculator rates remained at £4.40 below the minimum grade rate. The agreement, when viewed in the whole, gave the maximum possible increases under the government's pay guidelines and a deal weighted marginally in favour of the NGA's lower-paid members.

In February 1979 the NGA submitted a claim for a revision of the 1978 agreement. In doing so the main priority was to secure the largest possible increase in the overall earnings of the members. Negotiations were concluded in March 1979 and the proposed agreement accepted in a ballot of NGA members. The agreement, which operated from 24 April 1979, provided for a provincial grade rate of £53.25 and £54.17 in London, with a flat-rate supplement of £8.96, making a new minimum earnings level of £62.21 in the provinces and of £63.13 in London. The agreement also provided for all 'operation extras' to be increased by 25 per cent, but excluded photocomposition and machine classification 'extras', which were to be the subject of separate negotiations. The employers finally conceded the NGA claim that the bonus calculator rate should be established at the level of the appropriate minimum grade rate. The evening newspaper 'extra' increased from £4.84 to £6 and improvements were obtained for journeymen engaged on morning newspaper night shifts which end after 6.00 pm, in that they would receive 25 per cent of the minimum weekly grade rate calculated on an hourly basis for all shift hours worked after that time.

The BPIF and the NS reaffirmed that during the life of the new agreement there would be negotiations about a shorter working week, restoration of differentials, introduction of a national sick pay scheme and 'constructive solutions' to the problem of lower-paid members. Agreement was also reached with the employers on a new overtime limit based on 24 hours in any consecutive weeks, on a disputes procedure which for the first time provided a status quo clause and for differences not resolved at house level to go to the national level, and on a joint statement on work from unrecognised sources.

The 1979 settlement increased the minimum grade rate for all classes by 24.1 per cent, and provided new money increases of £8.49 for craftsmen. It gave across-the-board rises of 15.8 per cent, in answer to the NGA's original 20 per cent claim. Although it was not possible to reduce the flat-rate supplement to £7.98 as had been claimed, it was reduced to £8.96 for craftsmen. For the first time since March 1975 agreement had been reached on the basis of free collective bargaining. However, there was no way in which the NGA could in one fell swoop escape from the straightjacket of four years of pay policy. The settlement was the first step towards the achievement of the union's objectives of the establishment of a respectable basic rate, the complete consolidation of 'flat' payments, the elimination of low pay, and a reduction in the working week.

THE 1980 DISPUTE

In January 1980 the NGA presented a two-pronged claim to the BPIF and the NS for a new agreement from 24 April 1980. A claim for a standard working week of 37½ hours for day, double day and night shift workers was backed up by a wage increase claim for a new minimum grade rate in the provinces of £75 and in London of £76.18. In addition, the NGA requested the discontinuation of the flat supplementary payment of £8.96 and its replacement by a new flat supplementary payment of £5 to give minimum earnings levels for craftsmen of £80 in the provinces and £81.18 in London. The proposals also claimed a new provincial daily newspaper 'extra' of £8.45 above the minimum grade rate, and a rise from 33.28p to 50p per hour in the 'extra' paid to members on morning newspaper night shifts ending after 6.00 pm.

The NGA's two key objectives were a wage increase to protect members against inflation and a shorter working week. The claim for a standard working week of 37½ hours was to be a step towards an eventual 35 hour week which the NGA saw as offsetting the likely adverse employment effects in the industry of the implementation of technological changes and deteriorating trading conditions stemming from the economic policies introduced by the Conservative government in 1979/80. The wage increase was justified on the grounds that inflation was running at 20 per cent and was expected to rise further in the coming months. It was also thought the time was right to begin eliminating the irrelevant outstanding supplements and to eliminate low pay from the printing industry. The claimed new minimum earnings levels would bring a minimum new money increase of £17.95 (or 28.5 per cent) over existing levels.

The NGA had first claimed the 35 hour week in 1975 but there had been no meaningful discussions between the employers and the NGA on the subject. The NGA told the BPIF and the NS that the 37½ hour week was an issue on which its members would stand firm. The claim was not merely to safeguard and benefit the existing membership but also to bring security and well-being to its future membership. The NGA told the employers:

> the establishment of a respectable basic rate, a reasonable minimum earnings level and the move towards a shorter working week, as outlined in our claim, is going to go some way to restore printworkers to a standard of living in accordance with their commitment to a successful industry.[24]

In February the BPIF and the NS replied to the NGA's claim. They offered an increase of £7.79 a week in the provincial minimum craft rate, but were insistent that the existing flat supplementary payment should continue. This offer would have given a £70 minimum earnings level and 12.5 per cent new money on the minimum rate. However, conditions were attached to the offer; these included productivity improvements, new manning levels, revision of the apprenticeship agreement, and provisions for retraining and transfer of craft workers. The employers rejected the 37½ hour claim, but said that any reduction in hours would have to be linked to the conditions outlined above.

In March the employers offered a wage increase of £10.79 and 1 hour off the standard working week from 31 March 1981, with a further 1½ hour reduction from 1 November 1982. When the NGA rejected this offer, the employers offered revised proposals of a new money increase of £12.79 a week, a continuation of the existing £8.96 supplementary payment, and a phased introduction of a shorter week, with a 1 hour cut from 5 January 1981 and a further 1½ hour cut from 5 July 1982. This offer was also unacceptable to the NGA. One of its main objections was that the new money represented only 15.68 per cent more on average earnings compared with an existing inflation rate of 19.1 per cent, which was expected to rise even higher during the lifetime of the proposed agreement. The employers said their final offer was a £3.96 partial consolidation of the existing £8.96 flat supplementary payment, but this would not count for bonus calculations. This final offer meant a new provincial craft rate of £70, a new flat supplement of £5 and a new minimum earnings level of £75. For the NGA negotiators this offer was insufficient to offset the fundamental changes to the existing NGA working practices which the employers were seeking.

Deadlock had now been reached. To break this, the NGA launched a campaign of industrial action in March 1980. However, it exempted firms that would agree to an 'interim agreement', to operate from 24 April, which provided for an £80 per week minimum earnings level, a £75 per week basic rate, and the phased introduction of a 37½ hour standard working week, via a 1½ hour reduction in April 1980 and a further 1 hour reduction in April 1981. Firms signing such interim agreements could absorb up to £5 per week of the £17.79 increase from existing house rates and merit money. The deals were to last until the dispute had been settled and then firms would revert to the agreement finally reached by the NGA and BPIF and the NS. By 19 April the NGA claimed that 25 per cent of BPIF and NS members were exempt from industrial action as they had signed interim agreements.[25]

The industrial action designed to get the employers back to the negotiating table included chapel meetings of up to twenty-four hours' duration, the withdrawal of flexibility, overtime bans, reducing running speeds and chapels sending home key staff at peak production times and paying them. In addition, coordinated action led to a series of twenty-four-hour stoppages in provincial newspaper groups and commercial printing. One other component in the campaign was indefinite stoppages covering 1,100 members in selected BPIF firms. In retaliation the BPIF advised its members to lock out NGA members as from 28 April. Where this happened, members received national and local financial support from the NGA. However, in reality the BPIF's attempt to lock out the NGA was a fiasco from the start. Firms employing 75 per cent of the workforce ignored the instruction. Picketing of BPIF and NS firms was undertaken and thirty-five NGA pickets – including national officers Bob Tomlins, John Ibbotson and Brenda Philbin and branch officials – were arrested outside the *Wolverhampton Express and Star* as they protested against the management's continued publication. There were other arrests of NGA members on picket lines at Bradford and Portsmouth. Support was also received from Slade and the NUJ, which ordered their members not to cross NGA picket lines if management tried to introduce 'blacklegs'.

To ensure that financial support was available to NGA members during the dispute, a levy payment of £6.20 per week was imposed on all full members not directly involved in the dispute. The levy remained in force for four weeks and raised £1,024,242, which to some extent compensated for the £1,345,357 paid out in dispute benefit. Undoubtedly, this magnificent response shown by the members contributed greatly to the eventual outcome of the dispute.

With the BPIF lock-out policy in disarray, an increasing number of firms signed interim agreements. By the end of May 1980 the vast majority of NGA members, who worked under the BPIF agreement, were covered by interim deals which met the union's claim. On 29 May an ultimatum was issued to firms which had not already made an interim agreement that unless they did so their NGA members would go on strike and receive NGA dispute benefit of £50 a week. When the NGA announced that it would only consider re-opening national negotiations on the terms of its exemption policy the BPIF's clear lack of strategy came under severe criticism from its members. However, the BPIF felt there was no option but to advise member firms to negotiate independent agreements with the NGA since many of those opposing signing interim agreements had in fact done so earlier in the dispute and incurred no disruption of production. By early June independent agreements had been secured with these firms. The BPIF was in total disarray and the BPIF/NS National Wage Basis Agreement dismantled. There was now no formal national agreement. NGA members working in BPIF houses were covered by interim agreements negotiated between individual employers and the NGA, which aligned with the NGA claim for an £80 per week minimum earnings level, a £75 per week basic rate and a 37½ hour standard working week by 23 April 1981.

At the end of April the Newspaper Society members locked out

NGA members. Two weeks later, on 11 May 1980, a basis for a settlement to the dispute was agreed when the NS sought negotiations with the NGA separately from the BPIF. The agreement, which was ratified by 7,941 votes to 1,784, provided for an £80 minimum earnings guarantee, an uplift in the weekly basic rate from £53.25 to £70 by the minimum payment of £12.79 new money and by a £3.96 consolidation of the £8.96 flat supplementary payment. The £70 basic rate was to remain until 2 November 1980, after which it would increase to £72.50. The bonus calculator rate was established at £66.04 and the evening newspaper 'extra' increased to £7.89. The morning newspaper night shift hourly premium increased to 43.75p per hour and further increased to 44.87p per hour on 5 January 1981. Hours of work were reduced from 40 hours to 39 from 5 January 1981 and to 37½ hours from 2 November 1981. The agreement also contained productivity proposals permitting flexibility of labour in origination and printing machine departments and allowed the retraining of NGA craft workers where a vacancy could not be met by normal recruitment within two months of its notification to the NGA branch.

The industrial muscle of the NGA allied to the determination, loyalty, discipline and sacrifice of its members had achieved a significant victory in its dispute with the BPIF and the NS. The £80 minimum earnings level represented a 28.5 per cent increase for the lowest-paid NGA members, while the £72.50 basic rate increase amounted to 36.15 per cent. Its members had protected their standard of living from the effects of inflation, thus achieving one of its key aims in the negotiations. The size of the wage settlement was well in advance of that being achieved in other industries in the first half of 1980. The BPIF had been reduced to a state of disarray such that it had advised its members to make the best deal they could with the NGA. The Newspaper Society had locked out NGA members, yet within two weeks it was making an agreement with the NGA for a 37½ hour working week by November 1981, an £80 minimum earnings level and a new minimum grade rate of £72.50 by November 1980 – just £2.50 less than had been claimed.

The NGA had become the first union to negotiate a 37½ hour standard working week across a whole industry, thereby maintaining its position of being the pacesetter in social advances in working hours. The NGA's achievement was without parallel not only in British industry but also in the Western European printing industries. However, the NGA's success did not spread to the rest of British industry as had happened with its previous breakthroughs on working hours, since the early 1980s were years of deep economic recession and heavy redundancies in British manufacturing industry. Although in the Newspaper Society areas the 37½ hour standard working week was to be implemented six months later than in the BPIF areas, the NGA had every reason to be proud of its success. It saw the breakthrough in hours as a significant contribution to protecting its existing and future membership against what the General Secretary, Joe Wade, described as the 'twin tidal waves' – new technology and unemployment – presenting the greatest challenges to the NGA in the 1980s.

Another success for the NGA in the 1980 dispute was that it secured significant changes to the original productivity proposals presented by the BPIF and the NS at the beginning of the negotiations. The NGA regarded the employers' productivity proposals to be a blatant and cynical attempt to remove control over recruitment and training from the NGA. It was particularly concerned about the employers' demands for complete flexibility throughout all origination and machine room departments, for an immediate reduction in the period of apprenticeship, for trainee recruitment whereby if the NGA could not fill a vacancy within one month employers could recruit whoever they wanted to do NGA jobs, and for the upgrading of other workers in the industry. In the final NS agreement, these proposals were amended in a radical way and in some cases to the positive benefit of NGA members. In the BPIF area the NGA agreed in the individual settlements to no more than some flexibility in the machine room and the origination areas. If the employer's proposals had been perceived by the NGA as being really about productivity they would have been given a very different reception. The NGA told the employers at the beginning of the negotiations that it agreed with the employers' own description of the British printing industry, namely 'This is an industry which should be proud of its performance; is high in the output league table; has a good sales record; has a favourable trade balance, and loses little time in industrial disputes.'

A further result of the dispute was that the NS had agreed that, in future, negotiations would be conducted with them alone and not jointly with the BPIF as in the past. The NGA had traditionally regarded such separate negotiations as logical and sensible. The provincial newspaper sector was more profitable than the general trade. Product market competition had been less severe and the NGA members in provincial newspapers consistently argued that, by negotiating jointly with the BPIF, NS members were conceding lower improvements in terms and conditions than if they negotiated separately. The achievement of separate negotiations with the NS was expected to be of benefit to all its members employed in Newspaper Society firms. However, this was not to be the case. Separate negotiations with the NS were commenced at the very time when the balance of bargaining power in the industry was to tip very much in favour of the employers because of the 'tidal waves' of new technology and the Conservative government's industrial relations legislation of the early 1980s.

There were, however, downsides to the NGA's victory. The BPIF had effectively disintegrated. No national agreement now existed. The NGA faced the prospect, when the independent agreements required review, of negotiating separately with potentially some 3,600 firms. The time this would require would leave little over for the national councillors and the national officers to service the rest of the membership. To depend on house agreements would be impractical. Having caused the break-up of the BPIF, the NGA now had an interest in ensuring its resurrection. The NGA maintained day-to-day contact with the BPIF, recognising that it was in the interests of all members within the industry to re-establish a national agreement in 1981.

Unlike the BPIF, the Newspaper Society was not in disarray. On the contrary, its member companies had locked out NGA members on a large scale. Some had continued to produce newspapers with the aid of management and other non-NGA personnel. If the NGA had not reached an accommodation with the NS, many more of the latter's members would have been producing newspapers in this way. The dispute had shown clearly to Newspaper Society members that papers could be produced without the need for NGA labour – a lesson that was not forgotten by NS members when they set about implementing new technology in the mid-1980s. In addition, many provincial newspapers were part of large and wealthy organisations with sufficient financial resources to assist them in producing newspapers without NGA members. The NS negotiators, who had at the last moment conceded almost everything the NGA had claimed, recognised from the outset that what they were agreeing were minimum terms and conditions. High rates and good conditions were generated more by house agreements than national agreements. The NS had not come back to the negotiating table cap in hand. It had come back in an eleventh hour attempt to salvage a national agreement in the knowledge that, if it did not succeed, its members would exploit new technology to produce newspaper with non-union labour and to remove the NGA from their establishments. These facts and realities of the 1980 Newspaper Society settlement were not hidden from the members by the General Secretary, Joe Wade.[26]

The 1980 dispute was to be the only NGA 'victory' in a major industrial dispute in the decade of the 1980s. Its bargaining power in the newspaper industry in the 1980s was turned on its head relative to previous periods by the 'tidal waves' of unemployment, new technology and the government's employment legislation, particularly the restrictions on secondary industrial action. Some of the tactics used by the NGA in the 1980 dispute, for example stoppage of the national press, were now made illegal. Had the NGA not given preference to the achievement of a shorter working week in 1980, then the opportunity to do so would not have arisen at any other time in the 1980s when the highest priority had to be given to other issues, especially employment security in the light of economic recession, and the introduction of new technology.

WAGE MOVEMENTS, 1981–9

The BPIF

Although there had been day-to-day contact with the BPIF between May 1980 and February 1981, no national agreement existed. Recognising that the interests of its members would be best protected by the re-establishment of a national agreement, representatives of the NGA, Natsopa and Sogat met the BPIF in February 1981 to present a claim for a national agreement to operate from 24 April 1981. The claim submitted by the three unions included a £12 new money increase to establish a minimum grade rate of £87, with a £5 flat supplementary payment, a minimum earnings level of £92 and a bonus calculator rate of £83.04. Agreement was eventually reached with the BPIF for additional new monies of £7.50 per week for craftsmen to be added to the existing grade rates and minimum earnings levels, which were to be calculable for shift and overtime premiums. The existing bonus calculator levels remained unchanged until 28 September 1981, when rates increased by £3.75 for craftsmen. On hours the agreement provided that existing arrangements in firms would continue to apply, thereby underwriting the NGA's success in achieving a 37½ hour week under interim agreements during the 1980 dispute. In return, the NGA accepted flexibility of labour in the origination and machine departments and arrangements to enable full cooperation at national, branch and local level in changes necessary to achieve increased output and lower unit costs through the most effective use of people, material and machines. The BPIF guaranteed that no NGA member would be made redundant as a direct result of these flexibility arrangements. In addition, the BPIF and the NGA confirmed their commitment to establish a new agreement on all methods of recruitment and training, including provision for retraining and upgrading within the industry. The NGA members endorsed the 1981 national agreement by 32,648 votes to 10,922.

The 1981 agreement was reviewed in early 1982 and revised with effect from 24 April 1982. The amendments provided for craftsmen to receive cash increases of £6.25, calculable for shift and overtime calculations. This provided a new basic rate of £88.75, a £5 flat supplement and a minimum earnings level of £93.75. During the period of the agreement there would be no change in the level of 'extras' laid down in the machine classification and photocomposition agreements, but from 24 April 1983 these 'extras' were to be linked to the agreed percentage increases in basic wages. The agreement also provided for a joint BPIF/NGA working party to consider means of removing the remaining link between incentive bonus calculator rates and basic wage increases provided in national agreements.

The negotiations in 1983 for a revision of the BPIF national agreement took place against a background of a severe economic climate which was affecting British industry in general and the printing industry in particular. However, the NGA claimed a new money increase of £9.00 per week, consolidation of the £5 flat supplement and a minimum earnings rate of £102.75. The claim also sought a 35 hour working week for all day and shift workers, 5 weeks' holiday entitlement payable at time and a half of the weekly rate and a double day shift premium of 25 per cent. In addition, the NGA claimed that the two weeks' minimum notice for the termination of double day shift should be extended to three months, and sought an equal opportunities clause and the establishment of working parties to consider all facets of pensions and parental responsibilities respectively.

Difficulties arose during the negotiations when the NGA would not support a Sogat (82) proposal for the abolition of the Class 3 grade because of its impact on established differentials in the industry.

However, so that a satisfactory settlement could be achieved, the NGA made a proposal which, whilst going towards meeting the Sogat (82) position, ensured that NGA interests would be taken into account in any discussions on changes in relativities and differentials. The eventual amendments to the agreement provided for new money increases of £5.33 for craftsmen to be added to existing rates to give a new minimum earnings level of £99.08. The BPIF conceded one additional day of annual holiday, to make a total of 4 weeks and one day. In future, the machine classification and photocomposition payments were to increase by the same percentage increase as the basic rate increment, but were to be determined in future at the house and not the national level. The BPIF insisted on a termination of the photogravure agreement, which it claimed was now irrelevant to the industry, but agreed to give four weeks' notice of termination of shift to NGA members who had worked shifts continuously for two years or more. A BPIF/NGA/Sogat working party was established to examine the feasibility of a pension scheme and a second working party was to consider whether the existing equal opportunities clause in the national agreement could be usefully extended.

In 1984, in presenting its claims to the BPIF for revisions to the 1983 national agreement, the NGA concentrated on three main elements: an increase in the minimum earnings level to £108.99, a 35 hour working week and five weeks' annual holiday. In intensive negotiations little progress was made on a reduction in the working week or a fifth week's annual holidays. To facilitate a settlement, the NGA withdrew these items from its claim. Revision to the agreement, to operate from April 1984, was eventually reached and provided for a new money increase of £5.92 for craftsmen and the consolidation in three stages of the £5 flat supplement into the minimum rate by April 1986. The machine classification and photocomposition rate was raised to £94.08. A National Joint Efficiency and Productivity Committee was established to guide and advise on efficiency and productivity issues not settled locally, and to review the wider issues of the industry's competitiveness and job security.

The 1985 discussions with the BPIF for the revision of the National Wage Basis Agreement took place against a continued background of economic stagnation. The NGA sought a new money increase of £20 per week to provide a new minimum earnings level of £125 per week, a fifth week of annual holiday, a 35 hour working week, a minimum of three months' notice for the termination of shift working, that the working of treble shifts be on a voluntary basis, and a daily paid meal break of 30 minutes per shift for all NGA members working a shift system. The 1985 agreement provided new money increases of £6.45 per week, an extra day's annual holiday entitlement and six weeks' notice of termination of shift working for employees who had worked shifts continuously for two years or more. During the negotiations the NGA pressed the BPIF to concede the introduction of a 35 hour week and a paid meal break of 30 minutes for double day shift workers. However, the Federation was adamant that it could not trade these items as there were severe competitive market pressures to keep cost increases to the minimum.

The 1986 claim to the BPIF centred around eight issues. There was a demand for an increase of £10.19 per week on the basic craft rate together with a continuation of the current 'linkage formula' for machine classification and photocomposition payments. In addition, the NGA sought a fifth week's holiday, a 35 hour working week, a minimum of three months' notice for the termination of shift working, and a daily paid meal break of 30 minutes per shift to be available for all NGA members working a shift system. Two new items appeared in the Association's shopping list relative to claims made in the immediate past. These were a claim for comprehensive paternity leave arrangements and an understanding that, in view of proposed parliamentary impending legislation to remove statutory restrictions on working hours of women and young people, no local change in conditions of these groups of workers would take place without reference to the NGA nationally.

The NGA negotiators were unable to achieve the claim in full, but did conclude an agreement giving a number of improvements in the terms and conditions of NGA members. These included a new money increase of £6.85 (6.2 per cent) per week for craftsmen, increases of 6.4 per cent in the machine classification and photocomposition payments, and the 'linkage' formula between these extras and the basic rate to continue for a further three-year period until April 1989. The agreement also provided for improvement in the length of notice for shift termination and a greater range of retraining and employment opportunities for NGA members, especially those likely to be affected by the implementation of technological change on the origination side of the industry. However, the most significant advance in the agreement was the establishment of five weeks' annual holiday for NGA members (see Chapter 13).

Negotiations aimed at achieving £12 a week new money and a new minimum earnings level of £130.30 per week for NGA members working in BPIF firms began on 3 February 1987. The claim also included rationalisation of the existing letterpress, provincial, litho, electrotypers and stereotypers and London agreements into one agreement, double day shift premiums to be at no less than time and a third, with time and a half for night work, the payment of 150 per cent of normal rate of pay or average earnings – whichever was the greater – for annual holidays, the provision of minimum sick pay arrangements and paternity/maternity leave arrangements and a review of the machine classification and photocomposition banding structure. Any new agreement was to operate from 24 April 1987.

The negotiations were at times fraught with difficulties. Agreement was reached whereby the BPIF offered £6.85 a week new money for craftsmen, taking the basic rate from £118.30 to £125.15 a week. Although the offer fell short of the £12 claimed, the NGA negotiators felt that, bearing in mind that it was above the then inflation rate and compared with or exceeded settlements being made in other sectors of the industry, it should be accepted by the members. The agreement also continued the 'linkage' formula for 'extras' and contained important clauses covering sick pay (see Chapter 13), efficiency, productivity and rationalisation of separate agreements. The agreement reaffirmed clauses on 'efficiency and productivity' and the parties agreed to 'encourage regular discussions on means of improving all aspects of performance' and that 'any problems would be dealt with quickly and expeditiously'. As a separate issue the BPIF was prepared to issue a set of 'guidelines' to its members covering paternity/maternity leave, bereavement arrangements and women's health issues.

In February 1988, after six negotiating sessions, the NGA and the BPIF signed a revised agreement to operate from 24 April 1988, which gave £7.97 new money per week. Other important parts of the deal included the BPIF's commitment to encourage its members to introduce plant-level sick pay schemes, the granting of three days' bereavement leave on the death of parents, spouse, legal guardians and children, the provision of on-site facilities or paid time off for cancer screening for women members, and the consolidation of some BPIF/NGA agreements into a single comprehensive agreement. In return for all these advances, the NGA accepted methods to improve efficiency, productivity, flexibility of labour, manning levels and arrangements of working hours. The BPIF refused to concede time and a half for all holidays, an improved shift premium, and a minimum earnings guarantee.

The 1988 agreement was revised with effect from 24 April 1989. Under this, NGA members received £10 new money (7.5 per cent), to take the basic rate to £143.12, and the machine classification and photocompositioni extra rate 'linkage formula' was to run for another three years. There was also agreement to two working parties. An NGA/Sogat/BPIF European Action Group was to examine the implications of the Single European Market in 1992 for printing firms and employees. The second working party was to examine childcare facilities in the industry. The 1989 agreement also included the acceptance by the employers of accrued holiday during maternity absence, that more emphasis be given to trainee recruitment and retraining, a drive to recruit and give equal opportunities for disabled people, and measures to improve the existing flexibility of labour and manning arrangements. Outside of the agreement, the Joint Training Council was to agree a minimum trainee intake figure and to discuss wage rates to be paid to trainees, whilst there would also be talks about the disputes procedure, including the role of the independent chairman.

The Newspaper Society

During February 1981 the NGA for the first time submitted a claim solely to the NS. It sought an uplift of £14.50 to the existing £72.50 minimum grade rate. Of the £14.50, £12 was to be new money; this would bring the minimum grade rate up to £87, which together with the then existing flat-rate supplement would give a new minimum earnings level of £92. Additional claims were made covering the bonus calculator rate, the evening news 'extra', the morning news night shift premium and revisions to the photocomposition 'extra'. Improvements on overtime payments for members working rota days/nights on provincial newspapers, as adopted by the 1980 Delegate Meeting, were also forwarded as part of the claim.

In March 1981 the NGA accepted an agreement with the NS which provided a two-stage application to take effect on 24 April 1981 and 4 January 1982. On 24 April the minimum grade rate increased by £7.50 new money from £72.50 to £80, whilst the flat-rate supplement increased from £5 to £6 to raise the minimum earnings from £77.50 to £86. However, throughout the agreement there was to be a minimum earnings guarantee of £88.80, £2.50 above the minimum earnings level.

It was further agreed that on each implementation date there would be appropriate percentage increases in the evening news 'extra' and the morning newspaper night shift hourly premium. During the agreement, the bonus calculator rate would be £70.54, representing an increase of £4.50 over the existing bonus calculator rate of £66.04.

The application of the 1981 agreement created interpretation difficulties. The problem revolved around the acceptance of the exclusion of £3.96 of the basic rate from the bonus calculation in the 1980 agreement. The NS claimed that the NGA had established a bonus calculator rate for all types of schemes, even those previously based on the minimum grade rate and, therefore, it intended in the 1981 agreement for the bonus calculator rate to continue to apply, irrespective of the type of scheme in existence in individual companies. The NGA denied it had agreed to this proposal and challenged the NS interpretation. At the request of a number of chapels, a reconvened meeting of the national wage negotiating panels was held in July 1981. However, no agreement was reached and the NGA authorised its chapels to pursue industrial action within the individual offices until the companies involved conceded to the NGA claim for the 10.34 per cent increase in the minimum grade rate.

In the 1982 negotiations the objective in revising the NS National Wage Basis Agreement was a settlement that would produce sufficient new money to protect the members' real wages against rising inflation but which at the same time would not have detrimental effects upon employment levels. The eventual agreement provided a new money increase of £6.75 per week (8.3 per cent) calculable for all overtime working, and a new minimum grade rate of £87.75 per week. The 8.3 per cent increase was also reflected in the evening news 'extra', which became £9.54 per week. The morning news shift hourly premium was raised to 56.3p an hour. The £5 per week flat-rate supplement was retained, to give a new minimum earnings level of £92.75 per week. The bonus calculator rate was increased by £3.45 per week, to £73.99, but would apply to not only all schemes currently related to the bonus calculator rate but those related to the minimum grade rate.

The 1983 negotiations with the NS were conducted against a background in which the provincial newspaper industry was undergoing severe economic recession, which was exemplified by falls in circulation and a decreasing advertising revenue. The eventual agreement provided a new money increase of £9.00, consolidation of the £5 flat-rate supplement, a minimum earnings guarantee of £104.25, and a minimum grade rate of £101.75. The claim also included a 35 hour working week, five weeks' annual holiday payable at time and a half of the weekly rate, a new bonus calculator rate of £87.99, an evening news 'extra' of £11.06, a morning newspaper hourly premium of 72.67p, and all other 'extras', including the photocomposition extra, to be increased by 9.7 per cent. An equal opportunities clause and the establishment of a working party to consider pensions and all facets of parental responsibilities were also sought.

Throughout the negotiations the NS stressed the parlous state of the industry and took a firm line on the holiday demand. To facilitate an agreement, the NGA withdrew the holiday claim but in doing so made it clear that it would be pressed in future negotiations. The revised wage basis agreement provided for a new money increase of £5.50 per week, raising the minimum grade rate to £93.25, the minimum earnings level to £98.25 and the minimum earnings guarantee to £100.75. The agreement also raised the bonus calculator rate to £78.63, with an evening news 'extra' of £10.14 and a morning news hourly rate premium of 60.5p. It was also agreed to establish one joint working party on equal opportunities and another on paternity-maternity arrangements.

In presenting the claim for the 1984 NS wage basis agreement, the NGA focused on three demands: a 10 per cent increase in new money after consolidation of the £5 flat rate supplement and pro rata increases on all extras, a 2½ hour reduction in the working week, and five weeks' holiday. The final agreement did not achieve all these objectives, but after detailed negotiations a half hour reduction in the working week for members who worked a 37½ week on night shifts was achieved. In addition the annual holiday entitlement was increased from four weeks per year to four weeks and one day. The settlement also provided an increase in the minimum grade rate to £99.50, in the minimum earnings level to £104.50 and in the minimum earnings guarantee to £107.00. The £5 flat rate supplement was consolidated into basic rates in five annual stages, commencing on 23 April 1985. The bonus calculator rate increased to £83.80 and the evening news 'extra' to £10.87. The morning news night shift hourly premium rose to 64.67p, with a guarantee of a minimum weekly premium payment of £24.21. Local discussions would take place on flexibility of labour between the origination and pre-press departments.

One of the causes of the 1985 NGA–*Wolverhampton Express and Star* dispute (see Chapter 14) was that company's introduction of changes in working practices in contravention of the industry disputes procedures. The NS refused to respond to the NGA request that it should make a member firm abide by the disputes procedure. In the light of this, the NGA refused to negotiate a national agreement for 1985 and undertook a campaign of achieving common agreements with individual firms. The claim included demands for a new money increase of £6.57 a week, to give a new grade rate of £107.07, a flat supplement of £4 per week to achieve minimum full-time earnings of £111.07, and a minimum earnings guarantee of £113.57 per week. The claim also included a phased consolidation of the flat supplement over a four-year period commencing from April 1986, an extra day's holiday, a 66 per cent increase in 'extras', and clauses relating to the introduction of new technology and a dispute procedure. Ballots were conducted at provincial news houses and, with only two exceptions, authority was given by NGA members to seek agreements in line with the policy. Westminster Press was the first of the major provincial groups to conclude a satisfactory agreement with the NGA and within a short space of time became the 'model' which was quickly concluded with other individual newspaper employers. These agreements in some cases following limited industrial action, provided for increases to photo-composition, web-offset and plate-making 'extras', and contained clauses covering the introduction of new technology and an improved disputes procedure to deal with disagreement over technology.

The NGA attempted to re-establish a national agreement for 1986. It submitted an eleven-point claim to the NS, the chief features of which included a 10 per cent increase on all earnings, a fifth week's holiday, a 35 hour working week, paternity leave arrangements, and the minimum notice to terminate shift work to be three months. The eventual agreement for 1986 provided for a new money increase of £6.29 per week, the phased consolidation of £1 of the flat-rate supplement, a new minimum grade rate of £114.36 with effect from 24 April 1986, and a new minimum earnings guarantee of £119.86. The evening news 'extra' increased to £12.43 and the morning news/night shift hourly premium became 74.57p. A controversial part of the agreement was that there would be no automatic increase in any bonus/house earnings, however based and calculated, unless local arrangements at chapel/branch were made. The annual holiday entitlement was increased to four weeks and three days from 1 October 1986. The agreement also contained a new technology clause, which provided that where negotiations on the implementation of new technology failed to result in agreement, and were referred to the disputes procedure, the installation of new systems could be carried out pending final settlement. However, the introduction was confined to installations and was not to involve training of employees. A comprehensive disputes procedure dealing with new technology implementation as well as normal disputes was also part of the agreement. Finally, the agreement provided that, where shift working was terminated at two weeks' notice, and where the employee had worked shifts for two years or more, they would be paid the shift rate for a period of four weeks from the date on which the notice of termination was given.

On 17 February 1987 the NGA submitted a claim for a revision to the national agreement involving a 10.5 per cent pay increase on all earnings, a fifth week's holiday, a 35 hour working week, premium payment of 150 per cent of normal rate of pay or average earnings for all annual and public holidays, a minimum of three months' notice before termination of shift working, overtime rates for rota day working of the first four hours at time and a half and thereafter at double time, abolition of late-night working in weekly newspaper offices, comprehensive paternity/maternity leave arrangements, and sick pay provisions. On 20 March the NS tabled what it described as its 'full and final' offer, which involved £5.14 a week new money, which was to count for the morning and evening news 'extra', overtime and shift premia. It offered one more day's annual holiday on condition that it be implemented locally at no additional cost. The NS also said any agreement must contain clauses about no automatic increases in any bonus/house earnings and the need for local discussions if adverse economic conditions led to serious difficulties about the agreement's implementation.

Following a meeting of branch secretaries and FOCs from regional and provincial newspaper firms, the NGA National Council 'reluctantly recommended' that its members accept the agreement, which they subsequently did in a ballot.

In February 1988 a claim for 10 per cent new money on all earnings from 24 April 1988 was made by the NGA to the NS. This would give a rise of £12.05 on the minimum grade rate. The eventual agreement provided for £5.14 new money on the minimum grade rate, taking it to £126.64, proportional increases in the morning and evening news 'extras', overtime and shift pay, and one additional day's holiday from 1 January 1989 to make a total of 5 weeks of annual holidays. Terms about work from unrecognised sources and cancer screening for women members were covered by an exchange of letters between the two sides.

The negotiations had been difficult and again the amount of new money obtained was less than from the BPIF.

In February 1989 the NGA, jointly with Sogat, presented a claim to the NS for £18 new money on the minimum grade rate payable from April 1989. Other items on the 'shopping list' were a 35 hour week, six weeks' holiday, 150 per cent of normal or average earnings for annual and public holidays, re-examination of differentials between weekly and daily hours, double time and a lieu day for Boxing Day working, payment of overtime undertaken without a specified finishing time, a sick pay scheme, maternity, paternity and bereavement leave and the provision of creche facilities. The negotiations were again very difficult. The main problems were the reluctance of the NS to consider a joint claim on union recognition and its insistance on an integrated press room clause, which would give the employers *carte blanche* to impose new working arrangements across the press and publishing rooms. The NS made an offer on pay which was considerably less than the rate of inflation, and rejected the NGA claim for a 35 hour week, six weeks' holiday, holiday pay at 150 per cent of normal pay, examination of the differentials between weekly and daily newspaper houses, double time and a lieu day for Boxing Day work and an extra hour's pay for overtime undertaken without a specified finishing time. The NS said that its aim was to pare back the national agreement to cover only 'core' employment terms, such as hours, holidays, minimum rates and disputes procedures. All other matters, it argued, should be settled at house level. A further sticking point was an NS proposal to remove union membership provisions from the agreement.

Eventually a deal was negotiated which the NGA advised its members to accept as 'undoubtedly the most that can be achieved by negotiation'. The final cash offer from the NS was £7.43 (5.9 per cent) on the minimum grade rate with a proportionate increase in other rates and extras. The NGA, however, managed to safeguard its position on training and retraining and resisted attempts by the employers to introduce a clause which would allow managements unilaterally to impose new working arrangements. The NS wanted to delete from the agreement the clauses on training and retraining craft workers. However, a compromise was reached on, instead, a new clause which meant that chapels and managements must mutually agree on retraining. On integrated press rooms the NS retreated from its *carte blanche* position and agreed that if flexible working was proposed it would be the subject of local negotiations. If there was a failure to agree, national officers were to be involved. The NGA claims for a 35 hour week, six weeks' holiday and holiday pay at 150 per cent of normal pay remained firmly rejected by the NS. The negotiations had tested whether the NGA should maintain a national agreement. Whilst what had been achieved might not have been ideal, the duty of the NGA to protect the interests of its weaker members meant that a national agreement should be maintained, as it was clearly the best method of doing this.

NOTES

1. The conciliation procedure had been amended after the 1956 dispute to provide for reference of national disputes ultimately to outside arbitration. During the 1959 dispute the union accused the employers of failing to observe the spirit of the JIC conciliation machinery in that they refused to negotiate with the unions and then sought to invoke the machinery. The unions saw the employers using the conciliation machinery as a substitute for, and not an adjunct, to negotiations.

2. The unions told the employers that the clause had previously proved of little assistance to Natsopa and was hardly likely to prove more so in the future. On the issue of the organisation of clerical workers, the unions were prepared to 'let sleeping dogs lie'.

3. During this time the JIC Apprenticeship Authority had continued to function. It met quarterly to consider reports from JIC district committees and to offer assistance or advice where necessary. It also played a prominent part in many spheres in connection with technical education and the welfare of apprentices.

4. Matters were made worse in that the TA had been involved in 1922 in a bitter dispute to prevent wage cuts. Musson records: 'TA members could not forget that while they had fought the printing trade unions' battle in 1922 the others had stood watching and that it was only after they had weakened the employers' forces that the London sections and the stereotypers were able to get more favourable terms . . .' See A.E. Musson, *The Typographical Association*, Oxford University Press, 1954, Ch. XVI, p. 402.

5. Under the 1919 agreement, TA branches were classified into six grades according to the size of the town, its importance as a printing centre, the industrial character of the neighbourhood and the local cost of living. There was a 15p differential between each grade. In 1942 the number of wage grades was reduced from six to four.

6. See J.E. Rawlins, 'A Review of the LSC–LMPA Dispute', *London Typographical Journal*, December 1950.

7. See *Report of a Court of Inquiry into the Causes and Circumstances of a Dispute between the London Master Printers' Association and the London Society of Compositors*, Cmnd 8074, HMSO, London, 1950.

8. ibid., p. 18, para. 64.

9. The pressure for one grade continued, however. The 1957 Delegate Meeting carried

a Warrington branch motion that when the 1951–5 agreement ended the Executive Council should be instructed to include in its manifesto the establishment of one minimum grade rate for TA members. This was included in the TA's 1955/6 wage demand.

10. See *Report of a Court ot Inquiry into the causes and circumstances of disputes between the London Master Printers' Association and the London Typographical Society and the Association of the Correctors of the Press*, Cmnd 9717, HMSO, London, 1956.

11. The employers described these demands as 'astonishing'.

12. At the same time as this dispute there were difficulties regarding the supply of ink to national newspapers. A breakdown in negotiations on wages and hours between Natsopa and the Society of Printing Ink Manufacturers led to a stoppage of ink supplies. To prevent the closure of national newspapers the unions agreed that the limited stocks be shared by the newspapers. Arrangements were subsequently made which enabled national newspapers to continue production though the number of pages were reduced. General print and provincial newspaper firms were exempted because they had accepted the unions' interim terms and were to notify their ink requirements to the P&KTF, which passed the information to Natsopa, which arranged for ink supplies.

13. See *Annual Report, 1959–1960*, Printing and Kindred Trades Federation, p. 34.

14. The collective movement of nine unions became ten on 22 June 1959 when Natsopa accepted an invitation from other unions to join them. From that date Natsopa took full part in negotiating the final settlement.

15. The settlement was rejected by the Society mainly because of a proposed clause for the introduction of auxiliary workers into the foundry. A satisfactory resolution to the difference was agreed on 7 December 1959.

16. At the same time, sixteen NUJ members also struck whilst four Slade members were sacked.

17. See *8th Annual Report, 1962*, London Typographical Society, para. 2, p. 4.

18. This would give the following new basic craft rates:

Date	London (£)	Grade 1 (£)	Grade 2 (£)
April 1965	15.15	14.47½	14.35
April 1966	15.80	15.35	15.22½
April 1967	16.65	16.22½	16.10

19. See *Prices and Incomes Policy*, Cmnd 2639, HMSO, London, 1965.

20. *Wages, Costs and Prices in the Printing Industry*, National Board for Prices and Incomes, Cmnd 2750, HMSO, London, August 1965.

21. Subsequently approaches were made to the Thomson Organisation and the British Printing Corporation. Both replied in September 1967 that they did not consider separate agreement with the unions feasible at this time and that it would be in the best interests of all that discussions resumed between the unions and the BFMP and the NS.

22. The NGA protested to the BFMP and the NS about their insistence that they would

pay the increases only on and from 5 August, although all the unions had notified them of the ballot results either by 1 August or almost immediately afterwards.

23. See *Print*, vol. 11, no. 1, January 1974, p. 1.

24. See *Print*, vol. 17, no. 2, February 1980, p. 3.

25. See *Print*, vol. 17, no. 5, May 1980, pp. 1 and 3.

25. See *Report of the Delegate Meeting, 1980*, National Graphical Association, p. 83.

CHAPTER 13

THE GENERAL PRINTING TRADE AND PROVINCIAL NEWSPAPER EMPLOYERS: (2) OTHER EMPLOYMENT CONDITIONS AND TRAINING

The wage basis agreement with BPIF and the NS provided for extras, for example the evening news and daily news 'extras' to the minimum grade rates. These agreements also incorporated payments under the machine classification agreements and the photocomposition agreements. The former provided a series of flat-rate machine extra payments, based on the type of machine being operated, and composition machine extras relating to extra skill and responsibility associated with linotype, intertype and monotype operations. The photocomposition agreements provided supplementary flat-rate payments to NGA members wholly engaged on photocomposition.

MACHINE CLASSIFICATION AGREEMENTS

The acceptance by the TA in the 1949 national agreement of the downgrading of all 'extras' led to demand for this to be reversed and that extras be paid on a percentage basis relative to the basic grade. The 1953 TA Delegate Meeting, for example, carried a St Albans branch motion:

That this conference regards the agreement reducing extras for

430

machine operators in both machine and composition departments as a betrayal of the interests of a section of our
membership. It calls upon the EC to reverse their present policy
and to pursue a policy designed to obtain extra renumeration for
extra responsibilities and skills in all TA departments on a
percentage basis equal to that operating in 1939.

In 1956 the TA secured a major revision of the machine classification
agreement, but did not achieve a percentage of the basic rate basis for
their payment. Although the membership continued to press for this,
the executive gave the highest priority on 'extras' to getting such
payments for the jobbing compositor. It considered this objective would
be adversely affected if the TA committed itself at the same time to
seek additional objectives on the 'extras' issues. The 1963 TA Delegate
Meeting nevertheless approved a motion from the Derby branch 'that
the Executive Council be requested to press for all machine extras to be
based upon a percentage of the agreement's basic rate'. At the time of
the formation of the NGA the payment of machine 'extras' on a
percentage basis and 'extras' for jobbing compositors had not been
achieved.

The TA's attempts to gain 'extras' for jobbing compositors went back
to at least 1956. The 1960 Delegate Meeting referred to the Executive
Council a Manchester branch motion 'that this conference views with
concern the "time lag" in reaching agreement with the BFMP and the
NS on the graded extras for jobbing compositors and instructs the
Executive Council to take the initiative in commencing the negotiations
at the earliest opportunity'. The claim for 'extras' for jobbing
compositors was based on three arguments. First, the whole trade
hinged on the jobbing compositor, who was the lowest paid of TA
members but whose pay could be increased if management paid merit
money. Second, TA members in the reading, lino and mono keyboard
departments received extra payment for their skill whilst machine
managers received 'extras' for their ability to operate and manage
different machines. Third, compositors doing specialised work, for
example colour or display setting, received only the same rate as
members engaged on envelope flaps or letter headings.

A major cause of the delay in raising jobbing compositor 'extras' with
the employers was that the TA could not agree what it would ask for. A
further problem was that 'extras' were easier to assess in the machine
room since there one could measure something, for example a

measurement of the machine to establish the sheet size that the press would take. In the composing room, however, there were no clear-cut measures. The problem was not a lack of skill on the part of the compositor, but the complexity of his work which made the 'extras' issue more difficult. By the time of the amalgamation with the LTS, the TA had concluded that the best approach to jobbing comps 'extras' would be to link this issue to introduction of new techniques, particularly film-setting.

By 1966 the NGA had accepted the need for a rationalisation of the machine classification agreement for London and the provinces. However, in the late 1960s the degree of manoeuvrability available to achieve these objectives was limited because of an incomes policy which required any changes to the agreement not to involve significant new money increases. The 1969 National Wage Basis Agreement, however, contained provisions for a review of machine classification. Although both sides wished the exercise carried out as expeditiously as possible, they recognised that any new formula should be soundly based and stand the test of time.

The 1969 agreement established a joint BFMP/NGA working party comprising of two representatives for each organisation together with an independent person on each side trained in job evaluation and work study. The working party undertook individual studies to determine the degree of extra skill and responsibility required to be exercised by NGA members normally engaged on each machine relative to the skill and responsibility normally exercised by a craftsman in charge of machines classified at the minimum rate, and recommended the extra money, if any, appropriate for such extra skill and responsibility. The working party, which began its work in 1970, soon realised that to cover the range of studies involved adequately, including as it did letterpress, aniline, photogravure and litho, the members of the joint panel must be knowledgable about these techniques.

Slow, but positive, progress was made and the long drawn out negotiations resulted in an agreement being made with BPIF to operate from 31 March 1975. A great deal of pressure had been exerted on the BPIF to put money values on the machine 'bands' that had resulted from the intensive work undertaken since 1970 by the joint working party. These machine 'bands' had been devised from a formula which took account of three elements in the machine managers' normal duties, namely preparation, responsibility and production speed. The employers were reluctant to commit themselves to money values for this banding and the NGA concluded that it was the employers' intention to delay any final settlement until the next wage negotiations took place. To bring matters to a head the NGA gave notice to the BPIF that after 3 February 1975 the machine classification provisions that had operated since 1956 would no longer be recognised as being either applicable or relevant. At the same time, machine chapels were advised to take steps to secure the necessary redress in machine rates within their own establishments. The NGA recognised that gaining upward adjustments in the machine rate by this method would not achieve the original objectives of the machine review exercise, namely rationalisation of machine rates in BPIF agreements, the removal of anomalies arising from the 1956 revision, and the establishment of a recognisable relationship between machine 'extras' applicable to all the printing techniques covered by the NGA.

The chapel instructions were withdrawn when the BPIF signified its willingness to continue negotiations, and the final settlement on a new machine classification was reached on 4 February 1975. Two sectors involved in the machine classification, however, were dealt with after the main settlement had been reached. In the case of counter check book, continuous stationery and reel-fed platen machines, the terms of settlement that were ultimately agreed became effective from 31 March 1975. The discussion regarding litho plate-making machines and other litho craft operations took longer to bring to finality but were finally implemented as from 13 August 1975. The 1975 machine classification agreement covered all machines with points value of up to 39.999, leaving those above this capacity outside the terms of the agreement. The agreement was to be reviewed in June 1978.

The revision of the 1975 agreement was delayed first by pay policy and second by the need to revise the absorption clause. The BPIF argued that, having raised the current rates by 10 per cent (66p per band) in the 1978 wage basis agreement, no further improvement was possible given the government's pay policy. For the NGA this was a less than realistic response to its claim for £1.20 increase (2.2 per cent) per band. From 1 June 1975 the NGA adopted the policy that any new machines installed after 1 August 1978 should be paid in accordance to its claim and local agreements should be made to this effect. On the absorption issue the NGA's position was that increases in rates should only be absorbed from the individual's merit payment provided the new total wage did not fall below the basic craft rate or departmental or house rate plus the extra specified.

However, this deadlock was subsequently broken and, following fresh negotiations, agreement was reached. This up-dated those 'extras' first established in 1975, including the restoration of their 'real' purchashing power. The NGA was disappointed that it had not been able to extend the 39.999 points so as to embrace the larger presses, particularly those in the periodical photogravure houses. The agreement allowed absorption of increased extras only from payments specifically made for the operation of particular machines or attachments. Any disagreements over absorptions were to be referred to the disputes procedure.

Between 1980 and 1982 the economic difficulties within the industry made it impossible to up-date the machine classification agreement. The NGA, however, made every effort to have payments index-linked to the basic rate and such a linkage formula was achieved in the 1983 BPIF wages basis agreement when it was agreed that in future machine 'extras' should be increased by the same percentage increase as given to the national agreed craft/class 1 wage rate.

The formula devised between 1970 and 1974 for calculating the value of the press has stood the test of time and remains of considerable value to the industry. The NGA continues to send delegations to view installations whenever difficulties are experienced, though issues of this kind normally centre around manning and the payment for attachments not covered by the agreements rather than the rating of the machine. New developments are carefully monitored by the National Council. Nevertheless, the 1988 Delegate Meeting rejected a Sheffield branch motion that the machine classification agreement should be renegotiated in order to establish a banding structure which recognised the changes that technological developments had brought to the machine room.

In the light of the 1975 machine classification agreement, the NGA sought some improvement to the machine 'extras' contained in the NS agreement. A decision not to proceed was reached on the grounds that it would be a difficult task given the accepted relativity of 'extras' in provincial news between machine, composing (including readers), stereotypers and telecommunications and electronics. The NGA accepted that in the NS field there was a wage structure which could be decimated if repercussive claims arose from one 'extra' being increased.

In 1976 the NGA examined ways of establishing 'extras' for jobbing compositors based upon the 1975 machine classification agreement. However, again the association could not devise practical proposals because in concluding the revised machine classification agreement it implicitly agreed that there would be no consequential claims from other NGA departments. Equally compelling reasons were that not all offices had machine rooms, while others were equipped with only small machines that would not produce the desired improvement in compositors' pay. The NGA saw that the logical way to enhance the position of compositors was via improvements to the BPIF/NGA photocomposition agreement when it was reviewed in July 1978.

THE PHOTOCOMPOSITION AGREEMENTS

The Newspaper Society

Protracted negotiations took place with the NS for a national agreement on photocomposition. The negotiations eventually resulted in 1971 in supplementary payments being made to NGA members wholly engaged on photocomposition. These payments were: to perforator keyboard operators – £1.25 in addition to the TTS operator rate; to photocomposing unit operators – £1.25 in addition to the compositors' rate; to qualified keyboard-operated headline machine operators – £1.25 in addition to the compositors' rate; to operators of other headline machines – 88p in addition to the compositors' rate. The agreement became operative on 29 August 1971.

The 1974 Delegate Meeting gave instructions that approaches should be made to the NS to bring photocomposing payments into line with those in the BPIF photocomposition agreement. In 1976 the NS rejected NGA claims in this regard, arguing that, whereas in the BPIF areas payments were restricted to the equipment, in the news field they were made over a wider area. However, it offered to increase the keyboard rate to £3 above the basic rate in the national agreement and to include readers in the agreement for the first time, who would receive an extra of £1.75 when they were reading from computer printouts, but £2.12 above the normal reading 'extra' when using a keyboard associated with a VDU. The rate offered for computer operatives was £1.75 (an increase of 50p), but a sticking point was payments to be made to NGA members engaged on paste-up. The NS refused to increase the 88p at present being paid. Although the NGA initially rejected the offer, the eventual agreement brought the NS photocomposition agreement very much into line with that of the BPIF. The implementation of the agreement was vetoed by the Department of

Employment as incompatible with income restraint policy grounds. Given this and further developments in technology, the NGA decided to renegotiate the agreement, taking into account present-day values, responsibilities and the productive capacity of the equipment. In the meantime, branches were advised that, if agreements could be reached with individual companies on the basis of the terms held up by the Department of Employment, they should operate on an interim basis until a new agreement was finalised. Several such agreements were approved by the National Council.

The NS refused to renegotiate a new agreement. Although several meetings took place in 1978 these did not result in any agreement that was acceptable to NGA news members. In January 1979 the NGA instructed all branches that £11 should be paid across the board by all companies installing new, additional or replacement photocomposing equipment and that the payment should be calculable for shift and overtime premia. This local campaign led to further NGA/NS talks, which resulted in a national photocomposition agreement under which an across-the-board payment of £11 was made for the use of equipment up to, but not including, full-page screen make-up. Certain weekly news offices using limited equipment were to receive an £8 photocomposition payment.

The 1984 wage basis agreement provided that discussions should take place over the photocomposition and web-offset 'extras' and whether they should be absorbed into the basic rate or continue as 'extras'. Many NGA members felt that since the rate had been set out many years before it must be part of the basic rate. However, no discussions in relation to the photocomposition and web-offset 'extras' took place during the life of the agreement. The NGA was not prepared to conclude a national agreement with the Newspaper Society for 1985/6 because of the society's inability or unwillingness to put pressure on the *Wolverhampton Express and Star* management to end their attempts to introduce direct entry technology without an agreement with the NGA. Instead, a non-negotiable claim was lodged by chapels at local level with their own individual employers, which included a demand for a 6.6 per cent increase in 'extras'. The agreements that were secured provided, *inter alia*, for increases to photocomposition, web-offset and plate-making 'extras'.

In 1986 the NGA again entered into a national agreement with the NS, but the price was agreeing that there would be no automatic increase in any bonus/house earnings, however based and calculated, unless local arrangements at chapel/branch level were made. The NGA accepted this as it saw that the key challenge in the 1990s in provincial newspapers was the implementation of new technology and whether the union could maintain a presence in the industry, rather than retention of bonus schemes and knock-ons. The photocomposition 'extra' was frozen at £11 and remains at that level today.

The General Printing Trade

The 1969 wage claim to the BFMP included supplementary payments based on three categories of equipment for NGA members engaged on film-setting. It was agreed that film-setting should be dealt with outside any national pay agreement. Early in 1970 negotiations for a film-setting agreement began. In October 1970, after long and hard negotiations, the BFMP and the NS offered 87½p 'extra' to employees described as 'all rounders'. The NGA rejected this as being derisory. The NGA's argument for a supplementary rate for film-setting was not only based on increased skill and responsibility but also that the new technique represented an insurance for the future and therefore the employers should expect to pay higher premiums. However, little further progress was possible and the employers were told that the NGA now intended to approach the matter on a house-by-house basis. This was a tremendous task but a pattern slowly began to emerge based on the conditons in each individual office with respect to the equipment installed, the use made of it and payments already made in respect of film-setting. The vexed question of merit money was also involved and in some instances chapels agreed to a measure of absorption in order to establish the supplementary payments included in the 1969 wage claim. In November 1970 chapels were further instructed that new equipment should not be operated until a rate had been agreed.

These local negotiations proved fruitful. By June 1972 film-setting agreements existed with over 101 establishments, with a further twenty-two in the pipeline. The guidelines laid down by the 1969 Delegate Meeting placed machines into three main categories of supplementary payment – £5, £3 and £1.50. In the cases of the last two categories, the average level of payment received in these house deals exceeded those figures. With the highest category, the average level of settlement was only marginally below the £5 figure. In 1972 the BFMP approached the NGA again with the aim of negotiating a film-setting agreement. Armed with the 'case law' of the house agreements, the NGA stressed that it was not seeking an 'extra' but a film-setting rate which should be expressed as a percentage of the basic rate – 20 per cent in the case of the £5 category, 12 per cent in the case of the £3 category and 8 per cent in the case of the £1.50 category. The NGA realised that the introduction of film-setting techniques offered a chance of advancing the position of the compositors by linking improvements in the conditions of compositors to the introduction of new equipment.

The negotiations opened in 1969 and reached fruition on 2 July 1973 when the long-awaited new national photocomposing agreement became operative. Under the agreement, photocomposing equipment was divided into three categories for which rates of £5, £3 and £1.50 per week were to be paid. In return, there was to be flexibility of labour within the photocomposing department and the agreement was to be reviewed in July 1978. The negotiations had been difficult and protracted but the NGA had been assisted by the case law it had established in house agreements in over 100 companies. The photocomposition agreement was sufficiently simple to have general application and represented a fair reflection of the NGA house-to-house endeavours.

The agreement broke new ground and the NGA'S objective was to extend the agreement as new equipment came into the industry. The NGA had found it necessary to depart from tradition and the agreement facilitated flexibility of working which required a common rate. In the agreement, therefore, whilst the operator and the reader had had their traditional 88p extra built into the photocomposition rate, the compositor now moved alongside them at the same rate. The photocomposition agreement provided an opportunity for jobbing compositors to elevate themselves from the relatively lowly paid position they had occupied for so long. The NGA intended to build upon this to gain due recognition for the compositors' skills.

When the BPIF/NGA photocomposition agreement ended on 2 July 1978, the NGA had been unable to secure any improvements on its terms, other than 10 per cent extra as part of the 1978 National Wage Basis Agreement. This had raised the three rates to £5.50, £3.30 and £1.65, but they were a long way below the NGA's claim for new rates of £5.37 (10 per cent), £13.43 (25 per cent) and £17.89 (33.5 per cent) plus a reduction in the working week to 35 hours. The NGA announced that all new installations would now be the subject of local agreement between branch, chapel and management, and these would provide a rate of £10 per week for the operation of headliner equipment, make-up of photocomposed matter, the operation of photocomposing keyboards and reading, together with £14 per week for operating visual display units, terminals and film-setters. It was recognised that it would be difficult to achieve the 35 hour week other than within the context of a major photocomposition installation. The BPIF argued that due to pay policy there was no point in opening negotiations since nothing further could be done above the 10 per cent improvement to the rate in the 1978 wage agreement.

It was not until the NGA undertook industrial action that the BPIF agreed in early 1979 to meet with it and a new agreement was reached. The agreement, which was backdated to 25 June 1979, provided for new supplementary payments of £7 for keyboards, £10 for keyboards capable of editing previously prepared material, £14 for using general-purpose computer programmes for composition, £7 for mechanical phototypesetters, £10 for electronic phototypesetters and £14 for high-speed electronic ones. There was £7 for photocomp make-up, £10 for compositors operating more specialised systems and £7 for readers. This new agreement expanded the number of rates from two to three, whilst still maintaining the separate rate for the simplified headliner machine. As with any complex and technical agreement, a number of criticisms were levelled against the manner in which rates of payments were distributed.

The early 1980s saw a steady growth in the number of photocomposition installations and witnessed the introduction of second- and third-generation equipment with a greater degree of sophistication and potential. However, in the early 1980s, faced with economic recession and the implementation of new technology, the NGA considered it inappropriate to re-open negotiations on the photocomposition agreement. The mid-1980s saw the installation of third- and fourth-generation phototypesetters, which created anomalies within the photocomposition agreement. To alleviate potential problems the 1982 BPIF National Wage Basis Agreement established a working party to make recommendations by 31 December 1982, to consider a relationship between nationally agreed basic wage increases and photocomposition payments, and to examine the anomalies within the photocomposition agreement as a result of technological developments since the 1979 review of the agreement. A formula was agreed with the BPIF in the early part of 1983 which established a percentage linkage formula based on a calculator rate of £88.75. The calculator rate was to be increased by the craft rate increases during the period 24 April 1983 to 23 April

1986, and photocomposition payments were to be increased by the same percentage that the calculator rate increased as a result of the national settlement each year.

Despite detailed and lengthy discussions, agreement could not be reached on changes which the NGA felt were necessary to encompass technological change and to alleviate current and future anomalies. The NGA thereafter adopted a policy that anomalies relating to payment for photocomposition equipment should be settled at local level. Where companies introduced more sophisticated phototypesetting systems the NGA was able in some instances to establish improvements in terms and conditions over and above those in the BPIF/NGA photocomposition agreements. Such arrangements were generally concluded after substantiating that the installation of the new equipment would secure improvements in productivity for the company.

HOLIDAYS

The 1980 Delegate Meeting accepted a Liverpool branch motion calling for a fifth week's holiday to enable members to gain maximum benefits from new technology. The 1982 Delegate Meeting backed a Stockport motion, which was amended by Manchester, proposing that the entitlement of a minimum of five weeks' holidays for all members should be 'the major priority' in negotiations with the employers. This call was justified on the grounds that it would help create employment in the face of technological change. The 1984 Delegate Meeting also discussed extra holidays in terms of tackling unemployment. A London motion, amended by South and West Wales, calling for the progressive negotiation of an extra day's holiday each year until an extra week had been achieved was carried. A Liverpool motion instructing the NGA to make a fifth week's annual holiday a priority in the 1985 wage negotiations was also approved. The 1986 Delegate Meeting approved a Stockport motion calling for a 35 hour week and five weeks' holiday, which argued that, in the past, hours and holiday claims had taken second place to demands for more money and 'extras' but priority should now be given to reductions in hours and longer holidays, as advances in these areas would create more jobs, were inflation proof and once agreed were difficult to take away.

In addition to the length of annual holidays, NGA members were concerned as to when these holidays could be taken and what would be the basis of calculation of holiday pay. The 1980 Delegate Meeting overwhelmingly carried a Manchester motion calling for the discretion of employers to have the final say on when employees could take their holidays to be removed from the hours and holidays agreement; whilst four years later the Delegate Meeting decided, on the basis of a Mid Anglia motion, to resist demands by the BPIF or any other employers' organisations to amend hours and holiday agreements to prevent members from obtaining the full benefit from their holidays. This decision did not relate to the winter and summer holiday periods, both of which were well known, but to the remaining holiday entitlement. The NGA members were seeking through the motion to ensure that these holidays were taken by mutual consent. Although for some time the NGA's objective had been to achieve holiday pay at time and a half, it was not until the 1988 Delegate Meeting that a Stockport motion formally committed the NGA to this policy.

In the 1980s the NGA sought to keep its lead amongst trade unions in enhancing the working life of its members by securing five weeks' holidays, an entitlement to take holidays outside the main winter and summer periods by mutual agreement with the employer, and holiday pay at the rate of time and a half. In the 1983 wage negotiations with both the BPIF and the NS the NGA claimed five weeks' holiday entitlement per annum and holiday pay based upon time and a half of members' weekly rate. These claims were resisted and, although the NGA eventually forced the BPIF to concede an extra one day's holiday, it found itself having to withdraw the annual holiday claim in order to secure an agreement with the NS. The NGA 1984 annual wage claim to the BPIF and the NS also sought the establishment of five weeks holiday. However, to secure a wage agreement with the BPIF the NGA withdrew the five weeks' holiday claim. In doing so the BPIF was told it would be presented again in future negotiations. By 1984 the holiday entitlement for NGA members in both the BPIF and the NS areas has become four weeks and one day.

The NGA did not make a national claim to the NS in 1985. It did so to the BPIF and the claim included a demand for five weeks' paid holiday. In the negotiations it was only able to extract one further day's holiday. The 1986 negotiations with the BPIF and the NS again saw the NGA's shopping list include a demand for five weeks' paid holiday. The eventual settlement with the NS included an increase in the annual holiday entitlement to 4 weeks and 3 days from 1 October 1986. The most significant advance in the agreement with the BPIF was the establishment of five weeks' annual holiday for NGA members.

Although this was not to be implemented until 1 January 1989, it maintained the position of NGA members towards the top of the league table for industry-wide holiday entitlement. The 1987 wage claim to the NS included a demand for a fifth week's holiday and payment at time and a half or average earnings – whichever was the greater – for all annual and public holidays. The claim to the BPIF in that year included only this latter claim. Both the NS and the BPIF rejected the 150 per cent holiday pay claim but the NS offered one more day's annual holiday on condition that it be implemented locally at no additional cost. In 1988 the NS offered one day's extra holiday from 1 January 1989 to make the minimum annual holiday entitlement in the provincial newspaper industry five weeks. In the same year, however, the BPIF again refused to concede time and a half for all holidays, as did the NS in the following year.

INDUSTRY-WIDE SICK PAY SCHEME

The 1980s also saw revived interest amongst NGA members in the establishment of an industry-wide sick pay scheme. The 1980 Delegate Meeting unanimously backed a Stockport branch motion proposing the establishment of a sick pay scheme with the BPIF and the NS. The NGA leadership asked delegates to remit the motion but they refused and instructed the national council to secure an industry-wide sick pay scheme as soon as possible, taking any steps it thought necessary to do so. The 1982 Delegate Meeting also unanimously backed a Stockport branch motion to make a national sick pay scheme a priority for negotiation.

However, it was not until 1987 that the establishment of an industry-wide sick pay scheme was included in the annual wage claims to the BPIF and the NS. The latter body rejected the claim outright and at the close of this history an industry-wide sick pay scheme for the provincial newspaper industry does not exist. The majority of NS members offer their own sick pay schemes. The BPIF, however, agreed as part of the 1987 revision of the wage basis agreement to consult with its members to obtain up-to-date information on the extent and coverage of sick pay schemes throughout the general printing trade. Following the completion of this, the BPIF said it would discuss the results of the survey with the NGA as well as the possibility of an industry-wide fallback sick pay scheme. The BPIF survey showed that 85 per cent of its members provided locally based sick pay schemes. The NGA, in its 1988 annual negotiations with the BPIF, was unable to persuade the employers to force the remaining 15 per cent of its members to introduce a sick pay scheme. The NGA achieved a clause in the 1988 revision of the wage basis agreement to the effect that 'both parties will encourage the introduction of sick pay schemes'. This remains the situation in BPIF areas at the close of this history.

PENSIONS

Following the 1980 Delegate Meeting, an ad hoc committee was established to examine relevant matters affecting the retirement of NGA members. A policy document on this issue was approved by the 1982 Delegate Meeting. Included in the document was the possibility of an industry-wide pension scheme, but the general view was that in the economic conditions of the early 1980s it was unlikely the NGA would convince employers of the need for it. The policy statement committed the NGA to consider an industry-wide pension scheme jointly managed by the unions and employers and funded by an insurance company. It also argued in favour of shop floor representation on management, advisory, investment or trustee boards of pension funds. The NGA sought the establishment of an industry-wide transferable pension scheme with the direct involvement of the employers' organisations, initially in an arrangement managed and administered by an insurance company.

The 1983 wages claim to the BPIF and the NS sought the establishment of joint working parties to consider all aspects of pensions. The NS refused to negotiate on the subject, claiming that the provincial newspaper industry was suffering from poor economic circumstances and could not afford any additional cost increases. The BPIF, on the other hand, agreed to examine the introduction of a pension scheme to which companies and employees would subscribe on a voluntary basis. Discussions were also held with the administrators of the Newspaper and Printing Industries Pension Fund, a voluntary arrangement that had existed for many years in the provincial newspaper industry and which had an element of transferability. However, these were not pursued on grounds that the NPIPF would not give full joint control.

In November 1984 the Sogat/NGA/BPIF working party on pensions reached agreement on the basis of an industry-wide pension scheme. This was to be a money purchase pension scheme and would be an addition to the state pension scheme. It was to provide a pension of 20 per cent of salary after a term of forty years and for a death-in-service benefit of twice annual salary together with a spouse's pension of about one-third of annual salary. The cost of the scheme would be 7 per cent of the payroll and the employers accepted the Sogat and NGA position that these costs be shared on a 2 to 1 ratio. The scheme was to be initially managed by an insurance company but under the control of a Sogat/NGA/BPIF board of trustees.

Towards the end of 1985 a number of companies expressed an interest in managing the scheme on behalf of the working group. Of these the Prudential Assurance Company was appointed to run the scheme under the direction of the trustees, of which the BPIF would appoint four and the NGA and Sogat two each. The chairmanship would rotate between the parties. The Printing Industry Pension Scheme (PIPS) was established in June 1986. The scheme is a voluntary, industry-wide, transferable, money purchase scheme with attractive benefits but administration and death costs kept to a minimum. It does not replace or affect existing pension arrangements in the industry but gives additional benefits on top of state basic pension and earnings-related payments. Benefits are determined in direct relationship to the combined employer/employee contributions made on behalf of each individual member and are dependent upon when the contributions were paid and the age at which the pension starts. Normal retirement age in the scheme is 65 for men and 60 for women. Good protection is provided for scheme members who die while in service or who have to retire early because of incapacity. The scheme is controlled by the industry, with the day-to-day running being taken by the Prudential Assurance Company.

The establishment of PIPS is something of which the NGA and the industry are proud and which will stand the membership in good stead for the future. Of its kind, it is a first-class, efficient and effective scheme which represents good value for money. By mid-1988 the scheme covered 683 lives, with forty-one deferred members and thirteen members covered for life assurance only. An indication of the scheme's potential can be seen in that from such a number of lives the annual premium income is £480,000. However, the launch of PIPS was adversely affected by two factors. The first was the agreed procedure of working through the BPIF regions to obtain members, using only a small specialist pension consultant sales force. The second, but more important, was the Social Security Act (1986). PIPS is a scheme whose benefits are paid in addition to both the state basic pension (SERPS) and the 1986 Act's reduction of the future value of SERPS reduced the attraction of PIPS. A further influence was the government's statement that money purchase schemes would, in future, be allowed to contract out of the state scheme, coupled with their intention to encourage individuals to set up their own personal pension scheme. This new legislation gave uncertainty to employers in casting proposals, and many who were interested in PIPS decided to delay decisions until 1988 when the legislative fog had cleared.

The 1986 Social Security Act led to changes in PIPS. The trustees decided that the scheme should offer employers and members three choices: first, the existing contracted-in scheme; second, a contracted-out scheme which can take advantage of the government inducements for such schemes; and, third, a minimal pension scheme similar to personal pension arrangements being offered by other pension providers. The changes were intended to enable PIPS to compete in terms of costs and value for money with other pension schemes being offered to employers and workpeople in the industry whilst retaining the advantage of direct control by organisations representing those working in the industry.

WOMEN AND EQUALITY

Participation in NGA Decision-Making Bodies

The forum for the representation of women's interests within the NGA's decision-making structure has been described in Chapter 7. In 1980 the NGA for the first time sent a delegation to the TUC's Women's Conference, and the 1980 Delegate Meeting agreed to send a delegation to the TUC's Women's Conference on a regular basis.

The Women's Committee initially examined the TUC Charter 'Equality for Women within Trade Unions', which was concerned that there should be no obstacles to women attaining positions at all levels within the trade union movement. In 1982 the recommendations of the Charter were adopted by the NGA and the terms of reference of its Women's Committee were extended to monitor continuously the progress of women's participation in the union. The NGA continues to publicise its desire to increase female participation in its activities at all levels, as it believes that it can only be an effective and democratic union if all members actively participate in its affairs and activities. The union is constantly taking active steps to increase the awareness of its male members of the different industrial problems facing their female colleagues.

An examination undertaken in 1982 of the NGA's decision-making structure revealed no formal barriers to women reaching decision-making bodies, but attitudes could be improved by stimulating discussion at chapel and branch meetings on the subject. Advice on time off for meetings and childcare facilities were suggested to encourage wider female participation in the union. To this end, recommendations, including holding meetings in working hours if possible, and negotiating time off without loss of pay where possible, were circulated to branches in 1983. Greater participation by women at the biennial delegate meeting was to be encouraged by the provision of nursery facilities. These were first provided at the 1984 Delegate Meeting and then at every subsequent delegate meeting. Women member participation has also been encouraged by positive discrimination in favour of women on the NGA chapel official training courses. In the light of the detailed 1982 examination of its structure, the NGA rejected the creation of women-only seats on its decision-making bodies. Reserved seats for women on the National Council was rejected by the 1988 Delegate Meeting.

The policy of the NGA is, and remains, to encourage participation of women on an integrated basis at all levels, thereby ensuring that the problems of NGA members, be they female or male, are problems of common concern which can be eliminated by united effort. In 1982 the NGA also neutralised the workings of its rulebook and other publications, including the monthly journal *Print*.

Equal Pay

On the question of equal pay the NGA policy has always been that there is a 'rate for the job' and that members doing that job, regardless of sex, should get that rate. It has consistently taken the view that, should 'equal pay' problems arise, normal negotiating machinery should be fully utilised and only where this fails should consideration be given to using the Equal Pay Act (1979). One result of these policies is that equal pay is not a problem for the NGA as it is for some other trade unions. In the traditional area of NGA organisation, in the few cases where pay discrimination against women has been discovered, the

NGA, through negotiations and not the law, has successfully resolved the issue. Despite the NGA's success in achieving equal pay through industrial representation, the Women's Committee did make representation, through the NGA's sponsored MPs, over the 1984 changes to the Equal Pay Act (1970). These changes gave individuals the right to claim equal treatment in pay and other contractual matters with employees of the opposite sex if they considered their work to be of equal value. The Women's Committee felt that the government had made the absolute minimum of changes to comply with the EEC Directive to provide for the concept of equal pay for work of equal value and that the government should have used the opportunity to eliminate weaknesses in the 1970 Act.

Equal Opportunities

In the early 1980s the NGA issued a model equal opportunities clause, which was to be included in all agreements made with employees. The clause committed the parties to an agreement to develop positive policies to promote equal opportunity in employment regardless of workers' sex, marital status, creed, colour, race or ethnic origins. This principle applies to all conditions of work, and management draws opportunities for training and promotion to the attention of eligible employees. The 1983 wage basis agreements with the BPIF and the NS provided for the establishment of a working party to examine equal opportunities in the printing industry. Today this model equal opportunities clause is to be found in almost all the major collective agreements to which the NGA is a party.

November 1988 saw, following on an initiative by the Joint Training Council, the launch of a statement entitled *Achieving a Balance* to provide equal opportunities in the printing industry. It was a statement by the BPIF, the NGA and Sogat that it was 'morally wrong' to exclude women and ethnic minorities by concentrating on recruiting white men. The statement reaffirmed the equal opportunities clause in the National Wage Basis Agreement, but in addition committed the three parties to actively promote equal opportunities for all applicants and employees in the industry irrespective of race, religion or gender. Managements and chapels were urged to promote and encourage applications from all groups, but in particular women and ethnic minorities, to provide equal opportunities to all applicants for jobs in recognised skilled occupations in the industry. *Achieving a Balance* was also a response to the expected

447

decline in the number of school leavers in the mid-1990s. The NGA considered that the printing industry had either to broaden the area from which it recruited, as recognised by the statement, or to accept that work would be lost to European competition, particularly after the introduction of the Single European Market in 1992. It was yet another example of how the NGA and the BPIF were working together for the good of the industry by attempting to prevent potential labour supply problems from adversely affecting the industry.

The document was also further recognition by the NGA of the increasing importance of its growing female membership. By the beginning of 1989 the NGA's female membership represented some 7 per cent of its total working membership. The demographic and structural changes expected to take place in the industry in the 1900s meant that the upward trend would inevitably continue. A major breakthrough had been made in 1983 when the NGA and the BPIF signed the recruitment, training and retraining agreement, which based training on acquiring and updating skills when they were needed, not on time serving. The NGA had hoped that the agreement would be of particular value to women in that it should assist the problem of maternity leave since women could be retrained when they returned to work, thus avoiding companies losing talented employees.

With respect too entry into the industry, the Women's Committee recommended that there should be balanced entrance into the industry of male and female school leavers. If this is to be achieved, the NGA will have to influence not only its own members but also employers, employers' organisations and the career information provided in schools. Surveys by the Women's Committee show that there are not as many girls applying for apprenticeships and traineeships as boys. However, in adopting a policy of balanced entrance to the industry, the Women's Committee recognised that it was no good women believing that they could solely take up the better-paid jobs in attractive environments.

Maternity/Paternity Leave

In May 1983 the NGA adopted a compassionate leave policy which included provisions for maternity and paternity leave and was to be adopted in collective agreements. On paternity leave, the policy called for two weeks' paid leave to be available to male employees at the time of confinement of their partners. The main features of the maternity policy are that the qualifying period for maternity leave should be six months, that members with twelve months' service or more should be paid eighteen weeks' maternity leave with the right to return to their job within a period of up to fifty-two weeks, that the calculation of a week's pay should be the contractual earnings plus any unconsolidated payments normally made, that service should be calculated to include employment at all workplaces within a company or its subsidiaries where such employment is continuous, and that maternity leave should be available to adoptive parents. The policy also proposed that, where reasonably practicable, a woman who had previously notified her employer that she did not intend to return to work but whose circumstances changed should be able to return (for example where a woman miscarried or her baby was stillborn), that all employees should have the right to return to their previous job under previous conditions of service, that in the event of the previous job disappearing due to redundancy or reorganisation, suitable alternative employment with no less favourable terms and conditions should be provided, and that employees should not remain on duties which are laborious and/or a danger to the foetus. In addition, it is NGA policy that that legal right to fully paid time off for antenatal care should be included in agreements and that such agreements should also contain fully paid leave for postnatal care for women who return to work earlier than the agreed maximum leave period.

The 1983 wage demands to the BPIF and the NS included a claim that a working party be established to examine all facets of parental responsibility. Both employers' organisations agreed to this request. The NGA's 1986 claim to the BPIF for a revision of the wage basis agreement included a claim for comprehensive paternity leave arrangements, as did its 1987 claim to the NS. Little advance was made in the 1986 negotiations, but in the 1987 annual wage negotiations with the BPIF it was agreed that a set of 'guidelines' would be issued to BPIF members covering paternity/maternity leave, bereavement arrangements and women's health issues. The 1988 wage agreement saw the BPIF granting up to three days' bereavement leave on the death of parents, spouse, legal guardians or children. No progress has been made with the NS, with which not even a 'set of guidelines' has been agreed. This NGA policy on maternity has been incorporated into many house agreements, particularly in repro houses. In addition, there are some agreements in other areas of NGA operation covering some, if not all, elements of the NGA's maternity/paternity policy.

Restricted Hours of Work

For many years there had been restrictions on the hours of work that could be worked by women and young persons. In 1986, instead of tightening these laws, the government amended the 1975 Sex Discrimination Act to relax these restrictions so that women could now work evenings, Saturday afternoons and Sundays. The TUC opposed this legislation, and the general thrust of its policy is to prevent women, who are already carrying heavy domestic, as well as work, responsibilities, from being pressurised into working longer hours and nights. The NGA generally supported the TUC policy on hours of work but considered that where an employer sought to change NGA members' (whether male or female) hours of work it would defend existing conditions. However, if a member wished to consider a change in hours then the NGA policy was that the member should consider a number of factors in addition to normal premium payments, such as the availability of transport to and from work, flexible working arrangements for those with heavy domestic responsibilities and the threat of attacks and physical violence against women travelling out of normal working hours. In response to the government's proposed changes to the Sex Discrimination Act (1975), the NGA's 1986 annual wage claim to the BPIF included an understanding that no change in the existing working hours of women and young NGA members would take place without reference to the NGA nationally.

Sexual Harassment

It was only in the 1980s that the NGA gave serious consideration to the issue of sexual harassment and formulated a policy, which utilised existing grievance machinery to resolve such difficulties whilst recognising that it can be a delicate and sensitive problem. The NGA believes that the resolution of alleged sexual harassment via use of existing grievance procedures encourages members suffering from harassment to use their union to help them articulate the problem with some confidence. The NGA's approach to sexual harassment involves chapel officers suggesting to victims of harassment that they note details of any subsequent occurrences and that officers should establish whether the same offender has subjected other members of the chapel or employees in the workplace to harassment.

There are two other important aspects to the NGA policy on this issue. One is that the member should make clear to the offender that the behaviour is unwelcome and unwanted. The other is that the member alleging sexual harassment can bring along a friend employed at the firm in addition to the representatives permissible under the normal grievance machinery.

Health Issues

Women's health also received increasing attention within the NGA in the 1980s. Particular concern centred on women working on VDUs, and in 1987 the NGA issued a comprehensive set of guidelines to help chapel officials monitor the introduction and operation of such equipment. The union is concerned that its women members have time off with pay for cervical smears and screening for breast cancer, with employers publicising the arrangements and encouraging their women employees to attend the clinics. In May 1983 the NGA adopted these aspirations, along with an additional one of its women members having the right every three years to be screened during working hours.

A major breakthrough on women's health issues was achieved in 1988 when the BPIF agreed to provide paid time off for women to attend cervical and breast cancer screening on site or at an appropriate clinic. Similar arrangements also exist outside the BPIF areas in house agreements. However, welcome though agreements are, the NGA's view is that they are not in themselves enough. The important thing is that female members take advantage of the cervical and breast cancer screening facilities because, in the overwhelming majority of cases, these conditions are curable if treated early enough.

The NGA's interest in women's issues stems from its increasing female membership. By 1988 the union had 8,700 women members, of whom 5,000 were in origination areas, 1,000 in clerical and administrative positions and 1,000 in the machine area, divided between the general printing industry and provincial newspapers. The increasing number of women members reflected the increasing number of women entering the industry and working in industries in direct competition with the traditional printing industry and in which the NGA needed a foothold if it was to have some control and influence in a new and emerging industry. These developments stemmed from the implementation of new technology in the traditional printing industry, which affected not only the production process but also the employment structure as more jobs were created in areas where females were the majority of employees. Art studios and advertising agencies, both of which employed significant numbers of women, became an industrial threat to the NGA, thus making organisation in these areas essential if the NGA was to gain some control in this competitive area.

Another factor making the recruitment of women necessary to the NGA if it is to maintain industrial influence is the demographic trends of the 1990s. By 1995 the majority of employees will be women. If the NGA is to be attractive to these employees it will have to not only concentrate on the protection and advancement of wages and conditions but show that it is aware of, and capable of delivering on, industrial problems affecting particularly women, for example childcare facilities.

A further factor in the NGA's development of its policies towards women's issues is its need to change its image of being an anti-female union. If the current amalgamation talks with Sogat fail and the NGA decides at some time in the 1990s that industrial control and influence can be retained only through an amalgamation, then the unions with which it is likely to merge will have significant numbers, if not a majority, of members who are female.

APPRENTICESHIPS AND TRAINING

1948–83

General
For the LSC, LTS, TA and NGA during this period the traditional apprenticeship system was a cardinal feature of their control of entry into the occupations they organised in the industry. The system performed two major functions. First, it was a system of training by which individuals acquired the skills necessary to perform certain crafts in the industry. Second, it was a mechanism for controlling the supply of labour to the industry, first by limiting the numbers of people who could gain access to the training via an apprenticeship quota which established a ratio of apprentices to journeymen, and second by restricting the age at which individuals could gain access to an apprenticeship, namely as a young boy leaving school. If an apprenticeship was not gained at this age then there were no opportunities later in life when access to training for skilled jobs could be achieved. Competence to perform a craft was related not to approved standards but to time serving.

The apprenticeship operated by the NGA and its constituent unions was the only way in which craft skills could be acquired and the only way these could be passed on was by those who already had the skills. Employers could not recruit an alternative workforce, since a relatively long period of time was required to acquire the skill. The apprenticeship quota was used to ensure that the demand for labour exceeded its supply. Over the period 1948–66, wage negotiations with the BFMP and the NS were characterised by wages increases being traded by the unions in return for increases in the labour supply, including apprentices (see Chapter 12). The constant fear was that if entry into the industry was not limited then in times of recession a disproportionate number of members would be claiming the union's unemployment benefit. Uncontrolled entry into the industry would undermine not only the craft print unions' control but also their financial viability.

There were also other ways in which the supply of labour to printing employers was restricted over this period. National newspaper employers were not permitted apprentices on the grounds that they could not provide training in sufficient breadth to produce an adequately trained journeyman. Craft apprenticeships were permitted only in provincial newspapers and the general printing trade. National newspapers had to 'poach' their skilled labour from other parts of the printing industry. The NGA and its constituent unions also refused to accept adult promotion, which was a constant demand of the non-craft unions. The former Natsopa had an agreement with the TA, and subsequently the NGA, whereby its members filled vacancies for newspapers rotary press minders on an alternate basis. Natsopa argued that its members were capable of managing any type of cylinder machine in the newspaper field and that the apprenticeship system in the machine room should be replaced by promoting semi-skilled members, after a probationary period, to skilled status. The TA would not visualise promotion based on experience of only one particular press, and insisted that any adult promotion scheme should be based on wider experience than managing rotary presses in provincial newspapers.

The 1975 reform of the apprenticeship system
Even at the time of the formation of the NGA there were those who were questioning whether a system based on time serving entry as a young person, and training for a specific craft relating to hot metal techniques in the composing room and letterpress printing techniques in the machine room was relevant to the changing needs of the industry in the light of the growth of lithographic printing and the increasing use of

453

film in the composing room. The first delegate meeting of the NGA, held in 1966, carried a motion from the London Region calling for an enquiry into the structure and functioning of training in the graphical industry with a view to framing proposals for a training system more suited to the current and future needs of the industry.

In its early days some in the NGA envisaged an apprenticeship system in which apprentices were indentured to the industry and not to individual employers. A Birmingham branch motion to this effect was remitted by the 1966 Delegate Meeting, but a call for apprenticeship to the industry was made in a successful Colchester branch motion to the 1969 Delegate Meeting at which:

> This Conference considers that with the technological changes taking place within the printing industry the time has arrived for a fundamental change in apprenticeships. It, therefore, calls upon the National Council to consider an apprenticeship to the industry and not to a particular craft, with specialisation to be considered at a later date of apprenticeship training. Conference also considers that the apprenticeship period could be reduced with a more streamlined training programme.

By 1969 many compositors and machine managers had moved on from traditional hot metal processes and were engaged on web-offset presses, film make-up and a whole range of new processes. In addition, the school leaving age was increased to 16 in 1971 with the expectation that the educational standards of those entering the industry would continue to rise.

The 1972 wage agreement between the NGA and the BFMP and the NS provided for a major review of the apprenticeship system, with particular reference to recruitment and selection, standards of training, periods of apprenticeship, apprentice ratios, percentage wage rates and qualifications for journeymen status. The review was to produce a new apprenticeship system more in keeping with technical developments and the future manpower requirements of the industry. The eventual outcome was a new apprentice agreement between the BPIF and the NS and the NGA, which came into operation on 4 August 1975. It radically changed the existing system.

From 4 August all apprentices, irrespective of the age they left school, would serve a four-year apprenticeship. However, if the required standard of training had been completed satisfactorily, the four-year apprenticeship could be reduced to three and a half years. If this happened the apprentice received an increased rate of pay but did not count as a journeyman for quota purposes until the original four-year apprenticeship had been reached. The agreement also provided that if, for any reason, an apprentice fell behind with their training the apprenticeship could be extended to five years. The agreement also broke new ground in that training received was to be monitored. Each apprentice was issued with a log book to ensure that specific training objectives were achieved and that there was a record of them. In-firm training was backed up by attendance at college, on either full-time or block release courses. The agreement also increases the wages of apprentices. A first-year apprentice received 50 per cent of the journeymean's basic rate compared with 35 per cent previously. When an apprentice reached the fourth year of training, 85 per cent of the journeyman rate was received instead of 70 per cent.

Further major changes brought about by the 1975 apprentice agreement related to apprenticeship quotas. For the first time there was to be a common quota for apprentices in London and the provinces. Just as important was that, in composing departments, the apprentice quota and the training covered composing, machine composition, reading, monotype casting work and stereotyping. No longer would there be separate quotas for jobs like stereotyping or monocasters in the provinces, and all composing apprentices were to receive training throughout their department.

The operation of the agreement was supervised by a Joint Apprenticeship Panel (JAP) made up of five representatives from the BPIF and NS and four members of the NGA National Council. The national Joint Apprenticeship Panel had the overriding authority in relation to the application of the agreement. Regional panels had the day-to-day responsibility to ensure that the agreement was complied with and for the monitoring of the trade testing requirements for apprentices seeking early release from their apprenticeship. The terms of reference of the JAP meant that for the first time the NGA had the right to discuss questions concerning the recruitment and training of apprentices directly with the employers. Any questions of dispute about apprenticeships were to be resolved by the JAP.

The negotiation of the agreement had taken three years but was seen by the NGA as breaking new ground. For many years apprentices had felt badly treated, but the 1975 agreement now meant that all young people who entered NGA areas of the industry would receive comprehensive training and reasonable wages. For the NGA as an institution the agreement meant that it was at long last able to have an effective say on how, where and when apprentices should be trained. The JAP kept the system of recruitment and training of apprentices under review and could recommend improvements to ensure that the industry's manpower needs were met. Although the Printing and Publishing Industry Training Board existed and its advice was sought on many matters, the BPIF, the NS and the NGA always made it clear to the ITB that training was a subject for decision by the industry itself and not for a statutory board like the Training Board.

The 1983 Reform of Industrial Training

As new technology was implemented within the industry, the issue of apprentice training remained a high priority on the NGA's agenda. Delegates to the 1978 Delegate Meeting urged that future apprentice training should enable the NGA to control new technology and that apprentices should be trained to maintain, programme and control the whole of an emerging new communications industry. Some delegates saw that in the immediate and longer term the future of the NGA would best be safeguarded by investing in an apprenticeship system which would give younger members, and future members, the strength and ability to control the industry.

Against the background of the rapidly changing nature of jobs, the 1978 Delegate Meeting remitted from the Norwich branch a motion 'that this Conference recognises that the apprenticeship system is quickly outliving its usefulness and instructs the panel negotiating amalgamation with other print unions, to seek to have included in their terms of reference alternative recruitment and training procedures'. It was argued that the apprenticeship system had stood the test of time but the late 1970s were witnessing the disappearance of craft jobs and the entry into the industry of young people to train in skills which were now redundant. The completion of an apprenticeship now invariably meant no job was available or retraining in other skills had to be undertaken. The movers of the motion also argued that training on a full-time basis should be available as a right when needed throughout a person's working life and not just in an apprenticeship period.

Both the employers and the NGA realised that the 1975 agreement was in need of radical change. Although this agreement had, for the first time, provided real NGA involvement in the apprenticeship system, it was fair to say that there had been a lot of criticism of the agreement from the branches, which disliked trade testing being carried out by regional joint apprenticeship panels with little or no say from them in the results of these tests. The 1980 wage negotiations with the BPIF and the NS dealt not only with wages and hours but with the employers' demand that radical amendments be made to the 1975 apprentice agreement. A commitment to carry out a fundamental review of entry to and training for the industry was embodied within the national agreement reached with the Newspaper Society in 1980. The commitment was reiterated in the 1981 agreement with the NS and was also underwritten in the 1981 agreement with the BPIF. The employers' initial proposals, however, were far from aimed at improving training and education provision, but were directed at reducing their obligations to finance apprentice training and to remove NGA control, not only over the number of entrants to the industry but over the quality and standards of education and training within the industry. The employers' main proposal was to reduce the period of apprenticeship to three years. The proposal was made without regard to the feasibility of completing a course of print education in that period. By removing the means of jointly regulating standards and qualifications, the employers' proposals would have rendered the 1975 agreement a dead-letter. The employers' proposals would also have made it difficult to regulate the number of apprentices.

The NGA was not encouraged by the BPIF and the NS approach but decided to continue to operate the mchinery and principles of the 1975 agreement until such time as it was possible to replace it with new understandings. The NGA recognised some considerable time before the employers raised the issue that there existed within the apprenticeship system a degree of inflexibility which in certain circumstances might prevent the industry and the NGA adapting smoothly to the changes being brought about as a result of technology. Although the NGA played a major strategic role in the industry and covered a diversity of occupations throughout the UK and the Republic of Ireland, it was only in the traditional skilled areas that any attempt had been made to control entry into the industry. Only in England, Wales and Northern Ireland had joint regulation been established to ensure training to specified standards. A serious limitation of the NGA apprenticeship was that it covered a limited spread of occupations and subsequently systematic training of any breadth and duration was restricted almost exclusively to craft occupations. No proper training programmes were laid down for NGA tin printers, those members who operated small offset machines, and NGA-organised jobs in clerical, administrative, advertising and art studio fields. It was areas not covered by proper training schemes that were expected to grow in importance within the printing industry in the 1980s and 1990s.

The 1975 apprenticeship agreement was criticised by some NGA members on the grounds of ease of entry into the industry through other doors, that the training programmes applied only to a restricted number of occupations, and that no clear provision existed by which training standards could be enforced. The machinery established under the 1975 agreement was also criticised as unduly cumbersome and inflexible.

The NGA had become critical of the 'youth factor' of the apprenticeship system as totally inadequate at a time when the march of technology showed that members might have to retrain possibly three or four times during their working lives. It was also critical that parts of the apprenticeship system laid too much stress on skills required in the past rather than those needed in the future. There was the constant problem that the training element in the apprenticeship varied from firm to firm and it was often necessary to enquire where newly qualified journeymen had been trained to get some idea of their ability.

It was these weaknesses in the apprenticeship system which led the NGA to propose a radical new training system for the printing industry based on a different philosophy of approach to the apprenticeship system. In doing so the NGA was determined not to discard what was good and useful in the apprenticeship system, for example its broad-based training, but to adapt these to fit in with the advances in training knowledge, social change and technological innovation which had overtaken the existing apprenticeship system. The cornerstones of the NGA's new training system were to be flexibility and control. It was designed to meet four criteria. First, the provision of training would meet agreed standards in all the skills involved in the printing processes. Second, the scheme should accommodate systematically planned periods of training for those occupations which would require a lengthy period of skill-development. Third, the scheme should be flexible on age of entry and provide opportunities for the acquisition, and the updating, of skills during one's working life. Finally, the NGA was involved at every stage in the scheme from constructing its mechanics through to the design and allocation of training modules, and the monitoring and assessment of training standards. The new scheme was to provide training and further education opportunities for all entrants into the industry, with further opportunities throughout their working lives to update those skills and acquire new ones under the guardianship of the NGA.

The NGA favoured a modular system of training to replace the apprentice system and as a long-term solution to the problems of training in the industry. The modular system was to be designed not only to guarantee the younger entrants a broad-based training in primary occupations but also to provide, under NGA control, the means for inter-occupational mobility for those workers already employed in the industry. A modular system of training would be based not on time serving but on the attainment of agreed training objectives. Coupled with appropriate further educational facilities, it also provides a practical approach to retraining needs in the light of industrial development and the introduction of new technology. It would also be a more effective training method for adult workers who in future entered into the area of NGA operations.

The NGA envisaged that if it were possible to achieve new and separate training arrangements with the BPIF and the NS this would assist it to achieve similar objectives in other sectors of its operations. Separate talks began in late 1980 with the BPIF and the NS about a new method of training to replace the apprenticeship system in BPIF, non-federated and NS firms. The NGA impressed on the employers that the industry needed a training system relevant to the industry's needs and one which would equip people to face the challenges of new technology. Training was required which was comparable with VDUs and laser plate-making rather than Gutenberg and Caxton.

Despite prolonged discussions with the NS, it proved impossible to reach agreement for the new training system the NGA was seeking. The NS found the concept of manpower planning totally unacceptable, as the information required to be given to chapels in this exercise might lead to breaches of commercial confidentiality as well as being an interference with management prerogatives. Following the breakdown of negotiations the NS insisted, under the 1980 National Wage Basis Agreement, on the introduction of a three-year apprenticeship, which became operative in the provincial newspaper field as from 1 August 1984. A joint NGA/NS standing committee administers the scheme, though it has met only once.

Negotiations with the BPIF were more successful and in 1982 the NGA concluded a recruitment, training and retraining agreement which became operative from 1 August 1983, following acceptance of its terms by NGA members by 28,027 votes to 6,924. The agreement accepted the principle of a modular system of training for five different categories of trainees – young trainees entering the industry under the age of 18, adult trainees, skilled NGA workers undergoing further training, other NGA workers undergoing skills training, and other workers undergoing skills training. For all new entrants, whatever their age, three modules of training are undertaken before skilled status is achieved. First, there is an induction module, which introduces the trainees to the way their own particular company carries out its work. This is followed by the basic skills module, which is also available to qualified NGA members changing primary occupation, and is designed to provide a broad-based skills training for each of the primary occupations. After the basic skills module has been completed, the trainee takes the skill development modules at their place of work; these are also available to skilled workers undergoing further training. These modules are designed to enable the trainee to reach experienced worker standard in a particular job in the firm where they work and on the equipment used in that firm. Where agreed between management and chapel, the trainee is required to complete additional skills development modules. The number of skills development modules which a trainee takes depends upon the equipment and/or machines in the department where the trainee works. When a trainee has completed all the required training modules their log book is endorsed by the chapel and management. Trainees acquire skills to agreed standards at their own pace. Some take longer than others, but there is an incentive for trainees to complete their modules as soon as possible since only when they qualify do they receive the full rate of pay for the job they are to do.

These nationally agreed modules lay down standards to be implemented when any training or retraining takes place. However, further education, particularly for young trainees, is an integral part of the 1983 agreement. In fact, further education is compulsory for young trainees and provides an opportunity to develop an understanding of the principles and techniques involved in printing and specialisation. Although further education is not compulsory for adult new entrants, it is permissible if agreed jointly by the parties.

With respect to recruitment, the 1983 agreement requires management and chapel to develop manpower plans to meet the needs of the company. On the basis of this plan a decision is taken on how many recruits are needed in NGA areas. These plans must be reviewed annually to ensure flexibility and to cope with unforeseen changes in circumstances. Agreement on the manpower plan must be reached by no later than 1 June each year. This need for an agreed manpower plan gives NGA chapels greater involvement in industrial training than ever existed previously and means that firms must tell the chapel about their future plans. After agreeing to a manpower plan, a training agreement must be drawn up by management and chapel for every agreed trainee and/or recruit and must state the category in which training or retraining is to be given and specify the training modules and related further education to be completed. The length of training period varies between trainees and depends on the time required to complete the training objectives set out in the modules to company standards of performance. If agreement on a manpower plan cannot be reached, a fallback apprenticeship quota applies based upon the origination department (covering all pre-press operations) and the machine printing department. If this quota is applied, it incorporates a time serving element of three years and new entrants recruited under the fallback quota count as trainees against the quota for three years. The agreement ensures that a fallback quota arrangement cannot be more advantageous than a manpower plan.

The pay of trainees is a percentage of the appropriate skilled rate for the occupation they are to follow. Young trainees receive 60 per cent of the basic rate for qualified NGA members, whilst adult trainees receive 80 per cent. Qualified worker trainees receive the rate for which they have previously qualified. Young trainees who have reached the age of 18, and completed the in-company training modules to the satisfaction of management and the chapel, are entitled to 80 per cent of the basic rate for qualified NGA members for any period required to complete the further education course.

The 1983 recruitment, training and retraining agreement is supervised by the Joint Training Council, which comprises an equal number of representatives from the BPIF and the NGA. The Council keeps the operation of the agreement under review and makes recommendations to the BPIF and the NGA for improvements and changes to ensure that the industry's labour supply and training needs are met. In addition, it develops, updates and improves the required training modules and deals with any disagreements between management and the individual or chapel on training, further education or the award of qualified status matters. The JTC keeps an independent record of the training and qualifications of individuals.

The 1983 agreement was a major breakthrough for the NGA. It was recognition that, if it wished to retain a large and positive say in the future in who entered the industry and how they were trained, it had to take on board that technological developments were undermining, and would continue to do so, the NGA's ability to maintain its traditional control of the labour supply based on an apprenticeship system the characteristics of which were time serving, quota restriction and access to training as a youth. The accelerating rate of technological change anticipated in the 1980s and 1990s meant an entirely different type of printing industry would emerge. If the NGA and its members were to be a really effective influence in this 'new' industry, the NGA had to accept the need for a new training system based on continual training and retraining throughout its members' working lives. The 1983 agreement, which is jointly administered by NGA chapels and branches and employers, puts the union and its members in a position to meet the challenges of training that new technology brings, which can be developed into other NGA areas given the development of its organisation and the trend of technological developments. The whole concept of the recruitment, training and retraining agreement was to give the NGA control not only of the intake of labour but also over the opportunities of retraining and redeployment within the printing industry. Continual training and retraining under the control and influence of the NGA were the cornerstone of the 1983 agreement.

In 1984 the NGA conducted a comprehensive survey of the operation of the 1983 agreement since its inception. The survey's conclusions indicated that, whilst the majority of chapels were aware of the agreement, a considerable number did not understand how the agreement should operate. In fact, many chapels were not achieving manpower planning either because management refused to disclose the necessary information or because of a reluctance by chapels to seek it. It also showed that, whilst many members were undergoing further training and retraining, little was being carried out under the provisions of the Joint Training Council modules. Despite these problems, the NGA succeeded in extending the terms of the agreement from 1 January 1986 to cover its members who work in the Irish Master Printers' Association Northern Ireland Alliance Area. However, the BPIF continues to resist NGA pressure to extend the agreement into the small offset areas.

The recruitment, training and retraining agreement was criticised at both the 1986 and 1988 Delegate Meetings. The Manchester branch, for example, unsuccessfully moved, to the 1986 meeting, a motion which stated: 'This Conference recognises the failure of the current Recruitment, Training and Retraining Agreement', on the grounds that despite much publicity by the NGA over the introduction of the agreement the vast majority of the membership, and indeed employers, did not even know what the agreement was, that the number of manpower plans had been virtually nil, and that nobody would acknowledge that the agreement was not working. The National Council defended the agreement by pointing out that, although it was not perfect, it could not be described as a failure. Underpinning the whole agreement was the provision of comprehensive, systematic and proper training to agreed standards for all NGA members, and as such it was the most progressive, far-reaching and comprehensive package of training in any British industry. At the 1988 Delegate Meeting, delegates were told that the main problem with the agreement was that it was simply being ignored by a large number of employers, whilst chapels did not make sure the agreement was complied with. It was pointed out that the 1986–7 Report of the Joint Training Council showed that just 614 companies had registered trainees under the agreement, whilst of the NGA's 4,000 trainee members only 1,600 were following the new training agreement.

In response to these criticisms the NGA approached the BPIF. It was agreed that there was a need for a more effective presentation of the agreement's objectives to employers and members. To this end, in November 1988 the NGA, Sogat and the BPIF training councils launched a comprehensive information pack about the recruitment, training and retraining agreement. Entitled *Training for Change*, it had a video, fact sheets and presentation notes. In 1987 the NGA agreed to discuss a request from the BPIF that the 1983 agreement be extended to former Slade members working in BPIF firms. However, despite some initial progress, the talks eventually reached an impasse when the BPIF representatives tabled proposals on fallback quota arrangements and trainee wage rates which the NGA decided it could not accept.

The National Training Centre Initiative

At the 1988 Delegate Meeting arguably the most important decision was the one which pledged £1 million of the members' money from NGA funds to establish a national training centre if a feasibility study showed such a venture was practicable and viable. The background to this initiative was the NGA's success in pioneering the recruitment, training and retraining agreement, which was a remarkable agreement in that it saw one of the oldest craft unions in British industry amending its apprenticeship system to replace apprentices with trainees. There is no other industry in Britain today that has a set of training arrangements that are as positive and as flexible as provided under the recruitment, training and retraining agreement.

Given its long and consistent record of placing training towards the top of its agenda, the NGA saw its national training centre initiative as providing a solution to the acute skill shortages that hit the industry in the late 1980s. By 1988, in high-tech areas, such as scanner and page-planning systems and in the machine rooms that had invested in sophisticated multi-colour sheet and web-fed presses, there was a frightening shortfall in the number of skilled people available to meet the recent, and expected to be sustained, upturn in demand for printed products. The NGA saw nothing to be gained from laying blame for this skills shortage, but considered positive ways of moving forward to ensure that the right skills became available at the right time, otherwise an advantage would be given to foreign producers in the home and overseas market with a consequent loss of jobs to UK printers and to NGA members.

The NGA's initiative for a national training centre was an imaginative and practical approach towards overcoming labour supply problems in high-tech areas. The traditional printing colleges or printing depart-ments and further education colleges would continue to provide a core curriculum and the broad-based training that all new entrants would require, but the specialist and specific high-tech skills required to meet the acute skills shortages could not be acquired and developed adequately in the colleges alone. The answer was to establish a national training centre, which would be a consortium of eight to ten of the largest printing employers, the NGA and the printing machine equipment suppliers. The centre would undertake the retraining of NGA members from one skill to another, and provide skills development training, thus helping to overcome the shortage of skilled labour. This high-tech training centre is to be established in an appropriate venue within the UK and will be .equipped with a range of 'state of art' sheet-fed and web-offset machines and high-tech repro equipment. The centre will be funded by the three parties. The NGA is to assist in funding the centre to the extent of £1 million, subject to obtaining the cooperation and involvement of major printing employers and machinery and equipment suppliers. In addition, the three parties are also to look for substantial government and/or EEC funding for the centre.

The national training centre will also undertake retraining and training of employees of the participating companies and sell its services to non-participating companies, thereby making the centre available to the whole industry. In addition it is hoped participating companies will provide instructors, seconded from their companies, and support the retrainees/trainees in terms of salary so that trainees return to their companies and, after familiarisation, perform to satisfactory production standards. It is proposed that the centre is also to be available to retrain NGA unemployed members, and in these cases the union will contribute to the training costs. The NGA envisaged the proposed centre being independent, as many of the appropriate employers, whilst linked to the national skills centre, would not be members of the BPIF. The centre could be administered by an appointed independent organisation such as PIRA (Printing Industries Research Association) who will be accountable to a board consisting of employers, equipment suppliers and NGA representatives. The General Secretary, Tony Dubbins, told delegates to the 1988 Delegate Meeting,

> What these new NGA initiatives will provide is a second tier of training which will be capable and flexible enough to meet the desparate shortage of high-tech skills that the industry urgently needs now. It will be an investment in the skills of our members and the future of our union.
>
> Because of its flexibility and because of the way in which we hope that such a centre could have state of the art equipment, with state of the art trainers, seconded from industry, the proposal comprises not merely a short-term solution to the problems of skills shortages but a medium and long term solution also.

Following the Delegate Meeting the NGA held talks with its financial, legal and property advisers who confirmed that the national training centre concept needed close investigation. This was followed by an approach to a number of prominent printing employers, who were invited to participate in a consortium with the NGA to carry out a feasibility study, which, if successful, would lead to a training centre being set up. The employers, all leaders in the high-tech field, were De La Rue, Norton Opax, Ben Johnson, Hunterprint, St Ives Group,

Aspen Communications and Watmoughs. After discussions with these employers, key machine and equipment suppliers were approached during the 1988 IPEX Exhibition and all expressed a willingness to cooperate in a feasibility study. Early in 1989 the PA Consulting Group was appointed to investigate, report and make recommendations about the skill needs required in the high-tech area of the printing industry, the practicability of a national training centre, the cost of establishing a centre, and the budget and running costs for its operation. It was also asked to look at alternative options. In October 1989 PA Consultants presented a report to the three consortium parties showing that a national skill training centre was a feasible proposition, and the close of 1989 saw the parties seeking a suitable location for the centre, which if finally brought to a successful conclusion it is anticipated to be operative in 1991 just prior to the challenge of the Single European Market in 1992 and the demographic 'time bomb', both of which will reinforce the need for training facilities if the printing industry is to meet these challenges.

The Industrial Training Boards

In 1964 the government passed the Industrial Training Act which had three main aims, namely to see that there are enough trained people, to improve training and to spread the cost of training more evenly through the provision of a levy grant system. The Act was designed to combat a national shortage of skilled labour. The NGA welcomed the Act because, with technological developments taking place so rapidly within the industry, proper training was more essential than ever if redundancies amongst NGA members were to be avoided. The NGA, therefore, supported the establishment of the Printing and Publishing Industry Training Board (PPITB), which became operative on 29 May 1968. The NGA General Secretary, John Bonfield, and its General President, Fred Simmons, were appointed to serve on the Board. Mr Norman Fisher was appointed chairman of the Board, which covered some 400,000 printing employees. Its terms of reference were 'to assist the Printing and Publishing Industry to increase its efficiency and prosperity through effective training; thereby developing the industry's potential for the benefit of those who own it, those who work in it, and its customers.'

The emergence of the government's Training Services Agency (TSA) in 1975 resulted in significant changes in the nature and operation of the

PPITB. This Agency was given overall authority over the work of all industrial training boards. The structure of the PPITB remained unaltered but its plans and action were now required to be sanctioned by the TSA, which in turn was accountable to the Manpower Services Commission. The TSA also approved the Board's financial budget, since the boards were now funded from the Exchequer. One of the differences between the Employment and Training Act (1973), which established the Manpower Services Commission, and the Industrial Training Act (1964) was that the former required training boards to exempt from the levy all firms which met acceptable standards of training. In 1975 the PPITB introduced an exemption scheme. In that year, 1,000 of the 3,887 establishments paying the levy to the Board applied for exemption and about half were approved.

The Board developed a thirty-six-week full-time integrated first-year basic course for production workers, comprising industrial training and related further education for new entrants to the industry. It was NGA policy to get people on the integrated course. The Board always gave a high priority to retraining and developed retraining programmes to meet the demands of new technology. The NGA played an active part in the work of the PPITB to protect the interest of its members. With the transfer of engagements of NUWDAT to the NGA in October 1979 the NGA gained representation on the Paper and Paper Products Industry Training Board.

In 1981 the future of industrial training boards was placed in jeopardy when the government planned to reduce its spending by decimating the existing boards and their staff to skeleton proportions and withdrawing their statutory status. The NGA totally opposed the proposal whereby voluntary training arrangements would replace statutory boards. Voluntary arrangements removed the employers' obligations to finance training via the levy system and would adversely affect the quality and standard of education and training in the printing industry. The NGA, along with other printing unions, supported the retention of a statutory industrial training board. However, this policy could not be sustained. When the Secretary of State for Employment, Mr Norman Tebbit, withdrew Exchequer support from the administrative costs of the industrial training boards, the NGA, and other print unions, were unable to persuade the print employers to levy themselves to compensate for this loss of income, and both the Printing and Publishing Industry Training Board and the Paper and Paper Products Industry Training Board were wound up in 1982.

CHAPTER 14

DISPUTES: NEW TECHNOLOGY, LEGISLATION AND DE-UNIONISATION

Over the period 1968–89 the NGA was involved in a number of industrial disputes over the implementation of new technology. The bulk of these disputes were in the newspaper field and some of them, particularly the Messenger and Wapping disputes, were the focus of heavy national media attention. One of the effects of this has been the creation of the impression in the minds of the general public that the NGA is predominantly a newspaper union. This is and was far from the case. At the height of its influence in newspapers, out of a total membership of 125,000 only some 3 per cent (13,000) were employed in provincial newspaper houses and about 5 per cent (5,000) in national newspapers. One consequence of newspapers being a minority of its membership was that the NGA was able, despite being unable in the mid-1980s newspaper technological revolution to maintain its influence against the backcloth of the 'war', to find itself at the close of this history with more members and financial resources than a decade ago.

This chapter is concerned with seven new technology disputes in which the NGA was involved. Their common feature was that the employer was attempting to remove the NGA from all or parts of the company. In 1968 the NGA was involved in a dispute with Parrett and Neves Ltd, which introduced web-offset machinery and sought to operate with non-union labour. In 1973 the NGA was in dispute with T. Bailey Foreman Ltd, Nottingham, over the introduction of optical character recognition (OCR) and photoresponsive plates. Two years later the NGA became involved in a dispute with Sharman's of Peterborough, which wished to produce an evening newspaper using OCR machinery without an agreement with the NGA. In 1979 the union entered a twelve-month strike with Times Newspapers Limited

(TNL) over two principal issues. The company insisted that the NGA first negotiate against arbitrarily imposed deadlines and, second, surrender its control of the original keystroke.

In 1983 the NGA entered a dispute with the Messenger Newspaper Group over wages, security of employment, union recognition and the honouring of agreements. In 1985 the NGA began a bitter dispute with the *Wolverhampton Express and Star*, when that company unilaterally, and in breach of the provincial newspaper industry's disputes procedure, introduced direct input from the advertising department. In January 1986 the NGA found itself involved in a major dispute with News International over that company's transfer of the production of four of its newspaper titles from Fleet Street to Wapping in East London. This bitter dispute was to last thirteen months.

PARRETT AND NEVES

Under the terms of an agreement between the NGA and the ASLP, a joint delegation had to be sent to any managements contemplating the extension or the introduction of web-offset machines. With one exception these joint visits enabled agreements to be reached with the management concerned for web-offset machines to operate with agreed rates and manning levels. The exception was Parrett and Neves (Chatham) Ltd, which in February 1968 received a joint NGA/ASLP delegation which sought to negotiate a rate for the job and manning levels. Negotiations broke down when the company refused to concede any extra rate for a new web-offset press, so on 7 March the NGA instructed its members not to operate the new press until an agreement had been reached.

On 2 May 1968 NGA machine managers were instructed by the company to proceed to a new factory at Sittingbourne, some miles from their existing place of employment, to operate the new web-offset press. When this instruction was not carried out the NGA FOC was summarily dismissed, as were twenty-three other members who decided to remain loyal to the NGA. Management staffed the press and computer and TTS equipment with non-union labour. The dispute was aggravated by management's offer of a wage rate £5 in excess of the agreed NGA/NS rate plus a job for life to those who ignored the NGA instruction.

Meetings with the Newspaper Society to resolve the dispute were to no avail. The NGA laid down four conditions for a return to normal working at Parrett and Neves. First, the twenty-four dismissed NGA members must be reinstated. Second, those members who accepted the company's terms and continued to work must be dismissed. The third condition was that all departments at Parrett and Neves must become 100 per cent union organised, and the fourth that the wages and manning issue that sparked the dispute must be settled. These conditions were unacceptable to Parrett and Neves, which was willing to take back five of the NGA members on condition that it had the right to select the five. The Newspaper Society rejected a demand from the NGA that it expel Parrett and Neves, after which the NGA ceased co-operation with the Society.

In an attempt to bring the dispute to a successful conclusion the NGA sought the assistance of unions both inside and outside the printing industry, paid the twenty-four members involved their basic grade rate as dispute pay, maintained constant picket lines at Chatham, attempted to prevent deliveries of newsprint, ink, chemicals and plates, etc. from reaching the firm, and held two mass demonstrations – 1,500 NGA members turned up to the second one held in May 1969. However, the company continued to produce its two papers. Attempts to curtail supplies to the company were hindered by Parrett and Neves having a riverside quay at the back of its premises. This unique geographical position gave the company direct access by sea to newsprint, which was crucial to its being able to produce its newspaper.

Towards the end of 1969, a formula was agreed by the NGA/NS joint standing committee as a basis for settlement of the dispute. The formula contained six principles. First, the dismissed NGA members should be reinstated by the company; second, present employees of the company engaged on work in NGA areas should remain in their present employment as long as necessary to meet production requirements; and third, in the event of redundancy arising, for any reason, employees not in membership of the NGA would be the first to be declared redundant. The three remaining principles were that the company observe all national agreements between the NGA and the NS, including the web-offset agreement, that the company extend recognition to the appropriate printing trade unions, and that in the event of any difficulties arising from the implementation of any settlement there would be an immediate reference to the NS/NGA joint standing committee.

Subsequently negotiations were opened with Parrett and Neves on the formula. However, it became apparent that the NGA Medway Towns branch and the Parrett and Neves chapel would not accept the second principle of the formula even as a basis for resuming negotiations. It was probably in the light of its knowledge of the branch and chapel's attitude that the management turned a complete somersault and went back on the formula. Further efforts by the joint standing committee to find a solution were rejected by the company, which insisted that 'practical difficulties' meant it could only reinstate eight members and could not guarantee when the remainder would return to work – or even if they would return at all. In addition, Parrett and Neves also wanted assurances from the NGA that the expelled members would not be required under any circumstances to leave the firm. The NGA and NS representatives on the joint standing committee unanimously agreed that these counter-proposals were totally unacceptable and must be regarded as a rejection of the committee's plan for a settlement of the dispute.

The dispute continued and the NGA maintained its picketing. However, in July 1970 the union advised its members involved in the dispute that it was clear that pickets could no longer be effectively utilised in the prosecution of the dispute and that, whilst the dispute would continue, it was in the members' best interests that they be found alternative employment. Little progress was made in this direction, so the NGA made a payment of £500 to each of the members concerned. It also provided financial assistance, including resettlement grants, retraining opportunities, interest-free loans for housing deposits and rail fares home during resettlement periods, to members accepting employment in other areas. By the summer of 1972 all members dismissed by Parrett and Neves had found alternative employment. The NGA continued in dispute with the company but in 1978 following approaches from the NGA, the company agreed to recognise the NGA again and become fully organised.

The NGA was unable to successfully prosecute the Parrett and Neves dispute. The London Region moved a successful motion to the 1972 Delegate Meeting which congratulated the Parrett and Neves members for their stand in support of union policy, and expressed concern 'at the apparent lack of action and intention on the part of our National Officers and Council in pursuing this dispute, and that in future disputes the National Council utilise the full resources of the NGA to promote and protect the interests of its members'.[1] The NGA leadership was criticised for not involving the chapel in the negotiations which led to the formula outlined above, for accepting that those members who had continued to work at Parrett and Neves should not be dismissed and for not calling NGA members to undertake secondary action. In their defence the General Secretary, John Bonfield, stressed that four officers were engaged on the dispute, that it had cost the union over £100,000 to run the dispute, and that since the company had left the Newspaper Society there would have been little point in stopping the provincial newspaper industry, the general printing trade and national newspapers. This would have hit every printing employer in the country except the one with whom it was in dispute.

The Parrett and Neves dispute was not about the manning of web-offset presses but about trade union recognition. Before the NGA members were dismissed the firm employed non-union female typists, and directly the NGA members were sacked these people began to operate computer typesetting equipment. In the machine room non-union labour was also employed. What, however, had the NGA achieved from the dispute? It had illustrated to employers that it was a fighting union which had organisational strength. It could back its members financially and would not walk away from attempts by other employers to copy the Parrett and Neves behaviour. The NGA saw its main gain from the dispute being that other firms that might have been contemplating taking similar action to that of Parrett and Neves had been effectively deterred. Delegates to the 1969 Delegate Meeting were told,

Parrett still manages to get out his weekly newspapers. However we are convinced that any newspaper proprietor who may have been tempted to follow the example of Parrett has been given a salutary lesson and if nothing else has come out of this dispute that in itself is enough.[2]

T. BAILEY FOREMAN LTD

This company owned the *Nottingham Guardian Journal* and the *Nottingham Evening Post*. Problems arose with the company in 1972 when, without NGA knowledge, OCR equipment was installed and the copy-preparation of small ads undertaken by tele-ad staff. This copy was placed direct into OCR equipment, bypassing the composing room. Since classified advertising was traditionally a Natsopa (clerical) area there was the prospect of inter-union conflict. OCR combined previously separate processes of receiving advertising copy (Natsopa territory) and the setting of advertisements (NGA territory). An agreement as to who was to be responsible for producing advertising copy was necessary.

Despite an agreement between the NGA and T. Bailey Foreman that NGA members would set adverts, the company would not abide by it. This resulted in a 'crunch' meeting with the company on 6 January 1973 at which a further agreement was reached whereby the NGA would prepare the small ads even if this meant duplicating the setting. Again T. Bailey Foreman would not honour the agreement, and the matter was referred to the NS/NGA joint standing committee, whose findings were that the agreement reached on 6 January 1973 was acceptable to both parties, and must be implemented. However, the culmination of these problems came in June 1973 over a completely different issue.

The management, knowing that Slade and NGA were in negotiations for an agreement over the production of photoresponsive plates, were not prepared to wait to see if the two unions could reach an agreement but precipitated events by insisting that NGA members produce such plates. Slade objected and the company responded by sacking the Slade members. This led the other unions in the company to refuse to handle work which would normally have been done by trade unionists. A complete lock-out, involving significant numbers of NGA and Slade members, occurred on 18 June 1973. The dispute lasted six weeks.

The NGA involved its other members employed in NS offices in the dispute, to bring pressure on the NS. When told of this, the NS agreed to set up a subcommittee of the joint standing committee to visit Nottingham and produce a settlement acceptable to all parties. The demarcation issue between the NGA and Slade was resolved, but the main obstacle for a return to work was T. Bailey Foreman's insistence that no punitive action be taken against twenty NGA or other print union members who remained working after the majority were locked out. The return to work agreement had provided that all staff, whether employed on the morning or the evening paper, were reinstated and if following this step there were staff surplus to requirements the issue would be dealt with on the basis of voluntary redundancy or voluntary early retirement.

Although a return to work took place on 31 July 1973, talks proceeded between the unions and the management over the interpretation of the settlement. In reality the company refused to implement the return to work agreement. The NS/NGA joint standing committee reconvened to give rulings on several points, but T. Bailey Foreman refused to implement them and stressed that unless all the union members expelled were re-admitted without an entrance fee the company was not prepared to discuss any issues. Matters were not helped in that the company insisted that any meetings with the unions could not be held on the company or unions' premises and must take place after office hours.

T. Bailey Foreman had succeeded in ending the closed shop at the *Nottingham Evening Post*, removing the NGA and other print unions from its departments, refusing to recognise the printing unions, and not implementing the OCR agreement of January 1973 so that NGA members were not setting classified advertisements. The problem for the NGA was that, if it did not try to re-establish its position in T. Bailey Foreman, there was the possibility it would find itself involved in similar disputes with other provincial newspaper companies endeavouring to do the same. However, a successful resolution to the problem required the cooperation of every union with members in the company with additional help from other TUC-affiliated unions, but this was easier said than done since it was clear that some print unions did not want to get involved in the dispute. By mid-1976 the dispute was still continuing but little in the way of effective action, other than meetings of those involved, was being taken.[3] Expelled NGA members were continuing to work alongside NGA members who had been recommended for expulsion eighteen months previously but against whom nothing had been done. NGA members working at the *Nottingham Evening Post* made it clear that they would not support another strike instruction as this would simply lead to their dismissal. The NGA's remaining ineffectual organisation at T. Bailey Foreman meant that the company put into operation for the first time in this country a direct on-line VDT terminal with input coming from journalists and advertising staffs. The company claimed that the system worked effectively and that its staff requirements, particularly in the composing department, had reduced dramatically.

In 1976 the TUC Printing Industries Committee took over the task of coordinating joint action by the printing unions to restore recognition at T. Bailey Foreman. In an attempt to change the company's attitude towards recognition, on 20 March 1978 the NGA and Slade instructed members not to handle work going to or emanating from T. Bailey Foreman Ltd, T. Bailey Foreman (Plate Makers) Ltd, T. Bailey Foreman (Printers) Ltd, Notts Free Press, and the Huthwaite Printing Company Ltd, which had the then most up-to-date web-presses in Europe. This last named company unsuccessfully sought an interim injunction in July 1978 ordering the NGA and Slade to refrain from this action. However, the NGA 'blacking' campaign to gain recognition at T. Bailey Foreman suffered a setback in March 1979 when a High Court order was granted to a number of national and provincial newspaper groups and some advertisers instructing the NGA to stop 'blacking' firms which advertised in the *Nottingham Evening Post*. The NGA lifted its 'blacking' instruction but lodged an appeal against the High Court order.

In May 1979 the NGA's appeal was unanimously rejected by Lord Denning, who ruled that the NGA was not involved in a trade dispute with T. Bailey Foreman and could not therefore claim legal immunity for its action. The Court heard that the NGA had ordered a nationwide blacking campaign against sixteen firms after they had refused a request to stop advertising in the *Nottingham Evening Post*. The NGA justified its action on the basis of its rule banning members from handling work going to or coming from an unrecognised source. This argument was rejected by Lord Denning, who argued that a trade union had no right to use its industrial strength to invade the freedom of the press and to interfere with the freedom of commercial firms to advertise their wares. Lord Denning accepted that there was evidence of a trade dispute between the NGA and the company in 1973, 1976 and 1977, but it was now arguable that the dispute was not about union recognition since the remaining NGA members at T. Bailey Foreman were content with their wages and conditions. This was a puzzling decision, since it was accepted that the NGA was in dispute with the company in the early and mid-1970s about recognition and that it still had not obtained recognition in 1979. How could it no longer be in dispute about the issue?

Even though the NGA ended the advertisement blacking in May 1979, the dispute with T. Bailey Foreman continued and more than 1,000 trade unionists attended a demonstration organised by the TUC Printing Industries Committee against the *Nottingham Evening Post* on 16 June 1979. Following demonstrations and picketing in Nottingham it became clear that, because of the police action in preventing effective picketing at the *Nottingham Evening Post*, the print unions would have to develop alternative strategies. A subcommittee of the TUC Printing Industries Committee recommended to the full committee that there should be a one-day stoppage across the entire provincial press. T. Bailey Foreman was still in membership of the NS, despite recognition by many NS members that the company was in breach of the original return-to-work formula, and was still refusing to grant recognition to the printing unions.

However, apart from the NGA and the NUJ, the other print unions would not support a one-day stoppage or any other form of industrial action in the provincial newspaper industry. The NGA now saw no prospect of effective action from the other print unions and decided to instruct its remaining members to withdraw their labour from the *Nottingham Evening Post* from 30 June 1980 and to remove the firm from the list of recognised NGA offices. The Assistant General Secretary, Tony Dubbins, told delegates to the 1980 Delegate Meeting,

> In my opinion we have really got no alternative except to face up to the fact that we really have a Parrett and Neves type of situation here, and it is one that we are going to have to pull away from and we are going to have to recognise that this is one that we have lost and in time, try to get back and get it organised as we have done with Parrett and Neves on a proper trade union basis.[4]

SHARMAN'S OF PETERBOROUGH

Sharman's, which produces a series of weekly papers in the Cambridge-shire and Huntingdonshire areas, announced early in May 1975 its intention to publish an evening paper in September 1975 and to produce it with OCR equipment with or without agreement with the NGA. Journalists were to keyboard editorial copy, while tele-ad staff were to handle advertising copy for direct input to the OCR equipment. NGA members would be confined to coding copy and making corrections. The NGA protested at the plan but the company refused to consider a compromise settlement. In an effort to meet Sharman's position the NGA was prepared to reach reciprocal agreement with the NUJ to cover editorial keyboarding, but Sharman's would not budge on the issue of NGA members undertaking the work connected with advertisements. The NGA concluded that the firm intended producing its new paper with cheap, non-union labour.[5] Eventually NGA members stopped work on 15 May 1975 and several who attempted to remain on the premises were physically removed by management. Letters from the company were sent to members' homes offering the choice of staying loyal to the union or loyal to the firm.

Attempts to reach a settlement with the help of ACAS failed. At one stage agreement had been reached providing for a return to work with discussions commencing on the use of OCR to be followed by the return of the remainder of the chapel. The NGA mounted pickets and succeeded in turning back lorries belonging to outside suppliers, whilst advertisements which were due to appear in Sharman's papers were blacked by NGA members. However, Sharman's continued to produce its weekly titles with the help of some NGA, Slade, and NATSOPA members who had continued to work, tele-ad staff who produced advertisements for direct paste-up, and journalists operating OCR equipment in defiance of an NUJ instruction that they should not prepare copy handled by non-union labour.

Following over eleven hours of talks on 24 July 1975, an interim formula, to operate until a national agreement had been reached covering OCR equipment, was agreed for the operation of such equipment at Sharman's. Towards the end of the dispute events moved rapidly. The NS/NGA joint standing committee met three times and put proposals to both sides. Whilst these were being considered the dispute reached new heights on 2 July when some several hundred NGA members formed a picket line in support of the members in dispute. On the following day the company attempted to bring out one of its publications but immediately many of the pickets present sat down on the road in front of the vehicle. The police moved in and arrested twenty-five NGA members for obstructing the police in the course of their duty, but publication of the newspaper was halted.

As a result of these events and many telephone calls between the NS and the NGA, the company agreed that no more papers would be produced until after a meeting of the Joint Standing Committee Panel, to be held on 4 July in Peterborough. At this meeting a formula for a return to work was accepted by both sides and the NGA members involved in the dispute returned to work on 8 July 1975. The formula allowed an NS/NGA panel into the factory to carry out an investigation, which eventually produced a possible solution to the dispute to both sides. All copy produced by journalists in the editorial department using IBM typewriters was to be accepted direct to the OCR scanner by the NGA, thus maintaining the single keyboarding principle. All copy originating outside the editorial department would be set by NGA members on either perforator keyboards or IBM typewriters. It was to be management's prerogative to decide whether written or retyped copy was supplied to the keyboard operator. Under the proposed settlement formula the principle of single keyboarding also applied to advertising copy. All copy that was not received by tele-ad staff was to be set by NGA members on either perforator keyboards or IBM typewriters.

The major issue of OCR at Sharman's had been satisfactorily resolved for the NGA, pending agreement at national level. OCR did not spread in the industry as anticipated and was overtaken by technological developments. However, this was not to be known at the start of the dispute and it was important that the NGA should be successful. As with Parrett and Neves and T. Bailey Foreman, management had introduced technological change unilaterally. That the NGA was successful in the Sharman dispute was due to a number of important factors. First, unlike at Nottingham, the NGA had the loyal support of the chapel, which stood firm in a situation that must at times have seemed fraught with danger to their future employment. Second, magnificent support was given by many members from many branches. Many were harassed, some prosecuted by the police and all at various times risked physical injury on the picket line. Third, the resolute, determined and controlled mass picketing was a crucial factor. Sharman's, despite a seven-week strike, had managed to produce every edition of its paper without the involvement of NGA compositors or machine men. The way that Sharman's was eventually prevented from publishing its paper had little to do with the withdrawal of NGA labour. It was the fact that the NGA mass picketed the factory and managed to stop the distribution and not the production of the paper.[6] Fourth, there was the discipline of other NGA members, in support of their fellow members directly involved in the dispute, in refusing to handle advertisements bound for Sharman's paper.

The dispute had been bitter but shorter than at one stage seemed likely. The bitterness arose from the dictatorial way the company introduced new technology and its denial of the union's right to defend the interests of its members involved. The relative shortness of the dispute was the result of the determination of the NGA not to accept this position and the support received from its wider membership. The NS also made a major contribution to the settlement. The longer-term significance of the dispute for which the NGA hoped was that it would dissuade other 'maverick' companies from being tempted to impose new new technology on NGA members, accompanied by the cry 'to hell with the union'.[7]

The Sharman dispute also saw the media distort the NGA's attitude towards new technology. The NGA was projected as being anti new technology when the union's approach was the exact opposite for three reasons. First, history shows that resisting technological change is not viable in the long run. Second, the NGA accepted its responsibility to the community that the printing industry serves to utilise the most economical methods of providing that product. Third, if the NGA wanted a soundly based and profitable industry – on which improved living standards can be based – it was in the long-run interests of its members not to resist technological advance.

THE TIMES DISPUTE[8]

This dispute developed into one of the most fundamental disputes in which the NGA has ever been involved during its history. The disagreement centred around two principal issues. The company insisted that the print unions negotiate against arbitrarily imposed deadlines and that the NGA surrender control of the original keystroke. At the time, this latter issue was the most serious threat to the print craft unions since the introduction of hot metal casting machines at the turn of this century.

Negotiations with Times Newspapers Limited (TNL) actually began in 1977, at which point the NGA made it clear that it accepted as inevitable the introduction of new technology but would not concede its traditional function to other unions or employees. TNL insisted on direct input from both editorial and advertising sections, reductions in staff in all departments, guarantees of continuous production, a new disputes procedure, and an improved company-wide wage structure. The General Secretaries of the printing unions were told that if these requirements were not forthcoming the company would cease publication of *The Times*, *Sunday Times* and *Times Supplements* on 30 November 1978 and from that date start to issue notices of termination of employment.

The NGA refused to participate in any further negotiations until the TNL lifted its threat to suspend publication of its newspapers, since the issues involved could not be negotiated by an arbitrary fixed date. The NGA 'Fleet Street' chapels committed themselves to raise a voluntary £5 a week levy to assist NGA TNL members should the suspension of TNL publications take place. FOCs working in Thomson regional newspaper offices also pledged chapels to give financial, moral and industrial support at the appropriate time to NGA members working at TNL. On 30 November TNL ceased publication of *The Times*, *Sunday Times* and the *Times Supplements*. No negotiations took place immediately before or after the suspension date, but following an intervention by Mr Albert Booth, the Employment Secretary, the two sides met for 'talks about talks' on 13 December 1978. A second meeting followed two days later and after five hours of talks the Employment Secretary announced a formula for a resumption of negotiations, including talks without preconditions on the crucial issue of new technology. However, 15 December was the date on which TNL was due to send out dismissal notices to 3,100 staff. The company had delayed sending out notices for fourteen days in the hope that further talks might take place. When the company refused to lift the 15 December dismissal notices, the unions refused to enter negotiations; 620 NGA members were dismissed.

In March 1979 the Employment Secretary again intervened in the dispute. A breakthrough came on 8 March when the print unions and the TNL management agreed a peace formula. This provided for immediate negotiations, for the re-engagement of all dismissed regular staff, for publication to resume following agreement with all unions, for dismissed employees to receive compensation for lost earnings, and for a disputes procedure. Means of maintaining continuous production, efficient working arrangements and the application of new technology were to be matters for negotiation in accordance with an agreed timetable. The peace formula provided for any side to seek advice or help from the TUC and for issues unresolved by 7 April 1979 to be referred to ACAS. Detailed negotiations were to take place without preconditions imposed by either side and 17 April was set as the target date for the resumption of publication. TNL had conceded joint discussions about new technology without preconditions, the re-engagement of dismissed staff and a target date for resumption of publication.

The NGA made every effort to find a solution. The major problem was the composing area. The NGA told TNL it was prepared to accept the introduction of new technology with all of its consequences, including a staff cut of some 40 per cent, to allow tele-ad staff to direct input all commercial information and to accept dead keyboards in the editorial department solely for the purpose of checking stories. This package was to be the basis for a three-year agreement with a review jointly with TNL management in the last six months of the agreement without prior commitment on either side. The company rejected this offer and insisted on the NGA conceding direct input. Negotiations broke down again and NGA members were dismissed for a second time from midnight on 17 April 1979.

During the months that followed, picketing took place at the offices of *The Times* and *Sunday Times* in Gray's Inn Road, whilst TNL tried to produce *The Times* at an office in Germany with effect from 30 April 1979. Due to the efforts of the German print union, Druck und Papier, and the IGF, the TNL failed to get *The Times* printed in Europe. In June 1979 the NGA advised its 620 members directly involved in the dispute to seek jobs at other firms, as there seemed no likelihood that Times publications would resume given the NGA's policy of resistance to direct entry by journalists and advertising workers and the direct opposite policy of the TNL.

During these many months of frustration the General Secretary, Mr Joe Wade, attempted to secure a meeting with Lord Thomson, owner of the Thomson Organisation which controlled TNL. In June 1979 Lord Thomson heeded an appeal for his intervention in the dispute by Joe Wade and agreed to meet the NGA. At this meeting the Thomson organisation agreed that the issue of direct input should be negotiated over a twelve-month period, initially with the NGA and subsequently with the NUJ and Natsopa. Against this hopeful background, peace talks opened at the Charing Cross Hotel on 4 July when TNL tabled a nine-point document entitled 'Republication and Return to Work at Times Newspapers'. However the print unions took exception to parts of the document and on 17 July 1979 put forward counter-proposals, to which the TNL management responded three days later with demands that went further than the original document.

To circumvent this management stance, the print unions took their proposals to the parent company, where on 27 July they negotiated a peace formula with Gordon Brunton, chief executive of the Thomson Organisation. This formula met most of the unions' conditions for a resumption of work. The dismissed employees were to be reinstated, republication would commence four weeks after the reinstatement of the dismissed employees, lump sum payments up to £500 would be made to compensate for the weeks of lock-out, reinstatement would be on pre 30 November 1978 wage rates, plus the NPA 1978 wage award, plus 10 per cent, and a 72-page *Sunday Times* would be produced. After reinstatement, negotiations would begin on the introduction of photocomposition, an 80-page *Sunday Times*, a new disputes procedure, guarantees of continuous production and other issues. To prevent a recurrence of breakdown in the republication negotiations, a committee composed of senior management and union leaders was set up to which disagreements threatening progress would be referred. The return-to-work formula removed the question of direct input and gave the NGA jurisdictional rights over the input of all matter on TNL titles.

The peace formula contained a clause that the conditions had to be accepted by all unions before a return to work could be effected. Although endorsed by the Natsopa National Council, some of its chapels refused to accept the terms. The NGA negotiators returned to the Thomson Organisation and secured reinstatement of the members involved in the dispute from 16 September 1979. The company was told that, unless NGA members were taken back in line with the 27 July formula, pressure from chapels to find alternative employment would become irresistible. Following their reinstatement, the NGA members were given training on the new systems and equipment they would be operating when republication began. A final settlement to the TNL dispute was not reached until Sunday 21 October 1979, less than three hours before the final deadline set by Lord Thomson for total closure of TNL titles and the dismissal of 3,700 employees if agreement were not reached.

The final brinkmanship in the dispute arose just after the reinstatement of the NGA members. The TNL management, after negotiating a return-to-work formula with General Secretaries, conceded Natsopa chapel demands for a full operating agreement before republication. These agreements, particularly that covering machine assistants, eroded the NGA machine manager differentials to an unacceptable level. The NGA considered that management's action justified withdrawal from the original return-to-work formula and that full operating agreements should be negotiated with the NGA before the relaunch. These negotiations took place over a four-day period against yet another deadline – midnight 17 October – but broke down. Both sides agreed to give the negotiations one last chance. Against this sombre background, negotiations to agree full operating arrangements covering manning, pay and working methods began. Deals were reached for NGA members in the composing room, the reading department, the foundry and the telecommunications and electronics sections. In the machine room, agreement was reached on operating procedures, including shift times and working practices and pay, although this fell far short of the NGA demand for £250 a week to restore the differential over Natsopa members. In the photocomposition area, compositors were to receive £227.50 for a 34 hour, four-day week. The only outstanding issue was manning in the machine room, but this was referred to an adjudication panel composed of equal management and union numbers and chaired by the chairman of ACAS. *The Times* reappeared on 13 November 1979 and the *Sunday Times* on 18 November 1979.

The agreement represented a significant climb-down by TNL and the retention of the keystroke for the NGA, which hoped the dispute would be a marker to all employers, whether they be in the national or provincial newspaper industry or commercial printing, that new technology can only be introduced with the consent and cooperation of the trade unions, and that the NGA could not be bludgeoned into surrender.[9] It is worth re-emphasising the important issues involved in the Times dispute for the NGA. First, it was clear that TNL was determined to implement new technology in a unilateral manner and without the agreement of the NGA if necessary. Second, the company's initial objective included pushing the NGA and its members into surrender by threats of closure and dismissal. TNL sought to introduce direct entry from the editorial and advertising areas on its own terms, to undermine the NGA's national and chapel bargaining power and control of the production process, to reduce the job opportunities of NGA members, and to impose arbitrary conditions on the negotiations. Due to the loyalty of NGA members at TNL, the leadership of the General President, Les Dixon, and the support received from other NGA members working in 'Fleet Street' and in other Thomson regional newspapers, the company did not achieve these objectives.

In the dispute the NGA was opposing not the introduction of new technology but the manner in which the company wished to implement it. The dispute was not an attempt on the NGA's part to destroy new technology on the anvil of TNL, nor was it an attempt to put the clock back to the days of Caxton. It was a battle to ensure the survival of the NGA and its members and to embrace new technology in a realistic and socially just way. The NGA was willing to accept new technology at TNL to improve the efficiency and competitiveness of the company, but at the same time it sought to protect the interests of its members and to ensure that they shared some of the benefits of the new technology.

The NGA realised that 'Fleet Street' and provincial managements were watching its reactions to TNL's attempt to introduce direct entry. The General Secretary, Joe Wade, told the 1980 Delegate Meeting, 'If we had conceded direct input there, if we had allowed the *Times* management to walk all over us with their arrogant demands and threats, does anyone doubt that the other vultures would have pounced in no time at all?'[10]

What were the lessons for the NGA from the dispute? First, the NGA demonstrated that it could keep control of the keyboards provided it maintained a united and disciplined front in the face of pressure from individual employers or groups of employers. However, 'the price' to win the dispute had been high in financial terms. The 620 members involved in the dispute received a weekly dispute benefit from the NGA of £40 per week. The total cost to the union over the duration of the dispute was over £500,000. In addition to the £40 per week from the union, the 620 members also received a further £30 per week from the £5 per week levy paid by other NGA members working in national newspapers in London.[11] But that was the price that had to be paid because the benefits which were likely to accrue from the NGA keeping control of the keyboards were immeasurable. In holding the line in the Times dispute, it had saved thousands of jobs in composing departments all over the country.

However, the NGA was under no illusion that because it had won the TNL battle it had won the war over new technology. It realised that sooner or later employers, in both the national and provincial press, would want to introduce direct entry systems from the editorial and advertising areas. The pace of technological change within the newspaper industry was quickening and the problem would return. The NGA realised that coming to terms with direct entry systems was inevitable. It was appreciated, especially by the NGA leadership, that the TNL victory had at worst delayed this day.

The second lesson the NGA learned from the TNL disputes was the importance of keeping its members involved in the dispute fully informed and having the maximum consultation with them. The NGA realised that it could not assume that members would become involved in long disputes over issues that had implications for the wider membership unless the union was prepared to pay them reasonable dispute benefit. The heavy involvement with those directly involved in a crucial dispute and the provision of meaningful levels of dispute benefit have characterised the NGA's approach in all the disputes considered in this chapter. They are important ways in which the union has assisted its members and limited the influence of political groups whose motivation is the achievement of political and economic change by revolutionary methods. The acceptance of these responsibilities by the NGA has made a significant contribution, in all the major disputes in which it has been involved in over the past forty years, towards the maintenance of morale and solidarity of those directly involved in the dispute.

A third lesson from the TNL dispute was that the whole membership needs to be kept involved with such issues and not just those who are immediately involved. That is why the NGA had a series of meetings with its members employed in Thomson regional newspapers who were willing to become involved in industrial action in support of their colleagues at TNL and in support of the vital principles over the introduction of technology involved in that dispute.

A fourth lesson from the dispute was the value of the NGA's international contacts. The support the union received throughout the dispute from the IGF, and in particular from Druck und Papier, effectively prevented TNL from producing a newspaper in Frankfurt and elsewhere on the continent. As a result of its action, Druck und Papier was fined the sum of £15,000 by the German Labour Court. The NGA however agreed to pay this fine.

THE MESSENGER DISPUTE[12]

This dispute was of such fundamental nature to the union that at one stage all the NGA's industrial national officers were instructed to concentrate solely on the prosecution of the dispute. The issues at stake were fundamental for not only the NGA but the TUC and the wider labour movement (see Chapter 10). The use of the 1980 and 1982 Employment Acts in the dispute illustrated how it was almost impossible to run a successful lawful dispute in the printing industry.

In early 1982 a dispute arose between Fineward Ltd, a subsidiary of the Messenger Newspaper Group, and the NGA over a new wages agreement. Nobody would have predicted that this was the seed of a dispute which exploded into national importance some eighteen months later. It became a dispute in which the Employment Acts of 1980 and 1982 were tested, the NGA's funds sequestered, and differences emerged within the TUC over its policy of opposition to industrial relations legislation. Both sides viewed themselves as defending fundamental principles. The NGA's position was that typesetting should remain a unionised activity, that employers should abide by agreements, and to defend, by all industrial means, its members 'victimised' by an employer. The Messenger Group's central position was the right of individual employees to join or not to join a trade union and that unions behave within the law.

In 1974 Mr Eddie Shah, owner of the Messenger Newspaper Group, began to publish the Sale and Altrincham free paper, which was printed at Cumbria Newspapers, Carlisle, by NGA members under closed shop agreements. In 1979 Mr Shah opened his own typesetting company, Fineward Ltd, in Stockport. He hired eight NGA members and signed a closed shop agreement with the NGA in January 1980. The agreement provided for a 37½ hour working week, and earnings of £155 per week. Meanwhile the Messenger Group opened negotiations with the NGA over conditions for a new typesetting plant at Bury. In March 1982 the company signed a closed shop agreement for this establishment, but failed to reach agreement on hours and pay vis-à-vis Stockport. The NGA wanted parity of conditions, fearing that otherwise there would be an incentive for the firm to switch work from Stockport to Bury. The company wanted to pay £40 per week less at Bury than at Stockport. In April 1982 the company reneged on the closed shop agreement at Bury and began to recruit non-union labour. The company also opened a printing plant at Warrington and in 1982/3 began recruiting labour for the plant. The NGA was concerned over the recruitment of non-union labour at these two establishments. The Messenger Group arranged for the NGA to meet with these non-unionists, but these meetings held in April 1983 proved fruitless. The NGA claimed that the employees had been hired only after their anti-union credentials had been established. In June 1983 Bury and Warrington employees of the company voted unanimously to reject representation by the NGA.

The existence of non-union typesetting and printing was viewed by the NGA as contrary to the operation across the provincial newspaper industry of an industry-wide closed shop and the obligation on its members not to handle work going to or coming from non-union sources. It also feared that the continuation of this situation might give encouragement to other employers. Following unsuccessful attempts to resolve the problem and the union's discovery that the company was advertising the jobs of the existing NGA employees at Stockport, the union wrote to the Messenger Group on 9 June 1983 saying that if agreement could not be reached by 22 June than it would enter into an official dispute with the company, withdraw its eight members from the Stockport establishment and instruct all NGA members to 'black' work emanating from or intended for any of the companies in the Messenger Group. On 4 July 1983 six NGA members at Fineward Ltd – Phil Daniels, Neil McAllister, Stan Hart, Alan Royston, John Noble and Kevin Shervin – withdrew their labour and were dismissed. The Messenger Group continued to produce its publications with the assistance of non-unionists, management personnel and, initially, NUJ members.

During talks with ACAS, the NGA indicated a willingness to accept an initial 50 per cent membership at Bury and Warrington with a post-entry closed shop arrangement for all new employees. This was a major concession by the NGA since it meant that the union would tolerate its members working with non-unionists. ACAS, however, suggested that the NGA consider a 50 per cent membership across all three of the company's establishments. The company rejected both these proposals. The NGA's reaction was to ask the NUJ to instruct its Stockport members to refuse to supply editorial copy to non-unionists. When the NUJ did this, the Messenger Group obtained a writ under the 1980 Employment Act instructing the NUJ to inform its members to supply copy to non-unionists. Although the NUJ refused to comply with the injunction, its members employed by Messenger worked normally.

The next development in the dispute was the Messenger Group's legal action against the NGA for exerting pressure on its advertisers and suppliers and for its instruction to its members to 'black' all origination work to the company. The NGA had written to advertisers and suppliers to the Messenger Group on 5 September asking them to refuse to advertise in and to refuse to supply goods to the group during the dispute. Using one of these letters to an advertiser, the company obtained a writ to restrain the NGA from continuing such behaviour. On 14 October 1983 the High Court issued two injunctions against the NGA. One ordered the union to stop pressurising advertisers to withdraw from advertising in the company's papers and to cease 'blacking' origination work to the company. The second was granted against secondary picketing by NGA members at Bury and Warrington since they were picketing away from their own workplace, a practice that was outlawed by the 1980 Employment Act.

The NGA did not comply with the injunctions. On the contrary, it intensified picketing outside the Messenger Group premises at Warrington. The company responded on 9 November 1983 by obtaining a writ of sequestration against the NGA for its breaching of the October injunctions. The Court would not grant a writ, but fined the NGA £50,000 for contempt of court. ACAS intervened in the dispute and on 21 November an agreement was reached providing for a post-entry closed shop throughout the group, for the NGA to be allowed facilities to recruit existing non-unionists, for all present employees to have the right not to join the union and a moratorium of eight weeks during which pay and conditions would be examined, especially in those areas where the NGA claimed non-unionists were receiving less than the recognised rates of pay for the provincial newspaper industry. The sticking point, however, was that the Messenger Group refused to reinstate the six dismissed NGA members. The union was convinced that the recognition issue was now resolved and that the only issue was the reinstatement of its six dismissed members. In an attempt to resolve this outstanding issue, the union intensified its picketing at Warrington. Nevertheless, the Messenger Group continued to print and distribute all its newspaper titles.

In late November the company brought a writ of sequestration against the NGA for its continued contempt of court. On 25 November the High Court fined the union £100,000 and ordered the sequestration of its total assets. In response to this, NGA members employed on national newspapers took 'spontaneous' industrial action and no national newspapers were printed over the weekend of 25/26 November. The national newspaper owners considered this induced action and issued dismissal notices to all their NGA employees. In the event, only six papers carried out the threat. Four papers broke 'ranks' and published normally on 28 November.[13] Notwithstanding this disunity, all the national dailies and Sunday newspapers sought writs for damages against the NGA for loss of their editions on Saturday and Sunday. However, over a period of some years these writs were subsequently all withdrawn. Following the 'Fleet Street' stoppages, ACAS brought the two sides together, but talks broke down when the NGA refused to accept the Messenger Group's proposal that the reinstatement issue go to binding arbitration, which would also consider the views of the company's non-union staff.

Although the night of 29/30 November saw a picket of some 4,000 people outside the Warrington plant, police ensured that there was little disruption to the distribution of the group's papers. The company returned to the Court, ACAS again intervened and the NGA offered to call off picketing for seven days to allow time for a negotiated settlement if the company would drop its proposed Court action. Although the company refused, the Court agreed to an adjournment of the hearing on condition the NGA lifted mass picketing for the same period. The Messenger Group agreed to talks but only on the condition that they were conducted in writing. Despite thirty-seven hours of negotiations, they broke down on 9 December. In an attempt to resolve the issue of the six dismissed employees, the company proposed to give them all the equipment owned by Fineward Ltd to operate a typesetting and artwork business as a cooperative, to provide for a period of twelve months some work for the firm and to provide assistance in setting up appropriate management/administrative control systems, etc. As an alternative it proposed the sale of Fineward Ltd and the re-engagement of the six by the new owner. Both proposals were unacceptable to the NGA since they would not achieve the reinstatement of its members by an employer who had dismissed them for carrying out NGA policy.

On 9 December 1983 the Court case proceeded and a further contempt of court fine of £525,000 was imposed on the NGA. The NGA called upon all its members to undertake a twenty-four-hour stoppage throughout the printing industry on Wednesday 14 December and asked for a 'statement of support' from the TUC (see Chapter 10). The TUC Employment Policy and Organisation Committee (EPOC) pledged its support, but on 14 December the General Council rejected the recommendation. In light of the TUC's refusal to provide even a statement of support, and the industrial and legal implications this decision carried with it and the subsequent confusion this caused, the NGA called off the proposed twenty-four-hour strike.

On 18 January 1984 the NGA agreed to purge its contempt of court and abide by the injunctions imposed on it. The union reluctantly took this decision but knew that without funds it could not maintain its essential work or protect the interests of the whole membership of the union. Limited picketing resumed at Stockport in January and moral and physical support of the 'Stockport Six' was given by national officers and national councillors joining them. However, on 24 May 1984, and with the full agreement of the members concerned, the NGA concluded that no useful purpose could be served by continuing the picketing at Stockport. The six members were placed into alternative employment in the industry. The Messenger Group went back to Court in February 1984 claiming compensation for damage to its business as a result of the NGA's actions. It was subsequently awarded £131,000 in damages, of which £10,000 was for 'aggravated damages' and £25,000 for 'exemplary damages'.[14]

The Messenger dispute was about industrial issues. The NGA was seeking the reinstatement of six members who had been sacked for upholding union policy, recognition from the company, that the Messenger Group honour the agreements it had made with NGA until they were changed by mutual consent, and the defence of wages and conditions established in the provincial newspaper industry. The General Secretary Elect, Tony Dubbins, told the 1984 Delegate Meeting:

This was a direct attack upon the NGA and it was brought about by Shah's refusal to honour signed agreements, his victimisation of our six members who had the audacity to defend their employment, their wages and conditions and his willingness to use the Tory anti-union laws. What started out as a small local dispute was, by Shah's use of the Tory laws, turned into a dispute of national proportions and ended up with High Court writs and the sequestration of the union's funds and assets.[15]

The dispute was not about a confrontation with the law in that the NGA deliberately set out to test the Employment Acts of 1980 and 1982, about challenging an elected government or about forcing employees to become union members. If this had been the case the NGA would not have made the concession to the company that NGA members work side by side with existing non-unionists. The NGA was defending fundamental trade union principles and utilised every possible industrial sanction to defend these principles. If the proposed one-day strike had failed in its objective, the NGA would have had to reconsider its objectives, but it was the view of the NGA that the 24 hour stoppage would demonstrate the NGA's determination to the industry, and bring with it immense pressure on the Messenger Group for a negotiated settlement. In the event, as we have seen, the General Council felt unable to support the NGA's proposed action because the TUC funds would be put at risk and there was no point in supporting 'illegal' industrial action if it was unlikely to achieve its industrial ends.

The issues in the Messenger dispute were too fundamental for the NGA to ignore, yet it was entering the unknown. The dispute was conducted by use of the traditional industrial practices of the NGA, which clashed with the provisions of the Employment Acts of 1980 and 1982. The three injunctions against the NGA obtained by the company – against secondary picketing, against the union's instruction to its members not to supply origination work, and against pressure on advertisers – went to the heart of its traditional industrial practices. The dispute illustrated how the Employment Acts of 1980 and 1982 could be used by a small employer to introduce, and maintain, non-union members, to dismiss trade unionists and to undermine the ability of a trade union to restrain an employer.

A fear of the NGA was that other employers, particularly in the newspaper field, would use the legislation to reduce NGA influence and/or de-unionise their plants. This was particularly so given events happening in the provincial newspaper field where, in 1982, the Newspaper Society launched its 'Project Breakthrough' initiative designed to introduce single keystroking in the provincial press by the end of 1984. Single keystroking would transfer origination work from the composing room to editorial and advertising areas, which were largely unorganised or had few union members. Some NS members were threatening that if single keystroking was not introduced by 1984 they would set up new plants employing non-unionised labour. Against this background the NGA saw no alternative but to pursue the dispute against the Messenger Group with all its resources. A successful outcome was important, as otherwise there would be an incentive to NS members to follow suit. If there was not to be a successful outcome, the NGA had to demonstrate to other employers the 'price' they would have to pay for such an outcome. In the Messenger dispute the NGA illustrated the cost implications to other employers of following the Messenger Group's behaviour. It had demonstrated that the union would, and could, deploy all its resources to support those directly involved in a dispute and could call upon assistance from the whole membership. Immediately following the end of the Messenger dispute, few newspaper employers sought to de-unionise their plants. The way in which the dispute had been conducted by the NGA influenced the less hawkish members of the NS and was a factor in the 'Project Breakthrough' objective of a national enabling agreement for the introduction of new technology being abandoned in favour of a company-by-company approach.

The Messenger dispute demonstrated that no one union, however big and strong and however loyal and determined its members might be, could adequately defend itself in isolation from other trade unions both within and outwith the printing industry. Nevertheless, the NGA did not fight in total isolation. It received support from the T&GWU, which kept the NGA afloat financially when its funds were sequestered, the NUJ and Sogat, and a number of other unions also. Whilst many other trade unionists came to Warrington to demonstrate their support for the Stockport Six and were at times brutally attacked by the police. However, it was important that the NGA's proposed one-day strike throughout the printing industry in December 1983 was not done in isolation from the wider trade union movement. A statement of support from the TUC was very important symbolically. Unfortunately for the NGA, this was the very point when the TUC's policy towards the Employment Acts of 1980 and 1982 became compromised.

It was the use of the Employment Acts which gave the Messenger Group/NGA dispute, otherwise minor in terms of numbers of workers involved and working days lost, its importance. It illustrated that, by the use of injunctions, contempt of court fines and sequestration, etc., an employer could act successfully even against a trade union like the NGA, which was perceived amongst employers and trade unions as a powerful trade union that more often than not was successful in its industrial disputes. The law had been used to substantially curtail the degree to which unions could lawfully ask other NGA members and other trade unions to take sympathetic action. Sequestration had been shown to be an effective way of tying up union funds. The NGA could not function properly. The commissioners administrating the sequestration order froze all traceable assets from the smallest chapel bank account to its trust funds. The sequestration order was rigidly applied and the NGA, in addition to being responsible for paying the commissioners' weekly expenses of up to £20,000, was unable to have access to funds to pay staff, pay provident benefits or continue legitimate industrial activities. The NGA survived under sequestration through the inventiveness of its members in the branches, together with financial and administrative assistance from other unions.

The dispute was also significant in other respects. The police had been more effective than in previous mass picketing situations in ensuring that the employer received essential production supplies and got its product to the market place. At Warrington the police used Police Support Units (PSU) to undermine the effectiveness of mass picketing. These techniques were to be used with equal effect in the coal mining dispute of 1984/5 and the Wapping dispute of 1986/7. The dispute also showed the imbalance of the 1980 picketing laws, which permitted employers to transfer work from an establishment where a dispute existed to another establishment which it then became unlawful to picket. In the Messenger dispute the only place the NGA could legally picket was the company's empty factory at Stockport. The key to imposing effective sanctions on the company was its Warrington plant, into which went supplies and out of which came newspapers.

THE *WOLVERHAMPTON EXPRESS AND STAR* AND *KENT MESSENGER* DISPUTES[16]

Early in 1982 the Newspaper Society launched 'Project Breakthrough', the aim of which was to secure a national enabling agreement with the print unions by 1984. The agreement was to provide for the introduction of new technology at chapel level in line with nationally agreed guidelines. Although acceptance of direct entry was a priority objective for the NS, its wider aim was to give the industry freedom to implement all innovations that would improve its competitiveness. The NGA challenged the economic basis of Project Breakthrough and argued that any agreement on the implementation of direct entry systems required guarantees on reductions in hours, improvement in holidays, sick pay and pension schemes and the maintenance of the closed shop. The NGA wanted the unions to develop a common approach to the acceptance of the introduction of technological change as the means of preventing NS members from introducing changes on the employers' preferred terms. To this end, in March 1984 the NGA produced a document entitled *The Way Forward – New Technology in the Provincial Newspaper Industry: An NGA 82 Initiative*, based on the principle that where new technology is introduced the entire origination area should be viewed as a single entity and the total workforce should be distributed equally amongst the three trade unions involved, i.e. NGA, Sogat and the NUJ. The document stipulated that typesetting should remain unionised and that only members of the three unions should be allowed to operate typesetting equipment. In the document, the NGA was saying that it would accept the introduction of new technology if the employers would accept a continued unionised industry.

In July 1984 the NS rejected the *Way Forward*, arguing that it was a denial of human rights, contrary to the law, an attempt to establish a tripartite closed shop, and an effort by the NGA to preserve its institutional existence. It also strongly rejected the proposal that only unionised labour should work the new technology. At the same time, the NS presented its draft enabling agreement, which sought local negotiations for the introduction of new technology, for duplicate operations to be eliminated, for revised disputes procedures, for employee redeployment if the company's economic circumstances warranted it, and for transferred employees to receive the pay and conditions of the area to which they were relocated. The proposed enabling agreement contained none of the safeguards for the introduction of new technology which the NGA and other print unions were seeking. In December 1984 both sides accepted that the circumstances of individual newspapers varied so much that negotiations over the implementation of new technology should shift to the plant level.

By this time the NGA had not succeeded in getting the NUJ and Sogat(82) to agree a common approach with it to the implementation of new technology. Talks with Sogat(82) had produced an agreement in November 1984 over membership rights in advertising departments as a condition for joint acceptance of new technology (see Chapter 6). However, this was rejected by the Sogat(82) national executive. Attempts by the NGA to persuade the NUJ to agree to a joint understanding on the introduction of new technology were rejected by the journalists.

At the beginning of 1985 the NGA found itself having to protect its own interests and make agreements with employers on new technology independently of the NUJ and Sogat. The two provincial newspaper groups ready to implement direct entry equipment in early 1985 were Portsmouth and Sunderland Newspapers and Midland News Association, which was the owner of the *Wolverhampton Express and Star*. Following the inability of the NGA to persuade the other unions to adopt a joint policy, and therefore forced to protect its own interests independently of those of other printing unions, in early 1985 the NGA signed at Portsmouth and Sunderland Newspapers the first editorial direct entry agreement in the provincial press. It provided for no compulsory redundancies amongst NGA members and some redeployment into the editorial area where they would retain membership of the NGA, which would continue to negotiate for them. The NUJ objected to NGA negotiating rights in the editorial department and called its members at the company out on strike. NGA members crossed NUJ picket lines. The dispute ended on 30 March 1985, but the NGA retained its bargaining rights.

The NGA dispute with the *Wolverhampton Express and Star* was expected by the provincial newspaper industry to be an important, if not *the*, dispute that would test the NGA's ability to influence the method and rate of introduction of new technology. The company's management style was aggressive and confrontational. In November 1984 it announced it would produce an all-electronic newspaper by 1986. In subsequent negotiations it became apparent that its objective went far beyond the elimination of the second keystroke. Its proposal included the end of the closed shop, severe limitation of the NGA's right to represent its members, significant reductions in earnings for many members, with limited alternative jobs being offered. Even before the chapels had time to consider these proposals, the company precipitated the dispute in February 1985 by imposing direct input from the advertising department at the *Wolverhampton Express and Star*. When 100 NGA members refused to handle the work, they were locked out, as subsequently were a further seventy-two members at the Midland News Association's other businesses, the *Shropshire Star*, Ketley, and Precision Colour Printers, Telford. The NGA invoked the disputes procedure and sought a return to the status quo. The company rejected this and attempts to involve the NS resulted in that organisation advising the NGA that it considered the disputes procedure to be voluntary. The company insisted that direct input material be handled whilst talks were held. It was on the fundamental principle that the NGA would not accept that major changes in working practices could be made without consultation and agreement that talks finally failed.

The subsequent involvement of ACAS failed to resolve the dispute and the NGA continued to picket the company. NGA attempts to persuade the *Wolverhampton Express and Star* to negotiate an agreed basis for the introduction of direct entry systems were undermined in three ways. First, the NUJ, resentful of Portsmouth, and Sogat refused to respect its picket lines. Second, in April 1985 the NUJ members working on the paper agreed a deal with management providing additional wage increases to operate direct entry from the editorial area. Third, nineteen NGA members returned to work following an ultimatum from the company that the alternative would be dismissal. When they were dismissed, the NGA paid them a dispute benefit of £160 per week in light of the implications for the NGA's whole provincial newspaper membership in terms of the methods and conditions by which employers introduced direct entry systems.

A further problem was that the dispute again brought the NGA into dispute with the law. Press Computer Systems (PCS), a subsidiary of the Midland News Association, obtained an injunction ordering the NGA not to take any action against PCS or its products. Midland News Association also obtained an injunction that the NGA should hold a secret ballot after chapel meetings had voted overwhelmingly to refuse to handle work from non-union sources without agreement. The NGA was fined £500 for this breach. Considerable pressure was placed on the NGA when it was fined £7,500 for each of two breaches of an injunction restraining secondary actions.

Throughout the dispute the company continued to produce its publications. In the autumn of 1985 the NGA decided that continued picketing at Wolverhampton, Ketley and Telford would not assist in obtaining a satisfactory conclusion to the dispute. It lifted the picketing and placed the 172 members involved in alternative employment.

Another important 'new technology' dispute involving the NGA was at the *Kent Messenger*. In December 1984 negotiations were proceeding with the company for the introduction of a PCS advertising system. The company were insisting that contributed copy should be input by advertising staff. It went ahead with its installation and, when the NGA chapels objected, 144 members were dismissed by the *Kent Messenger*. The company continued to produce its titles and the NUJ and Sogat failed to respect NGA picket lines. Whilst the NUJ members performed their normal duties, Sogat members deliberately went out of their way to undermine the NGA position in the dispute. They performed typesetting jobs and distributed work that had been produced by non-union printers, including the Messenger Group. The prosecution of the *Kent Messenger* dispute continued with picketing and demonstration until January 1986 when the NGA decided to cease picketing and place the 144 members involved in alternative employment.

These two particular disputes were seen by many employers as crucial tests of the NGA's ability to influence the method of introduction of new technology in the provincial newspaper industry. Although the NGA had not 'won' the disputes, some gains flowed from them. The NGA had shown other employers that it was prepared to back its members with all its resources in resisting unilateral imposition of new technology. The NGA paid out nearly £5 million in dispute and unemployment benefit to those involved in the *Wolverhampton and Express and Star* dispute and £1.1 million to those in the *Kent Messenger* dispute. The NGA had demonstrated to other employers 'the costs' they could incur if they were to follow the *Wolverhampton Express and Star* and *Kent Messenger* examples. In considering the introduction of front-end systems, provincial newspaper employers would have to take these costs into account. Events showed that few employers immediately copied Wolverhampton and Kent, but it later became apparent that this was because they were not at that time as prepared as those companies were.

A second gain from these two disputes was that they illustrated to NGA members that no one print union on its own could determine the manner and conditions by which new technology would be introduced into the provincial newspaper industry. They saw that the support of the other print unions was essential. The General Secretary, Tony Dubbins, told the 1986 Delegate Meeting.

> Our members in newspapers I believe, realise that it is now not possible to successfully prosecute an industrial dispute in isolation. It is no good the NGA being 100% solid if their colleagues in Sogat/NUJ are going to step in and do their jobs.[17]

A further gain from these two disputes was that the NUJ realised what the NGA had long argued, namely, that if the two unions could not agree a joint basis for the introduction of new technology then provincial newspaper companies would simply play them off against each other to management's advantage. The bitterness caused by the NGA crossing NUJ picket lines at Portsmouth and the journalists in turn crossing NGA picket lines at Wolverhampton and Kent was considerable. The disputes had been salutary lessons to both unions. However, although painful, the experiences did more than anything else to bring about in October 1985 the 'Joint Accord' between the NGA and NUJ, under which both unions agreed that direct entry from the editorial department would be accepted on the basis of a prior joint agreement with an employer and that negotiations would be undertaken jointly by both unions at national officer level with branch and chapel involvement (see Chapter 6).

Following the 'Accord', many employers peacefully negotiated the introduction of new technology and by May 1987 the NGA and the NUJ had jointly signed sixty-seven direct entry agreements with provincial press employers. Their main features included an acceptance by the NGA that the number of compositors would be reduced, no compulsory redundancies, direct inputting by journalists and advertising staff, that contributed copy be typeset by NGA members, that displaced compositors be retrained and redeployed in the editorial department, earnings protection for transferred NGA members, and in some instances improvements for remaining compositors.

However, the downside of the two disputes could not be ignored, especially the defeat at the *Kent Messenger*. Although it had been expected that the *Wolverhampton Express and Star* dispute would be the one that would determine the outcome of the new technology battle in the provincial press, this turned out not to be the case. It was an important dispute, but the company was not a typical provincial newspaper employer. Its management was aggressive, had no compunction about using, if necessary, the 1980s' employment legislation and had the support of being part of a wider group – the Midland News Association. The Wolverhampton management sensed the strained NUJ/Sogat/NGA relationships of the early to mid-1980s and realised the weakness of the NGA chapel in that it contained many long-serving employees most of whom were more management- than NGA-oriented and who accepted the management's paternalistic approach. *Wolverhampton Express and Star* anticipated that these features would reduce the ability of the NGA to be effective amongst its members. The NGA also recognised that it might be difficult to get some of the Wolverhampton chapels to take action. Indeed it is possible that support was given only because management overstepped the mark by issuing an ultimatum to long-serving and loyal employees that if they did not accept direct entry from the advertising area on the following Monday they would be dismissed.

The *Kent Messenger* was quite different. An important aspect of this dispute was that the PCS the company wished to introduce were made by a subsidiary of Midland News Association. In order to put pressure on the *Wolverhampton Express and Star* there was a view within the NGA that the union should refuse to make agreements on PCS throughout the industry and that this would encourage employers to use alternative systems. There was an alternative view that this approach was too optimistic and employers would continue to buy PCS systems in support of Wolverhampton. The former view prevailed and so *Kent Messenger* was to be a test case on this issue for the whole industry. The company was a typical small provincial newspaper producer of the kind that dominated the industry. It was not part of a larger group and its management had no initial apparent desire to push the NGA out of its plant or to use the new employment laws. The NGA chapel at the *Kent Messenger* was strong and every member answered the industrial action instruction. The Kent branch was also a strong organisation. In short, the NGA organisation in Kent was almost the complete opposite to that at Wolverhampton, as were the attitudes of the two employers. The *Kent Messenger* dispute showed that a typical employer in the provincial press even where strong NGA chapels existed, could produce its newsapers and produce them without any NGA labour. In this sense the *Kent Messenger* defeat was far more significant for the NGA than that at Wolverhampton. Of all the industrial defeats of the NGA in both national and provincial newspapers in the 1980s the most significant was undoubtedly its loss at the *Kent Messenger*.

A major factor in the defeat had been the behaviour of the NUJ and Sogat. The Accord subsequently dealt with the NUJ problem, but the failure to conclude a similar understanding with Sogat with respect to direct inputting was always going to be a problem for the NGA in retaining contributed advertising and editorial copy for its members. Things were made additionally difficult in that Sogat was prepared to assist employers in undermining this NGA objective. The failure to reach agreement with Sogat was also responsible for reducing the number of agreements whereby contributed advertising copy was retained by the NGA. The NGA/NUJ Accord came under challenge from a number of provincial newspaper groups, including the *Liverpool Post and Echo*, encouraged by the agreements that Sogat was prepared to reach and supported by assurances from Sogat officials that they would assist companies that found themselves in difficulties with the NGA and the NUJ.[18]

Armed with these assurances from Sogat, provincial newspaper employers began to challenge the NGA's retention of contributed copy, which they had initially conceded to the NGA to eliminate double keystroking. This led to a number of unsuccessful disputes in support of NGA retention of contributed copy under the terms of the NGA-NUJ Accord. These setbacks, exampled by the *South Wales Argus* dispute, led the NGA to review this policy. It concluded that, if employers could impose a cut-rate inputting section with Sogat's support, it would be better to accede to the demands for the establishment of NGA inputting sections, which would at least maintain an NGA influence and involvement. Initial agreements established NGA membership as an employment requirement and limited the number and role of inputters. Unfortunately, the NGA was unable to maintain these standards in the face of opposition from certain employers.

Companies used the possible implications of equal pay legislation as justification for reducing NGA wage rates. This action by companies was designed to limit the ability of new – usually female – non-union employees in the origination area to identify NGA rates as the benchmark for equal pay claims.

In a number of houses, managements imposed wage cuts. For

example, at the *Oxford Mail*, part of the Westminster Press Group, NGA members were given notice of their house agreement being terminated and were offered enhanced 'voluntary' severance terms. At the same time, an alternative workforce was recruited at rates some £100 a week lower. Those who did not 'volunteer' not only were to be paid at lower rates when the notice of termination of the house agreement expired but were advised that they would be made redundant on the minimum state terms. Not surprisingly, when faced with this choice, the majority of NGA members saw no alternative but to 'volunteer'. It was clear that NGA inputting sections would not satisfy employers that were also seeking deunionisation and wage cuts as protection against equal pay claims, and the NGA decided to drop its policy on inputting sections. The *Oxford Mail* events are just one example of what became a common occurrence in the provincial newspaper industry.

The *Wolverhampton Express and Star* and the *Kent Messenger* disputes had enabled the NGA to secure the retention of contributed copy for its members when direct entry systems were introduced from the editorial and advertising area. However, the failure of the NGA and Sogat(82) to make an accommodation with each other over the conditions for the acceptance of technological change considerably lessened the ability of the NGA to sustain this policy in the longer run. By 1988 it was clear that the NGA could not sustain the provincial newspaper new technology battle. With it went a considerable change in the balance of bargaining in favour of the employer, a reduction in the terms and conditions of employment of the NGA members, acceptance of changed working practices that would have been unbelievable a decade before, a reluctance on the part of NGA provincial newspaper members to take any industrial action to protect their own employment and an even greater reluctance to consider taking supportive action for their colleagues elsewhere. The General Secretary, Tony Dubbins, summed up the situation when he told the 1988 Delegate Meeting.

> Regrettably we have been proved right. The Newspaper Society's 'Project Breakthrough' was not, and never was, about the introduction and use of the 'single keystroke'. It was about cutting wages and conditions, to produce more profit, and the deunionisation of the origination side of the industry. NGA members who have had the same employer for 20, 30 or 40 years were sickened by the callous way in which they were forced out of work – not because of redundancy or even work

transferred to other areas, but because employers were looking to replace them by cheap, and usually female, labour receiving up to £100 below the negotiated rate.

Mr President, it gives me no pleasure, it has to be said, that many employers relied on the co-operation of other trade unions and trade unionists to undermine the NGA and to transfer traditional NGA work to other poorly paid areas that usually were non-union, or trade union in name only.[19]

THE NEWS INTERNATIONAL DISPUTE

In 1985 the question of a move of the printing of the *News of the World* and *Sun* to Wapping was discussed on an informal basis on a number of occasions with News International management, despite the company's complaints about its inability to reach agreements regarding Wapping and its Glasgow plant for the printing of the *Sun*. The main complaint as far as the Wapping plant was concerned was Sogat's attitude to staffing in the publishing room and that of the NGA in respect of claims for involvement in day maintenance in the *Sun* machine room. Even when the NGA's claim to day maintenance in the *Sun* machine room was dropped, News International showed no inclination to discuss seriously with the unions moving to Wapping. The situation was clouded by a dispute that arose in the *Sun* machine room in April 1985 concerning plate breaks.

By mid-1985 concern was growing about the situation at Wapping and there were rumours of staff who were not traditional printers being recruited to the plant. In response to questions about this the management said there were specialist installation, building and maintenance people who were preparing the plant for use. Rumours grew stronger but in July 1985 Rupert Murdoch, head of News International, said that while he was in the country in September he would talk to the unions about the Wapping plant. However, beyond that point, when meetings were held with News International management it was denied that there were arrangements in hand to operate the Wapping plant without members of the printing unions. The company consistently said that the people there were electricians on short contracts rewiring and wiring in new controls on the printing machines and Goss engineers making ready the machines.

On 30 September 1985 Rupert Murdoch informed the print unions that Wapping would produce a new London evening paper, which, if successful, would be expanded into a national twenty-four-hour daily paper. News International entered into immediate negotiations with the print unions with the aim of reaching an agreement covering the production of the *London Post* by 25 December 1985. The negotiations actually began in October 1985, when News International presented a document that contained four fundamental points that were not negotiable. These were a legally binding agreement, no industrial action in any circumstances, the unfettered right to manage, and no closed shop. In the subsequent discussions, management explained that the unfettered right to manage meant that the management could make any decision without consultation with anyone's views on the unions' side or any relevant agreements.

It was also made clear that NGA members currently employed at TNL and in Bouverie Street on the *Sun* and the *News of the World* would not automatically transfer their employment to Wapping and that the management would have the sole right to select the staff. The agreement was simply to give the NGA recognition, leaving it to recruit the employees engaged by the management. This was underpinned by the demand that there be no closed shop and that the agreement be legally binding, with its provisions being written into individual contracts so that, should unconstitutional action take place, not only could the union be held liable but also so would the members involved in the action. The negotiations continued, but it was clear that nothing the unions offered would enable an agreement to be reached.

During this period evidence started to come to light indicating that a very significant recruitment exercise was underway for non-traditional staff for the Wapping Plant. This was being secretly undertaken through the Southampton branch of the electricians union, the EETPU.

A further meeting took place with Rupert Murdoch, following a meeting with the TUC General Secretary, who had already warned the electricians' union not to sign any single-union agreement with News International. He also advised the unions to draw up proposals for a joint approach to News International. In the course of the meeting with Mr Murdoch the unions learned that the EETPU had broken ranks and had no objections to News International's demands. In a final effort to reach agreement, the General Secretaries met with Bill O'Neill, but during the meeting the company requested to see EETPU national officials, as it felt that, on the issue of management rights, sufficient progress had been made to warrant further meetings. These were clearly developments against the advice of the TUC General Secretary. After the Christmas period, the NGA, Sogat and the Amalgamated Union of Engineering Workers (AUEW) agreed to ballot their members for industrial action, and these were held on 13 January 1986.

At the same time, the unions, in conjunction with the TUC, agreed fresh proposals for an agreement with News International. The basis of these was recognition of the unions involved in Wapping with provisions for a new disputes procedure containing binding arbitration, unilaterally triggered. On 19 January 1986 News International rejected these proposals and two days later the result of the ballot for industrial action was announced as:

	For	Against
NGA	843	117
Sogat	3,534	752

On 23 January came a bombshell. Mr Murdoch told the unions that, of the 5,500 jobs in News International, only 'several' hundred would be kept in Gray's Inn Road and Bouverie Street and then only until the existing agreements terminated at the end of July 1986. Additionally, the unions were told that the company would only pay statutory redundancy terms to those people who would no longer be required. On 24 January 1986 the strike began and the company issued letters of dismissal to all union members. The company threatened the journalists employed on its four titles with instant dismissal if they did not go to Wapping, but to sweeten the pill it offered them an increase of £2,000 per year. At the same time as picketing started at Gray's Inn Road, Bouverie Street and Wapping, the complaints against the EETPU put forward by the NGA, Sogat, AUEW and the NUJ were considered by the TUC (see Chapter 10).

During the first phase of the dispute, News International attempted to get its normal 2 million copies of the *News of the World* printed by Express Newspapers in Manchester, but NGA members there refused to handle the work. The company then made arrangements to print the *News of the World* in its plant at Kinning Park, Glasgow, which had also been staffed by people recruited for the company by the EETPU. The NGA, together with other unions, mounted demonstrations at Kinning Park. The print unions also called upon trade unionists to boycott the *Sun*, the *News of the World*, *The Times* and the *Sunday Times*.

Although efforts to halt the printing of the *Times Supplements* were initially successful, the NGA was unable to sustain the 'blacking' when on 14 February 1986 the union was fined £25,000 for not stopping the boycott, even though it had been lifted shortly before the hearing. An injunction granted by the Courts against Sogat for action taken against the distribution of News International's titles through the wholesalers was ignored and on 10 February all Sogat's assets were sequestrated, added to which they were fined £25,000 for contempt of court. On 4 March the Court ordered the seizure of all Sogat officials' cars and at the same time threatened to close all its offices.

The combined activity involving demonstrations and picketing at TNT depots[20] and newspaper wholesalers in the provinces led on 12 March 1986 to an informal meeting between the unions and News International. This meeting was followed by several others, and at one on 4 April News International offered the unions the old Thomson House part of the building in Gray's Inn Road together with most of the equipment it contained. The offer included the transfer of the contract that would run until January 1988 to print the *Guardian*. At the meeting the unions put forward proposals for recognition and employment in Wapping. A further meeting took place on 14 April when the unions enlarged upon their proposals. The unions wanted an agreement whereby the company vested trade union recognition in the News International national joint committee, an annual comprehensive agreement, a conciliation and arbitration procedure providing for binding arbitration at the request of one party, and a commitment to avoid breaks in production, to flexibility, to consultation machinery and single-status agreements.

The company took the proposals away but on 17 April revised its own offer on the old Times printing presses. The premises would print any newspapers but News International would retain ownership, leasing the plant to the unions at a peppercorn rent. The company offered to pay minimum statutory redundancy pay to those dismissed amongst the 5,500 who did not find employment at Gray's Inn Road. The unions' response to the original offer of the printing plant was to allow it to remain on the table as part of the negotiations but not as a substitute for the jobs of the dismissed workers or for union recognition at Wapping and Kinning Park. The company unilaterally set a deadline of 7 May for the unions to accept its offer and made clear that the offer of minimum state redundancy money was an *ex gratia* payment and not an acceptance by the company of any legal or other obligations. On 22 April News International rejected the unions' proposals of 14 April but extended its offer of Gray's Inn Road, plus compensation, to 30 April.

One of the problems throughout the dispute was that necessary support did not materialise, despite the efforts of the various union officials. In the first eighteen weeks of the dispute 100 journalists left Wapping but, despite the efforts of officials of the T&GWU, their members at TNT continued to cross picket lines in both London and

Glasgow. Throughout the dispute the morale of the NGA members involved remained high. They regularly attended picket lines and mounted demonstrations during the evening and early hours of the morning at Wapping, Gray's Inn Road and Bouverie Street.

Over the weekend of 23–25 May detailed talks between News International management and the unions involved, with the assistance of the TUC General Secretary, produced an offer for settling the dispute described by the company as its 'final' offer. It was to pay four weeks' earnings to all dismissed workers for each year of service with the company, with £155 being the maximum weekly earnings figure for the calculation. The minimum to be paid to any of the employees was to be £2,000. All legal actions over the dispute, including claims for compensation, would be dropped, as would outstanding legal actions against the trade unions. Union recognition at Wapping and Kinning Park was to be 'reviewed' in a year's time and the unions would be given the Gray's Inn Road building. The final date for acceptance of the 'final' offer was 6 June. The company estimated that this offer would cost £50 million. However, the NGA members involved in the dispute rejected the offer by 648 votes to 165 following advice from national officials to do so.[11]

The News International response was to obtain writs against the NGA and Sogat to ban effective picketing and demonstrations at the company's printing plants and distribution centres. The EETPU, however, agreed to use 'their best endeavours with their members at Wapping and News International generally to bring about a resumption of talks between the company and the unions'. Nothing came of this and the Court heard the company's case for banning the print unions from marching and unlawfully picketing Wapping. The unions endeavoured to show that the company's claims were an infringement of a union's right of assembly and to demonstrate, and of the right of individuals to demonstrate and to picket. The Court ordered the maintenance of the six pickets on the gate to convey information, but defined limits that made the pickets and the unions vulnerable if they were exceeded. The Court had not completely banned demonstrations, but had made the unions responsible for any actions taken by individuals or groups that would constitute a breach of the law. This action was followed by TNT obtaining orders restraining NGA members from picketing its various distribution depots up and down the country.

In September 1986, talks with News International recommenced and a further 'final' offer was put forward by the company on 17 September.

Redundancy payments to the dismissed employees were to be four weeks' pay for each year's service at a ceiling of £205 per week. Wages, conditions and grievances would be dealt with by a 'works committee', which would have the sole bargaining rights for the workers in the plant. This committee would be elected on a plant-by-plant basis from the staff currently employed in Wapping. In a "works council' the works committee would be joined by management representatives. A News International joint committee, composed of bona fide trade union representatives and News International representatives, would deal with individual grievances at Wapping and Kinning Park. The dismissed employees would not be entitled to their jobs back but the company promised that they would have the opportunity to apply for future vacancies, although it would not guarantee them appointment. The NGA was sceptical of the offer, believing that further discussions would have improved what was on offer, particularly in regard to jobs which formed no part of the second package. On 8 October, NGA members rejected the 'final offer' by 556 votes to 116. Sogat members rejected the offer by 2,372 votes to 960, whilst the AEU rejected it by 107 votes to 47.

Following the rejection of the News International's second 'final' attempt to buy out NGA members' rights to jobs, union recognition and negotiated severance pay, the company put the offer to each individual through ACAS. Only a tiny minority of dismissed members accepted the offer. On 20 January 1987 the company returned to the High Court claiming damages against the NGA and Sogat for costs of security and of transporting dispute-breaking staff to Wapping. On Saturday 24 January a large demonstration was mounted at Wapping to mark the first anniversary of the dismissal of the 5,500 print workers. The march was well ordered with large numbers of stewards involved. For the people listening to speeches the rally was marred by unprovoked attacks on them by police on foot, in riot gear and on horseback, who charged the crowds unable to gain access to a nearby small park and who had been left standing on the highway. After the initial charges the police ranged far and wide in the streets around Wapping to break up the rally. As a result of these events, calls were made for an independent public inquiry to consider the events of the night, but they fell on deaf ears. An internal police enquiry was set up, and its report, 'leaked' to the BBC in January 1990, was highly critical of police behaviour on 24 January 1987.

The consequences of the demonstration were more far-reaching in that it led News International to threaten to go back to Court to argue that the unions had acted in contempt of previous High Court decisions with regard to picketing and demonstrating outside the plant. This threat had to be considered against the background of whether it would be possible for the unions to continue the dispute, given that they would be likely to be subjected to sequestration by the Court. The NGA was in an extremely difficult position in that it had always held the view that it could not 'win' the dispute alone. Whilst the NGA was considering its position, on 5 February 1987 Sogat decided to end the dispute and accept a settlement based on the offer made on 17 September 1986. This led to a traumatic meeting on 6 February of the NGA National Council, which at the end of the day accepted that the dilemma facing it at that time could not be resolved and that the ending of the dispute could not rest solely on the outcome of a ballot of the members concerned. The position had been reached whereby the union could no longer in isolation sustain the dispute, which was reluctantly ended on the compensation terms of the News International's offer of 17 September. The thirteen-month long News International dispute was over.

The NGA ended the picketing and demonstration at Wapping whilst the company offered compensation for individuals, payments to the dependants of people who had died during the period of the dispute, no discrimination in future employment opportunities at Wapping and Kinning Park against former employees, and security of pension rights. The company called off threatened legal action against the NGA that could have led to large fines and sequestration. After a great deal of difficulty, money was secured from the Manpower Services Commission to which was added resources from the NGA, which in conjunction with the BPIF acting as a training authority, enabled retraining courses to be set up for NGA members who had been involved in the dispute. In addition, the London Region, with the help of many branches outside of London, set about finding jobs as soon as possible or making arrangements with individual employers for retraining for those involved in the dispute.

The News International dispute was significant because of its national importance, its impact on the NGA and the national newspaper industry and its implications for the type of trade unions in terms of their functions, etc. that could emerge in the UK in the late 1980s and the early 1990s. The popular press portrayed the dispute as involving a group of workers who wished to resist the introduction of new technology, defend the right to a particular job for life and whose trade unions refused to negotiate. This, however, was not the case. The NGA

507

had accepted and never questioned the introduction of direct input from the editorial and advertising departments at Wapping. The dispute was about union recognition, wages, jobs, compensation and the non-negotiable conditions that News International insisted must be included in any agreement. In return for recognition at Wapping, the NGA and other print unions offered no industrial action without a membership ballot, binding arbitration that could be triggered by either party, a profitability, efficiency, productivity and job flexibility commitment, fewer collective bargaining units and joint union comprehensive agreements. The company had rejected these, stating that any agreement must be legally binding, must contain a no-strike clause, must involve no closed shop and that management must have the total unfettered right to manage. The NGA took these four non-negotiable conditions to mean that the company did not want an agreement and was at best seeking a unionised plant in name only, which in reality did not contain effective trade unions.

As in all the other disputes considered in this chapter, the NGA could not walk away from the situation in which it found itself. The timing of the dispute was not of its own making and there was no other course of action open to it but to withdraw labour even though it suspected that this was what the company wanted. What it did not know, although it suspected it, was that News International was moving machinery into Wapping and was recruiting an alternative workforce with the assistance of the EETPU. The company had made a strategic decision to establish an alternative production unit, to divest from its relationships with the print unions and their members and to replace them with a more compliant trade union and workforce. To achieve this objective it had been prepared to 'provoke' the print unions into taking strike action, to break off negotiations and blame the 'intransigence' of the unions, to take advantage of inter-union rivalries, to dismiss employees whilst participating in a strike and to use the Employment Acts.

The dispute, like that with the Messenger group, illustrated the lack of balance in the Employment Acts of 1980 and 1982. The company had been able to use legal means to restrain the unions' picketing activities because Wapping was not the workplace of the 5,500 dismissed print workers. That had been Gray's Inn Road and Bouverie Street, but the employer had closed those establishments and picketing was thus only legal under the 1980 Act at these empty workplaces. An employer had extended a dispute and the unions had at great risk decided to picket the employer's new establishment. However, the News International dispute also showed how an employer could take advantage of company law to gain legal advantages vis-à-vis secondary industrial action under the 1980 Employment Act, which allowed unions to extend industrial action to employers with whom they had no dispute so long as the employers were a first customer or a first supplier of the company where the primary dispute was taking place. News International recognised that newspaper wholesalers, which were 100 per cent Sogat organised, would be first customers of its four titles and that Sogat would be able to instruct its members in the warehouses to refuse to handle News International newspapers without the fear of legal consequences. The company overcame this problem by creating a series of shadow companies – e.g. News International Supply Limited, News International Distribution Ltd and News International Advertising Ltd – so that the warehouses ceased to be a first customer. It was on this basis that in early February 1986 News International gained an order banning Sogat from instructing its members in newspaper distribution warehouses to black its papers. When this order was ignored, Sogat suffered a £25,000 fine and sequestration of its funds. Although the company had achieved its objective, many observers felt that management and the courts, had grossly extended the intentions of the 1980 legislation on secondary industrial action.

The role of the EETPU in the News International dispute was crucial to the company's success. Without the cooperation of the EETPU it would have been difficult, if not impossible, for News International to recruit an alternative workforce to print its papers. Plate-making and machine managing needed experienced workers, and the printing machines at Wapping were far from high-tech, being some twenty-five years old. The print unions presented first-hand evidence to the TUC inquiry into the electricians' behaviour of that union's direct involvement in recruitment for News International. An unemployed AEU fitter from Glasgow explained the EETPU role in his recruitment to Kinning Park, whilst evidence was also produced that the Southampton EETPU area organiser had been involved actively in recruiting for the Wapping plant. The General Secretary of Sogat, Ms Brenda Dean, described this evidence as the EETPU having 'been caught with their fingers in the till of our members' jobs'.[22] Nevertheless, the print unions at that time were unable to prove conclusively that the EETPU at national level was aware of the activities of its Southampton and Glasgow area secretaries. The national officers of the union repeatedly gave assurances that there was no question of taking over the work of the print unions. Nevertheless, the NGA always suspected that, in a union as centrally controlled as the EETPU, it was inconceivable that no word of the activities in Glasgow and Southampton reached national officials.

Why had the EETPU behaved in this way? The union's membership fell from some 420,000 in 1980 to 320,000 in 1986. It already had a presence in the newspaper industry as a maintenance union. Wapping offered the EETPU the opportunity to become a production union in the newspaper industry and if it could establish itself there it could challenge the NGA and Sogat in the machine rooms of the provincial and national newsapers. If the EETPU had been successful at Wapping then, given the terms it was prepared to concede to employers to gain recognition, there is little doubt that other national newsapers and large provincial newspaper groups would have welcomed the EETPU into their plants. It was important to the NGA that the electricians' union did not succeed. The NGA had shown employers that, if they followed the News International line, an inter-union problem would exist. For the same reason it had no option but to keep the pressure on the TUC and other unions to take action against the EETPU. A gain for the NGA in the News International dispute was the prevention of the EETPU from establishing itself as a production union within the national and provincial newspaper industry. In addition, the behaviour of the EETPU dented its image with the wider trade union movement and, more importantly, probably with employers outside the printing industry.

What of the immediate impact of the dispute on the NGA? Some 900 of its members had been involved in a thirteen-month long dispute and many suffered periods of personal distress and unemployment after the dispute. Over £2.5 million was eventually paid out in dispute benefit, to which had to be added unemployment benefit payments, contempt of court fines, and legal costs. The financial cost of the dispute was high and, along with the costs at *Kent Messenger* and *Wolverhampton Express and Star*, led the NGA to introduce a Dispute Fund designed to remove the financing of industrial action from the General Fund. There was also a psychological short-term impact of the dispute. National newspapers had been viewed by the wider membership as *the* area where the NGA probably had its greatest strength and influence. It was a heavy blow for some members that the NGA had been defeated in this area since, if the 'marines' could not stand their ground, was there a future for the union and its members? For others, however, this was not the case, as they had always considered the power of 'Fleet Street' to be a myth rather than a reality and, apart from the 620 members involved in the Times dispute in 1979, many of whom were again involved at Wapping, the national newspaper membership was over many years untried and untested in a lengthy large-scale dispute. For some, the exposure of the myth of 'Fleet Street' power could only be beneficial to the union in the longer term. Although at times during the dispute the wider membership's lack of sympathy with Fleet Street occasionally surfaced, in terms of Fleet Street being perceived as having too much attention from the national union, they were easily contained. The wider membership, when asked, always replied that they would not accept in their own agreements the four non-negotiable conditions being sought by News International. It was thus easy for the national leadership to reply by asking why the London membership should then.

In previous disputes the NGA members not directly involved in the dispute always loyally responded to calls for industrial action in support of those members directly involved. Traditions of discipline and solidarity have been hallmarks of NGA members' behaviour. However, the News International dispute witnessed groups of NGA members not taking action in support of those directly involved in a major dispute.[23] Members working at Bemrose, which printed the *Sunday Times* colour supplement and is part of News International, refused to 'black' this work because they were fearful for their jobs as the company threatened to close it down. Again, NGA members at two plants in Northampton and London, which printed the *Times Supplements*, voted not to black this work when the company issued individual writs against members, and in one factory the management drafted in an alternative workforce, even while the ballot was taking place, in case the members voted to black work.

Another immediate impact of the dispute on the active members of the NGA, when taken against the TUC treatment of the NGA in the Warrington dispute, was an increasing degree of disillusion and despair about the effectiveness of the TUC to control its affiliates. An affiliated union had colluded with an employer to put 5,500 members of other affiliated unions out of work. NGA activists could not understand why the TUC did not tell the EETPU to instruct its members in Wapping and Glasgow to stop performing work previously undertaken by print workers and not to cross print worker picket lines. Respect for the TUC in the eyes of NGA activists declined, and some have concluded that if the TUC is never going to recommend that a union behave unlawfully, then affiliates would be able to behave in any way they like and still keep their gains.

The News International dispute was not just about Fleet Street. It was also about the future place and role of trade unionism in society. The NGA is a union prepared to change, to negotiate and to reach agreements which take on board new conditions and working practices. It is a union which provides substantial servicing, democracy and benefits to its members. It is not one that will disregard its members' interests but it is opposed to the uncontrolled introduction of new technology where all the benfits go in one direction, particularly to the employer. For the NGA these are basic trade union principles along with those of hard bargaining and delivering deals. The trade unionism the EETPU was offering to News International employees was one of undermining fellow trade unionists, of recognition on the employer's terms, of acting as an employer's recruiting agent, of allowing members to do the work of other trade unions, of refusing to accept the advice of the General Secretary of the TUC and the procedures and rules of that body, and of conspiring and collaborating with an employer. Within twelve months of the dispute ending, the Wapping employees had not had a pay increase and the union situation was in the untidy position left by the EETPU. The employees held a union membership ballot which split three ways – those in favour of doing nothing, those in favour of staying with the EETPU and the overwhelming majority who favoured seeking membership and representation by print unions. The company's response was simple and direct. It gave each individual a new contract of employment and stated that after 13 December 1987 the company would no longer recognise the workers' council. Wapping still remains unorganised, but the EETPU vision of future trade unionism has been rejected there.

The News International dispute had repercussions throughout the national newspaper industry, in both London and Manchester. By the end of 1989 the exodus from Fleet Street was complete and most national newspapers had decentralised their printing arrangements in a number of different ways. In addition, virtually all newspapers had separated their editorial and origination departments from the actual printing process. The editorial and origination offices are now widely spread across London, with the *Daily Mail* moving to Kensington, the *Telegraph* to the Isle of Dogs and the *Daily Express* to the south side of Blackfriars Bridge. These decentralisation trends brought a number of unwelcome developments as far as the NGA was concerned. The overall reduction of union and chapel influence in the industry. The elimination or reduction in some areas of collective recognition. An extension of working hours and a return to a 5 day week. Large-scale redundancies, and the break-up of what was regarded by many as the NGA's powerhouse, the national newspaper industry.

These moves, all of which were made easier by the outcome of the News International dispute, were accompanied by the introduction of direct input, which created a loss of jobs across composing areas. This change has brought in its train changes affecting the process, the telecommunications and electronics and the former stereotyping areas in the national newspaper field. Direct input changes were not confined to the composing area, because in the main they were also accompanied by far-reaching changes in the printing of national newspapers. In composing rooms the introduction of direct entry has reduced staffing levels by a half to two-thirds of their previous size. Although work has been lost to NGA members in the telecommunications area – such as the punching of copy between different sections and the monitoring of wire copy and news agency services – the transmission and receipt of complete pages has, to a large extent, not only offset the loss of work in the wire rooms but added to the work in the plate-making area. An ongoing development affecting the NGA in the telecommunications area is the increasing use of the editorial electronic picture desk. The introduction of portable negative transmitting equipment used by photographers has eliminated the use of the mobile picture transmission unit, normally operated by NGA T&E members.

The impact of direct entry in national newspapers has borne more heavily on the Manchester branch than elsewhere. The centralisation of editorial departments in London has in turn brought with it the elimination, with one exception, of all the composing rooms that previously existed in Manchester. Direct input gives the ability for stories printed in Manchester to be entered directly into the editorial computer base in London, aided by the transmission of copy by fax, thus eliminating the requirement for the double setting of newspapers previously done in Manchester. The loss of jobs has gone beyond the composing room. Where composing ceased to exist, the process departments were similarly affected.

Throughout 1985 and into 1986 the national newspaper market was hyped up on the view that the introduction of new technology would see an expansion of the overall market, since it would make it possible for almost anyone to start up a national newspaper. The outcome of the News International dispute was expected to accelerate this trend and bring about a more diverse press with a wider spectrum of ownership and control. The view that new technology would herald a flood tide of new newspaper titles has proved optimistic. Britain now has only a marginally greater choice of newspapers. If anything, the very opposite to a wider spectrum of ownership and control appears to be happening. News International has taken over *Today*, originally launched by Eddie Shah, whilst the *Sunday Sport* has linked up with United Newspapers. The *Independent* has flourished, but the *London Daily News*, and *News on Sunday* – all new-technology launches – disappeared only a few months after being born. The NGA remains convinced that its objective of a more diverse newspaper industry will not be achieved by new technology alone. It considers that this situation will be created only by the election of a Labour government committed to introduce reforms on press ownership, such as a limit on newspaper ownership to one title, a nationally owned production facility for hire, an advertising levy and a requirement of UK citizenship.[24] This envisaged legislative regulation of press ownership is an important by-product of the NGA experiences during the News International dispute and a future Labour government would need to positively consider press ownership reform.

NOTES

1. See *Report of the Delegate Meeting, 1972*, National Graphical Association, pp. 370–6.
2. See *Report of the Delegate Meeting, 1969*, National Graphical Association, p. 109.
3. See *Report of the Delegate Meeting, 1976*, National Graphical Association, p. 216.
4. See *Report of the Delegate Meeting, 1980*, National Graphical Association, p. 316.
5. See *Print*, vol. 12, no. 6, July 1975, p. 1.
6. See *Report of the Delegate Meeting, 1978*, National Graphical Association, p. 247.
7. See *Print*. vol. 12, no. 7, August 1975, p. 4.
8. For more detailed accounts of this dispute see R. Morton, *New Technology and Industrial Relations in Fleet Street*, Oxford, 1981, Ch. 7, pp. 254–301, and E. Jacobs, *Stop Press: the Inside Story of the Times Dispute*, André Deutsch, 1980.
9. See *Report of the Delegate Meeting, 1980*, National Graphical Association, p. 11.
10. ibid., p. 86.
11. This London voluntary levy was estimated to be bringing in over £25,000 per week.
12. For a fuller account of this dispute, see John Gennard, 'The Implications of the Messenger Newspaper Group dispute', *Industrial Relations Journal*, vol. 1, no. 3, Autumn 1984.
13. The six papers were the *Daily Express*, the *Daily Mirror*, the *Daily Star*, the *Sporting Life*, the *Sun* and *The Times*. These four papers were the *Mail*, the *Telegraph*, the *Financial Times* and the *Guardian*.

14. The NGA took a decision not to pay these damages voluntarily, and subsequently the company was served with what is called a garnishee order, which is virtually an attachment order placed against the NGA's funds or assets.

15. See *Report of the Delegate Meeting, 1984*, National Graphical Association (1982), p. 129.

16. See also John Gennard, 'The NGA and the Impact of New Technology', *New Technology, Work and Employment*, vol. 2, no. 2, Autumn, 1987.

17. See *Print*, August 1986, p. 4.

18. See *Report of the Delegate Meeting, 1988*, National Graphical Association (1982), p. 16.

19. ibid., p. 77.

20. TNT was a road haulage firm in which Rupert Murdoch had a major shareholding. It was used to distribute the four titles produced at Wapping and Kinning Park. News International knew that it could not use the British Rail network for the distribution of its papers as the rail unions were likely to be reluctant to handle them.

21. Sogat voted by 2,081 to 1,415 to reject the 'final' offer, whilst the AEU made the same decision by 112 votes to 57.

22. See *Print*, November 1986, p. 4.

23. See *Report of the Delegate Meeting, 1986*, National Graphical Association (1982), p. 103.

24. See *Report of the Delegate Meeting, 1988*, National Graphical Association (1982), p. 78.

CHAPTER 15

NATIONAL NEWSPAPER EMPLOYERS

The major employers' organisation for national newspapers was the Newspaper Proprietors' Association (NPA), which changed its name in 1968 to the Newspaper Publishers' Association. It came into existence in 1906 when the LSC threatened a 'general strike' of compositors in response to Hampton's, a London firm, deciding to become non-union and giving notice to all union members. Alarmed at the industrial consequences of a general strike of compositors, a group of daily newspaper owners approached the LSC and agreed to withdraw from the LMPA and to conduct separate negotiations, providing the union excluded the daily newspapers from any general printing industry dispute. Daily newspapers claimed that their product was so perishable they could not afford the risk of a stoppage. They saw themselves as vulnerable to union action in a way that did not apply to the provincial press and the general printing trade. As competition between national newspapers increased in the 1960s and 1970s, the NPA became less influential in industrial relations and in 1986 closed its industrial relations department. The major employers had withdrawn from it for industrial relations purposes.

WAGES

1950–64

The 1951 agreement
In 1951 the print unions collectively met the NPA, which offered a graded increase of 60p for employees earning over £9 per week, of 52½p for those earning between £7.50 and £9 per week and of 45p for

those receiving less than £7.50 per week. The NPA proposed that any agreement should be stabilised for five years and that there should be a cost-of-living bonus related to movements in the Index of Retail Prices. However in the end it proved impossible to proceed on a collective union basis. Nevertheless the TA and the LSC reached agreement with the NPA on the pay offer outlined above. The agreement was to run until 31 October 1954.

The 1955 agreement

The LSC refused to participate in any collective movement to amend the 1951 agreement, and claimed a percentage increase, a new cost-of-living agreement and stabilisation. Following the formation of the LTS, an agreement was made with the NPA which provided a cost-of-living bonus based on the Index of Retail Prices as at June 1955, stabilisation until 30 November 1957 and an increase of 12.5 per cent on the combined figure of the minimum rate plus the cost-of-living bonus as it existed on the date of termination of the 1951 agreement. As a result of the 1955 agreement, LTS comps and machine managers became the highest-paid groups of workers in the national newspaper industry. It was also the only union in the 1954/5 negotiations to retain a cost-of-living bonus scheme.

The 1951 agreement covering the wages of TA members in Manchester on the production of northern editions of national newspapers also expired on 1 November 1954. The TA claimed a basic weekly wage rate of £12.65 and the ending of the cost-of-living bonus. The NPA wished parity of wages between national newspaper production in London and Manchester. For this reason the NPA offered to the TA, as an interim measure, that 80p of the existing cost-of-living bonus should be consolidated into the basic rate. TA members eventually accepted an offer of wages of £9.67½p plus a cost-of-living bonus of £1.05 to be increased by 12.5 per cent to give a basic rate of £11.99, on condition that the employers resumed negotiations within three months, payments were retrospective to June 1955 and if a final settlement was not reached the matter would be resolved by conciliation. The agreement established a 72½p London/Manchester differential for time rate compositors, thereby ensuring both the TA and the LTS had a common interest in the news compositors' time rate.

The 1957 agreement

In 1957 the LTS and the TA made a joint approach for the first time to the NPA for a revision of the 1955 agreement. However, without consulting the LTS, the TA took unilateral action on the claim, which led the LTS to withdraw from joint negotiations. The LTS then made an agreement with the NPA which consolidated 75p per week of the cost-of-living bonus, introduced a new cost-of-living bonus of 10p per point change above the index figure of 104, retrospective payments to 1 December 1957, and stabilisation to 30 November 1959. The agreement established a minimum rate for compositors of £16.40 on morning papers, £16.07½p on evening papers and £14.47½p on Sunday newspapers. For machine managers the figures were £15.65 (morning papers) and £13.10 (evening papers). The time rate compositors were to receive extra payments ranging from 90p to £1.25 per week, whilst piece-rate compositors received enhanced piece scale rates. In Manchester the TA secured a new basic rate of £15.36 together with two years' stabilisation from 1 December 1957 and a new cost-of-living bonus calculated on 10p per point rise or fall in the Index of Retail Prices, based on the index figure of 104 and adjustable at three-monthly intervals.

The 1960 agreement
In previous wage negotiations the LTS and the TA' had presented claims, whilst the other print unions had pursued a collective claim. However, in anticipation of the expiry date of the 1957 agreement, each union decided to present its own claim separately. The TA's claim included three weeks' holidays, a 7.5 per cent wage increase and an increase in the compositors' overtime rate for Sunday newspaper production. The main items in the LTS claim were a wage increase of 10 per cent, an annual holiday of three weeks, and a cost-of-living bonus. Realising that the lack of a collective claim would make concluding an agreement longer than on previous occasions, the NPA made an interim offer, which was accepted by both the TA and the LTS, of a 2.5 per cent increase on minimum rates with consolidation of the 50p cost-of-living bonus from 1 December 1959.

A final agreement was reached in early 1960 to operate from 1 April 1960 to 31 March 1964. For the LTS it provided a third week's holiday with pay and minimum rates for time rate compositors of £17.50 on morning papers, £17.12½ on evening papers and £15.42½ on Sunday newspapers. For machine managers on the morning papers the minimum rate became £16.05 per week and for those on evening papers £14.07½. The TA agreement provided for a third week's holiday, a wage increase of 21p paid retrospectively to 1 April 1960, and the restoration of the London/Manchester basic rate differential to 72½p.

The TA settlement gave an increase of about 4 per cent 'new money', a basic rate of £16.43 and a cost-of-living bonus.

Although the TA and the LTS 1960 agreements were to run for four years, the form of stabilisation was different from what had operated in previous agreements. Under these agreements stabilisation meant that no issues whatsoever could be raised with the NPA during the life of the agreement. Under the 1960 agreements only wages were stabilised. The unions were free during stabilisation to raise any other matters with the employers. The 1960 agreements also set up a joint standing committee to consider matters of mutual concern to the NPA and the unions, particularly efficiency and new techniques and processes.

The Incomes Policy Years, 1964–79

The 1964 agreement

One of the first tasks of the NGA was the preparation of a claim, later submitted by the P&KTF to the NPA, for a wage increase on behalf of national newspaper members. In April 1964 the NPA, in spite of the difficulties in respect of its memorandum 'Efficiency of Production' (see below), felt that a joint board should be established to examine problems of mutual interest. The union representatives, led by the NGA General Secretary, John Bonfield, indicated that if a satisfactory wage settlement could be agreed they would recommend participation in the joint board. The agreement subsequently provided a 10 per cent increase on all basic rates, whilst maintaining the existing London/ Manchester differentials, continuance of the cost-of-living bonus, consolidation of 50 per cent of the existing bonus into basic rates and stabilisation to 30 September 1967.

Implicit in the settlement was acceptance by the unions of the establishment of a joint board for the national newspaper industry consisting of equal numbers of union and management representatives. The joint board was to examine the publication and production of national newspapers and make recommendations to the NPA and the printing unions whereby increased efficiency could be achieved. The joint board could also recommend the methods by which the benefits accruing from increased efficiency could be shared between managements and employees. At the inaugural meeting of the board, held in January 1965, Lord Devlin became the board's independent chairman. One of the Board's first acts was to commission the Economist Intelligence Unit to undertake a comprehensive survey of the industry in relation to its capital structure, revenue, raw materials, productive and managerial efficiency and employee benefits such as pensions, sick pay schemes and redundancy arrangements.[1] However, the board disappeared in 1967 without having made any significant contribution to solving the industry's problem.

The 1968 agreement

Before the expiry of the 1964 agreement due in September 1967 the NPA chairman warned the unions that the industry was in a parlous state, that it would seek stabilisation and that it wished to abolish the cost-of-living bonus. The P&KTF convened a meeting of NGA, Sogat and Slade, as a result of which the following proposals were agreed: consolidation of the current cost-of-living bonus, continuation of the cost-of-living bonus scheme, stabilisation for two or possibly three years, and a 5 per cent increase per year of stabilisation. The collective approach did not last long. Sogat withdrew and Slade followed suit. The NPA response to the NGA claim was to submit three documents for its consideration. Two of the documents covering P&KTF agreements and work study applied to all three unions, but the third centred on NGA agreements. Implicit in the NPA's proposals was that savings should be subject to a 50/50 distribution between management and chapel. The NGA accepted all three documents in principle, but in the case of the work study document only if there were safeguards for the members concerned.

This background meant that the negotiations were protracted in the extreme, but eventually the NPA modified its documents, particularly that on work study, and proposed an increase of 3 per cent from 1 September 1968 and a further 2 per cent from 1 September 1969. The latter would be recoverable by the NPA from savings arising from productivity agreements, after which any further savings would be divided on a 50/50 basis. The cost-of-living bonus at this time was £2.20 and the NPA agreed to consolidate £1.10 into basic rates with the remainder being a priority in any future agreement.

The 1970 agreement

Although the national agreement was not due to expire until 31 August 1970, the NGA found itself involved in June of that year just prior to a general election in a difficult situation owing to the action of other print unions. Whilst the NGA was formulating its claim to the NPA, Natsopa, Sogat and Slade presented an interim claim to the NPA. The NGA found itself involved in a dispute from this interim claim and the halting of the production of newspapers in Fleet Street and Manchester. During the negotiations preceding the dispute, the NGA made it clear to the other printing unions and the NPA that it was honouring the existing agreement and to that extent it did not consider itself involved in the dispute. However, the NGA participated in the talks aimed at achieving a return to work. The eventual agreement gave NGA members an increase of 5 per cent on earnings from 1 July 1970, with a guarantee that no one would receive less money than the equivalent of 10 per cent of their basic rate. An additional week's holiday was negotiated and piece workers had 5 per cent added to all their earnings, with the exception of the outstanding cost-of-living bonus. The agreement operated until 30 June 1971.

The 1971 agreement

In May 1971 the unions again started negotiations on a collective basis. Once again a number of problems arose, not least of which was pay differentials, and once again production in Fleet Street and Manchester stopped. This resulted from the NPA carrying out its threat to close all national newspapers in London and Manchester should disruption of production caused by NGA chapel meetings continue. These meetings were held in association with the presentation to individual managements of the NGA claim for a percentage increase in wages. Following a breakdown of national negotiations when the NPA rejected the NGA demand for a percentage wage increase, this claim was in response to the employers' offer of a flat-rate increase of £1, which would have eroded NGA members' pay differential over other workers in the machine and reading rooms. The serious situation brought about the intervention of Mr Victor Feather, General Secretary of the TUC, and, following three days of continuous negotiations, agreement was reached on 22 September 1971.

The agreement, to operate from 1 July 1971 until 30 September 1972, was in the form of two options from which each could chose. Option 1 provided for either a 5 per cent increase on earnings or 10 per cent on the basic rate, whichever was the greater. The £1.10 cost-of-living bonus was consolidated into the basic rate in two stages – 55p on 1 January 1972 and 55p on 1 April 1972. Option 2 gave either £1.12½ on the basic rate or 10 per cent on the basic rate, whichever was the greater. The cost-of-living bonus was consolidated as in Option 1. The purpose of the 10 per cent on the basic rate was to protect the lower-paid worker. In addition, the NPA undertook to ensure that implementation of the agreement would not result in a reduction of the current 12½ per cent differentials in the machine and reading rooms. NGA members voted for Option 1.

The 1972 agreement

The print unions met in August 1972 to formulate a collective claim for a new agreement. The unions were prepared to consider a two-year agreement providing wage increases of 12½ per cent for the first twelve months and 10 per cent for the second twelve months could be gained. These percentages were to be additions on total earnings and written into the basic rates. To protect their members from inflation, the unions agreed to seek a 'threshold' clause similar to that obtained from the Scottish Daily Newspaper Society (see Chapter 16). They also sought in principle a shorter working week and commitment to discuss pension and sick schemes during the lifetime of the agreement.

In comparison with previous negotiations, those of 1972 were concluded in a speedy manner. This was due partly to it being clear that at this time that the government was to introduce a prices and incomes freeze. The unusual course was therefore taken of seeking acceptance of the offer from NGA members at meetings held in London on 3 November 1972 and in Manchester on 5 November 1972. On the following day, the government announced that a wage freeze would apply from 6 November, but would exclude any agreements accepted before 6 November 1972, which meant that NGA members received the negotiated increases.

The agreement was to operate from 1 October 1972 and to be terminable by six months' notice by either party at any time after 31 March 1974 or as determined by special arrangements. From 1 October 1972 an 8 per cent increase on all earnings and basic rates came into effect. On 1 October 1973, or as determined by the threshold arrangements, there was to be a further 8 per cent increase on all earnings and basic rates. The first and second increases both related to an 11 point increase above the threshold of the Index of Retail Prices for September 1972. In the event of the Index rising by over 22 points from the base figure of mid-September 1972, then the agreement became subject to renegotiation. Due to an unprecedented increase in the cost of living, the threshold figure was reached in July 1973, which meant that NGA members were due to receive the second stage of the increase in July instead of October. However, the NPA refused to bring forward the agreement, stating that it was prevented by the government's statutory prices and incomes policy. The NPA initially suggested that the money be paid into a trust fund, but this was unacceptable to the NGA. Eventually the unions accepted an offer to pay threshold payments in line with the government's incomes policy after a categoric assurance from the NPA that any threshold monies up to a ceiling of £2.80 would be absorbed in any subsequent agreement made after October 1974.

The 1974–79 agreements

The NGA claimed an 8 per cent increase on earnings from 1 October 1974. Threshold payments were seen as an interim arrangement until that date, since the government's prices and incomes policy did not permit the claim to be processed earlier. The NGA did not know at that stage that it would become involved in a major dispute with the NPA over threshold payments.

Initially the NPA stated that the economic circumstances of the industry meant that it was not in a position to make an offer, but it was prepared to pay four more threshold payments and review the position in March 1975. The NGA immediately rejected this offer, as flat-rate payments under threshold payments would only exacerbate potential problems over differentials. The NGA negotiated separately with the NPA but, just when it looked as though the problem over differentials would be overcome, NGA members took to industrial action in one office and the NPA refused to meet the NGA. Whilst the NGA was persuading its members to return to work, the other unions received an offer from the NPA designed to improve the position of their lower-paid members. However, the offer proposed that the then £2.80 threshold payment would from October 1974 be paid as a fixed house bonus. The £2.80 became a house payment and would not in future be a subject for national negotiations. There was to be a second-stage payment of a 2 per cent increase on all earnings and basic rates. The agreement would be for twelve months from 1 October 1974. The NGA rejected the offer, arguing that it would create differential problems and that the NPA had reneged on its promise to absorb threshold payments in subsequent agreements.

The NPA refused to amend its offer and overwhelming support was given to the NGA's recommendation that chapels should take whatever action was necessary to gain a percentage increase. When ACAS failed to resolve the dispute, NGA members undertook industrial action, which was suspended following an intervention from the Employment Secretary, Mr Michael Foot. No progress was made and the industrial action resumed. The NPA called upon the NGA to restore normal production and said if the NGA failed to do this its members would have terminated their employment. The NGA applied to the High Court for an injunction restraining the employers from carrying out their threat. The High Court, and subsequently the Court of Appeal, refused the injunction, but this legal action, apart from being unique, provided valuable breathing space and the employers were deterred from implementing their threat.

To break the deadlock the NGA balloted its members on a recommendation that they reject the NPA offer. If members accepted this recommendation, further meetings would be held with the NPA and if these proved abortive then the NGA would take appropriate action, including strike action to maintain differentials. If, on the other hand, members voted against the recommendation, the NGA would advise the NPA that its offer had been accepted, but that the restoration of differentials would be the priority in the claim for a new agreement. The ballot result was close. On a turnout of 96 per cent some 47 per cent voted to reject the NPA offer and 53 per cent voted to accept.

In the light of the government's July 1975 White Paper on inflation, the NGA submitted a claim to the NPA for a £6 flat payment, but with the proviso that it would require discussions during the lifetime of the agreement to rectify differential problems when government policy permitted. The October 1976 agreement between the NGA and the NPA was strictly in accordance with government pay policy and consisted of an increase of 5 per cent on earnings with a cash minimum of £2.50 and an upper limit of £4. However, the 1977 negotiations took a different turn. Initially, negotiations were delayed to await the determination in September 1977 of TUC policy on a further period of wage restraint and clarification of the NGA's attitude towards that policy. Following the TUC and NGA's decision not to accept the government's 10 per cent guideline for income movements, strenuous efforts were made, without success, to move the NPA from adherence to the policy. It offered a 10 per cent increase on all earnings, with pro rata or percentage payments to casual workers, juniors and apprentices. This was accepted by the NGA in an agreement to operate for one year from 1 October 1977. At the end of that agreement, new conditions were negotiated providing for a 7.5 per cent increase on all earnings from 1 October 1978, with a further increase of 2.5 per cent from 1 May 1979. This agreement was to terminate on 31 December 1979.

The 1980s agreements

Prior to the termination of the 1979 agreement the NGA claimed a 20 per cent increase on all earnings, one additional week's holiday, the removal of the Bank Holiday agreement from the main wage negotiations and the removal from the agreement of the self-financing overtime. Although this was achieved, the basic rate in national newspapers continued to bear little relationship to actual earnings, which were boosted by a proliferation of comprehensive and new-technology agreements plus the London scale of piece charges. The wide disparity between basic rates and actual earnings was one factor which persuaded the NGA post-1980 to make a priority claim of additional holidays, which would generate additional employment opportunities for NGA members in the national newspapers. By the early 1980s another cause for concern was the continuing tendency for the NPA wages and conditions agreement to generate sizeable retrospective payments. The NGA stressed to the NPA the need in future for new agreements to be finalised before existing ones terminated. A third cause for concern to the NGA in the NPA areas was that, in the past, a majority of newspapers were not parties to the wages and conditions negotiations. The *Mirror*, the *Express*, the *Guardian*, *The Times* and the *Morning Advertiser* now preferred to negotiate their own agreements. The NGA began questioning the value of the NPA as an organisation.

In the 1981 negotiations the NPA sought a disputes procedure that would place financial penalties upon all trade union members regardless of whether they were involved in a dispute or not. The NGA rejected this, although it recognised that under the existing procedure the parties quickly found themselves at ACAS when this was not the intention. Over the two years to 1984, in national negotiations the NGA received a minimal wage award and no improvement in the working week or holidays. The NPA effectively asked for a wage freeze, but the NGA pressed for reductions in working time as it considered this the best way to generate work for unemployed national newspaper workers in London and Manchester.

The negotiation of the NPA agreement for 1985 was a difficult and time-consuming exercise. It started early in 1985, with the aim of reaching a settlement before the end of the year. The NGA hoped to arrive at a position where its members could objectively consider the NPA offer without there being a considerable amount of back pay due, which had in the past affected any ballot on an agreement with the NPA. By the end of 1984 the situation was that other unions had been offered an increase on all earnings of 5 per cent coupled with a fallback figure for lower-paid workers. The NPA and the NGA finally agreed a 5 per cent increase on all earnings, fallback and a commitment to discuss a fifth week's holidays. The NGA members, however, considered the wages offer inadequate.

In the light of this situation the NGA balloted its members with a recommendation that the NPA offer be rejected and in doing so to empower the NGA to make individual approaches at house level to achieve its original claims. When the members voted to reject the NPA offer, the NGA approached individual houses in both London and Manchester, but, in the main, it was rejected. The NGA's position became even more difficult, as all other unions, except the AUEW, had by now accepted the NPA 1985 offer. The only real success in the house-level campaign was at the *Guardian*, where a fifth week's holiday was achieved from 1 October 1985.

The negotiations for the NPA agreement in 1986, although spread over a fairly lengthy period, involved only two meetings. They took place against a background of consistent change and the lowest number of newspapers ever covered by the negotiations.[2] Despite efforts to get further meetings with the NPA, it was clear that there was going to be no improvement in the 3.5 per cent offer that the NPA had put to the NGA. The offer was subsequently accepted.

At the end of 1986 the NPA announced that it no longer wished a national agreement, that its whole involvement in industrial relations in the national newspaper industry would end and that its industrial relations department would close. Whatever arrangements were made to extend or prolong any part of the NPA agreement with individual national newspapers, including the disputes procedures, were matters between each individual newspaper and the unions. This even led, in late December 1986, to the NGA seeking a 6 per cent increase in wages across all newspaper houses, but every national newspaper would only negotiate increases in wages in exchange for changes in methods of operation and production.

DIFFERENTIALS AND MANNING

The differentials that existed within the national newspaper industry were many and varied and existed not only between different groups of NGA members but between the NGA and other unions. There was always a differential between piece-work compositors and time rate compositors under hot metal production, and on the introduction of new technology the NGA sought always to establish one NGA rate, using as a basis an equation of all generated earnings. This policy led to the acceptance of the buying out of the London Scale of Prices as a compensation for loss of future earnings to piece-workers.

A traditional differential in national newspapers was that between the composing and pre-press areas and the rate established in the machine room. However, the differential problems that received the widest publicity were those between NGA machine managers and machine assistants who were members of another union. During the last forty years, several dispute situations have developed over the disturbance of the machine manager/machine assistant differential. The NGA invariably sought to resolve these problems by the establishment of joint press room agreements that allowed members of other unions to achieve their aspirations but at the time protected NGA manning levels and pay differentials. Examples of such disputes occurred at the *Daily Mirror* in 1968 and 1970, the *Sunday Times* in 1981 and the *Financial Times* in 1982.

The Mirror Group, 1968–70

The Imperial chapel at the *Daily Mirror* supported NGA machine managers, who argued that a recent agreement between the *Daily Mirror* and the then Sogat (Division 1) had disturbed the traditional differentials between machine managers and machine assistants on both the night and the day maintenance shifts. Approaches were made to management, who insisted that any increase in the machine managers' rate under the productivity scheme must be fully matched by productivity measures, including a reduction in the number employed.

The NGA members undertook industrial action, but management refused to accept that differentials should automatically be adjusted and reiterated that concessions on manning and productivity must balance increases in pay. Disruption of production assumed serious proportions and the NPA issued an ultimatum on 19 September that unless normal production resumed NGA members would be dismissed at 6.00 pm on

Monday 27 September. The NGA pointed out that it had repeatedly warned the employers of the impending dangers if adequate safeguards were not built into any agreement on wage structures. The NGA sought the assistance of the TUC, which secured a withdrawal of the NPA statement and a resumption of negotiations, during which a formula was evolved which it was hoped would end the dispute. However, when it was put to the *Mirror* machine managers' chapel, it was unanimously rejected.

The dispute dragged on. In March 1970 the chapel and the London Region examined management proposals for a new comprehensive agreement. The NGA was to submit counter-proposals but none were forthcoming. It told the *Mirror* in April 1970 that their proposals were unacceptable. Given the NGA's previous statements to the NPA and the *Mirror* about the implications of piecemeal productivity bargaining for differentials and that the issue at the *Mirror* had been outstanding for some considerable time, the *Mirror* management was informed that unless the differential was restored *within two weeks* the NGA would regard itself as in dispute with the company and its members would follow a policy of non-cooperation.

The reaction of the NPA was to threaten to shut down all national newspapers in London and Manchester. Resenting this threat, the NGA repeated its notice to withdraw all NGA members from the London offices of the *Mirror* unless the pay differential dispute was resolved within the next fourteen days. These events resulted in Mr Victor Feather, General Secretary of the TUC, intervening in the dispute. A settlement was reached on 15 May 1970 by a joint committee chaired by Mr Feather. Having considered evidence from both sides on the disturbance of differentials since April 1968, the joint committee unanimously decided that an additional payment of £2 should be made to night machine managers at the *Daily Mirror*. However, it also said that it would be appropriate for the NGA machine chapel to enter negotiations with a view to offsetting the £2 payment by improvements in productivity. A major contributory cause of the dispute had been the complex negotiating procedures within the *Daily Mirror* machine room.[3]

In November 1970 the first joint press room agreement in the history of the national newspaper industry was reached at the *Daily Mirror*. It laid down staffing levels for various sizes of *Daily Mirror* and *Sunday Mirror*, defined working arrangements, including sickness cover and holiday arrangements, and detailed various productivity and flexibility measures. Importantly, in view of previous difficulties, the agreement embodied a clause which stated 'the Sogat Grade 1 rate shall be 87½% of the NGA machine managers' rate and that this differential shall be maintained unless negotiations at national level establish some different percentage differential or some other method of wage calculation'.[4]

The Sunday Times Dispute, 1981

In autumn 1981 a dispute involving machine managers started at the *Sunday Times* when the NGA demanded restoration of machine room pay differentials. The dispute was referred to ACAS, which recommended the appointment of a mediator, who in turn recommended that the company meet urgently with the NGA 'in respect of working practices and duties in the machine room in the light of the recent disturbance of pay differentials'. The mediator recommended that the company deal with the NGA claim as a matter of urgency.

The company rejected the recommendations and then demanded an official assurance of normal working. When this was not forthcoming, the company suspended the paper, locked out 101 NGA machine managers and then 1,300 members of other printing unions. NGA members at *The Times* refused to cross *Sunday Times* picket lines and the company threatened to suspend the 2,500 staff employed by that paper. After hours of talks a formula was agreed under which all suspensions were lifted. The company agreed to tripartite talks with the NGA and Natsopa with the aim of establishing a joint press room agreement. In return, the NGA lifted the picket line and gave an assurance of normal working. The machine managers at the *Sunday Times* did not want this signed by their FOC, Vic Dunn, because they thought it would diminish his authority in future negotiations. However, after an intervention in the dispute by Mr Len Murray, General Secretary of the TUC, a separate document was signed by him drawn up by Mr Murray. The 101 machine managers returned to work in the interests of the wider workforce rather than their own sectional interest. The reaction of the *Sunday Times* was to seek immediate negotiations with all the major unions securing improvements in efficiency.

The Financial Times Dispute, 1983

This dispute dated back to 1979 when the *Financial Times* machine managers entered negotiations to revise their existing comprehensive agreement, which had remained static for nine years. In those negotiations the NGA gave priority to proper staffing, differentials and securing a realistic press agreement. The NGA gave six months' notice of termination of the agreement but, after a reference to ACAS, agreed in December 1980 that there should be a major review of the comprehensive agreement which 'would take full account of the merit and justification of NGA claims'. In May 1981 in further discussions at ACAS it was agreed that the NGA should have a 19.5 per cent differential over the then Natsopa rate in the press room.

Subsequent attempts to conclude the matter were unsuccessful. The NGA felt that the *Financial Times* had not moved sufficiently on the fundamental issues of staffing, differentials and work responsibilities. Matters were further complicated when the company reached an agreement with machine assistants defining new duties and responsibilities, which management then sought to impose unilaterally on the NGA. The NGA could not accept this as it conflicted with its right to negotiate, as a sovereign union, rates and conditions for its members. It could not be committed to agreements made independently by management with other unions. For the NGA, a joint press room agreement meant an agreement negotiated with both NGA and Sogat not with one union and then imposed on the other.

On 1 June 1983 the *Financial Times* failed to be published and did not return to the streets for nine weeks. The dispute involved 270 NGA members, and the union initially paid a dispute benefit of £40 per week but later raised this to £75 per week. Following an intervention by ACAS, a three-man mediation panel was established, but when they reported the NGA did not accept their recommendations. The TUC intervened in the dispute and recommended on 27 July 1983 that the NGA accept the mediators' ruling, giving the NGA a week to consider its response and inviting its representatives to appear before the General Council on 4 August. The NGA refused to change its position and complained that the General Council had made its decision before the NGA had presented its case to them. However, the possibility that the TUC might suspend or expel the NGA for not complying with the General Council's recommendation became academic when intensive talks between the *Financial Times* management, senior ACAS officials and the NGA resulted in an agreement for a return to work.

The NGA had achieved its prime objective of upholding its right to negotiate, as an independent union, rates and conditions for its members and not to have agreements struck independently by other unions imposed on it. The defence of this principle had led the NGA into confrontation with the TUC, which was only avoided when the company conceded, at the end of the day, to the NGA's aspirations. The NGA had accepted Sogat's long-standing request for an 87½ per cent differential in the machine room. The NGA believed a joint press room agreement was the most viable way in which leapfrogging claims between itself and Sogat over differentials and manning levels in the machine area could become a thing of the past. However, the return to work after the nine-week stoppage saw the NGA again in dispute. Within one week of the return to work, in spite of management's statement to the NGA and ACAS that there was no more money and no possibility of additional staffing, the company entered negotiations with Sogat over a claim for additional staff on the basis of the formula agreed with the NGA as part of the return-to-work formula. When the *Financial Times* agreed to twelve additional Sogat staff in the machine room the NGA was perturbed. Its members had returned to work on the ACAS formula and they were now being expected to accept an increase in Sogat's staffing levels when the NGA's staffing aspirations had not been met under the ACAS formula.

These concerns rumbled on and in January 1985 the *Financial Times* machine managers were instructed not to produce any issues over forty pages, because the company had not properly followed the peace formula drawn up during the 1983 dispute. ACAS intervened, indicating that the peace formula on NGA staffing had not intended to carry staffing implications for Sogat machine assistants. The NGA therefore insisted that the *Financial Times* adhere to the formula, warned that there could be no moves towards a joint press room agreement until this happened and that it would be unwilling to cooperate in overtime working whilst the dispute remained unresolved. It was 1986 before a joint press room agreement at the *Financial Times* was finally secured based on an NGA differential of 12½ per cent and an agreed equal number of NGA and Sogat staff in the machine room.

EMPLOYMENT SECURITY

National Newspaper Closures

October 1960 saw the closure of three national newspapers – the *News Chronicle*, the *Star* and the *Empire News*. This was followed by a fourth closure – the *Sunday Graphic* – in December 1960. These four closures resulted in some 200 LTS members becoming redundant, but by the end of 1960 only a handful had not been placed in alternative employment. In 1961 another national newspaper ceased publication when the *Sunday Dispatch* merged with the *Sunday Express*. Early in 1964 the TUC severed its remaining formal links with the *Daily Herald* by selling its interest in the paper to International Publishing Corporation (IPC), which announced that it would close the paper and replace it by the *Sun*. However, this paper was eventually saved from closure when it was taken over by Rupert Murdoch in 1969. In 1966 the Economist Intelligence Unit report for the Joint Board for the National Newspaper Industry predicted the closure of four more national newspapers unless there were radical changes in the industry. In March 1971 it was announced that the *Daily Sketch* was to cease publication and merge with the *Daily Mail* no later than mid-May 1971.

The threat of newspaper closures still remained in the 1980s. In the autumn of 1980 the employment situation in national newspapers worsened with the announcement that the Thomson Organisation was pulling out of national newspaper publishing in Britain. With 1,750 jobs lost by the closure on 31 October 1980 of the *London Evening Times*, another 4,000 were now under threat by Thomson's announcement that *The Times*, *Sunday Times* and its three supplements would close in March 1981 unless a buyer for the titles was found. The chief reason given by the company for its decision was the 'continuing troubled history of industrial relations which goes back over many years'. The titles were subsequently bought by Mr Rupert Murdoch's News International group, which already owned the *Sun* and the *News of the World*.

Of the national newspaper titles that survived, many only did so because they obtained production and manpower economies and/or rationalisations via mergers and takeovers. In 1966 the *Guardian* notified the P&KTF that its financial position was critical and there were doubts about the form in which it would survive unless economies could be achieved. Fortunately, in February 1967 the newspaper announced that it had reached agreement with the unions on savings in its production departments and it was now confident that it could continue publication in London and Manchester as 'a strong, viable and independent newspaper'.[5] In 1971 the *Daily Mail* announced that, despite its incorporation of the *Daily Sketch*, it would require 1,700 redundancies if it and its stable paper, the *Evening News*, were to survive. In 1975 the *Observer* sought a 30 per cent cut in its total wage bill as a means to profitability, whilst the *Evening News* told its chapels that reductions in staff were necessary if the paper was to survive.

Sufficient economies were achieved at the time for these papers to remain viable.[6]

The national press, radio, television and the printing unions were all anxious about the closure of national newspapers and the emergence of mergers and takeovers in the industry, with their consequent concentration of newspaper ownership into fewer and fewer hands and the disappearance of a balanced and diverse press. Prior to October 1960 the national newspaper industry had enjoyed full employment. Although there had been cases of a few firms in the general printing trade closing down or moving from London, there had been no large-scale shut-down of a printing establishment in London. Why was employment security in national newspapers lessened from 1960 onwards? The LTS, the TA and the NGA were in no doubt as to the cause and consequences of the closures of, and reduction in the number of, national newspapers. They rejected the view that Fleet Street's problems were the result of high wages, overmanning and restrictive practices, and argued that they were due to declines in circulation and advertising, the high price of newsprint and inefficient management. Before the Second World War newsprint sold for £10 per ton. By the early 1960s the price had reached £60 per ton and by the mid-1970s was as high as £90 per ton. The NGA and its constituent unions considered that there was a direct link between the high cost of newsprint and the high concentration of ownership of newsprint mills.

The NGA was concerned about the influence of advertising revenues on the survival of newspapers. Sales of papers and advertising space are the main sources of revenue for national newspapers. The 'quality' press relies on advertising for a greater proportion of its income than does the 'tabloid' press. There is a link between sales (circulation) and the amount of money allocated by advertising agencies to national newspapers, particularly the tabloids. The greater the circulation of a newspaper, the greater the amount of advertising revenue it will attract. This factor had been complicated from the mid-1950s by the emergence and development of commercial television. The 1960s and early 1970s saw declines in newspaper circulation and falls in the advertising revenues received by national newspapers, whilst increases in the cover price were insufficient to offset the decline in revenues from these sources. Once a newspaper's circulation falls, then its advertising revenue falls, and the newspaper can be on the 'slippery' slope to closure.

The NGA has been concerned that national newspaper closures have concentrated ownership into fewer and fewer hands, a trend which the

1949 Royal Commission on the Press said it would deplore if it were to happen. The NGA's worry has been that the continuation of the concentration of the ownership of the press has resulted in substantial groups being deprived of a public voice, which endangers the effective functioning of democracy. The union fears the creation of a monopoly of control over the freedom of expression, which it sees as a vital part of liberty. The NGA believes that national newspapers must provide not only adequate channels of information to the public but also adequate means of expression for a variety of currents of serious opinion.

Measures to improve employment security

Compensation for redundancy

Following the 1960 closures, the P&KTF met with the NPA to discuss four issues: first, that there should be a collective agreement with the NPA for compensation for redundancy; second, that the problems of finding work for those made redundant as a result of a newspaper closure should be taken up by the NPA immediately there was redundancy; third, that, if a newspaper is facing difficulties that might lead to closure, management should meet with the union General Secretaries before any decision is taken; and, fourth, even if a decision to close has been made, that consultation should take place with the union General Secretaries before any public announcement is made. It was decided to establish a small joint subcommittee 'to examine the possibility of avoiding redundancy and of providing compensation to those concerned in the event of redundancy arising'. Both sides recognised that the words 'to examine the possibility' applied to the phrase 'of avoiding redundancy' and not to 'providing compensation', which had been given as a more definite undertaking. On the other issues the NPA agreed to recommend to its members that, where a newspaper was in difficulty, there should be consultation with the General Secretaries, and that when a decision to close a publication had been made the maximum practical period of notice should be given of the decision to the General Secretaries. The unions accepted this.

In the joint subcommittee meetings the print unions pressed the NPA to insure against the payment of compensation as a result of closure. However, the employers were advised by insurance brokers that this route was impossible since the likelihood of a newspaper closing down was not a risk capable of actual assessment. The unions then pressed the employers to establish a redundancy fund, but they refused to do this. The most the NPA was prepared to do was to suggest that a clause be inserted in the union agreeements with the NPA providing compensation for redundancy. The unions sought compensation of one month's wages for each year of service, whilst the NPA would not consider anything beyond one week's wages in each year of service. Anything in excess would have to be negotiated in the light of the particular circumstances of each closure.

The NPA and the P&KTF were unable to negotiate a redundancy compensation agreement. However, the Royal Commission on the Press which reported in 1962 recommended that the NPA and the unions should consider reforming the negotiation procedure and the introduction of redundancy compensation and pensions. The Commission had suggested a central negotiating body, but after consulting its affiliated unions the P&KTF concluded that this was not a practicable proposition since unions were not prepared to change their autonomous positions and negotiations for the various sections of even one union were so complex that it would be impossible for them to be handled by another body than the union itself. The P&KTF felt that the unions' present method of negotiations by voluntary collective association through the Federation on matters of broad general application, followed by separate union discussions with the NPA on 'domestic' matters affecting the individual unions, could not be improved upon. The Federation agreed to approach the NPA on compensation for redundancy on the basis of one week's wages for each year of service where total service was less than five years, two weeks' pay for each year of service for between five and fourteen years' service and three weeks' pay for each year of service from fifteen years or more. On pensions it was decided to approach the NPA for a contributory industrial scheme with transferable rights to provide for a pension of up to half wages on retirement. However, before a meeting could be arranged to discuss these matter, events were overtaken by the NPA's memorandum 'Efficiency of Production'.

NPA Memorandum 'Efficiency of Production'

In 1962 the NPA presented a memorandum 'Efficiency of Production' setting out how it considered the national newspaper industry could recover competitiveness. It argued that existing staffing arrangements should be subject to scrutiny by a firm of industrial consultants briefed by a joint P&KTF/NPA committee, who should submit proposals 'from staffing to fringe benefits'. The NPA envisaged a smaller but higher-paid labour force, resulting in greater efficiency, and savings shared between management and employee. It also sought realistic staffing in all departments but no displacement of regular employees, since agreed staffing levels would be achieved over a period of time by natural wastage. The NPA also desired a reduction in the number of wage categories in the industry and that the basic wage should be more closely related to 'take-home money'. It also proposed a reduction in the amount of casual working and stabilised regular staffs to handle all sizes of paper in all contingencies. Within this context of a reduced labour force, schemes would be implemented to provide redundancy compensation, sick benefits and pensions.

The P&KTF considered 'Efficiency of Production' on 19 August 1963. The unions recognised that, if they were to be successful in their claims to the NPA for schemes for compensation for redundancy and transferable pensions, they would have to concede increases in productivity. There was also general agreement that the unions needed to examine the questions posed by the employers on matter such as staffing. However, there were varying opinions as to the procedure to be adopted. One view was that adjustments should be the subject of direct negotiations between the separate unions concerned and the NPA. Others considered that the employers' suggestion of an enquiry by management consultants was contrary to their policy. Whilst there was some support for an enquiry, it was thought that it should be conducted not by professional consultants but by those with a sound knowledge of the industry, appointed by both sides. Others, however, were not averse to consultants providing they were not simply time and motion study experts. There was general agreement that the enquiry should include the quality of management and that the attention of the NPA should be drawn to the forces operating against the newspaper industry which were outside the control of the unions, for example the dependence of newspapers on advertising, and the selling price.

The P&KTF decided to consult its affiliated unions on agreement to independent management consultants providing they were under the control of a joint P&KTF/NPA committee, which would select them, draw up their terms of reference and jointly pay for their services. The consultants would report to the joint committee, which would consider any report before submitting it to the NPA and the P&KTF, which would then send it to their constituents for them to take any appropriate action. The LTS and the TA were agreeable to an investigation into the national newspaper industry on this basis. However, other unions objected to the use of industrial consultants and the NPA was informed that an independent investigation into all departments was not possible, although the unions were prepared to participate in collective talks on the future of the national newspaper industry and to examine the NPA's reference to sick pay, redundancy payments and pension schemes.

In October 1963 the NPA decided to issue a press statement expressing regret that the P&KTF, after eight months, had been unable to agree to a collective approach to the proposals submitted to it in February. However, the Federation later postponed this decision and on 1 October the two sides met. After a lengthy meeting the unions told the NPA that they had a contribution to make to improve the efficiency of the industry and were prepared to act on the problem. The unions differed, however, on the method. At a meeting held on 29 November 1963 the NPA reported that its object was to inject into the industry a degree of productive efficiency as near to the optimum as possible. For this reason it felt it necessary that outside consultants should review the situation under joint control and establish what was needed to achieve a maximum possible efficiency of the industry. It did not wish to achieve this by imposing the burden of making improvements on those employed within it and that was the reason the guarantee of no redundancy was in its memorandum. However, the unions were unable to agree a method of enquiry and told the NPA that they would be unable to proceed on a Federation basis so long as the employers persisted with their proposals to use industrial consultants.

In January 1964 the NPA wrote to the Federation saying that it intended to approach each union individually. Three months later it suggested to the unions the establishment of a 'high powered Joint Board advising, guiding, and encouraging lines of inquiry in the interests of the future of the newspaper industry'. The board would not have mandatory powers but the employers hoped it would acquire such an influence that no section of the industry would disregard its pronouncements 'without thinking twice'. The board would consist of union General Secretaries and NPA directors and have an independent chairman. The NPA reassured the unions that it was not proposing an arbitration forum, as it would deal only with questions of general application. The print unions indicated that they would participate in the proposed joint board provided suitable terms of reference could be agreed and there was a satisfactory settlement to the 1964 wages claim. When these two conditions were achieved the board was established.

The Joint Board commissioned a research report on the industry from the Economist Intelligence Unit and, following the report, established a Joint Management Committee to 'take the question of labour supply and demand out of the field of collective bargaining'. This failed and the main stumbling block was deciding how savings from improvements in productivity should be shared amongst the members of the trade unions or between trade unions and management. The Joint Board disappeared in 1967 without having made any significant contribution to the problems of the national newspaper industry.

The Joint Standing Committee for the National Newspaper Industry

On 2 May 1974, in reply to a question by Eric Moonman, the NGA-sponsored MP, the government announced the establishment of the third Royal Commission on the Press since 1945. Included in its terms of reference were management and labour practices and security of employment in the newspaper and periodical industry. In March 1975 the Commission published an interim report, setting out ways to assist the national newspaper industry. Its brief had been to enable as many national papers as possible to survive, by minimising production costs, by improving industrial relations and securing stable employment and proper remuneration for permanent employees, and by making reductions in manpower and changes in methods of working in a socially acceptable way.

The interim report pointed out that national newspaper plans would mean the loss of 4,500 regular jobs in the machine, publishing, clerical and ancillary areas plus 2,000 casuals. Up to a further 2,500 jobs were estimated to disappear from the composing and related areas as a result of new techniques. The Commission anticipated that these savings would be of the order of £35 million. It concluded that the financial position of the national newspaper industry was poor, that the only adequate means of cost saving was higher productivity through reductions in manpower and the introduction of new technology, and that some financial help from outside the industry was necessary but not as a general subsidy. The report saw the establishment of the Joint Standing Committee for the National Newspaper Industry as offering the best opportunity for achieving the necessary changes. The main recommendation of the interim Royal Commission on the Press report was that financial help should be made available, so far as possible from the private sector, to enable the industry to finance manpower reductions and new technology. Loans totalling £55 million to help the national newspaper industry were proposed, of which £35 million was to be for redundancy payments and £20 million for investment in new technology.

However, it did not follow that, if the interim report recommendations were implemented, this would enhance employment security in the national newspaper industry. Joe Wade, the NGA General Secretary, warned members:

> What we have to be careful about now that the Interim Report has been published and the Joint Standing Committee has been set up, is that we do not allow ourselves to be carried away with the idea that financial assistance, new technology and manpower reductions are going to provide a universal panacea for all the industry's ills.
>
> Even if agreement is eventually reached on manpower and the introduction of new technology, this in itself is not going to cure the fundamental malaise of the national newspaper industry which manifests itself in falling circulations, escalating newsprint prices, the effects on advertising of the current recession and, in one or two instances, thoroughly bad products.[7]

New technology was now seen as the saviour of employment security in the national newspaper industry.

THE IMPLEMENTATION OF NEW TECHNOLOGY IN NATIONAL NEWSPAPERS[8]

Industry-wide Initiatives

In the autumn of 1975 the NGA asked to meet with the NPA to discuss technological change in the industry. The NGA told the NPA that rationalisation of manning levels and the introduction of new technology were not only desirable but necessary and could be achieved without compulsory redundancy. The background to this NGA initiative was that all but two national newspapers had approached it about financial problems or new technology or both. Whilst detailed discussions would have to take place with each of the newspapers concerned, the NGA felt it desirable to agree a number of general guidelines between the unions and the NPA for the implementation of new technology. The alternative to a controlled implementation of new technology, the NGA argued, would be newspaper closure and large-scale redundancies.

In February 1976 the Joint Standing Committee (JSC) for the National Newspaper Industry, made up of union and management representatives, was established to monitor developments generally and new technology entering the industry. In November 1976 it produced a plan entitled *Programme for Action* covering redundancy compensation, pensions, decasualisation, retraining, disputes procedures and the vetting of management plans for new technology. Under these proposals all companies were required to table a manpower plan to the Committee in which they had to state when they expected to submit their new technology proposals, the timetable envisaged for the introduction of new technology, the date on which they envisaged being able to implement proposals on optimum staffing levels in areas affected by new technology and an indication of what problems had been met or could be anticipated. At the planning stage managements were expected to indicate where demarcation problems might arise and the union side would then meet separately to consider them and report to the JSC. A special disputes procedure was to be drawn up to deal with demarcation issues. When company proposals were submitted they were to contain *inter alia* an exploration of why new technology and manpower reductions were needed, a summary of the company's economic prospects, including their broad strategy on investment, pricing and advertising policies, and a detailed retraining programme.

On redundancy compensation the JSC recommended that any scheme would have to be attractive to 'individuals across the spectrum of ages and lengths of service' to the industry, as only in this way would a balanced labour force be maintained. It put forward a plan under which redundancy payments would be calculated on three scales, relating to age, length of service and wages, added together to give the total sum. Some newspapers were expected to be able to offer only this scheme, but others would have the option to compensate employees under 60 years of age on a straight four weeks' pay for each year of service. On pensions the JSC's target was for a pension equal to 1 per cent of final pay for each year of service after the introduction of the new scheme, plus two years' gross pay for a married man who died in service, payable as a lump sum or a pension or a combination of the two, whilst widows of retired workers who died would get a widow's pension of 50 per cent of the employees' pension. Existing schemes would not be expected to change to the new basis, but the total value of benefits payable under them would have to be at least equal the minimum level under the new scheme.

On decasualisation the JSC agreed to establish a register of bona fide casuals wholly employed on national newspapers and to determine the number of workers in each office needed to be taken into a regular labour force. When this had been completed a comprehensive plan for decasualisation was to be presented to the JSC. A new system of joint house committees and a new disputes procedure were proposed. The latter was to apply where meetings between management and national union officers could not resolve a dispute. The parties in dispute were to decide whether the disputes committee would conciliate, mediate or arbitrate.

Programme for Action was a comprehensive plan for redundancy pay, pensions, training, disputes procedures and planning the introduction of technological change. When the programme was put to a ballot of NGA members, it was decisvely rejected. Only 889 members were in favour of the proposals, whilst 3,778 were against. Members of Sogat, Natsopa and the EEPTU also voted against *Programme for Action*. The union leadership were disappointed at the result but were quick to point out that the vote should not be construed as NGA national newspaper workers being against new technology. They realised that the implementation of new technology was necessary if the national newspaper industry was to survive. The General Secretary told the members, 'So it's clear to me that it is not the technology they are opposed to or, indeed, a rationalisation of the manpower situation but the methods proposed by the Joint Standing Committee.'[9] It was decided that the JSC should remain in being but no further meetings were held. It simply faded away, as did the joint board before it.

Individual Company Initiatives

In the summer of 1978 the Mirror Group announced a £2.8 million investment in new technology such that by October 1976 it planned to produce all its national titles with photocomposition. Although the plan involved some reduction in staff, it was hoped that this could be dealt with by a combination of voluntary redundancy and early retirement.

The *Daily Mirror* was the first national daily to change over to a fully integrated computerised photocomposition system. The NGA maintained control over all input into the system and saw the agreement setting the pattern for other national dailies that were about to introduce direct input systems. This was followed in early 1979 by agreements being reached between the NGA and Express Newspapers and the *Observer*. Both these agreements gave complete jurisdiction to the NGA for the keyboarding into the computer of all copy, whether editorial or advertising. The NGA considered that these agreements gave the lie to the story that it was adopting a Luddite attitude to new technology.

Although, in the *Observer* case, agreement had been quickly reached regarding the NGA's sole right to input into the system, negotiations became bogged down as to the management's future intentions in respect of mid-week printing, which had been introduced to cope with the increased circulation and larger-size papers produced whilst the *Sunday Times* was off the streets. At the same time as the discussions were being held in respect of new technology, management were conducting parallel negotiations with NGA machine managers to provide the flexibility to accommodate the larger-size paper and increase circulation on one night's production. Eventually the *Observer* management took the decision to cease mid-week printing and shortly afterwards agreement in principle was reached with the NGA in respect of hours, holidays and basic pay rates to cover the introduction of new technology in the graphic area. Although the machine chapel reached agreement with management in respect of additional holidays and staff to cover the additional production requirements sought by management, deadlock was reached on the issues of money, hours and machine speeds. Eventually management agreed to pay additional money when large-size papers were produced, but their offer in this regard was not acceptable to the chapel. A period of intensive negotiation and discussion followed when, in spite of all the efforts of ACAS and the TUC and during which the chapel modified their attitude, management's only response was to issue ninety days' notice of closure. The chapel had rejected recommendations to accept the management's previous offer on three occasions despite the concern felt at the extensive job losses which would follow from the threatened closure. Finally, conscious of the situation facing other trade unionists, the NGA instructed the chapel to accept the agreement and this was accepted by the chapel, albeit reluctantly.

The development of photocomposition continued in national newspapers in the early 1980s. Agreements were subsequently made with the *Telegraph*, the *Financial Times*, at which the NGA sought the return to the London office of origination work that was initially agreed should be produced in Frankfurt when the European edition was first projected, and *The Times*, although only after a number of disputes and the intervention of ACAS.

The mid to late 1980s were most traumatic for NGA members in national newspapers. The entry of News (UK) Ltd onto the national newspaper scene to produce the *Today* newspaper, and its single-union, no strike agreement, had implications not only for the NGA but for other unions in the industry. However, *Today* was not a success and was taken over by News International. The events surrounding the closure of Thomson Withy Grove, when NGA members perceived themselves as being used as pieces in some kind of monopoly game, were humiliating for them. The events surrounding the year-long dispute with News International have been described in Chapter 14. The close of this NGA history sees the exodus from 'Fleet Street' complete. All the nationals have moved their origination and/or printing centres to London's Docklands. These moves were accompanied by the introduction of direct entry and the consequent reduction in the number of NGA members employed by these companies. The effects have also been felt in Manchester and the number of members employed in national newspapers in that city has been greatly reduced. The last few years have seen the publication of a number of new titles, including the *Independent*, which have been accompanied by a new trend in the production of national newspapers, namely contract printing at a number of sites throughout the country.

NOTES

1. *The National Newspaper Indsustry*, Economist Intelligence Unit, 1967.

2. Not involved in the negotiations were News International, the *Daily Telegraph* and the Mirror Group of Newspapers.

3. See *Print*, vol. 7, no. 6, June 1970, pp. 1 and 24.

4. See *Print*, vol. 7, no. 12, December 1970, p. 24.

5. See Printing and Kindred Trades Federation, *Annual Report, 1966–67*, p. 8.

6. See *Print* vol. 12, no. 8, September 1975, p. 1. Although the period 1960–4 saw the closure of five national newspapers, it also witnessed the birth of a new newspaper

(the *Sunday Telegraph*) and the printing in London, for the first time, of an existing newspaper (the *Manchester Guardian*, which changed its title to the *Guardian*).

7. See *Print*, vol. 13, no. 4, April 1976, pp. 4 and 20.

8. For a fuller account of this up to the early 1980s, see R. Martin, *New Technology and Industrial Relations in Fleet Street*, Oxford University Press, 1981. See also K. Sissons, *Industrial Relations in Fleet Street*, Blackwell, 1975.

9. See *Print*, vol. 14, no. 4, April 1977, p. 4.

CHAPTER 16

RELATIONSHIPS WITH OTHER EMPLOYERS

Over 55,000 NGA members are employed in firms that are in membership of the BPIF, or are covered by the BPIF agreement. At the height of NGA influence in provincial newspapers, some 15,000 were employed in firms in membership of the NS. Some 6,000 at the same time were employed in national newspapers. Today, the number employed in newspapers, both national and provincial, is around 15,000. The remaining 25,000 NGA members are employed in firms in membership of employers' associations in Ireland, the Channel Islands, Scotland, trade setting houses, litho plate-making, tin printing, wallcoverings, news agencies, art and advertising agencies. Some former Slade members are covered by the litho/process house agreement policy.

IRELAND

The TA, and subsequently the NGA, organised printing craftsmen in Northern Ireland and the Irish Republic provinces. The NGA did not have a presence in Dublin until the transfer of engagement of the National Union of Press Telegraphists. Its membership in Dublin expanded with mergers with the ASLP and Slade, but competition with the Irish Printers' Union was a constant problem. However, there were a multiplicity of employers' asociations with whom negotiations were conducted. In Northern Ireland, there was the Northern Ireland Alliance of the Irish Master Printers, in the provinces of the Republic the Irish Master Printers, in Cork the Cork Master Printers and the

Cork *Examiner*. In Dublin the NGA dealt with the Irish Printing Federation.

Northern Ireland

Separate negotiations took place with the Northern Ireland Alliance of the Irish Master Printers' Association independently from those with the IMPA or with the BFMP (later BPIF) and the Newspaper Society.[1] The TA, and subsequently NGA, approach to wage negotiations in Northern Ireland was to reach agreements the same as or similar to those made with the BPIF and the NS. This policy was in general successful. The terms of the 1977 wages agreement with the BPIF were also made with the IMPA Northern Ireland Alliance but were rejected by a small majority on a membership ballot vote. Further negotiations were opened and the claim submitted included a demand for a sick pay scheme and the introduction of a transferable pension in line with that already operating in Southern Ireland. The employers agreed to give serious consideration to both of these schemes but no conclusions were reached. Although the 1977 wages agreement was never signed, all NGA members in Northern Ireland received Phase 2 increases.

In 1979 the Northern Ireland branch submitted a claim for an increased payment to be made having regard to the additional costs being incurred by NGA members in Northern Ireland and a claim for the introduction of a transferable pension scheme in line with that operating in Southern Ireland. The IMPA remained adamant in refusing to concede anything outside the terms agreed between the NGA and the BPIF/NS. In 1981 the NGA again submitted to the IMPA Northern Ireland Alliance a claim for terms slightly in excess of the BPIF. However, the employers made an offer of £5, stressing that in the economic situation and the recession affecting printing firms in Northern Ireland there was no possibility of increasing that offer beyond that particular point. This offer was rejected, but following further negotiations and discussion the IMPA made a final offer of £7.50 new money to be applied to both the minimum grade rate and the minimum earnings level. In the 1982 negotiations the NGA claimed an additional allowance of £473.20 per annum to cover the higher cost of living in Northern Ireland, which at the time was some 7 per cent higher than in the UK. However, the employers refused to concede any additional money in respect of the Northern Ireland allowance.

The Irish Republic (except Cork and Dublin)

In 1951 the TA and the IMPA concluded an agreement that wages in Eire should be brought into line with those laid down in the National Wage Basis Agreement in England and Wales and included provision for a cost-of-living bonus to be determined at six-monthly intervals by the Eire Interim Cost of Living Index. In 1956 the TA and the IMPA agreed that any new wage agreement should operate from the same date as that from which the new English and Welsh agreement operated, provided that date was not earlier than 1 March 1956. However, a problem arose over the Dublin/provincial differential, which in Eire was the counterpart of the London/provincial differential. This was resolved by the 1956 IMPA agreement providing for a grade 1 rate of £9.56 (25p below the Dublin rate), a cost-of-living bonus, three years' stabilisation, the abolition of grading at the end of the three years, and, if during the agreement the Dublin rate increased to more than 50p above the grade 1 rate, negotiations could re-open for restoration of the differential to 50p.

In 1957 the TA decided that its negotiations panel for a new wage agreement to replace that expiring in April 1959 would be constituted differently from in the past. In future the negotiating panel would be Eire branch secretaries plus Executive Council representatives. This change in procedure stemmed from the system of graded towns in Eire being abolished in April 1959. In the past, practice had been to call all the grade 1 branch secretaries to join the EC representatives. With the abolition of grading this practice could not continue.

In 1965, arising from the settlement of a dispute in Dublin which widened the Dublin/provincial differential, the NGA lost no time in presenting a consequential claim to the IMPA. The result was that from 25 October 1965 the basic provincial rate in Eire was increased by £1.05 to £15.82½ and the employers accepted in principle a third week's holiday, and this was implemented in 1966. A £1 increase in Dublin rates again disturbed the differentials, but the employers opposed any provincial wage increase so soon after the October 1965 settlement on the grounds that the stability of the printing industry in Southern Ireland would inevitably be endangered. Nevertheless, an agreement was subsequently made which established the Dublin/provincial differential at 25p.

An industrial pension scheme with transferable rights was introduced in the Eire printing industry in 1968. In September 1967 the NGA put in a claim for such a scheme but two obstacles had to be overcome. One was that a large number of employers had yet to be persuaded to accept the idea of a pension scheme, and the second was the need for the NGA to state clearly its policy on the question of priorities. A draft industrial pension scheme was put before delegates at the 1968 All Ireland Conference, which decided that a pension scheme should be the first priority in the negotiations. The terms of the proposed pension scheme were put to a ballot and approved by Southern Ireland members in May 1968. Although there were many practical difficulties to be resolved, upwards of thirty firms registered with the Irish Pensions Trust, which was to administer the scheme, which was inaugurated on 1 November 1968.

A general movement for increased wages was seen in 1968 in Southern Ireland industry, of which a wage increase of £2.40 over eighteen months from 8 July 1968 to commercial printers from Dublin was a significant part. There were increases in the basic rate of £1.17½ from 26 August 1968, a further 50p from 1 March 1969 and another increase of 50p from 1 March 1970. The effect of this agreement was to give, over a period of eighteen months, an overall increase in the weekly basic rate of 13.5 per cent to provide a basic rate of £18.85 at 1 March 1970. The employers also agreed to be responsible for the additional amount of weekly pension contributions needed to ensure that, on retirement, NGA members would receive a combined pension from the state and from the industrial pension scheme of not less than half the wage rate then prevailing.

In June 1970 the NGA met the IMPA over its claim for a substantial wage increase, for the first five hours of overtime to be paid at time and a half, for an extra week's wages to be paid when the summer holiday was taken, and for an upward adjustment of machine 'extras'. The employers were shocked at the magnitude of the overall claim and considered that the NGA was being unrealistic in pursuing a claim which disregarded the necessity of maintaining a realistic comparison between the provinces and Dublin. Eventually an agreement was made which provided a craft minimum rate in Southern Ireland of £23.42 by 1 March 1971. With the approval of the Southern Ireland government, the Irish Congress of Trade Unions and the Southern Ireland employers entered a new national agreement in 1972,[2] which provided for a two-stage wage increase spread over a maximum period of eighteen months.

Although the NGA was opposed in principle to interference by government in wage bargaining, the majority of unions affiliated to the

Irish Congress of Trade Unions consistently supported the idea. Short of withdrawing from the ICTU, the NGA had no option but to accept the national agreement. However, in practice the wage improvements resulting from the application of the national wage agreement undoubtedly measured up in money terms to anything that might otherwise have been achieved. None the less, there were limitations attached to the national wage agreements. Unions were precluded from submitting individual claims, which meant the NGA could not pursue its claim for a fourth week's holiday to which its Eire membership attached the highest priority. However, in 1978 the IMPA conceded the fourth week's holiday to be introduced on a phased basis – two days in 1978, a third day in 1979 and the full five days in 1980 on the condition that the Irish Printing Federation, which covered firms in Dublin and Cork, also conceded this principle. The NGA was the first trade union in Southern Ireland to achieve the fourth week's holiday.

Following the decision of the special ICTU conference in July 1979 to accept a new national pay agreement, negotiations took place with the IMPA from which emerged an agreement which lifted the basic rate for the Southern Ireland provinces to £75.39 plus percentage increases in respect of machine classification and photocomposition agreements. Talks between ICTU and the employers for a further national agreement broke down in 1981. Consequently NGA members experienced free collective bargaining in Ireland for the first time in eleven years. The NGA used the opportunity to claim a wage increase of 25 per cent and a 37½ hour standard working week. These negotiations were long and protracted. The employers finally offered a three-stage increase in pay over a fifteen-month period to give a minimum grade rate up to £114.54 and a reduction in the standard working week to 39 hours from 10 January 1982.

Wages claims to the IMPA in 1983, 1984 and 1985 were against a background of the extremely serious economic conditions existing in the Republic and many employers' organisations insisted on pay pauses. Indeed, in 1984 the NGA failed to reach an agreement with the IMPA and its members attempted to negotiate an 8 per cent increase on a house-by-house basis. Many branches, however, secured agreements for periods in excess of twelve months and up to fifteen months and in some cases these agreements were for more than 8 per cent. In 1985 an agreement was made for a fifteen-month period to give a basic rate of £147.52 by 1 March 1986.

Following discussions between the Eire government, the ICTU and various employers' bodies, a *Programme for National Recovery* was published in October 1987. It provided for measures to regenerate the economy and improve social equity and a formula for pay increases in the public and private sectors. A special conference of the ICTU held in December 1987 accepted the *Programme for National Recovery* and its associated pay agreement by 181 votes, although the NGA delegation voted against the programme. The pay agreement associated with the national recovery plan provided for pay increases, calculated annually, over the next three years of 3 per cent on the first £120 of basic weekly pay and 2 per cent on any amount of basic weekly pay over £120, with the minimum increase to be adjusted to £4. These increases were to be applied through existing industrial relations machinery.

Cork

The TA, and then the NGA, dealt with two groups of employers – the Cork Master Printers' Association and the Cork *Examiner*, which was the only office in Eire, outside Dublin, that published a morning and evening paper. Wage claims to the *Examiner* were almost always based on the Cork jobbing rate plus the news differentials provided for in the BPIF/NS agreements. In the Cork general printing trade the bargaining objective was to maintain parity of basic rate with the jobbing industry in Dublin. The Cork Master Printers agreed in principle to the introduction of a third week's holiday for 1966–7 and that the commencing rate for overtime should be time and a half, and in 1968 that they would participate in the Southern Ireland industrial pension scheme. The transferable pension scheme was inaugurated in Cork on 1 January 1970 and provided similar benefits to those applied to NGA members in the Irish provinces, namely a combined benefit from the employers' scheme and from the state social welfare retirement arrangements equal to 50 per cent of the negotiated basic wage rate applicable at the time of retirement.

The national wage agreements that operated in the Republic in the 1970s meant that the position in negotiations with the Cork Master Printers and the Cork *Examiner* was similar to that prevailing in the Irish provinces. Wage increases were maintained in accordance with the terms of the ICTU/employers' national wage agreement on the basis of comparability with the Dublin position. The successful conclusion of the NGA's claim in the Irish provinces for the restoration of its wage relativity sparked off an NGA claim to the Cork Master Printers for similar treatment in respect of the Cork jobbing members. This was challenged by the employers and no progress could be made until, in August 1974, the Labour Court recommended the resumption of talks between the parties on the basis of productivity. Further negotiations resulted in a settlement in August 1974 which advanced the minimum basic rate in the Cork jobbing industry by £2.50 per week retrospective to 13 May 1974, the 50p difference between the Cork and the provincial position being in recognition of the increased holiday allowance already being received by the Cork members and also to the late-night working that applied in some provincial newspaper offices but was not relevant in Cork.

In 1981, when free collective bargaining returned, the NGA approached the Cork Master Printers for a 25 per cent wage increase and a reduction of 2½ hours in the working week. Following rejection of the employers' offer of 16.6 per cent, industrial action was called to try and improve the offer. Employers agreeing to meet the NGA's claim were excluded from the dispute. Eleven firms agreed to meet the claim and were excluded from the dispute. The NGA members remained solid, refused to accept the intervention of a Labour Court, but after several weeks finally agreed to attend a conciliation conference under the chairmanship of the Labour Court. The settlement achieved at this conference included a fifteen-month agreement giving a 10 per cent increase on the basic rate with effect from 1 December 1981 and a further increase of 6 per cent with effect from 1 October 1982, a reduction in the working week from 40 hours to 39 with effect from 1 March 1983, and an increase in annual leave entitlement from twenty days to twenty-one days in the 1982/3 leave year. This reduction of the working week, albeit only one hour, meant that the NGA was the first industrial union to achieve this breakthrough in Eire. This Cork dispute was the first dispute of its kind in the previous forty years.

The 1983 agreement with the Cork Master Printers' Association agreed to abolish the differential between the Cork Master Printers' Association agreement and the IMPA agreement in three phases over three years. In 1985 the NGA sought a 12 per cent increase in gross wage rates on and from 1 September 1985, a reduction in the working week to 35 hours, five weeks' annual holiday and a holiday bonus increase from 78 per cent to a full week's pay. The employers, due to the serious economic situation in the industry and as a result of competition from other areas, said they were only prepared to discuss the pay element of the claim. They rejected outright a reduction in working hours, increased holidays or an increased holiday bonus. The final agreement increased the basic rate in the Cork jobbing industry from £137.31 to £148.51 over the fifteen-month period 1 September 1985 to 30 November 1986.

Dublin

The transfer of engagements of the NUPT to the NGA in 1965 took the union into Dublin, where the main printing employers' organisation was the Irish Printing Federation. In the late 1960s NGA T&E members in Dublin felt strongly on two issues, namely parity of basic rates with Dublin compositors and an additional payment for Sunday paper working. Satisfaction was reached in 1968 in relation to Sunday paper working, but it was 1970 before the T&E members' basic rate was lifted to obtain parity with lino operators in Dublin and an assurance given that any future increase in the lino rate would be paid to NGA T&E members.

Another major issue with the IPF concerned NGA members working in the London offices of Dublin-based newspapers. These members did not come under the national agreements applicable to NGA members in Dublin. Discussions were held with the IPF to examine ways of including these London members in the IPF agreement either directly or in the form of an appendix or in a separate agreement. The stumbling block was that Eire legislation precluded agreements reached in Dublin being extended to members in London. The IPF eventually accommodated the NGA by agreeing to negotiate in each of the London-based offices in the light of the wage rates paid in Dublin. This was not entirely satisfactory, but it went as far as possible to satisfy members' aspirations given the difficulties over a geographical situation where two governments were involved.

THE CHANNEL ISLANDS

Jersey

The main employers' organisation on the island was the Jersey Master Printers. In 1956 the TA succeeded in establishing the principle that agreements should be the same as on the mainland in so far as grade 2 town wages should prevail on the island. In short the Jersey basic rate should have parity with grade 2 towns on the mainland.

This policy was continued by the NGA. The November 1969 Jersey agreement had a specific provision written into it that after twelve months there would be an opportunity to review the position if the inflationary trends on the island were of such significance as to justify it. This provision was later to be the subject of a challenge from the employers. During the first six months of 1970 wage rates in other Jersey industries rose substantially. However, unlike the UK employers, the Jersey employers insisted that the NGA should adhere to the precise terms of the existing agreement. They also made it clear that they were not prepared to accept a settlement which would maintain the minimum NGA grade rate on the island at a higher level than the mainland grade 2 rate. Although the employers' final offer of a £2 increase from 1 December 1970 meant a basic rate in Jersey of 50p above the UK grade 2 rate, it was equally apparent that the relative position of NGA members on the island had been barely maintained. The NGA reluctantly accepted this final offer, which established a Jersey basic rate of £20.75.

At the time the agreement ended in August 1971, the grade 2 basic rate in the UK was £1 above the Jersey minimum, but an application for a substantial increase met with strong resistance from the employers, whose response was to offer, on a take it or leave it basis, an increase of £1 to restore the grade 2 relativity. This was unacceptable to the NGA, which was seeking a basic rate of £24 to maintain their Jersey members' living standards and their relative position in the Jersey wage league, which had suffered because of the unprecedented inflation rate on the island. In September 1971 the employers offered a basic rate of £23 but this was rejected by the NGA members, who were instructed to give a fortnight's notice of the withdrawal of labour unless the NGA's claim was met. This led the employers to offer a basic rate of £23 from 1 September to be followed by a further increase of £1 from 1 March 1972. This was accepted by NGA members on Jersey.

In 1973, the NGA members on Jersey were involved in strike action. From the commencement of negotiations for a new agreement to replace that terminating in February 1973 the employers put up strong resistance to any settlement which would put the basic rate for Jersey above the UK level. They were not moved by evidence from the NGA showing that the cost of living on the island had risen faster than on the mainland and was likely to continue to do so. The NGA sought a basic rate of £30, but the most the employers were prepared to offer was £27.75 with a cost-of-living escalator paid quarterly. NGA members gave notice that in the absence of a satisfactory settlement being reached they would withdraw their labour as from 5 March 1973. There being no reaction from the employers, strike action was taken on the appointed day. During the three weeks of the dispute there was 100 per cent support throughout. Towards the end of the third week, as a result of the offer from a member of the Jersey government to act as a convenor of a meeting between the NGA and the employers, negotiations were resumed on 24 March 1973. The settlement which resulted from these talks, and which was subsequently accepted by NGA members on the island, included a basic rate of £28.75 on return to work with a further increase of £1 at 4 March 1974 and a fourth week of holiday to be taken from 1 July 1974.

In August 1976 the NGA secured an agreement with the Jersey employers which provided for improvements in the basic rate, a continuing link with the cost of living bonus and a rate of payment for annual holidays of time plus 25 per cent of their normal weekly wage. This was the first time the NGA had managed to achieve this holiday pay objective in a national agreement. A reduction in the working week was achieved in 1980. From April 1981 the standard working week was to be 39 hours, but from 7 December 1981 was to be 37½ hours. In accepting the 1980/1 settlement NGA Jersey members were obliged to trade the end of the mid-term cost-of-living adjustments within their agreements. A fifth week's holiday was achieved on the island in 1989, again in line with the NGA policy of ensuring that the Jersey agreement related to that on the mainland.

Guernsey

The TA faced many problems on Guernsey, including the absence of any form of employers' federation, that the form of indenture entered into by apprentices came within the jurisdiction of the island's Labour Office and that membership, in spite of continued efforts to organise, remained a very small minority of the eligible journeymen on the island. These meant that wages, hours and working conditions varied from office to office and the TA was unable to exercise control over the number of apprentices entering the industry. The low level of TA organisation on the island made it difficult, indeed impossible, to achieve a wage agreement for the island. The Guernsey employers made it clear that only when the TA could speak for a substantial proportion of printers on the island would they seriously consider entering into a collective agreement to provide wage levels equal to grade 2 towns on the mainland. By the time the TA merged with the LTS to form the NGA it had still not secured a basic wage agreement for the island.

It was not until 1977 that the NGA managed to establish a branch on Guernsey and in early 1978 began negotiations for an island agreement within the Guernsey Printing Industries Federation. As a result of these negotiations, a basic rate of £63 was established in an agreement to operate for fourteen months from 1 March 1978. A fourth week of holiday was also established in the agreement, as was appropriate payment for overtime, shifts, machine classification, photocomposition and evening newspaper production. The 1979 negotiations established holiday pay at 25 per cent above the island basic rate. Negotiations in 1980 and 1981 with the Guernsey employers proved tough on both occasions. In 1980 a settlement was reached only after the NGA members had decided to take industrial action. In 1981 negotiations, the Guernsey employers were only prepared to offer a reduction to 39 hours and were not prepared to bargain on wages unless this was accepted. However, last-minute negotiations eventually moved the employers to offer a new craft basic rate of £95 per week, a reduction in the standard working week immediately to 39 hours, and a further 1½ hours' reduction from 26 April 1982.

During the 1982 wage negotiations the employers' organisation in Guernsey collapsed. To obtain recognition on Guernsey the NGA had had to agree not to enforce the closed shop. In the 1982 negotiations the NGA sought the removal from the agreement of that assurance, as it wanted the opportunity, which was available to all other trade unionists on the island, to pursue a 100 per cent trade union organisation should it wish to do so. The employers were not prepared to comply with the general provision on the island of Guernsey and made it a major issue to such an extent that little progress could be made.

The difference between the two sides were registered with the state industrial disputes body and the NGA undertook to go to arbitration on the issue. The employers refused to do this and, rather than go to arbitration, they disbanded their association. The result was that the NGA's weakness in the Guernsey Press, the main print employer on the island, was exposed and that company took the attitude that it would break the NGA organisation in its factory. It established a house union and enforced upon NGA members the terms which it was prepared to agree with the house union. The NGA members of Guernsey Press, being a minority, were obliged to accept these terms and return to work. They went back to work together, not as individuals, and retained their NGA membership with the objective of eventually creating a trade union shop.

Subsequently the NGA negotiated house agreements with Flowline and Paramount Lithoprint. Flowline, while continuing a separate agreement with the NGA, integrated its commercial printing operations with those of *Jersey Evening Post* to create a company called Channel Islands Printers. Paramount Lithoprint was taken over by Croydon Printing Company, which has other establishments in London. Since 1982, printing establishments on the island have been covered by individual agreements. However, in 1989 the Guernsey Press remains essentially non-union.

SCOTLAND

Daily Newspapers

The Scottish Daily Newspaper Society represented producers of daily papers in Scotland, for example the *Scotsman* and the *Glasgow Herald*. In Scottish newspapers the NGA covers only the reproduction department, plate-making and the telecommunications areas. The SDNS was disbanded with regard to wages and conditions in 1981, after which such negotiations were conducted in Glasgow, Edinburgh and Aberdeen. Prior to the disbanding of the SDNS, the NGA sometimes approached that organisation collectively with other print unions, with the P&KTF acting as the coordinating body, or independently. The main achievements in negotiations with the SDNS included the introduction of the fourth week's holiday in the 1970 agreement and payment at average earnings in respect of the five days in lieu of public holidays in the 1972 agreement. Following the introduction of separate negotiations, a major breakthrough was achieved at the *Daily Record* in Glasgow when a new wages structure covering craft and non-craft rates was agreed by all unions. At the Scotsman Publications in Edinburgh, a new-technology agreement in the plate-making area was established with some difficulty and wage awards in this area fell below 5 per cent.

In the mid to late 1980s Scottish newspapers suffered the wind of change equally with those of the rest of the UK, although the developments and change-over from photocomposition to direct input came a little later. Nevertheless it still had considerable effect on the employment prospects of NGA members in Scotland. The switch to offset plate-making led employers to seek the creation of combined process/plate-making departments involving the production of colour. However, there has been no adverse effect through these changes on general employment conditions, as there have been in other national papers. In some respects wages have been improved through changes that were brought about in new agreements.

The General Printing Trade and Newspapers other than Dailies

The main employers' association in this section of the Scottish printing industry is the Society of Master Printers of Scotland.[3] In October 1967 the Society, whilst retaining full membership of the BFMP, made a separate agreement from that organisation with NGA electrotype and stereotype members. The NGA continued this separate agreement approach, believing this to be the best means of accurately interpreting the wishes of its stereotyper and subsequently litho members in Scotland. In the 1970 agreement the NGA secured average earnings for holidays, whilst the 1972 agreement provided for a fourth week's holiday and for the first time in many years increases in machine classification 'extras' for lithographers and the rotary and trade 'extras' for electrotyper and stereotyper members. The 1975 agreement saw the introduction of paid leave for a bereavement for a period of up to three days and the introduction of a Litho and Stereotyper basic weekly rate of £40.70. The 1977 and 1978 agreements were influenced by the government's anti-inflation policy and were similar to those sections in agreements with the BPIF and the NS. However, the 1977 agreement provided for all members to receive one-third of their normal weekly wage after two weeks' certified illness for a period of six weeks. Thereafter each case was to be reviewed individually.

Major features of the July 1979 agreement were the establishment of a new minimum earnings level of £44.95 for journeymen and the reduction of the standard working week from 40 hours to 39 hours with effect from 1 February 1980, which was subsequently reduced to 37½ hours. The 1983 agreement saw the securing of an additional day's holiday. The maximum level of sick pay entitlement increased by £4 to a maximum achievable level of £63 per week, and an accommodation over

557

continuous stationery machines. The 1985 agreement established *inter alia* an £86.49 minimum wage level for craft employees and a maximum level of sick pay entitlement of £71. However, the SMPS refused to make any concessions on the demand for a 35 hour working week and for three months' notice to terminate shift. In June 1988 an industry-wide money purchase contracted-in pension scheme for the printing industry in Scotland was launched. The scheme mirrors the Printing Industry Pension Scheme. The NGA continues to have the minority of print workers in Scotland. Nevertheless, the NGA Edinburgh and Glasgow branches have representation on the apprentice training forum set up by the SMPS, which includes Sogat, Scottish educational authorities and the Manpower Services Commission.

THE TRADE SETTING HOUSES

APEF/ATFEF

Both the LSC and the LTS had aspirations to secure a separate agreement for their members working in advertisement-setting houses from that covering members in BFMP. In these houses work was highly specialised and had peculiarities separate from the rest of the general printing trade. Both the LSC and the LTS had an agreement with the national newspapers that they would not involve advertising-setting houses in any industry-wide general printing dispute. However, in the 1950, 1956 and 1959 disputes the national newspapers were affected because members in ad-setting, being in the general trade, stopped work. On each occasion the NPA complained to the LSC/LTS that they had failed to keep their word.

During the 1959 wage negotiations the LTS again suggested that the ad-setting employers make a separate agreement with them. The LMPA would not consider this but after the dispute a number of ad-setting employers indicated their willingness to talk to the LTS about such an agreement. Out of a total of twenty-eight advertisement-setting firms twenty-two formed the Advertising Production Employers' Federation (APEF) and negotiated an agreement with the LTS to operate from April 1960 for a period of five years. The agreement adopted a new approach in a number of aspects. First the LTS–LMPA agreement minimum rate of pay bore little relationship to wages actually paid in the ad-setting section of the industry. The agreement would now enable a realistic rate to be negotiated rather than an artificial one based on other sections of the industry. Second, the 40 hour week had been achieved in the agreement by peaceful negotiation and without the necessity for intervention by an outside body. Third, the agreement dealt with the apprentice question on the basis of two considerations, namely the requirements of the section concerned and the opportunities available for the proper training of an apprentice. Finally, the agreement made provision for a joint board to which either side could refer matters in dispute.

In 1967 there was a merger between the two employers' organisations covering the separate interests of foundry and composing departments to form the Advertising Typesetting and Foundry Employers' Federation (ATFEF). The same year also saw the NSES transfer its engagements into the NGA. These two events were used to negotiate a new and all-embracing agreement in 1968 covering all NGA members employed in advertisement production houses, based on a 'productivity package deal' to include flexibility between composing departments and foundries. In 1972 the NGA submitted a claim to the ATFEF for a 36 hour week to be spread over four days and for an increase in the day rates with 50 per cent extra for night workers. The employers considered a four-day week impractical, but NGA chapels commenced a policy of working to rule, which finally brought about the employers' acceptance that a 37½ hour week could be implemented from the start of the new agreement, which was to operate from October 1972. The 36 hour week was established during the 1974 wage negotiations.

During the 1976 negotiations the NGA secured a sickness scheme and a wider night over day differential. Nevertheless, the NGA would still have to make further advances if it was to achieve its long sought objective of a night rate 50 per cent higher than the day rate. There were dangers in this policy. It was important to have a high night rate when virtually half the NGA members in this section of the industry were working shifts. However, it militated against ever establishing a high day rate, to which one day NGA members might be obliged to return.

On 1 December 1977 ATFEF became part of the Graphics Reproduction Federation (GRF). Although in the mid to late 1970s the number of offices operating under this agreement declined, its terms remained amongst the best in the printing industry. By 1979 the standard working week had been reduced to 35 hours and the NGA had established a day rate of £100 and a night rate of £125.35. In the early 1980s the future of the GRF(ATFEF)/NGA agreement covering typesetting companies came under increasing doubt as the employers' organisation continued to lose members due to companies either closing or resigning their membership. By May 1984 the GRF had only two small typesetting houses still in membership and the NGA concluded that it could no longer justify the continued renegotiation of the GRF(ATFEF)/NGA agreement. Both parties accepted that this agreement had regrettably to be terminated and that in future the terms and conditions of NGA members in this area would be determined by the NGA/RAGA agreement, although a better conditions provision would prevail in those areas where the GRF agreement was more advantageous than the RAGA agreement.

RAGA

During the 1972 negotiations with ATFEF the industrial sanctions applied by NGA chapels resulted in the creation of a new employers' organisation – the Reproduction and Graphics Association (RAGA) – consisting of firms previously referred to as non-federated. The NGA lost no time in seeking an agreement with RAGA and, whilst the terms were basically the same as the ATFEF agreement, there was one very important difference, namely the introduction of a 36 hour week in October 1974. The NGA policy towards the RAGA agreement was to keep its terms and conditions in line with the GRF(ATFEF) agreement, but it was not always able to achieve this and had to accept certain departures. However, in the RAGA area the NGA was faced with the same problem as in the GRF(ATFEF) area of maintaining an adequate day rate whilst recognising the importance of a high night rate when half the members were employed on nights.

The 1979 negotiations resulted in a fifth week of annual holiday being introduced on a phased basis that would reach fulfilment in December 1981. During the 1983 negotiations it was jointly agreed that the NGA and RAGA would meet outside the wage negotiations to seek to establish provisions covering the NGA's policy relating to equal opportunities and compassionate leave. Eventually the NGA secured a new clause in the agreement covering equal opportunities, bereavement and training and retraining of NGA members employed by RAGA companies, which gave a commitment that where NGA recruitment was concerned, where retraining was required then the recruitment would be subject to consultation between the company, the chapel and the NGA branch officer.

Unlike the GRF(ATFEF) position the number of offices operating under the terms of the RAGA agreement increased, though not all of them joined RAGA. Most of the new companies were small and in order to install the latest photocomposition techniques have become highly geared. Although originating from the advertisement production side of the industry, many RAGA employers now have highly sophisticated typesetting equipment and are widely involved in many facets of origination from the individual advertisement to full page production. By 1988 the bulk of RAGA companies were to be found in London, but there were also companies in membership covered by the NGA's Birmingham, Chiltern and Thames Valley, Kent, Lea Valley and Newcastle branches. The increasing practice of studios to install their own typesetting equipment and of magazine and periodical publishers introducing full-page make-up in-house, with tapes and discs being sent to contract typesetters, has created difficulties for some RAGA employers and their NGA employees. This led in December 1989 to an agreed joint statement on page make-up by the NGA and RAGA designed to protect the jobs of NGA members in typesetting houses.[4] The statement provides a basis for the handling of such material and for any difficulties to be referred to the RAGA/NGA disputes procedure. It recognises that publishers may undertake keyboarding and make-up of their own magazines and periodicals, but both the NGA and RAGA believe that, when publishers recognise that they have underestimated the difference between word processing and desk top publishing, they will realise that it is inefficient to undertake their setting and make-up in house. The NGA established a 35 hour week in its agreement with RAGA, and although at times difficulties have arisen, the overall relationship between the two organisations has been built on cordiality and mutual respect.

PHOTOGRAVURE

The inter-war years witnessed rival claims for the control of photo-gravure machines between the letterpress and the litho unions. This was resolved in 1938 when the BFMP and the TA signed an agreement giving the TA exclusive control over the manning of photogravure machines and establishing wages, manning and apprenticeship conditions. These conditions were supplemented by local negotiations. By 1950 the 1938 agreement had become outdated, and pressures built up amongst the membership involved that a new photogravure agreement should be negotiated, bearing in mind the anomalies that had arisen and would arise with the further expansion of the gravure process. A new agreement was not reached until 1955 and was to operate for a period of five years. A new agreement negotiated in 1960 was also to operate for five years, although if certain circumstances arose the agreement could be reviewed after two and a half years. These agreements involved three companies – Odham's Press, Sun Printers, Watford, and Bemrose of Liverpool. When the 1960 agreement expired in August 1965 there was a considerable delay in negotiating a new agreement because the three employers in question decided that they no longer wanted a collective agreement and preferred to have three separate house agreements. In the light of this continued disinclination of the three firms previously associated with the photogravure periodical agreement to negotiate new terms on a collective basis, the NGA decided in 1967 to conduct separate agreements in future with each of the three individual managements.

In 1954 the NGA had been involved in an industrial dispute with E., S. and A. Robinson Ltd of Bristol over the manning and rating of certain photogravure machines. The JIC conciliation machinery could not resolve the dispute and a number of TA members were dismissed for refusing to operate unclassified machines. The company claimed that their photogravure presses came within the 1938 agreement, whilst the TA claimed this was not the case as that agreement dealt with machines with fixed cylinders whilst the machines concerned in the dispute had detachable cylinders. The TA gave a fortnight's notice that if agreement was not reached by 8 February 1954 on the manning and rating on the machines it would instruct all rotary gravure minders employed in Robinson's and its associated companies not to operate unclassified machines as from that date. At the end of the first week of the dispute, notification came that the Ministry of Labour, at the request of the employers, had referred the matter to the Industrial Disputes Tribunal. The TA declined to appear before a Tribunal and recommended that all TA members employed by Robinson companies in Bristol tender notice in support of their colleagues.

The Industrial Disputes Tribunal report said that it would be to the advantage of both parties if they made a further attempt to reach a settlement. The TA agreed to re-open discussions, but the employers made it clear that, unless the TA was prepared to instruct its photogravure minders to return to work and work the new machines under pre-dispute conditions, they would refuse to discuss the matter.

When the TA refused to accept these conditions, the attempt to resolve the dispute failed. The Industrial Disputes Tribunal again considered the matter and published an award on 20 April 1954 in which it concluded that it was not, on the evidence before it, able to make a definitive award but that a case had been established for payment to the minders in charge of the machines in dispute of wages higher than those paid previously and for a scale of manning in excess of that which had operated hitherto.

Following the Tribunal's award it soon became clear that the main obstacle to a resumption of work was the question of how three new machines were to be operated pending negotiations. Eventually a two-point formula was agreed. The first point provided for a single arbitrator of national repute to decide on the manning conditions of the three machines and the second for the establishment of a joint panel of the JIC. The unanimous award of the arbitrator and the assessors was that, for the period during which negotiations would take place to reach a final settlement, each of the three machines should be manned by two minders. On 17 May 1954, TA members returned to work. The award of the joint panel of the JIC, under the chairmanship of Sir John Forster, KBE, QC issued in August 1954, removed some anomalies from the old agreement but created some new ones. The TA found it hard to understand the decision not to award extra rates for machines with more than four cylinders, as it considered responsibility must increase with each colour added. However, it took heart from that part of the award which indicated that 25p extra should be paid for cutting, scoring or even punching. It regarded the award to be, by and large, reasonably satisfactory.[5]

OTHER

News Agencies

The NGA agreements with British and foreign news agencies were initially on a company-by-company basis. In 1967 an approach was made to all the news agencies with a view to their forming one organisation. Six of the larger news agencies eventually formed the News Agency Liaison Committee (NALC), enabling the NGA to deal mainly with one body instead of individual managements. Overtures to persuade other larger news agencies to join the NALC proved abortive. The NGA continued to negotiate with NALC until 1981, when the latter decided to disband itself as a negotiating body. The NALC advised the NGA to seek separate agreements with each individual agency and this remains the situation today.

Agencies and Studios Agreement

Following the recruitment campaign conducted by both Slade and the NGA in advertising agencies and studios, a number of house agreements were established which eventually led to the original joint NGA/Slade Agency and Studio Agreement which was implemented from 1 July 1977. Since the original agreement was established the number of members covered by the terms of the agreement has grown to the current day where some 25 NGA branches have members working under the terms of the agency and studio agreement. Whilst it is a national agreement, the employers are represented by three Associations: the Association of Midland Advertising Agencies, the Association of Northern Advertising Agencies and the Association of Scottish Advertising Agencies.

Since the original agreement a 35 hour week has been established as well as five weeks annual holiday and annual improvements to salary. The agreement also provides a comprehensive sick pay arrangement. Additionally, pension provisions are available to employees working in agencies and studios who are not only in membership of the appropriate Agency Association but also in membership of the Institute of Practitioners in Advertising. The NGA held an agreement with the Northern Ireland Association of Advertising Agents until late 1987 when the agreement was terminated as a result of the lack of employer membership of the NIAAA.

Art Studios and Photographic Laboratories Association

From 1st August 1976, Slade established an agreement covering members working in ASPLA member companies in London, Manchester and Newcastle. This followed the 70s recruitment campaign in studios. However in recent times there has been a deterioration in the number of employers in this area and currently the agreement only covers member companies in London and Newcastle. Member companies of ASPLA are under increasing technology pressure from traditional repro houses and have had to move closer into that sector of the industry by investment in new equipment. The agreement itself provides for a 35 hour week, five weeks holiday and comprehensive sick pay arrangements.

The Metal Packaging Manufacturers Association

The ASLP as a constituent part of the NGA previously held agreements in the Tin Printing Section of the Industry, or that known as Metal Decorating prior to its amalgamation with the NGA. This section of the printing industry is not generally recognised in the public domain as being part of the printing industry but nonetheless the level of skill involvement in this area was generally recognised under the ASLP agreements as having a greater premium than those printers involved in the paper or board sections of the industry. They were in fact the 'aristocrats' of the litho printers.

There is not a single company, whether they evolved in can printing, making metal caps, making biscuit tins or celebratory metal decorated boxes for national occasions, who were not part of the employers organisation, who apart from major wage negotiations involved themselves in the general control of the industry and in recent times having a major input into the recycling basis due to environmental pressure.

It was also a section of the industry which, because of its relationship to metal and more particularly the drawn wall iron canning process, generated enormous health and safety problems with regard to noise levels and the drying processes using infra-red and ultra-violet. It has been necessary therefore to be very vigilant with regard to the health and safety problems of NGA members involved in this area.

While the MPMA still negotiates on wages and conditions with the Association there are noteable exclusions from the wage area, namely Metal Box, Nacanco, Continental Can which has recently been acquired by Crown Cork who also have a separate agreement. Although these are separate agreements they closely relate to the MPMA main area. It is perhaps indicative that the agreement between the Association and the employers organisation is still identified as the Tin Section Agreement, although the MPMA changed into its current structure in 1977.

Litho House Agreement Policy

The Litho House Agreement programme has been in existence since 1968. The need for a policy requiring agreements to be reached with individual companies at local level stemmed from the 1968 BPIF/ Slade wage negotiations, particularly that part of the negotiations that covered craftsmen employed in litho reproduction across a wide area of the industry at that time. The decision to embark on house agreements was taken against the background of the BPIF asking for the introduction of assistants into reproduction areas. The role of the assistants was broadly to help the craftsmen in their work. This move was resisted. It proved impossible to reach any accommodation with the BPIF with regard to their aim. It was against this background that the negotiations were broken off and attempts made to reach agreements at house level.

The effect of this was, in the long term, to create an increasing number of trade reproduction houses, as opposed to the maintenance, as they existed at that time, of large reproduction studios attached to printing houses. The policy took something like two years to achieve the position whereby agreement with the BPIF was no longer relevant. Although not every litho house was covered by a house agreement. Most people had come to terms with the policy and that this would catch up with them as employers sooner or later.

The longer term effect of what had happened was to effectively remove reproduction from being an integral part of litho printing houses. At this time, litho was beginning to take off quite rapidly, and although wages and conditions of employment were probably going ahead in this part of the industry faster than elsewhere, large printers were not prepared to concede some of the things that Slade were seeking at that time, because of the knock-on effect elsewhere in the company. Obviously, this change was not brought about without there being difficulties, but eventually the aims of the original policy were not only achieved, but exceeded most people's expectations.

It never was the aim of the policy to stand still simply on negotiation being taken on a house basis. It had always been expected, particularly following the example that came out of the dispute in Leicester in 1971/72, that the policy would be developed into area, town agreements or group agreements, and at a later date the facility be built into the policy to enable this to be achieved, subject only to the agreement of the chapels involved. This policy never worked. The group agreement in Leicester was never looked upon favourably by NGA members, coming as it did at the conclusion as part of the settlement of a dispute, and the agreement with the BPIF Alliance in Leeds subsequent to the amalgamation taking place in 1982. At that point the Leeds Branch returned to negotiating straightforward house agreements.

The Litho House Agreement Policy itself, both prior to and since the amalgamation of Slade and NGA, has involved firstly the National Council as being the body responsible for deciding the ultimate policy lines to be followed in any given year. In order to help the National Council arrive at this policy, branches are invited to table proposals that are considered by a committee of the Council. The programme that is then drawn up is endorsed by the National Council, and put to a national meeting of Litho FOCs and Branch Secretaries for approval. In more recent years, the discussion that takes place at the FOCs' and Branch Secretaries' meeting has been limited to consideration of alternative proposals coming from branches that have not been adopted by the Council in their initial review of the programme in any particular year. The effect of this has been that the FOCs' meeting has the ability to propose amendments to the policy adopted by the Council. At the end of the day the House Agreement Programme in any particular year is based on the final decision of the National Council.

NOTES

1. In 1970 the Northern Ireland employers were prepared to forgo separate negotiations and to offer NGA members the terms of settlement with the BFMP and the NS in their entirety. This proposal was a departure from the procedures adopted over many years, but it was accepted by the NGA that, providing this procedural departure was not to be taken as a precedent, the Northern Ireland employers' offer should be accepted forthwith without a meeting with the employers or a ballot of the membership.

2. An employer/trade union national wage agreement had been adopted in 1971.

3. The Scottish Alliance of Employers in the Printing and Kindred Trades was founded in 1911. It retained control of all matters affecting the industry in Scotland and of its own finances and conditions of membership. In labour matters, the Scottish Alliance reserved the right to vary any terms and conditions proposed in so far as they affected Scotland. In 1954 it became the Scottish Alliance of Master Printers and in 1961 the Society of Master Printers of Scotland. The 1961 change of name was made in the light of experiences in the 1959 dispute and the need to avoid further confusion between the BFMP autonomous organisation in Scotland and the Alliances in England and Wales, which were subject to the authority of the BFMP Council.

4. See *Print*, vol. 28, no. 1, January/February 1990.

5. See *Typographical Circular*, September 1954.

APPENDIX I

OFFICERS OF THE NGA AND ITS FOUNDING UNIONS

THE LONDON SOCIETY OF COMPOSITORS (1955)

General Secretary	Mr R. Willis	1955
Assistant Secretary	Mr F.G. Isaac	1955
Financial Secretary	Mr W.F. Potts	1955
News Officer	Mr A.N. Buchan	1955
Organiser	Mr H.J. Griffin	1955
Research and National Insurance Officer	Mr J.E. Rawlins	1949–55

THE LONDON TYPOGRAPHICAL SOCIETY (1955–63)

General Secretary	Mr R. Willis Mr P. Astins	Joint 1955–6
	Mr R. Willis	1956–63
Assistant General Secretary	Mr F.G. Isaac	1955–9
	Mr H.J. Griffin	1959–63
Assistant Secretary	Mr W.T. Borroff	1955–63
Financial Secretary	Mr A. Matthews Mr W.F. Potts	Joint 1955–63
News Officer	Mr A.N. Buchan	1955–60
	Mr J. Clifford	1960–3
Organiser	Mr H.J. Griffin	1955–9
	Mr E.T. Welham	1959–63

Research and National Insurance Officer	Mr J.E. Rawlins	1955–8
	Mr R.H. Stafford	1958–63

THE TYPOGRAPHICAL ASSOCIATION (1963)

General Secretary	Mr H. Riding	1954
	Mr F.C. Blackburn	1955–6
	Mr J.M. Bonfield	1957–63
General President	Mr H. Inglis	1949
	Mr F.C. Blackburn	1949–55
	Mr F. Simmons	1957–63
Financial Secretary	Mr H. Taylor	1961
	Mr G.C. Moore	1962–3
Assistant Secretaries	Mr H.E. Joseph	1956
	Mr J.M. Bonfield	1955
	Mr W.G.R. Hutchings	1956–63
	Mr J.F. Wade	1956–63
	Mr J. Jones	1957–63

THE NATIONAL GRAPHICAL ASSOCIATION (1964–82)

General Secretary	Mr R. Willis	Joint 1964–9
	Mr J.M. Bonfield	
	Mr J.M. Bonfield	1969–76
	Mr J.F. Wade	1976–82
General President	Mr F. Simmons	1964–76
	Mr L.S. Dixon	1976–82
Assistant General Secretary	Mr J.F. Wade	1967–76
	Mr A.D. Dubbins	1976–82
Financial Secretary	Mr A. Matthews	Joint 1964–8
	Mr G.C. Moore	
	Mr G.C. Moore	1968–77
	Mr J. Jones	1977–8
	Mr C. James	1979–82
National Officers	Mr J. Clifford	1964–8
	Mr H.J. Griffin	1964–72
	Mr W.G.R. Hutchings	1964–76
	Mr J.F. Wade	1964–7
	Mr J. Jones	1964–78

Mr R.H. Stafford	1964–76
Mr M. Clayton	1965–7
Mr O. McCarthy	1965–8
Mr A. Pearson	1967–82
Mr R. Harris	1968–76
Mr R.A.W. Emerick	1969–78
Mr K. Haughton	1969–82
Mr J. Broom	1971–7
Mr J. Willats	1971–82
Mr J. O'Conner	1977–8
Mr G. Colling	1977–82
Mr J.A. Ibbotson	1978–82
Mr G. Jerrom	1979–82
Mr F.G. Tanner	1979–82
Mr R.W. Tomlins	1979–82
Ms B. Philbin	1979–82
Mr C.W. Harding	1981–2

THE NATIONAL GRAPHICAL ASSOCIATION (1982)

General Secretary	Mr J.F. Wade	1976–84
	Mr A.D. Dubbins	1985 to date
General President	Mr L.S. Dixon	1982
	Mr J.B. Griffiths	1982 to date
Assistant General Secretary	Mr A.D. Dubbins ⎫	Joint 1982–4
	Mr J. Jackson ⎭	
	Mr J.A. Ibbotson	1985 to date
Financial Secretary	Mr C. James	1982 to date
Assistant Financial Secretary	Mr G. Richford	1982–6
National Secretary	Mr. A. Parish	1982 to date
National Officers	Mr C. Colling	1982 to date
	Mr C.W. Harding	1982 to date
	Mr K. Haughton	1982–6
	Mr J.A. Ibbotson	1982–4
	Mr G. Jerrom	1982 to date
	Mr E. Martin	1982 to date
	Ms B. Philbin	1982 to date
	Mr F.G. Tanner	1982 to date
	Mr R.W. Tomlins	1982–9
	Mr J. Willats	1982 to date

THE NGA NATIONAL COUNCIL, 1 JANUARY 1989 – 31 DECEMBER 1990

London Region (6 seats)
J. Beck
J. Clifford
D.J. Douglas
D. Marsh
R. Pritchard
P. Taylor

South Eastern Region (7 seats)
J. Anderson
D. Baker
M. Broomfield (Deceased)
K. Price
H. Capel
M.A. Chizlett
M.A. Duncalfe
M. Talbot

Irish Region (1 seat)
A. Kavanagh

Scottish Region (1 seat)
R.P. Hutchison

Northern Region (7 seats)
M. Appleby
W.G. Bailey
T. Burke
D. Hargreaves
T. Howley
T. Lyons
E. Saltmarsh

Midland Region (5 seats)
A. Carr
K. Gardner
R. Hughes
J. McHugh
E.G. Smith

South Western Region (3 seats)
S. Attwill
M.K. Griffiths
M.J. Holland

Welsh Region (1 seat)
A. Speed

INDEX

INDEX